Events Management

For tourism, cultural, business and sporting events

4TH EDITION

Events Management

For tourism, cultural, business and sporting events

Lynn van der Wagen and Lauren White

4TH EDITION

PEARSON

Pearson Australia
707 Collins Street
Melbourne VIC 3008
www.pearson.com.au

2018   2017   2016   2015
10 9 8 7

Acquisitions Editor: Lisa Railey
Project editor: Catherine du Peloux Menagé
Copy editor: Kathryn Lamberton
Proofreader: Nicole Le Grand
Copyright and Pictures Editor: Emma Gaulton
Cover and internal design: Pier Vido
Cover photograph: Glenn Pokorny
Typeset by Midland Typesetters, Australia

Printed in China

National Library of Australia
Cataloguing-in-Publication entry
Author: Van der Wagen, Lynn.
Title: Event management for tourism, cultural, business and
                 sporting events / Lynn Van der Wagen,
                 Lauren White.
Edition: 4th ed.
ISBN: 9781442534889 (pbk.)
Notes: Includes bibliographical references and index.
Subjects: Entertainment events--Planning.
                 Entertainment events--Management.
                 Special events--Planning.
                 Special events--Management.
                 Tourism.
Other Authors/Contributors:
                 White, Lauren.
Dewey Number: 338.4779

Pearson Australia Group Pty Ltd   ABN 40 004 245 943

PEARSON AUSTRALIA
is a division of

PEARSON

CONTENTS

PREFACE

As a professional field of practice, events management requires sophisticated skills in strategic planning, risk analysis, marketing, budgeting, cash flow planning and human resource management. There are chapters on all these topics and many others in this book. Indeed, more and more public events are appointing professionally trained staff to senior positions. The project nature of events, as well as the range of risks they carry (including financial risk), ensures that skilled and knowledgeable management staff are required. In fact, many major projects in today's corporate world are one-off events requiring these skills.

Events management, as a diploma or degree program, is a business course with a strong project focus. Topics covered include marketing, accounting and legal compliance. It also covers human resource management. A small event planning team can explode to a workforce of several hundred for the short period of an event, thus providing significant challenges for human resource management. The skills and knowledge gained in the study of events management can be used in diverse contexts. Events management covers a wide range of interest areas including business, sport and the arts. Most significantly, governments and local councils are developing policies and procedures supported by legislation, making legal compliance and risk management important roles for the professional event manager. The tourism impact of events is increasingly attracting the interest of governments seeking to maximise domestic and international tourism revenues. All these trends are working towards the development of events management as a professional practice.

Students emerge from this field of study with business and project management skills of the highest order, ready to face any business challenge. They can confidently apply for a wide range of positions (few titled 'event manager') for which this type of training has prepared them. Indeed, recognising the project orientation and customer responsiveness of most modern organisations, students are confident that they are developing skills for the future. Many events are also community focused and this has particular appeal for many entrants to such positions.

Several people played a direct role in the writing of this book. Ron Beeldman read the proofs and provided feedback. Anitra Walker, Robyn Spencer, Lesley Guthrie and Barry Hall gave me invaluable advice on several of the chapters. And Warwick Hamilton of Events Unlimited contributed many ideas and useful information included in the text. We would also like to thank the many people and organisations acknowledged throughout the book who made invaluable contributions by providing case studies, diagrams, photographs and discussion material.

This text is based on the Tourism, Hospitality and Events Training Package, copyright Commonwealth Department of Education, Science and Training (DEST). Training packages comprise nationally endorsed standards and qualifications for assessing and recognising people's skills. In order to accurately reflect the nationally agreed guidelines, a number of headings, paragraphs and lists from the training packages have been integrated into the text and the author hereby acknowledges the use of this copyright material.

Kathryn Lamberton has edited all my books. It has always been a pleasure working with her and with my publisher, Pearson Australia.

To loyal readers, students everywhere, thank you for your feedback. May all your events be successful!

Lynn van der Wagen and Lauren White

CHAPTER 1

EVENT INDUSTRY KNOWLEDGE

Unit descriptor

This unit describes the performance outcomes, skills and knowledge required to develop and update general knowledge of the events industry, including industry structure, legal issues and current technology. This knowledge underpins effective performance in all meeting and event organisation and management roles. By its nature, the unit acknowledges the concept of an event industry and the need for individuals who participate in the event management process to be able to source, develop and apply current and emerging information about the industry. The unit is relevant to those individuals working in an event support and management role.

More specialised and advanced event research and management knowledge is found in other units.

Elements

- Source and apply general information on the structure and operation of the event industry
- Source and apply information on ethical and legal issues for the event industry
- Source and apply information on event industry technology
- Update event industry knowledge.

Critical aspects for assessment

- Understanding of the ways in which industry knowledge can be applied to work activities to maximise effective performance
- General knowledge of the event industry
- Application of knowledge in specific event organisational contexts.

BRISBANE Convention & Exhibition Centre is working towards becoming a world-leading sustainable event facility. The Centre is committed to striving to achieve ecologically sustainable development (ESD) through a balance of environmental, economic and social/cultural factors in a way that will ensure that resource conservation and the environment is protected now and for future generations.

A recent initiative consolidates the Centre as champions for environmental sustainability. The services of our custom made Carbon Calculator deliver clients the opportunity to measure the carbon footprint of their events and to stage carbon neutral events.

Designed in conjunction with the Carbon Reduction Institute (CRI), the Carbon Calculator takes into account room occupancy, menu selection, event services and is applicable for all events. The online calculator is a free service provided by the Centre to assist clients in reducing the impact of their events on the environment.

If requested, the Centre will also source high-quality carbon credits to offset the emissions from your events through the Centre's two partners, Climate Friendly and Carbon Reduction Institute, for as little as $2 per person.

Sources: <www.bcec.com.au/venue-and-services/green-meetings.aspx>; <www.bcec.com.au/about-us/sustainability.aspx>
Copyright © 2010 Brisbane Convention & Exhibition Centre.

A number of initiatives are underway to ensure that events have limited environmental impact or, as this extract illustrates, are carbon neutral. Over time it will become quite commonplace for carbon credits to be offered as an option when you book tickets.

Running a sustainable event is just one of the many considerations for an event manager. Events can have positive as well as negative social impacts and, increasingly, governments want to attract events to their states, territories and regions due to the economic impacts associated with increased tourism.

The aim of this book is to assist you in your training to become an event manager of the highest calibre. Many of us have observed events, most of us have participated in events, but few of us have managed events. As an event manager, you are there to do far more than just observe, and you are definitely not there as a participant. You are there to ensure the smooth running of the event, to minimise the risks and to maximise the enjoyment of the event audience. The demands on an event manager are far greater than you would expect. The career path for a successful event manager does not involve running a party which turns into a riot, something that has happened on several occasions in Australia, involving police and damage bills in the hundreds of thousands of dollars.

Many events carry a significant risk to the safety of participants. Accidents and injuries sustained at soccer matches and music festivals are sometimes fatal. Concerns for safety are paramount and risk assessment forms a major part of any event proposal. Qualifications and experience in risk management, covering all facets of event organisation, are essential for the modern event manager, as is the ability to identify all legal compliance issues.

Financial risk is also an important concern of the event manager. Events are generally extremely expensive, with high expenditure required over a very short period of time, and there are far higher levels of uncertainty about revenue and profit than there are with the average business.

In the case of voluntary and charitable events, of which there are many in every community, the risk is that the time invested by individuals will be wasted and their objectives will not be achieved.

Finally, one of the most important things about an event is that it is often a highlight of a person's life. This is not to be taken lightly. A significant birthday, a wedding or a christening is so important to the main participants that nothing must go wrong. If something does go wrong, it cannot always be easily rectified. A wedding at which the power fails due to overloading of the electrical supply cannot be repeated. The offer to 'come back again at our expense' just doesn't work! The event manager therefore carries overall responsibility for ensuring that the event, however large or small, is a success as there is often only one chance to get it right.

From what we have discussed so far, events are characterised by the following:

★ They are often 'once in a lifetime' experiences for the participants.
★ They are generally expensive to stage.
★ They usually take place over a short time span.
★ They require long and careful planning.
★ They generally take place once only. (However, many are held annually, usually at the same time every year.)
★ They carry a high level of risk, including financial risk and safety risk.
★ There is often a lot at stake for those involved, including the event management team.

This last characteristic is crucial, since every performer, whether athlete or entertainer, wants to deliver their best performance. The bride wants the day to be perfect in every way. The marketing manager and the design team want the new product to be seen in the best possible light. Consider for a moment how much easier it is to run a restaurant (where you spread your risk over a number of days and a number of customers) than it is to run a one-off, big-budget product launch—particularly if the launch has 500 key industry players and the media in attendance, and is taking place at a unique location with unusual demands for logistics, lighting, sound and special effects.

Having pointed out the level of demand on the event manager and thus the possible downside of the profession, it is important also to point out that the event industry is one in which people (the event audience) tend to have the time of their lives. Making this possible and sharing this with them is extremely gratifying. The work is demanding, exciting and challenging, requiring a finely tuned balance between task management and people management. The team needs to be both organised and flexible. Events can be unpredictable and do require quick thinking, based on a sound knowledge of procedures and options. Decision-making is one of the most important skills of the event manager, and those with first-class analytical skills are highly sought after by most industries.

Professor Donald Getz (2005), a well-known writer in the field of event management, defines special events from two perspectives, that of the customer and that of the event manager, as follows:

• A special event is a one-time or infrequently occurring event outside normal programs or activities of the sponsoring or organizing body.

Festival crowd

- To the customer or guest, a special event is an opportunity for a leisure, social or cultural experience outside the normal range of choices or beyond everyday experience (p. 16).

Another well-known author, Dr J Goldblatt (2005), defines a special event as '... that which is different from a normal day of living' (p. 6).

In this book, the emphasis is on a wide range of events, including 'special events', as defined above, and more common events such as sporting events, meetings, parties, carnivals and prize-giving ceremonies, which may not meet the definition 'outside the normal range of choices'.

THE STRUCTURE AND OPERATION OF THE EVENT INDUSTRY

Internationally there is fierce competition for the staging of mega and major events. Countries compete against each other for the right to hold the Olympic Games, Rugby World Cup, FIFA World Cup and World Expo. In this competitive environment, Australia competes against other countries, such as France, Brazil and China. Australian cities also compete against each other for major sporting events, such as motor racing and major entertainment events. In the conference exhibition area, there are convention centres in all capital cities vying for business. Aside from the prestige that some of these events bring to a country or city, the wider social and economic impacts of staging such events is often the key reason why the competition is so fierce. As this chapter will show, events play a vital role in profiling a country as an attractive tourism destination and event tourism contributes significantly to a country's economy. While this is hard to quantify, we know that event-related tourism is an important export for Australia.

According to the Australian Bureau of Statistics (ABS) exports of tourism goods and services compare favourably with Australia's 'traditional' export products such as coal and iron ore. Tourism and events are sustainable, low-impact and environmentally friendly export industries; in other words, a 'clean' way for Australia to earn foreign income.

Events are often the trigger for spikes in the tourism industry, and this was the case for the Olympic Games, Commonwealth Games and Rugby World Cup. If events are scheduled for low-occupancy tourism periods this is highly advantageous for the economy. Regional councils are also highly supportive of festivals and other types of events as here, too, economic impacts are a valuable stimulus.

EVENT INDUSTRY STRUCTURE

Within events there are several key organisations and businesses which help to describe the scope and structure of the industry and the potential career paths that exist within it.

Government agencies

Many government agencies take responsibility for managing large events, such as the City of Sydney, which runs the annual New Year's Eve fireworks event. On a smaller scale, many local councils run Australia Day celebrations and other community festivals. As Figure 1.1 illustrates, the Manager Corporate and Community Services would oversee any events run by council or approved by council.

Governments operate at federal, state/territory and local council level. Organisers of smaller events would work mainly with the relevant council, while organisers of major sporting, arts or business events might work nationally with federal and state bodies.

Event organisations

In the case of some major events, specific organisations are formed, such as the Adelaide Festival Corporation, which was set up to run the Adelaide Festival. The Adelaide Corporation also manages another biennial event, the Adelaide Festival of Ideas (FOI), which is held in the alternate year to the Adelaide Festival.

Promoters

Promoters have a crucial part to play in the organisation and staging of certain major events. Chugg Entertainment is one of Australia's best known event promotion and production companies, having been responsible for the tours of Robbie Williams, Coldplay, Elton John, Keith Urban, John Fogerty (US), Santana (US), Feist (Canada) and, for the first time to Australian shores, Sinead O'Connor (Ireland). In early March 2006, Michael Chugg was awarded 'Promoter of the Year' at the International Live Music Conference awards in London, and in June of the same year, he received the Gentleman Jack award at the 3rd Annual Jack Awards for his service to live music in Australia.

Event service providers

Event services such as catering, cleaning and waste disposal are highly specialised,

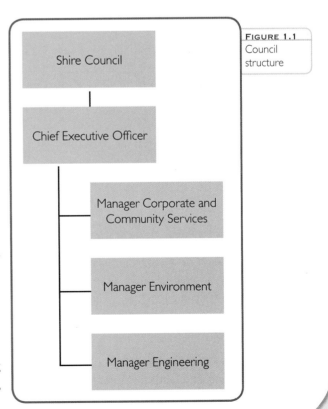

FIGURE 1.1
Council structure

Council-run food and wine and sustainability festival

and so too is event security. These services are generally provided by specialist organisations such as Cleanevent (now known as CE Property Services Group), or ACES (Australian Concert and Entertainment Security). In addition to providing staffing solutions, ACES security conducts risk assessment as a service to the event organiser. Management services can also be provided by businesses specialising in this area, including party planners and wedding consultants.

Event suppliers

Party and equipment hire companies can provide anything from chair covers to scaffolding. Stage equipment, lighting, sound systems, stages, props and seating are all supplied by event suppliers. While event suppliers generally provide these more tangible items, they also provide operational support such as information technology and catering. They are also known as 'service providers'.

Venues and sites

Conference and wedding venues likewise provide a range of services that support the delivery of an event, including catering, bar service, cleaning and security. In some cases the client hires the venue as a blank canvas and plans all aspects of the event. A venue is usually a built environment, such as a banquet room or sports centre, whereas a site is generally an outdoor space, such as a park, at which an event is held. A greenfield site refers to a site that has no buildings or other infrastructure, and all equipment needs to be brought in, including portaloos, kitchens, stages and seating. The most famous greenfield site for an event was the farm on which Woodstock was held in 1969. The organisers of Woodstock were expecting 50 000 people and 10 times that number turned up!

Non-specialist and in-house event producers

In addition to the above specialist organisations, there are many events staged in-house by companies (e.g. a large bank might run a product update for its clients). Corporate events include those run internally (e.g. staff training and awards nights) and those run externally. Often the external events have a marketing focus and may include trade shows, product launches and publicity stunts.

Many smaller private events are also organised informally by friends and family who may or may not call on some of the specialists mentioned for one or other facet of the organisation.

As these examples illustrate, there is a great deal of overlap between the above agencies, organisations and businesses.

Crossover industries

Several allied and crossover industries work alongside the event industry, including organisations involved in tourism, hospitality, arts and culture, sport and recreation. This is

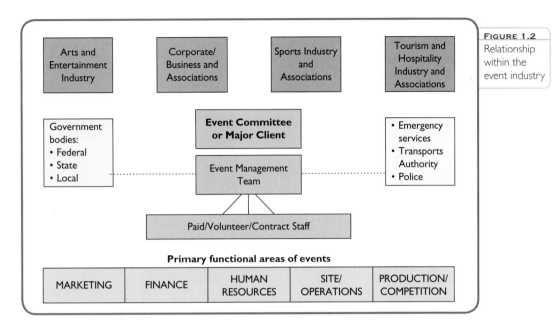

FIGURE 1.2
Relationship
within the
event industry

illustrated in Figure 1.2 in which all of the industries represented are set within a legal and business environment. This diagram illustrates the structure and functions in a simplistic way for an industry that is diverse and complex.

EVENT CLASSIFICATION

There are a number of ways in which events can be classified: in terms of the **size** of the audience; the organiser's **motivation** for running the event (raising money, selling products, providing entertainment); or in terms of the **event characteristics**, including the **profile of the event audience**. Events can also be **public** (open to everyone) or **private**. Private events are usually by invitation only; however, distribution of information about the event can sometimes lead to gatecrashers turning up. Another simple way to differentiate events is between those where **profit** is the motive versus those which are **not-for-profit**, such as charitable events.

Size

The largest events are called **mega events** and these are generally targeted at international markets. The Olympic Games, Commonwealth Games, World Cup FIFA and Superbowl are good examples. The Superbowl, for which in 1967 there were 30 000 tickets unsold, now sells out before the tickets have been printed and attracts 100 000 visitors to the host city. It is televised to an audience of 800 million and adds US$300 million to the local economy.

All such events have a specific yield in terms of increased tourism, media coverage and economic impact. While some cities are continuing to meet a legacy of debt after hosting an Olympic Games, Sydney was fortunate in meeting its budget due to a last-minute surge in ticket and merchandise sales, returning $10 million to taxpayers. However, as with all events

KUMBH MELA—WORLD'S LARGEST RELIGIOUS FESTIVAL

THE holy city of Haridwar is home to some of the most sacred Hindu rituals. All year devotees flock from all over the country to pray. Haridwar is known for the Kumbh and Ardh Kumbh festivals that are held to mark the 12-year solar cycle. Millions of devotees and visitors take a dip in the holiest of Hindu rivers at this time, to attain salvation. The Purna (complete) Kumbh takes place at four places—Prayag (Allahabad), Haridwar, Ujjain and Nashik—every 12 years, while the Ardh Kumbh Mela is celebrated every six years at Haridwar and Prayag.

These are some of the interesting statistics for Kumbh Mela 2010 at Haridwar:

- Pilgrims: 50 million
- Police: 20 000
- Toilets: 25 000
- Tents: 50 000
- Fatalities at Kumbh Mela: hundreds were crushed to death underfoot in 1954 and dozens also died in 2003; in 2010 seven people died in a stampede.

of this size, it is difficult to calculate the costs accurately with so many stakeholders (mainly government) involved. The budget for the Athens Olympic Games did not include a new tram network and a suburban rail line, which were both funded by the European Union's Third Community Support Framework.

While the size of the Olympic Games in terms of expenditure, sponsorship, economic impact and worldwide audience would undoubtedly put it in the category of mega event, it is worth comparing its size with, for example, that of the Maha Kumbh Mela ('Grand Pitcher Festival'), the world's largest religious gathering. The big Maha Kumbh Melas are held every 12 years, with lesser festivals held at stages in between. The celebrations—especially the Maha Kumbh and Ardh Kumbh—are the largest religious gatherings of people in the world, with about 60 million attending in 2007.

Hallmark events are designed to increase the appeal of a specific tourism destination or region. The Tamworth Country Music Festival, the Melbourne Cup and Floriade in Canberra are all examples of tourist destinations in Australia achieving market positioning for both domestic and international tourism markets through their annual events. The Edinburgh Military Tattoo and the Rio Carnival are international festivals with significant event tourism impact. In fact, Edinburgh has 16 key festivals that form the basis of its event tourism calendar. These events and their host cities become inseparable in the minds of consumers.

Events that attract significant local interest and a large number of participants, as well as generating significant tourism revenue, are known as **major events**. The National Multicultural Festival in Canberra and Chinese New Year celebrations fit into this category, as do many of the hallmark events described earlier. The three-week Chinese New Year festival in Sydney includes market stalls, food stalls, exhibitions, street entertainment, parades and dragon boat races. Friends and relatives of the Chinese community often visit at this time. According to Tourism NSW the New Year's Eve fireworks contributes approximately $150 million to the state's economy.

World Youth Day 2008, a major event—an estimated 400 000 people attended the final Mass

Governments are often called upon to enact special legislation in relation to major events such as World Youth Day 2008 when Pope Benedict XVI visited Australia. In New South Wales, the Major Events Bill 2009 removes the need to enact special legislation for major events, such as special requirements for temporary road closures, limiting use of airspace, and other security and crowd control provisions. Major events are of a large scale with a significant number of participants or spectators, whether of a sporting, cultural or other nature. Similar provisions exist in other states and in New Zealand. When an event is declared a major event, the cooperation and support of many government agencies is assured. An extract from the Bill is shown in Figure 1.3. From this it is evident that declaration of an event as a major event is an important consideration.

Without limiting any other matters the Minister may consider, the Minister may have regard to the following matters before determining whether to recommend the making of a regulation under subsection (1):
(a) the potential size of the event
(b) the likely number of spectators for the event
(c) the possible media coverage of the event
(d) the possible economic impact of the event
(e) the potential contribution to New South Wales's international profile as a host of major events
(f) the commercial arrangements for the event, if known
(g) the views of the event organiser, including the organiser's event management experience and expertise
(h) possible factors affecting the operational organisation of the event, such as the following:
   (i) preparation of road and transport plans
   (ii) the need for emergency management plans
   (iii) the need for security plans and consultation with police and emergency services
(i) if known, the views of local councils directly affected by the event in relation to the arrangements made or to be made for the event
(j) the possible need for consultation and agreements to be made between the event organiser and affected local councils in relation to the event, including any agreements about the restoration of event venues and facilities.

All legislative material herein is reproduced by permission but does not purport to be the official or authorised version. It is subject to Commonwealth of Australia copyright.

FIGURE 1.3
Extract from NSW Major Events Bill 2009

Most events, however, fall into the category of **minor events**, and it is here that most event managers gain their experience. Almost every town and city in Australia runs annual events. For example, the Broome area promotes the Pearl Festival, the Battle of Broome and the Mango Festival. A count of special events and festivals meticulously researched for the *Reader's Digest Book of the Road* reveals that nearly 2000 festival-type annual events are held around Australia. In addition to annual events, there are many one-off events, including historical, cultural, musical and dance performances. Meetings, parties, celebrations, award ceremonies, sporting finals, and many other community and social events also fit into this category.

Motives for running events

Business events are generally commercially motivated. They include meetings, incentives, conferences and exhibitions. This sector was previously known as MICE and continues to be labelled as such in many countries. There is a great deal of international competition for the business event dollar as the average daily expenditure of business visitors exceeds that of other tourists.

Table 1.1 shows some of the business events staged in Australia's major cities and the expected attendance levels. From this it is clear that there are competitive pressures between the major convention and exhibition centres, particularly between Melbourne and Sydney. Asian destinations also compete with Australia's convention centres. The bidding and planning processes for some of these events can take up to 10 years. The economic impacts of business events are most important, thus providing the impetus for government support of this sector.

Table 1.1 Business events and attendances

Business event	City	Attendees
International Surgery Week	Adelaide	2000
World Lottery Association Convention & Trade Show	Brisbane	800
XXIXth International Horticultural Congress	Brisbane	2000
International Plant Lipid Symposium	Cairns	250
Parliament of the World's Religions 2009	Melbourne	10 000
Australasian College of Dermatologists	Darwin	700
World Congress of the World Institute of Pain	Perth	2000
105th Rotary International Convention	Sydney	22 000

Source: Adapted from <http://www.businessevents.australia.com/rsc/AACB/International_assoc_events_Sept09.pdf>.

Festivals Australia is a government funding program designed to assist the presentation of arts and cultural activities at Australian regional and community festivals. The emphasis is on supporting new projects, which add to the quality and diversity of the arts and cultural programming. For the purposes of this program, a festival is 'a regular public celebration that is organised by members of the community, has clear, strong and broad-based community support and involves public outcomes such as performances, exhibitions/displays, film screenings, etc.' Table 1.2 describes the major arts festivals held in the capital cities. Festivals such as these have important social impacts, profiling the arts in many forms.

The annual Movie Extra Tropfest attracts large crowds

As Table 1.2 on page 12 shows, these festivals are fairly evenly spread across the year as it is pointless to compete on the domestic tourism calendar.

Charities usually run events on the basis that any funds raised in excess of operating costs are allocated to the charitable cause. In contrast, music producers who bring big name artists to the country or who run large annual music events such as Big Day Out are clearly motivated by profit. Neither can afford to run at a loss if the event or business is to be sustained.

EVENT IMPACTS

From the above, it is clear that the key motivations for running events are **economic** (including profit-making and flow-on effects to the wider economy), **social** (the main impact of celebrations of cultural, historical, religious or social significance) and **political** (major and mega events may have a political impact, in addition to their social and economic impacts) (see Figure 1.4 on page 13). For example, it was said that the Olympic Games in Beijing put China on the world stage as a modern economy. As Lee Sands (2008) writes in the *China Business Review*:

> The huge inflows of investment to support the Olympics and recreate Beijing have had an important ripple effect on economic growth, not simply in Beijing but in areas surrounding the capital. The Beijing Statistical Bureau estimates that spending on the Olympics has added 2.5 percent annually to Beijing's overall economic growth since 2002.

Likewise, the Edinburgh Festival—not just one festival but 10, including the Fringe Festival. Collectively, they are the jewels in the crown of Scotland's cultural scene, attracting hundreds of thousands of visitors and pumping £200 million into the nation's economy every year. In 2009, an estimated 19 000 performers took part in 34 000 performances and the Fringe alone generated about £75 million for the economy (McRae 2010).

Table 1.2 Festival calendar

Month	Festival
January	Each year the **Sydney Festival** offers a rich and diverse program spanning all art forms including dance, theatre, music, visual arts, film, forums and large-scale free outdoor events. For three weeks in January the festival hosts around 80 events involving upwards of 500 artists from Australia and abroad. In any given year, it makes use of most of the main theatres across the breadth of the city and also has a commitment to the presentation of quality, large-scale outdoor events.
February	The **National Multicultural Festival** is held in Canberra over two weeks and features the very best in local, national and international music, dance, food and creative arts. Festival favourites include the Food and Dance Spectacular, the Greek Glendi, Carnivale, the International Concert and the Pacific Islander Showcase. The Festival Fringe complements the mainstream festival, providing a full-on week of zany entertainment.
February	The **Perth International Arts Festival** is the oldest annual international multi-arts festival in the southern hemisphere and is Western Australia's premier cultural event. The first Perth Festival was in 1953. It has come a long way since then and now offers the people of Western Australia some of the best international and contemporary drama, theatre, music, film, visual arts, street arts, literature, comedy and free community events. Other events on the program include the Western Australian Indigenous Arts Showcase (WAIAS) involving Indigenous singers and songwriters, musicians, actors and comedians from all over Australia's largest state.
March	The **Adelaide Festival** has created a strong tradition of innovation since 1960, inspiring celebration and presenting diverse art from across Australia and around the world. Held in the warm South Australian autumn in every 'even' year, it is a large-scale multi-arts event of extraordinary richness and diversity.
March	Tasmania's flagship celebration of island arts and culture, **Ten Days on the Island**, boasts a multitude of events in 50 locations across the island. Events and activities range across all types of music, dance, visual arts, theatre, literature, food and film. Individual artists and companies come from all corners of the globe, and a number of local artists also take part.
July	**Brisbane Festival** is Brisbane's foremost international multi-arts festival, offering an outstanding program of theatre, dance, music, opera, multimedia and free community events for the residents of Brisbane and its visitors. Held every two years, it endeavours to include the entire community in its program of activities by having intellectual rigour, international artistic credibility and an extremely broad grass-roots support base.
August	The **Darwin Festival** is a celebration of the city's uniqueness, celebrating its multicultural community, youthful energy and tropical climate. The cultural program provides a feast of local, national and international performances to excite, inspire and entertain. It includes opera, cabaret, dance, music, film, comedy, the visual arts and workshops—incorporating music and dance from Indigenous, Indonesian and Pacific Island communities. There is also a strong visual arts component, with traditional land owners guiding visitors through the many galleries exhibiting Indigenous art.
October	**Melbourne International Arts Festival** has a reputation for presenting unique international and Australian events in the fields of dance, theatre, music, visual arts, multimedia, free and outdoor events over 17 days each October.

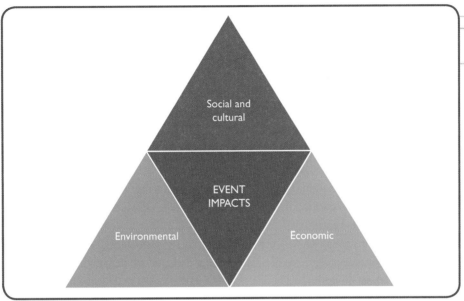

FIGURE 1.4
Impact of
events

Events such as the Australian Open Tennis Championships and the Melbourne Cup also have economic benefits, mainly through increases in domestic tourism and the multiplier effect. Tourism and events create jobs in the tertiary sector, and they also encourage growth in the primary and secondary sectors of industry. This is what is known as the multiplier effect, which in its simplest form is how many times money spent by a tourist circulates through a country's economy. Money spent at an event, attraction, restaurant or hotel helps to create jobs directly but it also creates jobs indirectly elsewhere in the economy. The restaurant, for example, has to buy food from local farmers, who may spend some of this money on other items. The demand for local products increases as tourists buy food, petrol, merchandise and souvenirs, which increases secondary employment. The multiplier effect continues until the money eventually 'leaks' from the economy through imports —the purchase of goods from other countries.

When researchers talk about the triple bottom line they are referring to economic, social and environmental impacts. Impacts can be both positive and negative; examples of negative impacts including:

★ gatecrashing, drug use at music events, drunken behaviour, parking inconvenience to locals (social impacts)

★ cost to taxpayers in provision of infrastructure and services such as policing (economic impact)

★ displacement of 'normal' visitors, e.g. at World Youth Day (social and economic impacts)

★ white elephants: new arenas and stadiums not being used enough (economic impact)

★ ill-defined careers due to the nature of the event industry and oversupply of graduates (social impacts)

★ waste, damage to environment, noise, etc. (environmental impacts).

There are of course many positive impacts, which is why events are supported and funded by many government agencies.

EVENT INDUSTRY BODIES AND ASSOCIATIONS

Support bodies and associations for the event industry include:

★ Business Events Australia—a specialist team within Tourism Australia
★ Meetings and Events Australia (MEA)—a national organisation representing members of the industry
★ Events Industry Association (EIA)—represents the events industry in Western Australia
★ Exhibition & Event Association of Australasia (EEAA)—the peak association for the exhibition and event industry
★ Regional Arts Australia (RAA)—the key national body representing the broad, complex interests and concerns of those working with and for the arts in regional, rural and remote Australia
★ Northern Territory Major Events Company—identifies and attracts major sporting and cultural events which have the potential to benefit the Northern Territory by providing substantial economic and social benefits.

Many other organisations fund and support events as well, including governmental bodies at federal, state and regional level.

EVENT CATEGORIES

Event categories help to explain the diversity of the industry and the scope of employment within it:

★ conference
★ symposium
★ exhibition
★ festival
★ promotional event
★ show (e.g. agricultural)
★ sporting
★ parade
★ cultural celebration
★ trade and consumer show
★ social event
★ private and public event
★ corporate event
★ charitable or fundraising event.

EVENT DIFFERENTIATION

When differentiating events, it is useful to look at the following variables:

★ purpose and objectives of the event (e.g. fundraising, product promotion)
★ scope of the event (e.g. single or multiple venues, road show)
★ nature of the audience (e.g. businesspeople, leisure tourists, locals)
★ marketing and distribution channels (e.g. online ticket sales, part of tourism product promotion such as Visit Melbourne, free entry/gold coin contribution at the gate)
★ key stakeholders (for major and hallmark events it is likely that government bodies will be key stakeholders)
★ key elements of staging (e.g. competition, display, parade, exhibition, conference).

Figure 1.5 illustrates these criteria using the Byron Bay Bluesfest as an example. As you can see, this event has clearly articulated aims and objectives and its position on sustainability is described in detail on the website, which also describes the audience and infrastructure required for the festival.

CAREER OPPORTUNITIES

There are many career opportunities in the event industry and these fall into two broad categories: the buyer and the supplier. The buyer is the person or organisation with financial responsibility for producing the event and as such the buyer calls the shots, organising venues, marketing, staging, etc. The supply side of the industry includes all those organisations that contribute goods and services, such as caterers, equipment hire companies, security services providers, etc. Event managers are known by many different titles such as Professional Conference Organiser, Race Director, Operations Manager, Logistics Coordinator and so forth.

An event manager is generally supported by a team which grows exponentially as the event draws near. A planning team of 12 that works together for a year can explode into a team of 500 for the short period of the event. This phenomenon was called the 'pulsing organization' by Alvin Toffler (1980), who coined the term to describe organisations that expand and contract in size. It is particularly applicable to organisations such as the Australian Open Tennis Championships, where staff numbers surge for a short period every year (Hanlon & Cuskelly 2002).

Aims and objectives	Scope	Audience	Marketing and distribution	Key stakeholders	Key staging elements
• Building institutional sustainability and management capacity • A culturally relevant festival • A festival that respects, transforms and grows local community • A zero waste festival • A carbon neutral festival • A festival site that is a functioning, healthy natural ecosystem	• 20th anniversary • Over 125 artists in a 5-day period • One of Australia's most acclaimed and respected festivals, despite size and audience numbers when compared to Big Day Out, Woodford, Tamworth Country Music Festival • Has won many awards	• 20 000 people will attend the festival each day • 6250 campers • Bluesfest prides itself on being an all ages family event, with female attendances in 2008 (54%) being slightly greater than males (46%), and approximately 28–30% of its audience being local	• Bluesfest website • Membership • Ticket sales, Ticketek • Ticket sales, other venues • Twitter • MySpace • Facebook	• Byron Shire Council • Charities • Sponsors • 1000 VIPs and guests • 50 festival staff • 100 stallholders and staff • Other contractors • Performers	• Permanent site at Tyagarah Tea Tree Farm • Camping • Temporary stages • Lighting and sound • Catering and waste • Security, fencing

FIGURE 1.5 Differentiating events, using Byron Bay Bluesfest as an example

Source: Based on information from Byron Bay Bluesfest website <www.bluesfest.com.au>.

It it is important to note that the event manager typically works with a number of contractors. These could include any or all of the following:

- ★ venue managers
- ★ stage managers
- ★ lighting, audio and video companies
- ★ decorators and florists
- ★ entertainers
- ★ employment agencies
- ★ rental companies
- ★ public relations and marketing consultants
- ★ security companies
- ★ catering companies
- ★ cleaning companies
- ★ ticketing operations
- ★ printers.

ETHICAL AND LEGAL ISSUES FOR THE EVENT INDUSTRY

Legal issues will be discussed in detail in Chapter 24. Here, we will briefly look at duty of care, safety, OHS, risk management and insurance, as risk is higher for the event industry than for many other industries.

LEGAL ISSUES

Duty of care is the responsibility shown by organisations to all people attending an event, whether staff, visitors or contractors on site. This responsibility is covered more specifically under OHS legislation in Chapter 9, which looks closely at occupational health and safety and establishing policies and procedures that must be implemented in all workplaces. Risk management is an approach used to identify potential risks, analyse and evaluate them, and implement risk treatments. Some treatments are preventive, such as the use of barriers and barricades or police on horseback, while other treatments apply when risks cannot be prevented, for example, first aid emergencies. Insurance, in the form of public liability insurance, is compulsory for all event venues, organisations and contractors in case of an accident involving a member of the public. Workers compensation insurance is also compulsory for all employers.

It is obligatory to ensure that where licences are required they are validated and up to date, and in the events business this includes licences for rigging, fork lift operation and use of fireworks.

Liaison and approval from local government

There are a number of local government acts and regulations that may apply to the event. These vary considerably from one area to another. Detailed guidelines are provided by some councils, whereas others are more informal. The size of the event determines to a large extent the detail required in the submission since smaller events tend to have low impacts on the community.

An event organiser may need to meet different requirements even if the event has been held in another council area with approval. Likewise, if the event covers more than one jurisdiction, more than one proposal may need to be submitted.

A development application for permanent structures is generally required. This links to the Local Environment Plan (LEP), which is the community's vision for the future of the area. Application for the use of premises and property for entertainment may be necessary. Plans for erecting temporary structures will need to be developed and application made to council. Approvals are required by most councils for:

★ using loudspeakers or amplifiers in public spaces
★ installing amusement devices
★ charging fees for singing or providing entertainment in public places
★ using a building or structure for entertainment (change of approval classification).

Of course, councils are most interested in the cleaning programs planned for during and after the event. They also demand that the site or venue be returned in the same condition as prior to the event.

Other relevant acts and regulations cover clean air, clean water and noise. Noise is a particularly troublesome problem for festivals and events since by their very nature they attract crowds. Entertainment events are particularly loud, so it is essential to check noise limitations in terms of decibels and times during which music is permitted. Discharge of sewage, oil and other waste into water systems is illegal and the waterways are protected by a number of acts in the states and territories.

ETHICAL ISSUES

Ethical industry practices may relate to:

★ procedures for payment of commissions
★ bookings at venues
★ confidentiality of contracts, personnel and performers
★ overbooking
★ subcontractors not meeting standards
★ exploiting volunteers
★ pricing and scalping
★ providing free of charge entry
★ tolerating unsociable behaviour.

When running events for under 18s, control of unsociable behaviour is vitally important. Many Schoolies Week destinations have put in place a broad series of risk management strategies to keep celebrating teenagers as safe as possible.

A search of the internet using the words 'ticket fiasco' will result in examples of ticketing problems at events, most notable being the Edinburgh Fringe Festival in 2009. An independent report concluded: 'Implementation suffered from inadequate project control, insufficient resources, overreliance on key individuals and insufficient independent scrutiny at key milestones' (Carrell 2009). Getting ticketing right is crucial, particularly where there are lots of young people in attendance, as party rage can erupt when ticket holders are barred from entering a venue because it has reached capacity due to overselling.

Careful appointment of contractors, ideally through an objective tendering and reference checking process, is also advised.

The International Special Events Society (ISES) has the following code of ethics, which is a useful guide for event managers:

★ Promote and encourage the highest level of ethics within the profession of the special events industry while maintaining the highest standards of professional conduct

★ Strive for excellence in all aspects of our profession by performing consistently at or above acceptable industry standards

★ Use only legal and ethical means in all industry negotiations and activities

★ Protect the public against fraud and unfair practices and promote all practices which bring credit to the profession

★ Maintain adequate and appropriate insurance coverage for all business activities

★ Maintain industry standard of safety and sanitation

★ Provide truthful and accurate information with respect to the performance of duties

★ Use a written contract stating all changes, services, products, performance expectations and other essential information.

EVENT INDUSTRY TECHNOLOGY

The event industry is similar to tourism in that most event products (tickets) are purchased online through an e-commerce option. Indeed, it could be argued that the anticipatory build-up to an event, which involves frequent visits to the event website to study the program, is part of the final fleeting marketing product. Thus the design and maintenance of the event's website is vitally important, as it is here that the consumer looks for the event line-up or the history of competition.

In addition to e-commerce, advances in technology allow many other activities to be carried out online. For example, event planners, including brides, can plan online the size of the function, the menus, the layout of the venue, and even develop a budget prior to contacting a salesperson.

Technological advances are also evident in audio and video production, offering larger and larger screens, better vision and remote conferencing. Security systems are becoming increasingly complex, and even banquet chefs employ computerised cooking and refrigeration processes.

The main technology solutions used by the industry include:

★ project planning software (Gantt charts and PERT charts used for critical path analysis)

★ venue booking systems (for leasing and contracting venues and services)

★ audience reservation and registration systems (used for concert ticketing, conference bookings, races and competitions)

★ identification and accreditation systems (to capture data about individuals attending exhibitions or race officials working in the field of play)

★ employee records and police checks

★ security systems (for managing assets, checking inventory, monitoring crowd movements)

★ CAD systems (for designing stages, stands and venues)

★ timing and scoring systems

★ broadcasting systems (e.g. big screen replays, closed circuit for judging)
★ communications systems (e.g. radio).

Given the wide range of applications used at a major event, a sophisticated IT team is needed for installation of computer networks, customisation of software and integration of the tasks performed by the software packages.

UPDATING KNOWLEDGE OF THE EVENT INDUSTRY

There are many ways to update event industry knowledge, for example, through supplier websites and the media. One important resource is the online publication of event planning guides by government organisations. These detailed outlines for planning and proposal development are exceptionally useful, as too are the extensive guidelines on event safety, risk management and emergency planning.

There are many opportunities to visit and observe events and to participate in industry seminars and training courses. Membership of industry associations such as MEA (Meetings and Events Association) can provide opportunities for professional development and informal networking. Industry journals, all available online, are another important source of current information.

By staying up to date with industry trends, you can take advantage of new technologies, stay abreast of legislative changes and monitor consumer trends. Legal issues that concern professionals working in the industry, such as public liability, duty of care, licensing, risk management, and occupational health and safety, are all newsworthy, with case studies emerging in the media almost daily.

Staying up to date can be done by:
★ reading newspapers
★ attending industry seminars
★ participating in training seminars
★ upgrading and extending qualifications
★ joining relevant associations
★ participating in industry association activities
★ networking with colleagues
★ reading industry journals
★ subscribing to industry magazines (e.g. *MiceNet*)
★ internet research.

As mentioned earlier, careers in the event business are extremely varied, few having the title Event Manager. Conventions, exhibitions, sports competitions, product launches, charity gala dinners, incentive tours and music performances all come under the umbrella of event management. The skills required are largely in the area of project management, covering the full range of traditional business skills, but applied in a more challenging, dynamic and deadline-driven environment. Continuing research and reading will enable you to develop a better understanding of this evolving professional field and the many players involved, ranging from government to business to community groups.

SUMMARY

This chapter has highlighted the important role played by events, particularly in relation to economic and social benefits to communities. Business events, in particular, have been singled out by governments due to the significant role they play in boosting tourism revenues. This is also the case for sporting events, large and small. And the area of arts and entertainment is clearly of interest to the younger demographic, with music festivals becoming increasingly popular. The importance of safety is indicated by the level of attention paid to compliance with legislation and regulation. Planning and monitoring of safety is undertaken using risk management as a tool. Deaths of young people at music festivals have prompted increasing concern among government bodies and event organisations, with many preventive measures being implemented. For all these reasons, it is important for all those working in this exciting industry to keep up to date with trends and developments in the industry.

Chapter review questions

1 The economic, social and environmental impacts of events can be both positive and negative. Give an example of both positive and negative impacts using specific events as examples.
2 Describe how new technologies have impacted on one sector of the event industry such as sport or music.
3 Explain why regional areas are keen to host events.
4 In some cases a careful balance is necessary to manage the impacts of an event on the surrounding community. Using a specific example, describe some of the concerns that the commercial operators and residents might have regarding an event in their neighbourhood.
5 Describe five key ways in which negative impacts of events can be managed effectively by councils and other government agencies.

Activity

Investigate two events (ideally two that are quite different) and describe them in detail. You might like to do your research on the internet, starting with one of the state or territory tourism websites such as <www.tourism.nsw.gov.au> or <www.mcvb.com.au>, or you could visit your local council. If you are attending an event, use the questions in Appendix A to guide you.

Case study

Student rave party

A group of university students decided to hold a rave party in the mountains in December and advertised it on the internet. Three bands attended the three-day party and there was 24-hour music. One young girl described it as living hell, although why she stayed is unfathomable. 'The dance area was in a valley and to get a drink of water you had to climb a steep hill. Even then, the water was dirty and brown. The toilets were so far away that

continued

Case study (continued)

nobody bothered to use them. The music pounded all night and the floor vibrated so you couldn't sleep. My friend was unwell and there was no medical help. The organisers didn't have a clue. They just wanted to make a fast buck.'

Questions

1 What are some of the things that could go wrong, or have gone wrong, at similar events?
2 List three ways in which the organisers were negligent.
3 List three ways in which the event could have been improved.
4 This event was described to the authorities as a cultural festival. Do you think this was accurate?
5 The legal compliance issues of such an event will be covered in a later chapter. However, what are some of the ethical issues involved in this and other events?

References

Anderson, S (2010), 'Oh what a sight … the highs and the lows', *Sydney Morning Herald*, 2 January.

Carrell, S (2009), 'Edinburgh festival: report slams Fringe ticketing fiasco', *guardian.co.uk*, 4 February.

Getz, D (2005), *Event management and event tourism*, 2nd edn, Cognizant Communication Corp., New York.

Goldblatt, J (2005), *Special events: event leadership for a new world*, John Wiley & Sons, Hoboken, NJ.

Hanlon, C & Cuskelly, G (2002), 'Pulsating major sporting events organizations: a framework for management personnel', *Event Management*, 7(4):231–43.

McRae, H (2010), 'The science of success', *The Deal*, March, <www.newsspace.com.au/www.newsspace.com.au_thedeal>, accessed 5 May 2010.

Ninomiya, K (2008), 'Olympic boon to trade with China', *Suite 101.com*, <www.suite101.com/search.cfm?searchType=1&q=Olympic+boon+to+trade+with+China>, accessed 5 May 2010.

Sands, L (2008), 'The 2008 Olympics impact on China', *China Business Review*, <https://chinabusinessreview.com/public/0807/sands.html>, accessed 4 May 2010.

Toffler, A (1980), *The third wave*, Pan Books, London.

CHAPTER 2

EVENT CONCEPTS

This unit describes the performance outcomes, skills and knowledge required to develop the overall concept, theme and format for a complex event comprising multiple components. This unit applies to the overall concept development process for any type of event. It may be relevant in any industry context, but has particular application in the cultural, community, hospitality, sporting and tourism sectors.

Concept development occurs at the commencement of the event management cycle and involves the application of significant analytical, creative and conceptual skills teamed with sound operational management expertise. Sometimes the concept development phase is undertaken as part of the event bidding process. An event manager or other individual often in the event sponsoring organisation undertakes this role in consultation with a range of event stakeholders and sometimes under the guidance of an event organising committee.

The unit does not include the specialist concept development undertaken by experts such as writers, technical specialists or lighting, sound, exhibition, set or costume designers. Consultation with relevant experts, however, may be a key aspect of overall event concept development.

Elements

- Establish overall event objectives and scope
- Establish event concept, theme and format
- Evaluate and progress concept to operational stage.

Critical aspects for assessment

- Ability to develop an event concept and format that are **operationally practical** and result in the achievement of event objectives
- Knowledge of typical formats and specific components for different types of events
- Development of a concept, theme and format for a **complex event** to meet a specified need

A complex event comprising multiple components must involve:

- need for a comprehensive and multifaceted event plan
- need for a formal internal or external communications strategy
- a dedicated and diverse event budget
- multiple administrative and operational components
- a wide range of stakeholders
- an event operations team.

WHY an Elvis Festival in Parkes? Parkes has a bunch of passionate Elvis fans—one local Elvis fan has even changed his name to Elvis by deed poll and another local couple operated 'Gracelands Restaurant' for many years. The Festival concept was conceived by these and other passionate community members, who saw potential for a fun event. January was identified as the perfect time to stage the event, being a slow time in local tourism and also coinciding with Elvis Presley's birthday (8th January). The first Festival was held in Parkes in January 1993. The Festival has sparked a boom in awareness of Parkes as a tourist destination. Since the Australian movie *The Dish* hit the big screen, Parkes  has been best known as the home of Radio Telescope, but now the town has become widely recognised as the 'Elvis Capital of Australia'!

Source: <www.parkeselvisfestival.com.au/about/index.htm>. Courtesy of 'Country Link Parkes Elvis Festival'.

The Elvis Festival in Parkes highlighted above has grown over the years, expanding from a few hundred people attending 10 years ago to the current level of 10 000 attendees. Many festivals and events grow in this way, often surprising their founding bodies. In other cases, the concept is carefully researched and linked to market trends, consumer behaviour and emerging fashions. Perhaps this is indicative of the art–science balance of the event business: it takes real flair to develop innovative, creative ideas and a lot of hard work and attention to detail to pull it off. Some events develop organically over time, while others are carefully planned and plotted, developing in a linear manner. As this chapter shows, the team that runs an event needs to attend to the creative core concept as well as the logistics of its implementation.

ESTABLISH EVENT PURPOSE, OBJECTIVES AND SCOPE

Before clarifying and agreeing on the purpose and key objectives of an event, it is necessary to take into account the different perspectives of the event stakeholders. It is most important to understand the concept of 'a stakeholder' in relation to event management. This is because there are generally multiple stakeholders who contribute to the development of the event concept and its implementation. There are various definitions of this term, ranging from the broad idea that a stakeholder is a person who can affect or will be affected by the event, to the more specific idea that a stakeholder is a person of influence but not directly involved in the work. Clearly, this definition could also include an organisation, such as a government authority.

Getz (1997) states that 'stakeholders are those people and groups with a stake in the event and its outcomes, including all groups participating in the event production, sponsors and grant-givers, community representatives, and anyone impacted by the event' (p. 15). Alternatively, the model developed by Allen et al. (2008) includes six major event stakeholder groups: the host organisation, host community, co-workers, event sponsors, media, and participants/spectators.

To clarify the concept of stakeholder, the best example is that of a wedding, where everyone has an opinion about how things should be done, including the mother-in-law. In the tradition of most weddings, the father is the client as he is paying for the wedding, and the bride and groom are the participants. Presumably the father would veto ideas that were too expensive and the mother-in-law anything that was too outlandish. There are also contractors, such as the celebrant, florist, caterer, etc. who have a stake in the planning as they too have limitations, not least of which is the budget. In all event environments there are many stakeholders, sometimes with conflicting opinions, ideas and objectives. There are also constraints that limit the scope of the event project, including the aforementioned budget, the size of the venue, accessibility, availability, and so on.

Thus, in developing an event plan, analysing event information and consulting with stakeholders to determine the broad scope of the event is the first step. As mentioned, these stakeholders may include (see also Figure 2.1):

★ event principal (key person in host organisation, or client)
★ organising committee
★ sponsors, donors
★ local community
★ local authorities (e.g. council, emergency services, environmental authority)
★ service contractors (e.g. staging, cleaning, catering, security)
★ suppliers
★ performers, entertainers, participants
★ spectators, audience
★ media.

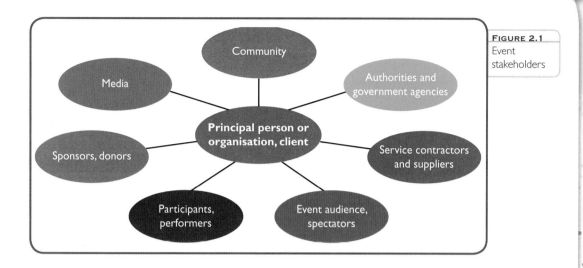

FIGURE 2.1
Event
stakeholders

PURPOSE OF THE EVENT

Numerous factors need to be considered in developing the event concept. The most important of these is the purpose of the event, although the purpose is also strongly linked to both the theme and the venue. In some instances, defining the purpose may be difficult. For example, a discussion with 10 people about the purpose of a wedding is likely to lead to many different ideas such as 'to formalise a relationship', 'to make a commitment', 'to show off to relatives', 'to have a big party', and these ideas do not even include a religious element. However, they will need to work out the purpose—the one thing that summarises the primary aim of the wedding—to ensure its success.

The purpose of the event should drive all planning and assist in sorting out differences of opinion and managing conflict. For example, if you were running a conference for financial planners, there could be two quite different purposes:

1. To facilitate an exchange of information, bringing participants up to date with the latest changes in financial planning software products.
2. To achieve a memorable out-of-body experience for financial planners in order to develop a positive association with a new software product.

Achieving the first purpose would be quite straightforward, as this would require a fairly standard meeting or convention. Fulfilling the second purpose, however, would be more difficult. For this unforgettable experience you would need a unique venue and carefully planned activities that the participants would enjoy. At the same time, the product would need to be reinforced constantly so that attendees would leave with an inescapable association with it. To have the fun without the positive association would defeat the purpose.

The focus of the first of these purposes is **information**, while that of the second is **entertainment**.

While for many events the main purpose is making a **profit**, for many it is not. The mission statement of the Maleny Scarecrow Carnival in Figure 2.2 is an excellent example of an event with a **community** purpose.

FIGURE 2.2

Example of an event with a community purpose

Maleny Scarecrow Carnival

Mission Statement (purpose)

To make this unique event an annual celebration of Maleny's rich cultural and social diversity. To present an opportunity for the community to unite and share creative energy, spirit and pride.

Background

The aim of the celebration is to enrich the social and cultural fabric of our community. Since ancient times, scarecrows have been used by almost every culture in a rural context; in most instances, in the belief that their presence would increase fertility and enrich the harvest.

The Maleny Scarecrow Carnival began in 1998 with the concept of a cultural event that would enhance Maleny's distinctive rural qualities and offer a unique opportunity for the local and wider communities to express their creativity. It is difficult to imagine a more perfect setting for hundreds of artistic and whimsical scarecrows than the rolling emerald green hills of Maleny. The event is based on the creation and display of scarecrows throughout the Sunshine Coast hinterland. It is comprised of four major facets:

- Scarecrow Masquerade
- Scarecrow Discovery Trail
- Scarecrow Contest
- Scarecrow Fiesta.

The Carnival coincides with the September school holidays to maximise the opportunity for families, the local community and visitors to participate in a wide range of activities.

The Maleny Scarecrow Carnival provides broad-based regional economic benefits consistent with community values and encourages involvement from all sectors of the community. In doing so, it heightens community awareness of various local groups and services as well as providing the opportunity for entertainers and artisans to showcase their creative skills. Most importantly, the Carnival is based on whole family participation, from toddlers right through to grandparents. Following on from the overwhelming success of the inaugural event in 1998, the organisers are building on the framework already in place. Interactive skill development workshops will add a new dimension and greater opportunities for members of the community to participate.

People involved include community and support groups, hospitals, libraries, Chambers of Commerce, schools, preschools and kindergartens, tour groups, garden clubs, retirement villages, businesses, sporting clubs, service groups and, of course, individuals. It is most interesting to note that 14 towns outside Maleny participated in the Scarecrow Contest; many well beyond the Sunshine Coast hinterland. We even received international involvement, including 30 miniature scarecrows sent by the children of the Australian International School in Singapore.

We have initiated relationships with other scarecrow festivals throughout the world, including Japan, Canada, USA and Europe, and our aim in the future is to seek international participation, with a view to expanding the cross-cultural elements available to the community.

OBJECTIVES OF THE EVENT

Planning for an event should also involve defining specific, measurable objectives. These might include targets for the following:

- ★ number of people attending
- ★ number of participants
- ★ contributions of sponsors
- ★ value of grants and donations
- ★ break-even or amount of profit
- ★ goals for charitable contributions
- ★ level of media exposure
- ★ number of repeat visitors
- ★ value of merchandise sold
- ★ value of food and beverage sold
- ★ number of exhibitors, stall holders.

Establishing objectives helps keep the organisers or the event manager focused on what they wish to achieve. Measuring the outcomes against the objectives assists planning of future events.

SCOPE OF THE EVENT

Related to the purpose and objectives of the event is its scope. This encompasses the date, time and duration of the event and its size. The scope of the event is dependent on available resources. Resources that may be required include human resources (e.g. the number of volunteers), physical resources (e.g. equipment or infrastructure) and financial resources (e.g. sponsorship)—there is nothing like a tight budget to get the committee focused!

Timing is another critical factor here. It is essential to ensure that the event does not clash with other similar events during a peak season. In almost every country, spring is the time when most festivals and sporting events are held. This creates a competitive environment as the general public have lots of options for the first week in September (or April in the northern hemisphere) and few for weekends in mid-winter. Clearly, a night-time outdoor event in mid winter would not be a sensible option.

Let's now look at some of the factors that may have a bearing on the development of the event concept.

ESTABLISH EVENT CONCEPT, THEME AND FORMAT

All of the above factors—the purpose, the objectives and scope of the event, available and potential resources, timing—will impose restrictions on concept development. The extent of the lead time may also impose limits on the concept. For example, a short lead time may mean that the performers or venues that the organisers were considering may not be available. Support by the management of potential host organisations, such as sporting associations or councils, may be withdrawn. But the most constraining factor, generally, is the extent of financial resources and/or voluntary commitment to the event.

Of course, there are events where money is no object. Many celebrity weddings immediately come to mind, as do elaborate corporate events. But with a little imagination, it is still possible to come up with an event concept that is innovative and appealing and does not break the bank. This may involve adapting existing ideas, developing new ideas, or incorporating or experimenting with new technologies.

Once the concept is clear, a suitable location needs to be found, bearing in mind that many event-specific environments provide ready-made decor and tried and tested services. However, the concept may be designed for a more exotic location or venue, requiring more complex planning, particularly if the event is to be held outdoors.

Risk management is an important consideration in both concept development and event planning. Risk management involves analysis of the likelihood and consequence of potential risks, such as threats to health and safety of staff and attendees, volunteers not contributing as much time as expected or a sponsor deciding to withdraw at the last minute. (Risk management is covered in depth in Chapter 26.)

A wide range of implementation factors also need to be considered, beginning with the theme and venue, which are closely tied to the event concept. These are discussed on page 28.

THEME

The theme of the event should be linked to the purpose. It should be completely compatible with guest/audience needs and consistent in all respects. Most events adopt a colour scheme that is repeated on all items produced for the event, such as tickets, programs, uniforms, decor, posters and merchandise. This helps attendees to identify with the theme.

Potential themes are endless, limited only by your imagination and the customer's pocket. Some examples include:

★ historical   ★ entertainment
★ geographical   ★ artistic
★ cultural   ★ food and wine
★ sporting   ★ objects (e.g. CDs, boats).
★ musical

When coming up with ideas for a theme, it is most important to consider the range of suitable venues available, keeping in mind the constraints of budget and other considerations.

VENUE

The event manager needs to carefully consider the planning implications of choosing an unusual venue in preference to a standard venue requiring decoration only to match the theme. Lighting, sound and catering also provide challenges in unusual settings. This will become more evident in the logistics section later in this chapter.

The following are examples of unusual venues:

★ demolition site   ★ amusement park
★ parking lot   ★ orchard
★ tunnel   ★ vineyard
★ museum   ★ aquarium.
★ research facility

The remaking of the Australian Open is an example of a fully integrated event venue and theme. The Australian Open is the only sporting event in the world boasting two retractable roofs at its venue. When not in use for tennis, retractable seating moves away to reveal a velodrome, which is used for cycling events.

Many venues provide enormous flexibility and can be readily transformed to meet the requirements of the theme. The range is extremely wide—from hotel banquet rooms, conference centres and theatres to sporting venues.

When considering the choice of venue, the event organiser needs to look at a number of factors, including:

★ potential to fulfil the purpose of the event   ★ built features (such as stages)
★ ambience   ★ cost of decoration, sound and lighting
★ location   ★ cost of labour
★ access by public transport   ★ logistics of setting up
★ parking   ★ food and beverage facilities
★ seating capacity   ★ safety.

There are many, many other factors that need to be taken into account in selecting an event venue, but the overall strategy should be to aim for the best possible fit with the client's and the audience's needs at the lowest possible cost. If all stages, props, carpets, seating, portable kitchens, refrigerators and so on have to be hired, the cost will be very hard to justify—even if the venue seems perfect in other ways.

EVENT AUDIENCE

When organising an event, the needs of all participants must be considered before finalising the concept. When one of Australia's best known athletes was invited to give a presentation at an event attended by approximately 200 people, the rental agency said that they were unable to provide a ramp to the stage for her wheelchair and wanted to compromise by asking members of the audience to lift her chair onto the stage. This was clearly unacceptable. In this situation, the response from the event coordinator is 'Find one!'

In the example of the entertainment-based event held for the financial planners (conservative stereotype!), an organiser would be wise to challenge normal behaviour and encourage participation in unusual activities. However, great care would need to be taken to ensure that such an audience were not pushed beyond its conservative limits. At a similar event, an event coordinator found that persuading the audience to wear unusual hats was all that it took to break them out of their normal patterns of interaction. Of course, every audience is different, and the event manager needs to go with the flow and direct the event to meet audience response. This can involve sudden changes in plan.

FINANCIAL CONSIDERATIONS

The topic of financial management will be covered in detail in Chapter 29. However, it is an important consideration at this early stage of event concept and design. Initial financial estimates can get out of control very easily, and the choice of event concept can certainly contribute to this. Otherwise good ideas should be knocked on the head at an early stage if they do not appear financially viable as it is possible to come up with concepts that are startling in their simplicity and also cost effective. This is where the creative and rational aspects of the event manager's abilities can come into conflict. Very often the creative aspect wins—sometimes at the expense of the company's profit on the event.

TIMING OF THE EVENT

The timing of an event is often linked to the season or weather. For example, a food and wine festival would be better programmed for early autumn than for mid-summer when the heat would be intolerable for both the audience and the stall holders. And mid-winter is certainly not the time to hold a flower show. While this might seem obvious, it is surprising how often events are programmed to occur at very unsuitable times. The timing of sporting events is, of course, limited by the sporting season and their traditional competitions. Broadcast to international audiences is another consideration. Television schedules for local and international events are tightly managed, and live television broadcasts need to be carefully planned. Not every sporting enthusiast is keen to stay up all night for a delayed broadcast and this is always a consideration for major sporting competitions held in one time zone and broadcast in another.

Evaluation of an event concept must take into account the following four time-related factors:

1 season   2 day of the week   3 time of day   4 duration.

Generally, mid-winter events are poorly attended, while event audiences are faced with an oversupply of events in spring.

Closely linked to this concept of timing (in the sense of scheduling on the event calendar) is the topic of lead time. This is the time available for planning and implementation. Last-minute requests are very difficult to manage. For the event manager, a long lead time is preferable, allowing adequate time to develop the event specifications and commence contract negotiation with suppliers and other contractors.

The duration of the event is another consideration, with multiple-day events providing the biggest challenges as the venue has to be cleared, cleaned and restocked between sessions.

EVENT TEAM, CONTRACTORS AND OTHER STAKEHOLDERS

The skills of the event team and, just as importantly, the contractors, such as lighting technicians and catering staff, are an important consideration in terms of concept development. Staff working at most events have very limited opportunity for training, making job breakdowns and task sheets essential aspects of planning. In addition, stakeholders such as the waterways police, the Environmental Protection Authority and the transport authority have all sorts of requirements that could challenge the feasibility of an event, and these must be investigated.

The following list is not exhaustive but provides an idea of the many people involved in staging an event:

★ talent/performer/team and manager
★ cast and crew
★ contractors (service providers)
★ suppliers
★ employees
★ volunteers
★ emergency services.

EVALUATE THE FEASIBILITY OF THE CONCEPT

The following elements are covered only briefly here since they are revisited in a number of later chapters. The aim of introducing them here is to raise awareness of the problems and pitfalls that can occur if they are not considered at this early stage of concept development. In addition, if not dealt with, they can have a negative impact on the event planner's creativity.

COMPETITION

Prior to involvement in any event, it is essential to conduct an analysis of your competition. This involves looking at the timing and duration of other events, even if they are unrelated. People have limited disposable income and festivals and events tend to be non-essential items in most family and tourist budgets. A wider study would include an analysis of the political, environmental, social and technological impacts, known as environmental scanning. This would place the event in a broader context.

REGULATIONS

A wide range of laws and regulations have an impact on the staging of events and these can severely limit creativity. As a simple example, releasing balloons into the atmosphere is considered environmentally unfriendly. Parking, traffic and neighbourhood impact, especially in terms of timing and noise, are all aspects that require the event manager's liaison with local or state government.

MARKETING

How to sell an event is a very important part of the initial planning, the timing of your marketing efforts being crucial. Do you advertise months beforehand or the day or week before? Will the audience turn up on the day? How can you encourage them to do so? Should you sell tickets in advance? (Many events actually have no advance ticket sales.) All these questions require the decision-making skills of the event manager or the event management team.

COMMUNITY IMPACT

The impact of an event on the local or wider community and others is a major consideration of the planning stage. Local traders and other lobby groups can raise hell for the unprepared event organiser, so it is absolutely essential that community benefits are explained and other impacts considered as part of the event proposal.

RISK

The weather is the greatest risk to attendance, enjoyment and success for most events. (You will be reminded of this at several points throughout this book.) Drought-breaking storms forced the evacuation of 400 campers at the 2004 Tamworth Country Music Festival, and created a muddy mess reminiscent of Woodstock at the Brisbane Big Day Out. However, participants were excited to see the rain at these events, which were both scheduled at times when heavy rain was least expected. Measures to counteract the impact of the weather are essential aspects of event feasibility planning. You must also be aware that insurance premiums will be linked to the perceived risk to the safety of participants.

There are many risks associated with events and Chapters 17, 18 and 26 cover this topic in detail. Risks may include, among many others:

- ★ cancellation by a key performer
- ★ non-arrival of equipment
- ★ technical failure
- ★ transportation crisis
- ★ accidents.

REVENUE AND EXPENDITURE

Losing money is the fastest way to get out of the event business. For this reason, the event concept (and the investment in event design) needs very careful analysis. So too does the topic of cash flow. In almost every case, contractors for catering, security and other services require deposits and payment in full prior to the event, which can cause cash flow problems if there are no advance ticket sales.

DESIGN THE EVENT

Consistency and links to the purpose of the event are all essential parts of the creative process in designing an event. The following are the main creative elements that must be considered.

THEME

As Goldblatt (2005) points out, the theme should ideally appeal to all senses: touch, smell, taste, sight and hearing. If the aim of the event is to transport the audience, appealing to all the senses will contribute positively to the outcome. Keep in mind, once again, the needs of the audience when planning, for example, what music will be played. As we all know, taste in music and desirable sound level vary enormously from one audience to another.

LAYOUT

This creative element is so often given far too little consideration. Consider events that you have attended in which you have felt socially uncomfortable. Your discomfort was generally the result of too much open space, too much light or the limited opportunity for people to mix. The worst scenario is being seated at a long, wide table where you are too far away to talk to those opposite and are stuck with people you have little in common with on your left and right. And to add insult to injury the venue is ablaze with light. Worse still is the cocktail party in a huge ballroom where a small circle develops in the centre—not small enough, though, for everyone to talk. The audience needs to comfortably fill the venue to create a positive ambience.

Event with an Australian theme

DECOR

Fabrics, decorative items, stage props, drapes and table settings can all be hired and it is generally worthwhile investigating these options before settling on the event theme as hiring items can reduce costs enormously. Floral arrangements need to be ordered from florists experienced in larger events. Australian native plants, some of them up to 2 metres high, can produce a stunning effect. In many ballrooms the floral arrangements are elevated above the table, on tall stands, so that guests can talk to each other more easily. The effect is quite dramatic, with the floral arrangements dominating the decor.

SUPPLIERS

Good relationships with suppliers of all commodities will ensure that only quality products will be received, including the freshest flowers and the best produce the markets can supply. During most large events, suppliers are pressed for the best quality from all their customers at a time when volumes are much larger than usual. This is when a good long-standing relationship with a supplier is invaluable. It was reported that at Atlanta during the 1996 Olympic Games you could not buy tissues or towels anywhere. The success of the Olympic Games in Sydney was due to early planning (especially of menus), allowing farmers and other suppliers to sign contracts well in advance. Consider for a moment that some of the flowers had to be planted years before the event! So, too, some of the fruit and vegetables, which were in good supply despite it being the off-season.

TECHNICAL REQUIREMENTS

Few people would have attended an event or meeting where there wasn't a single technical glitch. Speakers put their notes on the laptop and the screen starts changing at a phenomenal rate. Screensavers come on when the speaker goes on too long, the presentation is halted and file names appear on the screen. While none of these problems are caused by technical support, there are ways in which they can be reduced. Technical glitches by the contracted company are unacceptable. Microphones must have back-ups, the power supply must be assured, stages and video screens must be visible to all in the audience. There is no substitute for wide-ranging experience and this is a key attribute that should be sought when choosing technical contractors. New technology, especially anything used to demonstrate new products, needs to be tested thoroughly through many rehearsals. A back-up system is essential.

There are times when an event concept should remain just that because it is technically impossible.

STAGING

Many events require professional staging and there are companies which specialise in this. Staging Rentals, for example, has completed a wide range of projects over 20 years of operation, including product launches, road shows, fashion shows, exhibition stands, conferences, award presentations, media launches, concerts, gala dinners and fabulous parties, to name a few. Staging Rentals has a wide range of specialist skills resident in the company, including logistics and installation. However, technical effects, such as firework displays, may require other specific specialist skills.

ENTERTAINMENT

For some events, entertainment is central; for others, it is peripheral. The most important thing is that the entertainment suits the purpose of the event, not detracts from it. The needs of the event audience must be carefully considered when making this decision.

A clown creating balloon art is something one would consider for a children's party. However, the same idea (with different designs) could also work extremely well at a wedding reception while guests are waiting for the photography session to finish.

TALENT

Closely allied to the previous point, talent may come in the form of musical performers, dancers, athletes, golfers, conference speakers, etc. When the talent is the focal point for an event, management of the talent is exceptionally important. This includes meeting their essential needs as well as their many personal preferences for hotel rooms and unique foods! Most performers and top sports men and women have very clear requirements that must be obtained well in advance, particularly if there are staging needs for which equipment is specialised and perhaps not readily available.

CATERING

Nothing makes participants at an event more frustrated than delays in service and poor quality food—except, perhaps, lack of toilet facilities! While guests may have patience with other delays, they will become very agitated if hours are spent in queues, especially if these are away from the action. Food quality and selection are notoriously bad, and outrageously expensive, at many events and planning must take this into account. These days an espresso coffee cart can be found every few metres at most events, reflecting changes in the expectations of the audience and event managers' response to this. Creative event planning frequently requires unique or unusual food and beverage products and these can take time to find. They may even need to be imported. Time means money, as does importing, and both can contribute to an escalation in costs.

SERVICE

Finally, the service elements of the event need to be considered. As Matheson (2009) suggests, the intangible aspects of the event are vitally important. These include the atmosphere or ambience and the factors that contribute to the uniqueness of the visitors' experience. This is provided largely by staff and/or volunteers. Outsourcing to service contractors is a consideration, but these employees need to make their contribution to the event ambience. First impressions count, and being greeted by a surly security officer certainly won't enhance the atmosphere. The outfits worn by the event workforce also contribute to the atmosphere, as does their enthusiasm and energy. In some cases, actors are employed to ramp up the drama of the event experience still further.

Having given consideration to the above factors, the operational practicality of the concept, theme and format needs to be considered. For a banquet on a beach for example, catering provided the biggest challenges, the bluebottles being a secondary inconvenience. For this event, lifesavers were seconded to provide service despite their lack of training in this area. They were, however, able to respond knowledge-

Fine dining with a beach theme

ably to questions and no doubt contributed far more to the event experience than agency waiters.

Berridge (2007), the author of *Events design and experience*, stresses the importance of design having a focus and considering the use of space and flow of movement (p. 97). He gives the example of an exhibition in which the zones provided different experiences for the visitors. This is illustrated locally in the royal (agricultural) shows held in Australia and New Zealand. Clearly, there is more to design than just the visual impact of the event. Berridge's text is recommended for the creative aspects of event design.

PROGRESS THE CONCEPT TO OPERATIONAL STAGE

The next stage involves developing a summary of key logistical requirements based on the overall concept, theme and format. Accurate and complete information should then be provided to all relevant stakeholders, including councils and other authorities, so that any necessary formal approvals can be received before planning is too far advanced.

The following logistical elements must be taken into account when considering an event concept:

★ access to the site (Can vehicles come close enough for off-loading or parking?)
★ physical limitations (Will the size or shape of the stairs make it impossible to move heavy equipment?)
★ dimensions of the site (Is it too high, too low, too narrow?)
★ refrigerated storage (Is it sufficient?)
★ physical space for food preparation (Is it too small?)
★ toilet facilities (Are they fixed or portable?)
★ cleaning (Is it contracted?)
★ catering (Will there be any physical problems with transporting, storing and serving food?)
★ safety (Are patrols, exits, fire procedures, first aid, etc. all in place?)
★ potential damage to the site (Is there a danger of flowerbeds being trampled?)
★ provision of basic services (Are water and electricity laid on?).

This chapter illustrates the careful balance required between the creative and rational aspects of decision-making when considering an event concept. Brainstorming by the planning team will generate ideas but these then need to be considered as to their feasibility in terms of the issues raised in this and subsequent chapters.

SUMMARY

It is essential that the event concept is workable right from the start. In this chapter we have shown that determining the purpose/objectives of the event in conjunction with all stakeholders is critical in ensuring that the event concept will work. Early in the process, it is also necessary to identify the potential audience as well as the financial and other resources required to support the event. The event concept can then be further developed to include the theme and the decor, and a suitable venue can be selected. Any logistical requirements of the event must also be identified early in the planning process. The purpose, theme, audience and venue need to be compatible elements for the event concept to be successful.

Chapter review questions

1 From a financial point of view, many event concepts are influenced by the arrangements for financial underwriting of the event. Give three specific examples of existing event concepts that match the following financial outcomes: not-for-profit, for profit, and fully subsidised.
2 Explain five aspects of a venue that impact on concept development.
3 What does Goldblatt (2005) say about the appeal to the senses of an event concept? Use an event that you have experienced to illustrate the importance of engaging all the senses.
4 List the pros and cons of using an existing, fully functioning venue versus a unique but untested building for an unusual event where the aim is to create a WOW factor.

Activity

Start a collection of images that will inspire future event designs. These may come from a range of sources, including magazines, gift wrapping, table napkins, cards and posters. All will give you ideas for themes and colour schemes. You may also like to begin to investigate colours and textures by looking at fabric samples.

Case study

It's a wrap!

In many ways Mercedes-Benz Fashion Festival really is a circus. A gorgeous celebration of colour and movement, of the innovative and the unpredictable, that always generates excitement and wonder when it comes to town.

continued

Our models who, like the acrobats under the Big Top, have wowed us all week with their grace, their beauty and their poses. They performed at the Cloudland Wrap Party for free, which proves their beauty is much more than skin-deep!

To our designers who manage, each year, to conjure the remarkable and the mysterious, just like the travelling magicians of old. They have taught us to expect the unexpected—but even then, they still manage to surprise us.

To our retailers, the tightrope walkers who walk the highwire every day, seeking to strike a balance between the cold hard world of business and the ethereal and airy stratosphere of style.

To our sponsors who really are the strong men of an event like Fashion Festival, supporting our efforts, lifting our spirits and catapulting our dreams into reality, even when times are tough. A particular thanks to the strongest of them all, Mercedes-Benz, our naming rights sponsor and enduring supporter.

And, of course, to Brisbane City Hall, for this year providing a truly stunning Big Top for our circus.

To the Queensland Government Department of Employment, Economic Development and Innovation. This year they were the lion tamers, taking on the fiercest of economic conditions, staring down those who'd like to take a swipe at the value of a Fashion Festival, and generally taming the most conservative budget beasts.

To our fabulous volunteers. Because when any circus comes to town, there is always an army of people working away from the spotlight to get the Big Top up in time, to welcome visitors and answer questions, and generally to make sure the show runs smoothly. And our little army did it for free!

And to our team at MBFF. You are truly talented jugglers, keeping all the balls in the air, spinning the plates and dodging the flying knives, to put on a terrific show.

And finally, to you. Our fabulous MBFFashionistas, those who bought tickets, got involved, participated in events and proved how beautiful Brisbane really is.

Thank you for your support in 2009 and we look forward to sharing plans for next year in the coming months.

MBFF will further enhance Brisbane's positioning as a city of creativity and style and its reputation to stage a dynamic, consumer-driven event that will:

- boost retail sales and the city's economy by supporting another home-grown industry
- increase awareness for our local industry
- increase visitation to the city, and
- positively reinforce the city's ability to stage international standard events.

Source: Lindsay Bennett Marketing Pty Ltd.

Questions

1 What was the theme of the 2009 event?

2 How does the theme fit with the idea of a fashion festival?

3 What theme would you suggest for the next festival?

4 Who were the stakeholders who were thanked for their contributions? Draw a diagram to summarise these relationships.

continued

Case study (continued)

5 What are three operational or logistical challenges associated with running a fashion show?

6 If you were to develop some measurable objectives for this event, which elements could be chosen to develop these targets?

7 Choose or develop a single statement that summarises the purpose of this event.

References

Allen, J, McDonnell, I, O'Toole, W & Harris, R (2008), *Festival and special event management*, 4th ed, Wiley Australia, Brisbane.

Berridge, G (2007), *Events design and experience*, Butterworth-Heinemann, Oxford, UK.

Getz, D (2007), *Event studies: theory, research and policy for planned events*, Elsevier, Oxford, UK.

Goldblatt, J (2005), *Special events: event leadership for a new world*, John Wiley & Sons, Hoboken, NJ.

Matheson, V (2009), 'Economic multipliers and mega-event analysis', *International Journal of Sport Finance*, 4(1):63–70.

O'Neill, M, Getz, D & Carlsen, J (1999), 'Evaluation of service quality at events: the 1998 Coca-Cola Masters Surfing event at Margaret River, Western Australia', *Managing Service Quality*, 9(3):158–66.

3

EVENT VENUES AND SITES

Unit descriptor

This unit describes the performance outcomes, skills and knowledge required to undertake the venue or site selection process for a complex event comprising multiple components. This unit applies to the overall venue or site selection process for any type of event. It may be relevant in any industry context, but has particular application in the cultural, community, hospitality, sporting and tourism sectors.

Elements

- Analyse venue or site requirements
- Source event venues and sites
- Confirm venue or site requirements.

Selection of an appropriate venue or site for a **complex event** requires the application of significant analytical and research skills as well as sound knowledge of venue or site issues that impact on different types of events. Individuals working autonomously with limited guidance from others undertake this role. This may include senior event coordinators or event managers.

Critical aspects for assessment

- Ability to research and select an appropriate venue or site for a complex event
- Ability to develop, interpret and analyse the range of information used in venue and site selection and confirmation process
- Knowledge of different venue and site options within the local area
- Conduct of venue or site selection process for at least two events, one of which becomes an event managed by the candidate.

THE *Disability Discrimination Act* (1992) requires that people with disabilities are able to access and use places open to the public and to access any services and facilities provided in those buildings. People with disabilities can face barriers to attending and participating in public functions in a variety of ways. They may experience difficulty hearing what is said, seeing small print on an invitation, climbing steps to the venue, understanding signage or using a rest room in the building. Public events need to be planned to ensure they are accessible to all members of the community. Consideration of aspects such as the venue, a continuous accessible path to the venue, invitations, and hearing augmentation are important.

Source: <www.dsc.wa.gov.au>.

The terms 'venue' and 'site' are used almost interchangeably by event managers, with 'venue' used mainly for built structures and 'site' for outdoor spaces. 'Site' also has more general use for a range of locations, which in turn can be transformed into event venues. Events are also held at convention centres, hotels, clubs, restaurants and many other places. The term 'facility' is also used extensively, particularly in North America in the context of a 'sports facility' or 'convention facility'.

In this chapter the various attributes of event sites will be considered, particularly for outdoor events where all infrastructure has to be brought in and erected on site. This chapter will also look at disability access, since best practice in this area is likely to meet the needs of all visitors, particularly in the areas of signage, lighting, pathways and emergency exits.

ANALYSE VENUE OR SITE REQUIREMENTS

When evaluating the suitability of a venue or site, there are two main considerations: the functionality of the venue and the suitability of the site for the event's creative purpose. Natural features of some sites lend themselves well to creating an extraordinary event experience. Concerts held in caves and natural amphitheatres are good examples. In such situations, however, the event manager needs to be mindful of the costs of using unusual, untested sites and the functional problems inherent in using them, as well as their legal obligations for access to public places.

When planning an outdoor event, the onus is on the management team to ensure that the infrastructure meets the needs of everyone in the event audience.

For the event manager considering an established venue, a site inspection would determine whether the venue was suitable for the planned event, particularly from a functional perspective. Building codes ensure that most modern buildings comply with other aspects such as disability needs (e.g. that doorways are wide enough for wheelchair access).

The size and scope are considerations when looking for appropriate cities and venues for staging major events. When a major event such as the FIFA World Cup, Olympic Games or Commonwealth Games is planned, various cities bid for the event. During this process, the

Aerial photograph and customer circuit map of the Australian Grand Prix site, Albert Park

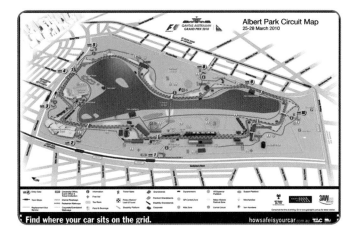

city presents the infrastructure available for the event, not only specific competition venues but also descriptions of transportation, accommodation, etc. The city must demonstrate that it has the full range of physical and human resources to support the bid, as well as the financial resources for the event to succeed. In bids for such international events, the infrastructure is promised but sometimes not delivered. For example, the steel and glass roof for the Athens Olympic Games swimming centre could not be finished in time for the Games. Bids also need to address the issue of accessibility for both athletes and audience. This topic is covered briefly in this chapter. The challenge of providing accessible public spaces is fairly easily met when the venues and transport networks are new; however, it is much more difficult when the event is held in an ancient city like Athens.

An old building provides an interesting but challenging venue

When bidding for a large conference of, say, medical professionals, the bid would again cover the city, its accommodation, entertainment options and attractions. Indeed, conference centres in Singapore and Melbourne would differ little in what they could provide as regards the conference venue and meeting rooms. Delegates arriving at the conference are more interested in the city that hosts the event and the attractions it has to offer.

Prior to selecting a venue or site, it is essential to analyse the overall venue or site requirements based on a detailed review of all aspects of the proposed event. Developing accurate venue or site specifications will facilitate the research process.

The role of the event manager as a walking, talking checklist will become evident in this chapter.

SOURCE EVENT VENUES AND SITES

In Chapter 2 we discussed the importance of analysing the feasibility of the event concept. Now we will consider the aspects of an event that must be taken into account when developing venue or site specifications. These include:

★ creative theme or image required
★ estimated number of attendees
★ audience composition
★ facilities and services to be provided
★ staging/competition requirements
★ budget parameters
★ location
★ capacity of site or venue
★ timing (including availability and access for set-up and breakdown)
★ accessibility.

The requirements of all stakeholders also need to be considered. Stakeholders may include:

★ attendees/delegates/guests/spectators (including those with a disability)
★ host organisation
★ sponsors
★ contractors
★ emergency services
★ regulatory authorities.

Imagine, for example, that a client has requested a small event, the purpose of which is to introduce newly appointed executive staff (and their partners) following a merger of two banks. The client wants to 'break the ice' and for this reason wants something a bit different from a conventional dinner, with more of a team focus. However, it cannot be a tacky team-building theme or an outdoor activity. Pretending to be spiders in a web, walking over logs, or something similar is absolutely out of the question.

This elegant solution could well meet the needs of this client:

A chef's table dinner in a five-star commercial kitchen where guests, guided by the executive chef, 'prepare' the food. A chef's table is usually located inside a commercial kitchen, providing a unique venue, surrounded by glimmering stainless steel and professional cooking equipment. Usually the chef invites selected people to dine at the chef's table and this is a privilege few enjoy. The food is generally unsurpassed in quality and creativity. This concept is unique in that guests at an event would never normally get their hands dirty. Guests would arrive expecting a conventional dinner, be surprised by the location, and further surprised when given a large apron and asked to assist. Since all ingredients would already be prepared, as on a television cooking show, none of the guests would find the situation daunting. Each guest would be involved, with movement around the kitchen and the table, observation, questions, congratulations and so on. No time for embarrassing conversational lapses when discussing the jobs people have lost in the merger process! Rather, an unforgettable dining experience that would really 'break the ice'!

The number of guests would be the major consideration when sourcing the venue. Only five-star commercial kitchens would be suitable and the size of the chef's table would be limited by the space available in the kitchen. The dining area would also need to be a safe distance away from the heat and flames! One solution would be a banquet table in a function room outside the kitchen but this would destroy the energy and creativity of the concept. For the concept to work, a dining table in the kitchen would be essential. Such a space could well be available in a convention centre on a Saturday night, but would be hard to find in a busy five-star hotel conducting normal peak business.

As this example illustrates, decor, availability, capacity, safety and access issues are all relevant when selecting an appropriate venue.

VENUE INFORMATION SOURCES

When looking for a venue, there are various sources that can be utilised:
★ local/regional/state tourism organisations
★ convention and visitor bureaus
★ venue publications and directories
★ destination brochures
★ trade journals
★ internet searches.

In conducting such a search, it is useful to compare services and specifications. Some venues have interactive websites that allow you to configure function rooms, depending on whether the event is a cocktail party, meeting or dinner function. These CAD designs are most useful in showing the space available (not forgetting any space needed for a stage and possibly wheelchair access). Clear communication of requirements is essential, particularly if the event is so large that it will be sent out to tender.

SITE INSPECTION—CONFERENCE

Figure 3.1 provides a checklist of the technical requirements for a small conference, as this is the most important consideration for an event of this nature. A more detailed analysis of the site for the conference would cover other fundamentals such as parking, public transport, accessibility and smoking areas, as well as registration, seating and catering.

FIGURE 3.1
Conference
technical
requirements

Registration desks	Flipcharts
Display screens	Lecterns
Staging	Speakers
Data projector	Audio equipment
DVD player	Laptop with presentation software
Remote controls	Sufficient power supply
Overhead projector	Accessible power outlets
Extra lenses and bulbs	Extension cords
Laser pointers	Lighting effects (including dimmer)
Projection screens	Microphones and stands
Projector trolleys	Radio microphones (hand-held and lapel)
Whiteboards	Technician on site

All elements of an event need to be itemised to ensure that even the smallest detail is given attention. For an outdoor music concert, for example, the site inspection checklist would run to many pages, including site elements such as perimeter fencing, lighting, signage, pathways, parking and so on.

SITE INSPECTION—ACCESSIBILITY

The Western Australian Disability Services Commission provides a checklist for creating accessible events, which is reproduced in Figure 3.2 on pages 46–47. This covers invitations and promotional materials, external access, internal access, communication and function space requirements. A more detailed planning approach to a major event might cover these elements and more:

★ way-finding
★ signage
★ transport
★ parking
★ footpaths
★ ramps
★ stairways
★ lifts
★ surfaces and finishes
★ entries and exits
★ doorways and doors
★ toilet facilities
★ emergency provisions (must comply with Australian Standards).

SITE INSPECTIONS—OUTDOOR EVENTS

For an outdoor event, significant considerations include:

★ access for emergency services
★ public access
★ service access and loading docks
★ parking
★ public transport
★ power supply
★ potable water (cold)
★ sanitation.

For a sporting competition, considerations include:

★ competition area cleanliness, maintenance and safety
★ competition area clearly marked

★ adequate lighting for competition area
★ spectator area cleanliness, maintenance and safety
★ marked out-of-bounds area
★ perimeter fencing
★ buffer between spectators and competitors
★ competitor change rooms
★ sports equipment of appropriate standard
★ all areas clear of non-essential equipment
★ exits and entrances clearly marked and unobstructed
★ electrical systems in good condition
★ waste containers provided
★ walkways clean and well-maintained
★ stairs non-slip
★ wheelchair access to all areas
★ compliance with fire safety regulations in all aspects.

Viewing platforms can be provided for people in wheelchairs

The checklists could be endless, including also loading docks, storage areas, access, refrigeration space, etc. In particular, the special requirements of large items such as stages and athletics equipment need to be considered to ensure that they can be brought into the event area, otherwise known as loading restrictions. The logistics of boat shows and car shows are complex and have to be linked to both space and scheduling, making sure that items arrive in an orderly and timely way.

FIT WITH AUDIENCE PROFILE

An overriding consideration in the choice of an event venue is the fit with audience needs. It is easy for an event manager to lose sight of this when inspired by a concept and unusual

Set-up for a half-marathon start

FIGURE 3.2

Checklist for creating accessible events

DISABILITY
SERVICES
COMMISSION

making a difference

Checklist for creating accessible events

External environment

People with disabilities require a continuous, even, accessible path of travel. An accessible path of travel means there are no obstacles in the internal or external environment such as revolving doors, kerbs or steps.

Location of the nearest:

Bus stop: _____

Train station: _____

	Yes	No
Accessible parking bays		
Does the venue have an accessible parking bay?	☐	☐
Is the accessible parking bay/s identified by the international symbol of access?	☐	☐
Raised sign	☐	☐
Ground markings	☐	☐
If the accessible parking is undercover is the roof a minimum of 2500 mm in height to allow the use of a car top hoist?	☐	☐
Is the distance from the car park to entrance less than 40 m?	☐	☐
Continuous accessible path of travel		
Is there a continuous accessible path of travel, including kerb ramps, to the building from the:		
Accessible parking bay/s?	☐	☐
Set down area?	☐	☐
If there are steps to the building:		
Is there a ramp available for wheelchair users?	☐	☐
Do all steps have handrails?	☐	☐
Is there a contrasting strip on step edges?	☐	☐
If there is a ramp to the building:		
Is the gradient no steeper than 1:14?	☐	☐
Does the ramp lead to the main entrance?	☐	☐

The building
Entrance

	Yes	No
Is the entrance threshold level?	☐	☐
If there is a step/s at the entrance of the doorway:		
Is there a ramp of not more than 450 mm in length and with a gradient of 1 in 8?	☐	☐
Is the entrance door easy to open?	☐	☐
Is the clear door space 800 mm (preferred)?	☐	☐

Internal environment

	Yes	No
Is the inquiry or reception counter low enough for a wheelchair user?	☐	☐
Does the venue have an accessible path of travel from the front entrance to all areas guests will use?	☐	☐

If there are internal steps:
    Do all steps have handrails? ☐ ☐
    Is there a contrasting strip on step edges? ☐ ☐
If there are ramps:
    Are they no steeper than 1:14? ☐ ☐
    Do they have handrails? ☐ ☐
Do all doors have a clear space 760 mm (essential) or 800 mm (preferred)? ☐ ☐
If there is only a side approach to the door, is there 1200 mm clear space in front of the door? ☐ ☐
Does the venue have a non-slip floor surface or carpets with a firm low pile of 6 mm or less? ☐ ☐

Visibility
Are facilities in the venue clearly signed? ☐ ☐
Is the venue well lit? ☐ ☐
Are there any areas of high reflection or glare? ☐ ☐

Toilets
Does the venue have a unisex accessible toilet? ☐ ☐
Is the toilet situated on the same floor as the function? ☐ ☐
Does the door have a clear space of 800 mm (preferred)? ☐ ☐
If there is only a side approach to the door, is there 1200 mm clear space in front of the door? ☐ ☐
If the door of the toilet opens inwards, is the space large enough for the person in a wheelchair to shut the door once inside? ☐ ☐
Is there 950 mm space at one side of the toilet pan? ☐ ☐
Is there a grab rail next to the toilet at 800 mm – 810 mm high, preferably in an 'L' shape? ☐ ☐

Signage
Does the venue have clear, directional signage to:
    The function room? ☐ ☐
    The toilets? ☐ ☐

Please note that disabled facilities in older buildings will only have a clear space of 760 mm. The standard has now been revised to a clear space of 800 mm.

Source: <www.dsc.wa.gov.au/cproot/270/2/CreatingAccessibleEvents.pdf>. © Disability Services Commission of Western Australia.

location or bogged down with checklists. Will the event audience travel to the venue? Will the venue provide too little or too much space for the number of people? This psychological factor contributes a great deal to the event experience. What is the event purpose? Being constantly mindful of the event purpose and the needs of the event audience is necessary throughout the venue selection process. Being able to think three-dimensionally in terms of height and decor is another beneficial attribute for an event manager.

VENUE SAFETY

The subject of venue safety has been mentioned several times and will be covered in more detail in Chapters 17 and 18. Safety is a crucial issue and the event manager cannot be too careful. Unfortunately, there are several examples of structural failure at large events that have led to fatalities.

Staging an event at a modern, state-of-the-art stadium, using professional contractors, is a low-risk option from a safety point of view as is running a conference in a purpose-built conference centre. Outdoor events using hire equipment present a much higher level of risk. Checking engineering and other certification, as well as contractor references, can reduce this risk. There are no short-cuts or savings in the area of venue safety—old buildings may not meet fire safety standards, for example—and attention to detail is essential.

Figure 3.3 outlines the type of detail provided to contractors to ensure the safe delivery of goods at the loading dock. Figure 3.4 opposite outlines the process for venue and site selection.

FIGURE 3.3
Detailed instructions for access and delivery

The Adelaide Festival Centre
Access Details

Vehicle access

Passenger vehicle access is via Festival Drive (off King William Street).
Height clearance is 2.1 metres.
Heavy vehicle access to dock is from North Terrace down ramp (in front of Casino).
Height clearance is 4.5 metres.

Loading dock

A 'Cab Over' prime mover is essential when manoeuvring a semi-trailer flush against the dock.

The Space, Dunstan Playhouse and STC Workshop, share a common dock. The dock is an 'end loading' facility service, one vehicle only at any time.
There is a 1500 kg capacity hydraulic lift platform from ground level to dock floor immediately in front of the dock. This lift platform is 2.75 metres wide × 1.5 metres deep.
The dock door is 3.15 metres high × 2.75 metres wide.
Scenery and equipment must be moved from the dock to the Space stage via a 4355 kg capacity hydraulic lift 7.3 metres long × 2.4 metres wide × 2.75 metres high. Scenery must then travel through the STC Workshop and onto the Space stage. The door from the STC Workshop into the Space is 3 metres wide × 5.5 metres high with full acoustic isolation.

Source: The Adelaide Festival Centre 2008.

CONFIRM VENUE OR SITE ARRANGEMENTS

On completion of the investigative and evaluation phase, and with approval from stakeholders for a site or venue, arrangements must be confirmed in writing with the venue provider. The contract may include estimated numbers, facilities and services to be provided, audience or delegate profile and location, event theme and image, and of course the budget. Other important considerations include access and timing for set-up and breakdown, size of the area and equipment, technical capacity or potential, and staffing.

Research potential venues and sites using appropriate information sources
⇩
Compare environment and services offered with event specifications
⇩
Evaluate venue and site capacity to deliver a range of quality outcomes
⇩
Negotiate and liaise with venue and site personnel
⇩
Identify risk management issues associated with specific venues and sites
⇩
Assess the need for tentative bookings and take action promptly
⇩
Coordinate multiple site or venue selections when required in a logical manner
⇩
Provide clear and accurate briefings on venue or site options to key stakeholders
⇩
Provide recommendations and rationale
⇩
Gain appropriate approval and confirm agreements

FIGURE 3.4
Venue and site selection process

Matthews (2008, p. 152) says that:

> The first point to bear in mind is that when in any venue or on any outdoor site, the event producer is a guest and not an employee or even a contractor for that venue. Certainly the event producer is usually a contractor of the client who is also a client of that venue or site, but that does not automatically allow the producer to demand whatever he or she wants of the venue.

He goes on to highlight the importance of maintaining good relations and understanding internal management hierarchies in hotels, convention centres and other venues.

In some cases, such as for touring events, multiple sites or venues are involved. In other cases, such as for a major festival, related events are held in multiple locations. Both require careful integration in the planning phase.

On finalisation of the contract, it is necessary to draft the physical dimensions of the event in order to develop more detailed equipment specifications. A scale map, plan or CAD drawing of the event and two- or even three-dimensional models help to clarify expectations to all stakeholders. Many events are set up at the last minute and the most difficult thing for all concerned is visualising the event and the work environment. Check all measurements, or you may not hire enough carpet! An example of the Formula 1™ ING Australian Grand Prix circuit map was shown at the start of the chapter.

On completion of the event, a report should be prepared, providing an assessment of the venue or site, the level of cooperation shown by venue personnel, and their willingness to negotiate on products, services and costs. The initial risk assessment should be reviewed for the post-event report as well.

CONDITIONS OF HIRE AGREEMENT

Between the VENUE MANAGEMENT and the hirer.

BOOKING PROCEDURE: Every person applying to hire the VENUE must provide a permanent address and contact details. This booking is unconfirmed until such time as a signed copy of the Conditions of Hire Agreement has been returned to us together with payment of the required deposit and other actions as specified within this and supporting document(s). Our return of this countersigned agreement with deposit receipt will provide formal acceptance of your confirmed Hire Contract.

CANCELLATION: Any cancellation after confirmation of this agreement, or part thereof, will result in forfeiture of the total deposit value, plus any other costs incurred.

SET-UP AND BREAKDOWN: Set-up and Breakdown (bump-in and bump-out) shall be agreed and stated within the Conditions of Hire Agreement. In the event of any performance or use continuing beyond these times, the Tenant shall pay to VENUE MANAGEMENT such further sum or sums as is specified in the Venue Rental Schedule. The keys of the Building shall be kept by the Caretaker or nominated deputy. Labour costs for access outside normal operating hours shall be payable by the Tenant.

SUBLETTING: The Tenant may not sublet the venue or any part thereof.

DEPOSIT: On the signing of this Conditions of Hire Agreement and receipt of the deposit invoice, the sum shall be payable to secure confirmation of this document.

The balance of the account as invoiced by VENUE MANAGEMENT shall be payable within seven days of the event date.

CATERING: VENUE MANAGEMENT, through their in-house caterers, retain sole and exclusive right to supply to persons attending the premises with food and beverages. A separate catering deposit may be required should there be any pre/post-performance catering required by the Tenant. Numbers and menu confirmation must be made not less than 72 hours (3 days) prior to the function date.

SMOKING: Smoking shall not be permitted in any part of the building. The Tenant shall be liable for any damages or costs should any person smoke within the venue.

FURNITURE AND EQUIPMENT: The Tenant shall be accountable for the replacement of all furniture and equipment to where it came from at the conclusion of the event unless set-up and dismantling fees are being paid as detailed in this agreement. The Tenant shall be accountable for damages or breakages. At the conclusion of the event, the Tenant shall be responsible for removing any furniture, equipment items or decorations introduced to the venue at that time, unless alternative arrangements have been made with VENUE MANAGEMENT.

LABOUR: VENUE MANAGEMENT can provide labour for the set-up and dismantling of your event. This is charged out at a $30.00 per hour per person (normal working hours) and $35.00 per hour per person (after hours). This does not include technical staff.

CLEANING: The Tenant is expected to leave the facilities in the condition they were found. If this is not so, additional cleaning charges will be incurred and charged on the final invoice. The final decision will be made by VENUE MANAGEMENT.

NOISE LEVELS: These shall be restricted to a maximum of 100 decibels within the venue, or less if determined by VENUE MANAGEMENT.

FIRE ALARMS: The Promoter/Tenant shall be liable for any charges incurred due to the activation of the fire alarm by 'false alarm' during the hire period.

EVACUATION PROCEDURE: As a requirement of the Fire Safety Regulations, the Tenant and their staff should familiarise themselves with the Venue Evacuation Procedure, copies of which are on display in all areas of the venue. If the Tenant and their staff are unsure of any part of the procedure please contact the Caretaker.

THE TENANT covenants with VENUE MANAGEMENT as follows:

(a) Not to infringe or breach, or permit to be infringed or breached, any copyright, performing right or other protected right by or in the conduct of any performance.

(b) Shall make no alteration to the structure, fittings, decorations or furnishings of the buildings without previous written permission of the Caretaker and shall after each performance or use leave the building in as good a condition as they were in before any permitted alteration to the satisfaction of the Caretaker. Any damages or costs associated with alterations, or other activities, shall be made right, with the full cost met by the Tenant.

(c) Shall not introduce, display, attach or suspend any equipment, fittings or furniture without previous written permission from VENUE MANAGEMENT.

(d) Shall meet all Australian standards in the use of electrical equipment.

(e) Shall pay the cost of any special electrical equipment installation or fittings which may be required for the purpose of the Tenant's event, and shall obtain written permission prior to any such work from VENUE MANAGEMENT.

(f) Shall permit the VENUE MANAGEMENT (or Caretaker) to visit at any time all parts of the premises.

(g) Shall ensure that they operate with current policies as required under the Occupational Health & Safety Act, Australian Standards for building evacuation and any other Acts or local by-laws as may be relevant. The Tenant will accept total liability, as the lessee of the facilities, for adhering to these laws.

(h) Shall provide certificate of currency for Public Liability Insurance Policy and Workers Compensation Insurance. Shall do likewise if subcontractors are employed.

VENUE MANAGEMENT agrees as follows:

(a) Shall provide such staff, equipment and services as are specified at the full cost to the Tenant, or as included within Venue Rental as determined within the Venue Rental Schedule.

(b) The Fire Safety Officer is a separate charge to the Tenant, to be present in the venue one hour before the doors are due to open, through until the building is vacated at the conclusion of the performance or use.

(c) Shall reserve the right to revise fees and charges from time to time as may be found necessary.

(d) Shall reserve the right of entry to any of our venues for our staff members or management at no charge.

(e) Shall have complete supervision and control over admission of the public, the Tenant or subcontractors.

(f) VENUE MANAGEMENT shall not be responsible for the loss or damage to any article of any kind brought to or left in the building.

SUMMARY

The creativity of an event concept is often tempered by the suitability and availability of a venue or site to stage the event. Of course, many venues and sites can be totally transformed if there are unlimited funds available to the event manager! As this is not the case in most instances, choosing the right venue for an event is crucial to its success. In this chapter we have covered what you need to know to develop accurate site specifications for different types of events and how to source suitable venues or sites. For the event manager, there are many aspects to consider when preparing site specifications, not least of which is safety. We have also stressed the importance of confirming venue arrangements in writing and reviewing and signing a venue contract for which an example has been provided.

Chapter review questions

1 Explain the difference between the terms 'venue' and 'site'.
2 When an overseas group is visiting for a conference, what are some of the considerations for the choice of venue?
3 List five key areas that need to be considered concerning accessibility to a venue or site.
4 How can the event manager ensure everyone's understanding of the proposed layout of the site or venue (two dimensional) and the concept (three dimensional)?

Activities

1 Visit a large convention centre in your state or territory (see links in Appendix E) and look at the facilities available. Obtain scale diagrams of meeting and function rooms and check the suitability of the convention centre for a two-day conference for 200 delegates, including a gala dinner.
2 Develop your own site inspection checklist and visit a public site often used for big events to look at disability access. Evaluate the site.

Case study

Researching the event venue

The Brisbane Convention and Exhibition Centre provides detailed specifications and guidelines for events held at the centre. These can be found at <www.bcec.com.au>. Any other large venue would do equally well. Use the information on the website to prepare a scale map for an event concept of your own to see how well the function space could be used. Read the general guidelines and discuss elements of this event that may be problematic.

References

Carlson, J, Getz, D & Soutar, G (2000), 'Event evaluation research', *Event Management*, 6(4):247–57.

Commonwealth of Australia (2008), Australian Flexible Learning Framework, Events Alive Flexible Learning Toolboxes, <http://toolboxes.flexiblelearning.net.au/series11/11_08.htm>.

Getz, D, Bowdin, G & Wunsch, U (2010), *Events management casebook*, Butterworth-Heinemann, Oxford, UK.

Matthews, D (2008), *Special event production: the process*, Butterworth-Heinemann, Oxford, UK.

Photo credits

CHAPTER 4

....

EVENT STAGING

Unit descriptor

This unit describes the performance outcomes, skills and knowledge required to manage the staging and operation of a complex event comprising multiple components. This unit applies to staging management for any type of event. It may be relevant in any industry context, but has particular application in the cultural, community, hospitality, sporting and tourism sectors. The unit focuses on the key knowledge and skills required to manage overall event staging from an organisational and contractor management perspective. It requires the application of advanced planning, organisation and communication skills combined with a detailed knowledge of the event management process and broad understanding of individual specialist services.

Elements

- Analyse event staging requirements
- Source and negotiate staging contractors
- Monitor staging contractors.

Critical aspects for assessment

- General knowledge of the range of staging services and related terminology to allow for informed planning and decision-making
- Ability to source, organise and coordinate multiple staging contractors as part of the overall event management process
- Management of the staging of at least one **complex event**.

THE BIENNIAL New Zealand Festival is presented by a charitable trust—The New Zealand International Festival of the Arts. Up to three hundred specialist arts administrators, communicators, production and technical staff are employed to help produce and present the Festival, but most are on short-term contracts, of between six weeks to eighteen months' duration. In the 'off' period between Festivals, a skeletal administration staff of only four is maintained.

The Festival operates on a financial knife-edge, with a mandate to break even at the end of each event, and the requirement to start from zero each time. It has 'core funding' by Wellington City Council, but relies heavily on public and private sector support for its existence; 62 per cent of income comes from ticket sales, and 31 per cent from sponsorship and grants. The Government, through its arts funding agency, Creative New Zealand, assists the development of new New Zealand work for presentation at the Festival.

Approximately 75 per cent of the Festival's operating budget is spent on buying, producing and presenting the events which make up the Festival, with the remainder split between administration and marketing costs.

Source: <www.nzfestival.nzpost.co.nz>. © New Zealand International Arts Festival.

The New Zealand Festival, with over 100 ticketed events, provides an introduction to the issues associated with staging. The staging of an event incorporates all aspects of the event that enable the performance to go ahead. Broadly speaking, by performance we mean entertainment: the sport, the parade, the ceremony. The topics covered in this chapter, such as theme, venue, sound and lighting, as well as all the essential services, are relevant to every one of the free and ticketed events of the New Zealand Festival. For every event in that festival, the organisers would have had to look at issues such as capacity, seating arrangements, emergency access, stage requirements and staffing.

Staging is an ancient concept: the Roman gladiatorial events were staged in spectacular, albeit gruesome, fashion, but these events certainly had the enthusiastic atmosphere every modern event organiser aspires to, although the modern audience would be unlikely to enjoy the same level of bloodshed.

One of the largest outdoor music events held in Australia illustrates the complexity and logistics of staging. In 2005, Robbie Williams entered the *Guinness book of world records* for the fastest, and largest, number of concert tickets ever sold in one day—1.6 million—when the European leg of his World Tour went on sale. Williams sold out five London shows, each with a capacity of 75 000. His Leeds concert sold

Robbie Williams concert, site set-up

Lighting effects transform the stage

Pyrotechnics offer particular challenges for both the event organiser and the specialist contractor

out in 90 minutes. Holland sold out four Amsterdam Arena gigs in a breathtaking 89 minutes. In Germany, a mass of 20 000 fans braved the cold to line the streets of Munich waiting for tickets to go on sale at midnight! Williams went on to tour in Australia in November 2006, playing in five Australian capital cities. According to promoter Michael Chugg, this was a rare occasion where Australia saw exactly the same concert as countries in the northern hemisphere. They brought two stage roofs and rigs from the UK, which ran in tandem and leap-frogged across the country. There were 57 semi-trailers on the road, 30 steel containers and 27 trucks to transport staging, production and the six 400-amp generators needed to power the pop-hunk's super-sized show. Lighting was designed by Al Gurdon. Lighting director for the tour was Rich Gorrod. The lighting rig contained 16 × B52 Syncrolites, 42 × VL3000 Spots, 88 × Mac 2k Washes, 28 × VL5a's, 122 × Martin Atomics Strobes, 8 × 2.5k Nova Lites, 14 × VL2000 Washes, 6 × DMX Dominators, 6 × Hungaro flashes, 8 × Coemar Supercycs, 18 × 8 lite DWE Moles c/w Wybron Scrollers, 8 × 18k Gargantrams, 24 × Thomas Pixel Pars, 80 × Colour Blocs, 129 × Colour Blasts, 1 × Virtuoso EX1. This was staging on a grand scale.

This chapter focuses on the key knowledge and skills required to manage overall event staging from an organisational and contractor management perspective. It requires the application of advanced planning and organisation and communication skills, combined with a detailed knowledge of the event management process and a broad understanding of individual specialist services. It does not, however, require a specialist knowledge of these areas.

Event staging requirements may relate to:

- ★ exhibition set-up
- ★ audiovisual requirements
- ★ display and decoration
- ★ furniture
- ★ temporary structures
- ★ special effects
- ★ entertainment
- ★ sound and lighting
- ★ stage design
- ★ rigging
- ★ catering and catering set-up
- ★ security
- ★ disabled and emergency access.

Special effects, for example, may include pyrotechnics, which are used at many outdoor sporting and entertainment events. An event or venue manager would need to know that there are specific requirements for the use of pyrotechnics (fireworks) and would need to contract a licensed operator to provide these special effects. Close-proximity pyrotechnics are smokeless and have no fallout, making them suitable for parties, weddings and awards nights where they contribute greatly to the WOW factor.

ANALYSE EVENT STAGING REQUIREMENTS

There are many factors to consider when staging an event, the primary consideration being the suitability of the venue for the production and the audience. The production could be a performance, but it could also be a marathon, a meeting or an exhibition.

THE STAGING ENVIRONMENT

Selection of an event venue must take the needs of all stakeholders into account. Stakeholders include emergency services, catering staff, entertainers, participants and clients. Performers and their promoters are particularly fussy about the configuration of the venue, including the stage and the seating as these can contribute to the success or failure of the performance. The sound qualities of the venue are equally important.

Frequently, the client has an unusual idea for a venue, but however imaginative this may be, selection of the site must be tempered with rational decision-making. While a parking lot could be transformed into an interesting place to have a party, it would have no essential services, such as electricity, and would present expensive logistical problems. An existing event venue, such as a conference centre, could more easily lend itself to transformation using decoration and props. Table 4.1 and Figure 4.1 illustrate useful information, such as hall size and capacity and layout of facilities, which is available from venues and convention centres on the internet.

Choosing a venue that is consistent with the event purpose and theme is essential. It can also lead to cost savings as there is far less expense in transforming it into what the client wants. The major considerations for selecting an event venue include:
★ size of the event (including the size of the audience)
★ layout of the site and its suitability for the event
★ stage, field of play or performance area
★ transport and parking
★ proximity to accommodation and attractions
★ supply issues for goods and services providers, such as caterers
★ technical support
★ venue management.

Table 4.1 Example of information, such as hall size and capacity, provided by venue providers on the internet

Capacities	Area (sq m)	Area (sq f)	Theatre	Banquet	Classroom
Hall A	430	4628	540	300	210
Hall B	430	4628	540	300	210
Hall C	430	4628	500	300	210
Hall D	430	4628	500	300	210
Halls A&B	860	9256	1080	650	420
Halls C&D	860	9256	940	650	400
Halls B&C&D	1290	13884	1540	720	N/A
Great Hall A&B&C&D	1720	18512	2330	1300	730
Hall 2 (Auditorium)	1470	15817	5000	N/A	N/A
Hall 2 (Flat floor)	1470	15817	N/A	1080	630

Source: Reproduced with permission. Cairns Convention Centre.

FIGURE 4.1(a)
Layout of halls and facilities of a convention centre available on the internet

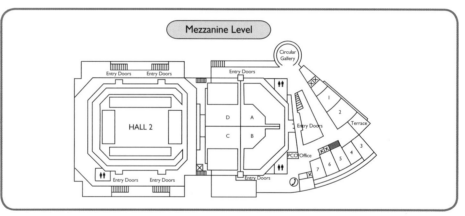

FIGURE 4.1(b)
Cairns Convention Centre Hall 2 used for trade exhibition

An inspection of the venue or site should reveal any limitations. The aspects to consider include:

* compatibility with the event theme
* audience comfort
* visibility for the audience (line of sight)
* sound quality
* entrances and exits
* stage area (where relevant)
* storage areas
* available equipment
* cover in case of poor weather
* safety and security
* access for emergency vehicles
* evacuation routes.

In viewing a potential event site, there are three major stakeholders who need to be considered and whose perspectives could be quite different: the **performers**, the **audience** and the **organisers**. By performers we mean those in the limelight, whether this involves providing an educational talk, dancing in a parade, presenting an award or scoring on a try line. Performers have specific needs that are fundamental to their success, such as the level of intimacy with the audience (often the result of the distance from the audience) or the volume of the sound. The audience also has needs, the primary one being to see what is going on! The level of lighting and sound, as well as access to and comfort of the seating, also contributes to audience satisfaction. Catering and facilities are generally secondary. Finally, from a management perspective, the venue must help to minimise risks, such as adverse weather, power failure, accidents and emergencies.

EVENT STAGING ELEMENTS

Once the venue or site has been selected, it is necessary to analyse the staging requirements for the event based on a detailed review of all aspects of the proposed event. Safety and risk management issues also need to be incorporated in planning for event staging. In order to plan an event involving a stage and set, it is necessary to know the types of props that will be required and the equipment needed to install them. Staging can involve one or more of the following elements:

Staging requirements for an exhibition.

* framed scenery (e.g. flats, profiles, doors, windows)
* weight-bearing scenery (e.g. rostra, ramps, steps)
* non-weight-bearing scenery (e.g. columns, trees)
* soft scenery (e.g. canvas legs, borders, cloths, gauzes, cycloramas)
* furniture and other set props
* revolves
* trucks.

Equipment to be used could include the following (which must be used according to regulation limits and licensing requirements):

* tallescope
* maxi-lift or genie-type lifter
* cherry picker
* mobile scaffolding
* ladders and A-frames
* scissor lift.

If working outdoors, staging requirements may include stages, tents, scaffolding, fences, ground covering and seating. All of these are available from suppliers of staging products and services. An event manager needs to understand product and service terminology, features and options, as well as current technology in key areas of staging. This knowledge is essential for contractor briefing and development of specification documents for:

* catering
* venue or site services and set-ups
* technical services (e.g. audiovisual, lighting, sound, rigging, special effects)
* entertainers
* registration requirements and set-ups
* physical elements (e.g. display, furniture and temporary structures)
* security
* media coverage
* safety equipment.

As we have mentioned several times, the theme of an event must be supported in every aspect, including the decor, lighting, sound and special effects. The theme may be quite subtle: for example, in the case of a high-tech theme for a conference, the audience would only be subliminally aware of aspects of the theme, such as the colour scheme. In more dramatic cases, guests might be asked to support the theme by dressing appropriately or participating in entertainment that is consistent with the theme. Themes may be tried and tested, or quite unique.

A theme can be reinforced through such creative elements as:

* colour
* landscape and/or location
* film/theatre/art/dance
* humour
* fantasy.

Following are important aspects of the theme that need to be carefully considered by the event organiser. As you will see, there are many decisions to make! Detailed staging specifications may relate to price, performance standards, timelines, technical specifications for equipment, and regulatory requirements.

Entertainment

A wide range of acts can be used to enhance the theme of an event, and corporate events, in particular, often employ interesting performers such as snake charmers, hypnotists and belly dancers. Entertainment companies have a wealth of ideas, which you can explore on their websites. They need to be briefed in the early planning stages so that they become familiar with the event purpose and the event audience. They can then look at the event theme and come up with a range of concepts to suit the theme. If a band is recommended, the specific technical requirements should be discussed at this stage. (One event organiser illustrated the importance of briefing the entertainment provider with her own experience in organising an event for a 21st. When the parents of the young woman celebrating her birthday heard that one of the band members had made indecent gestures, they were furious with the organiser!)

Decor

Lena Malouf is one of Australia's foremost event designers and her work has earned her two major awards, the first for Best Event Produced for a Corporation or Association (overall budget US$200 000 to US$500 000) and the second for Best Theme Decor (decor budget over US$50 000). Her guests were submerged in a magical 'underwater' world reminiscent of the fantastical journey in the children's classic, *Bedknobs and broomsticks*. Malouf's events are characterised by extravagant displays, including imaginative moving art pieces that tie in perfectly with the chosen theme, her main aim being to surprise and transport the audience. She has served as the Worldwide International President of the International Special Events Society (ISES).

Decor encompasses many things, from the colour scheme to the drapes, from props to floral arrangements. The challenge is to bring them all together into a cohesive theme. Staging rental companies can be extremely helpful with this task.

Layout

The layout of the event venue is clearly integral to the success of the event. Anyone who has worked on conferences and formal dinners knows that table layout is something that needs to be negotiated with the client well in advance. With large dinner events in large venues, all too often the audience at the back of the room has very limited vision of the stage. Where this is compounded by poor sound and too much alcohol, it does not take long before the presenter is drowned out by the clink of glasses and the hum of conversation. This can be very embarrassing.

When planning an event at which guests will be seated around a table, it is essential to plan the layout according to scale. If the dimensions of the tables and chairs are not considered, as well as the space taken by seated guests, there may prove to be no room for waiters or guests to move around. A number of common table and seating layouts are illustrated in Figure 4.2. For each of these, a scale drawing would be used to calculate the capacity of the room and the appropriate use of furnishings.

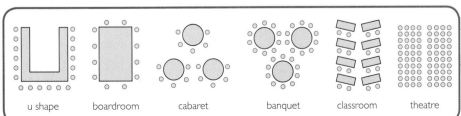

u shape　　boardroom　　cabaret　　banquet　　classroom　　theatre

FIGURE 4.2
Table and seating layouts

Lighting and special effects

Lighting can be used to spectacular effect, and for this reason events held at night provide the opportunity for more dramatic results than those held during the day. Lighting can be used both to create the general ambience and to highlight particular features. It is often synchronised with sound for special effect at dances and fireworks displays, and can also be used to highlight sponsor advertising. As with sound, lighting is used to create a particular mood, although it is important to remember that this must be consistent with the event theme. Subtlety is required, for there has been a tendency recently to use some of the latest patterning techniques too often. Professional advice from a lighting designer is recommended as lighting is more often than not one of the main contributors to staging a successful event.

Sound

Music is a powerful creator of mood. It can excite or calm an audience, while particular pieces can be highly emotive. The volume needs to be pitched at just the right level, and all members of the audience need to be able to hear clearly, particularly if the event is being staged in a large stadium. Professional sound engineers can be relied upon to give advice on equipment and the acoustic qualities of a venue. For example, a concrete venue with little or no carpeting or curtaining has a negative effect on sound, but this can be remedied by the incorporation of drapes in the design.

Vision

Vision incorporates all projected images, such as replays of sporting highlights on large screens or scoreboards. Video projectors, slide projectors and data projectors can project images onto screens for dramatic effect, and this can be extended to live broadcasts with satellite links. A wall of monitors can be used to project one large image across the whole monitor wall, achieving the effect of a large screen. The splitting of the image between monitors is done by computer programming.

Back-up projectors and duplicate copies of videos, slides and so on are essential. Most business and academic presentations use computer software packages to improve the visual quality of the images.

Stage

The stage is used for many reasons, including performances, prize-givings and presentations. Equipment rental companies can provide advice on the size and shape of the stage, as well as on screens and other devices on which to project images from the rear of the stage.

Stage set-up and rehearsal before the performance

However, the needs of the audience are the prime consideration, particularly the line of sight, which must be considered when deciding on the size and shape of the stage and the placing of lecterns or screens.

Set

The set includes all objects on the stage: props, flats, lecterns, stairs, curtains. Sometimes these are hired; at other times they must be built or made. The **cyclorama**, for example, is the curved white screen at the back of the stage used to create a sense of distance, special lighting of the cyclorama providing different coloured backgrounds. **Borders** are used to mask parts of the rigging system and to trim the sightlines so that only the set may be seen by the audience. A **traveller** is a type of curtain that moves along a track. Often it is used as the main stage curtain, being configured so that one operating line moves curtains from both sides of the stage simultaneously. Other staging terms are described in the box on page 64.

The stage specifications from the Adelaide Festival Centre shown in Figure 4.3 would be most useful in planning operations by the event organiser. Most larger centres provide this level of detail, as well as plans and drawings.

Tenting

Doug Matthews (2008) points out that a tent provides a blank canvas allowing for highly creative lighting and decor. Tents are also associated historically with circuses and entertainment, as well as providing an environment that many of the audience will not have experienced. In Australia, a tent is called a 'marquee' but in the USA this term refers to a canopy. There are many designs and colours of tents but the most commonly used is white. Movie goers will remember the breach of protocol of Indian wedding planner Vijay Raaz in *Monsoon wedding* when he erected a white tent rather than a red or orange one. In India, white is associated with mourning and death.

Field of play

Each sporting event has specific requirements. These may include gymnastic equipment, which must be properly set up to very clear specifications, or simply a good-quality pitch and wicket. In fact, there is nothing simple at all about a good-quality wicket, as cricket fans would know only too well! The quality of the grassed field is important for most sports. The 2000 Olympic Games soccer semi-final held in Canberra was threatened with cancellation due to the poor quality of the newly laid turf. Fortunately, the problem was solved in time for ticket-holders to enjoy the eagerly awaited match. Problems of this nature are not uncommon. For this reason, sporting fields are often covered when they are used for other events. However, while the cover protects the surface, it also blocks out the light so that damage can still be caused to the field. These days, professional grass specialists can replace the entire field within hours, but this is a very costly exercise.

The photos illustrate the installation of protective flooring in parts of a stadium. This included two layers: the first, a mesh to protect the grass and limit flattening; the second, a series of boards which were laid by hand by a team of 20 workers over 8 hours. This effort was repeated for each concert performance at the stadium as the flooring could not be left on the grass over a 24-hour period or the grass would not survive the heat and lack of light.

STAGING TERMS

PERFORMANCE

Management and agent	Take care of performers' interests
Talent	Performers (although sometimes used as a demeaning term to refer to the people who are not the main performers)
Green room	Area where performers wait and watch monitors
Dressing room	Area where performers dress and are made up
Wings	Area used for assembling performers and props
Stage-in-the-round	Circular stage allowing 360° views for the audience
Proscenium arch	Traditional theatre-style curtains at side and above
Thrust	Stage projecting into the audience, such as at fashion parades
Tracks	Fixed tracks used to move props
Lectern	Stand for speaker

LIGHTING

Mixing desk	Where the lighting engineer controls lighting effects, adjusting colours, brightness and special effects; also where the sound engineer controls sound, including volume and switchover between music and microphone
Rigging	Overhead truss
T-stand/tree	Upright stand for lights
Floodlight	Wide light
Spotlight	Narrow light
Fresnel	Circular soft-edged beam (can go from spot to medium flood)
Cyclorama	Curved white screen at the back of the stage for light projections
Parcan	Fixed beam with soft edge, cheaper than floodlight, usually above the front of the stage and usually used in groups of four
Lighting gels	Slip-over colours used to change the colour of spotlights and parcans
Wash light	General area cover
Key light	Used for highlighting an object
Back light	Rear lighting effect (should use for speakers)
House light	Lighting provided by venue

SOUND

Sound spec sheet	Specifies the sound requirements for a particular group or performance
Sound amplifier	Used to project the sound (microphones are plugged into amplifiers which power up the sound and send it to the speakers)
Out-front speakers	Speakers which face the audience
Fold-back speakers	Positioned on stage, facing the performers, to help performers hear themselves
Microphones	Include battery, stage (dynamic voice), headset and lectern

EXHIBITIONS

Floor plan	Two-dimensional layout of the venue
CAD drawing	Computer-generated, three-dimensional drawing of the design for a stand
Booth	Usually 3 m x 3 m stand at an exhibition
Corinthian	Walling covered with fabric to which Velcro will adhere
Pit	Service duct located in the floor, providing power and telephone cables (for some indoor and outdoor events, water and compressed air and gas can also be provided in this way)
Tracker/reader	Device for scanning visitor cards to capture their data

GENERAL

Pyrotechnics	Fireworks
Three-phase	Power for commercial use comes in three-phase (lighting, sound and vision equipment requires three-phase) and single-phase for domestic use

Stage specifications
Adelaide Festival Centre

FIGURE 4.3

Example of stage specifications

STAGE FACILITIES

Stage
Timber, covered with 6 mm masonite.
Painted: Matt black.

Traps
The Space has an understage trap in a T formation across the centre of the floor area. The trap is covered by a series of steel framed and timber covered lids, each measuring approx. 1.2 m × 1.8 m. Please refer to the 'Space Plans and Drawings' for further details.
The space also has a shallow audience seating trap with two levels. Please refer to the 'Space Plans and Drawings' for further details.

Power Supply
In addition to the Stage Lighting Power (distributed from the Drama Centre Rack Room) the Space has one 32 amp 3 phase outlet located in the grid.

Control Rooms
The Space Sound Control Room is at balcony level with a fully opening window. The Space Lighting Control Room is also at balcony level with a fixed, double glazed window. Some stage managers choose to call the show from the Lighting Control Room, although there is limited space.

Music Stands and Sconces
Music stands, sconce lights and orchestral chairs can be supplied out of the Festival Theatre stock subject to availability.

Pianos
Concert and rehearsal pianos are available by arrangement with the Production Co-ordinator. Moving and tuning charges apply.

Masking
The Space Theatre is stocked with the following masking items:

HARD MASKING

4 Flats	4500 mm high × 1600 mm wide	Wool covered ply
4 Flats	3000 mm high × 2000 mm wide	Wool covered ply
2 Flats	2300 mm high × 900 mm wide	Wool covered ply
2 Flats	3100 mm high × 600 mm wide	Wool covered ply
1 Flat	2700 mm high × 1500 mm wide	Wool covered ply
2 Flats	3400 mm high × 1400 mm wide	Wool covered ply (fit above balcony)
2 Flats	2800 mm high × 900 mm wide	Wool covered ply (fit below balcony)
1 Flat	2800 mm high × 1500 mm wide	Wool covered ply (fit below balcony)

SOFT MASKING

8 Curtains	5400 mm high × 3400 mm wide	Pleated velour (for hanging from bobbins on perimeter track)
6 Curtains	5400 mm high × 3100 mm wide	Flat velour (fair condition only)
7 Curtains	5400 mm high × 4000 mm wide	Flat velour (fair condition only)

Cyclorama
Cyclorama — approximately 36.57 m × 5.48 m drop (approx. 120 ft × 18 ft).
*Please note that one end of the cyc has visible water marks.

Source: The Adelaide Festival Centre.

Laying protective flooring in a stadium

This mesh layer protects the grass and limits flattening

Successful flooring products need to sit on the ground but still allow air, light and water to permeate. They also need to have an acceptable load-bearing capacity. Terraplas, the first turf protection product, was developed in the UK and is used widely in stadia accommodating audiences of 80 000 or more. An alternative product is PRO-FLOOR®. Unlike Terraplas, which is rigid and flat, this Australian product follows the contours of the ground, rolls up for storage and is easy to install and dismantle. This type of product allows light to permeate so it can be used for longer periods than the system illustrated in the photographs. It is commonly used for pathways at shows and festivals and in the queuing areas. When making a decision regarding turf protection, the labour required for installation and dismantling is a cost consideration.

Line of sight is another important consideration, and organisers cannot afford to sell seats from which the visibility of sporting enthusiasts is impaired. The placement of media equipment is often the cause of this type of problem, and discussions must be held before tickets go on sale to establish the proposed position of cameras and sound equipment. The same holds true for processions and street parades where an elevated position is preferable for camera crews. This may require authorisation by the local authority, and accreditation may be necessary for those eligible to enter the media area.

Finally, the use of giant screens with rear screen projectors, such as those used at the Mahler 8 concert at the Sydney Superdome, need to be considered for large venues where there is a risk that members of the audience will not be able to readily see the stage or field of play.

Rehearsals

The importance of rehearsal cannot be underestimated. This is the opportunity for all involved to integrate their efforts—everyone from the stage manager (who calls the shots for the presentation) to the technical support staff (who follow the appropriate cues for lighting and sound). A technical run-through allows the staff involved to test the set-up and to make sure that all elements work satisfactorily. Technical glitches at an event are unprofessional, to say the least, so a back-up plan for all aspects of the presentation is absolutely essential. This includes two copies of each video or sound clip, slide presentations in more than one format and multiple microphones. Every potential problem should have a ready solution. The final aspect, over which the event manager has little control, is the quality of the presentation given by the speaker, particularly at business and academic conferences. Giving some basic

Rehearsal leads to perfection

advice and encouragement beforehand can assist a presenter enormously. If rehearsals have been conducted and everything is under control, speakers are far less nervous and far less likely to feel uncomfortable under the spotlight. A 'ready room' where the speaker can set up and test the presentation before going on stage is recommended.

EVENT SERVICES

The supply of essential services, a communications network, and transport and traffic management are essential to the staging of most events.

Essential services

Essential services include power, water and gas. While the provision of these may sound simple, various different electrical sources are often required, including three-phase power for some equipment and power back-up in case of emergency. Providing the venue kitchen with gas can also be a challenge. The choice of a complex site can add to the difficulties of providing these essential services to the event venue.

Communications

Many events have particular requirements for communications, which may even include the installation of a complete telephone and communications network. Where there is a high level of demand on the communications network, the issue of bandwidth must be resolved, particularly if there is a significant amount of data being transmitted. A stadium often requires its own mobile phone base station owing to the number of people using mobile telephones, particularly at the end of an event.

Transport and traffic management

Transport to the event, including air, rail, bus, train and taxi, needs to be considered. So, too, does the issue of parking and its impact on local traffic. In some cases, streets have to be closed, traffic diverted and special permission sought for this purpose, the event plan being an important part of the submission to the relevant authorities. Thought must also be given to access for people with disabilities, marshalling of crowds and notifying of businesses affected by any disruptions. Most importantly, the stars of the show need to be able to find their way into the venue without any difficulty. Most large stadiums and convention centres have special entry at the rear or via underground tunnel for the VIPs, players and performers.

SOURCE AND NEGOTIATE STAGING CONTRACTORS

From a legal and business perspective, it is essential to develop accurate and complete staging specifications detailing precise requirements based on sound product and service knowledge for provision to contractors. (See Figure 4.4 for the types of technical specialists often required at events.) In turn, contractors should provide timely quotations for the provision of products and services, which should then be confirmed in writing showing details of the products and services and their costs. The legal nature of these arrangements is discussed in Chapter 9.

The organiser's aim is to:
★ identify and source appropriate contractors to provide services for the event
★ provide accurate briefings or specifications on precise staging requirements to contractors
★ obtain complete and timely quotations for the provision of services
★ analyse quotations and select contractors in consultation with key stakeholders
★ confirm agreements with contractors in writing, including details and costs of all services.

FIGURE 4.4
Technical specialists

THE TECHNICAL TEAM

The production, or staging, of an event involves many specialists. As an example, members of the technical team supporting a performance would include:

- Artistic Director
- Production Manager
- Technical Director
- Stage Manager
- Choreographer
- Scriptwriter
- Lighting Designer
- Lighting Operator
- Sound Designer
- Sound Operator
- Vision Designer
- Vision Operator
- Front of House Manager
- Floor Manager.

The following staff would support the performance indirectly:
- Venue Manager
- Operations Manager
- Logistics Manager
- Catering Manager
- Cleaning and Waste Manager.

When monitoring contract implementation, the organiser needs to:

★ monitor progress, including safety issues, at regular intervals through ongoing liaison with contractors and other stakeholders

★ identify the need for adjustments and organise appropriate changes, with confirmation in writing

★ negotiate adjustments to maintain the integrity and quality of the event

★ evaluate work completed against event requirements and time schedules, and take appropriate action to address delays.

The dynamic nature of the event environment generally brings about multiple additional requests or changes. For this reason, contract variations need to be negotiated and always documented in writing.

Safety is a major consideration in the staging area, and this work is generally done by licensed professionals. Staging contractors are able to interpret stage plans, and they have a detailed knowledge of:

★ types of control desks which operate stage machinery

★ techniques for working out load capacity of stage machinery

★ safe and efficient methods and procedures used in manoeuvring loads

★ techniques for handling scenic elements (e.g. toggling flats and pin hinging)

★ relevant legislative and/or organisational health and safety requirements (e.g. safe manual handling techniques, working at heights, moving loads safely)

★ safety issues associated with using ladders

★ signals to be employed when using stage machinery

★ safety procedures to be followed in the event of lifting, revolving or trucking emergencies.

Tum et al. (2006) point out that there are any number of potential causes for accidents including *direct damage* to the venue or equipment, *consequential loss* due to the venue being unavailable, *legal liability* through failure to perform, and *personal loss*, including financial loss by the event organiser (p. 152).

CATERING CONTRACTORS

A catering contractor usually does the catering for an event, taking care of food orders, food production and service staff. These contractors (or the venue catering staff) should provide menus and costings relevant to the style of service required. Photographs of previous catering and food presentation styles can be helpful in making a decision.

There are many approaches to event catering, the most common being:

★ set menu, with table service

★ buffet

★ finger food

★ fast food.

The style of cooking and the type of service have the main impact on cost. Food that is prepared off site and heated or deep-fried on site can be very cost effective. If fully qualified chefs are to provide quality fresh food with superb presentation, and the guests are to be served by silver service–trained waiting staff, then clearly the costs will escalate enormously.

When discussing catering contracts, the event organiser needs to be very explicit about food quantities, type of food required and speed of service. Despite expressions of interest in healthier food at sporting events, findings show that the old favourites, such as pies and chips, are still popular and that fruit salad and sandwiches do not sell well.

A food safety plan is another essential item when planning an event. Food safety involves protecting the customer from food poisoning by implementing a plan to prevent cross-contamination and other factors that cause bacterial growth. For example, food needs to be kept at the correct temperature all the way from the factory/market to the store, into the kitchen and onto the buffet. Food safety plans look at every aspect of food handling and, if well implemented, ensure the measurement of temperatures at key points in the process in accordance with the guidelines of the plan. The best kitchens have refrigerated delivery areas and separate storage for vegetables, meat, seafood and other products at the correct temperatures. Planned food production processes, including plating food in a refrigerated area, can further reduce the risk of bacterial growth. Finally, it is essential for the food safety specialist to consider the length of time taken for the food to reach the customer (perhaps at the other side of the stadium) and the length of time before it is consumed. Health authorities in the various states and territories monitor food safety.

Catering for an event is extremely demanding for those in the kitchen. Producing several hundred hot meals is not for the faint-hearted. The chef should be aware of the planned time for service of all courses and this should be confirmed at an early stage of the planning. Most floor managers will ask the chef how much notice is needed for service of the main course and they will monitor proceedings and advise the chef accordingly.

Beverage supplied at functions and banquets usually comes in the form of beverage packages ('packs') which are available in a range of prices, depending mainly on the quality of the wine. A pack includes a specific range of wines, beers and soft drinks, and does not generally include spirits. The client may choose a selection of beverages, but this will clearly be more expensive, and may also specify a time limit for an open bar.

The logistics of catering from a site that has no kitchen are quite daunting. All equipment and ingredients have to be transported to the site and, as discussed above, perishable food must be maintained at the right temperature. This often involves hiring a cool room. Workflow planning is particularly important: for example, certain ingredients must be pre-prepared ready for use when needed.

Queue management is another consideration, as customers waiting or needing to use condiments can hold up the process if appropriate planning has not occurred.

ACCOMMODATION PROVIDERS

For many conferences, exhibitions, shows and sporting events, accommodation is an essential part of the package. The packaging of air travel and accommodation demands that planning for such events occurs well in advance in order to acquire discounted airfares and attractive room rates. If such rate reductions are essential to favourable pricing of the event, it is preferable to hold the event in an off-peak season. However, as soon as an event such as the Formula 1 Grand Prix in Melbourne reaches a significant size, discounted rates are out of the question as accommodation in the destination city will be fully booked.

The following extract illustrates the response of many accommodation providers as soon as they get wind of an event, although this approach to pricing is generally counter-productive. The negative image created by overpricing can have an impact on tourism in the long term.

> The normally sleepy town of Mongu (in Zambia) is about to come alive this weekend for the Kuomboka ceremony. The ceremony stretches back several centuries and is about moving Lozi people from the flooded Zambezi Plains to the plateau. Hotel owners in Mongu say they immedi-ately hiked room rates as soon as the announcement of the event was made, by between 600 and even 1000 per cent in some cases. They are also quoting their room rates in United States dollars as they expect more than 5000 tourists to witness Zambia's foremost traditional event.
>
> The holding of the ceremony is dictated by the amount of rain that falls in a particular season. So much rain has fallen this year that staging the ceremony was never in doubt.
>
> *Sunday Independent*, South Africa, 25 March 2001

This is a most unusual event—most event organisers dread the prospect of rain, while those organising this event require rain to ensure its success!

WASTE MANAGEMENT SPECIALISTS

One of the legacies of recent mega events in Australia is an increased awareness of environ-mental issues. Biodegradable plates and cutlery are now commonplace at smaller events, replacing non biodegradable foil pie plates and polystyrene containers.

Methods for reducing the environmental impact of noise, air and water pollution should be part of the planning process and advice on these can be obtained from the Environmental Protection Authority which has offices in each state. With regard to air pollution, releasing helium balloons into the atmosphere has been shown to be environmentally unfriendly and this practice is slowly dying out around the world.

Waste management is another important consideration for event organisers, and is often contracted out to specialists. This will be covered in detail in Chapter 20. Professional contractors can advise on the correct disposal of cooking oils and other toxic waste that could affect the water supply. As we know, clearly marked bins should be provided for recycling of waste products. Waste management companies can provide the full range of equipment and services including installation and removal of bins.

The number and type of toilets to be provided at an event, including the number allocated to men, women and people with disabilities, must also be decided. The composition of the event audience—the number of men and women attending—and the average time taken by each also need to be considered! Theatre management has been working on this for years. Every woman has faced the problem of long queues at interval and there is in fact a formula for working out how many toilets are required! Too many events provide substandard toilet facilities that cannot meet the demand, so it is essential to discuss the requirements for any event you are planning with a toilet facilities hire company as they are the experts.

CLEANING CONTRACTORS

Some cleaning contractors specialise in events, including Clean-event, the company most widely used for events in Australia. In most cases, cleaning is done before and after the event. Maintaining cleanliness during peak times is challenging, particularly if there is only a short changeover time between event sessions. This means that you have to get one audience out, the cleaning and replenishment of stocks done, and the next audience in on time. The timing is part of logistics planning, which we will cover in detail in Chapter 16. Cleaning staff are part of the event staff and should receive appropriate training so that they can answer questions from people attending the event.

Hand-washing facilities are useful for guests and essential for staff preparing food. The temporary hand-washing facility illustrated is ideal for outdoor events. It provides soap and hygienic running water.

As you can see from the above, staging an event involves myriad tasks for the event organiser. With some events, the staging process may even include managing the fans who queue for days before the event for places at the event. At the Academy Awards, for example, the area designated for fans is occupied for up to two weeks before the big night, as one of the fans receives a free grandstand seat overlooking the red carpet. According to the *London Daily Telegraph*, 20 April 2001, 'The commitment of Oscar followers makes Wimbledon campers look like amateurs. A thriving industry has developed around their needs, from food stands to camping equipment.'

Overall, many events can be conceptualised as theatrical events. According to Martin et al. (2004), this conceptualisation embraces characteristics of authorship, 'performativity', spatial and temporal dynamics, and performance–audience relationships (p. 91). Lissa Twomey's opening to the New Zealand International Arts Festival in Wellington certainly comprised all these characteristics. According to the reviews (Sorensen 2010), thinking outside the box was not just a guiding principle but a leitmotif for Twomey's work as artistic director: 'Guided by her long experience with the Sydney Festival and her now shrewd understanding of the NZ audience, Twomey put together a triumphant program of calculated risk-taking.'

Temporary hand-washing stand, including soap and towels

MONITOR STAGING CONTRACTORS

The event manager needs to monitor the pre-event progress of staging components at regular intervals through ongoing liaison with contractors and other stakeholders and to evaluate work completed against event requirements and time schedules. Sometimes it is necessary to take appropriate action to address delays or other problems; these issues are more easily resolved if the specifications were clear in the first place. However, the event environment is a dynamic one and it is almost always necessary to make staging adjustments and changes. Staging adjustments may relate to changes in numbers, budgetary changes, demands by the performers, or unexpected difficulties with staging components. These, too, should be agreed in writing, however trivial they may seem at the time.

As will be shown in Chapter 10, it is essential to maintain good relationships with suppliers of event services and equipment as it is these contractors who may be needed to help with last-minute changes. If they are responsive, many crises can be averted

SUMMARY

In this chapter we have looked in detail at the staging of an event, including layout, decor, sound, lighting and vision. The staff and subcontractors have also been identified, and the services required at an event, including catering, cleaning, waste management and communications, have been discussed. Staging an event is probably the most creative aspect of event management and there is enormous scope for making an event memorable by using the best combination of staging elements. The selection of the right site for an event is essential as this can have a large impact on the cost of staging the event and the level of creativity that can be employed in developing the theme.

Chapter review questions

1 List and explain five staging challenges associated with the production of a concert.
2 List and explain five staging challenges associated with holding a marathon.
3 How can the capacity of a banquet room vary? Investigate the average space for different room arrangements by comparing layouts and tables provided by convention centres.
4 What are the issues associated with special effects and pyrotechnics?

1 Develop a checklist for a venue inspection and then visit two or three venues and compare their various merits and limitations. In order to do this, you will need to have a specific event in mind, for example, a sporting event, a party, a conference or a wedding.

2 Watch a video of *Gladiator* and review the staging and the audience response to the events portrayed.

Case study

Creating a stage set

As an introduction to an academic awards ceremony in the Town Hall, you have been asked to organise a performance by contemporary or Indigenous dancers. Unfortunately, the Town Hall is a large space, with limitations in terms of lighting effects. There will also be a significant difference between the requirements of the performance and the requirements of the awards presentation, which is a formal, traditional daytime event.

Task

Investigate the options for props and drapes and/or create a model of the stage set-up for the dance production. Remember that the set will have to be easily removed or somehow integrated with the awards presentation.

References

Malouf, L (1998), *Behind the scenes at special events*, John Wiley & Sons, Brisbane.

Martin, J, Seffrin, G & Wissler, R (2004), 'The festival is a theatrical event', in Cremona, V, Eversmann, P, van Maanen, H, Sauter, W & Tulloch, J (eds), *Theatrical events: borders, dynamics, frames*, Rodopi, New York, pp. 91–110.

Matthews, D (2008), *Special event production, the resources*, Butterworth–Heinemann, Oxford, UK.

Sorensen, R (2010), 'NZ festival puttin' on the risk', *The Australian,* 4 March.

Tum, J, Norton, P & Wright, J (2006), *Management of event operations*, Butterworth–Heinemann, Oxford, UK.

Photo credits

67:Source Reproduced with permission. Cairns Convention Centre.

QUALITY CUSTOMER SERVICE

Unit descriptor

This unit describes the performance outcomes, skills and knowledge required to manage customer service quality in a range of service industry workplaces. It requires the ability to develop and monitor management strategies to enhance and oversee the delivery of quality customer service. This unit applies to individuals responsible for managing and improving service quality in the service industries. It focuses on the need to research and develop proactive approaches to service quality issues with some strategic and leadership focus. Depending on the size and nature of the organisation, managers and some supervisors undertake this role.

Elements

- Develop approaches to enhance quality customer service
- Manage the delivery of quality service
- Monitor and adjust customer service.

Critical aspects for assessment

- Ability to develop proactive approaches to delivering and monitoring quality customer service within a specific workplace context
- Knowledge of quality service principles and processes
- Demonstration of skills
- Monitoring and evaluation of service delivery in a workplace context (e.g. managing an event).

OUR EVENT staff are the face of the Melbourne Cricket Ground.

This means whether you work as a car park attendant, ticket seller, turnstile operator or usher, you become the customer's first and last impression of their MCG experience. Events staff must accept the ongoing responsibility of being an ambassador and advocate for the MCG at all times.

Event work occurs on weekends or late afternoons to evenings. These hours differ week to week, depending on the fixture. Friday night availability is greatly preferred. To proceed in applying for work, it is important that your availability is flexible at most of these times.

The process of event staff recruitment is conducted intermittently during the year when additional staff are required. The process is not necessarily conducted at the same time every year or at the start of the football or cricket season. This page will be updated when the recruitment process is open.

Source: <www.mcg.org.au/About%20the%20G/Employment/Event%20Day%20Staff%20Recruitment.aspx>.
© Melbourne Cricket Ground 1853 – 2009.

As this extract from the Melbourne Cricket Ground (MCG) illustrates, frontline employees such as ticket sellers and ushers are ambassadors for the venue. The MCG is not only a cricket ground, many other sporting and entertainment events are held there. For this reason, the staff also need to be ambassadors for the event that is held at the venue, and this is not possible unless they are properly briefed about the football match or the entertainment event. The duality of roles—venue management (running the grounds) and event management (putting on the show)—is starting to become apparent as a customer service issue and this will be discussed further in Chapter 15. For this duality to be invisible to the general public, seamless integration is needed. Careful planning and countless meetings are required to ensure faultless service delivery. There are multiple organisations represented at most large events, over and above the two key players already mentioned. This provides increased challenges for managing customer service.

In order to understand some of the customer service issues that service providers experience at events, some examples follow of the kinds of things that can go wrong and which should be prevented:

★ V6 concert: Taipei fans were upset about the seating arrangements made by the concert organisers. On entering, fans were informed by staff that because extra filming equipment was needed, their seats had been switched. Arguments escalated and fans began complaining online to the Consumer Protection Commission. Disputes ensued as the visibility was poor.

Security staff play a role in customer service

★ Live Earth concert: Almost 150 people complained about the use of foul language during the Wembley concert.

★ Ashes Series: Demand was unprecedented. Just 30 minutes after tickets went on sale, the Cricket Australia website had 'maxed out', forcing technicians to shut down all non-ticket-related functions on the site. Cricket fans jammed phone lines and the official website, as Cricket Australia threatened to cancel those tickets bought through eBay.

★ Music festival: Fans spent two hours in a queue to see a headline act only to find out that the set times had changed and the band had played an hour earlier.

★ Field Day Festival, London: Revellers were forced to wait up to two hours to be served at the bar, while women queued for upwards of one hour for the women's toilets. Organisers of the festival apologised for the farcical lack of toilets and bars at its inaugural event and promised to provide double the number the next year.

★ Britney Spears: It was reported that hundreds of her Australian fans walked out, three songs in, during her second show. There was much debate about whether it should have been mandatory to declare on promotional material that Spears was not singing live for most of the show.

★ AC/DC: A concert by the heavy metal rockers AC/DC in Munich drew over 100 noise complaints by irate neighbours. Complaints came from a suburb almost 20 kilometres away from the stadium.

★ Soccer: A player allegedly sustained injuries from a head-butt from a member of the crowd. The crowd member, who was not a registered player, was found guilty of spectator or crowd violence by the panel and was suspended from any soccer-related activity, including watching games, for 10 years.

★ Wedding photography: The most frequent complaint is about late delivery of photographs. 'So far this year we have received complaints about 22 different traders,' Ms Driscoll of the WA Department of Commerce said. 'We have received numerous reports of couples waiting six months or more and incredibly, in some instances, delays of more than two years. In some extreme cases, the pictures or videos never arrive because the company engaged to undertake the work has gone out of business' (WA Department of Commerce 2009).

Registration systems are a core part of customer service delivery for ocean swim races

There are many more complaints about nightmare nuptials, ranging from the quality of the food to the lack of management sensitivity in showing the wedding party the door at 4 pm after a 'lunch' booking to make way for the 'dinner and dance' booking.

As these situations illustrate, customer contact begins at the point of planning the event (art exhibition) or purchasing a ticket (sporting event). There are numerous systems and procedures necessary for managing customers through the many stages of their event experience, for example, invitation or ticket issue, booking or reservation, special requests, transport, parking, arrival and greeting, entry and seating, performance/show, first aid, catering, toilet facilities, departure and transportation. For most event visitors, gaining easy access to the event is one of the important aspects of their experience, coming second only to the main purpose of the visit, enjoyment of the event itself—even if it is a match lost!

EVENT SERVICE COMPONENTS

In many other industries, such as hospitality, a great deal of research has been done on quality customer service. However, the event environment is quite different as events are generally run over a short time span with temporary staff, and there is little opportunity to develop service relationships with customers at a personal level. To understand the components of service in the event environment it is useful to use a popular diagram, the fishbone diagram. The fishbone diagram is also known as the cause and effect diagram, or the Ishikawa diagram, named after its originator Kaoru Ishikawa, the Japanese quality pioneer. In simple terms, the fishbone is brainstorming in a structured format. As Figure 5.1 for a wedding shows, the diagram assists with the planning process and clarifies the customer's expectations. Similar diagrams can be done for conference planning or a marathon. The traditional headings for a fishbone diagram are methods (processes), machines (equipment), manpower (people), materials, measurement, and environment. However, this tool is flexible.

These diagrams indicate how key components can be broken down into increasing detail. The aim of the diagram is to illustrate the scope of the customer's experience. Other planning tools, such as schedules and checklists, can assist with the project management of the event. These will be covered in Chapter 14. In this chapter, in particular, the emphasis is on the management systems used to present the event experience to the customer.

DEVELOP APPROACHES TO ENHANCE QUALITY CUSTOMER SERVICE

To obtain information on customer needs, expectations and satisfaction levels, both formal and informal research can be undertaken. Formal research is structured and can be analysed statistically if the sample is big enough. Informal research is also useful and often the only tool available to the event manager of a small one-off event. Formal and informal research on customer needs may both involve:

★ talking to customers
★ seeking feedback from service delivery colleagues

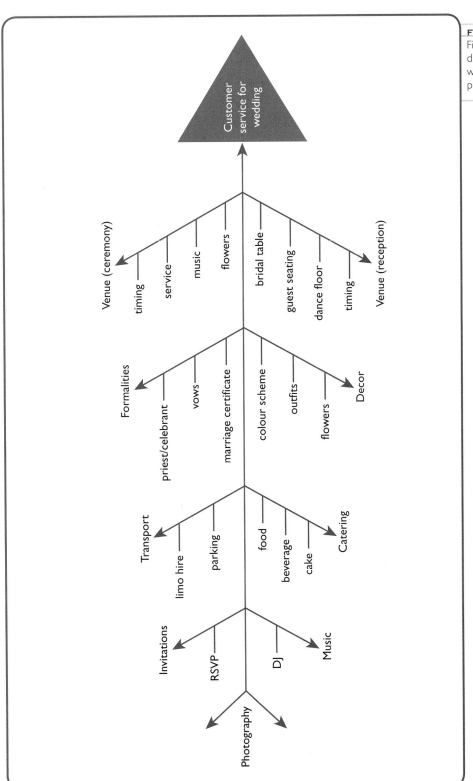

FIGURE 5.1
Fishbone
diagram for
wedding
planning

★ analysing the competitive environment

★ analysing industry and market trends.

For example, qualitative research can be done by talking to customer focus groups, while quantitative research may involve a ratings survey. Quantitative research can be presented both numerically and graphically. The mystery customer survey illustrated in Figure 5.5 includes both quantitative ratings and qualitative (open-ended) responses.

Customer service issues and standards may relate to:

★ response times

★ product quality

★ service guarantees

★ complaint management processes.

★ pricing guarantees

Face-to-face communication with the event customer is often limited, most of it occurring online, by email or by telephone. Planning a conference, for example, generally involves countless emails. Where the website is well designed, it is possible for the customer to play with a range of options, including choice of room set-up, menus, etc. These arrangements can then be confirmed in writing. The customer does not see the 'product' until the day of the event. This is why planning is so important. An event organisation has to develop standards to address key quality service issues such as provision of IT support or audiovisual services to exhibitors and conference presenters. Many of these ancillary services are provided by contractors and development of KPIs (key performance indicators) can assist in developing and monitoring quality service (see Figure 5.2).

FIGURE 5.2
Key performance indicators for quality audiovisual support

- Confirming timing for conference presentations 24 hours beforehand
- Arriving at least one hour before the first presenter's rehearsal
- Assisting conference presenters in the use of the audiovisual equipment
- Providing help with use of portable media (e.g. CDs, USBs)
- Connecting user laptops to the audiovisual system
- Helping with rehearsals of the presentations prior to the live presentation
- Ensuring issues that arise are actually with the supplied equipment, for example, by testing problems against the standard PC provided before the conference session commences
- Checking the physical security of the venue equipment
- Issuing and recovering microphones, laser pointers, etc. and ensuring batteries are replaced when required
- Ensuring that mobile contact numbers are prominently displayed if the technician is not present for any reason (this should not occur during the conference)
- Ensuring end-user instructions are available on the lectern
- Remaining on call from 7 am to midnight on the conference dates.

MANAGE THE DELIVERY OF QUALITY SERVICE

Service standards and expectations need to be explained clearly to colleagues in the event workforce, including employees of the event organisation, employees of the venue organisation, service and supply contractors, and volunteers.

These service standards should be monitored according to the venue organisation's policies, and feedback should be provided to contractors where necessary. The end user should also be asked to evaluate the service provided in the post-event evaluation survey.

Sureshchandar et al. (2001) point to the absence of focus on systematisation of service delivery, and this is highly pertinent to the event industry. They believe that if the primary service is not seamless from a systems point of view, customer satisfaction will not be achieved, no matter how convivial the service provider is. They refer to this as the 'content' of service (p. 115). For example, no matter how well treated, travellers will not be happy with airline service if the plane is late or judged unsafe. Likewise, event staff cannot meet the needs of customers through the force of their smiling personalities if the queuing system and security checks cannot allow them to reach their seats before start of play.

Sureshchandar et al. identify several dimensions for systemisation of service delivery: having a highly standardised and simplified delivery process so that services are delivered without any hassles or excessive bureaucracy; having a highly simplified and structured delivery process so that service delivery times are minimal; enhancing technological capability in order to serve customers more efficiently; providing adequate and necessary personnel for good customer service; and ensuring adequate and necessary facilities for good customer service (p. 118).

The concept of systematised foolproof procedures is highly relevant to the event industry where so little time is available for training. Procedures and control systems need to be carefully developed before the event, using checklists and run sheets. Also, the level of detail required in these systems, and in procedural training, is much greater, as customer demand is generally excessive over a short period.

Lashley's (1998, 2001) model for management of human resources in service organisations has been adapted in Figure 5.3 where the two variables forming the axes are variability (customised and standardised) and tangibility (high and low) of the service product. By way of explanation, marketers refer to the goods and services components of the product, goods being tangible (such as food items) and services being intangible (providing information and advice). Thus organisations can be positioned in one of the four quadrants. Most sporting events held at a stadium would be placed in quadrant 2 since many tasks, such as ticket taking, are simple and routine. However, in the high-budget, high-stakes, unpredictable arts environment, the event organisation would sit in quadrant 4. As events are predominantly characterised by a high service component, almost all would fall in the right-hand quadrants.

When applying this model to customer service management, event organisations would place themselves in the appropriate quadrant and develop policy and procedures according to the qualities that define the particular quadrant. For most events this would mean the development of highly specific, standardised work practices, with simple routine tasks for the majority of the event service workforce.

FIGURE 5.3
Approaches
to
management
of human
resources
in service
organisations

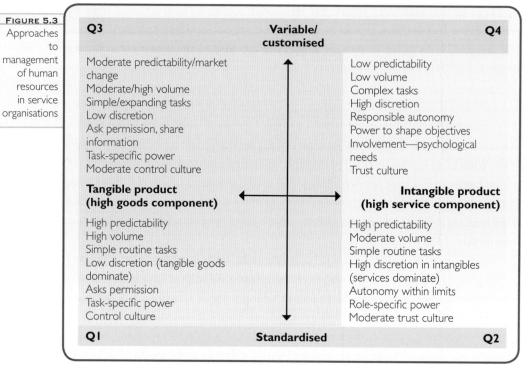

Q3	**Variable/ customised**	Q4
Moderate predictability/market change Moderate/high volume Simple/expanding tasks Low discretion Ask permission, share information Task-specific power Moderate control culture		Low predictability Low volume Complex tasks High discretion Responsible autonomy Power to shape objectives Involvement—psychological needs Trust culture
Tangible product (high goods component)		**Intangible product (high service component)**
High predictability High volume Simple routine tasks Low discretion (tangible goods dominate) Asks permission Task-specific power Control culture		High predictability Moderate volume Simple routine tasks High discretion in intangibles (services dominate) Autonomy within limits Role-specific power Moderate trust culture
QI	**Standardised**	Q2

Source: Adapted from Lashley, 'Matching the management of human resources to service operations,
© 1998, *International Journal of Contemporary Hospitality Management*, 10 1), 28.

MONITOR AND ADJUST CUSTOMER SERVICE

Many retail stores and fast food chains use mystery customers to evaluate customer service levels. This type of evaluation is effective in the event environment too. A simple questionnaire is illustrated in Figure 5.4. The quality of the feedback received can be further enhanced by giving more specific directions to the mystery customer (e.g. 'present yourself to a security guard asking for first aid assistance'; 'visit the toilet facilities at least three times to check for queues, cleanliness and supplies'; 'ask a volunteer for directions to the ATM machine'; 'ask a specific question about the event program or performer').

As with all aspects of event management, customer service planning is reliant on detailed planning and careful integration of the needs of the various stakeholders and the organisations that present the final event as a 'product' to the customer. Planning takes place over a long period, implementation is very brief and evaluation is essential for continuous improvement. For large events, such as New Year's Eve fireworks, the planning cycle can be as long as 15 months—a considerable time given that the 'show' usually lasts for only 15 minutes.

It is essential to monitor changes in the internal and external environments that may affect quality service planning particularly with events that are planned over many years.

Parking	Very good	Good	Average	Poor	Very poor
Was the parking clearly signposted?					
Were queues managed effectively?					
Were any staff present to give directions?					
How long did you wait to get into your car space from the main entrance to the car park?					
How long did it take to walk from the car park to the venue entrance?					
Could a staff member tell you the correct start time for the game?					

Entrance	Very good	Good	Average	Poor	Very poor
How long did you queue at the entrance?					
Were you greeted at the entrance?					
Was there a staff member at the ticket machine to assist if necessary?					
When inside the venue, how many uniformed staff could you see?					
Were you greeted by an usher?					
Were you shown to your seat?					
Was your ticket checked to see if you were in the correct seat?					
Were you encouraged to 'enjoy the match'?					
Were you able to gain access to an area for which you did not have a ticket?					

Seating	Very good	Good	Average	Poor	Very poor
Was visibility obstructed in any way?					
Was your seat comfortable?					
How would you describe the sound quality?					
How would you describe the behaviour of the crowd around you?					
How many security staff or police could you see from your seat?					
Did you feel that there were any threats to your comfort or security?					
Did you notice any customers with special needs (elderly, children, disabled) and were they given assistance?					

Show/match	Very good	Good	Average	Poor	Very poor
Did the match start on time?					
Did each part of the match concur with the description on the program (time and content)?					
How would you rate the response of the audience around you to the program elements?					

Catering	Very good	Good	Average	Poor	Very poor
How long did you wait for food service during the interval?					
How would you rate the hot food item you ordered (specify item)?					
How would you rate the cold food item you ordered (specify item)?					

Amenities	Very good	Good	Average	Poor	Very poor
Were toilets well signposted?					
How long did you wait?					
How would you rate the cleanliness of the toilet facilities?					
Were the toilets well stocked with toilet paper and other supplies?					

FIGURE 5.4
Mystery customer questionnaire

FIGURE 5.4
Continued

Security	Very good	Good	Average	Poor	Very poor
Were you searched on entry? Would you say that security staff contributed or detracted from the event atmosphere? Did you observe any security-related incidents? Please specify and describe how they were handled.					
Other services	Very good	Good	Average	Poor	Very poor
Was a staff member able to direct you to the lost and found facility? Was a staff member able to explain an aspect of the event program (specify question asked)? How many staff members or volunteers smiled at you in passing (without being approached)?					
Departure	Very good	Good	Average	Poor	Very poor
How long did it take you to get to your car? Were you farewelled by any of the staff when leaving? How long did it take to get out of the car park and into mainstream traffic?					

In the case of the Olympic games for example, external environmental change that might affect service planning includes cultural change, such as trends in music. The audience will be unhappy if the program does not meet their expectations. And a downturn in the economy can lead to cancellation or delay of business events. During such periods, competition for conferences and exhibitions is extreme both within Australia and with overseas competitors, and the quality of customer service and the expertise of the management team become even more critical in differentiating between one event organisation and another.

Because of the organic nature of the event environment and the exponential growth in staff numbers as the event draws near, policies and procedures need to be refined over time. Procedural planning can also occur on the spur of the moment when something unexpected happens, such as IT problems with ticket scanning.

The emphasis in this chapter has been on planning systems, policies and procedures for customer service since the nature of the service environment in events is quite different from that of most other long-life service organisations. While it is important to be flexible and responsive to client and audience needs, this should be done against a solid basis of documented systems and procedures.

There is no substitute for the personal touch, but good signage can alleviate the pressure on information officers

SUMMARY

This chapter has highlighted the complexity of the event environment, particularly the diverse nature of the workforce and the short duration of the performance, match or show, and thus the challenges in delivering quality service to the customer. Integration of the various operational functions, such as transport, security, policing, ticketing, catering, cleaning etc., is therefore essential if this is to be achieved. This requires detailed documentation of policies and procedures and, in turn, this information needs to be shared with all stakeholders, so that everyone attending to customer needs has the full picture. However, no matter how smoothly an event runs from an operational perspective, the customer is there for the event experience. Unless the quality of the product (the entertainment, sporting event, business conference) is outstanding, none of the friendliness or efficiency displayed elsewhere will count for very much. And last, but not least, this chapter has demonstrated the importance of evaluating the service provided to ensure continuous quality improvement.

Chapter review questions

1 Compare the *management* of customer service in a retail store with that of an event. In doing so illustrate the complexity of the event environment.
2 What are five common complaints from visitors to events? How can they be prevented?
3 How can the delivery of customer service in the events environment be enhanced by systematisation?
4 What are the pros and cons of using volunteers to provide additional levels of service?
5 Suggest two ways in which service quality can be evaluated in the event environment.

Activity

Using a fishbone diagram, brainstorm, discuss and map the customer service issues associated with the following three events:
- surfing carnival
- eighteenth birthday party
- soccer awards night.

Case study

Policy development
BIG DAY OUT CONDITIONS OF SALE AND ADMISSION
When this ticket is purchased subject to the following conditions from the Promoter, these conditions apply to that purchaser both as conditions of sale and as conditions of admission to the event; otherwise the following conditions apply as conditions of admission to the event:

1 All conditions shown on this ticket are to be read together with all other statements or directives either shown on this ticket or displayed on the premises.

continued

Case study (*continued*)

2　This ticket may not, without the prior consent of the Promoter, be resold or offered for resale at a premium over the face value of the ticket (including via on-line auction sites) or used for advertising, promoting or other commercial purposes (including competitions and trade promotions) or to enhance the demand for other goods or services either by the original purchaser from the Promoter or any subsequent ticket holder.

　　If a ticket is sold or used in breach of this condition, the Promoter reserves the right to cancel the ticket without a refund. This ticket is only valid when purchased from official agents. Tickets bought from other sources may be refused entry.

3　The Promoter reserves the right to enforce published ticket purchase limits and cancel any tickets obtained above said limits by any one customer.

4　If the event is cancelled by the Promoter for any reason, only the face value of the ticket will be refunded. If Promoter deems it necessary to abandon the event due to the forces of nature or any other reason, refund of the face value of the ticket is at the discretion of the Promoter.

5　Save as required by law, tickets will not be replaced nor money refunded after purchase. Duplicate tickets will not be issued for lost, stolen or damaged tickets. The Promoter does not offer refund in the event of lost, stolen or damaged tickets or where the ticket holder cannot attend the festival due to reasons beyond the Festival's control.

6　The Promoter reserves the right to change the lineup and/or the date of the event without prior notification. In the event of change of the date or lineup, refunds will not be available.

7　Please note there are restricted capacities at some Stages and other tented structures. Once the maximum capacity is reached in these areas there will be no further admissions. Your purchase of an event ticket does not guarantee admission to these areas in such cases.

8　We play rain or shine.

9　The Big Day Out is for Mature Audiences only (MA15). Children under the age of 15 are not permitted. All patrons entering the site must have a valid ticket.

10　The Promoter reserves the right to refuse a ticketholder admission to the event or to evict that person from the event in any of the following circumstances:

　　a)　if the ticketholder fails to produce appropriate identification as proof of age

　　b)　if the ticket has been sold or used in breach of condition 2

　　c)　if the ticket has been sold or used in breach of condition 9

　　d)　if the ticketholder refuses to make their clothes, bags, containers or other possessions available for search by the Promoter

　　e)　if the ticketholder is affected by the consumption of alcohol or drugs

　　f)　if the ticketholder participates in dangerous activities including aggressive dancing, moshing, stage diving, crowd surfing and climbing.

11　The words 'Big Day Out', and the Big Day Out logo and artwork are Registered Trademarks and are Copyrighted and cannot be used without the prior written consent of the Promoter.

continued

Case study (continued)

12 Entry is at own risk.

13 The Promoter and the owner and/or lessee of the Venue shall not be held liable for any loss, injury or damages sustained entering or within the Venue whether caused by the negligence of the Promoter or that owner or lessee or otherwise.

14 Small still cameras, including small digital cameras, are permitted but no sound or video recorders will be allowed inside the Venue. Professional cameras of any kind are not allowed on site without authority from the Promoter.

15 Bottles, cans, weapons, lasers, fireworks, umbrellas, illicit drugs and alcohol are prohibited items and will not be permitted into the Venue. All bags/containers are subject to a full search at entry to ensure the safety of patrons. Prohibited items that are confiscated will not be returned.

16 Ticketholders consent to filming and sound recording as members of the audience.

17 No pass outs will be issued unless otherwise advised.

18 Patrons who wish to consume alcohol must have photographic identification (except NZ). Anyone found to be supplying or buying alcohol for a minor will be evicted from the Venue and will possibly face criminal charges.

19 In the case of an emergency evacuation or situation, you must follow all official directives.

20 If you feel at any time your or anyone else's health or safety is threatened, you should contact the nearest security guard. There are St Johns Ambulance Officers on site at all times who can be contacted by security.

Source: <www.bigdayout.com/conditionsofsaleandadmission.php>. © Big Day Out.

Task

The above terms of sale for tickets to this event clarify the organisation's policies on a number of matters. Rewrite these terms as policy statements for the event organisation under the following headings:

1 Ticket scalping

2 Admission

3 Cancellation or changes to the line-up

4 Capacity and admission

5 Security and search

6 First aid.

References

Lashley, C (2001), *Empowerment: HR strategies for service excellence*, Butterworth-Heinemann, Oxford, UK.

Lashley, C (1998), 'Matching the management of human resources to service operations', *International Journal of Contemporary Hospitality Management*, 10(1):24–33.

Sureshchandar, G, Rajendran, C & Anantharaman, R (2003), 'The influence of total quality service age on quality and operational performance', *Total Quality Management & Business Excellence*, November, 14(9):1033.

Sureschchandar, G, Rajendran, C & Kamalanabhan, T (2001), 'Customer perceptions of service quality— a critique', Total Quality Management, 12(1):111–24.

Van Der Wagen, M (2008), 'An exploration of the notion of generic skills through a study of customer service training in two industry sectors', EdD thesis, University of Technology Sydney (UTS).

WA Department of Commerce (2009), 'No pretty picture results in wedding day blues', media release, 2 September, <www.docep.wa.gov.au/corporate/media/statements/2009/September/No_pretty_picture_results_in_w.html>, accessed 5 May 2010.

CHAPTER 6

MARKETING ACTIVITIES

Unit descriptor

This unit describes the performance outcomes, skills and knowledge required to plan and coordinate a range of marketing and promotional activities at an operational level. The unit incorporates knowledge of marketing principles. Coordination of marketing activities may relate to the promotion of any product, service or event; a group of products being cooperatively marketed; or even a whole city, region or event precinct.

Elements

- Plan and organise marketing and promotional activities
- Undertake a general public relations role
- Review and report on promotional activities.

Critical aspects for assessment

- Project or work activities that show the candidate's ability to plan and coordinate multiple marketing activities for a specific business operation and to prepare marketing reports
- Logical and detailed activity planning supported by relevant action plans
- Knowledge of marketing principles and their application to practical workplace activities
- Detailed knowledge of the industry, including structure and interrelationships, industry networks, information sources, and distribution and marketing networks
- Knowledge of the types of promotional activities commonly used within the event industry and specific major industry marketing and promotional events
- Project or work activities conducted over a commercially realistic period of time so that the planning, analysis and reporting aspects of this unit can be assessed.

PROMOTIONS work is not as glamorous as some might imagine—there is a lot less VIP entertainment and champagne involved! The daily role involves hard work and perseverance but is often rewarding. Ultimately, my role for our charitable fundraising event is to help bring our organisation and event to the attention of our target audience to increase donations.

In order to achieve this, extensive planning and research is required to identify the audience, key messages, communication channels and media opportunities to generate interest. The role involves extensive writing and requires strong communication skills.

Public relations activities are just one part of the broader marketing mix, which includes other communications disciplines and promotional activities. For example, direct marketing involves distribution of promotional materials directly to the customer. Personal selling involves meeting the customer face to face, or at the very least speaking on the telephone. It is all about strategic positioning of the organisation or event and communication of the right messages to reach and engage the target audience.

My role in assisting with the promotion of our fundraising event has involved begging family and friends to play rent-a-crowd for photo shoots. I have also helped prepare our spokespeople for media interviews, and speak with journalists to line up interviews in advance of the event, during the key promotional period. Lining up photo shoots and coordinating interviews are just some of the many tasks I perform to support the overall marketing plan.

EVENT MARKETING AND PROMOTIONS ASSISTANT

Promotion and public relations are a crucial part of the marketing of any event, as we have mentioned in previous chapters, and they will be discussed below in some detail.

Types of promotional activities commonly used in the service industries include trade and consumer shows, in-house promotions, advertising, public relations, familiarisations, signage and display, as well as web-based activities.

As part of the marketing strategy, event promotion involves communicating the image and content of the event program to the potential audience. Broadly, the aim of a promotional strategy is to ensure that the consumer makes a decision to purchase and follows up with the action of actually making the purchase. It is essential to turn intention into action and this is often the biggest obstacle of a promotional campaign.

PLAN AND ORGANISE MARKETING AND PROMOTIONAL ACTIVITIES

Promotional activities include far more than advertising. Indeed, most community events rely on free editorial publicity in the local media. Other forms of promotional activity include direct marketing, sales promotion and personal selling. All of these approaches will be discussed in detail later in this chapter.

Event promotion involves planning and scheduling marketing and promotional activities according to the overall marketing plan and marketing objectives. It is vital to identify

FIGURE 6.1
Marketing communications mix

relevant market information and use it to inform your short-term promotional planning. The market analysis may be based on marketing reports, sales reports, financial statistics, marketplace trends and competitive activity. A carefully crafted, integrated approach to communication with the client or customer is also needed to ensure that the marketing objectives are achieved in the established time frames (see Figure 6.1).

Having undertaken the market research, the marketing department is in a better position to decide how to promote a particular product or how to launch a new product. A number of activities are used for the marketing and promotion of event products and services, but not all will be applicable to every situation. Indeed, one key skill is the ability to determine which promotional activities are most appropriate, based on the current marketing focus and other relevant information.

Awareness of the different types of promotional activity is, however, essential. The most relevant of these are outlined below.

IMAGE AND BRANDING

The first step for most events is the development of a name, logo and image for the event. This includes the colour scheme and graphics that will appear on all event material ranging from registration forms to tickets to merchandise. Image and logo are closely linked and need to be agreed on well in advance. Together they are referred to as 'branding'. Where sponsors are involved, it is essential to obtain their approval of the branding, otherwise there could be conflict over the use of colour or the positioning and size of logos. The design must meet the needs of all stakeholders, as well as appealing to the event audience, particularly if the design forms the basis for merchandise such as T-shirts and caps. A slogan is sometimes developed as part of the image for an event and incorporated wherever possible. The result should be a consistent theme and colour scheme for all promotional material. In most cases, the colour scheme is also carried through to the decor, including signs, fencing, flags, table settings, banners and posters.

ADVERTISING

Advertising is paid communication, using one or more types of media to reach potential buyers. It can be extremely expensive, particularly radio and television advertising, and for this reason it is essential to accurately identify the market and target the advertising as cost effectively as possible.

Advertising is one of the most effective ways of raising awareness of an event or event business. However, from a marketing point of view, the aim is to achieve more than awareness. Awareness and interest need to be converted into sales and loyalty. The four steps to becoming a loyal customer are illustrated in Figure 6.2.

FIGURE 6.2
Stages in buyer behaviour

awareness (positive appeal)
⇩
interest and knowledge of product
⇩
testing and evaluating of product
⇩
becoming a satisfied, repeat or recommending customer

Whereas advertising might attract a potential customer to a convention centre as the possible venue for a wedding reception, a tour of the establishment and a display of photographs from previous receptions would create interest and allow the client to evaluate the product. An invitation to sample various menus, in consultation with the chef, would more than likely clinch the deal—provided the food was of an appropriate standard. The buyer has expressed interest, developed knowledge of the product and tested some elements of the product. For such an important decision, these steps are critical. Signing the contract is almost guaranteed and so, too, are the couple's expectation of the event's success and the possibility of recommendation to others.

In the event industry, expectation and anticipation are part of the product. Anything that can be done to enhance this is adding to the product benefit. A well-designed website, such as that of Big Day Out (see link in Appendix E), can help to develop loyalty, while a website for an agricultural show is an essential source of information for visitors wanting to see specific exhibitions. Full multi-page colour brochures and programs are used less frequently as more visitors access the required information online.

Various popular types of advertising are described in detail below.

Internet advertising

Website design and adequate listings with search engines (incorporating SEO (search engine optimisation) efforts to improve Google page rankings) are critical factors in the success of internet marketing and advertising. Security for online transactions and privacy of information given by customers are other very important considerations. The potential of this method of advertising is well recognised, with exponential growth expected in the coming years, many events being leaders in the field.

Internet advertising can assist with decision-making on all types of bookings by providing detailed knowledge of the facilities, such as accessibility for displaying large items such as cars and boats. Some convention centres have interactive planning available, so that when the customer chooses a type of function (banquet, conference) and identifies the number of guests, various room configurations are shown on-screen using CAD software. Most websites also offer email links to facilitate questions and answers.

Internet advertising has the potential to be more than advertising—it can translate interest into purchase with bookings made, paid and confirmed online.

Print advertising

Newspapers and magazines are the media most commonly used for advertising, although a *Yellow Pages* listing is essential for most small event operations. Cost is related to the medium chosen and to the size and positioning of the advertisement. The front and back covers and inside front and back covers are usually the most expensive spaces to purchase, followed by the top part of right-hand pages. Choosing the appropriate newspaper or magazine is essential, as wide coverage or untargeted advertising tends to produce a very limited response. The circulation statistics for the publication need to be analysed, including the demographic profile of readers, and matched to event target markets.

As part of the marketing plan, it is necessary to identify the market to be reached and then to establish where these people live and which of the print media would be most likely to reach them. When selecting the most appropriate media, cost is generally the biggest issue. Then you need to decide when to advertise—a month before, a week before or the day before? Faced with budget limits and potentially expensive advertising, these are all crucial decisions.

When preparing an advertising budget, you should be aware that different time slots on radio and television cost vastly different amounts, as do different positions on the pages of print media, as mentioned above. Local newspapers and local radio stations are always more cost effective than national ones and are generally a most effective way to reach a local audience. Larger events may aim to attract international audiences and, if this is the case, you will need to clearly identify the potential overseas audience and perhaps develop a tourist package to include accommodation and other attractions. Partnership arrangements can often be reached with travel companies and the assistance of state and national tourism bodies obtained to support and promote the event.

The content of advertisements must be informative but, most importantly, it must inspire decision-making and action to attend or purchase. Let's look at the following advertisement by an event company for their wedding hire products and services:

> We provide six-arm gold candelabra in the Victorian style, silk flowers, tea lights, fairy lights, table overlays (in organza, Jacquard and cotton), chair covers with sashes and ceiling drapes. We set up for you.

In this advertisement there is a lot of information but absolutely no inspiration. A number of descriptive adjectives would certainly have enhanced the text, as well as the possibility of customers buying their services!

In contrast, the advertisement for the unusual event in Figure 6.3 on page 94 is much more creative.

It would be very difficult to attract an event audience if only the facts of a blood donation were presented, and the promotional team has realised this by making this event into something not to be missed.

YOUR BLOOD!

Greendale Clinic Big Bleed Week

May 10–15 with the grand finale (don't miss this) on May 15

Greendale Clinic's last Big Bleed was a huge success. This year our target is 3000 units of blood. Sponsors have donated 10 major prizes as well as minor prizes for all other donors. The biggest prize, a trip to Cannes, will be presented at the grand finale. We will have free health advice, coffee shop and food stalls, a craft fair, children's entertainment, celebrities, races, a jazz band in the late afternoon and fireworks at the close each evening. Attendance is free and all donors receive a sponsor prize, plus go into the draw for the major prizes. Parking is available in Macleay Street. We start at 10 and finish at 9 pm.

The advertising message needs to meet the motivational needs of the audience, at the same time assisting the decision-making process by supplying the necessary facts.

Radio advertising

Radio advertising is effective if the message is clear. However, it is not possible to show images or provide very specific information and is thus used infrequently by all but the biggest event operators.

Television advertising

While the impact of television advertising is greater than for most other media, it is extremely expensive. Specific marketing objectives would need to be developed and an advertising agency fully briefed on the proposed campaign. The timing of the advertising campaign should be linked to consumer decision-making, which is generally possible only when market research has been conducted on similar previous events. Celebrity endorsement does not come free unless the event supports a charity. It costs around $2000 to $3000 for a minor celebrity and between $100 000 and $250 000 for a high-profile celebrity.

Direct mail advertising

A substantial client list is a valuable resource for direct mail advertising and selling. A client list can be developed rapidly if an organisation is promoted at trade exhibitions where

Signage—one form of advertising

the list of attendees is made available to exhibitors. If the market can be clearly identified, then direct mail is a most effective form of advertising, and one that is cost-effective too. Where customers are transient, the expense of direct mail is unwarranted. Of course an invitation is a form of direct mail advertising.

Displays and signage

Signs are one of the most effective ways by which small event businesses advertise, even though most councils place limitations on the size of signs. Lighting, too, is an important element of outdoor signage, and one that is often neglected. Sky writing is expensive: one display of up to 12 characters costs $2600. For a second display on the same day the cost comes down to about $1800.

Brochures and fliers

Brochures and fliers are essential advertising items for many types of small events, and they need to be descriptive, informative and colourful. The quality of any photographs or artwork used in them is most important too.

Advertising collateral

This interesting term covers a range of advertising media, from tent cards to billboards. Posters and billboards are often displayed in public places and tourist information centres.

PERSONAL SELLING

Personal selling involves face-to-face contact between seller and buyer. This enables the salesperson to talk directly to the buyer, and to persuade the buyer through negotiation to purchase the product. This type of promotion is most common for booking conferences, weddings, parties and incentive travel events. This is because the event details need to be planned and a quote provided.

For all personal selling, it is essential to prepare in advance by finding out as much as possible about the potential customer. Following are the steps and stages involved in meeting a potential client or making a sales call:

1 **Welcome**
   Give a friendly greeting.
   Open first.
   Observe body language.

2 **Explore**
   Ask about the planned event, including the purpose.
   Explore and listen to what the client needs or wants.
   Find out about the person's role in planning the event.

3 **Offer information**
   Clarify the client's needs—what they really mean.
   Focus on the buyer, not the product your company provides.
   Outline the product (e.g. function facility and catering) after
   clarifying the client's needs.

SALES CALL REPORT

Event venue details

Name of representative _____

Date and time of sales call/client meeting _____

Client details

Name of client, department and address _____

_____

Contact person's name and position/role _____

Person responsible for bookings and their department (if not as above) _____

Sales and promotions information

Purpose and type of event _____

Types of rooms/facilities required _____

Other services _____

Number of guests/attendees _____

Specific entitlements or limitations (e.g. budget) _____

Other facilities currently used (competitors) _____

Opportunities for preferred supplier status (tendering) _____

Other needs (e.g. sales meetings, training sessions, conferences) _____

Outcomes of meeting _____

Action required _____

4 **Close**

Agree the next step or action to be taken.

Work out the follow-up required to finalise the event details.

Complete a sales report form.

5 **Follow up**

Follow up in a timely manner.

Provide a quote to the client.

Review status periodically.

Completion of sales call reports is essential since face-to-face meetings are costly and business development managers need to show a return on the time invested. An example of a sales call report is illustrated in Figure 6.4.

SALES PROMOTIONS

Sales promotions are intended to persuade a buyer to purchase immediately, so they often include incentives or discounts. Sales promotions may follow the introduction of a new product or may be implemented during a slow period. Examples of sales promotions include discounted event tickets, discounted off-season function facilities, incentive meeting packages, and newspaper or magazine competitions to win prizes such as tickets to a premiere. Giveaways would also fit into this category.

The Australasian Promotional Marketing Association (see web address in Appendix E) provides a code of conduct for promotional activities, as well as advice to member organisations. For example, if a discount is available to only a limited number of customers, this should be clearly stated on all promotional material. In both Australia and New Zealand, gaming and trade practices acts outline specific rules for promotions offering prizes.

PROMOTIONAL EVENTS AND TRADE SHOWS

Hotel groups, casinos, resorts and convention centres frequently exhibit at promotional events where they distribute information to potential buyers, particularly in the area of incentive travel. So too do suppliers to the event business, such as staging and rental companies, event software companies and event planners.

Issues to be considered when assessing whether to participate in promotional events or trade shows may include:

★ consistency of the activity with the overall marketing direction of the organisation
★ level of exposure to be achieved by attendance at an event, or sponsorship of an event
★ matching of attendees to an organisation's target markets
★ available financial resources
★ human resource requirements
★ timing of the activity or event.

Travel show

UNDERTAKE A GENERAL PUBLIC RELATIONS ROLE

Public relations is stimulation of demand for a product or service by providing commercially significant news about the product or service in a published medium, or obtaining favourable editorial review in a medium, such as a newspaper, free of charge. The most commonly used form for public relations is the press release. Most major events have a press release page on their websites, although such releases would be sent primarily to specific contacts in the media. Editorial publicity in the form of an article or a story is highly sought after and valued. Of course this is not completely free as there is significant time cost involved in preparing and issuing press releases, following up journalists and producers by telephone, planning launches and so on. Thus while there is no cost associated with the space allocated to the story, a public relations budget (in the form of human resource requirements or outsourced supplier fees) must be factored into the marketing budget.

Publicity for an event can be secured by running a careful publicity campaign with the media. Sometimes photo opportunities and interviews with a spokesperson or celebrity will also be necessary to develop the feature.

There are different types of media materials:

★ backgrounder—providing general information about the event, history, previous success, etc.
★ press release—story, newsworthy information
★ media alert—invitation-style alert to the fact that the event is imminent.

There are several points of contact. In the print media, these include the editor, the feature writers, and the editors responsible for individual sections of the newspaper or magazine. In the broadcast media, the people to contact include the station manager, producer or news director who in turn provide the story to the news announcers and radio personalities. In each case, the first question asked will be 'What makes this event newsworthy?' and the answer to this must be clear.

The aim of a press release is to stimulate media interest in the event and thus achieve positive and cost-effective publicity. Many large event organisers post their press releases on their websites. For mega and hallmark events, a launch is usually held prior to the event to which the media and the stars of the show are invited. These occasions are used to distribute the press release. It is essential that a launch be well attended and that the media report the event in a positive way, otherwise it will be counterproductive. The launch must be staged for photo opportunities and interviews. In the case of smaller events, sending a press release to a local paper is generally the best option. Since the staff working on these smaller publications are extremely busy, it is advisable to provide them with a ready-to-go article, including quotes as well as photos and logos where possible. The example in Figure 6.5 is the sort of press release/article that would draw the attention of a local newspaper.

Media Release

WE HOST THE COUNTRY'S LARGEST CYCLE RACE

Thousands Pedal the Peninsula

This year's 54 km race will see 15 000 riders tackle the most scenic mountain and beachside race in the country. The race is the largest sporting event in the state and the largest bicycle race in the country. This indicates a trend towards competitive physical competition for all age groups and cycling is a popular choice. Contestants will be visiting from overseas countries including Japan, Korea, India and Holland. Some riders are fiercely competitive, while others ride as family groups. All age groups are represented, and last year's race was completed by an 84-year-old and his 7-year-old grandson. The race will raise funds for a community parkland project and will be run by 5 local clubs. An additional $3 million is the target for other deserving causes. To register for the event, contact Richard on 9879 6543 or register on-line at www.pedal.com.au.

FIGURE 6.5
Press release for a local newspaper

The following guidelines for preparing a press release will help to ensure that the reader sits up and takes notice:

★ There must be something newsworthy to appeal to the reader in the first two sentences: he or she must be motivated to read the whole press release.

★ All the facts must be covered: what, when, why and how. This is particularly the case for negative incidents. The reader wants to know what happened, when it happened, why it happened and how things will be resolved. When something goes wrong, the facts are important because unsubstantiated opinion is dangerous. If the press release is promoting an event, all information such as the venue, date, time and so on should be included.

★ The press release should be short and to the point.

★ Layout should be professional.

★ Contact details should be provided.

★ Photographs should be captioned.

★ Quotes from senior staff and stakeholders (including sponsors) must be included.

★ If the press release is promoting an event, it should describe all potential benefits for the audience.

★ An action ending for booking or registering should include all necessary information.

★ The style of writing should be appropriate for the targeted publication.

★ There should be no errors in grammar or spelling.

Apart from media attention, it is also possible to obtain exposure through a number of official tourism organisations, many of which are listed in Appendix E. They provide tourist information to visitors through tourist information offices or their websites at state or national level. Brochures distributed to such offices or listings on their event calendars can provide valuable information to the potential (and sometimes very hard to reach) event audience. Every effort should be made to ensure that the event is listed as widely as possible.

The role of public relations is to manage the organisation's and the event's image in the mind of the audience and the public. This is mainly done through press releases as described above. These up-to-date information sources, together with photographs, provide the media with the background information they need to develop stories about the event. Media briefings can also be conducted before and during the event, particularly if high-profile people such as celebrities, entertainers and athletes can enhance the publicity.

One of the most critical public relations roles is to inform the media if there is a negative incident of any description. For this reason, an incident reporting system needs to be in place so that senior members of the event management team are fully informed, including the Public Relations Manager, if this is a separate role. It may be necessary to write a press release or appear in an interview if such an incident occurs. In some situations it is essential to obtain legal advice regarding the wording used in the press release. The public relations role can be a highly sensitive one, and in some situations words need to be chosen carefully. A simple expression of regret, for example, would be more tactful than suggesting the cause of an accident before a thorough investigation or inquiry.

Another more positive public relations role is the entertainment of guests and VIPs attending the event, in some cases from other countries. In this public relations role you need to be:

★ attentive to the needs and expectations of your guests
★ mindful of their cultural expectations
★ flexible in your response to their behaviour
★ informative and helpful as a host
★ proactive in designing hosting situations to meet the required protocol
★ able to make easy conversation.

Particularly with overseas guests or guests of event sponsors, you need to know in advance who they are (official titles, correct names and correct pronunciation) and where they come from. Most importantly, you need to know the reason why your company is acting as host to these guests as often business objectives, such as sponsor product awareness or negotiations, are involved. Research is therefore essential to determine how to meet the needs of the guests and the expectations of, for example, the sponsors.

According to Roger Axtell (1990) the effective multicultural host is able to:

★ be respectful
★ tolerate ambiguity
★ relate well to people
★ be non-judgemental
★ personalise their observations (not make global assertions about people or places)
★ show empathy
★ be patient and persistent.

As you can see from the above, there are a number of roles for the Public Relations Manager, or indeed for any member of the event team. The opportunity to sell an event occurs every time the telephone is answered or an enquiry is made by a potential customer. Customer relations becomes the role of everyone involved in an event and for this reason training in this area is recommended. This training should focus in particular on the event information likely to be requested by the customer, which is more difficult than it sounds since plans are often not finalised until very close to the event. Training ties in closely with the planning process, and the distribution of information to all concerned right up to the last minute is very important.

There are a number of situations in which an event manager might become involved in public relations, including:

★ making travel arrangements by telephone or email
★ meeting and greeting at the airport
★ providing transport
★ running meetings
★ entertaining at meals
★ entertaining at events
★ providing tours and commentary.

If you had to lead a small group around a venue or an event, there are a number of additional recommendations:

★ plan the tour so that enough time is allocated to see everything.
★ advise your guests of your plan, however informal the group.
★ make sure that there is time for a break and refreshments.
★ provide maps so that people can get their bearings.
★ pause frequently so that the guests can ask questions.
★ be gracious—questions are never trivial or stupid.
★ make sure that everyone can see and hear.
★ treat everyone equally.
★ speak slowly and at an appropriate volume.
★ be patient and speak positively.
★ be flexible and change plans if necessary.
★ be attentive to fatigue or boredom and accelerate the tour if necessary.

In promoting an event, it is essential to analyse and understand the needs of the target market or markets. If, for example, one of the target markets were children aged 8 to 12, it would be necessary to understand the motivations of this group and to match the product to these motivational needs. It would also be necessary to keep in mind that the person purchasing the product might not be the consumer—in this case, it could be the parent and promotional efforts would need to assist with decision-making processes within the family. Likewise, a sponsor might be making a substantial investment in the event, and might have general, as well as specific, expectations of the event, which might or might not be consistent with those of the event audience.

To summarise, the task of promoting an event to the optimal audience at the most beneficial time is the first challenge. The second is to meet the needs of all stakeholders and to maximise public relations benefits to the satisfaction of customers at all levels.

CREATE PROMOTIONAL ACTION PLANS

Once the marketing and promotions strategy has been agreed, the following issues need to be considered when creating detailed plans for the various promotional activities outlined above:

★ objectives and nature of the activity
★ budget availability
★ public relations implications
★ staffing requirements and briefings
★ availability of brochures and other promotional materials
★ equipment requirements
★ contracting of other services (e.g. display)
★ travel arrangements
★ strategies to ensure maximum benefits
★ possible cooperative approaches (proactive or reactive)
★ need for external assistance
★ fulfilment of administrative and procedural requirements
★ available technology
★ potential e-commerce opportunities.

The promotional budget allocates funds to the various components of the promotional mix. This is illustrated for an event company in Figure 6.6.

FIGURE 6.6
Budget allocation to event company promotions

Type of promotion	Timing	Cost (including production, media and HR) $
Advertising		
Website management and search optimisation	Ongoing	1 700
Magazine	Quarterly	1 200
Direct marketing		
Mailing list	Quarterly	450
Publicity/PR	Linked to key events (est. 4)	8 000
Trade exhibition	June	950
Sales promotion	August	810
Personal selling	Ongoing	21 000
Contingency		550
TOTAL		**34 660**

The promotional effort is often closely linked to ticket sales. Box office software enables the capture of information on peak booking periods, profile of the audience, ticket yield, ticket sales in the various price ranges and group bookings, as well as providing addresses for direct marketing, allowing further promotions to be directed towards the areas of lowest sales.

For mega events, the post-codes of ticket holders are used to anticipate demand for public transport. Ticket sales can form the basis for domestic and international travel packages, including hotel accommodation and transportation. In some cases, large numbers of tickets are reserved for organising bodies and returned for sale if not utilised. The primary benefit associated with ticketing programs is the opportunity to manage cash flow. For events where tickets are sold only at the gate, it is impossible to monitor promotional efforts and extremely difficult to anticipate audience numbers, particularly if the event can be affected by inclement weather.

For an annual event, ticketing data—part of customer relationship management (CRM)—is a valuable source of information for planning subsequent years' events. Popularity of ticket grades, profiles of customers and timing of decision-making are a few of the trends that can be monitored through ticket sale data.

REVIEW AND REPORT ON PROMOTIONAL ACTIVITIES

All activities included in the promotional action plan must be able to be reviewed against agreed evaluation methods set during the planning stages. It is important to take 'learnings' from this review process to be incorporated into future planning to ensure that the most successful activities are used again, where appropriate, and activities that did not live up to expectation are either improved or avoided altogether in future planning.

Reports should be prepared according to organisation policy and within required time frames so that those within the organisation are informed in a timely manner. They should assess activities against the marketing and promotional goals set at the planning stage.

Measures that can be used to evaluate the success of promotional activity may include:

★ lift in customer enquiry levels
★ lift in event ticket sales
★ quality and quantity of media coverage
★ level and quality of exposure to target market (percentage of target market present at promotional/sponsored event)
★ consistency with the overall marketing direction of the organisation
★ ability to meet set financial resources
★ ability to meet set human resource requirements
★ activity executed in the time frame originally set
★ results of event feedback forms or anecdotal feedback from key contacts/customers/ clients or organisational representatives.

Blythe (2010) suggests that trade shows often waste promotional effort due to their sales-led approaches. He suggests that exhibitors need to rethink their management of trade fairs in terms of communication models and focus on creating dialogue rather than using one-way communication processes.

As previously discussed in this chapter, market intelligence gathered as the basis of planning the marketing and promotions plan is a key step in the early preparation stages, and it is important that all market intelligence gathered is reported in a clear and concise way to those responsible for planning sales and marketing. Providing informal reports and updates to relevant colleagues also helps to maximise the likelihood that team targets will be met.

SUMMARY

In this chapter we have dealt with event promotion in some detail, and have seen that branding or image is linked to the event purpose and theme, and that all of these aspects must be consistent and compatible in order to create the greatest impact on the consumer or event audience. There are many media options for advertising and these are often determined by the promotional budget available. Advertising and publicity need to be carefully planned to ensure the highest possible level of attendance at the event. We have also discussed the public relations role, communication with the media and other stakeholders being important during the planning phases and equally important when there are problems or incidents that threaten the success or reputation of the event. A more positive public relations role is the entertainment of guests and VIPs for which certain attributes are essential, including tolerance, patience, persistence, respectfulness and an ability to relate well to people of all cultures.

Chapter review questions

1   What is the difference between public relations and advertising?
2   Explain, using examples, three forms of advertising.
3   Give guides for personal selling when providing a quote to a conference customer.
4   List five key elements of a good media release.
5   What is a promotional action plan?

Activity

Select three advertisements for events and analyse the differences, deciding which has the most audience appeal in terms of:
- attraction
- development of interest
- assistance in decision-making
- ability to lead to action/attendance.

Case study

Preparing promotional material

The Garma Festival, one of Australia's major cultural exchange events and now a model for authentic, insightful Indigenous tourism, has won a major international tourism accolade—a Skål International Ecotourism Award.

    Mandawuy Yunupingu, the deputy Chairman of the Yothu Yindi Foundation, organiser of Garma, said today he was very proud the annual festival had won the 2005 Skål award, in the 'Educational Programmes—Media' category. 'Given that "Garma" is a Yolngu (Indigenous people of north-east Arnhem Land) word meaning "two-way learning process", this is great recognition of the Foundation's efforts in achieving its aims,' he said. 'It is recognition that you can have a major tourism event, bringing together Indigenous and non-Indigenous

continued

Case study *(continued)*

Australians, and international visitors, for real cultural interaction, and achieving real social, cultural and economic outcomes. Garma has a five-day line-up of entertainment, education and real cultural interaction, providing a unique cultural tourism and learning experience.'

Source: <www.garma.telstra.com/mediaspeeches/PRskal.htm>. Reproduced with the permission of Yothu Yindi Foundation.

Task

Use the above press release, and any other information you can find on the history of this event, to prepare the following materials:

- a travel brochure for a holiday that includes this festival
- a backgrounder to explain the history of the Garma Festival
- a press release designed for a feature story
- a list of media outlets that could be contacted regarding promotion of this festival.

Note: It is not necessary to contact the organisers to complete these tasks; there is sufficient information on their website.

References

Allen, J (2009), *The executive's guide to corporate events and business entertaining: how to choose and use corporate functions to increase brand awareness, develop new business, nurture customer loyalty and drive growth*, John Wiley and Sons, Canada.

Axtell, R (1990), *Do's and taboos of hosting international visitors*, Wiley.

Blythe, J (2010), 'Trade fairs as communication: a new model', *The Journal of Business & Industrial Marketing*, 25(1):57–62.

Hoyle, L (2002), *Event marketing: how to successfully promote events, festivals, conventions, and expositions*, John Wiley and Sons, New York.

Kemp, S (2002), 'The hidden workforce: volunteers' learning in the Olympics', *Journal of European Industrial Training*, 26(2-4):109–16.

Meerman, S (2010), *The new rules of marketing and PR: how to use social media, blogs, news releases, online video, and viral marketing to reach buyers directly*, 2nd edn, John Wiley and Sons, New York.

Parasuraman, A & Colby, C (2001), *Techno-ready marketing: how and why your customers adopt technology*, The Free Press, New York.

Pope, N (2001), *Sport and event marketing*, McGraw-Hill, Roseville, NSW.

CHAPTER 7

SPONSORSHIP

Unit descriptor

This unit describes the performance outcomes, skills and knowledge required to obtain and manage sponsorship for an activity, event or other organisational activity. This unit applies in any industry context where sponsorship is sought to support business or community activity. Sponsorship may relate to a one-off activity, such as an event, or to ongoing operations, such as sponsorship of a particular service.

Elements

- Determine sponsorship requirements and opportunities
- Source sponsorship
- Service sponsors.

Critical aspects for assessment

- Development of clear, concise and professional sponsorship proposals
- Comprehensive knowledge of practices and protocols in relation to accessing sponsorship opportunities
- Application of effective communication and negotiation skills in the context of sponsorship management
- Demonstration of skills by obtaining and managing sponsorship for at least one activity, project or event.

FOR SOME sponsors like Cadbury Schweppes, the decision to invest in an event is a natural one. Andrew Kelly, the company's sponsorship manager, explains: 'Cadbury Schweppes is the leading supplier of drinks and confectionery in the golf market in Australia and the Cadbury Schweppes Australian PGA Championship is the leading professional golf tournament in Australia so it's a perfect fit.'

Conrad Jupiters likes to boost its brand's own glamour quotient by linking it with that of another glittering name—the Magic Millions Carnival. Public Relations Manager, Donna Campbell, reveals what naming rights sponsorship can offer the company that traditional advertising cannot: 'It's specifically aimed at our target audience, not just in Australia but in Asia, which is a key market for us.'

Source: <www.queenslandevents.com.au/news/>.

As these extracts illustrate, the 'fit' between a sponsor and an event is critical. A sponsor seldom commits to an event on purely altruistic grounds. There is generally a motive, such as developing brand awareness in association with a particular product. For example, the sponsor will choose a sport that attracts an event audience that has the appropriate characteristics. This is why a beer company will select a sporting code (such as soccer) with a corresponding audience demographic and a car manufacturer will choose another sporting code (such as rugby union) with a different demographic. Most large organisations have long-term strategic plans for sponsorship that are closely linked with their marketing plans. This is again illustrated in the fit between sponsor and event for the Optus National Country Music Muster shown in Figure 7.1.

Inexperienced event organisers often assume that big companies will be generous with sponsorship for small events and often the first step suggested by the committee is to contact corporations. Unfortunately, this seldom works, because companies of this size already have well-established plans, with specific objectives to be achieved as part of their sponsorship deals. In fact, in most cases, the outcome is a joint marketing effort by the sponsor and the event organiser. Most large organisations also have policies with regard to sponsorship and for this reason will reject a request from a fringe arts festival, for example, if this is not consistent with their marketing plan and policy to support a sporting code.

Many organisations have corporate charity partnerships as a means of achieving corporate social responsibility (CSR) goals, one example being Australia Post and Merry Makers Australia, a dance troupe with intellectual or physical disabilities ranging in age from 6 to 56 (Williams 2010). Another example is that of the Telstra Business Women's Awards. The Commonwealth Bank is also a sponsor of these awards.

If a straightforward donation, or patronage, is made to an event, without strings attached (no logo, publicity, etc.), this is known as philanthropy. When seeking assistance for an event, it is important to identify whether the request is for a donation or a sponsorship arrangement. Sponsorship is defined as follows:

> A 'partnership' between an organisation and another organisation or event in which the sponsor publicly endorses an activity and ties its reputation with that of the organisation or event being sponsored.

Source: <www.murdoch.edu.au/cwisad/glossary.html>.

OPTUS NATIONAL COUNTRY MUSIC MUSTER

... 'there are no strangers at the Muster, just friends you haven't met yet ...'

The Optus National Country Music Muster is a phenomenal experience rooted in music and community, far removed from ties and clocks, suits and schedules. Thousands of patrons flock to this iconic event, attracted each year by the smorgasbord of diverse programs rich with our country's finest musicians, the bushland setting laced with inviting whiffs of campfire cooking and fresh bush eucalypt, the easy camaraderie created by convivial patrons all set to simply enjoy themselves.

As well as traditional and modern country, entertainment within 13 other stages and venues includes an aural collage ranging from folk, bluegrass, balladeers and gospel, to blues, bush poetry, clogging, linedancing, salsa and rock 'n roll ... there's even a theatre production, celebrity guest debate and the serious competition of the Maton Talent Search where future careers are established.

The Optus Muster's picturesque 50-hectare site is an ideal location for this great festival. The site, 2 hours' drive north of Brisbane, 40 minutes from Noosa and 1 hour from heritage listed Fraser Island, is easily accessible by large vehicles—just watch for meandering cows!

Over 50 community groups and 2000 volunteers annually help the event organisers, Gympie Apex Club Inc. to stage this non-profit community-based festival to raise funds to assist charities Australia-wide. Since its inception in 1982, the Optus Muster has raised over $12M for charities and community groups. The Optus Muster also raises funds through its Rural Aid Appeal, annually raising up to $100,000 for its nominated charity. Funds are raised through sales from a range of merchandise which includes CDs & DVDs, shirts, caps, leathergoods and Bundaberg Rum.

Source: <www.muster.com.au>. Optus National Country Music Muster.

Sponsorship is a business relationship between a provider of funds, resources or services and an individual, event or organisation which offers in return some rights and association that may be used for commercial advantage.

The key distinction between sponsorship and patronage is that no commercial advantage is sought or expected in return for the support of a patron.

Source: <www.sponsorship.co.uk>.

With these definitions in mind, it is clear that any hint of poor media exposure (e.g. drugs in sport, crowd safety issues) is likely to make the sponsor very edgy!

Potential sponsors may include:

★ individuals
★ private companies
★ corporations
★ government agencies

★ industry associations
★ educational institutions
★ community organisations.

Sponsorship may cover:

★ naming rights for events or event venues (e.g. Optus National Country Music Muster)
★ media coverage (e.g. a particular channel always broadcasting a particular series or event creating viewer loyalty)
★ staging or performances costs
★ telecommunications expenses (e.g. providing communications equipment and service for the event)
★ IT support (e.g. scoring, results processing)
★ overall sponsorship of the event (e.g. agricultural conference sponsorship)
★ physical items (e.g. satchels, prizes)
★ food and beverage (e.g. morning and afternoon teas)
★ travel for performers, artists or athletes
★ entertainment (e.g. new talent)
★ speaker sessions (e.g. supporting topical research such as salinity)
★ ongoing organisational activities (e.g. annual publications)
★ one-off promotional activities or projects.

However, planning a sponsorship program is not a haphazard process; it requires a targeted approach with specific outcomes for both the sponsor and the event organisation. Sponsorship arrangements can, in fact, make or break an event. For example, champion surfer Layne Beachley was recently thrown a financial lifeline by the Commonwealth Bank in a last-minute deal to save the Beachley Classic pro-surfing event. The five-day competition had been hanging in the balance as Beachley and organisers scrambled to find a major sponsor to plug an $80 000 funding gap (Bashan 2008).

DETERMINE SPONSORSHIP REQUIREMENTS AND OPPORTUNITIES

The first step in determining sponsorship requirements is to establish the amount of financial or other support needed; the second step is to identify items, activities or projects that may have sponsor appeal. Only then is it possible to identify potential sponsors for a particular activity and the fit with the sponsor organisation's profile.

When approaching a potential sponsor, it is essential to address the motivational factor(s) that will spark the potential sponsor's interest. (This is particularly important when making an approach in writing.) Motives for sponsoring events fall into five major categories, as outlined below. Once the sponsor's motives have been clarified, it is then a matter of developing (where possible) measurable objectives, so that when the event is over the benefits of the sponsorship arrangement can be demonstrated.

BROAD CORPORATE AND SOCIAL OBJECTIVES

Broad corporate and social objectives for a sponsor organisation include community involvement, promoting the organisation's image and linking the company's image to success. Any change in audience attitude to corporate and social objectives of sponsors is, however, hard to measure. Public perception of an organisation shifts very slowly and it is difficult to evaluate this shift over a short time span. Qantas, for example, promotes its corporate image by linking advertising to sporting achievement and national pride, thus cementing its image as the national carrier. Other organisations prefer to support local rather than national events.

PRODUCT/BRAND-RELATED OBJECTIVES

Many sponsors use events to promote a product. Examples of products include airline travel, beer, wine and communications products. Examples of sponsoring organisations include Qantas, Heineken, Lion Nathan, Lindeman's and Telstra. They in turn may have a number of brands. For example, Lion Nathan has several brands in Australia: Toohey's New, Toohey's Extra Dry, XXXX Gold, Hahn Premium Light, Heineken, James Squire Golden Ale and Beck's. The organisation may choose a specific event to promote just one of its products. In many cases, the brand can be sampled at the event (especially beer at sporting matches), hopefully leading to higher brand awareness and strengthening brand preference.

SALES OBJECTIVES

Sales objectives are far more specific, having to do with the sales force prospecting for new customers and strengthening relationships with current customers. Sales staff may circulate at an event. At one recent event a mobile telephone company built product awareness through personal selling. Roving sales staff took photos of spectators and then (with their permission) sent these photos to friends of the spectators using mobile phone technology.

Santos is a major partner for the Darwin Festival

Business-to-business relationships can result from networking between a number of sponsors for a particular event, in turn leading to long-term benefits to all sponsor organisations in the alliance. Events such as the Olympic Games offer exclusive rights and all sponsors must work inclusively with other sponsors, using only their products and services.

Data capture is of significant benefit to sponsors of trade exhibitions and conferences because the contact information of all attendees is available to sponsors to be used at a future date for direct mail purposes.

MEDIA COVERAGE

Gaining media exposure is one of the most obvious objectives of sponsors. Who has not seen the winning captain put on a cap featuring the sponsor logo before being congratulated on prime time television and thanking the sponsor in view of hundreds of thousands of television viewers? There are many ways that the sponsor organisation can gain media coverage before, during and after the event. Outdoor advertising, publicity activities, branded clothing items and extensive signage are all part of this package.

CORPORATE HOSPITALITY

Hospitality (in the form of corporate boxes) is often a key element of a sponsorship package. The guests are generally current or prospective clients who are entertained during the event. In some cases, the hospitality is also provided to key staff as an incentive for good performance.

SOURCE SPONSORSHIP

According to the ABS Business Generosity Survey, during 2000–01 businesses gave almost $1.45 billion to organisations and individuals, of which sport and recreation activities received $628 million (43%). This comprised $480 million of sponsorship, $109 million of donations and $39 million of 'business to community projects' funding. Activities associated with sport and recreation attracted the most business sponsorship compared with the other activities surveyed, namely community service and welfare, health, education and training, environmental activities, and arts and culture (ABS, cat. no. 1301.0).

The Bell Shakespeare Company has two leading partners, Optus and Westpac, as well as major sponsors, supporting partners, company partners, community partners and government partners. The organisation also relies on private giving. There are thus several funding sources supporting just one theatre company.

Some sponsors support events as part of their community profile. For example, McDonalds is the Founding Partner of Clean Up Australia and has been working with the organisation since the first Clean Up in 1989. Clean Up Australia also accepts donations and bequests.

A sponsorship proposal should outline the benefits to the sponsor and associated costs. Once a sponsor indicates interest in the proposal, a period of negotiation generally ensues. It is important to note that the timelines for sponsorship negotiation are generally significant. Three to five years should be allowed for locking in a major sponsor and, during this time, frequent contact should be made with the potential sponsor to maintain their interest in the proposal. Agreement to the sponsorship concludes with the signing of a written contract, including full details of the commitment made by both parties.

Finalisation of the sponsorship agreement has to occur before any of the following can be planned and implemented:

★ printing brochures and posters
★ developing a website
★ ticketing
★ merchandising
★ signage.

Sponsorship may include sponsorship packages, value-in-kind sponsorship and/or naming rights. These are outlined below.

SPONSORSHIP PACKAGES

Figure 7.2 illustrates the ways in which sponsorship packages can be developed to meet the needs of different types of sponsor; in this case there were six levels of sponsorship: platinum, gold, silver, bronze, trade and special. Sponsorship was for a regional conference, co-hosted by the Australian and New Zealand Societies for Horticultural Science (AuSHS and NZSHS), on 'Harnessing the Potential of Horticulture in the Asia-Pacific Region'. It was held in conjunction with the Fifth International Strawberry Symposium.

For smaller events there is often only one type of sponsorship or one sponsor.

FIGURE 7.2
Example of a sponsorship package

REGIONAL HORTICULTURAL CONFERENCE
PROGRAM OUTLINE & SPONSORSHIP OPPORTUNITIES

The Regional Horticultural Conference is a joint initiative of the Australian and New Zealand Societies for Horticultural Science in association with the New Zealand Society for Plant Physiology, and is proudly supported by the Horticulture Australia Ltd, Department of Primary Industries, Queensland and the University of Queensland.

The event builds on the synergies across the Tasman and to develop an effective network of horticultural scientists across the Asia-Pacific Region. The Conference is being held in conjunction with the Board, Executive and Council meetings of the International Society for Horticultural Science and the Fifth International Strawberry Symposium, also being held at the Hyatt Regency Coolum in August to September.

Program Outline
Details of the Conference program can be found on http://www.aushs.org.au/
The conference program is structured to provide for variety in presentation styles, including formal presentations, workshops and field activities:

Date	Program
Tuesday 31 Aug	Arrival / Welcome Reception / Pre-conference technical tour
Wednesday 1 Sep	Official Opening / Speaker Program 'Achieving commercial potential – Case Studies from discovery through to commercialisation', 'Harvesting the genetic potential', and 'Reaching the potential for sustainable horticulture' – papers, case studies or workshops / Taste of Australia – horticultural delights and wine/ Aussie barbecue
Thursday 2 Sep	Speaker Program: 'Building Bridges – unlocking the potential for international collaboration', and 'Education and Training – training the potential horticulturists of the future' / Poster Session / Annual General Meetings / Conference dinner
Friday 3 Sep	Speaker Program: 'Enhancing Economic Potential by Innovative Production Systems', and 'Harnessing the potential of sensory and postharvest technologies' – papers, case studies or workshops.
Saturday 4 Sep	Technical Tour of horticultural enterprises on the Sunshine Coast / Departure

Sponsorship Opportunities
Attached for your information are details of the wide range of sponsorship opportunities available to your company. Should you require further details please do not hesitate to contact:
Australia: *Jodie Campbell e-mail Jodie.ac@bigpond.com.au*
New Zealand: *Jill Stanley*

Sponsorship Registrations
We look forward to your early acceptance of this exceptional opportunity to capture high profile exposure for your goods and services. As they say, the 'early bird gets the worm'.

Jodie Campbell
Conference Secretariat

continued

FIGURE 7.2
continued

REGIONAL HORTICULTURAL CONFERENCE
SPONSORSHIP ENTITLEMENTS and OPPORTUNITIES
'PLATINUM SPONSOR' — $20,000 *

We are proud to offer the following 'Platinum' sponsorship entitlements:

- **Exclusive category** representation on a first come, first served basis (eg. no other sponsor will be accepted if they directly compete in the same market with same or similar products or services).
- Prime location mega-display booth of 6 metres x 3 metres with high exposure to delegates during the conference.
- Acknowledgment as a 'Platinum Sponsor' in the pre-conference brochures, magazines, and other promotional materials.
- Opportunity to make a five minute presentation during the main conference program.
- Naming rights to conference dinner.
- Public acknowledgment of support at the beginning, during and at the end of the conference.
- Unlimited opportunity to include promotional materials in delegates conference kits.
- Opportunity to display signage on auditorium stage during conference.
- Frequently repeated exposure of individual corporate logo on sponsor's screen via electronic display during all sessions.
- Be provided with contact details of all conference participants for post conference service.
- Five complementary conference session registrations with a complementary table for ten at the conference dinner.
- Allocation as 'host' sponsor to a specific session or room for the Conference program.
- Identification of your organisation on the Conference www site for the world to see.

Pre-Conference Publicity
As part of your sponsorship, you will also receive complimentary editorials in any trade magazines promoting the conference. You will be individually contacted to maximise exposure of your organisation as the major sponsor of this conference.

Other Opportunities
- Additional trade display space by negotiation.
- Additional conference registrations are available at $350 per person.
- The complete conference proceedings will be printed as an issue of *Acta Horticulturae*, and able to be purchased from the International Society for Horticultural Science (ISHS).

*All prices are quoted inclusive of GST.

REGIONAL HORTICULTURAL CONFERENCE
SPONSORSHIP ENTITLEMENTS and OPPORTUNITIES
'GOLD SPONSOR' — $10,000 *

We are proud to offer the following 'Gold' sponsorship entitlements:

- Prominent display booth of 3 metres x 3 metres with high level access to all delegates during the conference.
- Acknowledgment as a 'Gold Sponsor' in the pre-conference brochures, magazines, and other promotional materials.
- Opportunity to make a five minute presentation during the conference.
- Naming rights to Welcome cocktails, Aussie Barbecue or wine-tasting event.
- Public acknowledgment of support at the beginning and at the end of conference.
- Opportunity to include multiple items of promotional materials in delegatesî conference kits.
- Frequently repeated exposure of individual corporate logo via electronic display during main sessions.
- Be provided with contact details of all conference participants for post conference service.
- Three free conference session registrations, and three additional conference dinner tickets.
- Allocation as 'host' sponsor to a specific presentation in the conference program.
- Identification of your organisation on the Conference www site for the world to see.

Pre-Conference Publicity
As part of your sponsorship, you will receive complimentary editorials in any trade magazines promoting the conference. You will be individually contacted to maximise exposure of your organisation as the major sponsor of this conference.

Other Opportunities
- Additional trade display space by negotiation.
- Additional conference registrations are available at $350 per person.
- The complete conference proceedings will be printed as an issue of *Acta Horticulturae*, and able to be purchased from the International Society for Horticultural Science (ISHS).

*All prices are quoted inclusive of GST.

continued

FIGURE 7.2
continued

**REGIONAL HORTICULTURAL CONFERENCE
SPONSORSHIP ENTITLEMENTS and OPPORTUNITIES
'SILVER SPONSOR' — $7,500 ***

We are proud to offer the following 'Silver' sponsorship entitlements:

- Display booth of 3 metres x 2.4 metres.
- Acknowledgment as a 'Silver Sponsor' in the pre-conference brochures, magazines, and other promotional materials.
- Opportunity to include two items of promotional materials in delegates' conference kits.
- Frequently repeated exposure of corporate logo via electronic display during concurrent sessions.
- Naming rights to a conference lunch.
- Opportunity to make a five minute presentation prior to lunch.
- Two free conference registrations, plus two additional conference dinner tickets.
- Identification of your organisation on the Conference www site for the world to see.

Pre-Conference Publicity
As part of your sponsorship, you will receive complimentary editorials in any trade magazines promoting the conference. You will be individually contacted to maximise exposure of your organisation as the major sponsor of this conference.

Other Opportunities
- Additional trade display space by negotiation.
- Additional conference registrations are available at $350 per person.
- The complete conference proceedings will be printed as an issue of *Acta Horticulturae*, and able to be purchased from the International Society for Horticultural Science (ISHS).

*All prices are quoted inclusive of GST.

Source: Australia Society for Horticultural Science and New Zealand Society of Agricultural and Horticultural Science.

VALUE-IN-KIND SPONSORSHIP

In the examples illustrated so far, sponsors were asked to make a cash contribution. In many cases, however, sponsorship is provided as 'value in kind'. This means that the sponsor provides its goods and services free as part of the sponsorship arrangement. For example, air travel could be sponsored by Virgin Blue, vehicles provided by Holden and advertising could be underwritten by Fairfax Publications. A value is placed on this contribution and this value must be reflected in the event budget even though there is no cash contribution.

NAMING RIGHTS

The primary sponsor of an event is often able to obtain naming rights, for example, Rosemount Australian Fashion Week; GMC Australian Motorcycle Grand Prix; Billabong World Junior Championships; Ford Ranger One Day Cup.

In some cases, sponsors negotiate naming rights for event venues or facilities, such as the Etihad Stadium in Melbourne, ANZ Stadium in Sydney, First National Bank Stadium in Johannesburg and the Pepsi Center in Denver. These are generally long-term strategic agreements with associated sponsor benefits such as tickets, hospitality, parking, etc. The exposure of the sponsor's name in all media communications in relation to the facility is a key element of this negotiation.

SERVICE SPONSORS

Sponsorship often plays a crucial part in an event and therefore sponsors need to be 'massaged' by event management throughout the entire process leading to the performance—and beyond. Issues that sometimes arise include ambush marketing, incompatibility between sponsors or a sense of inequity in the profile achieved by other sponsors. In this last situation, one sponsor may feel that its company profile has been eclipsed by another because it has achieved more air time or its signage was of superior quality. Sponsors can become quite competitive, insisting that one or other has been given higher exposure, a more prominent logo, a taller flag, and so on. Logos must also be handled with care by the event coordinator with regard to correct reproduction in terms of colour and style, as there have been many occasions when a whole production run of T-shirts, banners and posters has had to be written off due to sponsor complaints. When sponsor logos are used in any public arena, a sign-off by the sponsor is an essential procedure.

Sponsors are always concerned about ambush marketing, which can occur when competitors muscle in on the media attention gained by the event. This may happen if T-shirts with a competitor's logos are distributed free or body paint is used to achieve similar exposure.

Incompatibility between sponsors is another issue, although it is fairly obvious that an approach would never be made to more than one organisation in a particular product category: never two beer companies, two soft drink companies or two breakfast cereal brands. Since some of these organisations are major conglomerates with many products and many brands this can be a minefield only avoided if the organisation and its products are carefully researched prior to negotiation. 'Who are the other sponsors?' is one of the first questions asked of the event manager. Sponsors want to be associated with appropriate partners, and this includes the event company as well as other sponsors. Athletes, models, actors and performers also have their own sponsors and they may not be compatible with the sponsors of the event. Rules about exhibiting logos and promoting competing sponsors must be very clear. For example, a competitor logo cannot appear in the event precinct, particularly if worn by a high-profile celebrity.

Ongoing evaluation of the sponsorship arrangements is essential. For most large events there is a dedicated sponsorship manager to manage these sometimes temperamental partners. They can be demanding and often the minor sponsors expect outcomes beyond their original brief. This delicate balancing act can be managed well if sponsorship documentation is maintained throughout. This includes:

★ agreed contract with detailed specifications
★ activity reports and schedules
★ financial records
★ minutes of meetings
★ records of correspondence and agreements.

Finally, sponsors want to be associated with success. Any hint of failure in the press causes major consternation. This can result from cancellation of acts, ticketing problems, accidents on site and other unforeseen problems that can crop up. For this reason, a risk management plan in relation to sponsorship is essential, with contingencies in place for every eventuality.

EVALUATE SPONSORSHIP

Evaluation is an essential component of the sponsorship arrangement. For a contract to be renewed there must be demonstrable gains made by the sponsorship organisation. These are measured in terms of the sponsorship objectives discussed earlier. The process illustrated in Figure 7.3 shows the process for sponsorship planning and evaluation. Unless evaluation in its various forms is carried out, it is impossible to demonstrate the success or otherwise of the sponsorship arrangement after the event. A warm glow is not enough to convince future sponsors that the event can produce tangible marketing benefits.

There are numerous measures for sponsorship evaluation, including:

★ value of 'free' TV or radio exposure (measured as minutes × advertising rates)
★ column centimetres in the press (publicity)
★ geographic scope of media reach (number and location of media exposure, such as five country radio stations)
★ consumption of sponsor's products at the event
★ purchase of sponsor merchandise such as caps and T-shirts
★ spectator figures
★ spectator demographics
★ sponsor name recall surveys
★ product awareness surveys
★ alliance with other sponsors (value of business generated)
★ increased product sales post-event
★ success of hospitality provided
★ analysis of corporate image (need pre- and post-event surveys).

Sales of merchandise can be a most effective form of measurement, providing that good estimates of sales are made beforehand. Merchandise is becoming increasingly popular with event spectators and audiences—the event audience wants a tangible reminder of their event experience. Big shows sell CDs, soft toys, caps, pens, posters, mouse pads and any number of other products. At sports events people buy hats, T-shirts, pins and stickers. However, these are generally beyond the scope of smaller events. For many events in the small to mid range,

FIGURE 7.3
Process of sponsorship planning and evaluation

Plan the sponsorship program/target potential sponsors
⇩
Develop specific, measurable sponsorship objectives
⇩
Negotiate and finalise the sponsorship plan
⇩
Implement the sponsorship plan
⇩
Evaluate the success of the sponsorship plan
⇩
Provide feedback to the sponsor

sponsorship is one of the largest risk factors to the financial outcome of the event, even if the target is break-even.

Brand recall or awareness are other measures used in evaluating sponsorship; however, some studies have looked at 'congruence' between the brand and the individual's profile or event personality (Close et al 2009; Lee & Cho 2010). The Lee and Cho study showed that the personality congruence between the sponsoring brand and the sporting event was the most significant attitude predictor towards the sponsoring brand. In other words, those individuals whose 'personality' matched the brand image were most likely to have a positive attitude towards the brand. However, for marketing purposes, more than a positive attitude towards a product or brand is needed: the positive attitude has to be converted to a purchase action. The impact of event sponsorship on brand use is hard to predict as there are so many variables involved in the purchase decision. The consumer process can be summarised in this way: sponsor awareness → sponsor attitudinal response → decision to purchase → purchase action.

Sports merchandise

Research is generally undertaken by a professional market research organisation in order to produce reliable and valid statistical information for reporting. Research consultants Sweeney Sports conduct regular surveys to provide information to sports sponsors, such as that presented in Figure 7.4.

Event organisations must ask:

★ Are we giving sponsors what they want?
★ Are they getting value for their investment?
★ Are we managing the relationship well?

Sponsors can withdraw funding if they do not perceive value for their investment or if they are not managed well. Ongoing attention must be paid to this important aspect of event management, with a proactive approach being taken to managing these important stakeholder relationships. Maestas (2009) highlights the importance of these measurements: return on investment (ROI) and return on objectives (ROO). The first measures the direct relationship between sponsorship and product sales or company profits. The second measures performance against objectives, such as sponsor recall or web hits. In both cases, plans need to be made and implemented to obtain the data necessary to make these evaluations.

FIGURE 7.4

Sports
sponsorship
report

Nike, Billabong solid as Uncle Tobys and Nutri-Grain slip — 3's cricket sponsorship makes ground

Nike and Billabong have consolidated their positions at the head of Australia's sports sponsorship awareness ladder largely because of a slide in the ratings by former long-time leader, Uncle Tobys. The 2006–07 summer edition of the Sweeney Sports Report shows that Nike and Billabong remain in first and second places, respectively, having last year, with Nutri-Grain, deposed Uncle Tobys. The Report — the current summer edition is the 21st — is recognised as Australia's most authoritative sports and sponsorship survey.

It shows that Uncle Tobys, while losing awareness during the past year, has not lost as much ground as Nutri-Grain, moving from fourth to equal third place with Ford.

High levels of focus were the key to Uncle Tobys' success in the 1990s — it concentrated for years on its Iron Man series.

In contrast, a range of executional strategies and tactics are now being used by the plethora of sponsors which are operating in a highly competitive sponsors' market place.

Hence, '3' has broken into the top ranks of sponsors in equal sixth place through its wide-ranging sponsorships of the Australian summer test cricket series, the national team and other sporting teams. It is not far behind the leaders and is closing fast.

Other increases in sponsorship association have been achieved by Telstra, on the back of its NRL sponsorship, Kia (Australian Open tennis) and the Commonwealth Bank (ODI cricket).

And Billabong, Rip Curl and Quiksilver — which have extended their footprints by becoming lifestyle brands — continue to feature among the leading sponsors.

Cricket sponsors such as '3', Emirates, VB, Ford and the Commonwealth Bank have picked a winner by investing in our main national summer pastime. Sweeney Sports data to be released shortly will show that cricket is now the most popular sport in the country with several of its key players among the hottest sponsorship 'properties' in the country.

(Statement by Martin Hirons, Director, Sweeney Sports)

Source: <www.sweeneyresearch.com.au/newsPDF/news_pdf_14.pdf>. Courtesy of Sweeney Research.

SUMMARY

Sponsorship is a partnership arrangement between the event organiser and the sponsor organisation, usually formalised in a legal contract. Developing marketing and publicity objectives as part of the sponsorship plan provides the opportunity to evaluate the success of the event from the sponsor's perspective. This is essential for maintaining ongoing relationships with primary and secondary sponsors from one event to the next. As we have seen in this chapter, all parties have expectations of these relationships and they need to be clarified before operational planning begins. Staff need to be briefed about sponsorship arrangements and activities (e.g. hospitality, signage, merchandising) must be organised in accordance with sponsorship agreements. Every opportunity to enhance the value to the sponsor/s should be taken and every effort must be made to keep sponsors involved and up to date with ongoing plans.

Chapter review questions

1 What is the difference between sponsorship and philanthropy?
2 What is value in kind (VIK)?
3 Explain how the impact of sponsorship can be measured.
4 What is ambush marketing?

Activities

1 Visit the websites of two major organisations to find out about their sponsorship arrangements. Then explain how the sponsorship arrangements meet their corporate objectives.
2 Visit a website that sells corporate merchandise and suggest which items would be suitable for a jazz festival on the beach.

Case study

Seeking sponsorship

You have just been appointed as sponsorship manager of a four-wheel drive motor show. In addition to exhibitors, there is a range of other organisations that may wish to be associated with the show, such as camping, clothing and wine companies.

Tasks

1 Develop a sponsorship package for various types of sponsor.
2 Identify 10 potential sponsors as targets.
3 For each potential sponsor, explain why the sponsor may be motivated to enter into this arrangement.
4 Write a letter of introduction to send with your sponsorship proposal.

References

Bashan, Y (2008), 'Layne gets cash lifeline', *The Sunday Telegraph*, 28 September.

Close, A, Finney, R, Lacey, R & Sneath, J (2006), 'Engaging the consumer through event marketing: linking attendees with the sponsor, community and brand', *Journal of Advertising Research*, December, pp. 420–33.

Close, A, Krishen, A & Latour, M (2009), 'This event is me! How consumer event self-congruity leverages sponsorship', *Journal of Advertising Research*, 49(3):271.

Latham, J (2006), 'Study proves live events have major impact', *Events Review*.

Lee, H & Cho, C (2009), 'The matching effect of brand and sporting event personality: sponsorship implications, *Journal of Sport Management*, 23(1):41.

Maestas, A (2009), 'Guide to sponsorship return on investment', *Journal of Sponsorship*, 3(1):98–102.

Neijens, P, Smit, E & Moorman, M (2009), 'Taking up an event: brand image transfer during the FIFA World Cup', *International Journal of Market Research*, 51(5):579–91.

Rowley, J & Williams, C (2008), 'The impact of brand sponsorship of music festivals', *Marketing Intelligence & Planning*, 26(7):781.

Williams, S (2010), 'Doing good', *The Deal*.

CHAPTER 8

PROTOCOL REQUIREMENTS

Unit descriptor

This unit describes the performance outcomes, skills and knowledge required to address protocol requirements in a broad range of business activities. The unit focuses on basic research skills to acquire a knowledge and understanding of protocol requirements within diverse business, social and cultural contexts, as well as the ability to use that knowledge in a practical workplace context. This unit applies to people working in different roles and at different levels in many industry sectors. It applies to event, hospitality and tourism operations and is particularly relevant to those involved in event management and operations function coordination, tour operations and tour guiding.

Elements

- Source information on appropriate protocol
- Integrate appropriate protocol procedures into work activities
- Update knowledge of protocol.

Critical aspects for assessment

- Knowledge of where to source accurate information on protocol for specific situations
- Knowledge of appropriate protocols
- Ability to apply protocol knowledge to a specific workplace requirement.

THE CEREMONY is a major state function, with the Royals granting an audience at the event, hence certain restrictions regarding the observation of the ceremony are unavoidably necessary. They apply to all persons who are not actual participants in the ceremony. The Royal Household requests the kind cooperation of all visitors to this ceremonial event to observe the following:

- Dress code for international media. Members of the Press are requested to dress in formal business attire with 'Press/Media' accreditation. For men: shirt, jacket and necktie. For ladies: blouse and skirt or dress. (Please refrain from wearing trousers or pants.)
- Photographers must have their cameras and accreditation passes checked by Security at approximately 9.00 am at tent number 19.
- Photographers who are authorised to take photos at the event must be dressed in a business suit with the appropriate press accreditation status. Other unauthorised photographers will be excluded.
- After 11.30 am guests and tourists must remain within the tents assigned.
- Photographers are not permitted to walk into or with the procession. Photographing is permitted only from both sides of the procession. Three specific locations with elevated seating have been prepared for photographers at the eastern side of the procession.
- Following the arrival of the Royals at the gala luncheon, guests and individuals without media accreditation are not permitted to take photos. Photographers are allowed to take photos from the designated vantage points.

The above example illustrates the protocol for a Royal ceremonial procession. If VIPs and dignitaries are present at an event, protocol is an important aspect of planning. Functions where protocols need to be used include:

★ civic receptions
★ formal parades
★ freedom of city ceremonies
★ national day receptions
★ citizenship ceremonies
★ private functions.

Visits by VIPs, celebrities and heads of state all entail protocol of one form or another: laying out of red carpets, meeting and greeting, seating and verbal acknowledgement. One of the most important protocols in Australia is 'Welcome to Country' which recognises the ancient roots of Indigenous culture and occupation in the region by Aboriginal and Torres Strait Islander peoples. Most formal ceremonies and increasing numbers of public events include this protocol at the start. This chapter will describe some of these considerations from an event management point of view.

SOURCE INFORMATION ON APPROPRIATE PROTOCOL

When planning an event, protocol considerations include the display of the flag, use of honorific titles and order of precedence. There are numerous sources of information on protocol, including:

- ★ libraries
- ★ internet
- ★ federal, state and local government protocol departments
- ★ Aboriginal Land Councils
- ★ Australia Day Councils
- ★ Office of the United Nations.

For example, if you visit the website for any of the state or territory governments, you will find all relevant information about the state, its government, emblems and icons. Accessing this information can assist the event planning team with issuing invitations, preparing running sheets, preparing briefing papers, liaising with dignitaries and officials, and providing services during an event.

The formalities outlined below are among those you might be called upon to put in place when managing events.

INTEGRATE APPROPRIATE PROTOCOL PROCEDURES INTO WORK ACTIVITIES

During the planning phase of an event, it is necessary to identify specific work activities that require appropriate use of protocol. These may include issuing of invitations, preparing running sheets and briefing papers, liaising with dignitaries and officials, and providing services during the conduct of an event, including on-site management and service of food and beverage. Liaison with colleagues and other stakeholders will help determine the appropriate protocol requirements.

One such consideration for more formal functions is the order of precedence, in other words: who is top of the pecking order?

ORDER OF PRECEDENCE

Outlined in Figure 8.1 is an abbreviated version of the order of precedence for Australian Commonwealth, state and territory dignitaries. Besides these basic requirements, there are additional rules for more complex situations, such as establishing order of precedence based on the date of taking or leaving office. Those dignitaries included range from the Governor-General to ex-ministers of state to those who retain the prefix 'Honourable'.

An event planner would consult the order of precedence in order to make seating and other arrangements, and would also need to contact state or federal government protocol officers for any specific information on protocol. The late Sir Asher Joel's book, *Australian protocol and procedures*, now in its third edition, has been updated by Helen Pringle and is a very useful reference on this subject.

In addition to government officials and members of parliament, involvement of any of the following personnel and officials at an event would require research into the necessary protocol requirements:

- ★ diplomats and foreign officials
- ★ religious officials

1   The Governor-General

2   a) The Governor of the State.
    b) The Governor of the other States according to their date of appointment.
    c) The Administrators of the Northern Territory and Norfolk Island within their own Territories.

3   The Prime Minister.

4   The Premier within his/her own State. The Chief Minister of the Northern Territory and Norfolk Island within their own Territories.

5   The President of the Senate and the Speaker of the House of Representatives according to seniority of appointment.

6   The Chief Justice of Australia.

7   a) Ambassadors and High Commissioners.
    b) Chargés d'affaires en pied or en titre.
    c) Chargés d'affaires and acting High Commissioners.

8   Members of the Federal Executive Council under summons.

9   The Administrators of the Northern Territory and Norfolk Island.

10 The Leader of the Opposition.

11 a) Former Governors-General.
    b) Former Prime Ministers.
    c) Former Chief Justices of Australia.

12 The Premiers of the States according to the population of their States and then Chief Minister of the Northern Territory and Norfolk Island.

13 The Lord Mayor within his/her city.

FIGURE 8.1
Abbreviated order of precedence for Commonwealth, state and territory dignitaries

★ military personnel
★ academics
★ nobility
★ royalty.

For events such as the visit of His Holiness, Pope Benedict XVI, one can only begin to imagine the protocol arrangements necessary within the Vatican and the Catholic Church in Australia and during meetings between His Holiness and his entourage and government ministers, premiers and the Prime Minister.

TITLES

Style guides, available in most public libraries, provide guidelines on the correct titles for people such as Prime Ministers ('Right Honourable') and Commonweath Ministers ('Honourable').

Red carpet under wraps awaiting dignitaries' arrival

If high-ranking overseas visitors were attending an event, an event organiser would contact the relevant embassy to obtain information on the order of precedence and the titles to be used.

STYLES OF ADDRESS

Styles of address for foreign dignitaries are summarised in Table 8.1. Again, style guides can assist you with this form of protocol, as well as with the correct form of address for the clergy.

DRESS FOR FORMAL OCCASIONS

The appropriate dress for formal occasions should be included on the invitation. This might include morning dress for formal day functions or black tie (or sometimes white)

Table 8.1 Styles of address for foreign dignitaries

Dignitary	Salutation	Final salutation	In conversation
A King/An Emperor	Your Majesty/ Sire:	I have the honour to remain, Your Majesty's obedient servant,	'Your Majesty' first, then 'Sire'
A Queen	Your Majesty/ Madame:	I have the honour to remain, Your Majesty's obedient servant,	'Your Majesty' first, then 'Ma'am'
A Prince/Princess With title 'Royal Highness	Your Royal Highness:	I remain, Your Royal Highness, Yours very truly,	'Your Royal Highness' first, then 'Sir/Ma'am'
With title 'Serene Highness'	Your Serene Highness:	I remain, Your Serene Highness	'Your Serene Highness' first, then 'Sir/Ma'am'
Without title 'Highness'	Prince: Madame:	Yours very truly, Yours very truly,	'Prince' first, then 'Sir' 'Princess' first, then 'Madam'
A President of a Republic	Excellency:	Yours sincerely,	'Excellency' first, then 'President' or 'Sir/Madam'
The President of the United States	Dear Mr President:	Yours sincerely,	'Mr. President' or 'Excellency' first, then 'Sir'
A Prime Minister His/ Her Excellency (full name) Prime Minister of (name) Address	Dear Prime Minister:	Yours sincerely,	'Prime Minister' or 'Excellency' first, then 'Sir/Madam' or 'Mr./Mrs./Ms./Miss (name)'
Ambassadors/High Commissioners of foreign countries	Dear Ambassador/ High Commissoner:	Yours sincerely,	'Your Excellency' or 'Excellency'

for formal evening events. Protocol also needs to be observed as to the correct insignia to be worn at ceremonial events.

PROTOCOL FOR SPEAKERS

Speakers need to be briefed in advance and provided with a list of the guests to be welcomed, in order of precedence. The timing and length of speeches need to be discussed with the speakers before the event and must also be canvassed with the chef so that food production coincides with the event plan and speakers are not disturbed by food service or clearing of plates.

SEATING PLANS FOR FORMAL OCCASIONS

Correct seating arrangements for occasions such as awards ceremonies and formal dinners must be observed by the event organiser. The guest of honour always sits at the right of the host unless the Governor-General or Governor is present, in which case the guest of honour sits at the left of the host. If other government dignitaries are present, the order of precedence outlined in Figure 8.1 is then followed.

The seating plan illustrated in Figure 8.2 is designed for an event at which all dignitaries are male and accompanied by their spouses. If some of the dignitaries are female, or some are unaccompanied, this adds to the level of difficulty in planning the seating. In modern times, the seating plan is more challenging as women fill the role of dignitaries and are accompanied by spouses or partners. In general terms, those with higher rank sit closer to the official party, and the guest of honour sits at the right of the host. As mentioned above, protocol officers based at federal and state government level are an invaluable source of information, as are their counterparts in other countries.

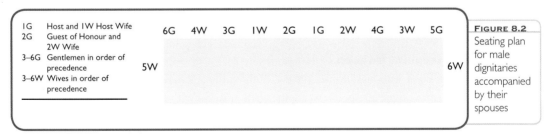

FIGURE 8.2 Seating plan for male dignitaries accompanied by their spouses

Source: Based on 'Protocol' from the Canadian Heritage website, < http://www.pch.gc.ca/pgm/ceem-cced/prtcl/index-eng.cfm>.

DINING

As an event manager, planning the style of food service also has protocol implications. Formal service for a sit-down dinner may be appropriate for an occasion involving local dignitaries. If, however, there are many visitors from overseas, the etiquette associated with Western fine dining may be too daunting and a buffet may be a more suitable option.

Plated food served to each guest

This style of service ensures that food preparation is streamlined as each guest is served their meal on the plate. In most cases, the system of 'alternate drop' is used, in which two meals are served alternately, usually a fish dish and a meat dish.

Limited à la carte menu

A limited à la carte menu with a few selections, such as you would have in a restaurant, is increasingly common, particularly for weddings. This allows guests to make their own choice from a limited range and to make requests such as 'medium rare' for the cooking time.

'French service'

This highly formal style of service involves attentive waiters who pour sauces and dispense various foods from platters at the table. This may extend to filleting, carving or preparing flambé dishes alongside the table.

'Russian service'

The idea of a tray of delicacies is not unique to Russia from which this concept supposedly originated. In India, for example, many different menu items and accompaniments may be served on a tray for each guest.

Yum cha

The popular Chinese style of roving waiters serving exotic dishes (which are selected in passing) is a way to encourage a shared meal with more conversation.

Long buffet

The traditional long buffet has several sections for different courses. The most elaborate of these have ice carvings and colourful food displays.

Station buffet

The idea of a station buffet (or grazing station) is that the smaller buffet tables are more accessible and people are able to help themselves without standing in line. Often a chef will man the station, shucking oysters, carving meats and assisting guests.

Centrepiece kitchen

For an event with high impact there is nothing like a kitchen that is central to the dining experience, where guests can watch the chefs at work. With the right lighting and flair this can enhance the event experience and provide a conversation point.

Marriott Hotels provide the following advice on planning meals:

- At events offering food and beverage service, allow enough time for guests to eat leisurely, network or socialise with colleagues or friends and family, and enjoy all presentations or ceremonies, if there are any involved.
- Generally allow 30–40 minutes for breakfast, 45–60 minutes for lunch, and 20 minutes per course for dinner. For refreshment breaks, allow a minimum of 15 minutes for up to 100 people, 30 minutes for up to 1000 people and 30–45 minutes for groups larger than 1000.
- Plan on two cups of coffee or tea per person for a morning break and one cup of coffee/tea or one soda per person during an afternoon break.

- Consider a luncheon buffet for small group working sessions. Buffets offer variety and faster service.

- Consider requesting one server for each table for more formal meals and/or VIP tables.

- Most facilities allow one server for every two tables, for standard, three- or four-course meals. Check with the facility to determine if there will be additional labour charges for the extra servers.

- Always plan to serve a variety of foods during cocktail receptions. The food should be healthy, appetising and visually appealing.

- Provide one bartender for every 75–100 people.

- Offer non-alcoholic beverages in addition to beer, wine and premium liquor.

- Consider donating leftover food to homeless shelters or distribution organisations for the needy.

Source: Courtesy of Marriott Hotels.

BUSINESS PROTOCOL

Many books and websites give advice on business protocol, particularly when meeting an international visitor. In Asia, for example, the business card carries far more weight than it does in Western countries and its design and presentation creates an important first impression, along with a formal business style of dress. This advice is provided as an example:

★ Keep your business cards in good condition by using a business card holder. Never use dirty, damaged or marked cards.

★ The visiting party is usually the first to hand over business cards and the correct way to do this is to present the card with two hands with your name facing towards the person you are greeting.

★ If possible, have your cards translated into the local language and present this side of the card.

★ Take time to read the other person's card carefully, giving it due attention.

★ Never produce a card from or return one to a back pocket.

★ Never write on another's business card.

★ Briefly study the card and, when seated, place the cards so you can see them clearly and address the person by name.

Making small talk and entertaining are important ways in which relationships are developed. Many business people from the Middle East and Asia complain that Australians and Americans are too hasty and too direct. Getting to the point is less important to them than developing a relationship based on familiarity and trust. The Executive Planet website listed in Appendix E provides detailed information on business etiquette for a number of different countries and practices, including:

★ arranging appointments

★ organising translations

★ understanding seniority

★ using correct forms of address

★ selecting topics of conversation

★ gift giving

★ negotiating and deal making.

Of these, forms of address are most important and may differ from country to country. In Japan, for example, care should be taken to use courtesy titles such as 'Mr', 'Ms', or the suffix 'san', in addition to last names. 'San' is an honorific attached to a person's last name. First names are seldom used in a business context. In China, names appear in a different order from Western names. Each person has, in this order, a family, generational, and first name. Here, too, first names are seldom used in a business environment.

When planning an event that involves international stakeholders or visitors, it is also useful to gain some background knowledge of the country in question. *The World Factbook* (see website in Appendix E) provides an up-to-date profile of all countries. Prior to a meeting, it is also useful to obtain a weather and current affairs update, which will provide topics for introductory conversations.

INDIGENOUS CULTURAL PROTOCOL

Many Australian events commence with a 'Welcome to Country' opening ceremony. This ceremony recognises Australian Indigenous culture and custodianship of country. The following guidelines from the Musicological Society of Australia illustrate its policy:

The policy

It is the policy of MSA to recognise the Indigenous custodianship of country where MSA public events are held, and acknowledge the continuing significance of Indigenous culture in Australia. This policy embraces the spirit of reconciliation between Indigenous and other Australians and reflects the national process of reconciliation as guided by the national Council for Aboriginal Reconciliation.

What is Welcome to Country?

Recognition is made through a formal process called Welcome to Country. It always occurs in the opening ceremony of the event, preferably as the first item. Welcome to Country is conducted by a representative (or representatives) of local Indigenous custodians who welcome the delegates to their country. Indigenous protocols in relation to Welcome to Country are wide and diverse and will vary according to region and locality. The form of the welcome is negotiated between the Indigenous people and the event organisers. For example, Welcome to Country may consist of a single speech, or it may include some kind of performance (a song, dance, didjeridu solo, etc.), or it may be a combination of these. It is important to remember that the Indigenous representative/s must feel comfortable with the arrangements. Rather than a gesture of tokenism and political correctness, MSA acknowledges that Welcome to Country is a right of the local Indigenous custodians and not a privilege.

Who performs Welcome to Country?

Who performs Welcome to Country is agreed between appropriate representatives (individual or organisation) of local Indigenous custodians and the event organisers.

Source: Musicological Society of Australia Inc., <www.msa.org.au/welcome.html>.

Welcome to Country, also known as the Traditional Welcome, allows the Traditional Owners of the region to give their blessing for the event to take place on their land. It must be done by a representative of the Traditional Owners of the location at which the event is taking place. If it is not possible to arrange a Traditional Welcome by a local representative or Elder of the community, a simple acknowledgement of Traditional Owners by other speakers is appropriate: for example, 'I would respectfully like to acknowledge the Traditional Owners of the land on which this event is taking place'.

There are also many considerations relating to the use of images, dance, songs (copyright) and the performing arts in general. For example, sometimes Indigenous artists are treated as one group, as the diversity of their cultures and traditions is not well understood. Very often, Elders of the community are asked to assist with Welcome to Country and other aspects of events and this is expected to be done free of charge. As a result, Indigenous artists miss opportunities to maximise financial benefit from their time and work. In a background paper on 'Indigenous intellectual and cultural property', Terri Janke and Robynne Quiggin (writing for the Aboriginal and Torres Strait Islander Arts Board of the Australia Council) suggest the following:

> One foundational principle underlies the development of Indigenous culture and arts. That is, the need for Indigenous peoples to control their intellectual and cultural property and to manage it in appropriate ways.
>
> In order to positively contribute to the integrity of Indigenous cultural life, arts infrastructure must support Indigenous control of Indigenous Cultural and Intellectual Property (ICIP) management. An essential part of this support is acknowledgement of local community authority, communal rights over cultural heritage material, and engagement of Indigenous people through consultation and prior informed consent mechanisms. This must be balanced with acknowledgement of the authority of individual artists and encouragement of creativity and innovation.
>
> Generally, protocols are appropriate procedures for interactions; they provide a basis for the way dealings occur within a particular situation, community, culture or industry. Agreeing to comply with the accepted protocols of other cultural groups promotes interaction based on good faith and mutual respect, thus encouraging ethical conduct. Over time, protocols also set standards and inform the development of laws. They also serve as what is acceptable practice in terms of reasonableness issues for moral rights. They can also be made legally enforceable under contract. For example, arts and film funding could be made contingent on the protocols being followed.
>
> *Source:* <www.lrc.justice.wa.gov.au/2publications/reports/ACL/BP/BP-12.pdf>.

Also see *Protocols for producing Indigenous Australian music* (2007) and *Protocols for producing Indigenous Australian performing arts* (2008) written for the Australia Council for the Arts., also available from the Australia Council website listed in Appendix E.

ACKNOWLEDGEMENT OF COUNTRY

According to Reconciliation Australia, there are no set protocols or wording for an Acknowledgement of Country. However, most statements take the following form: 'I would like to acknowledge that this event is being held on the traditional lands of the (appropriate group) people, and pay my respect to elders both past and present.' This acknowledgement can be personalised and localised.

RELIGIOUS AND CULTURAL PROTOCOL

Formalities attach to most religious and cultural ceremonies, although these may or may not be observed by the client. The event organiser may therefore be required to assist with the protocol for such an event or to provide advice if the client wants a more relaxed arrangement.

Following are examples of traditions associated with a number of wedding ceremonies from around the world.

Scottish wedding

The stag night is a tradition of Scottish—and Australian—weddings, male friends taking the groom out to celebrate with lots of drinking and practical jokes at the expense of the groom. Another old Scottish custom requires the groom to carry a basket of stones on his back until the bride can be persuaded to kiss him. The groom and his groomsmen often wear kilts to the wedding (traditionally with no undergarments), and the groom may present the bride with an engraved silver teaspoon on their wedding day as a pledge that they will never go hungry. A traditional sword dance is sometimes performed at the wedding reception.

Greek Orthodox wedding

There are two parts to this service: the betrothal ceremony and the marriage ceremony. During the marriage ceremony, the priest crowns both bride and groom three times and all three parade around the altar table three times. The entrance of the families of the bride and the groom to the reception area, as well as the arrival of the bride and groom at the reception, are greeted with a fanfare.

Japanese wedding

The bride's wedding gown is often a traditional wedding kimono. The first sip of sake drunk by the bride and groom at the wedding ceremony symbolises the official union of marriage. The ceremony is generally quite small and is held at a Shinto shrine or in a chapel. Guests invited to the wedding reception make gifts of money to the couple and they, in turn, are given a gift to take home.

Macedonian wedding

Prior to the wedding ceremony, an unmarried relative or friend of the family makes a loaf of bread and decorates it with sweets. Once the bread is cooked, the family members dance and sing, and then give the loaf to the best man who carries it to the reception. Towards the end of the reception the bread is taken apart by all the single males. The story goes that if they eat some and keep some under their pillow they will see their future wife.

The formalities for weddings of different nationalities can be found on the internet or from the many books on wedding etiquette available in bookstores.

For the modern bride and groom there are many variations on the old traditions and these must be discussed with them before the ceremony. For the organiser of the wedding,

THE DAY A SYDNEY WOMAN MARRIED A ZULU WARRIOR

When talk turned to ritual sacrifice, the Cogley family from Sydney wondered what kind of wedding they were in for. They had flown to South Africa to see their daughter, Sofi, 31, marry Robert Ntshalintshali, also 31, a Zulu from a small village in the foothills of the spectacular Drakensberg mountain range.

The night before the April 18 ceremony they were summoned to the spirit hut to witness the village chief call upon his ancestors. Three boys held down a bleating goat while a man slaughtered it, collecting the blood. With a piece of dried sage burning and the skinned goat strung from the ceiling, the chief called the names of his ancestors, one by one, telling them about Sofi, about the wedding and asking them to accept the couple into the family.

He sprinkled bile on Ms Cogley's forehead, arms and legs, then rolled a thin piece of goat skin around her wrist, a symbol that she was now a member of the family.

Custom dictated that Mr Ntshalintshali should give Ms Cogley's family 11 cows for her hand in marriage. Not surprisingly, both families were relieved to quietly drop the whole subject — not just because of the unwanted excess baggage for the Cogley family but because the cost is prohibitive for the average Zulu.

The Cogleys tried to get some idea of the number of guests who would attend the festivities, only to be met with a shrug. 'Maybe 100, maybe 300, maybe 1000 — it depends who hears about it', their daughter said. 'There are no invitations here. The word spreads and people start coming.'

Source: Danielle Teutsch (2001), *Sydney Morning Herald*, 13 May 2001.

the most crucial elements are the timing of the music, the speeches and the meal at the reception. From a planning perspective, there are many details which need to be agreed upon, including:

★ decor
★ seating plans for the bridal party (see Figure 8.3) and other guests
★ timing and duration of the reception
★ menu and special food requirements
★ beverages and payment for beverages
★ timing of food service, speeches, dancing, etc.
★ music, sound system and microphones for those giving speeches
★ rooms where the bride and groom can change.

| Chief Bridesmaid | Groom's Father | Bride's Mother | Groom | Bride | Bride's father | Groom's Mother | Best Man |

FIGURE 8.3 Seating plan for bridal table

A run sheet (see Chapter 14 for other examples) for a wedding reception would need to include the following steps and the timing of these steps:

★ music on arrival
★ arrival of guests
★ drink service commencement (generally champagne, wine, beer and soft drinks)
★ arrival of bride's and groom's families
★ guests seated
★ entry and introduction of the bridal party approximately half an hour later
★ entree served, starting with the bridal table
★ main course served, starting with the bridal table.

Approximately two hours after commencement:

★ all guests are served champagne in anticipation of the speeches and toasts
★ speeches by father of the bride, the groom and the best man (this may vary)
★ cutting of the cake
★ bridal waltz
★ dessert and coffee served
★ dancing
★ throwing of garter and bouquet
★ farewell of bride and groom through an arch formed by guests
★ close bar and music stops
★ guests leave.

Note that an open bar (which does not generally include spirits) may extend only for a number of hours, after which guests pay for their drinks.

PROTOCOL FOR SPORTING CEREMONIES

There are a number of formalities for sporting events, including the awarding of trophies, cheques or medals at the ceremony held soon after the event has finished. Traditionally, in team sports, the press interviews the team captain of the runner-up before the winner is announced. However, different sports have different conventions. For example, at motor racing events, champagne is sprayed over spectators by the winner and this ritual is followed by a press conference at which the drivers remain seated. Press interviews for a number of other sports take place in the locker rooms. Generally, there is a major presentation at the end of the season. An outline of the procedure at a sporting awards ceremony is illustrated in Figure 8.4. The briefing provided for the MC of such an event in Figure 8.5 lists the order of precedence of those attending so that the MC can make the appropriate introductions.

RULES OF FLAG FLYING

There are many conventions involved in flying the national flag and the flags of other nations. Take, as an example, an international sporting event staged in Australia. The Australian flag,

6.30	Guests arrive and are greeted by President.
6.55	Guests invited to be seated.
7.00	Formal welcome to the evening by MC; welcome to Guest of Honour.
	President's speech. Junior awards presented by President.
7.30	First course.
7.50	Referee of the year award presented by former President.
	Coach of the year award presented by former President.
	Club of the year award presented by Guest of Honour.
8.20	Main course.
8.50	Speech by Guest of Honour.
	Presentation of players selected for state teams by Guest of Honour.
9.30	President introduces Main Sponsor.
	Main Sponsor speaks.
	Sportsman and sportswoman of the year award presented by Main Sponsor.
10.00	Formal end to proceedings. MC thanks all presenters and Guest of Honour; Congratulates all winners and wishes good luck for next season.
10.10	Music. Informal part of evening continues.

FIGURE 8.4
Order of proceedings for a club sports award evening ceremony

Briefing notes for MC

Welcome

Welcome guests in order of importance:

- Major sponsor
- Guest of Honour
- Life Members
- President
- Former President
- Vice-President
- Board Members
- Athletes
- Staff
- Family and friends

Order for presenters

- MC announces title of award and welcomes presenter (unless already on stage).
- Walk to stage up centre steps to lectern.
- MC greets you and hands you the envelope.
- Open envelope and announce all nominations (pause for applause if this occurs).
- Announce the winner 'And the winner of this year's xxx Award is…'
- The assistant hands you the award.
- Greet the winner, shake right hands and present the award with the left hand.
- Official photographs – facing the front and shaking hands.
- Awards assistant ushers winner off-stage.
- Leave stage unless there is a second presentation.

Briefing notes for assistant

- Ensure all awards lined up in order on presentation table to right of lectern.
- Ensure envelopes with winners' names are under appropriate award.
- Hand envelopes to MC to give to presenter.
- Hand award to presenter after winner is announced.
- Give official photographer go-ahead for official photograph. When photographs are finished, usher winner off stage.
- Hand next award to presenter if there is a second presentation.
- When MC has thanked presenter, usher presenter off stage.

FIGURE 8.5
Briefing notes for presenters at a club sports award evening ceremony

as Australia's national emblem, should take precedence over all flags of other nations and should always be presented properly (it should not be used as a tablecloth or seat cover!). When flying with flags from other countries, the Australian flag should be in the position of honour, for example, immediately opposite the entrance to the stadium; when carried in procession, the Australian flag should lead. The Australian flag may be used for advertising purposes, although it must be displayed clearly and be unobscured by other logos or images (Joel & Pringle 2007).

EVENT-RELATED PROTOCOLS

The term 'protocol' is mainly used to describe traditional forms of behaviour in the context of ceremony, that is, forms of ceremony and etiquette observed by diplomats and heads of state. However, the term is also used to describe a code of 'correct conduct'. In this sense, there are a number of protocols followed in the event environment.

★ radio use ('over', 'over and out') ★ handling lost children
★ emergency evacuation ★ incident reporting.

Slightly more complex are issues such as managing child performers, dealing with bands and their 'friends' and managing celebrities, all of which require event organisers to develop protocols. The procedures developed for serious incidents and public relations issues associated with disaster management are also termed protocols.

Protocols of this sort are thus highly formalised procedures.

UPDATE KNOWLEDGE OF PROTOCOL

As followers of fashion would know, things change rapidly—none more quickly than the A-list of celebrities! It is therefore important to remain up to date with changes over time, including changes to dress codes and other forms of etiquette that are rapidly becoming redundant. However, as the organiser, it is essential to know when to hold fast to the rules and when to 'lighten up', particularly in the area of formal dress for official occasions.

SUMMARY

This chapter has dealt with the topic of event protocol. Protocol encompasses the traditions associated with government functions, official ceremonies, sporting events, weddings and the like. Such rules and guidelines assist event planners in working out seating arrangements, making introductions, and protecting the privacy and security of VIPs, such as overseas dignitaries. Our national symbols often form part of event decor and an event manager needs to be aware of the rules pertaining to their use. Awareness of the importance of protocol and the ability to locate the relevant information prior to the event will ensure that the event runs smoothly.

Chapter review questions

1 What is protocol?
2 What is the difference between 'Welcome to Country' and 'Acknowledgement of Country' in Australia?
3 Explain the order of precedence you would be likely to consider at a local citizenship ceremony.

Activity

You have been asked to run an event with an Australian theme for a senior American executive who is about to return to the United States after working in Adelaide for three years. This event will be held outdoors and up to 400 staff members will attend. The Australian theme should be evident in all aspects of the event, including the decor, music, food and beverage. Since this is a large multinational company and the media will no doubt attend the event, you must observe the correct protocol for use of Australian symbols. You also need to ensure that you do not breach copyright in your use of images, music, etc. and seek permission for usage or pay licensing fees as necessary.

Tasks

1 Expand on the approach to the theme of this event.
2 Explain how you will use Australian images and music.
3 Illustrate your use of the Australian flag.

Case study

Managing protocol for a multicultural event

Objective of the National Multicultural Festival:
The key objective of the annual National Multicultural Festival is to provide a platform for the celebration of the rich cultural diversity of the Australian Capital Territory through the participation by members of multicultural community groups showcasing their respective cultural traditions and heritage.

Purpose of the Participation Policy:
The dual purpose of this Participation Policy is to provide a framework that ensures that the opportunity exists for all members of Canberra's ethnic community groups wishing to showcase their respective cultural traditions can do so as stallholders or as performers as well as to ensure the financial viability of the event into the future.

Questions

As the coordinator for protocol of this event:
1 How would you prepare for the management of many different cultural protocols represented at this event?
2 How would you prepare for the management of visiting politicians and other VIPs?

References

Australian Institute of Aboriginal and Torres Strait Islander Studies (AIATSIS), Indigenous protocol, <www.aiatsis.gov.au/atsilirn/protocols.atsilirn.asn.au/indexbebd.html?option=com_content&task=blogcategory&id=23&Itemid=27>.
Joel, A & Pringle, H (2007), *Australian protocol and procedures*, 3rd edn, UNSW Press Sydney.

CHAPTER 9

EVENT REGULATORY REQUIREMENTS

Unit descriptor

This unit describes the performance outcomes, skills and knowledge required to assess the regulatory requirements that impact on a **complex event** comprising multiple components, and to incorporate appropriate responses into event planning and management. This unit may apply to individuals coordinating events in any industry context, but is particularly relevant to event specialists who operate in the cultural, community, hospitality, sporting and tourism sectors. A senior event coordinator or event manager would undertake this role.

Elements

- Evaluate event for regulatory compliance
- Develop plans and procedures to address regulatory requirements
- Establish strategies for working with regulatory authorities.
- Analyse regulatory issues that impact on event management.

Critical aspects for assessment

- Ability to analyse, assess and respond to the range of regulatory issues affecting an event to ensure event compliance
- Sound knowledge of the range of regulatory issues that affect different aspects of event staging, relevant networks and information sources
- Identify all sources of relevant legal and licensing requirements
- Practical demonstration of skills through development of plans and procedures to address the regulatory requirements of a specific complex event
- Determine the risks and consequences of failure to comply
- Assess the need for specialists in event management legal and regulatory requirements

WHILE the press reports would lead one to believe that the party was a disorganised, feral bunch of teenagers running an illegal rave party at which drug dealing was rife, this was not the case. The party had been carefully planned with approvals sought from police and council and had met requirements for liquor licensing, security and amenities. Showers, water and first aid were all provided. The event was supported by a range of sponsors and had taken two years of planning. Recreational drug use is widespread and difficult to control, although it is illegal.

EVENT ORGANISER

This case study clearly illustrates the dilemmas faced by event organisers of dance parties, whether at fixed or open venues. In this case, the organisers had sought all approvals and had the support of the police and St John Ambulance's first aid services. It is easy to see, then, why event organisers must ensure that they comply with the relevant legislation and regulations. For example, if you were organising a music event, it would be necessary, among other things, to contact the two bodies responsible for music licensing and to pay fees to satisfy copyright agreements with all artists. There are numerous authorities that need to be notified of an event. As every 18-year-old running a birthday party at home knows, it is a good idea to notify the police in case things get out of hand. In fact, every state has substantial penalties for anyone who serves alcohol to under 18s at a function, even if that function is held at home.

This chapter covers all the necessary requirements for event regulatory compliance and will be followed up by a later chapter on legal knowledge (Chapter 24), which deals with legislation in more detail, as well as contract management and insurance. For the moment, however, the aim is to look at all the compliance considerations that need to be met to run a safe event which is approved by the authorities.

ANALYSE REGULATORY ISSUES THAT IMPACT ON EVENTS MANAGEMENT

Legal compliance in the event business is predominantly about health, safety and environmental factors. This chapter will focus primarily on occupational health and safety (OHS) as this legislation provides a useful framework for understanding how legal frameworks are developed in general and applied in practice, that is, compliance with Acts and regulations. Specific event regulatory issues that need to be considered for approval to run an event may also include food safety, security, responsible service of alcohol, use of licensed personnel, such as tradespeople and pyrotechnicians, crowd control and environmental regulations.

Legislation originates as a draft Bill which is introduced in Parliament. Once the Bill is approved, it comes into force as an *Act*. In addition to the Act, a *regulation* can provide more specific rules on more practical matters—regulations are delegated legislation not statute legislation. Regulations are the practical parts of legislation written by senior bureaucrats and not subject to the same controls as Acts of Parliament (Vickery and Pendleton 2006). For example, OHS regulations may have specific requirements for recording major accidents, near misses and security breaches. In the case of food safety, the regulations deal with specific matters such as labelling and storing food. Thus, a regulation is more specific than an Act and is developed by specialists to assist with the practical application of the Act, which is more general in content.

Both Acts and their associated regulations are mandatory; in other words, they have to be strictly complied with. For example, under the *Collections for Charitable Purposes Act 1939* (SA), no person may, for any charitable purpose, collect any money or goods, sell badges, discs, flowers, tokens or other similar things without a licence, or charge for entertainment, unless the person, or the organisation to which the person belongs, is registered. Licences for charitable collections can be obtained from the Office of the Liquor and Gambling Commissioner. Raffles and lotteries, while seeming a good way to raise income for an event, are illegal without a licence.

Codes of practice, standards and guidelines are all instruments to help organisations meet their obligations. Industry codes of practice provide practical guidance and advice on how to achieve the requirements of the Act and regulation. Codes of practice are developed through consultation with representatives from industry, workers and employers, special interest groups and government agencies, For example, many guidelines for event management are provided by government agencies (see examples included in the resource materials on the text website). A code of practice or standard is not law, but it should be followed unless there is an alternative course of action that achieves the same or better outcome. Employers, workers, service contractors and suppliers should use the code of practice in conjunction with the Act and the regulation. However, a person is not liable under an Act or regulation simply because of a failure to observe a code. Clearly, then, the best approach is to take note of the Act, regulations and any other relevant support documents such as event industry guidelines, codes of practice or standards. This text and support resources on the companion website will assist in this regard.

In summary, an event industry *code of practice* for OHS:
★ is based on the Act (statute law) and the regulation (delegated legislation)
★ applies to a specific industry context (e.g. a public event)
★ gives practical guidance on how the required standard of health, safety and welfare can be achieved in the area of work
★ should be followed, unless there is an alternative course of action which achieves the same or better standard of health and safety in the workplace
★ can be used in some instances to support prosecutions for failing to comply with or contravening the Act or regulation.

There are many instances where prosecution may result, other than breaches of OHS legislation. The most likely one results from failure to comply with liquor licensing laws where there will be fines and penalties imposed on several parties: the licensee, the server and the buyer if underage. There are also situations where breaches of the responsible service of alcohol requirements can occur. In this regard, every person serving alcohol at an event must hold a current responsible service of alcohol (RSA) certificate and it is a responsibility of the event organisers to ensure that this provision is complied with. Breaches can lead to the event being closed down and the licensee losing their liquor licence. There are also strict legal controls on the sale and promotion of tobacco products, as well as laws that cover smoking in enclosed public places. Event organisers or promoters have important responsibilities under these laws, and must ensure compliance at any event where tobacco will be sold or consumed. Failure to do so may result in prosecution of offenders. Noise and other environmental impacts are covered by environmental protection acts.

The following introduction to *Guidelines for the management of public health & safety at public events* (2006) describes the scope of the public event guidelines for South Australia. The complete Guidelines are included in the resource materials on the text website.

> There are many aspects of an event which can be potentially hazardous to the general public if not planned and managed correctly. For an event to be successful, it is essential that event organisers provide venues, access and egress points, which do not put the health and safety of the public at risk or cause environmental harm.
>
> Event organisers and major participants need to understand the health and safety implications of staging a public event and be aware of the precautions that must be taken to minimise health and safety risks.
>
> This guideline addresses ways in which stakeholders such as event organisers, major participants, the relevant health authority and relevant agencies can reduce risks to health and safety. The primary recommendations are sound planning and management, including comprehensive risk assessment and mitigation processes.
>
> These guidelines address South Australian requirements, focusing on environmental health issues such as food safety, infectious disease control and waste disposal, with references to other areas of relevance that should be addressed by event organisers. These guidelines should be read in conjunction with the Manual, *Safe and Healthy Mass Gatherings*, published by Emergency Management Australia, which provides a comprehensive overview of issues to be addressed during the planning, management and operations of a public event.
>
> *Source:* Guidelines for the Management of Public Health and Safety at Public Events, Department of Health South Australia.

The manual mentioned above, *Safe and Healthy Mass Gatherings*, is included in the resource materials on the text website.

At the time of writing there were nine separate OHS jurisdictions. However, OHS Acts are generally consistent across states and territories. The national reform agenda is directed at implementing uniform OHS legislation by 2011.

Now that the hierarchy of legal and other industry compliance requirements has been explained, a short history of OHS legislation in Australia will explain how the approach to offences under the OHS Act has changed. In earlier times it was expected that an Act and regulation would be sufficiently specific for inspectors to visit worksites and prosecute the **observed practices** for non-compliance. However, in more recent times there has been a much greater emphasis on **process**, as this recognises differences between workplaces, and many of the unique attributes of different industries. This process is similar to that of ongoing quality improvement, and is called risk management.

Risk management underpins most aspects of event management planning, from financial planning to health and safety. Risk management is a carefully **documented process** that can be described as follows:

> Risk management is a process of thinking systematically about all possible risks, problems or disasters before they happen and setting up procedures that will avoid the risk, minimise its impact, or cope with its impact.

In terms of compliance, it is therefore essential that event and venue managers use the risk management process to analyse and evaluate risks before deciding on priorities and actions. This is an ongoing process throughout the planning and implementation period. This documentation will be illustrated in detail in Chapter 17 (Safety and Security Risks) and Chapter 26 (Business Risk). For the moment, it is important to understand that, when assessing risks, employers should also identify the factors that may be contributing to OHS risk, including:

★ the work premises and the working environment, including their layout and condition
★ the capability, skill, experience and age of people ordinarily undertaking the work
★ the systems of work being used
★ the range of reasonably foreseeable risk conditions.

The example of OHS compliance has been used here for illustrative purposes, but the same principles apply to other compliance issues. When planning an event, particularly one that is held at a new outdoor site, the event organiser needs to analyse the event concept to determine the scope and nature of regulatory issues to be considered as these will impact on the feasibility of an event. Following this, they need to research and assess the impact of specific event regulatory issues on event operations and establish and assess the roles of different stakeholders in relation to regulatory issues. After investigating and contacting these stakeholders, the risk management process can be applied to the identified regulatory requirements and incorporated into overall management planning. In some cases there is a need for specialist planning and operational advice or assistance to address regulatory requirements. Examples are crowd control and fire safety, both areas being highly specialised.

ESTABLISH STRATEGIES FOR WORKING WITH REGULATORY AUTHORITIES

Consultation and communication with regulatory authorities is an ongoing process, the first point of call being the authority or organisation responsible for the site or venue. An outdoor site would be likely to come within the scope of a local council, this being the first point of call. An event venue such as a hotel, function centre or exhibition centre would provide the benefit of ready-made policy and procedure for many aspects of the event's operation. This does not mean, however, that the event organiser can abdicate all responsibility to the venue operator. The roles and responsibilities of event organiser and venue operator need to be spelled out clearly.

For example, the exhibitors at a particular venue would be required to:

★ ensure that the relevant federal, state or territory workplace health and safety regulations are met, and appoint a qualified person as workplace health and safety officer

★ account for the safety and conduct of their staff and subcontractors in the venue

★ be responsible for all structures, displays, vehicles, demonstrations and personnel associated with their event

★ display appropriate safety alert signage at all loading docks and entrances.

All parties must ensure compliance, including venue manager and event organiser

In applying the risk management approach to the problem of non-compliance, the implications and consequences need to be considered (fines, closure, etc.), accountability discussed and clarified (event organiser versus specific contractors), and safety issues addressed. Clear communication and reporting protocols will assist with this process. You must also take into account insurance problems that will clearly arise if your risk management is defective. This can lead to an insurance company refusing claims made as a result of injuries to persons or property where it is clear that management did not effectively consider the risks that resulted in the claim.

DEVELOP PLANS AND PROCEDURES TO ADDRESS REGULATORY REQUIREMENTS

The next step is to integrate regulatory issues into planning, including the broader event management structures (committees), processes (meetings, agendas, minutes, briefings) and constraints. Responsibility needs to be assigned for developing and documenting specific procedures that address event regulatory requirements. Critical tasks need to be identified and allocated, with timelines for completion. As with all risk management planning, contingency and critical incident procedures in relation to all regulatory requirements should be completed. Briefings to staff, stakeholders and volunteers are essential forms of communication which should occur on an ongoing basis. The event operations manual

Safety is ensured through numbered seating, ready access and staff monitoring

discussed in Chapters 15 and 16 should demonstrate compliance with Acts, regulations and guidelines.

The scope of compliance is extremely broad. Figure 9.1 shows the table of contents for the ACT *Guide to risk management of public events*, which provides a good idea of potential areas for consideration.

This long list of items for consideration, while including safety in cattle handling, does not mention issues relating to the environment, including noise associated with sporting matches and music events. Decibel levels also need to be carefully monitored.

Stakeholders involved in an event may include any of the following:

★ industry bodies
★ professional associations

FIGURE 9.1
A guide to the scope of compliance

Table of Contents

1. Introduction
2. Duty of Care—Public Event Organisers
3. Hazard Management
4. Electrical Safety
5. Gas Safety
6. Animals
7. Side Shows
8. Fireworks Displays
9. Communications
10. Emergencies
11. Temporary Structures
12. Permanent Buildings
13. Staff Training
14. Vehicle Movement
15. Personal Protective Equipment
16. Alcohol
17. Disability Access
18. Accidents, Incidents and Dangerous Occurrences

Source: ACT WorkCover (2006), *A guide to risk management of public events*, December, pp. i–ii, <www.ors.act.gov.au/workcover/pdfs/WorkSafe/Guides/Guide_Public-Events.pdf>. This material has been reproduced with the permission of WorkSafe ACT.

- ★ government authorities, including:
    - – sport and recreation
    - – facilities
    - – parks and public places
    - – transport
    - – licensing
    - – traffic
    - – waste management
    - – utilities
    - – information services
    - – police
    - – emergency services
    - – convention and event sections
- ★ tourism authorities and organisations
- ★ unions.

Specialist planning and operational advice or assistance may be needed from technical experts such as staging or catering contractors. Useful advice following approval to run an event can also be obtained from local authorities. Some events are so simple that minimal involvement of stakeholders is necessary. The scope and complexity of liaison will be impacted by the scope of the event, the nature of the event in terms of complexity and number of attendees, the associated regulatory issues, the level of safety risk and the impact of the event on the physical environment. Thus a surfing carnival may be run under the auspices of the Surf Lifesaving Association which has over many years developed policies and procedures to ensure compliance with regulations. However, to run an ocean-based event without such support would be a daunting prospect! The government agencies most likely to be involved include WorkCover (OHS), licensing authorities, government departments (such as the Roads and Traffic Authority) and the aforementioned local councils.

The following areas of statute law are those most likely to require compliance. The names of the legislation may vary according to state, territory or region; however, the key aims of the legislation can be summarised as follows:

- ★ Local government (managing the local government region or area in a way that promotes the effective, efficient and economical management of public resources, provides excellence in service delivery and affords continual improvement in local services)—approvals for events in public spaces controlled by local councils is usually obligatory
- ★ Food Act (to ensure food for sale is safe and suitable for human consumption; to prevent misleading conduct relating to the sale of food; and to apply the food standards code)
- ★ Environmental Planning (use of land, building approval and temporary projects; includes protection of the environment and noise regulation)
- ★ Disability Services Act (infrastructure and services for the disabled)
- ★ Occupational Health and Safety Act (health and safety in places of work)
- ★ Waste Management and Pollution Control (waste disposal, such as oils and needles)
- ★ Trade Practices Act (consumer protection)
- ★ Road and Traffic (road closures, parking and diversions)
- ★ Major Events (crowd management; safety)
- ★ Security Industry (training and licensing)
- ★ Liquor (responsible service of alcohol and specific licensing requirements for events).

The Australasian Legal Information Institute provides details of Acts and regulations (see Appendix E for website).

EVALUATE EVENT FOR REGULATORY COMPLIANCE

When evaluating regulatory compliance requirements, the following information will be needed by stakeholders such as the local council or emergency services:

★ general nature of the event
★ event management structures (organisation charts)
★ level of government involvement
★ location (general area, site, venue)
★ dates and times (including bump-in)
★ duration of the event
★ number of activities, sports or individual events
★ details of performers, athletes
★ numbers attending or audience
★ scope of physical staging requirements
★ traffic and parking requirements
★ security and crowd control
★ control of alcohol entering the event area
★ evidence that there will be no breaches of gambling or lottery laws
★ insurance requirements of all subcontractors or participants.

Having obtained the necessary permissions and developed the broad organisational plans for the event, it is necessary to develop very specific procedures and checklists. Again, many of these tools are included in the resource materials on the text website. A food safety checklist for stallholders selling food is one example. Figure 9.2 illustrates another—specific guidelines for electrical wiring. In this case, most activities would require a licensed electrician to do the work. This is very important as, even for the smallest event, power supply can be problematic and a safety concern.

Having identified and included elements of compliance into all aspects of the event operational plan, it is necessary to maintain documentation on an ongoing basis. Compliance documentation may include pre-event reports and requests to authorities, details of licensed personnel, activity logs and incident reports.

This chapter has not mentioned the topic of insurance, which is covered in detail in Chapter 24. However, it is important to note that there are three types of insurance that are

Electrical safety is a concern for all event organisers and venue managers

All extension leads, plug-in electrical equipment, RCDs and power outlet devices should be tested regularly in accordance with AS/NZS 3760 *In-service safety inspection and testing of electrical equipment* by a competent person. RCDs should also be tested daily or each day they are used, by means of the in-built test button.

All electrical wiring and equipment installed in areas exposed to the weather or other adverse conditions must be suitably protected in accordance with AS 60529 *Degrees of protection provided by enclosures (IP Code).*

Underground wiring within public event sites should, where possible, be installed where pegs or anchor stakes are not likely to be driven.

Electrical cables that are buried (regardless of how temporary) in areas where pegs or stakes are likely to be driven must either be at a depth of 1.5 metres or, alternatively, 0.5 metres deep and mechanically protected in accordance with AS/NZS 3002.

Cables installed on the ground, in areas frequented by the public, must be suitably mechanically protected and installed in such a way that the cable will not be damaged.

Consideration must be given to whether foot traffic or vehicles will pass over the cable. In some cases, heavy-duty rubber matting over cables laid on the ground will be sufficient; other cases may require cables to be protected by suitable steel piping, rigid planking or purpose-made ducts. In many situations, the mechanical protection will need to be secured in position to avoid any damage to cables.

FIGURE 9.2
Electrical safety

Source: ACT WorkCover (2006), *A guide to risk management of public events*, December, p. 10, <www.ors.act.gov.au/workcover/pdfs/WorkSafe/Guides/Guide_Public-Events.pdf>. This material has been reproduced with the permission of WorkSafe ACT.

essential: **public liability insurance** to cover anyone injured within the event site; **product liability insurance** to ensure that anyone consuming or buying any product at the event is covered against defective products; and **workers compensation insurance** for anyone working on the site. Certificates of currency are needed from all contractors to ensure that their employees are covered, and that in case of a claim by the public, they too have public liability insurance. Attention to detail in this area of documentation is vitally important. If an incident were to occur, there would be several legal actions that the person affected could take against several of the stakeholders, contractors and obviously the event organiser.

Raising awareness of these important issues is usually done during briefings for staff, volunteers and contractors and includes:

★ information on regulatory requirements
★ specific procedures to follow in different situations
★ contacts and procedures for emergency situations
★ roles and responsibilities charts
★ blank copies of documentation to be completed.

SUMMARY

Is this a Pandora's Box of potential problems? Certainly there are many considerations for event regulatory compliance as we have indicated in this chapter. Authorities alarmed at the deaths of teenagers attending music events, bad behaviour exhibited by sports fans and damage caused to the environment, wish to ensure that events are safe and happy for all concerned, including the neighbours. Fortunately, there are many supporting guidelines for event organisers to ensure that they meet their obligations, and in this chapter we have outlined a couple of them and given details of how to access the complete guidelines. The alternative is to run low-key events in safe and tested venues where all policies and procedures provide at least a foundation for event operational planning.

Chapter review questions

1 Briefly explain the scope of each of the following types of compliance:
   (a) Food service
   (b) Environmental planning
   (c) Occupational Health and Safety Act
   (d) Waste management and pollution control
   (e) Trade Practices Act
   (f) Security
   (g) Liquor service
2 There are compliance issues associated with playing music at a venue or event. What are they?
3 Give examples of three regulatory authorities in your state or territory.

Activity

Search the internet for event or festival guidelines for your region, state or territory. List the inclusions in the table of contents, such as that provided in Figure 9.1 in this chapter. Explore two aspects in detail (e.g. service of alcohol and food safety) and summarise the compliance requirements.

Case study

As an event organiser for an incentive group travelling to the outback you have the option of staging an outdoor dinner for 100 people in the desert or using an indoor venue such as a hall. From a legal compliance perspective, what are the five key differences you should consider?

References

Abbott, J & Geddie, M (2000), 'Event and venue management: minimizing liability through effective crowd management techniques', *Event Management*, 6(4):259–70.

Cordato, A (2006), *Australian travel and tourism law*, 4th edn, Butterworths, Sydney.

Goldblatt, J (2008), *Special events: the roots and wings of celebration*, John Wiley and Sons, Hoboken, NJ.

Tarlow, P (2002), *Event risk management and safety*, The Wiley Event Management Series, Wiley, New York.

Vickery, R & Pendleton, W (2006), *Australian business law: principles and applications*, Pearson Education, Frenchs Forest, NSW.

10

BUSINESS RELATIONSHIPS AND MEETINGS

Unit descriptor

This unit describes the performance outcomes, skills and knowledge required to manage business relationships with customers or suppliers. It requires the ability to establish and maintain business relationships with customers or suppliers. It requires the ability to conduct formal negotiations and make and manage agreements or contracts. This unit also describes the performance outcomes, skills and knowledge required to plan and conduct structured meetings involving multiple participants. It requires the ability to write and distribute agendas, chair meetings and write minutes.

Elements

- Build business relationships
- Plan, prepare and conduct meetings
- Conduct negotiations
- Make formal business agreements
- Foster and maintain business relationships.

Critical aspects for assessment

- Project or work activities that show the candidate's ability to successfully establish and maintain business relationships, conduct formal negotiations, and make and manage agreements and contracts for a specific business operation
- Detailed knowledge of KPIs for the industry, industry structure and interrelationships, industry networks, information sources, and distribution and marketing networks
- Knowledge and understanding of role of contracts within a given business operation
- Project or work activities conducted over a commercially realistic period of time so that the planning and relationship-building aspects of this unit can be assessed.

WHEN you plan to use a venue you should start your negotiations early, at least six to nine months before the event. If you schedule the event for a quiet period, such as during holidays or weekends (for a business hotel), or during the low season, you will save thousands of dollars. This gives you opportunities for leverage in your negotiation for function room, hotel rooms and other venues. Your leverage is enhanced by the size (number of people attending) and duration of the event. You can also negotiate services, upgrades, complimentary hotel rooms (at least one for every 50 rooms) and other value additions if you are booking in a low season. It is essential that you shop around as hotels are highly competitive when it comes to group bookings. However, be cautious about food and beverage, as this is the most important aspect for most people attending meetings as savings here may lead to many complaints. For example, sandwiches for lunch will not meet the expectations of most conference attendees. When negotiating food and beverage compare the price charged with the cost of taking your group to a nearby restaurant. Whatever the nature of the event that you are running, indoors or outdoors, shop around for value; that can involve anything from an extra day to set up or provision of support services.

ANON

BUILD BUSINESS RELATIONSHIPS

In many sectors of the event industry, the consumer or client is a large corporation, association, government body or artist promoter. People working in event management can be on either side of this negotiation (as client or supplier) or they may sit in the middle. For example, a professional conference organiser (PCO) manages the planning of an event with the client on one side and the hotel or conference centre on the other. Of course, the ultimate customer is the person attending the event.

The following general guidelines are provided to aid event managers who often need to enter into detailed discussion and negotiation with a client about aspects of an event: the event concept, the parameters of the event, its feasibility. As the extract above illustrates, the event organiser can often negotiate favourable accommodation rates and venue prices for events to be held in the off-peak season, if these discussions are held a considerable time before the event.

In preparing for a business negotiation, it is necessary to understand the goals and positions of both parties, as these goals are often contradictory. Price is a good example. If price is being negotiated for a conference, the client will require the best outcomes for the lowest price while the event organiser (or professional conference organiser) will want the highest possible profit margin, particularly if working on commission. Ultimately, it is necessary for both parties to identify their bottom line so that the process of negotiation can continue. Chapter 22 will deal with budgeting, which informs this aspect of the negotiation.

It is also important to ensure that the appropriate people are conducting the negotiation. Ideally, the event organiser should negotiate with the owner or manager of the company or a person in the organisation with delegated authority. The event organiser should likewise have the authority to close the deal when the correct price and other conditions, such as conference specifications, have been agreed.

The ice cream vendor is a supplier

Taking the widest scope of definition, suppliers to the event client can include:

★ host countries and host cities (competitive forces often result in considerable VIK)

★ conference and exhibition centres

★ venues (e.g. sporting, cultural, unique).

The more usual suppliers of services include:

★ party, conference and wedding planners

★ audiovisual experts

★ sound and lighting technicians

★ tradespeople

★ caterers.

Suppliers of goods include those supplying:

★ merchandise

★ food and beverage

★ signage

★ equipment.

The most successful event managers are capable negotiators whose dealings are tough but friendly. During a career in events, you are likely to encounter the same venue managers and suppliers so these relationships are vitally important. Of course, word of mouth will enhance your profile as a cool, calm and delightful person to work with even in the most stressful of situations!

As has been illustrated in previous chapters, the event business is complex and this chapter raises the question: who is the client? For example, a council could be the client or simply a stakeholder. However, unless the event is fully funded by the bodies on the left-hand side of Figure 10.1, they are referred to as stakeholders.

Clarification of the hierarchy of organisations involved in the event is absolutely essential. All parties carry a certain level of risk and responsibility. For legal and business reasons, it is essential to know who, or which organisation, sits at the top of the hierarchy—and takes

Stakeholders	Suppliers
• Arts council	• Hire company
• Regional tourism body	• Staffing agency
• State tourism body	• Catering organisation
• Major sponsors	• Security company
• Local council	• Bus company

FIGURE 10.1
Identifying stakeholders and suppliers

the most risk. In some cases this is unclear, while in others there is a fairly clear delineation (e.g. between venue management and the event producer when staging a concert at a stadium).

In the next section, we will consider the skills, techniques and tactics of effective negotiation.

CONDUCT NEGOTIATIONS

Active listening and questioning are essential negotiation skills, particularly when used in conjunction with one or more persuasive negotiation tactics. Active listening involves confirming and clarifying what the person has said by paraphrasing and checking assumptions.

Negotiation techniques may include:

★ undertaking preparatory research of the facts of the business situation or parties to the agreement
★ identifying goals of the negotiation and limits to the discussion
★ clarifying the needs of all parties, including third-party stakeholders such as suppliers and contractors
★ identifying points of agreement and points of difference
★ actively listening and questioning to clarify points of discussion
★ using non-verbal communication techniques to reinforce messages
★ using appropriate language, avoiding jargon, acronyms and colloquialisms
★ using appropriate cultural behaviour
★ adopting bargaining strategies, including attempts to achieve win–win outcomes
★ developing options and alternatives using brainstorming
★ confirming agreements verbally and in writing.

Where those involved in the negotiation exhibit a wide range of individual differences, particularly in language or culture, some strategies can help to develop effective communication. These include identifying specific information needs of all participants in the negotiation, using plain English, developing sub-teams, using graphics, and providing all individuals with opportunities to participate.

Figure 10.2 outlines the five main steps in the negotiation process.

FIGURE 10.2
Stages in the negotiation process

Planning and preparation
⇩
Definition of ground rules
⇩
Clarification and justification
⇩
Bargaining and problem solving
⇩
Closure and implementation

Many books have been written on the many different types of strategies that can be used, but here we will outline just a few:

★ *We will beat our competitors.* 'Name any price you have been given and we will beat it' is a common sales technique.

★ *Try it out.* Once the customer or client has committed to trying a product (such as sampling the menu for a banquet), the deal is as good as done.

★ *Take it or leave it.* Starting at a ridiculously high price, the aim is for the other party to feel that they have 'won' when the price is negotiated lower.

★ *Pressed for time.* Creating pressure for a decision by creating an artificial deadline, 'by this date for this price', it is possible to force an early commitment.

★ *Worn out.* Constant communication using different channels and reinforcing customer benefits can work in some situations.

★ *Compromise.* The most common approach is to identify the extremes of, say, price and reach a mid-level compromise.

Each technique works in some negotiating situations and not in others. For the most part, a successful negotiation is one in which both parties strive for a win–win outcome (Kenworthy 2010), with the aim of ensuring the long-term commitment of both parties to the business relationship.

Cultural sensitivity is also important. As mentioned earlier, different cultures approach bargaining and negotiation in different ways. In some cultures, the aim is to get straight to the point, while in others relationship building is seen as more important than the specifics of the final agreement. It is always best to negotiate face to face than indirectly over the telephone or via email.

Following agreement, the details should be confirmed in writing. Agreements should be monitored over a period of time, since it is much more difficult to find new customers than it is to retain existing ones. Existing customers or clients with whom relationships have been developed should also be closely monitored to gauge their satisfaction level with the products or services supplied.

A study by Ogden and McCorriston (2007) of supplier management by conference venues in the UK highlights the benefits that can accrue from good supplier management within this sector:

> A survey of venue managers covering a cross-section of venue types was used. A significant proportion of venue managers report having long-term supplier relationships, placing considerable value on the non-financial benefits that can accrue from long-term supplier relations featuring mutual trust and good working relationships. These include consistency, responsiveness and flexibility in service delivery. Additionally, the familiarity of regular suppliers with the venue and its procedures can lead to seamless service delivery to the customer and free up venue managers' time.

The results indicated that there were both financial and non-financial benefits of establishing and managing supplier relationships effectively.

Make formal business agreements

While the scope of this text does not allow a full explanation of contract law, the following summary may be useful. A **simple contract** is an agreement made between two or more parties, which is generally supported by a document expressing that agreement in writing, but can be made orally. A **formal contract** is a deed, or a contract under seal. Clearly, a dispute over an agreement that has been written up and signed is easier to resolve than a verbal contract. For a simple contract to be enforced it must meet the following conditions:

★ The **offer** must be made with the intent to be binding; in other words, it must be a definite promise and not merely an enquiry. A court will not enforce an agreement if the material terms are vague or absent. In the case of hotel rate agreements, while it may not be possible to quote specific rates for the years to come, the offer should at least include a definite formula, or method, for setting rates for the future.

★ There must be unqualified **acceptance** of the exact terms of the offer for an agreement to exist. Usually this means both parties signing the agreement. There can be no additions or deletions unless these are agreed to and signed for by both parties.

★ An **exchange of money** for goods and/or services is the normal transaction for a business agreement. **Consideration** is the payment for, or cost of, the performance promised in an offer. An example in the event industry would be a hotel's promise to deliver a function space and a wedding organiser's promise to use that space and pay for its use.

★ There must be an **intention to create a legal relationship**. In most business agreements this can be assumed. However, an agreement to buy drugs for distribution and sale at a nightclub would not be an intention to create a legal relationship in any sense!

At the higher levels of contract negotiation and exchange, such as for a major sponsorship agreement or a long-term lease on a venue, professional legal advice would be necessary for both parties. However, in most business negotiations carried out by an event manager, a letter of agreement is all that is necessary to formalise the terms of the negotiation.

A letter of agreement should stipulate the goods and/or services to be provided, the prices agreed, payment conditions, and in some instances delivery guarantees. Conditions regarding cancellation of bookings for rooms or food orders also need to be included in agreements with, for example, hotels and food suppliers respectively. Note that all written agreements of this nature are contracts, even if they are referred to as 'letters of agreement' or 'confirmation letters'.

The agreement should contain certain information that is important for tax reasons because it establishes a business relationship (contract for service) as opposed to an employment relationship, particularly for service providers that work for the event company quite frequently, such as fitters, plumbers and electricians. This information includes:

★ names and ABNs (Australian Business Numbers) of both organisations
★ a statement that it is a fee for service or a purchasing agreement
★ obligation by service provider to use their own tools and equipment
★ obligation by service provider to meet business legal requirements, including taxation, workers compensation insurance and public liability insurance
★ payment for completed work (not hourly)
★ control over work and delegation to staff where necessary (this may be implied).

As much as possible, the language of the letter of agreement should be simple, so that both parties are clear about their expectations. This allows the partners in the relationship to build trust and conduct their business in a professional manner. Variations to the contract should also be in writing.

Matthews (2008) suggests that the event details included in a contract should also include:
★ venue details (time and location of event, specific room, times for bump-in and bump-out)
★ specifics of services and/or products to be provided (lighting, audio equipment, menus)
★ specifics of additional services (change rooms, food and beverage for staff and suppliers)
★ compliance with regulations and standards.

Where the standard or form contract is only one or two pages, these pages are too short to contain all necessary information. A rider or appendix that details all services provided can be added as an attachment. For events, the phrase 'the devil is in the detail' is quite true—small things in plans, schemes and contracts that are overlooked can cause serious problems later on.

Commercial negotiation of wedding catering is interesting in that there are expectations on the part of the whole wedding party, not just the client paying for the event. These expectations can also change on a daily basis and, for this reason alone, both specifications and variations to the specifications need to be carefully documented. The provision of photographs of the floral arrangements, decor and menu items by the caterer can help to clarify the expectations of the wedding party and avoid conflict.

STANDARD CLAUSES OF AN EVENT CATERING CONTRACT

As mentioned above, there are a number of clauses that are found in a typical contract or agreement. Those typically in a catering contract are provided here as an example:
★ *Parties to the contract.* These are the parties entering into the contract. Business names and ABNs should be specified. While the contract will list the parties involved, such as the two businesses, the caterer and the client, it may be useful to nominate who in these organisations has the authority to vary the terms of the contract.
★ *Deadline and deposit (prepayment).* Each contract needs to include a start and completion date. Any deposit or prepayment should be stipulated in the contract.

A deposit or prepayment is generally required as expenditure is usually incurred prior to provision of the service.

★ *Specifications.* Inclusion of specifications and performance standards ensures that the parties to the relationship have clear expectations of the service to be provided. In the case of a catering contract, a menu could be included as an appendix. Inclusion of food safety plans would illustrate the performance standard for food hygiene.

★ *Attendance figure (number of guests).* For a catering contract the number of guests must be specified and agreed in advance to ensure that the appropriate amount of food and beverage supplies are ordered. In addition, a final date and time should be included for the finalisation of numbers. The customer has to pay for that number regardless of attendance. This is vitally important as business functions often experience a large number of last-minute cancellations or no-shows.

★ *Beverage licence and arrangements.* The liquor licensing arrangements need to be clearly stated, as do arrangements for meeting bar costs. Some customers meet bar costs until a certain time or amount is reached after which guests pay for their beverages.

★ *Licences and permits.* It may be necessary to seek council approval for an outdoor event, and permits may be needed for some locations. Responsibility for lodging applications and payment must be clear in the contract.

★ *Services.* This section specifies the level of service to be provided, including the number of wait staff and bar staff.

★ *Special requirements.* This clause covers special requirements such as disability access for guests.

★ *Schedule of payments.* Payments are scheduled from the time of the deposit. In many cases the full amount for the catering is paid prior to the event.

★ *Insurance.* Currency of public liability and workers compensation insurance needs to be specified.

★ *Cancellation.* Terms of cancellation need to be specified.

★ *Termination/non-performance.* What measures would be in place if the service provider could not deliver on the contract as a result of illness, accident or other misadventure must be stipulated. This can prove particularly problematic if entertainment is part of the agreement as the client may have to find another provider at a higher cost. Some contracts include penalties for non-performance.

★ *Confidentiality.* The terms of a contract are generally confidential.

★ *Arbitration.* Arrangements should be specified in the event that a dispute occurs.

★ *Warranties.* Warranties are guarantees by the service provider (e.g. about the quality and suitability of equipment).

★ *Signatories and date.*

A sample contract for venue hire is provided in Chapter 3.

INCLUSION OF KEY PERFORMANCE INDICATORS IN CONTRACTS

Pearlman (2008) conducted research into Key Performance Indicators (KPIs) for several international convention and visitor bureaus (CVBs). While it was difficult to find adequate comparative data, the study highlighted measures used within the industry, such as economic impacts, net square footage of convention space, occupancy of hotels and convention centres, and number of attendees. Clearly, these KPIs were relevant to those centres, while the KPIs in the following example apply to a specific contract between the exhibitors at an international IT exhibition to be held in Brisbane and a logistics company, and focus on how performance would be monitored and evaluated.

As the overseas exhibitors would need to send their state-of-the-art technology to the exhibition, along with cartons of marketing collateral (brochures, business cards, CDs, etc.), this would need to be cleared by customs (and in some cases quarantined) and it would have to be stored until the exhibition infrastructure was assembled and then delivered safely to the exhibition hall. In signing up with the logistics company to handle this part of the exhibition, the exhibitors (with your help) would need to develop KPIs, which would specify the service levels required for the following tasks:

★ import documentation for exhibition equipment and displays
★ international transportation
★ loading and unloading
★ customs clearance
★ local transportation
★ warehousing
★ delivery
★ operation on site.

Following the exhibition, the process would occur in reverse as the equipment would need to be packaged and sent back to the home country.

As the exhibition organiser, you would be the broker in the relationship between the company providing logistics support and the exhibitors, your clients. In negotiating performance standards with the logistics company, timelines would clearly feature at all stages. Key performance indicators might specify:

★ accuracy and reliability at all stages
★ care in storage
★ insurance for any damage incurred
★ timelines for pick-up and delivery
★ operational support during the exhibition
★ troubleshooting.

PROVISION FOR BREACH OF CONTRACT

When negotiating contracts, it is essential to consider the possibility of cancellation of services at a critical time and the financial and logistical ramifications of trying to find another contractor at short notice. A caterer not arriving on time to set up the kitchen and prepare the food would have disastrous consequences for an event. Such possibilities need to be covered by a clause in the contract for breach of contract, detailing the penalties for non-performance. Contingency planning for such a possibility should also form part of the risk analysis.

PLAN, PREPARE AND CONDUCT MEETINGS

When planning meetings with clients and stakeholders, the style of meeting and the required level of formality vary according to the meeting purpose, occasion, nature of participants and organisational procedures. In the author's experience, the best format is the 'standing meeting', which only lasts long enough for attendees' legs to get tired. This is a popular approach in the event business.

An agenda that reflects the purpose of the meeting should be prepared in advance after asking participants for agenda items. This should be distributed well before the meeting in case preparation of documents or other material is necessary prior to the meeting.

The chairperson should follow organisational procedures and meeting protocols. The primary task of the chairperson is to keep the meeting on track. Open and constructive communication should be encouraged. In order to avoid an aimless discussion, participants should be encouraged to present information and ideas clearly and concisely so that agreement can be reached on the meeting's goals and required actions documented.

Minutes of meetings should be prepared, including unresolved issues and actions for which people should be assigned responsibility (see Figure 10.3).

FIGURE 10.3 Differences between positive and negative meetings		Substance of the meeting	Relationships in the meeting
	Negative	• Lack of agenda • Lack of focus • Background information missing • Lack of action items • Lack of minutes	• Angry • Impatient • Distrustful • Time wasting
	Positive	• Clear agenda • Agreement on price, terms, conditions, etc. • Operational schedule agreement • Action outcomes • Minutes of meeting	• Listening • Finding common ground • Participation by all parties • Taking responsibility for outcomes

FOSTER AND MAINTAIN BUSINESS RELATIONSHIPS

Ethical behaviour is of supreme importance in maintaining business relationships. The code of conduct below is for a person whose primary role is that of procurement, but it could equally be used by anyone in the event industry:

★ conduct yourself at all times with objectivity, honesty and integrity.

★ act in accordance with laws and regulations.

★ perform your duties with care and diligence.

★ respond to stakeholders equitably, courteously and in a timely manner.

★ maintain confidentiality.

★ avoid conflicts of interest.

★ do not take advantage of your position in order to seek or obtain benefit (including gifts or other financial benefit) for yourself or for any other party.

Ongoing communication with clients and customers is an informal way to gauge the success of these relationships. This can be done by telephone, email or face to face. More formal methods of monitoring client satisfaction and performance standards involve structured qualitative and quantitative research. Chapter 23 covers the evaluation of events in more detail. Evaluation can be done only when the event concept has been clearly defined and its feasibility tested. Following this, more detailed plans can be developed involving negotiation with clients and stakeholders. Once KPIs have been agreed, these can be used as the basis for evaluating the services provided during the process of event planning and implementation. When the event is over, an evaluation report is written by the event organiser for the major clients, such as business partners or sponsors, thus fulfilling its role in closing the management cycle, beginning with planning and finishing with evaluation of both process and production of the event.

SUMMARY

In this chapter we have covered the skills and knowledge required to establish, manage and maintain business relationships with customers and suppliers. In any business relationship there will always be issues that require negotiation, and guidelines for conducting successful negotiations have been provided. Considerable attention has also been given to preparation of written contracts which formally document the outcomes of negotiations between client and supplier on such aspects as price, delivery and quality. Contracts are essential in ensuring that both parties are legally protected. Finally, we have discussed four key attributes of a well-run, productive meeting: preparation (e.g. agenda), focus, constructive participation, and action (e.g. minutes and follow-up).

Chapter review questions

1 Explain the term 'stakeholder' using an example.
2 Explain the term 'supplier' using an example.
3 What are the core elements of a contract that make it legal?
4 Provide guidelines for effective negotiation.
5 In a meeting there are task elements (substance) and relationship elements. Explain how these work together for effective meetings.

Activity

In business, people talk about Business-to-Business (also known as B2B or B-to-B) relationships. This is the area of marketing and commerce in which a company sells to other businesses as opposed to individuals. They also talk about business-to-consumer (B2C or B-to-C) relationships, which involve companies selling to individuals as opposed to other businesses.

Describe two different events, one that facilitates B2B relationships and another that facilitates traditional business relationships, B2C.

Case study

As the newly appointed Film Festival coordinator, you will have the opportunity to screen 20 ten-minute films developed by graduates of the state's high-profile Film and Television School. This event has attracted an enthusiastic audience in the past, has achieved media attention and has launched some young artists into stellar careers.

Task

Using a diagram, illustrate two different ways in which the event could be structured, one where the Film and Television School is the main client and the other where the major client is a sponsor. In addition, show on the diagram the other stakeholders involved and their relationships with one another.

References

Kenworthy, A (2010), 'Service-learning and negotiation: an educational "win-win"', *Journal of Management Education*, 34(1):62–87.

Kim JH & Boo, S (2010), Dynamic Capabilities and Performance of Meeting Planners, 15th Annual Graduate Student Research Conference in Hospitality and Tourism, Washington DC, 7–9 January.

King, C (2010), 'Beyond persuasion: the rhetoric of negotiation in business communication', *Journal of Business Communication*, 47(1):69–78.

Matthews, D (2008), *Special event production: the resources*, Butterworth–Heinemann, Oxford, UK.

Ogden, S & McCorriston, E (2007), 'How do supplier relationships contribute to success in conference and events management?', *International Journal of Contemporary Hospitality Management*, 19(4):319–27.

Pearlman, D (2008), 'Key performance indicators of the MICE industry and the top 25 United States and Canadian CVBs', *Journal of Convention and Event Tourism*, 9(2): 95–118.

11

STAFF AND VOLUNTEERS

Unit descriptor

This unit describes the performance outcomes, skills and knowledge required to recruit, select and induct staff within the framework of existing human or staffing resource plans or policies. It requires the application of significant planning and organisational skills combined with sound knowledge of current recruitment, selection and induction practices.

Depending upon the sector and organisation, dedicated specialist staff, operational supervisors or managers undertake this role. A more strategic approach to recruitment and selection may be found in specialist human resource management units from the Business Services Training Package. The unit also applies to the whole process of volunteer management, including confirming need, establishing the recruitment program and monitoring implementation. It requires a range of critical thinking, communication and people management skills combined with sound knowledge of specific volunteer management issues.

Elements

- Identify recruitment needs
- Administer recruitment
- Select staff
- Plan and organise induction programs
- Research, determine and define needs for volunteer involvement
- Undertake volunteer recruitment
- Maximise volunteer retention
- Ensure a positive experience for volunteers.

Critical aspects for assessment

- Knowledge and understanding of recruitment and induction processes and procedures used within the event industry
- Ability to administer the total recruitment and induction process for staff and volunteers
- Ability to develop job specifications and selection criteria for recruitment, conduct fair interviews and make selections based on agreed criteria
- Conduct of a complete recruitment and induction process involving multiple applicants to meet a specific event industry need
- Conduct of interviews with multiple applicants as part of the recruitment process
- Ability to research, evaluate and implement a volunteer management program
- Development and management of at least one volunteer program for a business or community activity.

THERE were two training sessions for volunteers. The first was very general and did not answer any of my questions. In fact, I was so confused I almost didn't return for the second session. All I really wanted was a realistic idea of where I would be and what I would do. Instead we were told about reporting relationships, incident reporting and emergency evacuation. When they started to talk about the VERP and the chain of command I was totally lost. The final straw came when the manager talked about the contractors 'attempting to claw back service in response to price gouging'. I had absolutely no idea what he was saying. All I really wanted was a map and my job description.

EVENT USHER

This comment, made by a newly employed usher, illustrates the importance of effective communication and understanding the listener's needs and expectations. In this chapter we will look at two important staff planning processes: developing organisation charts so that people understand their reporting relationships and developing job descriptions so that people understand their specific roles, thus avoiding situations such as the one outlined above. The human resource functions of recruitment, selection, training and performance management will then all fit into place.

IDENTIFY RECRUITMENT NEEDS

When planning for optimal staffing, the first consideration is the number of full-time, fully trained and competent employees the business can afford. These are the mainstay of the event enterprise—the core members of the team—who will establish and maintain the ambience and efficiency of the business. Therefore, it is sometimes advisable to offer special incentives to key personnel, such as senior managers, based on the success of the event business or project. Recognising employees' critical role in the success of an event encourages long-term retention of those employees. Even in the smallest event business, there is generally at least one person who carries a valuable knowledge resource with them, such as the names of regular clients, detailed knowledge of an ancient and tricky software package or contacts for suppliers of staging equipment. For all of these reasons, and many more, employers are increasingly recognising the importance of investment in selecting, training and retaining their permanent and even temporary staff, who may be inclined to leave at a critical time just before an event deadline. For most event projects many of the workers are contractors, and outsourcing is another consideration at the recruitment stage. This has the advantage of involving experts in a particular field on a specific event project. On the other hand, loyalty does not generally develop in this short time and can only be established if there is a preferred provider relationship with these contractors. This was discussed at length in Chapter 10. Finally, the event management team has to decide whether the involvement of volunteers is appropriate. This, too, will be discussed in this chapter. In summary, the composition of the event workforce needs to be decided at an early stage of the planning process. Possibilities include:

★ full-time paid staff, permanent or temporary
★ temporary paid staff
★ agency personnel
★ contractor organisation staff (as a result of outsourcing elements such as catering)
★ volunteers.

For most large public events the workforce also comprises the many stakeholder personnel who are involved, such as emergency services or employees of sponsors. These members of the workforce, while not recruited specifically for the event project, need to be taken through the induction process. Most events of this nature require occupational health and safety (OHS) induction prior to entry to the site as well as a general overview of the planned proceedings.

Let's now turn to another issue that will have a big impact on recruitment—the new employment standards recently introduced by the federal government.

THE INDUSTRIAL CONTEXT

In many industries, such as hospitality, the pay and award conditions are highly structured. In the rather organic event environment, however, arrangements are often more ad hoc, providing that minimum guidelines are met. It is essential to know what these are before embarking on recruitment drives.

From 1 January 2010, employers and employees in the national workplace system are covered by the new National Employment Standards (NES). Under the NES, there are certain minimum conditions for employees. Together with pay rates in modern awards (which also generally took effect from 1 January 2010) and minimum wage orders, the NES acts as a safety net that cannot be altered to the disadvantage of the employee.

In addition to the NES, an employee's terms and conditions of employment may come from a modern award, agreement, an award and agreement–based transitional instrument, minimum wage orders, transitional minimum wage instruments, or state or federal laws.

The NES entitlements are set out in the *Fair Work Act 2009* and comprise 10 minimum standards of employment. In summary, the NES covers the following minimum entitlements:

1 *Maximum weekly hours of work*—38 hours per week, plus reasonable additional hours.
2 *Requests for flexible working arrangements*—allow parents or carers of a child under school age or a child under 18 with a disability to request a change in working arrangements to assist with the child's care.
3 *Parental leave and related entitlements*—up to 12 months unpaid leave for every employee, plus a right to request an additional 12 months unpaid leave, plus other forms of maternity, paternity and adoption-related leave.
4 *Annual leave*—four weeks paid leave per year, plus an additional week for certain shift workers.
5 *Personal/carer's leave and compassionate leave*—10 days paid personal/carer's leave, two days unpaid carer's leave as required, and two days compassionate leave (unpaid for casuals) as required.
6 *Community service leave*—unpaid leave for voluntary emergency activities and leave for jury service, with an entitlement to be paid for up to 10 days for jury service.
7 *Long service leave (LSL)*—a transitional entitlement for certain employees who had certain LSL entitlements before 1 January 2010 pending the development of a uniform national long service leave standard.
8 *Public holidays*—a paid day off on a public holiday, except where reasonably requested to work.
9 *Notice of termination and redundancy pay*—up to four weeks notice of termination (five weeks if the employee is over 45 and has at least two years of continuous service) and up to 16 weeks redundancy pay, both based on length of service.
10 *Provision of a Fair Work Information Statement*—must be provided by employers to all new employees, and contains information about the NES, modern awards, agreement-making, the right to freedom of association, termination of employment, individual flexibility arrangements, union rights of entry, transfer of business, and the respective roles of Fair Work Australia and the Fair Work Ombudsman.

Enterprise agreements can potentially include a broader range of matters than modern awards and, together with the National Employment Standards (NES), are intended only as a safety net of minimum terms and employment conditions. Enterprise agreements can also contain entitlements (or terms and conditions) *specific to the workplace*. The Gold Coast Convention and Exhibition Centre Enterprise Agreement 2009 is one such example (see the Fair Work Australia website, listed in Appendix E).

CONTRACTOR ORGANISATIONS AND THEIR EMPLOYEES

Turning now to the other significant component of the event workforce, the contractor organisations and their employees, there are a number of considerations for human resource planning that need to be taken into account.

Independent contractors can provide more flexibility and can bring specific expertise to an event. From a legal perspective they:

★ decide how to carry out the work and what expertise is needed to do so

★ bear the risk for making a profit or loss on each job

★ pay their own superannuation and tax, including GST

★ should have their own insurance (workers compensation and public liability)

★ are contracted to work for a set period of time (e.g. two months), or to do a set task

★ decide what hours to work to complete the job

★ generally submit an invoice for work completed or are paid at the end of the contract or project

★ do not receive paid leave.

It is essential that these matters are given due consideration and are clarified in contractual arrangements in order to prevent later claims for missing pay or injuries.

Deciding on the optimal mix of paid staff (permanent, temporary, full time or part time), contractors and volunteers is an important process. The principal (usually the event organiser) is also potentially responsible for remuneration, workers compensation and payroll tax for any defaulting subcontractor. For this reason it is essential to obtain an undertaking from all contractors and subcontractors that these obligations have been honoured. Completion of a form known as a Subcontractor's Statement (available from WorkCover NSW and similar organisations in other states) is recommended. This form states in part:

- In completing the Subcontractor's Statement, a subcontractor declares that workers compensation insurance premiums payable up to and including the date(s) on the Statement have been paid, and all premiums owing during the term of the contract will be paid.

- In completing the Subcontractor's Statement, a subcontractor declares that all remuneration payable to relevant employees for work under the contract has been paid.

- In completing the Subcontractor's Statement, a subcontractor declares that all payroll tax payable relating to the work undertaken has been paid.

    Source: <www.workcover.nsw.gov.au/formspublications/publications/Pages/WC05483_SubcontractorsStatement.aspx>.

From the above discussion, it is evident that human resource management for events is far more complex than for most long-life organisations.

ORGANISATION CHARTS

When planning for staffing needs, it is helpful to draw up separate organisation charts for each different stage or task.

Pre-event charts

Prior to the event, the focus is on planning and, as we know, this lead time can be quite long. The charts required during this period show:

★ All those responsible for the primary functions during the planning stage, such as finance, marketing, entertainment, catering and human resource management. For example, the core event team for the Melbourne Comedy Festival includes the Festival Director, General Manager, Marketing Manager, Development Manager, Marketing Executive, Marketing Coordinator, Ticketing Manager, Office Manager, Production and Technical Manager, Artist Coordinator, Senior Producer and Producer's Assistant.

★ Small cross-functional teams which manage specific issues such as safety and customer service.

★ The stakeholders committee (including external contractors, suppliers and public bodies).

The graph in Figure 11.1 shows the cumulative recruitment of full-time staff for the Commonwealth Games in Manchester. In this case, the organisation chart would change every month as more and more people were employed. However, for the purposes of most small events a pre-event organisation chart showing the planning structure in the early days is adequate. Figure 11.1 also illustrates the steady increase in the number of people being taken on as the Games approached. Most business organisations have a much more stable and long-serving workforce.

Charts during the event

When staffing levels for an event expand to the requirements of a full-scale operation, the size of the organisation generally increases dramatically. In some cases, there may be more than one venue involved, so each of the functional areas, such as the catering manager for each event venue, needs to be indicated on the chart. Charts should show:

★ full staff complement, together with reporting relationships for the overall event operations

★ emergency reporting relationships (simplified and streamlined for immediate response).

Post-event chart

After the event, the team frequently disperses, leaving only a few individuals and a chart showing key personnel involved with evaluation, financial reporting and outstanding issues.

An organisation chart can also include a brief list of tasks performed by individuals or the people performing each role. This clarifies roles and improves communication. An

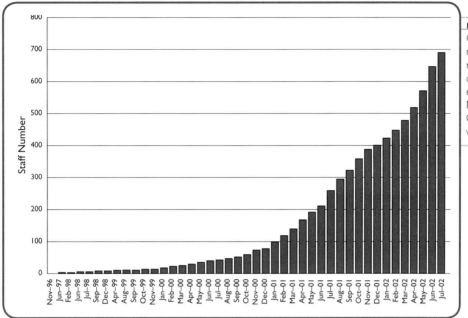

Source: Reproduced with permission of Commonwealth Games Federation, London

FIGURE 11.1
Cumulative monthly recruitment of full-time employees, Manchester Common-wealth Games

organisation chart for a team involved in a product launch is illustrated in Figure 11.2 and an organisation chart for a fun run is illustrated in Figure 11.3.

Figure 11.4 shows the organisation chart for Clean Up Australia. More than 300 000 volunteers turned up for the first Clean Up Australia Day and this number continues to rise each year.

PREPARING JOB DESCRIPTIONS

A job description, outlining the tasks that need to be performed, is required for each role. This document should show the position title, the reporting relationships and the duties. A position summary is optional. In addition to the sections shown in the job description for a Catering Services Manager in Figure 11.5 on page 169, there should be a section showing the terms and conditions of employment. This job description would indicate the salary applicable, while those for many other positions would show the award and the pay rate under the award or agreement. As this position is likely to be a temporary one, the job description should also show the start and finish dates.

As you can see from the job description, this person would not have a direct role in catering. Instead, he or she would be managing catering subcontractors. This means that experience in selecting organisations to tender for the catering contracts and managing supply of the products promised in the contracts would be essential.

Once the job description is complete, a person specification is developed, as shown in Figure 11.6 on page 170. This identifies the skills, knowledge and experience required for the role. This is used to inform the selection process. In this case, experience in a similar role, particularly in relation to tendering and contract management, would be required. In

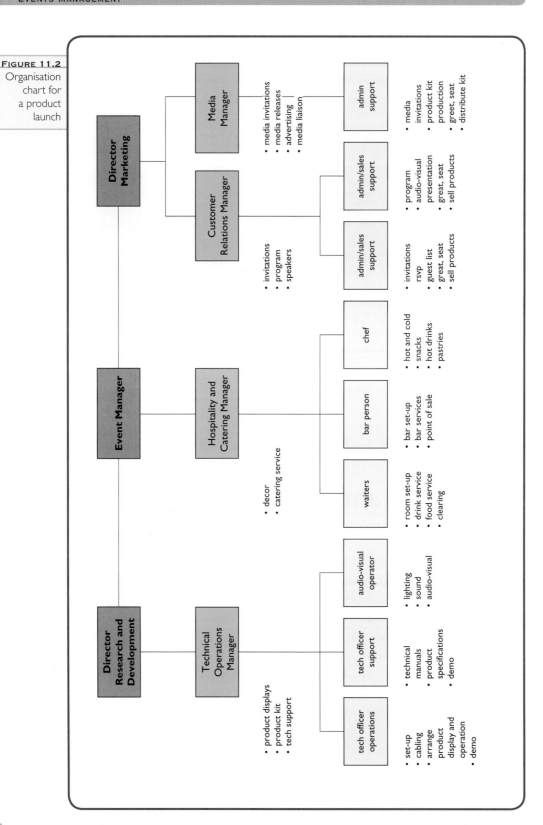

FIGURE 11.2
Organisation
chart for
a product
launch

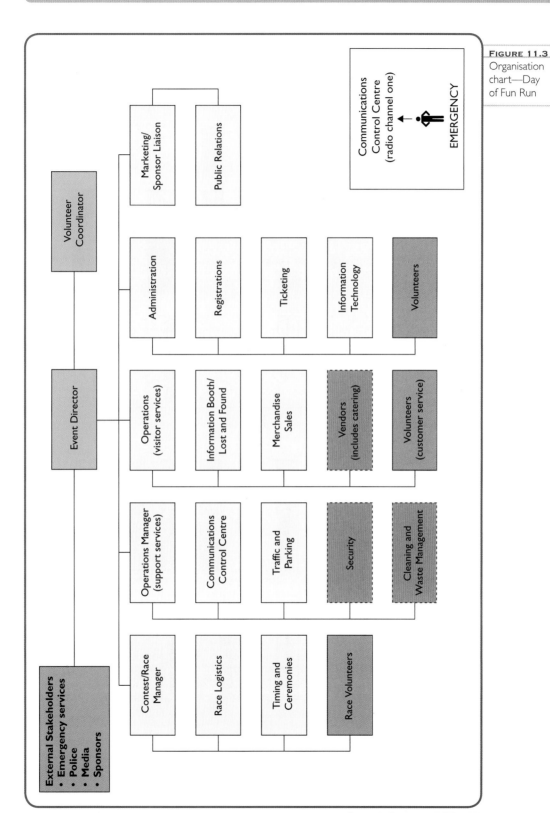

FIGURE 11.3
Organisation chart—Day of Fun Run

External Stakeholders
• Emergency services
• Police
• Media
• Sponsors

Volunteer Coordinator

Event Director

Marketing/ Sponsor Liaison

Public Relations

Administration

Registrations

Ticketing

Information Technology

Volunteers

Operations (visitor services)

Information Booth/ Lost and Found

Merchandise Sales

Vendors (includes catering)

Volunteers (customer service)

Operations Manager (support services)

Communications Control Centre

Traffic and Parking

Security

Cleaning and Waste Management

Contest/Race Manager

Race Logistics

Timing and Ceremonies

Race Volunteers

Communications Control Centre (radio channel one)

EMERGENCY

Source: Van Der Wagen (2007), p. 223.

FIGURE 11.4
Organisation
chart for
Clean Up
Australia

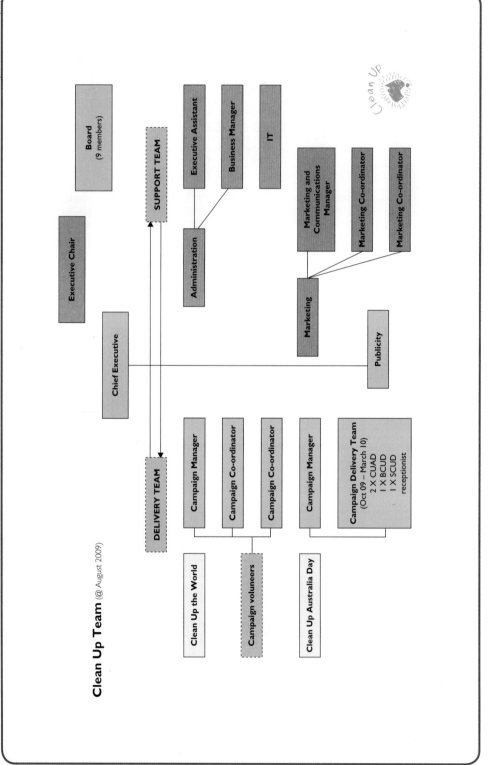

Clean Up Team (@ August 2009)

Job Description

Position title: Catering Services Manager

Reports to: Venue Services Manager

Responsible for: Subcontracts with caterers/concessionaires

Position summary:

To meet the food and beverage needs of all customer groups through the selection and management of appropriate subcontractors and concessionaires. To ensure compliance with the negotiated agreements regarding menus, pricing, quality and service.

Duties

- Develop tender documents for provision of food and beverage, including bars, fast food, coffee stalls, snack bars, VIP and staff catering.
- Select subcontractors and confirm agreements regarding menus, pricing, staffing and service levels.
- Develop operational procedures with special attention to integration of services, food hygiene plans, supply and storage of food and beverage, staffing and waste management.
- Work with venue operations on the installation of the required facilities and essential services (including power, water and gas) for food and beverage outlets.
- Monitor performance of contractors.
- Deal with daily operational and customer complaint issues.

FIGURE 11.5
Sample job description

addition, knowledge of menu planning and costing would be essential, as would knowledge of food hygiene planning.

As you can see from the requirements for the position, experience in an event environment is desirable. However, experience in managing multiple contracts, such as in a resort, hotel or catering organisation, may be relevant in the absence of event experience.

The actual position description for a volunteer for a music festival in Figure 11.7 is an excellent example.

ADMINISTER RECRUITMENT AND SELECTION

Once the job description and person specification have been completed, they can be used to develop advertisements and interview questions.

The most common approach to recruitment is to advertise the position in local or major newspapers, on the event's website or event-related sites, or on notice boards. Employment agencies can also provide event staff—for a placement fee. This is an attractive method of recruitment as it cuts down your work by providing you with a shortlist of suitable applicants, as well as managing the administrative side of employment, such as taxes and insurance.

The best places to look for volunteers are volunteer organisations, schools, colleges and universities.

FIGURE 11.6
Sample person
specification

Person Specification

Position title: Catering Services Manager

Reports to: Venue Services Manager

Responsible for: Subcontracts with caterers/concessionaires

Position summary:

To meet the food and beverage needs of all customer groups through the selection and management of appropriate subcontractors and concessionaires. To ensure compliance with the negotiated agreements regarding menus, pricing, quality and service.

Knowledge:

- Legal contracts (with professional advice where necessary)
- HACCP (food hygiene plans)
- RSA (responsible service of alcohol)
- Catering for large numbers
- Installation and management of bar and kitchen facilities

Skills:

- High level negotiation skills
- Verbal and non-verbal communication skills
- Preparing budgets and planning
- Development of operational procedures
- Problem solving

Experience:

- Managing large-scale catering subcontracts, multiple subcontractors, concessionaires
- Menu planning and catering control systems for large-scale catering
- Operational planning for new installations

Desirable:

- Experience in an event environment

ADVERTISING THE POSITION

By creating an advertisement that is positively worded, the event business is likely to achieve a good response. However, if the positive features of the job are not balanced with realistic requirements, such as the necessity for qualifications or a requirement to work on weekends, an overwhelming response from poorly advised applicants can waste a lot of time.

An employment advertisement must create strong appeal for a number of readers, but deter applicants who do not meet the minimum requirements. In some cases it is necessary to actually limit the response. By stating the selection criteria developed in the person specification, only those with the appropriate qualifications, knowledge and skills who are interested in the position will apply.

In general, an advertisement should include:

★ job title

★ necessary qualifications

VOLUNTEER JOB DESCRIPTION

RESPONSIBLE TO:
- Event Coordinator
- Volunteer Coordinator

LOCATION: Central Park, Wendell Street entrance; meet at the volunteer tent.

DATE & TIME: Friday 25th (12.00–17.00) AND

Saturday 26th (9.00–14.00 or 13.00–18.00 or 15.00–20.00 depending on shift allocation OR

Sunday 27th (9.00–14.00 or 13.00–18.00 or 15.00–20.00).

POSITION OBJECTIVE: To assist in a community event set-up, and provide customer assistance on the day to enhance audience enjoyment.

ACTIVITIES AND TASKS: **During bump-in/set-up**
- set out barriers
- set up backdrops
- set up chairs and tables
- put up sponsors' signs
- set up equipment for sound
- assist stallholders
- set up traffic, parking barriers signage
- place signs around festival—directional, parking
- place no-smoking signs around site

During the event
- check tickets at the entrance
- ensure patrons have valid tickets
- meet and greet patrons with enthusiasm
- supervise the queue
- conduct general minor security (e.g. ensuring patrons are not going through artists entry, etc.)
- assist with tidiness and cleanliness of the event site
- look out for lost children
- assist disabled and elderly patrons into the venue
- in the event of fire or emergency, assist with safe evacuation of patrons
- hand out and collect patron surveys

In general
- assist the Event Coordinator and Volunteer Coordinator as directed to deliver the festival
- follow directions as given to effectively carry out tasks
- present a positive image of the festival
- respect other volunteers and performers
- provide assistance to performers
- provide assistance to the public
- identify safety hazards
- report all incidents (including 'near miss')
- assist with customer complaints
- escalate issues to your supervisor if in any doubt

FIGURE 11.7

Excellent example of a position description

(continued)

FIGURE 11.7
Continued

ATTRIBUTES:	• Excellent time management skills
	• Good service ethic
	• Self-motivated
	• Able to relate well to others and follow directions
	• Prepared to promote the festival
	• Willingness to support the Coordinator and other team members
	• Trustworthy and a reliable team member
	• Show understanding of safe work practices
	• Desire to meet people of all ages and backgrounds
	• Ability to assist with physical but not arduous tasks
	• Previous event experience is desirable but not essential
SELECTION CRITERIA:	The applicant should:
	• have a genuine interest in the festival values
	• be available for a minimum of 5 hours on each day
	• be flexible and comfortable taking on role(s) as required, especially minor lifting and carrying
	• demonstrate verbal and non-verbal communication skills for assisting customers of all ages and backgrounds
	• be trustworthy and reliable
	• show ability to work unsupervised and as part of a team
	• demonstrate absence of a criminal record
	• show agreement to undergo a police check
	• demonstrate ability to apply OHS and safety procedures
	• have the ability to stand and walk for long periods (up to 6 hours)
ORIENTATION AND TRAINING:	An orientation session will be held one week beforehand to familiarise volunteers with their roles
REWARDS:	THESE POSITIONS ARE VOLUNTARY AND SUCCESSFUL APPLICANTS WILL NOT BE PAID A WAGE.
	They will however enjoy the following benefits:
	• festival T-shirt and festival cap
	• other event merchandise including music CD
	• pass to the event during leisure time, and non-work day
	• one hot meal break and one short tea break
	• opportunity to meet with performers
	• increased knowledge of festivals and music
	• meeting people from different walks of life
	• future work experience
	• a reference will be provided for each volunteer
	• a get-together will be held to celebrate the success of the event
THE WORKING ENVIRONMENT:	• work independently and as part of a team
	• work in a busy, noisy and sometimes hot environment
	• wear comfortable shoes, neat casual attire and sun protection
	• demonstrate safe work practices
	• show concern for the safety of others

★ required skills and experience
★ essential attributes, such as the ability to work shift work
★ location
★ wage/salary and any other benefits.

SELECTING THE BEST APPLICANT

The selection process involves reviewing applications, shortlisting applicants, checking their references (the job description and person specification can act as a guide for asking relevant questions) and interviewing shortlisted candidates. Interviewing is carried out with reference to the selection criteria and to Equal Employment Opportunity (EEO) guidelines, which indicate that selection and promotion should be made on merit.

During interviews there are a number of questions that should not be asked of the applicant as they are discriminatory:
★ Where were you born?
★ Have you changed your name?
★ Do you have any children?
★ What language do you speak at home?

The following questions should not be asked of the applicant because they are irrelevant to the job:
★ What do you do in your spare time?
★ What sports do you play?
★ What does your spouse do?

As a general rule, questions should be directly related to the position requirements and to applicants' behaviour and reactions in previous positions and allow the candidate to demonstrate their previous experience and its relevance to the position. Consider, for example, the following questions:
★ Can you tell me how you would handle a customer complaint?
★ Can you give me an example of a situation in which a customer experienced a problem or wanted to make a complaint and explain what happened?

The first of these questions is hypothetical, and most people would find it easy to answer. The second question, which asks about previous experience, is much more difficult to answer but would provide more information about how the applicant has dealt with complaints in the past.

Once the interview questions have been developed, the same questions should be asked of all candidates in order to maintain equity. Using behavioural questions allows the interviewer to rate the performance of applicants against specific and relevant selection criteria. This greatly assists the process and formalises the documentation of the selection process. Many interviewers start off with good intentions, but by the time they have interviewed the fifth candidate they cannot remember the first. Careful record keeping is therefore essential. If the questions have been prepared well, there is little risk of a claim of discrimination. Essentially, selection is a process of careful discrimination. A manager must be able to show that the process of selection was based on relevant criteria, not irrelevant criteria, such as hobbies, or discriminatory criteria, such as sex or marital status.

MAKING AN OFFER TO THE SUCCESSFUL CANDIDATE

Once the candidate has been decided, it is time to make an offer in writing in accordance with enterprise policy and industrial/legislative requirements. The employment offer is a contract like any other and should include the following details:

★ position offered
★ compensation/pay
★ benefits
★ trial period
★ start and finish date (if project or temporary)
★ reference to the attached job description for duties and responsibilities
★ reference to the attached employee handbook for policies and rules
★ signatures of both parties.

A signed copy of the acceptance letter, as well as clear and complete details of the selection process, should be kept on record.

All unsuccessful applicants should be contacted promptly and appropriate colleagues should be informed of the decision. If necessary, recommendations for improvements in the recruitment process should also be communicated to appropriate colleagues.

VALIDATING CANDIDATE INFORMATION

In the process of assessing the individual's suitability for the position, a number of checks may need to be carried out:

★ visa and other requirements for official employability status
★ licences and permits (e.g. to drive a forklift)
★ educational and other qualifications (e.g. responsible service of alcohol certificate, food safety training and first aid certificate need to be checked for currency)
★ police check (mainly for major events)
★ training and register of offenders (for positions involving work with children)
★ references from past employers.

PLAN AND ORGANISE INDUCTION PROGRAMS

Event staff must be trained in three basic areas:

★ *General outline.* Staff should be presented with a general outline of the event, including its objectives and organisational structure, and they need to be motivated to provide reliable information and outstanding service to every member of the event audience.
★ *Venue information.* A tour of the venue enables staff to become familiar with the location of all facilities, functional areas and departments, and the spectator services provided. This is the ideal time to cover all emergency procedures.

★ *Specific job information.* Event staff need to know their duties and how to perform them. Maps and checklists can be extremely useful for this purpose, while rehearsals and role plays help to familiarise staff with their roles before the onslaught of the event audience. Most trainees would rather move from the specific, which is more personally relevant, to the general. However, in some cases, access to the venue is only permitted at the very last minute and training has to focus on the more general aspects first.

Training days provide an ideal opportunity for team building. Team building activities, such as quizzes, games and competitions, should be included in all training so that comfortable relationships develop. Such activities should be relevant to particular tasks. Event leaders need to accelerate all processes as much as possible in order to hold the attention of the trainee group and develop team spirit.

Reinforcement is essential and, at the end of training, the event manager should be confident that all staff have achieved the training objectives for knowledge, attitudes and skills. Too often these sessions are a one-way process, trainees becoming bogged down with an overload of information. Training materials need to be prepared in a user-friendly, jargon-free format for participants to take home. An illustration of how to use a stopwatch is provided in Figure 11.8 to show how effectively simple training aids can support learning. A hotline staffed by volunteers who can answer staff questions about everything (e.g. rosters, roles, transport) is also a good idea.

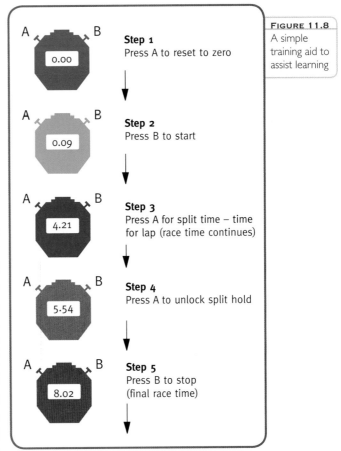

FIGURE 11.8
A simple training aid to assist learning

The following checklist covers the type of information that might be included in training manuals and training sessions:

Shift routine and specific tasks
★ location of check-in area and check-in procedure
★ reporting for shift and briefing
★ uniforms and equipment
★ incident reporting system

- ★ supervision
- ★ specific roles
- ★ breaks and meals
- ★ debriefing and check-out

Venue operations

- ★ venue organisation and support operations
- ★ staffing policies/rules
- ★ emergency procedures
- ★ radio procedures
- ★ other relevant procedures

General event information

- ★ event outline and objectives
- ★ event audience expectations
- ★ transport
- ★ related local services information
- ★ contingency planning.

Customer service training is a key component of all event training. As the general principles of quality service are well known, the focus should be on specific information required by staff in order to properly assist customers rather than on general skills. Most event staff rate training on specific event information for the event audience as being the most relevant to their training needs and to providing quality customer service. Staff, however well intentioned, find themselves helpless and frustrated when asked questions that they cannot answer. Figure 11.9 shows the attributes of staff that event customers value.

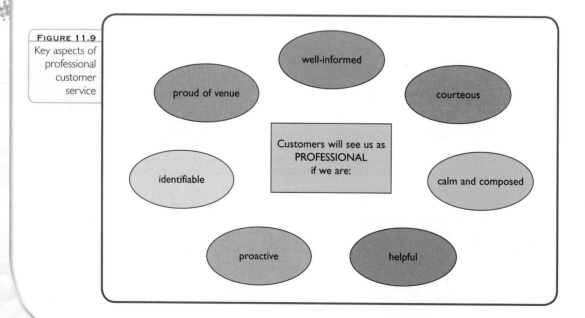

FIGURE 11.9
Key aspects of professional customer service

Briefing staff prior to every shift is essential. It is an extension of the training sessions and allows the venue or event manager to impart important, relevant information to staff before they commence work. Some information may be new, such as changes to spectator transport arrangements, while other elements may be a reinforcement of key information, such as incident reporting or emergency procedures.

Briefing volunteers

DETERMINE AND DEFINE NEED FOR VOLUNTEER INVOLVEMENT

When determining the need for volunteer involvement, it is necessary to consider the benefits, costs and risks of using untrained or partially trained staff. On the positive side, volunteers are generally keen and add to the sense of community at an event. It is not generally considered appropriate to use volunteers for paid roles, particularly in such areas as security and cleaning. Volunteers have a place in public, community, not-for-profit and fundraising events. They should not be exploited by commercial operators.

The Australian Council of Volunteers provides training in volunteer management and the following guidelines summarise the main principles of its management and training:

★ Volunteers have the right to be treated as co-workers.
★ They should be allocated a suitable assignment, task or job.
★ They should know the purpose and ground rules of the organisation.
★ Volunteers should receive continuing education on the job, as well as sound guidance and direction.
★ They should be allocated a place to work and suitable tools and materials.
★ They should be offered promotion and a variety of experience.
★ Volunteers should be heard and allowed to make suggestions.
★ They must be adequately insured.
★ They should be given a reference at the end of the event.

In return, the event organisation can expect:

★ as much effort and service from a volunteer as a paid worker, even on a short-term basis
★ conscientious work performance, punctuality and reliability
★ enthusiasm and belief in the work of the organisation
★ loyalty to the organisation and constructive criticism only
★ clear and open communication from the volunteer.

The organisation has the right to decide on the best placement of a volunteer, to express opinions about poor volunteer performance in a diplomatic way and to release an inappropriate volunteer.

The roles most commonly performed by volunteers include:

- ★ usher
- ★ marshal
- ★ time-keeper
- ★ results coordinator
- ★ referee
- ★ administrator
- ★ media coordinator
- ★ protocol/public relations assistant
- ★ logistics coordinator
- ★ transport officer
- ★ information officer
- ★ customer relations officer
- ★ first aid officer
- ★ physiotherapist/sports medicine
- ★ access monitor
- ★ shift coordinator
- ★ uniform/accreditation officer
- ★ safety officer.

CLEAN UP AUSTRALIA DAY

The first Clean Up Sydney Harbour Day in 1989 achieved an enormous public response with over 40 000 Sydneysiders donating their time and energy in an attempt to clean up their harbour. The next year Clean Up Australia Day was born, after Ian Kiernan, AO, and his

committee thought that if a city could be mobilised into action, then so could the whole nation. Over 300 000 volunteers turned out on the first Clean Up Australia Day and the numbers have risen ever since.

The subsequent challenge was to take the concept of Clean Up Australia Day to the rest of the world. After gaining the support of the United Nations Environment Programme (UNEP), Clean Up the World was launched in 1993. The success of Clean Up the World (an estimated 35 million people take part in over 120 countries annually) has shown that environmental effort in Australia has been noticed and the environment is a concern to all people globally.

Every official clean up site needs to have at least one supervisor on Clean Up Australia Day. Site supervisors must be over 18, and should be responsible people who are happy to commit their services for the entirety of the clean up activity. Site supervisors are volunteers who report to the national coordinator of the event.

Site supervisors are responsible for:

- Ensuring they have read the Clean Up Australia Day Site Guide
- Selecting and surveying a site
- Registering the site with Clean Up Australia
- Correct registering of volunteers
- Volunteer briefing and ensuring volunteers are aware of safety requirements
- Distributing Clean Up bags and gloves
- Reporting back to Clean Up Australia.

It is easy to organise a Clean Up Australia Day site in your local area. Once you register your interest in joining the national campaign, Clean Up Australia will provide you with a step-by-step guide explaining exactly what you need to do to get involved! Simply register on-line at www.cleanup.org.au or contact Clean Up Australia by telephoning us today on CUADAY 1800 282 329.

Source: Clean Up Australia Limited. Permission for reference to Clean up Australia Day is granted by Clean Up Australia Limited.

The contribution of volunteers needs to be recognised: not only customer relations volunteers but also volunteers working for other organisations such as the first aid provider.

A survey by the Australian Bureau of Statistics (cat. no. 4441.0) showed that 2 639 500 persons, or roughly 15% of the Australian population, performed some form of voluntary work. Two fields of voluntary work claimed almost half of all volunteer hours: sport/recreation/hobby (24%) and welfare/community (24%). The personal benefits, as perceived by volunteers, were:

★ personal satisfaction
★ social contact
★ helping others in the community
★ doing something worthwhile
★ personal or family involvement
★ learning new skills
★ using skills and experience
★ being active.

Another ABS survey (cat. no. 4172.0) into cultural trends, showed that 200 000 people Australia-wide were involved each year in organising cultural festivals. (Note that this does not include events from other categories as discussed in Chapter 1.) The following data revealed by the survey is also interesting: 28.5% of festival involvement was for a duration of one to two weeks and 24.9% involved three to four weeks work. Most people were not paid for their involvement—only 14.2% received any payment for their work.

These findings are useful in understanding the contribution and motivation of volunteers and the importance of developing recognition strategies to meet their needs. In the job description for volunteers earlier in this chapter, a number of benefits are listed that would meet the stated needs of volunteers for social contact and being active. These volunteers also received rewards in the form of merchandise and meeting musicians. After the Sydney Olympics, IOC President Juan Antonio Samaranch described Australia's volunteers as the 'most dedicated and wonderful volunteers ever'. This was a richly deserved accolade for a country in which volunteering is part of the social fabric. Furthermore, Kemp's (2002) evaluation of volunteer satisfaction with the Sydney Olympics and the Winter Olympics in 1994 showed that all volunteers in Sydney and Lillehammer were very positive about their participation as a volunteer. The mean satisfaction score for Lillehammer was 7.7 and for Sydney it was 9.2 (on a Likert scale of 1 to 10).

However, during the Sydney Olympic Games, it was not only volunteers who embraced the Olympic spirit. An experiment by one of the radio stations showed that a person posing as an American tourist with a map and a puzzled look was offered immediate assistance by those who witnessed his dilemma. The average response time to offer help was 66 seconds (Column 8, *Sydney Morning Herald*, 18 September 2000). This illustrates the positive attitude of most Australian citizens towards tourism and the importance of the role of events in increasing tourist numbers.

Better access for people with disabilities, targeted volunteer opportunities for young people and more respect for other cultures are some of the legacies of the 2006 Commonwealth Games held in Melbourne, with all Victorians 'equal first' in their involvement in the Games. The OCGC (Office of Commonwealth Games Co-ordination) was established within the Victorian public service with a staff of around 600 at its peak. At Games time 13 150 volunteers assisted, 74% from Melbourne; 14% from regional Victoria; 11% from interstate and 1% from the Commonwealth.

This event was evaluated in terms of the 'triple bottom line', which considers the economic, social and environmental impacts of an event. In this case, the objective of a lasting social impact was achieved, with over half the volunteer workforce stating that they would volunteer again. According to the Games' organisers, 'without their contribution it is difficult to see how events of this kind could successfully be delivered within a reasonable budget' (Insight Economics 2006).

MAXIMISE VOLUNTEER RETENTION

Recognition of the work of both paid and volunteer staff can have a huge impact on motivation and retention. One of the most effective strategies is the development of realistic goals for staff as this allows individuals to see that their work has contributed to the success of the event.

Intangible rewards include:

★ goal achievement through individual and team targets and competitions
★ job rotation
★ job enrichment
★ meeting athletes, stars, musicians and artists
★ working with people from overseas
★ providing service and information and performing other meaningful tasks

A volunteer at work at a community event

★ praise and verbal recognition
★ training and skill development
★ opportunities for building relationships and friendships
★ media recognition.

Tangible rewards include:

★ merchandise
★ tickets
★ post-event parties
★ recognition certificates
★ statement of duties performed
★ meals and uniforms of a high standard
★ badges, memorabilia.

Linking performance to individual or team goals should be considered carefully by those in charge of motivating staff. When recognition is given to individuals, it needs to be done with caution, otherwise it can lead to accusations of inequity. Team targets are more likely to improve team performance and to develop camaraderie.

PREPARE STAFFING POLICIES

Staffing policies should be developed as part of any human resource planning strategy and should cover such aspects as health and safety, misconduct, poor performance, sexual harassment and contravention of safety procedures. These policies are then simplified and summarised as a code of conduct for all paid and volunteer staff and should be clarified at induction:

1 Work in a safe manner.
2 Do not endanger the health and safety of others.
3 Report all accidents and incidents.
4 Protect the confidentiality of the event organisation and sponsors.
5 Do not say anything derogatory about any aspect of, or person involved in, the event.
6 Refer media questions to the correct person.
7 Look after equipment, uniforms and other assets.
8 Act in a polite and courteous way to spectators and team members.
9 Use and abuse of alcohol or drugs while on duty is prohibited.
10 Act in a financially responsible manner.
11 Follow reasonable instructions of supervisors and senior event staff.

The policies can be discussed during induction, and issued to all members of the event workforce. It is useful to assess understanding of these matters, especially OHS, through the use of a questionnaire. This provides evidence that the induction process has been thorough. For an example of online OHS induction, see Playbill Venues Safety Centre safety induction on the website listed in Appendix E.

DRAW UP ROSTERS

Staff planning also includes the development of work rosters. This can be quite difficult, particularly if multiple sessions and multiple days are involved and interrelated tasks have to be considered, as sufficient time needs to be factored in for each task. For example, if the site crew has not completed the installation of essential equipment for a particular session, work cannot begin on related tasks. Staff scheduled to be on duty will stand idle and become frustrated, knowing that deadlines are slipping. Having got out of bed at 3 am to arrive as scheduled at 4.30 am to set up for the day will contribute further to their frustration. In the event environment there is often limited time for transition from one session or show to the next and there are usually many interrelated jobs to be done, requiring extremely detailed planning and scheduling. A staffing crisis in the hours preceding an event can also contribute to the risk of accidents and poor service, again emphasising the importance of effective planning.

SUMMARY

Staffing is a very important part of event management and crucial to the smooth running of an event. To cover this adequately, we have discussed many topics in this chapter, from identifying recruitment needs to planning and organising induction programs. Recruitment and selection help to bring staff on line, while induction and training prepare them for their event roles. We have also looked at the types of events that lend themselves to recruiting volunteers, how to maximise volunteer retention and strategies for recognising their involvement. The event manager needs to be able to prepare human resource policies, job descriptions and person specifications, prepare organisation charts to enable employees to understand their reporting relationships, and manage workforce and occupational health and safety issues.

Chapter review questions

1 Discuss the pros and cons of outsourcing services such as catering and security.
2 What are the minimum entitlements of workers under the National Employment Standards?
3 What are the responsibilities of the primary or principal contracting agency (the event organiser) in relation to staff working for subsidiary contractors (subcontractors)?
4 How does induction and training for the event environment differ from induction and training in traditional long-life organisations?
5 Explain EEO and its application to recruitment and selection.

Activity

Investigate the OH&S legislation in your state or territory by visiting the NOHSC website. In the process of this investigation, identify the particular problems related to workplace health and safety facing employees and their employers in the event industry.

Case study

You have been asked to run a tourism destination promotional forum. The aims are to raise the profile of your region as a tourist destination, provide a platform for the public and private sectors of the local tourism industry, discuss and address regional tourism issues, and help to expand marketing networks and opportunities to promote local tourism destinations and events.

The Buyers and Sellers Business Session of the forum will enable delegates to network and conduct business with high-level government officials, national, state and local tourism organisations, representatives as well as entrepreneurs, hoteliers, travel agents, tourism operators and media. Open break-out sessions will aim to generate ideas and solutions. Issues such as standards, product ranges, joint promotional efforts, and marketing opportunities and strategies will also be discussed.

Tasks

1 Develop an organisational chart similar to the one illustrated in Figure 11.2 in this chapter.
2 Develop your own job description as Tourism Forum Event Manager.

References

Bryden, L & Madden, K (2006), 'Bounce-back of episodic volunteers: what makes episodic volunteers return?', working paper, Centre of Philanthropy and Nonprofit Studies, QUT, Brisbane, <http://eprints.qut.edu.au/4450/>, accessed 5 May 2010.

Costa, C, Chalip, L, Green, B & Simes, C (2006), 'Reconsidering the role of training in event volunteers' satisfaction', *Sport Management Review*, 9(2):165–82.

Cuskelly, G, Taylor, T, Hoye, R & Darcy, S (2006), 'Volunteer management practices and volunteer retention: a human resource management approach', *Sport Management Review*, 9(2):141–63.

Insight Economics (2006), *Triple bottom line assessment of the XVIII Commonwealth Games*, p. x, <www.sport.vic.gov.au/web9/rwpgslib.nsf/GraphicFiles/Final_Report_Executive_Summary/$file/Final_Report_Executive_Summary.pdf>, accessed 5 May 2010.

Kemp, S (2002), 'The hidden workforce: volunteers' learning in the Olympics', *Journal of European Industrial Training*, 26(2–4):109–16.

Nankervis, A, Compton, R & Baird, M (2008), *Human resource management: strategies and processes*, Thomson Learning Australia, South Melbourne.

Van Der Wagen, L (2007), *Human resource management for events: managing the event workforce*, Butterworth–Heinemann, Oxford, UK; Burlington, MA.

12

PEOPLE MANAGEMENT

Unit descriptor

This unit describes the performance outcomes, skills and knowledge required to lead and manage teams of people in the workplace, including volunteers where appropriate. The unit focuses on modelling high standards, developing commitment and managing team performance through effective leadership. It requires the application of highly developed communication, interpersonal and leadership skills with a strong focus on team development

Elements

- Model high standards of performance and behaviour
- Develop team commitment and cooperation
- Manage team performance.

Critical aspects for assessment

- Knowledge of leadership, motivation and teamwork principles
- Ability to build positive team spirit and effectively manage overall team performance within a specific workplace context
- Project or work activities conducted over a period of time to allow the candidate to play an ongoing team-leading role.

THE VOLUNTEER took one look at the uniform, refused to wear it and walked off the job. Of the twenty people I had in my team on the first day, only six remained by day five. Three of my best people were reassigned to another team on the second day. Some of those who remained beyond the second day found the work too hard; others found it too boring. People assume that when they work at a major event they will be directly involved in the action. We were long gone by the time the bike race began each morning, rushing ahead to set up the next night's camp. In reality, most event employees work behind the scenes, handling difficult situations such as spectators trying to gain access to secure areas. In our case, drunkenness, aggression and general horseplay by both riders and spectators were hard to handle. The work was physically hard too. Holding a team together is a real challenge, especially when there are many other opportunities for them, or nothing to hold them.

CYCLING EVENT MANAGER

This story illustrates the problems that face many event managers. Staff are often hard to come by owing to the short-term or unpaid nature of the work. In the above scenario, the event manager is struggling to keep the event team together for the duration of a six-day, long-distance bike race. While her team may have been enthusiastic to support the charity involved in the race, as well as excited to be on the road with the cyclists, the harsh realities are often quite different from the team's expectations.

Although the event planning team may work together for months or even years, the bulk of the event team works together for an extremely short period, ranging from one day to about one month. Staff expectations are hard to manage under these conditions, and there is little time for building relationships and skills. Therefore, the focus of the event leader should be on giving clear guidelines, facilitating efficient work, energising people and celebrating successes. The event must be extremely well planned and the event leader must concentrate on developing tools for organising and controlling activities, as well as on innovative ways to inform, lead and motivate employees and volunteers who may need to reach job maturity within minutes or hours.

MODEL HIGH STANDARDS OF PERFORMANCE AND BEHAVIOUR

Much has been said about the challenges of the event environment. However, from a human resources point of view, it is also necessary to consider the long and stressful planning period leading up to an event. For a major event, this can be for a period of a year or more. Due to the number of uncertainties that need to be resolved and the diverse range of contractual and stakeholder relationships that need to be negotiated during this period, stress management is an important consideration. It is at this time, and during the event execution, that supervisory and management staff need to model high standards of performance and behaviour. In this of all industries, charismatic leadership goes a long way to maintaining motivation. Open and supportive communication is also extremely helpful. This includes:

★ planned and informal exchanges of information
★ open access to documents, including operational plans
★ using technology to support effective communication (e.g. email groups)
★ involving others in developing solutions
★ being prepared to declare own need for assistance
★ providing constructive feedback.

In this chapter we will look at the all-important topics of team development, motivation and leadership. In the next chapter we will cover individual motivation and performance management.

DEVELOP TEAM COMMITMENT AND COOPERATION

The leadership model on which this chapter is based is shown in Figure 12.1. The two main dimensions of this model are task management and people management, the basis for many other models used in organisational behaviour.

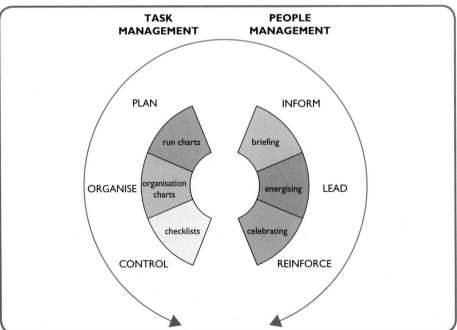

FIGURE 12.
Leadership model for temporary teams

TASK MANAGEMENT

Task management involves the skills of planning, organising, coordinating and controlling work processes, using tools such as run charts, organisation charts and checklists.

Plan

Planning is probably the most important aspect of event management. It encompasses the development of policies and procedures to cover all situations, from disputes over ticketing/seating to summary dismissal of alcohol-affected employees. Planning is necessary for the development of staff rosters and the provision of meals for paid and volunteer staff, as well as for restocking, careful scheduling of stock being essential for multi-session events. When a venue is still under construction, architectural drawings are used in logistics planning to ensure, for example, that materials and equipment can be unloaded and set up easily.

There are a number of useful tools which can facilitate the planning process. A simplified version of a run chart (see Chapter 14) is helpful for all team members, and charts and maps should be displayed and discussed during training. Sometimes it is necessary to modify them so that they can be easily understood by all event staff. While the event management team needs to focus on the macro level of the event (the big picture), the micro level must not be ignored. It is essential that all members of the team be clear about the specific jobs that they are expected to do, otherwise they will become frustrated and their performance will deteriorate.

Organise

Organisation charts were covered in Chapter 11 and will also be covered in Chapter 14 on project management. You will notice that including the main tasks of those involved has enhanced the chart illustrated in Figure 11.2 on page 166. An organisation chart enhanced with task lists is a useful tool for providing everyone with a more accurate idea of roles and responsibilities at a glance. There should be no ambiguity as to who is responsible for what. In addition to the organisation chart, every person should have a job description listing their duties.

Job rotation is an important organisational task, particularly where paid or volunteer staff are required to man remote locations. Change from one role to another during a shift can alleviate boredom and reduce feelings of inequity.

Control

Checklists are useful control mechanisms. They can be used to check cleanliness, monitor the temperature of food, check for safety or security risks, and to ensure that procedures are followed for setting up and shutting down. A completed checklist is also intrinsically satisfying for the person carrying out the tasks, especially if their job has no visible output. Most events are high risk, making control measures absolutely essential for risk and hazard minimisation. Tours of the venue (both front and back of house) to check that everything is safe are invaluable. Frayed carpets, loose wiring and chairs stacked in fire exits can all be dealt with using simple control tools such as checklists.

PEOPLE MANAGEMENT

The three skills shown in Figure 12.1 that are required for good people management are informing, leading and reinforcing. Briefings, energising strategies and celebratory activities can achieve closure on short-term targets and are necessary for keeping staff interested and motivated.

People management is one of the most significant challenges for the event manager. Due to the short-term nature of events, the frontline staff do not have the commitment of employees embarking on careers with traditional organisations. A volunteer or casual employee who finds the work boring, the location unappealing, the weather unpleasant or the food unsatisfactory may simply not return the following day. Indeed, he or she may not return from a meal break! The ability to keep people informed, to inspire and motivate them through positive leadership, and to reinforce the attainment of specific results is the key to successful people management in this fast-paced environment.

Inform

Briefings before and after shifts provide the opportunity to advise staff on the order of proceedings and to clarify issues of concern. If a single important piece of information is left out, and several hundred spectators ask the same question about it, it is frustrating for everyone involved and a mistake most event managers make only once in their career. If staff understand why they are performing what appear to be unnecessary tasks, such as checking accreditation or photocopying results, they are far more likely to understand how they fit into the big picture. Well-informed staff members, including all uniformed staff who are always the target for questions from customers, regardless of their role at an event, also respond well to positive feedback from guests and spectators.

Lead

Most event staff expect to have some fun at an event and most look forward to joining in the atmosphere. Positive actions on the part of management, including good verbal and non-verbal communication and the initiation of a range of activities to energise the team, can help to create positive staff morale. Event managers who are burnt out before an event begins are unlikely to provide inspired leadership or to solve problems with tact and diplomacy. Time and stress management are vital for everyone involved. As role models, event leaders demonstrate to their staff how to provide quality service to customers. Depending on the level of formality of the event, the service provided will vary in subtle ways. Staff look to management for these cues.

Finally, it is important that each staff member has accurate expectations of his or her role, especially the more mundane tasks. (Sometimes, jobs will be oversold and underdelivered, or undersold and overdelivered.) This provides the opportunity for the event manager to encourage the staff member to go beyond initial expectations by introducing motivational strategies such as job rotation, viewing the performance, meeting the stars and athletes, or assisting the public. Accurate expectations of the less exciting parts of the job, combined with a positive team spirit, are the outcomes of good leadership.

Reinforce

Positive reinforcement of key messages can enhance safety and service, two essential responsibilities of the whole event team. The range of ways in which core messages can be reinforced are outlined in Table 12.1. Event staff are well known for their capacity to celebrate success at every stage of a project, so recognition strategies for individuals and groups, including parties and prizes, are essential in this industry where people work under tremendous pressure to pull off an event.

In summary, event leadership is about:

★ planning for short-term assignments
★ organising and simplifying work processes
★ developing checklists and other control processes.

It is also about:

★ briefing and communicating with the team
★ motivating and energising on an hourly or daily basis
★ reinforcing key messages and targets
★ celebrating success.

The work of the event leader may extend to some or all of the following challenging contexts quite unlike those of the traditional business environment:

★ one shift for one day
★ single or multiple venues
★ single or multiple session times
★ a team separated by physical distance
★ routine and dull jobs away from the action
★ busy, pressured and high-stress roles in the midst of the action.

And the team itself may include all or any of the following:

★ contractors
★ volunteers
★ temporary workers
★ students
★ committee members
★ police and other stakeholders.

Table 12.1 Communication strategies

Verbal	Visual	Written	Behavioural
Briefings	Photographs	Training material	Videos
Meetings	Displays	Memos	Working practices
Radio conversations	Models	Letters	Role modelling
One-to-one discussion	Demonstrations	Email	Non-verbal communication
Instruction	Printed slogans	Handbooks	
Telephone conversations	Posters	Staff newsletters	
Training	Videos	Reports	
Word-of-mouth messages	Internet	Information bulletins	
		Checklists	

MANAGE TEAM PERFORMANCE

The characteristics of short-term groups differ dramatically from those of long-term groups. Long-term groups are able to focus on quality improvement initiatives, with quality teams contributing to ongoing improvements over a period of time. This is seldom the case for short-term teams. The differences are summarised in Table 12.2.

Not only is the event team temporary, it is also, as a rule, extremely diverse. The general approach to managing a diverse workforce is to assimilate everyone into a strong organisational culture. When individuals share common codes of behaviour and communication, and solve problems in routine ways, the positive benefit is consistency and this can be achieved in the normal organisational life cycle. However, this is hard to achieve in the dynamic event environment where there tends to be more on-the-spot decision-making and a wider acceptance of diverse standards of behaviour. With limited time, an event leader simply does not have the opportunity to assimilate the team into a strong organisational, or group, culture. Working with a diverse range of people with wide-ranging needs and interests is inevitable, but there are strategies that can be put in place to enhance team performance.

Let us now look at the main theories of group development and how these can be adapted by the team leader to enhance the performance of their team.

GROUP DEVELOPMENT

Studies by B W Tuckman as far back as 1965 and subsequently revised are still applicable today. They have shown that groups tend to go through five defined stages in their development:

1 *Forming.* This is the period during which members grow used to one another and tentatively formulate goals and behaviours that are acceptable.
2 *Storming.* In this stage there is generally some conflict over control and leadership, including informal leadership, known as sorting out 'the pecking order'.

Table 12.2 Differences between long-term and short-term teams

Long-term teams	Temporary teams
Commitment to organisation's mission	Commitment to task
Decisions by consensus	Leader solves problems and makes decisions
Group cohesion over time	Limited relationship building
Career development within organisation	No career/organisation orientation
Intrinsic satisfaction	Tangible rewards
Empowerment	Limited responsibility
Lifelong learning	Limited learning
Positive performance management	Positive reference

Briefing a security team, which is essential at most events

3   *Norming.* Once the hierarchy and the roles of all group members have been defined, the group tends to adopt a common set of behavioural expectations.

4   *Performing.* During this productive stage, members focus on performance within the framework of the team.

5   *Adjourning.* Faced with disbandment, successful teams share a sense of loss. In this stage, feelings of achievement are tempered by sadness that the group will be disbanding.

One limitation of the model is that it makes team building appear linear and sequential. Although it's a useful analytical tool, we must remember that some teams may not follow this pattern, particularly where there is some form of disruption, such as new members joining the team. However, this analysis of group development is useful to those in the event industry because the process of group formation does require special attention in this environment. Sometimes, the early stages of group development can be accelerated so that the performing, or productive, stage is reached quite quickly. This can be done effectively by using ice-breakers in team training sessions.

Where group members exhibit a wide range of individual differences, particularly in language or culture, the following strategies can help to develop effective communication between them:

★   Identify specific information needs of group members.
★   Use plain English.
★   Allocate buddies or develop sub-teams.
★   Use graphics to impart information.
★   Rotate roles.
★   Provide all members with opportunities to participate in the group.
★   Develop group rituals and a group identity.

Geert Hofstede (1980), well known for his work in cross-cultural communication, has identified the following value dimensions in communication.

The first value dimension he termed **power distance**. This indicates the extent to which a society accepts differences in power and authority. In some cultures, employees show a great deal of respect for authority, so Hofstede suggests that these employees have a high power distance. They would find it difficult to bring problems out into the open and discuss them with senior staff. The low power distance prevalent in other cultures encourages closer relationships at all levels, and questions and criticism from employees are more readily accepted. As you can imagine, if employees in an event team were to come from both high power and low power distance backgrounds, the first would be aghast at the audacity of the second when they brazenly pointed out problems and the low power distance employees would find it difficult to understand why the others did not speak up.

The second value dimension identified by Hofstede was **individualism/collectivism**. Some societies have a strong sense of family, and behavioural practices are based on loyalty to others. Such societies display higher conformity to group norms, and it follows that employees of these cultural backgrounds would feel comfortable in a group. In contrast, employees from highly individualistic societies would defend their own interests and show individual (as opposed to group) initiative.

These are just two cultural dimensions. There are many other variations in people's responses to situations, for example, their different attitudes towards punctuality.

Hofstede suggests that the main cross-cultural skills involve the capacity to:

★ communicate respect
★ be non-judgemental
★ accept the relativity of one's own knowledge and perceptions
★ display empathy
★ be flexible
★ take turns (allow everyone to take turns in a discussion)
★ tolerate ambiguity (accept different interpretations of what has been said).

IMPROVING COMMUNICATION

While the topic of event briefings has been covered briefly above, here are some additional guidelines for improved communication in the event team.

Establish the level of priority

It is important to establish the level of priority straightaway. Emergency situations are of course the highest risk for any event and communication about an incident or potential incident should be given top priority.

Identify the receiver

By identifying the receiver, you will be able to match your message to the receiver's needs, thus demonstrating empathy. Your message will also reach the correct target.

Know your objective

Clarity in communication is often linked to the development of an action objective. If you know what you want to achieve, you will be able to express yourself more easily and clearly. Stating a problem and its ramifications is often only the first stage. By indicating what needs to be done, you can more easily achieve your objective and reach an agreed outcome.

Review the message in your head

In preparing to send a message, you should structure your communication effectively. It is also useful to review the receiver's likely response.

Communicate in the language of the other person

If you use examples and illustrations that the receiver will understand, your message will be more easily comprehended.

Banquet teams await the onslaught of 300 guests

Clarify the message

If the receiver appears from their non-verbal behaviour not to understand your message, clarification is essential.

Do not react defensively to a critical response

Asking questions can help you to understand why your receiver has responded defensively and can diffuse the situation. By seeking feedback you can ensure that you have reached a common understanding.

Think about what this event staffing manager has to say:

In most event situations you are running on adrenalin from the start. There is never enough time. You have to deliberately stop yourself, focus on the person, look them in the eye and use their name. It is so easy to forget to do this when you have a hundred unsolved problems and the urge is to be short with them. Something as simple as using the person's name makes the difference between a good event leader and a mediocre one. The worst event leaders are so stressed they can't remember their own names!

Event Staffing Manager

TIME MANAGEMENT

As mentioned previously, the event environment is busy, noisy and often stressful. To work effectively with event teams, which may be together for a very short period of time, an event manager needs to:

★ plan effectively
★ build relationships quickly
★ identify critical issues and tasks
★ analyse and allocate tasks
★ manage work priorities
★ make quick, informed decisions
★ provide timely information

★ remove barriers
★ simplify processes
★ solve problems immediately
★ manage stress for self and others
★ develop creative, flexible solutions
★ constantly monitor performance
★ reward the achievement of outcomes.

From this list, it is clear that outstanding time management skills (on a personal and a group level) are required in order to gain maximum benefit from the planning phases. An ability to develop instant rapport with new people is also essential when time is limited.

PLANNING AND MANAGING MEETINGS

Meetings are an important feature of the management of events, starting in the early planning phases and building to pre-event briefings and post-event evaluations. Meetings can be highly productive, or they can waste an incredible amount of time. In fact, a poorly focused, poorly managed meeting will simply confuse and frustrate everyone. One event management company introduced the idea of a standing meeting to curtail the length of meetings.

Time lines should be set and an agenda for discussion distributed beforehand with all relevant material so that everyone is prepared. During meetings a chairperson should manage the pace and outcomes of the meeting and someone should be designated to keep notes for the record. The most important aspect of note-taking is the recording of actions and deadlines for those attending. Documentation from the meeting should be distributed and actions identified, prioritised and included in the planning process.

Information from the wider environment which may affect the team and need to be covered at meetings includes:

★ overall organisational objectives
★ rationale for management decisions
★ changes in organisation policies
★ marketing information and targets
★ business performance information (including financials)
★ technology updates
★ plans for new equipment
★ training developments.

In addition to focusing on tasks at event meetings, focusing on people should be a priority. Meetings can be an excellent venue for relieving stress, building team spirit and motivating all involved.

EVALUATING STAFF AND VOLUNTEER SATISFACTION

Gina and Jeffrey Pauline (2009) in their study of volunteers at a professional tennis event showed that volunteers were strongly motivated by material and purposive factors, and that volunteer satisfaction was higher when their motives were met. Gordon and Erkut (2004) in their study of volunteers at a music festival showed that, while people were enticed to volunteer by perks such as tickets, T-shirts and meals, their retention and willingness to return to the next event depended on intangible factors. One of these was a scheduling process that allowed for individual preferences.

In reality, the frenetic event environment does not provide the same context for performance management as a traditional long-life organisation. For most event managers, retention of staff is a pressing issue. This is achieved by charismatic leadership, good project planning, achievement of milestones, and a sense of camaraderie, teamwork and commitment to the event purpose. For events such as the Olympic Games volunteers are strongly motivated by pride in their country and culture (Kemp 2002).

SUMMARY

In this chapter we have discussed the time constraints in staging an event and the temporary nature of the event workforce, both of which have a major impact on event leadership. The event staff manager must be able to plan, organise and control tasks in such a way that all concerned are able to see their contribution to the aims and objectives of the event. In managing these temporary, and often diverse, teams, the event staff manager also needs to accelerate group development processes, communicate effectively, lead constructively, motivate team members, and develop recognition and reward programs.

Chapter review questions

1 How does the event leadership environment differ from that of a conventional long-life organisation?
2 Make three suggestions for team development in the event environment.
3 Select one theory of leadership and apply it to the event context.
4 List 10 elements of an effective volunteer management program.

Activity

Select an event and develop a list of pros and cons of working in three different roles at the event. Describe the leadership challenges and your solutions for the management team of this event.

Case study

Volunteer management
I knew what I had to do. I had to stand at an access gate all day on my own and check staff passes. I was prepared for the boredom but I didn't bring my thermos or a portaloo! Can you believe it? I wasn't given a break for six hours! By then I was really looking forward to some relief. You would think that these managers would learn something about people's basic needs. In this situation I needed to keep warm and dry. A folding chair would have made all the difference. A drink and an opportunity to go to the toilet would have been welcome! In terms of the hierarchy of needs, I wasn't expecting self-actualisation but I was hoping to have my physical needs met by being given scheduled breaks and possibly having my job rotated. In fact, by the time my shift was over for the day, my supervisor had long left the scene. It's good for some.

Event volunteer

Questions

1 How could this person's needs have been better catered for?
2 Are there any strategies for helping to motivate this volunteer?
3 What leadership approach would you take to managing your event team?
4 Is a different approach needed for managing paid staff and volunteer staff? Explain.
5 Explain one way in which you would energise your staff or celebrate success.

References

Gordon, L & Erkut, E (2004), 'Improving volunteer scheduling for the Edmonton folk festival', *Interfaces*, 34(5):367–76.

Grönfeldt, S & Strother, J (2006), *Service leadership: the quest for competitive advantage*, Sage, Thousand Oaks, CA.

Hofstede, G (1980), *Culture's consequences: international differences in work related values*, Sage, Beverly Hills, CA.

Kemp, S (2002), 'The hidden workforce: volunteers' learning in the Olympics', *Journal of European Industrial Training*, 26(2–4):109–16.

Nichols, G & Ojala, E (2009), 'Understanding the management of sports events volunteers through psychological contract theory', *Voluntas*, 20(4):369.

Pauline, G & Pauline, J (2009), 'Volunteer motivation and demographic influences at a professional tennis event', *Team Performance Management*, 15(3/4):172.

Robbins, S (2010), *Organizational behaviour*, 14th international edn, Prentice Hall, Upper Saddle River, NJ.

Robbins, S & Coulter, M (1996), *Management*, 10th edn, Prentice Hall, Upper Saddle River, NJ.

PEOPLE PERFORMANCE

Elements

- Allocate work
- Assess performance
- Provide feedback
- Manage follow-up.

Critical aspects for assessment

- Documented performance indicators and a critical description and analysis of performance management systems from the workplace
- Techniques in providing feedback and coaching for improvement in performance
- Knowledge of relevant awards and certified agreements.

IN ORDER to ensure that a volunteer is matched to the right role, the volunteer must have a clear understanding of what the role involves, what skills will be required to undertake the role and what standards are expected. The position description is a brief written summary of the duties and responsibilities of volunteers and ensures the aims and objectives of the program are being met. It is not a detailed record of every task and duty but a focus of expected outputs of the role and protects the rights of the volunteers. Role descriptions will be forwarded to volunteers once rosters have been set. Unlike paid workers, volunteers do not work under an award system and do not enter into an agreement based upon the provision of labour for a prescribed payment, which is protected by law. However, volunteers do enter into a contract with Council where they agree to perform certain tasks which are of benefit to the organisation and the community.

Source: Frankston City Council Festival Volunteer Manual, p. 3. © 2010 Frankston City

The importance of ensuring that both staff and volunteers have a clear expectation of the duties that they will perform at an event cannot be emphasised enough. While the event environment is an exciting one for the audience, the workforce (paid staff, contractors and volunteers) seldom has the opportunity to enjoy the event. For example, an event operations manager may sit behind CCTV monitors for the whole event, providing radio instructions to staff on the ground who may be dealing with spectator problems. The cornerstone of performance management is careful recruitment, selection and induction, all of which contribute to a better understanding of the performance levels expected.

In this chapter we will focus on techniques management can use to get the best from staff and volunteers in the fast-paced event environment, including motivational and performance measurement tools and utilisation of feedback. The final section will cover the important topic of workforce retention.

But, first, let's look briefly at work allocation.

ALLOCATE WORK

When allocating work in the early stages of event project planning, decisions have to be made regarding outsourcing various elements of the event plan, and in some cases work-force planning itself is put out to tender. If the workforce includes volunteers, their roles need to be allocated according to their skills but with their motivation levels in mind as well. Some volunteers may prefer to stay in one position for the duration of the event, while others need variety to maintain their interest. This may involve redeployment from one position to another. For large events, a stand-by team of volunteers is recommended, so that absentees can be replaced with minimum effort.

In Chapters 4, 11 and 12 we have stressed the importance of workflow planning, which is essential to the allocation of work and resources. In the next chapter you will see how project management tools can be used for scheduling work and monitoring performance. Critical path analysis also needs to be applied to meet critical dates and times in order to make the ultimate deadline. A critical path consists of that set of dependent tasks (each dependent on the preceding one) which together take the longest time to complete, thereby identifying the earliest possible time a project can be completed. And risk analysis is utilised to identify potential staffing problems that might occur and prevent attainment of the event objectives. Imagine the management issues of Shanghai Expo 2010 for which 1.7 million volunteers were trained—and this event ran for six months! The logistics of staffing an event of this size and of this duration are far more complex than that of an Olympic Games which is over in a relatively short period of two weeks.

Imagine also the huge task for management in keeping a workforce of this size motivated to turn up to work every day.

MANAGE PERFORMANCE

Performance management is the process of creating a work environment in which people are enabled to perform to the best of their abilities. Performance management is a whole work system that begins when a job is defined as needed. The steps are:

★ Develop a clear work breakdown structure and job descriptions.

★ Select appropriately skilled and experienced people.

★ Negotiate requirements and accomplishment-based performance standards, milestones and deliverables linked to project planning.

★ Provide effective orientation and training.

★ Provide ongoing coaching and feedback.

★ Conduct quarterly performance development discussions.

★ Design recognition systems that reward people for their contributions.

★ Provide promotional/career development opportunities for staff.

Performance appraisal is a specific part of this process. It is a formal evaluation of an individual's performance against performance standards, deadlines and deliverables associated with their job role (see Figure 13.1). In the best of situations, this is an opportunity to acknowledge effort and commitment and congratulate the individual for achieving the objectives established. In the worst of situations, it involves a process of managing unsatisfactory performance, with the possibility of termination of employment.

Non-performance or unsatisfactory performance in an employment context usually means that an employee who has the capacity to perform their duties is not performing them or is performing them unsatisfactorily. Non-performance of duties includes situations where an employee has been absent from work without approval and it is no longer reasonable for the employer to continue the employment relationship. Unsatisfactory performance includes situations

1. Review of current duties and scheduled tasks
2. Quality and timeliness of project deliverables
3. Areas of skills/strengths
4. Communication and teamwork
5. Areas of suggested performance improvement
6. Training and development needs
7. Long-term career development needs
8. Level of satisfaction
9. Action plan including timeline

FIGURE 13.1
Generic items on a performance appraisal form

in which the employee is not meeting required standards or is creating a safety risk to self and others, or where they are in breach of a code of conduct. If the latter is the case, it is important that in all but the most exceptional circumstances (such as intoxication, drug use or gross misconduct, which would result in summary dismissal) due process is followed, which means investigating the performance issue and providing the employee with opportunities for improvement.

PERFORMANCE MANAGEMENT TOOLS

Certain tools are used by organisations for managing the performance of their staff. One of the most useful and widely used tools today is the key performance indicator (KPI). Key performance indicators help an organisation define and measure progress towards organisational goals. KPIs are quantifiable measurements, agreed to beforehand, that reflect the critical success factors, or key result areas, of the organisation. They differ depending on the organisation and departments within the organisation. Customer Service may have as one of its KPIs percentage of customer calls answered in the first minute, while Human Resources may have an acceptable (pre-established) rate of turnover of staff. For the event organisation, however, KPIs are often harder to pin down.

Once KPIs reflecting the organisation's goals have been defined, they are used as a performance management tool. KPIs give everyone in the organisation a clear picture of what is important, of what they need to make happen. KPIs can also be used as an incentive. Letting employees know through various communication channels what the target is for each KPI and the progress that is being made towards that target is an excellent way of motivating people.

In long-life organisations, KPIs are usually long-term considerations. The definition of what they are and how they are measured does not change often. This is not always the case for events, with their short life and large component of contract and casual staff and volunteers.

One of the most important outcomes for the event industry is efficient and effective operations (zero complaints may be the KPI measure), so that the production (theatrical, sporting, concert) can go ahead as planned. A KPI for the artistic merit of a theatrical event may then be the number of positive reviews published in the media, while the organisers of a sporting event would be content with seamless operations regardless of whether the home team won. For all events, the most critical KPI is the show starting on time. This is more easily said than done!

MOTIVATIONAL TECHNIQUES

In common business operations, such as real estate and banks, most employees are permanent and motivational considerations are quite different from those in the dynamic and

The set-up team is soon to be replaced by the operational team

project-focused event environment. Here, the workforce is made up of contract, casual, temporary and volunteer labour and a small team of event staff who generally work much more flexible (and longer) hours than the norm.

Event employees are motivated by a wide range of factors, from hours compatible with study in unrelated fields to the potential for promotion and career development in the event industry. The first type of employee is probably looking for a position in which the tasks are simple, the work is routine and well paid, and the problems are few. The second is looking for a challenge: variable and complex work and new learning experiences. This diversity is matched by diversity in cultural expectations. Some employees are comfortable in a society in which individual effort is acknowledged, while others are more accustomed to a group-oriented environment in which social harmony is more important than competition.

With these challenges in mind, the modern event manager needs to evaluate contemporary theories of motivation to understand how best they can motivate their own work teams. A number of these theories are summarised below.

Three needs theory

David McClelland (1985, 1989) suggests that there are three motivating needs: the need for achievement; the need for power; and the need for affiliation. Those motivated by achievement are goal oriented and focus on career development. Those who are motivated by a need for power prefer to influence others, either through formal or informal leadership. Where such influence occurs informally, it is essential that leadership skills are harnessed for the good of the organisation. If the informal leader is a troublemaker, then their goals will not be compatible with those of the organisation. Finally, those who are motivated by affiliation look for a friendly, group-oriented workplace where there is positive social interaction.

Equity theory

In the workplace, people make comparisons between the effort they make and the rewards they receive and the effort and rewards of others. If there is a perception that other employees or volunteers are better rewarded or make less effort, this will result in a lack of

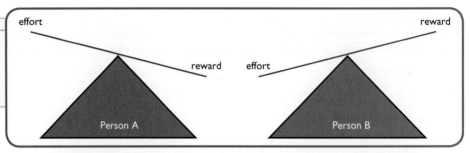

FIGURE 13.2

Perceived
imbalance
between
effort and
reward

motivation. To redress the issue, the person who feels that their treatment is inequitable is likely to become less productive or to leave. Inequity can be perceived by teams as well, with employees at one venue comparing their rewards and effort with those of employees at another venue. 'Not fair' is the usual comment made in this situation and is applicable to any number of rewards, including meal breaks, shift allocation, uniform design, and allocation of new equipment or incentives. The perceived imbalance between effort and reward is illustrated in Figure 13.2.

When evaluating the benefits and equity of rewards, another consideration is whether it is best to reward individuals or teams.

Opportunities for individual recognition, development and reward may include:

★ internal training/professional development
★ external training/professional development
★ change in job responsibilities
★ opportunity for greater autonomy or responsibility
★ formal promotion
★ contests and prizes
★ rewards for loyalty
★ incentives.

Goal-setting

Edwin Locke et al. (1984) suggest that achievable goals are highly motivating. However, as well as being achievable, goals must be specific and relevant. Goal achievement is an *intrinsic* (internal) motivator, while prizes and other tangible rewards are *extrinsic* (external) motivators. Many events with social impacts attract volunteers who are intrinsically motivated, because their efforts are directed towards fundraising for charities and other social causes. If this is the case, these goals need to be well articulated, and communication of the milestones towards achieving these goals needs to be timely and encouraging.

Reinforcement theory

The origin of the theory of reinforcement is the work of B F Skinner (1953). Reinforcement theory, more recently badged as incentive theory, is based on the premise that people's behaviour is determined by feedback. In the simplest sense, positive feedback is likely to enhance behaviour. So it follows that productivity will improve if the correct behaviours are identified, monitored, recognised and rewarded, often by praise, which is most effective when linked to specific behaviours and goals.

It is important to remember that unacceptable behaviour, too, can be reinforced by positive feedback or actions. For example, a lazy employee who arrives late to find that everyone else has set up the function room is being rewarded for laziness, and an employee taking credit for the work of others is being rewarded if management gives him or her a bonus. Managers need to be aware that they may be positively reinforcing the wrong behaviour. 'Let me do it' can encourage future demonstrations of incompetence!

Another outcome that can follow certain behaviours is punishment. In the event industry, this often involves criticism, and sometimes yelling. The effect is demotivating, even though the behaviour that provoked the outburst may be eliminated.

The use of rewards, including encouragement, can have wide-ranging benefits. A positive working environment can have a dramatic impact on motivation and, in turn, on customer satisfaction. Thus, there is a *customer benefit* associated with a positive environment. When an individual is rewarded for learning new skills or for working efficiently, this can have a direct, constructive effect on the reinforced behaviour. It can also have a spin-off benefit, by *influencing other positive behaviours*. Indeed, psychologists have shown that rewards do not have to be given every time the behaviour is exhibited. A variable ratio of reinforcement, given at random, can be even more effective. This principle is evident in the behaviour of gamblers. While gamblers may only win, say, once out of five times, that win is sufficient to encourage them to gamble again and again. Similarly, a manager can have a powerful influence over an employee's behaviour if the rewards follow the desired outcomes, even if these only occur from time to time. In addition, *positively reinforced behaviours are stable*, even in the absence of the reinforcer.

In contrast, when a manager has a punishing, critical style, employees may comply when he or she is present, but will take the opportunity to misbehave in his or her absence— 'While the cat's away the mice will play'. For many managers in busy event workplaces, the temptation is to notice errors and omissions. 'Your attitude towards customers is bad' is a negative, punishing reaction that will do little to improve performance. It takes a shift in thinking to provide constructive feedback and encouragement of good performance.

The challenge for the manager is to explain to the employee what a 'good attitude' looks like. 'Stop what you are doing, smile and acknowledge the customer, greet the customer and take time to listen' are some of the signs of a positive attitude towards the customer. Once these behaviours have been established, practised and understood, the employee can be encouraged for exhibiting a positive service ethic. The customer may also reward this orientation with an enthusiastic response. As mentioned, rewards can take many forms. However, in everyday life, simply noticing effort and complimenting it is often all that is needed to create an upbeat event environment which everyone on site can enjoy.

Role modelling

Role modelling is often used in training in the service industries. At events where the ambience is created by senior staff, the tone is set for subsequent relationships with clients and colleagues. For this reason, behaviour by senior personnel should demonstrate best practice, and employees who model this type of behaviour and uphold the service vision of the organisation should be appropriately rewarded. This may sound very simple, but in practice far too many managers in event workplaces exhibit autocratic, egocentric styles of behaviour that are not conducive to a positive service ethic.

Expectancy theory

This theory, developed by Victor Vroom (1973), looks at the motivators of performance and the outcomes of performance. It also considers the important issue of perception and how the balance between effort and reward is perceived by the individual, thus combining elements of some of the preceding theories. If the expectation is high, but the performance target is achievable, the individual or team will achieve the outcome, providing that the outcome has sufficient appeal.

Expectancy theory is one of the most comprehensive explanations of motivation, and identifies three variables:

★ expectancy (effort linked to performance)
★ instrumentality (performance linked to reward)
★ valence (attractiveness of rewards).

Expectancy theory stresses the importance of the individual's perception: their perception of effort leading to performance; their perception of the likelihood of rewards being delivered as promised; and their perception of the rewards promised.

CONFLICT MANAGEMENT TECHNIQUES

Many factors, including cultural background, language differences and previous experience, can have an impact on communication between members of the event workforce and, indeed, between the workforce and the client or the customer. Conflict will occur—contractors will complain about delays; customers will complain about waiting, their seat allocation, the sound level, sometimes in an unpleasant way; and team members will come into conflict while working in this noisy, frantic and highly pressured environment. Diplomacy and empathy are essential requirements in managing all these types of situations.

Conflict management differs from country to country. Some cultures are more prone to complain, others to suffer in silence. Differences also exist in how problems should be resolved. Some only want to air their grievances, while others want solutions. On the whole, clients don't want to hear excuses or to see blame being shifted.

The interactionist approach to conflict management proposes that there are two types of conflict: functional conflict, which is constructive; and dysfunctional conflict, which is destructive. Functional conflict occurs in a healthy, competitive environment where the goals of the organisation are being achieved and diverse management styles are represented.

When dealing with a conflict situation, managers can use a range of techniques: avoidance, accommodation, forcing, compromise and collaboration. These conflict management strategies are useful for day-to-day management of performance issues.

Some conflict is trivial and may be best ignored, with intervention escalating the conflict rather than resolving it. For example, when work pressure causes a flare-up, it is likely to be resolved when everyone relaxes after the event. Accommodation involves giving way to the other party in the conflict, while calling upon formal authority means forcing a resolution. The latter is often appropriate in a crisis situation where there is no time for compromise or collaboration. Compromise occurs when everyone in the situation gives way to a degree to reach a mutually agreed solution, while collaboration involves brainstorming and nego-tiation to reach a solution which is advantageous to all involved.

While collaboration would seem to be the 'best' conflict resolution technique, this is not always the case. Situational factors, such as the time and risk involved, the gravity of the issue, the personalities and formal authority of those involved, all contribute to the decision as to which approach to take in resolving conflict.

In the high-pressure event environment where stress levels are generally high, conflict is almost inevitable. As a result, managing conflict and stress are key elements of managing people performance in this environment.

PROVIDE FEEDBACK

As this discussion regarding motivation theory shows, feedback is necessary to ensure that people are motivated and continue to meet targets and deadlines. And research on the moti-vation of volunteers has indicated that everyone wants to understand the big picture (Van Der Wagen 2007).

Most feedback given in the event environment is informal, occurring during briefings and debriefings. Sometimes feedback requires individuals to receive on-the-job coaching to improve their performance. It is important to document substandard performance and corrective measures being undertaken in accordance with organisational performance management systems.

Most importantly, it is essential to provide feedback on excellent performance, either formally or informally. Most events celebrate their successful conclusion with a staff party once the audience has left. More novel ideas include having the workforce celebration before the event as a kind of bonding process, accelerating the 'mourning' phase described in the last chapter. In other cases, success is celebrated a few days after everyone has caught up on lost sleep!

MANAGE FOLLOW-UP

When individuals are not achieving the required performance outcomes, they need to be monitored and coached. The manager should agree the performance improvement required with the person, document this, and provide support services where necessary. If this proves ineffective, the manager needs to counsel the individual who is continuing to perform below expectations and implement a disciplinary process if no improvement occurs.

One of the most important principles in managing disciplinary measures is proce-dural fairness. In its fullest application, procedural fairness requires that the employee (or volunteer) is:

★ provided with an opportunity to put their case, and to hear the case against them
★ given clear reasons why the performance standard has not been met
★ told what the expectations are for improved performance
★ provided with a review date on which the situation will be re-evaluated.

In such circumstances, the action must be timely and consistent with the treatment of other employees. When serious misconduct occurs or ongoing poor performance continues, it may be necessary to terminate staff in accordance with legal and organisational requirements. This also applies to volunteers.

RETAIN STAFF

Management of people performance encompasses the all-important issue of staff retention. Retention of senior management personnel is vital. Hanlon and Jago's (2004) research into two major annual events shows that the period immediately following major annual events is typically flat in contrast to the adrenalin rush of the previous weeks. It is during this period that a number of retention strategies should be considered for permanent staff. In addition, organisations running annual events need to put effort into maintaining contact with seasonal workers who often return annually to these events.

Table 13.1 shows relevant retention strategies for full-time and seasonal workers before, during and after the event.

Lifelong friendships evolve from volunteers returning year after year to the same event

While there are few studies on retention in the short-life event workforce, there is anecdotal evidence of high absenteeism among volunteers on the second or third day of an event.

This chapter has illustrated the all-important differences between the event business environment and the event project environment from a human resource point of view. Managing people performance in these circumstances has special challenges during the often long lead-up to the event as well as during the event's execution.

Table 13.1 A recommended guide for retaining full-time and seasonal personnel at the Australian Open Tennis Championship and the Australian Formula One Grand Prix

Retention strategies for personnel categories		
Event cycle	**Full-time staff**	**Seasonal workers**
Lead-up	Event's status	Event's status
	Recognition	Recognition
	Ownership	Ownership
During an event	Team debrief	Team debrief
	Team activities	Team activities
After an event	Team debrief	Team debrief
	Thank you function	Thank you function
	Performance appraisal	
	Remuneration	
	Career management programs	
	Updated job descriptions	
	Re-establishing teams	
	Positive direction from management	
	Exit interviews	
	Loyalty payments	
During the year	Team meetings	Continuous contact (e.g. Christmas cards, birthday cards, organisation's newsletter, team meetings)
	Remuneration	Career opportunities
		Survey needs
		Employed for additional events

Source: Hanlon, C & Jago, L (2004), 'The challenge of retaining personnel in major sport event organizations', *Event Management*, (Cognizant Communication Corporation),9, 1–2:47..

SUMMARY

In most circumstances, the event workforce is likely to evolve from a small planning team to a large and diverse workforce comprising paid staff, contractors and possibly volunteers just prior to and during the event. As we have seen in this chapter, managing people performance in this complex environment requires a great deal of planning as well as the development of effective systems and key performance indicators for measuring performance. Systematisation and simplification of procedures can go a long way to ensuring that tasks are completed correctly and on time. Extensive checklists are not only good planning tools, but they also assist individuals on the frontline to understand what to do and how to do it. As with all other aspects of event management, the devil is in the detail. If all contingencies have been considered and plans made accordingly, the event will go without a hitch and everyone will be able to celebrate its success at the finish.

Chapter review questions

1 Sauer, Liu and Johnston (2001, p. 69) argue for improved project management, based on the success of a model used in the construction industry:

> Australian construction projects today are usually more successful than information technology (IT) projects. One reason lies in the way construction companies manage project management. Based on in-depth research of four successful construction companies, this paper describes a project management-centered organizational form. It describes the organizational and management arrangements that support project performance and the individual and organizational capabilities that underpin sustained project success. This particular form of organization is shown to be stable and effective because its constituent arrangements are logically consistent and mutually reinforcing. The authors show how many of these arrangements can be adopted by IT service firms and in-house IT organizations to improve their performance on projects.

Develop a similar argument for more professional project management (including the management of people) in the event environment.

2 Discuss five challenges for the management of senior personnel in event organisations.

Activity

Many workers feel that their annual performance reviews are pointless. 'It's a total waste of time. My boss never says what she really thinks and doesn't take any notice of what I say', said one person interviewed in a survey of 3000 workers. Almost half of those interviewed thought that their boss wasn't honest during the appraisal process, 29% said that reviews were pointless and 20% of workers felt that they had unfair performance appraisals.'

In light of this poll, discuss the value of annual performance reviews from both a positive and a negative point of view.

Case study

Keeping staff

As the Operations Manager for a major event, your current concern is a rumour that one of the contractor organisations is trying to poach your staff. Having worked with your team for many months and enjoyed a mutual understanding of the operational problems posed by this major event, you are worried that the loss of one or more of your staff will lead to a setback of several weeks. For you, retention is a priority. In preparation for a discussion with Fiona, the Human Resources Manager, about this rumour, prepare answers to the following questions.

continued

Case study *(continued)*

Questions

1 How are employee's expectations of their roles developed?
2 What sort of performance targets or goals can be set to motivate people in senior event roles?
3 How can feedback, both formal and informal, help to retain key staff?
4 If career development is important to an individual working on a major event, how can these aspirations be met, given the limitations of short-life organisations?
5 How will you approach this interview?

References

Hanlon, C & Jago, L (2004), 'The challenge of retaining personnel in major sport event organizations', *Event Management*, 9:39–49.

Hede, A & Rentschler, R (2007), 'Mentoring volunteer festival managers: evaluation of a pilot scheme in regional Australia', *Managing Leisure*, 12:157–70.

Sauer, C, Liu, L & Johnston, K (2001), 'Where project managers are kings', *Project Management Journal*, 32(4):39–49.

Syed, J & Kramar, R (2010), 'What is the Australian model for managing cultural diversity?', *Personnel Review*, 39(1):96.

Van Der Wagen, L (2007), *Human resource management for events: managing the event workforce*, Butterworth–Heinemann, Oxford; Burlington, MA.

Van Der Wagen, M (2008), 'An exploration of the notion of generic skills through a study of customer service training in two industry sectors', EdD thesis, University of Technology Sydney (UTS).

CHAPTER 14

PROJECT MANAGEMENT

Unit descriptor

This unit describes the performance outcomes, skills and knowledge required to manage all aspects of a complex project, including project planning, monitoring and evaluation. This unit applies to individuals who are responsible for the overall management of **complex projects** in the context of a broader job role.

Project management occurs across the full spectrum of business and community activity and may be extremely diverse in nature.

Elements

- Confirm project
- Plan project
- Administer and monitor project
- Evaluate project
- Select and use technology
- Process and organise data
- Maintain technology.

Critical aspects for assessment

- Ability to effectively plan, administer, monitor and evaluate an event-based project, including evidence of skills in planning, administration, financial management and leadership
- Ability to apply understanding of the critical aspects of effective project management
- Management of a multifaceted, complex industry-based project that reflects real industry practice and is completed within a specified time frame.

SUCCESSFUL event management involves many people undertaking separate tasks in a coordinated manner. In Mosman, this involves staff from every section of Council, staff in several other state agencies, staff of companies and clubs, as well as volunteers. Events must be managed in accordance with not only Council's own policies, but also various state laws and regulations.

ONLY a small portion of this effort is visible to the general public. Even if the event runs smoothly there will be some negative feedback as some degree of inconvenience is inevitable. If the event is poorly managed, however, the impact can be profound with damage to property and to the natural environment, with public safety threatened, and with widespread dissatisfaction by visitors and local residents alike.

Source: Mosman Municipal Council Special Event Management Operations Manual.

As this statement from a special event operations manual so clearly illustrates, planning and organisation are the key elements that determine the success of an event. For most event organisers, the first stop is the local council. The local council provides guidelines on the possible impact of events, such as the impact of noise. This may be a factor even if the event is not being held at a public venue. Another useful contact is the local tourism office. This office, with links to corporate offices in each state and territory, plays an important part in the strategic management of events and, in many cases, provides support in a number of other ways, such as listing events on their website.

However, before making these contacts, it is necessary to develop the event concept and project plan. As we learned in Chapter 2, this involves defining the event's purpose and aims, as well as the specific objectives on which the success of the event will be measured. Funding for the event may come from grants or from sponsors, but all stakeholders have to be provided with a good understanding of the event concept and project plan before proceeding further. If the client is the one funding the event, the provision of a clearly developed concept, plan and evaluation strategy will generally avoid problems down the line, including legal ones.

CONFIRM, PLAN AND ADMINISTER PROJECTS

The first phase in event planning requires the organiser to confirm the project objectives and scope in consultation with appropriate stakeholders. Stakeholders may include internal and external customers, organising committees, funding bodies, regulatory authorities and other government authorities. The second phase is to evaluate the financial viability of the project through analysis of the key factors and determine and develop a resource strategy for the project. The third phase involves confirming the administrative structure for the project and developing an integrated project management plan using appropriate project management tools to communicate the plan to appropriate colleagues. The administrative structure could be a steering committee, advisory or reference group, or a consultative committee.

Maps and models, Gantt charts, PERT charts, run sheets, organisation charts and check-lists are useful tools for presenting material and information to clients, members of staff and stakeholders. These are described and illustrated in the following sections.

MAPS AND MODELS

Maps are a useful way to represent an event, particularly to contractors who may be required to set up the site. It may be necessary to develop more than one map or plan, using CAD (Computer Assisted Drawing) software, since different parties involved in the event will require this material for different purposes. These parties may include:

★ builders and designers
★ telecommunications and electrical contractors
★ emergency response teams
★ spectator services hosts
★ artists, entertainers and exhibitors
★ event audience.

Models are also extremely useful, as most clients find it difficult to visualise three-dimensional concepts. A model can also assist in aspects of event management, such as crowd control. In this instance, bottlenecks and other potential problems can emerge from viewing a three-dimensional model. Most CAD software can present the information in this way, allowing the event management team to anticipate all design and implementation issues. Examples of models and maps are illustrated in Figures 14.1 and 14.2.

GANTT CHARTS

A Gantt chart is generally used in the early planning days and in the lead-up to an event. The Gantt chart, developed by Charles Gantt in 1917, focuses on the sequence of tasks necessary for completion of a project. Each task on a Gantt chart is represented as a single horizontal bar on an X–Y chart. The horizontal axis (X axis) is the time scale over which the project will span. Therefore, the length of each task bar corresponds to the duration of the task, or the time necessary for completion. Arrows connecting interdependent tasks reflect the relationships between the tasks they connect. The relationship usually shows dependency, so that one task cannot begin until another is completed.

The benefit of this type of chart is that the interdependence of the tasks can be clearly seen. For example, once you have plotted the process of recruiting, inducting, training and rostering staff for an event, you may realise that the recruitment process needs to start earlier than expected to enable staff to be completely ready for the big day.

Another aspect of planning is

FIGURE 14.1
CAD perspective views of an exhibition stand

Source: ExpoNet, <www.exponet.com.au>.

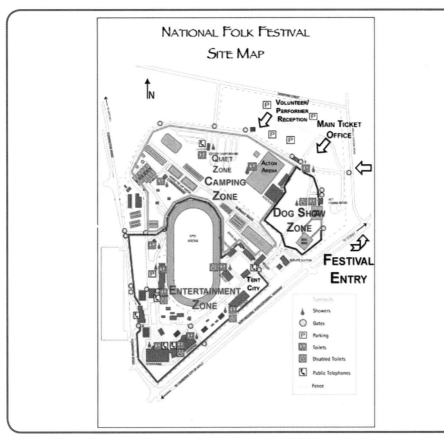

Source: <www.folkfestival.asn.au/index.html>.

identifying the critical path: those elements of the plan that are essential to the successful outcome of the event and therefore high priority. Critical path analysis is beyond the scope of this text; however, the general principle of identifying planning elements on which all else is dependent can be done with a Gantt chart.

In the case of arrangements with sponsors, for example, these need to be finalised before printing of promotional material can occur as sponsors need to approve the use of their logos. If one sponsor pulls out of the arrangement, this will have an impact on print production which will, in turn, affect promotional activities and ticket sales.

Project planning software, including specialised event planning software, is available, while for smaller events a spreadsheet is probably sufficient. The trick is to identify the tasks that can be clustered together and to choose the ideal level of detail required in planning the event. At the extreme, the chart can be expanded to a point where even the smallest task is shown (but at this stage it will fill an entire wall and become unmanageable). As with maps, the Gantt chart must be a user-friendly planning tool in order to be effective.

Another point to take into account is that change is an integral part of event planning and it may be necessary to make significant changes that immediately make all your charts redundant. An experienced event manager is able to ascertain the level of planning required to ensure that everyone is clear about their roles and responsibilities, while remaining reasonably open to change.

A high-level planning chart for an event is illustrated in Figure 14.3. It provides a broad overview of the main event tasks and a general timeline. Each of these major tasks could also be used as the basis for a more detailed plan. This has been done in Figure 14.4, which shows the planning process for recruiting and training staff for the above event. This Gantt chart is clearly an example of a fairly detailed level of planning although, even here, the training aspect is not covered fully as there would be many steps involved, including writing training materials and seeking approval of the content from the various functional area managers.

PERT CHARTS

The program evaluation and review technique (PERT) chart depicts task, duration and dependency information and is very useful in defining the critical path (see also Figure 14.10, page 221).

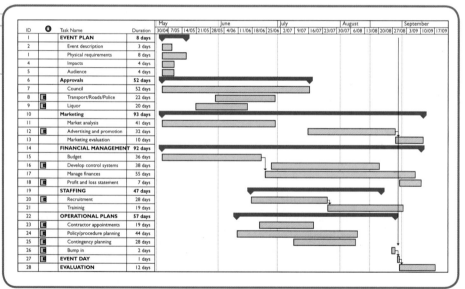

FIGURE 14.3
Sample Gantt chart for event planning

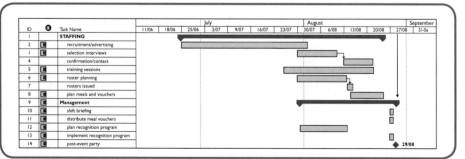

FIGURE 14.4
Sample Gantt chart for event staff planning

RUN SHEETS

The run sheet is an indispensable tool for most event managers. It is the program, or schedule, of events. In the preliminary stages of planning, the run sheet is quite simple, with times allocated only to specific elements of the event (see the run sheet for a gala dinner in Figure 14.5). This overview of proceedings forms part of the event concept briefing.

As planning progresses, however, the run sheet becomes even more detailed with, for example, timings for dancers, technicians and other staff. This is illustrated in Figure 14.6, in which bump-in and bump-out are also included. These processes will be discussed in much greater detail in Chapters 15 and 16.

From a project management point of view, correct sequencing, accurate timing and careful scheduling are the keys to good planning. Sequencing involves establishing the order of actions: what has to happen before another activity can start, and which activities can take place in parallel. For example, all mechanical handling equipment, particularly forklifts and scissor lifts, must be out of the site before seating can be laid out. Timing determines how long before the next action takes place. For example, how long is needed to clear the forklifts from the audience area to allow for seating layout to commence? Remember also that sometimes equipment such as chairs and tables will need to be delivered in several loads, and often the loading dock will be too busy for immediate offloading (in project management terms, this is a 'limiting step'). Now, having planned the sequence and the timing, scheduling can take place. This involves listing the order and timings for bump-in on a run sheet or production schedule. In both cases, the responsibility for each action should be clearly indicated. Experienced contractors can often offer valuable assistance and advice on the sequence and timing of many tasks.

1900	Guests arrive. Pre-dinner drinks in foyer.
1930	Doors to Royal open. Guests move to tables.
1935	MC welcome.
1940	Entrée served.
2000	First 'Championship' (demonstration dance routine).
2010	Main course served. Band starts playing.
2050	Band stops. Second 'Championship' (demo dance routine). Guests drawn onto dance floor at the end.
2115	Dessert served. Band plays.
2140	Band stops. ABTA Awards Presentation (1 award, with 2 finalists).
2225	Ms & Mr Sparkly awarded. Dancing for guests starts properly.
2355	MC announces final winners (all!) and last dance.
2400	Guests depart.

FIGURE 14.5
Preliminary run sheet for a gala dinner—concept stage

Source: Reproduced with permission of Events Unlimited.

FIGURE 14.6

Complete run sheet for gala dinner

0800	Lay dance floor and stage, and lower vertical drapes. Scissor lift ready. Audio subcontractor commences bump-in. Rear projection screen set.
0900	Dance floor and stage set. Stage designer bumps in for stage decoration.
1000	Production meeting.
1100	On-stage set-up commences (audio and video).
1230 (approx)	Band set-up.
1430	Technical set-up complete. Table set-up can commence.
1500	Technical run-through.
1730	All decorations complete.
1745	Rehearsal with MC and SM (probably walk through with music). Band sound check.
1830	All ready.
1845	External sign ON.
1900–1930	Guests arrive. Pre-dinner drinks in foyer.
1900	Dancers arrive. Walk-through and music check.
1915	Pre-set lighting ON.
1925	Walk-in music ON.
1930	Doors open. Guests move to tables. All dancers ready.
1935	MC welcome.
1940	Entrée served.
2000	First 'Championship' (Demonstration dance routine).
2010	Main course served. Band starts playing.
2050	Band stops. Second 'Championship' (Demo dance routine). Guests drawn onto dance floor at the end.
2115	Dessert enters and is served. Band plays.
2140	Band stops. Awards presentation (1 award, with 2 finalists).
2225	Ms & Mr Sparkly awarded. Dancing for guests starts properly.
2355	MC announces final winners (all!) and last dance.
2400	Guests depart. Bump-out commences.
Tue 0230	All clear.

Source: Reproduced with permission of Events Unlimited.

At this point, an even more detailed run sheet can be developed (at this stage called 'the script') to identify each person's role and cues. This is illustrated in Figure 14.7 where the timing of meal service and the cues for recommencement of the 'championships' after the main course are outlined in detail.

Suppliers waiting their turn to offload gear

Run sheets are an important tool for all stakeholders and participants, from the venue management team through to the subcontractors.

2010	Main course served.	
As main nearly cleared		MC and dancers stand by.
		Dance 2 music ready.
When clear 2050	Band stops and exits.	MC mic ON.
		Band OFF.
		MC spot ON.
		House down.
	MC: Welcome to our next championship, The Self-Booking Samba. Amazingly the finalists are our previous winners.	Vision — Self-Booking Samba.
	Please welcome them back.	Dance floor ON.
	Dancers run on.	MC spot OFF.
	(2nd dance routine 10 min).	Music 2 ON.
		MC mic OFF.
	Dancers pause at end.	When music 2 finished cue
	MC: And once again it's a tie,	music 3.
	isn't that fantastic! Now I know that	MC spot ON.
	there are some aspiring champions	MC mic ON.
	out there who are probably thinking	
	'I could never do that!' Well our	
	champions have graciously agreed	
	to teach you some of their steps, so	
	come on up and join in …	
	MC somehow coaxes people up.	
	When enough on dance floor he	
	cues music with: OK. Let's dance!	
	(About 10 minutes dance coaching)	House UP 1/2.
		Music 3 ON.
		MC mic OFF.
		Kitchen advised 10 min to dessert.
At end		Dance music 3 OFF.
		Cue march in — SB track 14.
		Kitchen 1 min to dessert.

FIGURE 14.7
Script for part of gala dinner

Source: Reproduced with permission of Events Unlimited.

FIGURE 14.8
Event
committee
structure

ORGANISATION CHARTS

An organisation chart is another important tool used in planning. Once all tasks have been identified and grouped logically, the staffing requirements for an event become much clearer and can be represented on an organisation chart. Figure 14.8 shows an organisation chart for an event committee. For more information on organisation charts and illustrations, see Chapter 11.

CHECKLISTS

At the most detailed level of planning, a checklist is indispensable. It is a control tool which ensures that the individual performing the tasks has not forgotten a single detail. For example, when checking fire-fighting equipment and emergency exits, it is imperative that a specific checklist be followed, and that it be signed and dated on completion. This is part of the record-keeping process, aimed not only at preventing potential problems, but also at reducing the risk of litigation if anything should go wrong. Detailed and correctly implemented plans reassure the client, allow the event team to work effectively and build confidence in achieving the objectives of the event. A safety checklist is illustrated in Figure 14.9.

UNDERSTAND PROJECT MANAGEMENT PRINCIPLES

As event management grows in professional reputation, more sophisticated project management techniques are used in the same way that they are in engineering and information technology. The standard system used is PMBOK (Project Management Body of Knowledge).

Daily Safety Checklist

Name		Today's date and time		
Task	Check ✓ ✗	Comment		Follow up required ✓
First aid kit fully equipped				
Flammable goods signage correct, storage away from combustible materials				
Extinguisher visible, free of obstruction				
Cleaning products labelled and stored correctly				
All electrical appliances tested and tagged within last six months				
Extension cords tested and tagged within last three months				
Extension cords not presenting a hazard over walkways				
Boxes, rubbish, etc. not obstructing exits or fire-fighting equipment				
Gas cut-off valve visible and not obstructed				

FIGURE 14.9

Daily safety checklist

The Project Management Body of Knowledge was originally developed in the early 1980s and has gone through at least three major revisions and updates since that time. It is an attempt to adapt generic project management principles for the special event environment.

There has been some discussion of whether or not special events fit within the project management definition of a project. Although special events are unique in having absolute deadlines given their very nature, it is generally agreed that they are projects which function as such. It would not be possible to develop a process specifically for special events since a process that applies to project management in general could also apply to a special event. The PMBOK and processes can be adapted for the special events industry to serve its own specific needs.

Below we discuss a number of concepts and terms that are used frequently in this system.

FEASIBILITY

In the world of project management, feasibility is tackled more scientifically than creatively (and this is the criticism that some event directors have of a 'pure' project management approach to event planning). Feasibility under this approach is reviewed largely in terms of realistic dates for completion of tasks and sub-tasks.

STAKEHOLDER ANALYSIS

Stakeholder input is a consideration at every stage of project management, stakeholders being required to 'sign off' at critical stages, which signals their agreement with the concept or plan. This is vitally important, and there are many examples of how this has paid off: a sponsor signing off on the use of their logo on the event poster may avoid a complete new print run if the colour is not 100% correct. As an event manager, it is comforting to be able to say, 'This is what you signed off on, if you want anything else it is going to cost you ...'

SCOPE

It is recognised that any project is limited by time, scope and cost. Time is allocated according to the work breakdown structure (WBS). This is very similar to writing job descriptions in the traditional business environment, but in this case the tasks are more specific and clustered according to function. Scope refers to the extent of the project. Anyone who has planned a wedding will easily understand the concept of scope creep, particularly the person paying for the wedding who finds that the bride and her mother frequently have new and more expensive ideas as the date draws near.

RISK MANAGEMENT

Risk management will be discussed in Chapters 16, 17 and 26; however, it is mentioned here to stress that risk is not only safety risk, but is any risk that can impact on completion of the plan by the due date.

DELIVERABLES

During the planning process, decisions are made about what is deliverable at each stage. These plans include ever increasing detail, for example, equipment details for procurement (purchasing). A sample uniform is a more tangible example of a deliverable.

MILESTONES

Within the framework of project management, a milestone is an element that marks the completion of a work package or phase. It is usually marked by a high-level event such as signing of a deliverable. Typically, a milestone is associated with some sort of decision that outlines the future of a project.

Project management involves disciplined planning and control. Many of the tools suggested in this chapter, such as Gantt charts and PERT charts, are utilised in project management. It is important that careful attention be given to the critical path for completion as often timelines are interdependent. However, as mentioned above, some of the more creative people in the event business argue that this approach constrains creativity and is too limiting for the 'organic' environment of event management.

Understanding the evolution of conceptions of the 'science' of project management from the use of tools and techniques on stand-alone projects to the conceptualisation of project management as an organisational capability is useful (Crawford 2006).

MAKE USE OF INFORMATION TECHNOLOGY

The role played by various different types of planning software for preparing plans, charts, run sheets and checklists has been illustrated in this chapter. Most events also have their own website, which plays a vitally important role in marketing and ticketing.

The PERT chart in Figure 14.10 illustrates the development process for a festival website. The numbered nodes represent tasks completed, deliverables or milestones. Diverging arrows indicate that tasks can be completed concurrently. Thus, in this example, after the concept for the website has been developed (1), one person can source the text and graphics (2) while another works on the website structure/design and storyboards (3). Directional arrows represent dependent tasks that must be done sequentially. Thus a direct arrow is drawn from uploading to website server (8) to the formal launch (9). Each of the arrows between the nodes shows how many days are needed for task completion. Since the critical path is the longest path, in this example the website cannot be launched in less than 45 days.

All graphical illustrations provide alternative ways in which to view processes. PERT charts, while not widely used, are particularly helpful in showing how a project's critical path can be shortened by developing as many parallel tasks as possible.

For many sporting events, technological solutions are needed for timing, scoring and results processing. The media place heavy demands on information technology systems including access to broadband internet for transmitting video and image files. Higher than usual demands are placed on outdoor events, particularly if the site does not provide intranet

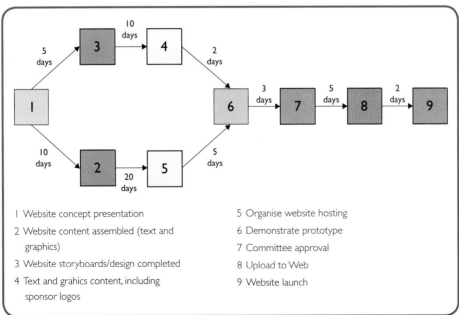

FIGURE 14.10
PERT chart for development and launch of a festival website

1 Website concept presentation
2 Website content assembled (text and graphics)
3 Website storyboards/design completed
4 Text and grahics content, including sponsor logos

5 Organise website hosting
6 Demonstrate prototype
7 Committee approval
8 Upload to Web
9 Website launch

and internet connections such as those provided at every stand at an exhibition centre as part of the venue hire agreement. A conference or exhibition needs tailor-made software for registration and dealing with the specific requirements of speakers, exhibitors and visitors.

In addition to these special requirements, standard office technology is required for administration. This includes software for word processing, spreadsheets and databases. Clearly, ongoing support and maintenance is essential, as is routine back-up of data.

IMPLEMENT AND EVALUATE PROJECTS

Effective communication is an essential feature of project management. Everyone involved needs to be aware of the goals and milestones and these have to be carefully monitored. In the stressful environment of event planning, trust and respect within the project team are essential. Ongoing consultation, in the form of meetings, telephone calls and emails, is one way to assess progress against project goals. Occasionally, additional resources will be required or the project timeline will need to be reviewed, but not the ultimate deadline, the event date, as that never changes! Actions must be agreed, with timelines and responsibility allocated. Everyone needs to be involved in ongoing communication—team members, colleagues and clients.

The nature of the event business is that most of the time is spent in planning and very little is spent in the execution phase. In fact, it often comes as a shock when the event is over so quickly. Things can go bad in an instant in the event environment but good planning can prevent this happening. In the best cases, the plans have been so thoughtfully developed that the event manager's role is simply to ensure that procedures are correctly implemented, resulting in minimal incidents and satisfied clients.

The two chapters that follow will cover the event implementation phase in detail, including installation of infrastructure and provision of event management services. Event evaluation strategies will be covered in Chapter 23. However, it is timely to point out here that unless the event manager develops clear aims and objectives and sets out to measure the outcomes against the objectives, there will be no legacy from all those many months of planning and no criteria to prove a successful outcome.

SUMMARY

In this chapter we have covered the important topic of project management and looked at various tools, such as maps, Gantt charts, checklists and run sheets, which are used to administer and monitor the progress of activities and timelines for events. Unlike most other projects, deadlines in event management cannot be postponed since the date of the event and the place where it will be held must be advertised. The planning tools described and illustrated in this chapter will help you meet those deadlines, particularly as each aspect of an event is generally contingent on another. Effective planning ensures the provision of all necessary services and amenities at an event. Nevertheless, planning needs to remain flexible since this is a very dynamic industry in which change is inevitable.

Chapter review questions

1 What is a project?
2 What are the characteristics of an event that make it a project?
3 Explain the meaning of the following project management terms using event examples:
   (a) Feasibility
   (b) Stakeholder analysis
   (c) Scope
   (d) Deliverables
   (e) Milestones.
4 Describe and illustrate four tools such as Gantt charts that can be used for event project management.
5 Discuss the pros and cons of establishing a unique project management model such as PMBOK for the events industry as opposed to working with the standard principles outlined in generic project management systems used by other industries.

Activities

1 The concept, 'chain of events', is very relevant to event planning. Review three different types of event (such as a product launch, fete and sporting competition) and identify potential weak links in the planning process that could jeopardise each event if they were not thoroughly considered. For example, the lack of a back-up system for electrical supplies at an outdoor venue could jeopardise an event.
2 Visit <www.travelsmart.gov.au/events/four.html> and compare two case studies of transport planning in terms of their travel solutions.
3 Using the checklist at the above website, visit a public event and analyse its transport arrangements, making observations and recommendations for the future.

Case study

Conference project management
Using the following approach, develop the remaining elements of the project plan to run a conference in your capital city. This part covers only the preliminary period.
Two-year event planner
Stage 1: 24–18 months ahead
Preliminary brainstorming, research, committees and budget planning

continued

Case study (*continued*)

Preliminary planning:				
Task	**Assigned to**	**Deadline**	**Contact details**	**Done? (Y/N)**
Plan the event dates				
Plan the event size				
Research conflicting events and adapt your planned dates if appropriate				
Discuss program structure and theme with key stakeholders				
Research, select and book an appropriate venue				
Appoint a professional conference organiser (PCO), if appropriate				
Confirm organising committee members				
Appoint any subcommittees				
Confirm social events and venues				
Prepare an 'accompanying persons' program				

Finance:				
Task	**Assigned to**	**Deadline**	**Contact details**	**Done? (Y/N)**
Set up event bank accounts				
Establish budget reporting methods				
Prepare the event budget				
Prepare a cash-flow chart				
Review the budget				
Set registration fees				

Source: Business Events Sydney, <www.businesseventssydney.com.au/plan-an-event/event-planning-toolkit/preparation/creating-a-timeline.cfm>. © Business Events Sydney.

References

Crawford, L (2006), 'Developing organizational project management capability: theory and practice', *Project Management Journal*, 37(3):74–86.

Locke, E A, Frederick, E, Lee, C, Bobko, P (1984), 'Effect of self-efficacy, goals, and task strategies on task performance', *Journal of Applied Psychology*, 694–9.

McClelland, D C (1985), 'How motives, skills and values determine what people do', *American Psychologist*, 40:812–25.

McClelland, D C, Koestner, R, Weinberger, J (1989), 'How do self-attributed and implicit motives differ?', *Psychological Review*, 96:690–702.

O'Toole, W (2009), 'Event project management system', <www.personal.usyd.edu.au/~wotoole/>, accessed 5 May 2010.

O'Toole, W (2002), 'Toward the integration of event management best practice by the project management process', <www.personal.usyd.edu.au/~wotoole/conf_paper.htm>, accessed 5 May 2010.

Project Management Institute (2000), 'A guide to the Project Management Body of Knowledge', *PMBOK Guide*, PMI, Newtown Square, PA.

Silvers, J (2003), 'Event Management Body of Knowledge Project', <www.juliasilvers.com/embok.htm>, accessed 14 December 2009.

Skinner, B F (1953), *Science and human behaviour*, Macmillan, New York.

Thomas, M & Adams, J (2005), 'Adapting project management processes to the management of special events: an exploratory study', *Academy of Strategic Management Journal*, 4: 99–114..

Vroom, V H (1973), *Research: A new look at managerial decision making*, Elsevier.

Vroom, V H & Yetton, P W (1973), *Leadership and decision-making*, University of Pittsburgh Press, Pittsburgh.

CHAPTER 15

EVENT INFRASTRUCTURE

Unit descriptor

This unit describes the performance outcomes, skills and knowledge required to coordinate infrastructure and facilities for a **complex event** comprising multiple components, where these do not already exist at a venue or site. It therefore builds on other Events units, such as SITXEVT013A Manage event staging. This unit applies to individuals managing events in any industry context. It is particularly relevant to the cultural, community, hospitality, sporting and tourism sectors.

Many events take place at outdoor venues or at locations where infrastructure and facilities are minimal. Significant event operations knowledge combined with organisational and management skills are required to establish that infrastructure and make it operational. This role is undertaken by an event manager working autonomously, but in consultation with suppliers, colleagues and broader event stakeholders.

Elements

- Identify event infrastructure requirements
- Establish and organise event infrastructure
- Monitor event infrastructure.

Critical aspects for assessment

- Ability to organise and monitor infrastructure for an event in a location with minimal existing facilities and services
- Knowledge of the issues that specifically impact on the organisation of events in venues without infrastructure, including requirements of relevant authorities, Australian standards and OHS regulations
- Demonstration of skills through the organisation and monitoring of the infrastructure requirements for at least one event where the candidate plays a key management role.

THE CONVERGENCE of two separate student research projects occurred when a comment made by one respondent linked the two themes. The research projects investigated, firstly, satisfaction with provision of toilet amenities at music events and, secondly, drug use associated with different music genres. The female respondent stated that the queues at events were so long that she did not drink anything so that she would not miss acts or lose her place. This has potentially serious ramifications, including death from dehydration due to ecstasy use, exacerbated by lack of adequate toilet facilities. While this risk may be overstated, the findings from the research showed high levels of dissatisfaction with toilet amenities at festivals and events among female respondents. On a satisfaction scale, this aspect of the event was rated as important as food/beverage and parking/transport and clearly deserves greater attention from event organisers.

Source: Van Der Wagen (2009).

In terms of waiting time to use toilet facilities, most respondents to this survey waited for 5–10 minutes. However, over 30% waited for 10–20 minutes, 8% waited for 20–30 minutes and 4% waited for up to 60 minutes. One respondent reported going home early as she could not face the waiting required. Just over 50% of respondents missed part of the show as a result of this wait and 24% said that this would impact on their decision to attend a future event.

Provision of toilet facilities is just one aspect of event infrastructure that needs to be considered and, judging from this research, needs to be considered more carefully than it has been in the past. While new products are available for getting around the problem of lack of facilities, the acceptance and use of such products is questionable. For example, the PWP Go Bag is a leak-proof bag containing a second bag with a polymer crystal pouch inside, in which the crystals are used to solidify urine and other liquids instantly into an odourless, spill-proof gel that is non-toxic and safe for disposal in any normal bin.

As well as toilet facilities, event infrastructure requirements include fencing, stages, catering facilities, provision of drinking water, data cabling, electrical cabling, etc. All need to be considered at the concept stage and installed just before the event opens. An event that is staged in a park, for example, requires more detailed site planning as many of the services need to be established (e.g. cloak room, first aid tent, information kiosk, ticketing booth, backstage area, site office). All of these involve the erection of temporary facilities.

The focus of this chapter is managing the set-up, operation and pack-up of the event infrastructure, which is the culmination of many months, at least, of careful planning.

IDENTIFY EVENT INFRASTRUCTURE REQUIREMENTS

The first stage of event operational planning involves establishing the event infrastructure requirements. These requirements could be for an indoor venue, such as a sports centre,

Effective planning ensures the provision of all necessary infrastructure and amenities at an event

community hall or an exhibition centre. They could also be for an outdoor site. Where the venue or site has been used frequently for events, this can be helpful, as the venue or site management team will have many more answers to the many questions organisers may ask. The planning challenges will be greater if the site or venue has never been used for the type of event you are planning.

The first step is to liaise with relevant authorities at the commencement of the event management cycle to ensure regulatory requirements are integrated into the planning process. The second step is to identify and analyse infrastructure and facility requirements based on a detailed review of all aspects of the proposed event and venue.

These requirements could include:

★ staging
★ power supply
★ water supply
★ heating or air-conditioning
★ public toilets
★ erection of temporary structures (in addition to staging)
★ scaffolding
★ emergency services
★ car and coach parking
★ transport systems
★ contractor access
★ camping sites or other temporary accommodation
★ signage
★ technology requirements (data cabling, internet access)
★ disabled access
★ waste management
★ security
★ any ecological, environmental or heritage requirements.

From this list it is immediately evident that many of these requirements can be met by existing, dedicated event facilities, providing a powerful incentive to use such a venue. However, there are also occasions where an untested site (such as a city precinct or a commercial building) is the most appropriate for the planned event.

Once a detailed list of the infrastructure requirements has been developed, it needs to be discussed with the approving authority or venue management. Relevant authorities may include local government, state or territory government, police, ambulance and fire services. At all stages it is necessary to incorporate safety, security and risk management issues into all planning documentation and processes as safety aspects are the most likely to lead to rejection of event plans.

ESTABLISH AND ORGANISE EVENT INFRASTRUCTURE

Following approval from the relevant authorities, site or venue manager, steps can be taken to establish and organise event infrastructure and contractors. This requires accurate requests for tenders or detailed briefing of contractors so that quotes can be obtained from suppliers of equipment and services. Chapters 9 (regulatory requirements), 10 (business relationships) and 24 (legal knowledge) also cover information relevant to this aspect of event management, including licensing requirements.

Licences may be required for:

★ building work
★ electrical work
★ plumbing work
★ gas fitting
★ handling hazardous materials

★ forklift operations
★ stage sets (e.g. fire retardant certification)
★ rigging
★ pyrotechnics and special effects
★ security.

The logistics of event management planning involves getting things organised, getting things (and people) in the right place at the right time and pulling everything down. Rock concerts and entertainment events featuring international artists present many logistical problems, particularly if the group is on a tour of several cities. Sometimes a complex array of musical equipment, some of which might have been airlifted into the country only days, or even hours, before the event, has to be set up. However, in most cases, the team supporting the artists would have identified specific requirements, at times down to the last detail, to be met locally. (These might even include requests for exotic foods, special dietary items and dressing room layouts.)

The most amusing example of a logistical dilemma was that reported by the organisers of an equestrian cross-country event. A decision had to be made as to how to manage 'comfort breaks' for volunteers deployed over an enormous open venue. Should a buggie pick up the staff member and take them to the facilities? No, it was decided that a roving portaloo on the back of a small truck was the answer. Take the toilet to the staff member, not the staff member to the toilet! This avoided redeployment of replacement staff. Naturally, also, the event organisers did not want to impact on the 'look' of the event on television by having temporary portaloos littered all over the cross-country course.

The level of difficulty associated with running an outdoor event at a temporary site cannot be underestimated. Each element of the proposed infrastructure must be discussed with key stakeholders and suppliers. Careful coordination and monitoring is essential, particularly during the bump-in phase when several contractors will be working simultaneously—as the expression goes, 'time is money', and contractors who

Operations staff ensure that dancers will be on time to go on stage

waste time during bump-in are not going to be responsive to later requests from event managers who have not planned the logistics of bump-in carefully enough to ensure an efficient process.

BUMP-IN (OR SET-UP)

Once final arrangements have been checked and staff and contractors have been briefed, the process of setting up all structures and facilities required for the event begins. Setting up can be a time-consuming process and a run-through must be built into planning. This is absolutely essential as it is imperative that all facilities and equipment work. For some tasks, such as installing sound and lighting equipment, the services of specialist engineers are needed.

For outdoor sites, an all-terrain vehicle may be needed to avoid damage to grass. This is illustrated in the photograph, in which first aid tents and ATM facilities can be seen in the background. Where an ATM is available on site, delivery of cash to the tent is a logistical issue: ideally there will be access from the rear for the armoured vehicle and also security guards. Perimeter fencing is another requirement for most outdoor events. Computer network and other cables are laid along the fence line, and these must be covered for safety reasons and tested to ensure that the network is up and running.

The collage of images from a food and wine festival on page 232 shows the many facets of bumping in such an event. Most infrastructure is installed on the day before the event (and there are safety issues with this if members of the public, including children, have access to the site). Food and wine vendors bump in early in the morning (so neighbours need to be notified) ready to commence sales mid-morning. Vehicles should be prohibited at this stage. While this should be obvious, vans driving through crowds is a common sight at many outdoor events.

All-terrain vehicles are useful for various purposes at outdoor events and are designed to avoid damaging the grass

Figure 15.1 illustrates the level of checking that needs to be done to ensure that the set-up of an event will run smoothly.

BUMP-OUT (OR BREAKDOWN)

Essentially, the bump-out sequence is the reverse of the bump-in. Timing, though, is usually a lot quicker. Again, a detailed schedule needs to be developed and agreed with contractors. This may include restrictions and/or scheduling of vehicle access to the site. All temporary structures and equipment need to be dismantled. If this has to happen immediately after the audience has left, sufficient staff will be required because at this stage everyone is generally exhausted, which itself presents a safety risk. If bump-out does not occur immediately, security staff will be needed to monitor the site until all equipment and materials have been removed. Some items are very expensive, and if they are

Establish contact with the nominated contractor personnel at the appropriate time and reconfirm and agree all requirements

⇩

Agree to and make any necessary adjustments with the contractor

⇩

Check all aspects of the event set-up against the pre-arranged agreements (materials and equipment, room set-up, staging, technical equipment, display and signage, food and beverage facilities, registration areas)

⇩

Check all areas of the venue, and equipment, are accessible and safe

⇩

Identify any deficiencies and discrepancies and take prompt action to rectify the situation

⇩

Brief any additional on-site staff on the full details of event operation (including communication and control mechanisms)

FIGURE 15.1
Overseeing event set-up

Oversee the breakdown of the event to ensure it is completed in accordance with agreements

⇩

Co-ordinate the packing and removal of all materials and equipment

⇩

Check the venue to ensure items and belongings are not left behind

⇩

Debrief with contractors to discuss any difficulties or suggestions for future improvements

⇩

Check and sign accounts in accordance with contractor agreements

⇩

Note any outstanding items requiring post-event action

FIGURE 15.2
Overseeing event breakdown

lost, stolen or damaged this can have a dramatic effect on the bottom line of an otherwise successful event.

Figure 15.2 shows what is involved in efficiently managing the breakdown of an event.

In most other industries, logistics involves managing the processes of manufacture, supply and distribution (including storage and transport) of the product to the ultimate consumer. The same general principles apply in event management, requiring an organised and structured alignment of key logistics functions. Procurement, transportation, storage, inventory management, customer service and database management are all examples of logistical aspects of such event activities as merchandise sales. In the same way, the supply of food and beverage to the event audience starts right back with the producer of the food and beverage products. For most events, food supply is unproblematic. However, in the case of a very large event, such as the Commonwealth Games, provision of sufficient stock of potatoes for fries may require importation of frozen fries, while ensuring an adequate supply of lettuce may mean the sourcing of an out-of-season vegetable. For events that run over multiple days, food storage is also an issue, as is the logistics of fresh supplies needing to be delivered

overnight, which has ramifications for staffing rosters and security. Often during a complex event there is the need to replenish stock or refurbish and clean areas. These activities must be planned and scheduled.

As the above illustrates, most perishable items and merchandise should be sold during the event, thus alleviating at least some of the burden of moving out. Always remember that at the completion of bump-out the venue or site must be handed back to the owner or operator and any damages checked. This will be stipulated in the contract, and this final check and handover should be carefully documented, no matter how tired the event team.

MONITOR BUILD OF EVENT INFRASTRUCTURE

During the bump-in process the event organiser needs to monitor progress with the infrastructure build. Specific times are allocated to this process in the exhibition industry and, for safety reasons, exhibitors are not allowed access to their stands until the build is complete. Ongoing liaison with contractors is necessary so that any need for adjustments to infrastructure can be identified and appropriate changes organised and confirmed in writing. This process is facilitated by well-prepared bump-in schedules, or run sheets, and a detailed operations manual. Sharing information with stakeholders, contractors and other staff is essential. One manager who did not follow this advice was seen on a children's scooter riding haphazardly from one part of the exhibition hall to another, leading to total meltdown when he could not cope with the hundreds of questions asked by stallholders. Keeping all plans in your head is not advisable.

Monitoring progress, by itself, may not be enough. A good event manager anticipates possible changes that might be required and develops positive action plans to keep progress on time and on budget. A delay in one area can cause a significant flow-on effect in many other areas. This proactive approach is called 'active monitoring'.

POLICIES, PROCEDURES AND PERFORMANCE STANDARDS

Every event requires policies. These describe the general principles, or 'what is to be done'. For example, policies may be drawn up to prevent accidents, avoid theft, or prioritise access to the site by emergency services crews. Having prepared the policies, the procedures for implementing them are then developed. The policy equates to 'what is to be done' and the procedure equates to 'how it is to be done'.

A procedure can take the form of a list of tasks or a checklist. Once procedures have been developed and integrated across the event functions, all the pieces begin to fit together. Sometimes, the timing of a procedure needs to be modified to meet the needs of another functional area. For example, if the grass surrounding the greens of a golf course were scheduled to be mowed the day before a golfing competition, it would not be possible to erect the crowd control fencing until this had been done.

Kitchen Safety Checklist

1 Food contact surfaces are clean and clear. ☐
2 Chopping boards for meat, chicken, vegetables are colour coded. ☐
3 Non-food surfaces clean and clear. ☐
4 Floors are clean and not slippery. ☐
5 Equipment is correctly cleaned and stored. ☐
6 Wiping cloths and cleaning equipment for different purposes correctly colour coded. ☐
7 Plumbing is functional. ☐
8 Refrigerator and freezer temperatures meet standards. ☐
9 Hand-washing facilities meet standards. ☐
10 Garbage disposal containers are labelled and covered. ☐
11 Storage areas are clean and clear. ☐
12 No evidence of insects or rodents. ☐
13 Lighting and ventilation is adequate. ☐
14 Gas supply is checked. ☐
15 All cooking equipment is functional. ☐
16 First aid box is fully equipped. ☐

A procedure for checking the safety of a kitchen could be outlined in a checklist, as shown in Figure 15.3. This procedure could also be shown as a flow chart or it could be based on a logical tour of the kitchen, with items re-ordered to match the kitchen set-up.

By establishing performance standards and inspection schedules, the operational success of an event can be more confidently assured. For example, in the case of a contract with a cleaning company, with clear expectations on both sides the result should be excellent customer service. In the case of the cleaning contractor, specific details about the level of service required would be outlined for the following:

★ pre-event cleaning
★ pre-event day cleaning
★ during session cleaning
★ turnover cleaning (between sessions)
★ post-event cleaning
★ removal of waste materials.

The criteria for performance standards may include efficiency (e.g. speed of set-up and breakdown—see Figure 15.4), accuracy (e.g. checklist 100%), revenue (dollar sales per outlet) or courtesy (customer feedback).

THE OPERATIONS MANUAL

An extract from the contents page from the Perth Convention Exhibition Centre's Event Operations Manual is shown in Figure 15.5. This is indicative of the level of detail required for a **venue operator**. (The full details of this manual can be found on the internet.) While this would form the basis for further operational planning for an exhibition, this is not the full picture. The **event organiser**—in this case the exhibition planner—is responsible for running the event. This requires negotiation with the tradespeople needed to build the exhi-

The band AC/DC has displaced The Wiggles as Australia's highest earning entertainers. The production, *Black Ice*, sold out nationally during their last tour.

Most rock tours are measured by the number of semi-trailers it takes to cart the show. U2 and the Rolling Stones use 40 rigs. AC/DC needs 80. It takes the 200 production crew five days to set up the show. AC/DC brings everything to the party, including speakers, lights, amplifiers, scaffolding and their own power generators. At the ANZ Stadium 10 000 square metres of terraplas were laid to protect the turf. However, after the show was over, it took only 24 hours to pack up and leave.

FIGURE 15.4
Effective planning ensures efficient set-up and breakdown

bition stands and development of run sheets for unloading and installing the equipment. Signage and other visual items hanging from the ceiling would almost certainly require the use of a cherry picker or scissor lift.

So, in this case, there are several bump-in phases: build for large infrastructure, build for exhibition stands, bump-in for exhibitors, and finally the opening. Thus, in addition to the plan for the layout of the exhibition, a run sheet for the build phase of the event would be required. The sequence would be as follows:

★ Equipment and contractor bookings confirmed.
★ Stakeholders fully briefed: staff, venue, suppliers, exhibitors.
★ Documentation checked and distributed.
★ Venue security briefed.
★ Venue clear and clean.
★ Production management team on site.
★ OHS officer on site.
★ Implement OHS induction and monitoring process.
★ Load in and install rigging (requires lift equipment).
★ Load in and install rigged lighting, audio, projection.
★ Load in and install aerially rigged signage.
★ Install and distribute power and Telstra cable.
★ Exhibition floor all clear.
★ Mark up floor.
★ Allocate subfloor services and install.
★ Load in and install flooring: carpet, floating.
★ Load in and install shell scheme and customised stands (inc. stand lighting and AV).
★ Load in and distribute graphics and signage.
★ Load in and distribute furniture and fittings.
★ Load in and install exhibitor materials.
★ Load in and set up food and beverage outlets.
★ All clear for doors to open for public entry.

FIGURE 15.5

Extract
from table
of contents,
event
operations
manual

CONTENTS

Source: Reproduced with kind permission of the Perth Convention Exhibition Centre

★ Exhibition commences.

★ Exhibition concludes.

★ Bump out commences (in reverse sequence).

Several event planning guidelines are included on the companion website to this text. These provide all the information needed to plan different types of events, indoor and outdoor, at dedicated venues and untested sites. It is a good idea for manuals to include copies of contractors' quotes and agreements as it is likely that the person who conducted the negotiation with the contractors will not be present at the time of bump-in. By keeping these quotes and specifications handy, problems can be more easily resolved and conflict avoided.

SUMMARY

This chapter has looked in more detail at logistics, including the often problematic bump-in and bump-out phases of an event. The task of identifying resources and equipment needed, bringing them on site and setting up in the required time takes careful planning. The emphasis in this chapter has therefore been on organisation and coordination to ensure that all functional areas work together smoothly and cooperatively through all phases of the event. The development of policies and procedures can assist in the fufillment of this goal by outlining the interrelationship between functional areas and will also help to ensure that the event performance standards and objectives are successfully achieved. The operations manual, including all plans, layouts and schedules, is invaluable in this regard.

Chapter review questions

1 What do we mean by the term 'infrastructure'?

2 List and explain 10 differences between a dedicated event venue and an untested site from an infrastructure point of view.

3 What are the safety issues for an event that is being built in a public space and how can these be managed?

4 Explain how policies and procedures can be used to streamline bump-in.

Activities

1 Use the montage of photographs of the food and wine festival on page 232 to develop a bump-in schedule for a similar festival.

2 Compare the infrastructure and services information provided to prospective event organisers by two venues.

Case study

Operational plans for race finish

You are organising a race for 20 000 runners. The biggest logistical problem you will face will be at the end of the race. At this time, runners crossing the finish line are exhausted and don't want to run or walk another step. Media wanting to take photographs and interview front runners compounds this problem. Enthusiastic supporters wishing to congratulate those who finish only adds to it. All runners need to get across the line without hold-ups, otherwise their times will be affected.

Task

You need to make plans to ensure that all runners cross the line, that they are advised of their times, and that they receive free sponsor products, retrieve their belongings and attend the prize-giving ceremony. Some participants and spectators will not wait for the final ceremony and will wish to take the transport provided back to the race starting point and go home.

Develop detailed operational plans for the end of the race, using estimates of finish times and crowd flow patterns for participants and spectators.

References

Getz, D, Andersson, T & Larson, M (2007), 'Festival stakeholder roles: concepts and case studies', *Event Management*, 10(2/3):103–22.

Goldblatt, J, Nelson, K & International Special Events Society (2001), *The international dictionary of event management*, 2nd edn, Wiley Events, Wiley, New York.

Kilkenny, S (2006), *The complete guide to successful event planning*, Atlantic Publishing Company, Ocala, FL.

Van Der Wagen, M (2009), 'Ecstasy, dehydration and inadequate provision of toilet amenities for female music fans', ACEM 5th International Event Management Research Conference, Gold Coast, 6–7 July.

CHAPTER 16

EVENTS MANAGEMENT SERVICES

Unit descriptor

This unit describes the performance outcomes, skills and knowledge required to coordinate the final preparation and set-up of a **complex event** comprising multiple components and to manage all aspects of the on-site operation. This unit applies to individuals managing events in any industry context, but it is particularly relevant to the cultural, community, hospitality, sporting and tourism sectors.

On-site management of a complex event requires considerable organisational, communication, negotiation and problem-solving skills as well as detailed knowledge of the range of issues and challenges that impact on event operations. Those with managerial responsibility undertake this role.

Elements

- Prepare for on-site management
- Monitor event operation
- Oversee event breakdown.

Critical aspects for assessment

- Ability to manage the on-site operation of an event, including all aspects of preparation, set-up, operation and move-out
- Knowledge of the range of issues and problems that may arise during the conduct of meetings and events
- Demonstration of skills in managing the on-site aspects of more than one complex event
- Presence of commercially realistic time pressures related to the operation of an event.

CHALLENGE Stadium is Western Australia's most versatile event venue. With a floor space of 2109 square metres and the flexibility to accommodate a wide variety of configurations, the Main Arena at Challenge Stadium is the perfect venue for entertainment events, exhibitions, trade shows, product launches, conferences, concerts, graduations, awards nights and banquets. The experienced and professional team in Challenge Stadium's Events Department can assist in every aspect of planning your event.

'The highlights of the games included the quality and closeness of the sports venues, involvement of volunteers, transport services … Your commitment to the Games and Australian University Sport was greatly appreciated,' said Tony Jermyn, Project Manager, Australian University Games.

'I would like to formally thank you and your staff for the assistance that was given before, during and after the event. I would like to make a special mention of Luke who completely exceeded my expectations. Nothing was too much trouble … What a fantastic venue you have. All the facilities were excellent, catering and beverage services fantastic, what more can I say? Brilliant, brilliant, brilliant.'

Thanks to the Challenge Stadium.

Source: Challenge Stadium <www.austadiums.com/index.php>.

Since opening its doors in 1986, over 10 million patrons have utilised the world-class facilities of Challenge Stadium for a wide variety of sporting, recreational and commercial activities. The centre has played host to numerous outstanding national and international sporting events, including the highly successful 6th and 8th FINA Swimming Championships. Challenge Stadium is firmly established as one of Australia's leading multipurpose venues. Each year over 1 million people visit the venue for a variety of events, activities and training purposes.

The $2 million headquarters of the WA Institute of Sport is located at Challenge Stadium, providing elite athletes with state-of-the-art training facilities and support staff. The stadium offers a wide range of services, making it an attractive option for event managers looking for a venue. The range of on-site services includes:

★ dressing rooms
★ change rooms
★ site office
★ ticketing facilities
★ scoreboards
★ telephone services
★ creche facilities
★ fitness centre
★ catering services
★ aquatic centre
★ ATM services.

The range of events held at Challenge Stadium extends beyond sport to cover concerts, awards nights and exhibitions. All of these have significant operational demands. First, there are the logistics of getting all equipment to the site and ready for set-up, as well as the athletes, participants or exhibitors. The bump-in period can take several days before the event is open to the public. At the end of the event, everything has to be dismantled and stored, as most items are valuable assets, and the venue restored to its original state for the next operation. With all events the cost of venue hire includes the period required for bump-in and bump-out. Between bump-in and bump-out there is an event to run and the event audience expects a range of services such as those provided by this venue.

In this chapter, therefore, the focus will be on managing operations while the event is in progress.

A music event at Challenge Stadium, WA

PREPARE FOR ON-SITE MANAGEMENT

Having built the physical infrastructure for the event, as discussed in the previous chapter, the next phase involves meeting the needs of the event **participants or performers**. These may be exhibitors, athletes, speakers, players or other talent. The **customers** may include the audience, spectators, visitors, ticket holders, delegates or media. For mega events the importance of meeting the needs of the media crews reporting live results around the world cannot be understated. However, for most events, the aim is to meet the needs of the more tangible audience.

The event organiser needs to develop plans and procedures for on-site management based on an assessment of overall event requirements and to collate materials to facilitate effective on-site management. The event operations manual, described in the last chapter, is once again the source document for the implementation phase of the event. Event briefings with operational staff and event production contractors prior to the event are essential and must include clarification of roles and responsibilities. Naturally, the infrastructure needs to complement the services provided. For example, for security to be effective at a music concert, appropriate fencing and entrances need to be provided. Where the event is of the type where fans may jump or storm the fences to get in free, the fence needs to be a sturdy structure, otherwise it creates a safety hazard (your author was once nearly flattened in just such circumstances). The fence also needs to be covered with a material that prevents outsiders seeing the performance at no charge. Security forces employed for this type of event have many specifications for managing their roles, including the set-up of the entry points, pass-out systems, lighting, etc. Thus infrastructure providers and services work closely together. During the briefing session some of these requirements may be revised or improved, for example, initiating additional crowd management measures.

Plans and procedures for on-site management are extensive. Depending on the nature of the event, they may include any of the following elements, all of which impact on the **talent** (i.e. the performers).

Technical services for performers

TRAVEL AND ACCOMMODATION ARRANGEMENTS

Speakers, athletes and entertainers some-times come from distant locations and their travel arrangements need to be organised, allowing for sufficient time for delays or missed connections. It would be most embarrassing for the event manager if the star of the show was still at the airport once the audience was seated! Accommodation bookings during a peak festival period are hard to come by and the performers need the best of these offerings, as close to the event venue as possible. Most major performers and players travel with a lot of equipment, some of which is potentially unsuitable for use with local electrical and other services, thus presenting further logistical challenges.

TECHNICAL REQUIREMENTS

Meeting technical specifications for technological and other equipment is another aspect of services management. The event manager generally has the role of organising all technical elements, including design, scheduling, staging, sound, lighting, audio visual, entertain-ment and decor for the production aspect of the event. The stage is replaced by the field of play for a sporting competition and there are quite different specifications for the prepara-tion of football fields and race tracks. In most cases, sporting venues are specialists in this area. The bigger challenges occur when a sporting stadium is used for a music event or other untested event.

ACCREDITATION

Accreditation badges limit access to various parts of an event site. At a music festival, for example, only people wearing the correct accreditation are allowed backstage. Lanyards are commonly used to display badges, tickets or ID cards for identification where security is required. When the accreditation system is designed, various zones are created and codes or colours allocated to the zones. As you can imagine, the Olympic Games has one of the most complex accreditation systems of any event, which is essential for security reasons. For major events it is quite common for staff to undergo police security checks and for them to wear photo identification on the lanyard. Once the system is in place, it is then necessary to post a security guard or volunteer at each entry to a zone. Tact and patience are required as many people try to breach the system, insisting on access to places for which they do not have the appropriate accreditation. The media often have one of the highest levels of accreditation, enabling them, for example, to take photographs front or back of stage. At less complex events, a black t-shirt with 'event crew' or 'media' on the back is sufficient.

BUMP-IN AND REHEARSAL

The bump-in and rehearsal process for performers (singers, speakers) or participants (athletes, cheerleaders, etc.) needs to be as smooth as possible, so that these participants can give their best performance. This is scheduled and run by the production team. All participants need to be briefed on their rehearsal schedules and the event program. The event is usually 'called' by the event producer and the stage manager executes these instructions, making sure people appear on stage at the correct time. All production elements need to be run on cue, including lighting, sound and visuals. A green room or change room should be provided for the performers.

SECURITY

Security staff play a role in both areas of the event, behind the stage area and front of house (FOH). Protecting talent, sponsors, VIPs and dignitaries is essential and once again accreditation processes come into play. Security also acts at the interface between the stage or field and the audience, watching for crowd-related problems. A security plan, which links with an emergency plan, is developed by the event manager in conjunction with venue/site management, security management and local authorities such as police, fire brigade and ambulance services.

Depending on the nature of the event, services for **customers** could include any of the following.

BOOKING AND TICKETING

Most tickets to larger events are sold on the internet or through ticketing agencies, bringing a whole range of efficiencies to booking and allocating tickets. A streamlined booking process is absolutely essential for all events, both commercial and not-for-profit.

FRINGE WAS WARNED OF BOX OFFICE DEBACLE MONTHS IN ADVANCE

A damning report into the failure of the Edinburgh Festival Fringe's box office has revealed how warnings of potential chaos were being made behind the scenes months in advance. Consultants have blamed a series of 'flawed' decisions by Fringe officials and board members for the ticketing debacle, which brought the world's biggest arts festival to the brink of financial ruin.

The review of last year's box office failure, published today, reveals how a new computer system was still not ready to be tested with a month to go before sales opened … The consultants have condemned a lack of proper planning, poor project management, inadequate risk assessments and a breakdown in communications both within and without the Festival Fringe Society.

Source: Ferguson, B (2009), *The Scotsman*, 4 February. Reproduced with permission.

A facility for lost tickets or badges needs to be in place if there is no ticket office on site. Mobile phone technologies are likely to bring many more changes to the booking and ticketing process as customers become even easier to reach and registering using their phones is now possible.

For many exhibitions, visitors register online. In the sphere of private events, responses to invitations are often slow to come in and this can be highly problematic when the venue is waiting for confirmation of numbers.

As mentioned earlier in the book, the anticipation of attending an event is part of the event experience and this is enhanced by an event's website featuring the line-up of artists or the current competition results.

REGISTRATION/ENTRY

With the advent of remote scanning devices, runners can now wear microchips that have their identity code and finishing time recorded as they pass the start and finish line. The identity of the runner is stored in barcode-like format which can be scanned over a short distance, the principle being the same as when a person uses a data card to swipe in or out of a building. Microchips that can be scanned remotely will no doubt replace the lanyard worn at exhibitions in future, and each exhibitor will have a report showing how long each visitor spent looking at their stand. Technology, both hardware (microchips) and software (databases), has solved many problems with registration of event participants.

For events such as exhibitions where visitors either register or pay, this process must be carefully planned to avoid delays and frustration. Where visitors register, the data to be collected must be agreed with the client. As with ticketing, registration is often performed online. Registration can be a complex action and consideration should be given to using a company such as Info Salons, which specialises in this area.

All staff need to provide customer service

USHERING

Security staff, volunteers and ushers all have the role of greeting visitors to an event, and they play an important role in customer service. By briefing contractors, such as security and cleaning staff, the level of customer service can be improved at all stages of the event. Then, as the guests stream out and thank the security staff for a great show, they too can feel that they have contributed to the event experience. Pass-outs or wristbands are an important consideration for facilitating on-site service.

Other customer service requirements at an event include information services, lost and found, cloakrooms/lockers and merchandising. First aid and automatic teller machines are essential if pass-outs are not permitted.

FUNCTIONAL AREAS

While the division of responsibilities into different functional areas has been discussed in previous chapters, it is useful to review the roles of these areas, known in most other businesses as 'departments'. Each of these functional areas develops its own policies, procedures and performance standards.

Procurement and stores

This area is responsible for purchasing, storage and distribution of all products required for the event. Such items may include radios, computers, sound equipment and drapes, and these are often hired from specialist suppliers.

If catering, for example, were contracted out to a subcontractor, the subcontractor would be responsible for food purchasing and storage, and the same would apply to other subcontractors. They, too, would be responsible for their product or equipment procurement and storage.

One of the main roles for this functional area during an event is the supply of event merchandise to the sales outlets.

Marketing

In the lead-up to an event, this functional area is responsible for the overall strategy for product, pricing and promotion. As the event draws near, image, sponsor liaison and sales promotion become priorities.

Ticketing

The ticketing area looks after ticketing in the lead-up to an event and during the event. In some cases this function is managed by the local tourism information office; in other cases, tickets are sold by charitable organisations. For most profit-making events, the ticketing function is managed wholly by a major ticketing organisation.

Registration

Most sporting events and exhibitions, particularly those with large numbers of participants or visitors, need a functional area to manage the registration of participants in the race or other event. This involves completion and processing of relevant forms by participants, as well as acknowledgement that participation is at their own risk.

Merchandising

The merchandising area is responsible for the sale of merchandise, ranging from caps and posters to CDs and DVDs. The range is frequently extensive and is sometimes advertised on the internet. Merchandising is usually subcontracted to one or more firms.

Finance

As the event draws near, the main concern of this functional area is to maintain control processes, minimise expenditure and manage cash during the event.

Legal

In most cases, legal advice is sought before the event and it is only with very large events that a specific functional area is established to cover this role.

Technology

Networks linking different reporting systems can be developed to include those for sales of tickets and merchandise, registration of attendees and athletes, and recording of results, as well as managing rosters and payroll.

Media

This functional area deals directly with the media, and during an event it needs to be constantly informed of progress. If a negative incident should occur, it is the media unit that writes the press releases and briefs the press. It also manages media interviews with the stars or athletes.

Community relations

Generally speaking, this functional area is only represented when there is a significant community involvement, for example, at non-profit events or those with a social or environmental impact.

Staffing

As the event approaches, the staffing area looks after training, uniforms, rosters and other schedules, and staff meal vouchers. Recognition of their efforts is needed to ensure that all are retained to the end of the event, particularly if the event runs over several days and fatigue is a factor.

Services and information

The provision of guest services and information to the event audience is obviously at its peak during the event, requiring staff to be extremely knowledgeable and resourceful. Most large event venues and sites can be confusing to the audience, so a clear traffic flow for ingress and egress, as well as routes, areas and facilities, should be planned with clear sign-posting.

Cleaning and waste management

Very often this function rests with venue staff who undertake cleaning as a routine operation before, during and after an event. For larger events, such as street festivals, the local council may ask current contractors to expand their role for the period of the festival. For other events, contract cleaners are often called in to manage this functional area. An important consideration today is to make the event as green or environmentally friendly as possible. Waste management is covered in more detail in Chapter 20.

Cleaning services are vitally important

Catering

In most cases, venue catering is outsourced to a catering company and there is generally a long-standing contract in place with that company. Sometimes, however, a decision needs to be made as to whether to employ one caterer to take on this role or several caterers, each offering different types of cuisine or beverages. Most event organisers leave this area to catering professionals. A food and beverage manager is often employed to oversee this aspect for complex events. Catering is covered in more detail in Chapter 19.

Venue operations

The management of the venue, in particular the operation of facilities and equipment, maintenance and the like, is the responsibility of the venue team. Health, safety and emergencies are the key areas of concern of this functional area. If the event is held at an exotic and unusual location, the appointment of a site manager is recommended to ensure that the obtaining of permits and such things as perimeter fencing, plumbing, cabling, gas and power are under control.

Production

Matthews (2008) points out that the term 'event producer' can be used interchangeably with 'event manager'; however, 'producer' generally refers to the role of coordinating and executing the technical side of the event: the production. This team usually comprises several specialist staging contractors.

Sports operations

All aspects of a sporting competition, including results management and award ceremonies, are managed by sports operations.

Medical

The medical functional area provides first aid to both attendees/spectators and performers/athletes. In some cases, this area is responsible for drug testing.

These functional areas, and their roles and responsibilities, should be spelled out in the operations manual, which should also contain emergency contact details for all event contractors. Run sheets, production schedules or running orders should be available to everyone who has responsibility for an action or actions included on these schedules. Some people will need only summaries, while others, such as the lighting engineers, will need minute-by-minute cues. Maps and layouts of the event overlay are also essential for event personnel. Exceptional personal skills in communication and people management assist in reducing the anxiety level of all concerned. Contractor communication mechanisms and protocols need to be put in place, including the appointment of a main liaison person for each contracted supplier. Two-way radios or walkie-talkies are recommended, as mobile phones are unsatisfactory tools for communication in the event environment. The benefit of two-way radio is that several listeners can be on the channel at one time.

Monitor event operation

Murphy's law says that if something can go wrong it will! Here are some things that can go wrong, and have gone wrong, in the event business:

★ All volunteer contact details and rosters are accidentally deleted two days before the event.
★ The sprinklers come on during an outdoor cocktail party.
★ The speaker is so short she cannot be seen behind the lectern.
★ There is no accessible toilet for someone in a wheelchair.
★ Fans find their way into the VIP area.
★ Beer runs out.
★ Children vomit in public.
★ The ATM is stolen.
★ The seat numbers are so faint they can't be read.
★ The prawns are left out overnight.
★ The toilets get blocked.

The event manager's role is to monitor event operations through observation and appropriate communication and control mechanisms and to identify and analyse operational problems, such as the need for additional services, as they arise and take prompt action to address them. As this chapter so clearly illustrates, careful contingency planning is absolutely essential. If all reasonable 'what if' questions have been answered, then there will be fewer problems to deal with.

Common deficiencies and discrepancies for business events may include:

★ incorrect room set-ups
★ incorrect staging
★ faulty or unavailable technical equipment
★ lack of equipment to manage displays and signage

★ shortage of food and beverage
★ insufficient or dirty toilets
★ inappropriate space in registration
areas.

Queues—the antithesis of quality customer service

Of these, the importance of sufficient food and beverage promptly served cannot be overstated. Nothing upsets a business client more than a long queue that leads to an almost empty banquet table.

Detailed run sheets are used for the timing of the actual event, irrespective of the type of event (sporting, concert, dinner, etc.). The actual implementation of these schedules is normally vested in one person, the producer/director/stage manager (depending on the type of event), who 'calls' the show using instructions to staff to ensure that all aspects are on cue. Under their direction may be performers, lighting, sound and vision. It is a very skilled and highly responsible role.

OVERSEE EVENT BREAKDOWN

When the event is over, the event manager has to ensure that event breakdown (bump-out) is completed according to contractual arrangements. This may involve supervising packing and removal of items (not before the audience leaves, please) and liaising with venue and site personnel to check the site before leaving, particularly making sure that everything has been turned off, lost property logged and a full inspection of any damage conducted. It may be necessary to debrief operational staff and contractors, with a view to future operational and service improvements. Finally, after a good night's sleep, accounts need to be checked against contractor agreements and any matters requiring post-event action assessed. Any legal issues are likely to emerge post-event, so careful analysis of duty logs and incident reports is recommended. For major events, the legal team is the last to leave the building as they have to deal with outstanding issues such as claims for compensation.

SUMMARY

This chapter has looked at operational management during the performance itself when a wide range of on-site services need to be provided to both the performers and the audience. This requires exceptionally careful planning and implementation, using checklists developed for previous similar events. Acute observation skills, quick thinking and problem solving are essential for the management team. Anxiety in the management team will transmit quickly through the whole production, damaging the ambience and inhibiting the enjoyment of the audience. Thus a cool head and gallons of charm are necessary when something goes wrong, as inevitably it will. However, careful planning for contingencies will ensure that most problems are likely to be minor. An upbeat management style contributes in a positive way to the event experience for all concerned.

Chapter review questions

1 Who do we refer to in this chapter when we talk about the needs of the performers?
2 Who do we refer to in this chapter when we talk about the needs of the audience?
3 Who are other potential customers?
4 Explain the following requirements of the performers using specific examples:
   (a) travel and accommodation   (c) catering
   (b) technical   (d) security.
5 Explain the following requirements of the event audience using specific examples:
   (a) booking   (d) problem solving
   (b) registration   (e) exiting the event.
   (c) ushering
6 What is a functional area? Give two specific examples.

Activities

1 Conduct your own survey titled 'The things I hate most about events' with 20 colleagues to see which aspects of customer service are most important.
2 Contrast these results with a survey about the things customers like most.

Case study

On-site services for awards night

You are running a graduation and awards night for a school. Using the concepts explained in this chapter, describe how you would provide event services for the following: (a) the graduates; (b) the award winners; (c) the parents and visitors; and (d) the school staff.

    You will need a layout diagram for the venue and a run sheet that includes tasks, timelines and responsibilities. The names and certificates will need to be checked against RSVPs more than once and a contingency put in place for a missing certificate.

    This should not be just like any other awards ceremony, so think about lighting, sound and other effects that could create the right atmosphere.

References

Matthews, D (2008), *Special event production: the process*, Butterworth-Heinemann, Oxford, UK.

Waters, K (2006), 'A practical step-by-step guide to organising successful events', *The British Journal of Administrative Management*, December, pp. 17–19.

CHAPTER 17

SAFETY AND SECURITY RISKS

Unit descriptor

This unit describes the performance outcomes, skills and knowledge required to identify hazards, assess the associated safety risks and take measures to eliminate or control and minimise the risk. It focuses on the processes necessary to control specific workplace safety risks. This risk management approach is central to compliance with OHS legislation, which imposes obligations on businesses (whether small, medium or large) in all Australian states and territories to manage the safety of their workers and anyone else in the workplace. In the service industries, the workplace includes any location where the business operates and 'others' includes customers.

Elements

- Identify hazards
- Assess the safety risk associated with a hazard
- Eliminate or control the risk
- Review the risk assessment process.

Critical aspects for assessment

- Project or work activities that show the candidate's ability to identify workplace hazards, and assess and control safety risks for a given service industry operation in line with regulatory requirements
- Ability to access and use appropriate template documents for hazard identification and risk assessment
- Ability to apply appropriate methods for hazard identification, and risk assessment and control
- Knowledge and understanding of the consultative approach to hazard identification, assessment of associated safety risks and implementation of controls
- Knowledge of OHS legislation requirements for hazard identification, and risk assessment and control
- Ability to implement and monitor OHS management practices within the context of an established system where policies and procedures already exist
- Knowledge of specific and relevant OHS legislative requirements
- Demonstration of skills in conducting risk assessments for different hazard scenarios.

THE WOMAN from Sydney's northern beaches was found clinically dead shortly after Limp Bizkit was forced to stop during its first song because of a crowd crush.

A witness said they carried the woman into a St John Ambulance area by the stage.

The witness said, 'It was like a war scene in the tent. There were 25 kids on their back. Drips were being connected to them. It looked like a mass resuscitation was going on. It was absolute pandemonium.

Source: Sun Herald, 28 January 2001

During this event, 12 people were taken to hospital and up to 600 treated, mainly for heat exhaustion. Prior to the event, the band had requested a T-style barricade through the centre of the audience to provide security access to the mosh pit, but the organisers had refused, saying that this measure was untested.

In the management of this type of event, careful analysis of crowd behaviour and the methods proposed for controlling crowds is required. Crowd management encompasses the steps taken to organise and manage crowds, while crowd control is the term used for dealing with crowds that are out of control. Security staff and security organisations play a major role in crowd control, particularly in events of this nature. First aid is also a necessity.

On the same day as the event described above, 220 000 people celebrated Australia Day with only a few minor incidents, none relating to crowd management. The behaviour of event visitors thus has an important role to play in the level of potential risk at a particular event and should form part of the analysis that begins with the risk management policy (discussed in Chapter 26) and follows through to the contingency plans for safety and security discussed in detail in Chapter 18.

Safety of the event audience, staff and subcontractors should be of paramount concern for every event manager, since all events carry safety risks which may result in anything from accidents to the evacuation of a venue.

Event worksites present numerous safety risks to workers

Another issue for consideration for most events is that of queuing. Queuing can be managed very well or very badly. The delays getting into events such as grand final matches are sometimes so long that the event manager has to direct staff to stop taking tickets and simply open the gates. Clearly this can lead to problems inside the venue if non-ticketed people manage to find their way in. On the other hand, if the grand final has commenced, and a goal scored while the spectators remain outside, there is little else that can be done. However, this would not be a viable option if there were numbers of people without tickets outside the venue and crowd crush was a possibility.

Orderly management of spectators leaving the venue is just as important, with clear directions and signage necessary to guide them to public transport. Sometimes revellers enjoy themselves so much at an event that they have to be marched out by security staff.

In this chapter we will deal with general security issues, occupational health and safety, hazard identification, assessment and control, and effective communication of incidents. Risks to audience and staff safety and the procedures used to manage these risks, including crowd control and emergency evacuation, will be covered in more detail in the next chapter.

SECURITY

Security is generally required for premises, equipment, cash and other valuables, but the predominant role of most event security staff is to ensure that the correct people have access to specific areas and to act responsibly in case of accident or emergency. Accreditation badges (generally a tag hanging around the neck, showing the areas to which staff, media and spectators have access) allow security staff to monitor access effectively. Security staff are also responsible for removing people who are behaving inappropriately, sometimes in cooperation with the police.

There are several considerations in the organisation of security for an event. First, it is necessary to calculate the number of trained staff required for the security role. Second, if the venue covers a large area, vehicles and equipment will most likely be required. (Four-wheeled buggies are usually used to deploy security and other staff to outlying areas.) And third, the level of threat needs to be determined to ascertain whether firearms are needed as would be the case when transporting money is involved.

In all cases, security staff should be appropriately licensed and the security company should carry the appropriate insurance.

POLICE

The police often provide some of the required support for security, generally at no cost to community events. However, with the growth of the event industry and the increased demands on police for spectator control, charges are now being levied by some police services for every officer attending a profit-making event. For major sporting events, about four police officers are provided free and the remainder are hired by the event organiser. The number of police required is negotiated by the police and the event manager, the number depending on any history of incidents and the availability of alcohol.

Mounted police are sometimes on duty at large street festivals and processions

SECURITY COMPANIES

Laws exist in relation to security companies and security personnel. The industry is well regulated and an event company must ensure that the appropriate licences are secured. A master licence is held by the security company, and there are various classes of licence for officers, depending on training and experience. All security officers are required to undergo a criminal record check.

The roles of security officers include:

★ acting as a bodyguard, bouncer or crowd controller
★ patrolling or protecting premises
★ installing and maintaining security equipment
★ providing advice on security equipment and procedures
★ training staff in security procedures.

Security companies must hold appropriate general liability insurance cover. General liability insurance cover is, in fact, a requirement of all contracts between event organisers and subcontractors. Subcontractors, including security companies, also need to cover their staff for work-related health and safety incidents.

OCCUPATIONAL HEALTH AND SAFETY

Occupational health and safety (OHS) legislation aims to prevent accidents and injury in the work environment and is of particular relevance to the event organiser. The duties of employers, people in control of workplaces and suppliers of equipment and services are all described in the relevant state or territory legislation. The following extract from *Making the workplace safe: a guide to the laws covering safety and health in Western Australian workplaces* (2002) gives a broad overview of these responsibilities:

Duties of employers (towards their employees)

General duties

Employers must, so far as is practicable, provide and maintain a working environment where their employees are not exposed to hazards.

General duties include:

• safe systems of work;
• information, instruction, training and supervision;
• consultation and co-operation;
• provision of personal protection;
• safe plant and substances. (Section 19)
• reporting of fatalities, injuries and disease. (Section 23J)

Duties of persons who have control of workplaces

General duties

People who have, to any extent, control of a workplace must ensure, so far as is practicable, that the workplace and all entrances and exits are safe so that people may enter, leave and use the workplace without exposure to hazards. (Section 22)

Duties of manufacturers, suppliers and others

General duties

Designers, manufacturers, importers and suppliers of plant for use at a workplace must comply, so far as is practicable, with the following:

- design and construct plant so that people who install, maintain or use it are not exposed to hazards;
- test and examine the plant before it is used;
- provide information; and
- ensure plant is installed or erected so it can be used safely.

Manufacturers, importers and suppliers of substances for use at workplaces must, so far as is practicable, provide information on the results of any testing and other safety and health information relating to these products.

Designers or builders of any building or structure for use at a workplace must ensure, so far as is practicable, that persons constructing, maintaining, repairing, servicing or using it are not exposed to hazards. (Section 23)

Source: Commission for Occupational Safety and Health. Reproduced courtesy of the Commission for Occupational Safety and Health, Western Australia, <www.worksafe.wa.gov.au>.

However, an independent panel has reviewed occupational health and safety laws in each state and territory and the Commonwealth and has advised on the optimal structure and content of a model work health and safety Act that can be adopted in all jurisdictions. It is expected that by 2011 a model *WHS Regulations* and a model *Codes of Practice* will be provided to jurisdictions to allow for a six-month education/transitional phase. Transitional and consequential legislation will be drafted by each jurisdictional Parliamentary Counsel. No doubt the acronym, OHS, will be replaced by WHS once the national legislation is fully implemented.

Returning to the current legislation, it requires that all employers must take out workers compensation insurance. This covers all staff for work-related accident or injury, including their medical expenses, payment for time off work and rehabilitation. Volunteers are not covered by this insurance because they are not, by definition, 'paid workers', but they are covered under general liability insurance. Workers compensation insurance generally covers the employee in transit to and from their workplace, provided that they travel directly to and from their place of work. The most important element of this legislation is the *responsibility placed on supervisors and managers* for ensuring that employees have a *safe place of work and safe systems of work*.

Policies and procedures in relation to safety are essential, and these procedures need to be part of all employee training. Standing on a wheeled trolley or on a box in high heels, as illustrated in the photos, are unnecessary OHS risks. Small ladders would solve these problems, but staff are often in a hurry and cannot go searching for safer options. It is also better to go the long way round than to take short-cuts on sites that provide limited access.

The Australian and New Zealand standard for risk management (AS/NZS 4360:2004 ISO 31000:2009 Risk Management) simplifies the process of systems development and is a useful resource for supervisors and managers in the event industry. Risk management

Provision of step ladders to these employees would have prevented this risky behaviour

plans for event safety can also be required from contract organisations working on site. This process is identical to that discussed and illustrated in Chapter 26 but is applied here at operational level. It bears repetition as the ability to plan all work using a risk management approach is one of the key attributes of professional employees in the event industry.

Risk management involves a five-step process:

1. Establish the context.
2. Identify the risk.
3. Analyse the risk.
4. Evaluate the risk.
5. Treat the risk.

This process allows the manager or supervisor to establish and prioritise the risks, to take steps to prevent problems occurring and to make contingency plans if problems do occur. The context for risk in this case is OHS in the event environment.

IDENTIFY HAZARDS AND RISKS

Identifying the risk or hazard involves ascertaining when and how a problem might occur. Hazards representing potential risk include:

* fire
* plant and equipment
* hazardous substances
* electrical equipment
* spills

* stacking of unbalanced heavy items
* moving vehicles
* hold-ups
* threats to visitor/spectator safety
* threats to staff safety.

Brainstorming by the event management team helps to identify potential risks and hazards.

People often confuse hazards, risks and outcomes. When documenting hazards, risks and outcomes in a register, the facilitator should attempt to define the three separately (WorkSafe Victoria, <www.worksafe.vic.gov.au>. 2006, p. 20):

Temporary structures and ladders present a safety risk

Hazards
★ Leaking LPG cylinder
★ Ignition source
★ Poor atmospheric circulation in confined area

Risks
★ Explosion
★ Crowd crush
★ Grandstand collapse

Outcomes
★ Burns
★ Smoke inhalation
★ Event reputation damaged
★ Financial loss on property claim/fine

ASSESS THE SAFETY RISK ASSOCIATED WITH HAZARDS

Once potential hazards have been identified, the risks associated with them and the consequences of these risks need to be evaluated. This process allows the management team to prioritise the issues for attention. It is a good idea to set up a committee to manage risk, safety and security issues, and to establish operational guidelines for hazards that pose risk. The following questions need to be asked:
★ What is the likelihood of this happening?
★ What are the potential consequences?
★ Who will be exposed to the risk/hazard?
★ What impact has this risk/hazard had in similar circumstances?
★ How will people react to this risk/hazard?

With hazards that might pose a risk to health and safety, the following three classifications are recommended:

★ **Class A hazard** This has the potential to cause death, serious injury, permanent disability or illness.

★ **Class B hazard** This has the potential to cause illness or time off work.

★ **Class C hazard** The resulting injury or illness will require first aid.

While this example refers mainly to incidents causing injury or illness, the potential consequences of fire, bomb threats, hold-ups, electrical failure, etc. can be evaluated in the same way. Tables 17.1 and 17.2 illustrate the use of measures of likelihood and consequence.

Having analysed the hazards, risks and consequences, the headings shown in Figure 17.1 can be used for the risk register.

Table 17.1 Qualitative measures of likelihood of an incident occurring

Level	Descriptor	Example
A	Almost certain	Is expected to occur in most circumstances
B	Likely	Will probably occur in most circumstances
C	Possible	Might occur at some time
D	Unlikely	Could occur at some time
E	Rare	May occur, but only in exceptional circumstances

Source: Based on Table 6.4, *Risk Management Guidelines: Companion to AS/NZS 4360:2004*.

Table 17.2 Qualitative measures of consequence or impact of an incident

Level	Descriptor	Example
1	Insignificant	No injuries, low financial loss
2	Minor	First aid treatment, on-site release, immediately contained, medium financial loss
3	Moderate	Medical treatment required, on-site release, contained with outside assistance, high financial loss
4	Major	Extensive injuries, loss of production capability, off-site release with no detrimental effects, major financial loss
5	Catastrophic	Death, toxic release off-site with detrimental effect, huge financial loss

Source: Based on Table 6.3, *Risk Management Guidelines: Companion to AS/NZS 4360:2004*.

FIGURE 17.1
Risk register

Risk no.	Hazard/ cause	Risk	Outcome	Current control	Adequacy of controls	Consequence	Likelihood	Risk ranking

ELIMINATE OR CONTROL THE RISK

Once the risks have been prioritised, the final step is to look at the most effective ways of managing them. Control measures include:

★ elimination plans (e.g. removal of dangerous children's equipment)

★ substitution plans (e.g. replacing slippery floor tiles in a wash-up area)

★ isolation plans (e.g. isolating dangerous or noisy equipment)

★ engineering controls (e.g. using fences to prevent access to waterways or busy roads)

★ administrative controls (e.g. warning signs, trained staff and well-developed procedures all help to minimise risk)

★ contingency plans (where risk cannot be completely avoided, contingency plans for, say, evacuation, need to be developed).

An example of a simple risk treatment plan is shown in Figure 17.2 on page 260. This plan shows the analysis of risk associated with an armed hold-up, the potential impacts, and the management strategies (or controls) and contingency plans put in place to control them. For a much more detailed analysis, visit the Australian Institute of Criminology website <www.aic.gov.au>.

Once controls have been proposed, you can revisit the risk matrix shown in Figure 17.3 and plot the intended changes to each risk based on the significance of the controls proposed, their reduction of likelihood and/or the reduction in consequence. For each of the combinations, there is an overall risk rating of low, moderate, high or extreme. As you can see from the matrix, two risks (6 and 9) have dropped from extreme to high as a result of improved control measures.

In the sections below we will discuss the safe handling of items and the safe performance of certain activities that otherwise may be a threat to the health and safety of workers in the event environment.

SAFE LIFTING TECHNIQUES

Lifting techniques are generally part of training for anyone involved in lifting, carrying or moving heavy objects, such as sporting equipment or display stands. A useful training aid for this purpose is illustrated in Table 17.3 on page 261.

The correct way to lift a heavy object is to squat close to the load, keeping your back straight. Do not stoop over the load to get a grip and pick it up. Test the weight of the object before attempting to lift it. Lift using your knees and legs (not your back) as leverage. Keep your back straight, not bent forwards or backwards. Do not twist or turn your body while carrying the object or putting it down.

The Commission for Occupational Safety and Health's Code of Practice for Manual Tasks provides the following guidance advice for implementing control measures in relation to manual handling which should include safe systems of work, work organisation and work practices.

Nature of risk	Likelihood of event A (almost certain) – E (rare)	Consequences of event 1 (negligible) – 5 (severe)	Preventative measures **NO SHORTCUTS, AVOID COMPLACENCY**	Contingency measures **MONEY AND PROPERTY NOT WORTH A LIFE, NO HEROICS**
Hold-up	D (unlikely)	4 (major)	• Develop procedures relating to cash handling • Assign responsibilities • Conduct training • Distribute standard hold-up form • Develop posters—'stay alert' • Report suspicious circumstances • Check doors and locks when opening • Lock rear entrances; monitor by CCTV • Monitor identification • Watch for bogus tradesmen • Remove excess cash and hold in strongroom • Check alarm systems weekly • Check CCTV monitors daily • Provide escorts for cash • Change routines and carriers • Alert employees to confidentiality requirements • Employ security when large amounts being handled	• Staff to stay calm • Staff to do as told by offender • Staff to stay out of danger • Observe bandits and vehicles • Avoid panic • Raise the alarm when safely possible • Phone police when safely possible • Provide name and address of premises to police • Provide offender's description to police • Provide vehicle description to police • Give travel directions to police • Close premises to public • Retain witnesses • Do not interfere with crime scene • Complete offender description form (all witnesses) • Avoid statements to media • Refer media to manager **Post hold-up** • Issue press release • Provide counselling for staff • Review procedures • Improve security for cash handling

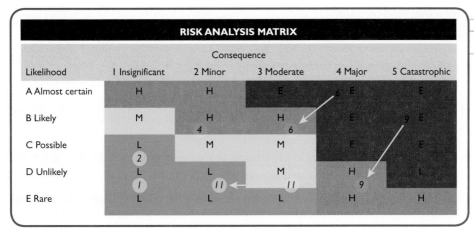

Source: WorkSafe Victoria, (2006) *Advice for managing major events safely*, p. 21. <www.worksafe.vic.gov.au>.

FIGURE 17.3
Risk analysis

Table 17.3 How to prevent injuries caused by lifting and moving heavy objects

Avoid	Common causes of injury	Common solutions
Lifting and moving	Lifting boxes from the floor	Do not store items on the floor.
	Carrying boxes or equipment	Use proper lifting techniques. Get help or use a lifting aid. Use a cart. Avoid over-reaching, twisting or lifting over head.
	Pushing carts	Maintain casters in clean, operating condition. Match the casters to the floor type.

Work area and layout

FOR example, select appropriate work areas to perform the manual task, increase the space designated for the task, alter the layout to improve work flow, redesign storage or alter the placement of items in the work area. These changes may reduce poor actions and postures such as twisting, reaching and stooping, and reduce the application of force required to complete the task.

Nature of items, equipment and tools

FOR example, alter the design or substitute the items, equipment and tools for those that allow the manual task to be performed safely and comfortably. The items, equipment and tools should be suited to the environment, reduce the effort required to perform the task, suit a range of users and be able to be used correctly with instruction.

Nature of load

FOR example, use a mechanical aid, handling device, or wheeled equipment, divide the load into smaller weights, change the size or shape of the load, apply handles to the load, make the load more stable or place labels on the load.

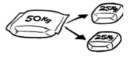

Working environment

FOR example, provide adequate space for handling objects, improve lighting, reduce the effects of adverse climatic conditions, improve floor surfaces, reduce noise and other distractions and provide adequate ventilation. Maintenance of the working environment and equipment is essential for safe performance of manual tasks. An adequate hazard reporting system and preventative maintenance program will help to ensure equipment and the working environment are kept safe.

Source: Commission for Occupational Safety and Health, Western Australia, (2010), *Code of Practice for Manual Tasks,*
<www.worksafe.wa.gov.au>.

This code of practice covers the full scope of risk management in relation to manual handling. It goes on to suggest that consideration should be given to safe duration and frequency of manual handling as well as safe work rates and demands. A definitive absolute safe lifting weight is not possible to determine and risk assessment needs to take into account factors such as load characteristics, the work environment and human characteristics.

SAFE USE OF ELECTRICAL EQUIPMENT

Electrical equipment is a significant hazard in the event environment, particularly in wet weather. All safety steps must be taken to prevent accidents involving electrical equipment, including routine tagging, lockout and inspection of equipment. Many venues are extremely rigorous in their demands for documentation demonstrating correct licensing and inspection. Electrical safety should be a priority for all outdoor event sites.

What is an RCD?

An RCD is a residual current device. RCDs (or safety switches) provide added protection when using electrical equipment. They cut the power supply to the electrical appliance if a current leakage fault is recognised (a current imbalance between active and neutral). They are designed to help prevent electrocution. RCDs should not be confused with lower cost circuit breakers, which cut power supply when the current draw exceeds a specified level (or in abnormal power conditions).

What types of RCDs are there?

There are hardwired RCDs such as those installed in homes. Householders also call them a 'trip switch' as they trip when safety is compromised. Portable RCDs, on the other hand, are plugged into power outlets and appliances are then plugged into the RCDs. Where hardwired protection is not available portable RCDs must be used with hand-held appliances. They should also be used where electrical appliances are in close proximity to water. This can occur at outdoor events particularly when it is raining. One can purchase portable power outlets with built-in residual current and overload protection such as the one illustrated.

What is AS/NZ 3760: 2003 'testing and tagging' standard?

This is a standard for safety inspection and testing of electrical equipment. It applies also to cord extension sets, portable electrical outlet devices, portable residual current devices and portable isolation transformers.

As you might recall from discussion about risk management, if elimination of the hazard is not possible, other controls should be implemented to reduce potential risks. These controls may include the use of residual current devices (RCDs) which need regular monitoring and testing.

SAFE USE OF MACHINERY

Regulations for safeguarding machinery in the workplace are provided in the Australian Standard, AS 4024.1-1996 Safeguarding of Machinery—General Principles.

Provision of temporary electrical systems requires monitoring by licensed tradespeople

This Standard identifies the hazards and risks arising from the use of industrial machinery and describes methods for the elimination or minimisation of them, as well as for the safeguarding of machinery and the use of safe work practices. It also describes and illustrates a number of safety principles and provides guidelines by which it is possible to assess which measure or method it is practicable to adopt in particular circumstances.

This Standard is intended for those who design, manufacture, supply, install, use, maintain or modify machinery, machinery guarding or safety devices, and identifies the existence of Standards for a number of particular classes of machine. It is also designed to be used by those concerned with information, instruction and training in safe work practices.

SAFE HANDLING OF HAZARDOUS SUBSTANCES

Because different chemicals have different safe use requirements, it is important for staff to know as much about hazardous substances used in the workplace as possible. Material Safety Data Sheets should be used to provide the following advice on these substances to staff members:

These cylinders contain a hazardous substance, requiring clear instructions for safe handling and storage

★ ingredients of a product
★ health effects and first aid instructions
★ precautions for use
★ safe handling and storage information
★ emergency procedures.

SAFETY SIGNS

Safety signs are particularly important in the event workplace since staff are generally only at the venue for a very short period, which does not allow much time for reinforcement of safety issues. However, these should be stressed during briefing sessions. Posters and safety signs, such as those reproduced below, can be used to reinforce key messages, helping to prevent many accidents.

FIRST AID

In most cases, first aid is provided by organisations such as St John Ambulance, although venue and event staff should also be trained in first aid procedures. Some of these procedures will be specific to the event in question. For example, at road races, common first aid emergencies that occur include exhaustion, collapse, dehydration, road burns, and bone and muscle injuries, and procedures should be in place for dealing with them. In addition, participants in races such as these sometimes do not wish to accept help and staff would need to be trained in the correct procedure for dealing with such an occurrence.

In more extreme circumstances, Tarlow (2002, p. 30) suggests the following four steps, known as APMC, as standard for serious and life-threatening emergency:

★ Administer triage for/to the injured individuals.
★ Plan the next steps (rescue).
★ Manage the scene.
★ Control (avert additional injuries or loss of life).

Risk management is an ongoing process, involving constant evaluation of the impact of change and the risk factors associated with that change. Analysis and consultation are essential when change in the workplace occurs, as is health and safety training relevant to any change. Most major events will not allow work to commence before safety and evacuation training has been undertaken.

HEALTH AND SAFETY TRAINING

All induction and training programs should include a component on health, safety and security, with a particular emphasis on duty of care. The topics that should be covered in training sessions include:

★ review of the risks to health and safety
★ magnitude of actual and potential problems
★ review of issues that could arise, such as public liability actions
★ specific job and individual risk factors
★ control strategies
★ reasons for procedures, rules and regulations
★ outline of the most prevalent areas of risk (e.g. slips and falls, manual handling)
★ responsibilities of all parties.

Every staff meeting should have health and safety on the agenda so that employees are able to identify risks and consult on procedures and systems. Both awareness and action are necessary, and when serious risks are identified, they should be referred to the organisation's occupational health and safety committee. The role of this committee is to:

★ help to resolve any health and safety issues
★ carry out regular safety inspections
★ develop a system to record accidents and incidents
★ make recommendations to management about improving health and safety
★ access any information about risks to health and safety from any equipment or substance or occupational disease.

All accidents and incidents need to be reported, even in cases where medical attention is not required.

INCIDENT REPORTING

For any event there are standard reporting relationships on all operational issues. On the whole, these reporting relationships concur with the organisation chart. However, there are many instances where communication is less formal and less structured, and this is the case in the event working environment where 'mayhem' or 'controlled chaos' may best describe it.

Despite some tolerance of rather haphazard communication just before and during the event, **any communication relating to an incident or emergency needs to be very clear**. (An example of an incident report card is illustrated in Figure 17.4 on page 266.) Reporting of an incident must follow a short and specific chain of command. Workers need to know what constitutes an incident and what constitutes an emergency. The chain of command, or organisation chart, for an emergency is seldom the same as the organisation chart for the event as a whole. Emergency reporting tends to go through very few levels, and all staff must be trained in emergency reporting. Many stakeholders may be involved—general staff, security staff, first aid personnel, police, emergency services—but absolute clarity is needed as to who makes key decisions and how they are to be contacted. These lines of reporting and responsibility will be reviewed in the next chapter.

INCIDENT REPORT CARD

Date   Time

Your name   Your position   Functional area/department

Names of person/s involved in the incident

Contact details of person/s involved in the incident

Name and contact details of witness/es if any

INCIDENT DETAILS

Time of incident

Location of incident

Cause of incident

Consequences of incident

Can any action be taken to prevent reoccurrence?

Date and time received and logged

Outstanding actions

Communication methods

Most event teams use radios as they are the most effective tool for maintaining communication. Different channels are used for different purposes, and it is essential that the correct radio procedures be followed. In Figure 17.5, radio links to the Event Operations Centre are illustrated, with Control serving as the link to the decision-makers. For example, in response to a request to remove a hazard, Control would ensure that the Site team responded to the call. If a spill were reported, Control would report to Cleaning, requesting that the spill be cleaned up. The Operations Centre also has links to emergency services which can be called if required.

At some events, mobile telephones are used, but the drawback of this method of communication is that the information transmitted can be overheard. Networks can also become overloaded if spectators are using their mobile phones, particularly during intermission and at the end of a match or concert.

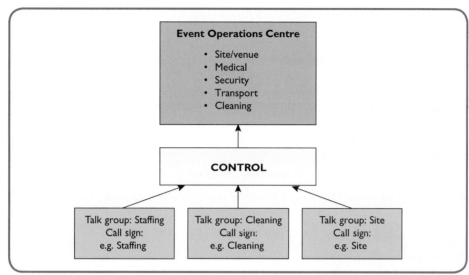

Event Operations Centre

- Site/venue
- Medical
- Security
- Transport
- Cleaning

CONTROL

Talk group: Staffing	Talk group: Cleaning	Talk group: Site
Call sign:	Call sign:	Call sign:
e.g. Staffing	e.g. Cleaning	e.g. Site

FIGURE 17.5
Channels of communication for radio incident reporting

Meetings between event staff, including security staff and emergency services, are necessary to plan and monitor security and safety, as difficulties can occur if the communications technology of the various services is not compatible. It is crucial that this issue be anticipated and that contingency plans be put in place to deal effectively with any communication problems.

A railway security officer in radio contact with Operations

SAFETY AT OUTDOOR EVENTS

The safety checklist for dance parties in Figure 17.6 on page 268 can be modified for any event, large or small. When staging an event, organisers need to consider all of the points outlined in order to demonstrate their duty of care to employees, contractors and spectators/audience, as well as additional considerations relevant to the particular event.

This guide also stresses that a person must be nominated as the 'event manager' and must remain at the event and be contactable at all times by emergency services and all individuals and organisations providing a service or working at the event.

An area must be designated as the event management centre or operations centre and must be staffed for the duration of the event. The event management centre must be able to communicate with the event manager, emergency services and crowd control supervisors at all times during the course of the event.

FIGURE 17.6

Checklist for planning and management of a dance party

- Pre-event site assessment for indoor and outdoor events
- Special requirements of outdoor venues
- Uninhibited access for emergency services
- Approvals for the use of private and state-owned land
- Compulsory notification of emergency services and hospitals
- Approvals and permits required and notification times
- Briefing and debriefing of staff
- Security and crowd control; regular patrolling in areas of high risk
- The need to have conditions of entry and a pass-out policy
- Communication systems for staff, management and partygoers
- Event management centre and contacts
- Public liability insurance
- Rubbish collection during the event
- Cleaning up after the event

Source: Code of practice for running safer dance parties (2004), Victorian Government Department of Human Services, Drugs Policy and Services Branch, Melbourne, <www.health.vic.gov.au/drugservices/downloads/dance.pdf>.
© Copyright State of Victoria 2004.

SUMMARY

The health, safety and security of staff and the event audience are very important concerns of the event management team. In this chapter we have focused on risk management, which involves identifying potential hazards, analysing and evaluating the risk of these hazards, eliminating or controlling the risk, and developing contingency plans for dealing with the risk. We have also discussed preventative measures such as the safe handling of heavy objects and hazardous substances and the safe use of electrical equipment and machinery. Not only must people be protected but also assets, and security personnel and the police are there to assist the event manager in managing these risks. Most importantly, an effective system of communication for reporting incidents helps to prevent their escalation and assists staff in dealing promptly with emergencies.

Chapter review questions

1 What are the essential duties of employers in relation to OHS?
2 What are the essential duties of employees in relation to OHS?
3 What are the steps involved in risk management?
4 Explain the difference between a hazard analysis form and an incident report form.

Activity

Identify some of the security issues at the following events and prepare plans to prevent or deal with these issues:

(a) Dance party with a mosh pit

(b) Street festival

(c) Private party for a celebrity

(d) Product launch

(e) Road race.

Case study

Occupational health and safety

The Gold Mining Company is a nightclub venue that is popular during the months of May, June and July for its Friday night dance events. The staff working at this venue are all casuals and turnover is high. During a conversation, two of the staff, Jason and Malik, find out that they have both been mugged on their way home from work in the early hours of the morning, but on different Friday nights. In both cases, the perpetrators waited in a nearby alley and threatened them with knives. Jason lost his wallet and $400 and Malik broke his ankle when trying to run away. Candice, another employee, has been harassed by patrons and was once burned deliberately with a cigarette by a particularly drunk and obnoxious customer. Management gave her some cash to get medical attention.

Task

Discuss the occupational health and safety issues in relation to the staff concerned. What were the responsibilities of management in each of these cases? Did management fulfil its OHS duty of care in relation to Candice? Explain your answer.

References

Participate in OHS processes (2010), Pearson Scope, Frenchs Forest, NSW.

Planning occupational health and safety (2009), 8th edn, CCH Australia, North Ryde, NSW.

Tarlow, P (2002), *Event risk management and safety*, John Wiley & Sons, Milton, Qld.

WorkSafe Victoria (2006), *Advice for managing major events safely*, <www.worksafe.vic.gov.au/wps/wcm/connect/b1acf6004071f4359a3bdee1fb554c40/major_events_organisers_advice.pdf?MOD=AJPERES>, accessed 10 May 2010.

CHAPTER 18

CROWD CONTROL

Unit descriptor

This unit describes the performance outcomes, skills and knowledge required to develop plans and procedures for the admittance, seating and dispersal of crowds. It includes procedures for emergency situations. Development of crowd management procedures in this unit requires the application of significant critical thinking, planning and organisational skills, combined with a detailed knowledge of risk management issues, crowd control techniques and relevant emergency procedures. Those with managerial responsibility undertake this role. The unit is generalist in nature and does not cover the specialised operational crowd management skills required by police or other security experts.

Elements

- Develop crowd management plans
- Analyse risks associated with large crowds
- Establish operational crowd management procedures
- Establish emergency crowd control procedures
- Evaluate crowd control plans and procedures.

Critical aspects for assessment

- Detailed knowledge of the factors influencing crowd management planning and operations
- Ability to analyse crowd risks and develop plans and procedures for crowd management
- Ability to determine and organise appropriate resources to address emergency situations
- Demonstration of skills through development of crowd management plans and procedures for event or workplace operation.

THE RUNNING OF THE BULLS is a well-known tourist attraction in Pamplona, Spain. People come from all over the world to test their bravery and enjoy non-stop street parties at this festival made famous by Ernest Hemingway's novel, *The sun also rises*. Last year, four people were seriously injured. Fourteen people have died at the Fiesta of San Fermin since record-keeping began in 1924. The last fatal goring was in 1995. The victim was Matthew Tassio, a 22-year-old American. In 2003, Pamplona native Fermin Etxeberri, 63, was trampled by a bull and died after spending months in a coma.

As this article illustrates, contingency plans need to be in place in case of emergencies at an event and, clearly, easy access for emergency services is one of the first aspects that needs to be considered. Crowd management and evacuation are others. In this chapter we will deal with all three topics.

The initial task of the event manager is to develop a crowd management plan.

DEVELOP CROWD MANAGEMENT PLANS

Following are the key things to consider when developing a crowd management plan:
★ number of people at the venue (event audience, staff and contractors)
★ likely behaviour of spectators (especially for events with a history of crowd behaviour problems)
★ timing of the event, including session times and peak periods
★ layout of the venue and/or other facilities
★ security services to be provided or contracted
★ legal requirements and general guidelines.

The last of these requires adherence to occupational health and safety legislation and the laws relating to fire egress (exits), as well as to a number of guidelines provided by Standards Australia, if applicable to the event, such as:

★ *AS 2187.4 Pyrotechnics—Outdoors*, which specifies the precautions to be carried out in storage, handling and use of pyrotechnics for outdoor displays.
★ *AS 2560.2.3 Lighting for Outdoor Football*, dealing with the level of lighting required for training, competition and spectator viewing for all football codes.

This sports stadium is not designed for concerts

★ *AS 1680 Interior Lighting—Safe Movement*, which sets out the minimum requirements for electric lighting systems within publicly accessible areas of buildings in order to provide visual conditions that facilitate the safe movement of people in the normal use of the buildings.

★ *AS/NZS 2293.3 Emergency Evacuation Lighting for Buildings*, providing building, maintenance and inspection guidelines for emergency evacuation lighting.

All of the above Standards, and many more that are relevant to building permanent and temporary structures, are available on the website listed in Appendix E.

There are also many considerations in relation to transport to the event site, parking and access to the venue. An outstanding website, TravelSmart, also listed in Appendix E, provides extensive guidelines in this regard and also lists the relevant legislative guidelines and policies for the states and territories. Special events involving street closures require careful planning and negotiation with the authorities (such as the Roads and Traffic Authority, local council and the police) many months before the event takes place. Events are classified as follows:

★ *Class 1 Event*—Impacts major traffic and transport systems, disrupts the non-event community over a wide area

★ *Class 2 Event*—Impacts local traffic and transport systems, disrupts the community in the area around the event

★ *Class 3 Event*—Does not impact local or major traffic systems, disrupts immediate area only

★ *Class 4 Event*—Small street event requires police consent only.

Consideration of event transport and access should cover:

★ pedestrian facilities

★ cyclist facilities

★ public transport facilities

★ access for people with mobility or visual impairments

★ car parking.

In relation to pedestrian facilities, for example, TravelSmart suggests asking the following questions:

1 Have you marked pedestrian routes on your access map?

2 Have you used walk times, rather than distances? Times are more effective in journey planning.

3 Are pedestrian routes good quality?

4 Are there any 'missing links', such as missing pedestrian crossings at busy roads?

5 Have you organised queuing facilities at stations, or other places where pedestrians may have to wait?

6 Could you arrange for staff to entertain and inform waiting pedestrians?

7 Could you provide televisions at queue points to inform and keep people relaxed? You may be able to subsidise these through advertising or sponsorship.

8 Do you have staff on hand to answer questions about public transport services and timetables? You could give staff an information sheet to help them answer questions.

9 Are queuing areas covered from the sun and rain?

10 Have you told people attending the event about the safest pedestrian routes?

11 Do you need to contact police about organising temporary crossing facilities?

Spectators at car festivals need to be monitored on the roads as they leave

12 Could you contact the state road authority to discuss temporarily making pedestrian crossing times longer at key intersections?

13 Do you need to provide mats or floor covers for outside areas?

14 Are pedestrian routes well lit if people will be walking to or from your event in the dark?

Source: TravelSmart Special Events Planning Resource Kit; <www.travelsmart.gov.au/events/eleven.html > © TravelSmart Australia is a joint initiative of Australian, State and Territory Governments

The crowd management plan covers readily available information, such as the dimensions of the venue or site, but it also goes further to encompass the probable number of spectators at particular times of the event and their flow through the site. Clearly the peaks are the most problematic from a crowd management perspective and the plan needs to address this and other challenges by carrying out the following tasks:

★ Estimate the level of attendance for specific days and times.

★ Estimate the number of people using public corridors, specific entrances, specific aisles and seating at particular times.

★ Estimate the number of ushers and service and security personnel needed for spectator management.

★ Establish the requirements for crowd control measures, such as barriers.

★ Identify the areas that need to remain restricted.

★ Develop accreditation plans for restricted access by specific staff.

★ Identify particular hazards (e.g. scaffolding, temporary structures).

★ Identify routes by which emergency services personnel will enter and leave the site.

★ Establish the means of communication for all staff working on the site.

★ Establish a chain of command for incident reporting.

★ Check safety equipment (e.g. the number of fire extinguishers and also that inspections have been carried out according to legal requirements).

★ Identify the safety needs of specific groups of people, such as people with disabilities, children and players/performers.

★ Identify first aid requirements and provision.

★ Develop an emergency response plan (ERP).

★ Develop an evacuation plan and initiate training and drills for the staff concerned.

As we know, there are many different types of event venue, each having specific features and some being safer than others. They range from outdoor environments, such as streets and parks, to aquatic centres, indoor facilities and purpose-built venues. The last of these is generally the safest since crowd management and evacuation would generally have been considered at the time these structures were built and rehearsed again and again by the venue team. However, a crowd management and evacuation plan would still need to be developed for each event held at the venue, as factors such as spectator numbers and movement would differ

Figure 18.1 summarises the broad considerations when developing a crowd management plan.

FIGURE 18.1
Tasks involved
in crowd
management
plan
development

- Establish and document maximum limits for admission based on analysis of risks and the venue.
- Estimate expected crowd numbers based on historical data and current trends or attendance information.
- Organise or confirm completion of any necessary work to ensure compliance with legal constraints and requirements.
- Determine and document human resource requirements for crowd management.
- Develop a plan that minimises identified risks associated with the venue and complies with legal constraints and requirements.
- Consult with and gain input from relevant stakeholders on crowd management approaches.
- Develop evaluation criteria for the crowd management plan in consultation with stakeholders.

ANALYSE RISKS ASSOCIATED WITH LARGE CROWDS

Particular risks associated with large crowds include alcohol consumption and drug use, alcohol being the most common and often the most serious as it can result in aggressive behaviour, which can exacerbate the difficulties in managing crowds effectively. Drug use is more likely to be an issue at music festivals. The age and sex of the audience will provide some indication of the likelihood of these issues emerging.

Crowd psychology and crowd frustration are two further issues that need to be subjected to risk analysis as they can sometimes lead to ugly scenes at sporting events or bands inciting their audiences into unacceptable behaviour.

From the above, it can be seen that a risk management plan specifically for managing large crowds is essential. This follows the approach covered in Chapter 17 and involves first identifying the risks and then analysing and evaluating the risks.

The major incidents that need to be considered in relation to crowd management and evacuation (the context) include:

★ fire, smoke

★ bomb and terrorist threats, threats to VIPs
★ flood, earthquake or other natural disasters
★ heat
★ failure of air-conditioning or lighting
★ gas leaks or biological hazards
★ crowd crush, overcrowding, congestion
★ riots, protests
★ vehicle accidents
★ collapsing fences and other structures.

Alcohol abuse is a common problem at cricket matches due to the length of matches

Once the risks have been identified, the circumstances that may lead to negative or destructive behaviour in these contexts need to be analysed and the likelihood of their occurrence must be evaluated. For each of the above risks, the response of the public to the emergency should also be evaluated so that the emergency team has procedures in place for preventing panic. Reassuring messages on the public address system is one way of reducing panic and ensuring orderly evacuation.

ESTABLISH OPERATIONAL CROWD MANAGEMENT PROCEDURES

The risks then need to be prioritised and plans put in place to avoid them (known as control measures) or to deal with them should they occur (known as contingency measures). An example of a preventive measure for reducing congestion at turnstiles would be to employ staff to assist spectators and to monitor the area. However, impatient crowds might simply jump over the turnstiles or knock them down, so there would need to be a contingency plan in place for dealing with this situation. Property damage by spectators would also need to be covered and procedures put in place for ejecting the offenders. At worst, the police may charge them. (Streakers who disrupt play during sports matches spring to mind in this instance.) The more serious risk, however, are non-ticketed spectators who gain illegal entry.

The following strategies (adapted from the Crowdsafe website listed in Appendix E) may help to prevent deaths and injuries suffered by fans at rock concerts and other large events:

The density of this audience illustrates the importance of appropriate crowd control measures

★ Review the behaviour of crowds attending similar past events.
★ Review crowd responses to specific bands and performers at past rock concerts.

★ Conduct an evaluation of all structures available for mosh pit management.
★ Obtain engineering and specialist advice.
★ Isolate the mosh pit from the general audience.
★ Limit mosh pit capacity and density.
★ Provide easy exits from the mosh pit area.
★ Ban alcohol and cigarettes from the mosh pit.
★ Station special first aid assistance near the mosh pit.
★ Ban stage diving, body surfing/swimming.
★ Provide specially trained private security and 'peer security'.
★ Provide special ventilation and drinking fountains for moshers.
★ Pad the floor and all hard surfaces, including barriers and railings.
★ Ban certain types of clothes and accessories worn by moshers in the pit.
★ Introduce mosh pit safety announcements in advance of the show and during shows.
★ Seek assistance from the performers in managing or preventing moshing.

In particular, consideration should be given to entrance management, barrier controls and exit management. Throughput capacities need to be calculated and crowd flows planned.

Another important consideration is first aid. The organisers of any event that involves people have a duty, both legally and morally, to provide a healthy and safe environment for participants and spectators, including a range of services to assist people who get into trouble or need help of some sort. In Australia, the Federal Government's Emergency Management Agency has produced an extensive manual called *Safe and healthy mass gatherings*, which is available from the website for Emergency Management in Australia (see Appendix E) and is also provided on the companion website to this text. This document lays down basic requirements for organisers to follow, in addition to specific occupational health and safety or local government planning legislative requirements. It requires organisers to have sufficient first aid facilities to cater for the expected size and nature of the event to meet their common and statutory legal obligations:

> Everyone who organises a public event which will be attended by a reasonable number of people and where there is any risk to health must have first aid or health services available to participants and spectators.

A number of services exist to cater for different levels of coverage. As part of the risk management process, you need to consider which type of service will meet your needs. For example, two volunteer first aid personnel would be nowhere near sufficient to cover a professional motor sports event. Equally, a team of six paid doctors and paramedics would definitely be overkill for a school sports carnival (and would probably never fit in such an event's budget).

The level of service available at an event is influenced by the number of first aid personnel on site and their qualifications. Whether they are paid or volunteer staff will also have an impact on service, as generally the more highly trained specialists are those working in a paid capacity.

UniMed, a first aid organisation supporting a range of major events, can assist with risk management planning, which is particularly useful for high-risk events such as those where alcohol consumption and drug use are expected and sporting events at which spectators sometimes behave inappropriately.

Responsible service of alcohol

A sophisticated operation would be required, say, for a rock concert attended by 35 000 people. In this case, roving staff would be needed as observers of risk areas such as front of stage or the mosh pit. These people would need to have reliable communication with the UniMed team, some of whom would also be present in spectator areas.

In the first aid zone, a triage area would be needed for quick initial diagnosis, enabling staff to prioritise treatments. The extent of the first aid facility and the supplies and treatment available differ markedly from one major event to another. After the event, reports of the medical incidents that occurred and the treatments given provide valuable information for future risk management planning.

UNIMED'S FIRST AID SERVICES

UNIMED provides services based on a risk management model. This allows us to work with the client to determine the best possible resourcing to provide the best services. UniMed references a range of national and international service standards. When you choose UniMed as your first aid provider, you get highly trained volunteer first responders and medical professionals equipped with the best equipment.

Our volunteers provide high quality services which will:

- ensure patrons receive prompt, effective care
- help organisers identify and control risks to the health and safety of patrons and staff
- reduce discomfort and inconvenience to patrons
- help ensure legal compliance with health and safety legislation and standards
- help organisers present the appearance of a safe environment for patrons
- reduce the risk of public liability litigation against event organisers.

Our volunteers are trained to some of the highest standards in Australia. All volunteers are provided with induction training as a standard component of their training and are required to undertake comprehensive continuing education. Event volunteers are trained to national standards from the Health Training Package. UniMed has a comprehensive clinical support and clinical quality assurance program.

After UniMed has provided services for your event, you will receive a comprehensive report with first aid statistics for your event and feedback from staff on how to make it even safer next time.

If you are interested in UniMed providing services for your event, please contact us on 02 4751 4200 or email us at info@unimed.org.au

Source: Reproduced with permission of UniMed, <www.unimed.org.au>.

ESTABLISH EMERGENCY CROWD CONTROL PROCEDURES

As mentioned above, Emergency Management in Australia has very useful guidelines for planning safe and healthy mass gatherings. This document also covers the psychology of crowds and is essential for anyone planning an event of this magnitude. Figure 18.2 outlines Emergency Management in Australia's recommendations for what needs to be addressed in an emergency response plan, from which procedures can be developed.

FIGURE 18.2
Outline of an emergency response plan

Different kinds of events may attract certain types of spectators who require special consideration, as follows:

- Rock concerts may have a higher incidence of problems with drug and alcohol abuse, underage drinking and possession of weapons.
- Religious/'faith healing' events may attract a significant number of ill and infirm people, which may increase the need for on-site medical care.
- Events for senior citizens may also require higher levels of health services.
- Certain sports events may attract over-reactive and violent supporters.
- Cultural events may require special arrangements, including the provision of interpreter services, special food services and multilingual signposting, brochures and announcements.

All public events should have a formal, written emergency response plan which should be developed in consultation with the appropriate authorities. The plan should:

- detail arrangements for on-site emergencies not requiring outside help
- specify arrangements to request further police and other emergency services assistance
- specify arrangements to hand over control to police and emergency services as required
- identify personnel who can authorise evacuation
- identify how the event will be interrupted
- provide a grid plan of the venue and all services
- identify access and evacuation routes
- identify evacuation areas for performers, employees and the audience
- establish an incident control centre, which should have back-up power and lighting
- provide details of coded messages to alert and stand down emergency service and security personnel
- identify the role event staff will take in supporting civilian services
- identify meeting points for emergency services
- identify triage and ambulance loading areas
- include details of hospitals prepared for a major incident
- identify access and egress routes and the security of these routes
- provide details of a temporary mortuary facility.

Note: In any major incident, for the purposes of the law, the venue is considered a crime scene and thus under total control of the police.

Emergency planning is Standards based. The following is a summary of the guidelines that are provided in AS3745 Emergency Control Organization and Procedures for Buildings, Structures and Workplaces (Standards Australia).

A committee called the Emergency Planning Committee (EPC) should be convened to:

★ establish the emergency response plan (ERP)

★ ensure that appropriate people are assigned to specific roles, such as Chief Warden, and that their responsibilities in the Emergency Control Organisation (ECO) are clarified

★ arrange training for all members of the ECO team

★ arrange for evacuation drills

★ review procedures

★ ensure that ECO staff are indemnified against civil liability in situations where they act in good faith in the course of their emergency control duties.

When developing the emergency response plan, specialist advice is recommended. Most security organisations offer this type of consultancy support. When developing the emergency procedures, the following should be taken into account:

★ peak numbers of people in the venue

★ assembly and evacuation routes, and signage

★ people with disabilities

★ lifts and escalators (assume that these are not used, except by fire authorities)

★ people check (making sure everyone has left)

★ marshalling points (especially for very large venues)

★ safeguarding of cash and valuables

★ communication systems (emergency warning and emergency intercom system—AS2220.1 and AS2220.2) as well as public address systems

★ emergency equipment

★ control and coordination point/s (location/s) for emergency response by the Chief Warden and liaison with emergency services

★ coordination with other agencies such as council and emergency services.

The Emergency Control Organisation is the team responsible for responding to the emergency. This team includes the following personnel:

★ Chief Warden   ★ Floor/Area Wardens

★ Deputy Chief Warden   ★ Wardens.

★ Communications Officer

During an emergency, instructions given by ECO wardens should override those given by any other person in the organisation structure.

The structure of the ECO and identifying features, is illustrated in Figure 18.3 on page 280.

Selection and training of emergency personnel should follow the comprehensive guidelines provided in the relevant Australian Standards document. It is essential that you read the full text of the Standards as this chapter provides only an overview of the Standards, roles and procedures.

In general terms, the people selected for roles in the ECO should be in attendance during the hours of operation, should show leadership qualities and sound judgement under pressure, and should be able to communicate clearly. The first of these attributes is the most problematic in the event business. For leased premises, the venue team is generally limited in number and few work for the full duration of an event. The question of availability during an event, especially one with multiple sessions, is a key consideration for the committee. There is no point in having a well-trained ECO that is not in attendance!

Following are the chief roles of each person in the ECO team.

Chief Warden

The duties of the Chief Warden include ascertaining the nature and location of the emergency and determining the appropriate action, ensuring that emergency services and floor wardens are advised, initiating evacuation, and briefing emergency personnel on their arrival.

Deputy Chief Warden

The Deputy will take on the roles of the Chief Warden if unavailable or assist as required.

Communications Officer

The duties of the Communications Officer include ascertaining the nature and location of the emergency, confirming that the appropriate emergency services have been notified, and notifying, transmitting and recording instructions and progress.

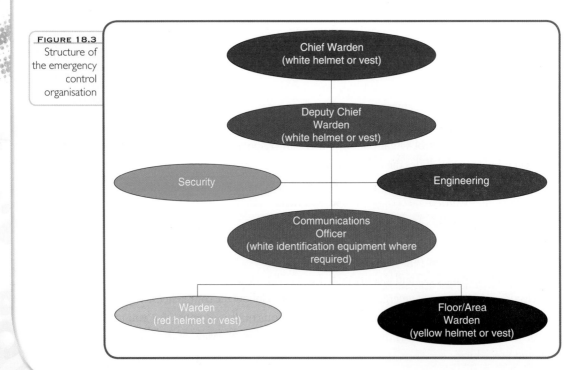

FIGURE 18.3
Structure of the emergency control organisation

Floor/Area Wardens

Implementing the emergency procedures for their area, checking the floor/area, and coordinating and communicating with the Chief Warden are all roles of Floor/Area Wardens.

Wardens

Checking, searching, giving instructions during an evacuation and reporting to the Floor/Area Warden are the tasks undertaken by the Wardens.

For all officers in the ECO, ensuring that emergency services have been notified is part of the job.

Full details of the roles and tasks of these officers are available on the Standards Australia website (see Appendix E), as well as a number of videos on this type of planning and training. Specialist assistance in this area is recommended, as well as the use of emergency warning and intercommunication systems (EWIS).

IMPLEMENT EMERGENCY PROCEDURES

In order to effectively implement emergency procedures, the following steps should be taken:

★ Review implementation issues and integrate them with all other event operational plans.
★ Ensure broad awareness of the procedures through wide dissemination of information and consultation with all concerned.
★ Use signage and well-designed communication materials in a simple format to provide information.
★ Train all staff.
★ Test the procedures by conducting evacuation exercises.
★ Review procedures to check effectiveness.

Emergency procedures for various threats are outlined below.

FIRE PROCEDURES

There are four major steps that ideally should be initiated concurrently in the case of fire:

1 Ensure the safety of everyone within the vicinity of the fire.
2 Call the fire brigade in any circumstance in which there is suspicion of fire.
3 Conduct evacuation.
4 Fight the fire with appropriate equipment (e.g. fire extinguishers) or retreat and close all doors.

Note that there is no need for anyone to give permission for a call to the fire brigade. This call can be initiated by anyone.

EVACUATION PROCEDURES

The evacuation procedure follows the same process for most venues: the Chief Warden uses the tone BEEP … BEEP … BEEP for alert and WHOOP … WHOOP … WHOOP for evacuation on the public address system.

The warden intercommunication phone (WIP) is used to advise the Chief Warden of danger in specific areas. All staff should be trained in their specific roles so that they are prepared for this situation.

In the event of an evacuation it is important for staff to:

★ remain calm
★ be observant
★ listen to and follow instructions
★ provide information and instructions to staff and spectators when advised to do so
★ maintain radio protocol (do not block channels)
★ follow all safety precautions (such as not using lifts in case of fire).

The emergency response plan is reliant on the warden system and the chain of command. Early warning means fast intervention.

BOMB THREAT PROCEDURES

As with fire and evacuation procedures, there is a recommended procedure for dealing with bomb threats. Details are available from the Australian Bomb Data Centre which publishes a handbook, giving standard guidelines that can be kept near all telephones. These include:

★ evaluation (deciding whether or not to take action, and whether to search, with or without evacuation)
★ notification (police should be advised)
★ search (the aim is identification of the suspicious object, which should not be touched or moved).

In Figure 18.4 is a checklist, which should also be kept near the telephone, outlining the questions to ask and information to secure about the caller.

EVALUATE CROWD CONTROL PLANS AND PROCEDURES

Crowd management is a feature of the whole planning process, encompassing transportation, entry (access), seating arrangements and orderly exit (egress) at the end of an event. It may involve the use of barriers, ushers, signage, and so on, and crowd controllers whose task it is to screen entry, monitor behaviour, remove offenders and maintain order. Crowd control is brought into play when there is an incident such as aggression, riot, injury or the like.

When evaluating crowd management plans, it is important to consider:

★ ease of access, including restricted areas, exits and aisles
★ evacuation procedures, training and simulation

Source: <www.afp.gov.au> The ABDC Phone Threat checklist may be obtained from the ABDC at a minimum of cost. Visit the AFP website or contact ABDC at <abdc@afp.gov.au> for further information .

★ special population needs
★ first aid arrangements
★ precise numbers and location of personnel
★ allocation of duties and rostering
★ placement of physical elements, such as barriers and staging
★ communication methods and protocols.

The state of Victoria has introduced the *Major Events (Crowd Management) Act 2003*, which is a useful reference for event managers. The purpose of this Act is to promote the safety and enjoyment of participants at major events. It deals with such issues as disruptive behaviour, searches, and penalties for entering restricted playing areas.

As this chapter has shown there are many variables that need to be considered when planning for crowd safety. For example, research by Zeitz et al. (2007) into events held in South Australia shows that weather is a primary determinant of police workload, and that collaboration with emergency services works best when planning is comprehensive and clearly communicated. This enables all stakeholders to prepare for and deal with contingencies relating to audience and participant safety.

SUMMARY

In this chapter we have dealt with one of the most problematic issues for event managers: crowd control. Unfortunately, there are many examples of events at which people have lost their lives through fire or riot, and there are many more examples of near misses. For this reason, it is necessary to prepare both a crowd management plan and a risk management plan for every event, as well as emergency response plans for crowd control and evacuation in case of fire or other major risks, all of which have been covered in this chapter. As indicated, these plans must comply with the relevant legislation and Standards and be properly implemented. All possible preventive measures and contingency plans need to be put in place prior to events, and appropriate staff training is essential.

Chapter review questions

1 What is the difference between crowd management and crowd control?
2 Differentiate between the roles of security personnel and the police.
3 Outline the steps involved in evacuation.
4 Outline the steps involved when a bomb threat is received.
5 What are five of the physical measures that can be used to manage crowds?
6 What are five of the staffing measures that can be used to manage crowds?

Activities

1 Visit the Crowdsafe website <www.crowdsafe.com> and list five major crowd control problems that have led to significant numbers of casualties at rock concerts.
2 Visit an event venue and evaluate the emergency plan in terms of:
   • the venue's physical features and likely emergency risks
   • the venue map, emergency equipment and access for emergency services
   • entrances and exits for the event audience
   • clarity of roles for staff involved
   • reporting relationships
   • communication technologies
   • record-keeping
   • other legal compliance or adherence to Standards.

Case study

Event safety

You are going to hire a venue for a fashion parade. The venue you have in mind is an old theatre that lends itself well to the event, with excellent sight lines for the audience. However, the decor and lighting planned by your Artistic Director for the fashion parade may compromise safety. Drapes over the ceiling area will obscure the normal lighting and prevent the fire sensors and sprinklers from working correctly. And there are a number of props that may hinder access to and out of the venue. On the other hand, the audience expected is quite small.

Questions

1 What are some of the safety risks associated with this event?
2 Who is responsible for the safety of the venue and the audience?
3 With whom should you discuss the risks associated with your event concept?
4 How could the risks be reduced?
5 What sorts of contingency plans could be developed?
6 What should the evacuation plan include?

References

Emergency Management in Australia (1999), *Safe and healthy mass gatherings: a health, medical and safety planning manual for public events*, <www.ema.gov.au/www/emaweb/emaweb.nsf/Page/PublicationsPublications_A_to_Z>.

Health & Safety Executive UK (1999), *Event safety guide: a guide to health, safety and welfare at music and similar events*, <www.hse.gov.uk>.

WorkSafe Western Australia (2002), *Making the workplace safe: a guide to the laws covering safety and health in Western Australian workplaces*, WorkSafe Western Australian Commission.

Zeitz, K, Bolton, S, Dippy, R, Dowling, Y, Francis, L, Thorne, J, Butler, T & Zeitz, C (2007), 'Measuring emergency services workloads at mass gathering events', *Australian Journal of Emergency Management*, 22(3), August.

CHAPTER 19

CATERING

Unit descriptor

This unit describes the performance outcomes, skills and knowledge required to plan the catering for an event or function. It involves developing the catering concept and planning and developing an operational plan to meet requirements. This unit is relevant to a caterer or other cookery specialist involved in event catering, but also to non-catering specialists like event managers. The skills to actually provide catering are covered in other cookery and catering units.

While catering is the major focus of the unit, it also refers to additional services that may be offered by a caterer, such as those related to decor and theme.

Elements

- Identify overall event objectives and scope
- Prepare the catering concept for an event or function
- Prepare and implement an operational plan for the catering of an event or function.

Critical aspects for assessment

- Ability to plan catering that reflects event objectives and is operationally practical
- Knowledge of the range of catering options to be considered for different event styles and contexts
- Knowledge of issues and challenges associated with event catering
- Project or work activities conducted over a commercially realistic period of time so that the planning, evaluation and monitoring aspects of catering for an event or function can be assessed
- Demonstration of skills through the planning of catering for at least two different styles of event.

AN OUTBREAK of food poisoning at the Darling Harbour Convention Centre that saw five ambulances, including a medical mini-bus, called to treat diners, is believed to have been caused by a rare mushroom toxin. Both NSW Health and the convention centre management are conducting investigations into the incident last Friday night.

Ambulance officers treated 17 diners, but no-one was admitted to hospital. The sudden onset of the illness saw some of the 700 guests at the NSW Master Builders' Association awards throw up at the table. A spokeswoman for the convention centre said a commercial laboratory report released yesterday afternoon showed there were 'no hygiene or food pathogen factors at fault'.

Source: Kirsty Needham (2003), 'Mushrooms blamed for poisoning', *Sydney Morning Herald*, 6 September 6.

Food safety is a major concern for event participants. In this chapter, food safety planning will be linked to the development of plans for catering at functions and outdoor events. In the above case, there were no food safety issues or, indeed, any fault found with food safety planning and implementation. This was instead a rare outbreak of mushroom poisoning similar to that experienced during a banquet for 482 people in Vancouver, British Columbia, in June 1991. Concerns of the public are no doubt reinforced by incidents such as that of a young man at an event stand blowing into hot dog bags to inflate them prior to packing them with hot dogs, and then leaving these in a heating unit for his germs to multiply in the packaging!

Knowledge of basic food safety requirements is absolutely necessary for all event catering staff. Most events involve bulk catering, and the risks associated with food safety are particularly significant for those staged at outdoor venues. In comparison with convention centre facilities, which use cook chill methods and state-of-the-art refrigeration, outdoor

Outdoor catering presents special challenges

venues seldom provide an ideal environment for food safety. Surveys conducted by Boo, Chiselli and Almanza (2000) show that foods served at outdoor fairs and festivals and fast food restaurants are considered the least safe compared with food served at other locations, such as in the home or at a restaurant. Insect and dirt or dust contamination was the major concern for customers eating at outdoor fairs and festivals. Food poisoning/spoilage was the major safety concern, while fat or cholesterol was the major health concern at all locations.

Before looking in detail at food safety planning, we will deal with the skills and knowledge required to plan the catering for an event or function. This is a specialised area for catering and function/banquet managers but an overview of the field is valuable for every event manager.

IDENTIFY OVERALL EVENT OBJECTIVES AND SCOPE

The functions and responsibilities associated with event catering generally follow similar lines. However, the level of specialisation differs between a large organisation, such as a hotel chain or convention centre, and smaller events where the catering team is likely to be quite small, with most roles undertaken by a few individuals. For most large outdoor events, catering is contracted out.

SALES

A Director of Catering is generally responsible for the catering sales team, which includes salespeople and administration staff. The sales staff have titles such as Convention Sales Manager, Banquet Sales Manager, Function Sales Manager, Convention Sales Manager, and Event Coordinator. The sales function involves negotiation with clients about their catering needs, preparation of quotes and finalisation of contracts.

SERVICE

Once all details of the proposed contract have been finalised, the details are handed over to the service staff for execution. The title, Functions Manager, is used to cover management of service for meetings, weddings, conventions and exhibitions, and is largely synonymous with the more old-fashioned title of Banquet Manager. The Functions Manager reports to the Director of Food and Beverage. Functions/banquet staff members are responsible for room set-up and food and beverage service. These employees have direct contact with the client, customers and guests at the event. In all cases where alcohol is served at least one barperson is also allocated to the event. The kitchen crew that prepares the food is likely to include the Executive Chef, a Banquet Chef, apprentice chefs and other kitchen workers. The senior kitchen staff are responsible for food safety and are supported by a purchasing department for food and beverage supplies. Figure 19.1 shows the functions and responsibilities of the sales and food and beverage staff and their reporting relationships.

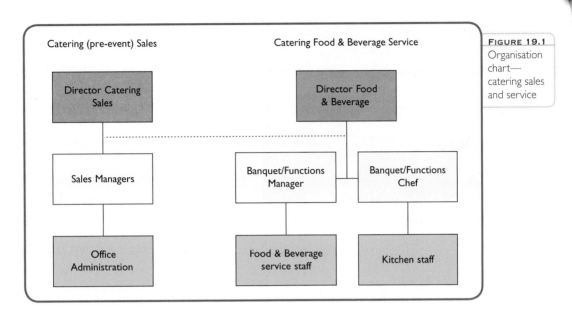

FIGURE 19.1
Organisation
chart—
catering sales
and service

Table 19.1 illustrates how performance standards can be developed for each of the tasks associated with catering provision.

Table 19.1 Procedures and performance measures for a Functions Manager

Standard procedure	Performance measure
Confirm bookings	• Acknowledge and confirm booking confirmation and reconfirmation within 24 hours by responding to catering sales manager • Liaise with chef regarding function catering in week prior to function
Plan function set-up	• Plan function layout two weeks prior to event • Check stock levels (e.g. tablecloths, cutlery) • Develop function specifications such as table layouts
Schedule and manage staffing	• Plan staffing requirements • Roster staff • Contact staff one week prior to function • Confirm rosters 24 hours prior to function • Brief staff immediately prior to function set-up
Supervise function set-up	• Monitor function set-up in progress • Check all physical specifications met two hours prior to function (e.g. tables, stage set-up) • Schedule service of food and beverage and confirm with chef three hours prior to function (timing of main course and dessert)
Manage customer requests on the day or refer to catering sales manager	• Respond to customer needs by meeting requests, or refer to catering sales manager immediately
Clear and clean up after the function	• Supervise staff clearing and cleaning up • Monitor occupational health and safety • Evaluate function and record outstanding or emerging problems • Where necessary, supervise function set-up for following day

Fast food—still a favourite at sporting events

As mentioned previously, catering is generally outsourced for outdoor or large events. This may involve one master caterer or several smaller caterers. In a large sports stadium, for example, there is likely to be one large catering organisation serving the needs of the corporate boxes and several smaller caterers servicing concession stands selling hot and cold food. The types of catering provided for most large events include:

★ VIP catering
★ sponsor catering
★ performer/athlete catering
★ staff catering
★ fixed concessions (fast food, beverages)
★ mobile concessions (coffee carts, ice-cream units, hot dog units).

Food and drink at Wimbledon is supplied by FMC (Facilities Management Catering Limited). The following statistics illustrate consumption levels at the most recent tournament: 32 000 portions of fish and chips, 22 000 slices of pizza, 28 000 kilograms of strawberries and 7000 litres of fresh cream. To ensure the utmost freshness, strawberries were picked the day before being served, arrived at Wimbledon at around 5.30 am, where they were inspected before being hulled. Visitors also consumed 300 000 cups of tea and coffee, 20 000 bottles of champagne and 100 000 pints of beer. About 1800 FMC catering staff were required to operate the catering outlets. These quantities are mind-boggling. For mega events, the purchasing process is commenced several years beforehand since supplies of potatoes, lettuce, etc. need to be planned in collaboration with farmers. Contracts must be signed in good time for planning, planting and production of raw foods. Flowers are another good example of a purchasing dilemma, particularly if large quantities of national floral emblems are required. Products such as eggs have to be imported since it is not worthwhile for producers to increase their number of laying hens for a short selling period.

In addition to planning and providing support to contract caterers, in some cases the Catering Manager is also responsible for managing environmental issues associated with catering, such as waste disposal. This job description is illustrated in Figure 19.2 opposite.

As this job description shows, the Catering and Waste Services Manager in this position has no direct involvement in catering. The primary role is planning, negotiating and overseeing contracts with the catering contractors. The process of negotiation would involve, for example, developing specifications for menus, prices and service levels. Following planning, the manager would then oversee all event catering, putting control measures in place to evaluate whether contractors were meeting contract stipulations. Problem-solving would be another feature of this job, as unusual requests and issues almost always arise as an event unfolds.

Catering and Waste Services Manager

FIGURE 19.2
Sample job description— Catering and Waste Services Manager

Job Summary

The Catering and Waste Services Manager is responsible for working with the venue Master Catering Organisation and relevant subcontracting caterers and concessionaires to finalise food and beverage specifications and control procedures in accordance with their contracts. Responsible also for working with the Cleaning contractor and Waste Management contractor for the best possible outcome for an environmentally friendly event.

Duties

- Establish operational specifications and procedures for catering, cleaning and waste management.
- Monitor day-to-day performance of contractors in accordance with contract specifications such as opening hours, service levels, quality, etc.
- Liaise with customers, including external customers such as sponsors and internal customers such as staff, to monitor satisfaction levels.
- Manage meal service for staff, contractors and performers.
- Liaise with Health Department and catering contractors in relation to food safety regulations, planning and control systems.
- Attend daily meetings with contractors, including Catering, Cleaning and Waste.
- Solve immediate problems or refer to venue or other managers as required.

Reports to: Venue Manager

PREPARE THE CATERING CONCEPT FOR AN EVENT OR FUNCTION

Food is an integral part of any event, so preparation of a catering concept is essential at an early stage in event planning. This is necessary to ensure that the catering concept complements and enhances the overall event or function concept.

Any experienced event manager knows that complaints about food are serious indeed and extremely difficult to remedy during or after an event. Conversely, where client expectations are surpassed, food quality can contribute to high satisfaction ratings for the entire event. Since, generally speaking, the cost of food in relation to all other costs is relatively low, food should always be served in reasonable portion sizes and reasonable quantities. Careful planning is essential, and advice must be given to the client on menu selection and service style to ensure that they meet the needs of the audience or spectators at the event.

STYLES OF SERVICE

There are several styles of service, ranging from plated meals to self-service buffets, from which a client may choose.

Buffet

A buffet style set-up offering a wide variety of foods will usually guarantee customer satisfaction. A major mistake often made with buffets is not providing sufficient vegetarian dishes.

As these appeal to non-vegetarians, too, it is common to find that dishes have run out before the vegetarians get to the front of the queue. Buffet queues are another matter of concern, but with careful planning and layout, queues can be avoided. If a queue forms, it can take some time for the last person to help themselves, by which time some dishes, such as seafood, may have run out.

Plated meals

For many functions and conventions, food is already plated and everyone gets the same meal unless a special dietary request has been made. Sometimes, there is a 50/50 drop, with different meals served to alternate guests. Guests at the table are then free to swap meals if they please. Again, demand for vegetarian meals is often higher than expected, even though guests are asked about special meal requests at the time of booking. One of the many menus offered by Suntec Singapore International Convention & Exhibition Centre is illustrated in Figure 19.3. This convention centre can organise events ranging from small cocktail parties for 10 people to weddings, corporate dinners, banquets, functions and other special events for 10 000 people. The centre's world-class chefs provide a gourmet selection of Asian, Western and Halal menus. In the competitive field of convention bidding, catering plays a big part in the decision-making processes of organisers.

FIGURE 19.3
Example of a gourmet menu offered by a convention centre

GOLDEN PEONY MENU

Sashimi on Ice
taro, deoduck clam, salmon and lobster

Buddha Jumps over the Wall
top broth with abalone, sea cucumber, shark's fin, scallops and fish maw

Stuffed Spiny Sea Cucumber
served with crab roe

Braised Abalone
served with Hong Kong kai lan

Pepper Beef Tenderloin
served with Oriental apple sauce

Imperial Pearl Rice
with crabmeat, dried scallops and prawns

Double-boiled Bird's Nest
with hasma, ginseng, red dates in young coconut shell

Suntec Singapore International Convention & Exhibition Centre

Source: Suntec Singapore International Convention & Exhibition Centre, <www.suntecsingapore.com>.

Healthy, nutritious food is becoming increasingly popular at functions

Grazing stations

A contemporary approach to function food is a grazing station—a small table with light snacks such as cheese and fruit. Healthier items are becoming increasingly popular, with fruit often being served for morning and afternoon tea. A large basket of red apples is a welcome change from a platter of processed biscuits.

Food stalls

Food stalls are commonplace at many events and here it is essential that food quality and food safety are carefully monitored. The caterers should be evaluated before the event, menu and food specifications agreed and food safety plans reviewed.

TYPES OF MEALS

All meals can form the basis for event catering, including breakfast, lunch and dinner. Refreshment breaks and cocktail parties also require catering. Whatever the event, the professional skills of a qualified chef are needed for planning purposes. Food can range in quality from frozen processed meals to sophisticated, unique gourmet offerings. In all cases, attention must be paid to nutrition, product quality, quantity, presentation, special dietary needs and food safety. Surpassing expectations by, for example, providing an espresso cart at an exhibition or serving hot snacks during a meeting break can contribute to the success of the event concept. Trends and themes are other considerations for menu planners.

Athletes provide a particular challenge for event caterers, and advice can be obtained from their managers or sports institutes. Food poisoning and food contamination are serious concerns for high-profile athletes—one memorable team blamed their host country for gastroenteritis and poor performance on the field!

A major consideration, linked to the bottom line, is the quantity of food necessary to meet demand. For many festivals and outdoor events, the audience is hard to predict and the number of meals purchased on the day can vary depending on the weather and other factors. On a cold day, hot foods and beverages are in high demand, while on hot days these stalls could have little business. Nearby storage facilities, such as refrigerated units, can be most useful for storing food until just before it is required.

LOGISTICS OF FOOD SUPPLY

Moving large quantities of food can be highly problematic, particularly if there is a full-scale accreditation system that limits access to the site. This means that only certain individuals and vehicles can deliver food. Traffic delays also have to be taken into account. Most large events have to develop a delivery schedule for the early hours of the morning, with limited times available for each operator. Supply chain analysis is useful in estimating the time needed for delivery and off-loading of supplies and equipment, which allows the venue hire period to be extended if necessary to ensure adequate delivery time. This also has implications for security of the site.

Storage is another logistical consideration, the importance of which is illustrated in the following example. It is not rare for an executive chef working at a stadium to have to supervise the preparation of 28 000 meals to be served in one day. Production of this number of meals would need to commence five days in advance, using cooking and storage methods to achieve a 7–21 day shelf life.

PROFITABILITY OF FOOD

For hotels, events such as meetings and weddings are more profitable than other food and beverage operations. However, food purchasing needs to be very accurate (little or no waste), the food component of the price quoted to the client should be low, and production and service should be tightly scheduled. Planning should occur well in advance, with menu engineering identifying the best items to include on menus for the highest profit margin. This generally means using products which are in season.

BEVERAGE SERVICE

There are many considerations for beverage service at events, not the least of which is the legislative requirement for responsible service of alcohol. The banning of 'beer wenches' has occurred in response to poor crowd behaviour at sports matches. Sponsorship arrangements generally have a major impact on beverages sold, with exclusive arrangements, for example, negotiated with sponsor beer and soft drink companies, including major promotional activities. This can involve changing the beer supply from one company to another at a sports stadium, a significant effort when the beer lines may run for 3.5 kilometres around the stadium to the various outlets!

Legislative compliance and profitability are the main considerations for beverage service.

Legislative compliance

In addition to all liquor-related responsibilities, such as correct signage, all staff must have RSA (responsible service of alcohol) certificates. This should not become a last-minute staffing issue. Poaching trained and accredited staff is a well-known feature of major events when staffing shortages occur. All sorts of non-monetary and monetary inducements are used to attract casual staff when outlets become desperate.

Profitability of selected beverages

Choice of brand and profit margin need to be considered when deciding what to stock and serve at events. House brands are generally selected on the basis of a regular, large supply with resulting discount. The quality of house brands is important as it must be acceptable to the guests. Some clients will require both regular and premium brands to be served and this must be negotiated before the event. Drink sizes should be monitored, and the correct glass used for each beverage. The temperature of beer and wine is also a consideration as is an adequate supply of ice for spirit-based drinks. This can be particularly problematic for outdoor events.

Prices for alcohol for functions such as weddings should be negotiated beforehand. This can be done on the basis of an open bar where the host pays for all individual drinks or a cash bar where guests pay for all their own alcohol. A compromise is an agreement by the host to pay for all beer, wine and soft drink but not spirits. In other cases, the host might set a limit on the budget, and once this is reached guests must pay for their own drinks. Or a full package deal might be negotiated where the establishment charges a flat rate based on average drinking at a similar type of function. This of course includes a margin for profit. In rare cases, the client may wish to provide the wine, in which case corkage rates need to be discussed before the event.

NEGOTIATING CATERING CONTRACTS

When outsourcing catering, or booking catering for an in-house event, the following questions form part of the negotiation process, leading to quotes and contracts with caterers:

1 What is the nature of the event?
2 Does the event have a theme?
3 Is it a one-off event?
4 How many people will attend (is this an estimate or a guarantee)?
5 When will the final head count be done?
6 What is the budget?
7 Where will the event be held?
8 Is there a properly equipped kitchen with hot and cold running water, cooking equipment, cool room and freezer? When can this be inspected?
9 Does the site have storage?
10 How easily can the site be accessed (accreditation and road closure)?
11 Can food be prepared off site and transported in?

12 How soon will the menu be finalised (impacts on costing)?

13 Are there preferred foods, items which must be avoided or special dietary or nutritional requirements?

14 Will alcohol be served? Who will pay for the alcohol?

15 What is the schedule for access to the venue and setting up?

16 When does the event run sheet (running order) allow for food service (e.g. after speeches)?

Prior to the event, the caterer's references should be checked, cooking and service facilities should be inspected, and staffing levels and qualifications should be discussed, along with menu planning. Food safety plans and registration are the most important control measures, requiring attention before the contracts are finalised.

PREPARE AND IMPLEMENT AN OPERATIONAL CATERING PLAN FOR AN EVENT OR FUNCTION

A detailed operational plan for catering should be provided to all stakeholders identifying steps, activities, sequence and responsibilities. All event details should be confirmed prior to the event, with any adjustments fully documented in the plan. In the following section on food safety planning, many elements of the catering plan are covered in detail. There are many operational constraints, such as limited space at the venue, small work areas, limited food storage and refrigeration space, and different climatic conditions. A risk management plan for catering is highly recommended and should follow the guidelines given in Chapter 26. This identifies the things that could go wrong (such as interrupted power supply to refrigeration units), and allows contingency plans to be developed to meet the most likely and the most serious possibilities.

Mobile cool rooms are essential for food safety

FOOD SAFETY PLANNING

Food safety planning involves identifying critical control points in food production and service. The process of purchasing through to food service is illustrated in Figure 19.4, along with the parallel processes of cleaning, garbage removal and pest control. At any one of these stages, raw

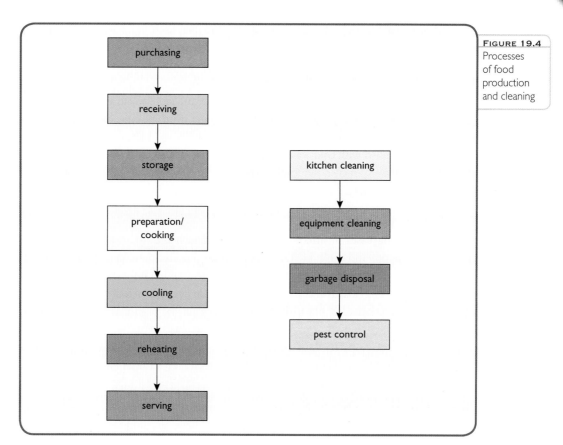

FIGURE 19.4
Processes
of food
production
and cleaning

materials or cooked food could become contaminated. For example, during the receiving process, long delays at the loading dock may result in all seafood being defrosted. Each control point must be identified as part of the HACCP (Hazard Analysis Critical Control Point) plan and the plan must form part of the tender and contract with the caterer/s. For catering operations at a large stadium, for example, there would be a scientific approach to food production, commodities delivery and storage, and procedures would be well documented for regular monitoring of food temperatures. However, in the more informal environment of a small event, such concerns require careful attention.

The following guidelines are adapted from information on food safety provided by the State Government of Victoria Department of Health on its website listed in Appendix E (click on Food Safety Program Templates).

Temporary premises

The event coordinator should ensure that a permit is obtained from the local council or relevant authority for setting up temporary food premises and that the following items are available:

★ benches or tables with smooth, easy-to-clean surfaces or plastic tablecloths
★ hand-washing facilities near the temporary premises, with water, a basin, soap and paper towels

★ a place to wash up cooking equipment, dishes and utensils
★ a fridge to keep cold food cold (below 5°C) and a freezer to keep frozen food frozen (a calibrated thermometer is needed to check temperatures)
★ facilities to keep hot food at 60°C or above
★ a sufficient number of rubbish containers to collect and store waste away from food.

There must also be a way of dealing with waste water from cooking, cleaning and hand washing. If there are no sinks near the food stall, these will need to be created by providing a drum with taps filled with cold water and a hot water urn. Detergent, food grade sanitiser and disposable towels are also required. Dishes should be washed in hot soapy water and rinsed before and between uses.

Cross-contamination

Most food poisoning cases are linked to **high-risk food** such as meat, seafood, poultry, dairy products, small goods and cooked rice, or any food that contains these foods such as pies.

Bacterial contamination can occur when germs contaminate food via physical food handling or via cutting boards and other utensils, or from one type of food touching another type (e.g. where cardboard boxes soaked in chicken juices are placed on food preparation surfaces).

In the right conditions, bacteria multiply rapidly—the **Temperature Danger Zone** is between 5°C and 60°C (see Figure 19.5). Thus hot foods left on a buffet for too long provide an ideal breeding ground for bacteria.

FIGURE 19.5
Temperature Danger Zone

Keep **High Risk Food***

HOT FOOD ZONE	100°C
	60°C
TEMPERATURE DANGER ZONE	
	5°C
COLD FOOD ZONE	0°C
FROZEN FOOD ZONE	-15°C

out of the **Temperature Danger Zone**

*HIGH RISK FOOD INCLUDES meat, seafood, poultry, eggs, dairy products, and smallgoods, and foods which contain these foods, for example: quiches, sandwiches and prepared salads. Other foods become high risk food when they are cooked, like rice and pasta.

Source: <www.health.vic.gov.au/foodsafety>. 'Food safety program template: food events', © Victorian Department of Health, 2007, p. 30.

More detailed guidelines are provided on the State Government of Victoria Department of Health website for specific purposes, such as product labelling and packing of food sold at market stalls, display and service of food, and temperature checking, but in general terms, food safety can be improved by:

★ safe and hygienic handling of food and beverages, including beer lines
★ regular hand washing (between, say, handling poultry and peeling vegetables)
★ use of gloves when appropriate
★ correct food storage (not on the floor)
★ checking manufacturers' labels for storage instructions (e.g. length of time permitted under refrigeration)
★ use of suitable containers for storage
★ correct labelling of items, including expiry dates
★ correct stock rotation (first in, first out)
★ appropriate and clean clothing (a damp apron is a perfect place for bacterial reproduction)
★ avoidance of cross-contamination (e.g. avoiding using the same preparation areas for fish and salads)
★ safe disposal of linen and laundry (especially when contaminated with bodily fluids)
★ appropriate handling and disposal of garbage
★ cleaning and sanitising surfaces (sanitising kills germs too)
★ cleaning and sanitising floors, etc. (environmental hygiene)
★ personal hygiene (including clean hair and wearing hair covering in the kitchen).

All of the above guidelines, as well as more specific ones for specific purposes, are generally developed as part of the HACCP plan. For event managers who contract out catering provision, an awareness of these issues is essential so that the implementation of food safety plans can be monitored by regular inspections prior to and during an event. It is also essential that the event organiser has a complete record of food providers so that sources of contamination can be traced should any food poisoning cases occur.

Waste management

Bulk waste resulting from catering operations is significant. By prescribing the use of biodegradable plates and cutlery (made from starch, not plastic), all food waste can go into a single bin and the contents used for compost. Depending on the waste stream, dedicated bins are generally allocated in the proportions indicated in Figure 19.6.

This topic is covered in more detail in the next chapter.

Waste stream	Estimated
Cans and bottles	20%
Paper and cardboard	10%
Food waste (for composting)	50%
Residual waste (non-recyclable)	20%

FIGURE 19.6
Allocation of dedicated bins

Sunshine Coast
Regional Council

ARTISTS IMPRESSION – MINIMUM STANDARDS FOR THE OPERATION OF A TEMPORARY FOOD STALL

Enclosed stall (Roof & three sides)
Please Note: Roofing may not be required where:
- Adequate roofing is provided when located within an existing structure; OR
- All food product is prepackaged (no taste testing)

Cooking equipment located to protect food from contamination & ensure public safety

Food Handler – see over

Dry Chemical Fire Extinguisher

Temperature Control for potentially hazardous and perishable foods – see over

Floor Covering – easy to clean, impervious material. *Please Note:* Must be provided if located on unsealed ground.

Utensil Washing Facility – see over

Hand Washing Facility – see over

Ensure a minimum distance of 10 metres separates food operations and any areas that are accessed by animals

Display of current Certificate of Food Licence for Temporary Food Stall (if applicable)

Food display, Food protection, Taste Testing - see over

Refuse Bin with lid and liner supplied

All food prepared inside stall. No food stored directly on ground. Overall clean condition.

Minimum hand washing facilities

20 litre water container with tap labelled 'Hand Washing Only'

Liquid soap and paper towels supplied for staff use

Container to catch waste water labelled 'Waste Water Only'. Disposed to sewer

Minimum utensil washing facilities

20 litre water container with tap labelled 'Utensil Washing Only'

Hot water and/or sanitiser available for emergency cleaning

Container to catch waste water labelled 'Waste Water Only'. Disposed to sewer

Two containers of sufficient capacity are to also be provided for adequate cleaning of utensils

Food Handlers

Money and food handled separately

Utensils and gloves used to handle food

Clean person, attire and habits

Hands must be washed whenever hands are likely to contaminate food

No smoking within temporary food stall

No cuts, illness, sores on food handlers

Food display, food protection, taste testing

Provide appropriate sneeze barrier

Signage must be provided to all taste testing stating 'No double dipping, single serve only'

Sauces, condiments and single serve utensils

Single serve utensils protected from contamination. Stored handle up.

Sauces, condiments in squeeze type dispensers or sealed packs

For further information on this topic, please contact Council

Temperature control of potentially hazardous food

Cold Food – ensure 5°C or below

Hot Food – ensure 60°C or above

Thermometer in use

SUMMARY

This chapter has looked at the catering element of events, with an emphasis on concept development and operational planning and implementation. This function can vary widely from in-house catering teams at major convention centres to small stallholders at local fetes. In all cases, the choice of food served is the critical factor as this can enhance or diminish the event concept, as well as customer satisfaction. Logistical issues of transport, storage, food production and service are particularly problematic at outdoor events, and such issues should be covered in the catering plans. There is nothing more frustrating for the event audience than a queue for food that is so long they cannot return to their seats before the end of intermission or half-time! Guidelines for food safety, a legislative requirement and an essential part of operational planning, have been outlined and sources provided for relevant authorities, for obtaining more detailed and specific information. While responsibility for this is generally delegated to a catering contractor, the event manager needs a good understanding of the general principles of food safety to ensure that procedures are implemented correctly.

Chapter review questions

1 Outline alternatives for pricing of alcohol at functions and events.
2 Outline alternatives to service of food and beverage at functions and events.
3 Explain the key elements of the HACCP approach to food safety.
4 Why is washing up a consideration for festival operations managers?

Activity

Visit the website of the State Government of Victoria Department of Health (Food Safety) listed in Appendix E and investigate the guidelines for product labelling and packing of food sold at events for charity or community causes.

Case study

One caterer or several?

You are planning an agricultural exhibition and the committee has asked you to weigh up the pros and cons of having one master caterer providing a range of food stalls with different types of food, or several small stallholders with their unique products. One of the purposes of this event is to showcase produce of the local area.

Questions

1 How can catering contribute to the event concept?
2 What would be the benefits of employing a master caterer for this exhibition?
3 What would be the benefits of having several small stallholders?
4 When selecting a caterer for this event, list five key questions you would ask them in the early selection process.

References

Boo, H, Chiselli, R & Almanza, B (2000), 'Consumer perceptions and concerns about the healthfulness and safety of food served at fairs and festivals', *Event Management*, 6(2):85–92.

Department of Environment and Conservation NSW (2007), *Waste wise events guide*, February, <www.environment.nsw.gov.au/warr/wwe_home.htm>, accessed 4 May 2010.

McVety, P, Ware, B & Lévesque Ware, C (2008), *Fundamentals of menu planning*, 3rd edn, Wiley, Brisbane.

Monash University Office of Environmental Sustainability (2009), *Greening up our catering: sustainable catering guide*, June, <http://fsd.monash.edu.au/files/MU%20 Sustainable%20Catering%20Guide%20On%20Screen_1.pdf>, accessed 4 May 2010.

ENVIRONMENTALLY SUSTAINABLE WORK PRACTICES

Unit descriptor

This unit describes the performance outcomes, skills and knowledge required to participate in environmentally sustainable work practices. It requires the ability to measure self-usage of resources effectively, follow predetermined environmentally sustainable work practices, identify and report on breaches and suggest improvements to work activities that will contribute to environmental sustainability and reduce negative environmental impacts.

Elements

- Identify current resources used within the workplace
- Comply with environmental regulations
- Seek opportunities to improve resource efficiency.

Critical aspects for assessment

- Project or work activities that show candidates' ability to identify and integrate environmentally sustainable principles into their work practices and to follow predetermined procedures
- Ability to participate in the improvement of environmental and resource-efficient work practices at own level of responsibility
- Knowledge of the principles of environmental sustainability and means by which they can be incorporated into the workplace.

THE LOW WASTE programs involved a number of initiatives aimed at raising awareness about waste minimisation among not only Games attendees, but also among suppliers and venue operators. Analysis by CES found that the goal of significant waste minimisation was achieved: 40 per cent less waste was produced at the venues than was projected to occur (only 598 tonnes of waste were produced compared to the forecast 1600 tonnes) and of this waste approximately 57 per cent was recycled (by weight). The Athletes Village recycled 60 per cent of its waste by weight, and the City of Melbourne recycled 52 per cent by weight. The Public Domain Waste Management Program was the only area to have underperformed substantially relative to its target, achieving a recycling rate of 26 per cent.

Source: Triple Bottom Line Assessment of the XVIII Commonwealth Games 2006, p. xii

Environmental issues are important considerations for all mega and major events, including Olympic and Commonwealth Games. These issues are also considered in competitive bids for major sporting events such as the FIFA World Cup and Rugby World Cup. Bid documents need to clearly spell out details of the intended plans for managing solid waste, sewage treatment and energy, and state how the organisers see this influencing the city and region in the future. Planning for even the smallest event must also consider the environment. Local councils are responsible for waste management and will look for a waste management plan. Councils demand assurances that the environmental impact will be minimal and that the area will be left in pristine condition. As mentioned in the previous chapter, environmentally friendly waste disposal is a major consideration of event organisers.

IDENTIFY CURRENT RESOURCES USED WITHIN THE WORKPLACE

This chapter deals with cleaning and waste management. Such services are most likely to be outsourced to companies such as Cleanevent, well known around the world for event and venue presentation and waste management consultancy services. This company can even provide, through a subsidiary, executive washrooms stocked with toiletries, perfumes and flowers—and every washroom comes with its own attendant.

Professional waste consultants can provide assistance in:

★ identifying the event venue's total potential waste stream
★ tailoring the waste stream to maximise the use of recycled materials
★ identifying biodegradable, cost-effective food and drink packaging
★ providing recycling collection, storage and transportation equipment
★ providing environmental audits post-event.

If waste management is not outsourced, it is the responsibility of the event organiser or local council to decide on the method of dealing with waste streams.

Standard colour codes and bin labels are recommended to simplify waste disposal for the event organiser and to educate the public. Other types of bins and recycling equipment, such as recycling cages, are also recommended where needed.

Medical and contaminated waste needs special care as these items must be collected, stored and disposed of in accordance with legal guidelines. This is particularly relevant where there is doping control at an event and blood tests are carried out. Oil used in catering also requires special treatment (in a restaurant a waste trap is used) and should not be disposed of in the sewage system.

Scheduled clearing of waste would avoid the problem of bins overflowing

In general terms, the goal of any event organisation is minimisation of environmental risks and maximisation of opportunities to improve business environmental performance. This may include minimisation of waste through implementation of the waste management hierarchy, which will be described in detail in this chapter. An additional role for all event staff is to model environmentally efficient work practices such as switching off lights and appliances when they are not being used or monitoring waste management streams to avoid contamination. Efficient water use is another area in which everyone working on site can assist. Seeking alternative sources of energy is, however, the role of organising bodies.

In order to comply with environmental regulations, the following practices are usually necessary:

★ Analyse use of resources such as individually packaged tomato sauce and overuse of packaging materials in general.
★ Discuss with suppliers how to minimise other packaging waste and use of items such as polystyrene boxes.
★ Examine invoices from suppliers and conduct resource audits to see if there are better alternatives.
★ Take measurements under different conditions (see measurement of waste streams discussed later in the chapter).
★ Monitor use of equipment.

COMPLY WITH ENVIRONMENTAL REGULATIONS

Compliance with the following is necessary to meet environmental standards:

★ federal, state or territory, and local government laws, by-laws and regulations including the key Commonwealth *Environment Protection and Biodiversity Conservation Act 1999* (EPBC Act), which came into force on 16 July 2000

★ requirements of industry codes of conduct to which the event organisation subscribes, such as the Waste Wise principles outlined later in this chapter

★ requirements of industry accreditation schemes to which the organisation subscribes.

The Restaurant and Catering Association, for example, has extensive guidelines for event caterers under their Green Table initiative. Most event venues describe their environmental credentials on its websites as this is an important consideration for organisations making bookings. The Australian Jockey Club and the Melbourne Convention and Exhibition Centre (MCEC) are two examples. The latter is recognised for its environmental attributes, having been named the winner of the Urban Development Institute of Australia (UDIA) Environmental Excellence Award. And the Sustainable Tourism Cooperative Research Centre (STCRC) has a useful tool for event organisers to use to calculate carbon impacts and therefore offer carbon offsets for travel. The carbon calculator can be found on its website (see Appendix E).

PLANNING FOR HEALTH AND SAFETY AT PUBLIC EVENTS

It is also important to consider all aspects of health and safety when planning a public event, particularly a large outdoor event such as a concert. The Department of Health in South Australia produces useful guidelines for the management of all important aspects of health and safety at public events, ranging from waste disposal to sewerage and waste water management for an event site which is not served by sewerage facilities.

WASTE DISPOSAL

Public events generate a considerable amount of waste including rubbish, wastewater and sewerage. A system for dealing with this waste needs to be adequately addressed by event organisers and must include clean-up after the event. Event organisers need to allocate enough resources to ensure that all waste is managed during and after the event to prevent insanitary conditions and environmental harm.

Event organisers should consult with the following authorities to determine who has legislative responsibilities and requirements for the management of solid and liquid wastes:

• the local council
• the Environment Protection Authority
• the Department of Health.

An accumulation of waste must not give rise to insanitary conditions, which are prohibited under the Public and Environmental Health Act. Premises are in an insanitary condition if:

- the condition of the premises gives rise to a risk to health
- the premises are so filthy or neglected that there is a risk of infestation by rodents or other pests
- the condition of the premises is such as to cause justified offence to the owner of any land in the vicinity
- offensive material or odours are emitted from the premises
- the premises are for some other reason justifiably declared by the relevant health authority to be in an insanitary condition.

Solid waste such as refuse and food waste are the biggest risk for nuisance and offensive conditions as well as infestation by vermin if not adequately controlled. Event organisers must provide an adequate number of refuse bins with lids with regular emptying as often as needed to prevent infestation and overflow.

Food businesses must implement a pest control program to ensure that:

- all practicable measures have been taken to prevent pests and vermin from contaminating food and/or entering food premises and
- all practicable measures have been taken to eradicate and prevent the harbourage of pests and vermin on the premises and vehicles that are used to transport food.

All temporary refuse, sewage and wastewater disposal sites constructed for the event must not create nuisance or offensive conditions. Disposal of refuse or liquid wastes must not result in the contamination of ground, surface or stream waters or provide breeding sites for rodents, vermin or insects. Special arrangements must be in place for the collection and disposal of decomposable and hazardous waste including food waste, clinical waste and waste from first aid and sharps.

SOLID WASTE DISPOSAL

Public events must have suitable and adequate facilities for the storage, collection and disposal of solid waste that:

- contain the waste
- prevent animal, pest or vermin access
- are easily identifiable and accessed by patrons, food vendors and waste collectors
- are able to be easily and effectively cleaned
- ensure that materials such as glass, cardboard, plastic, etc. are recycled through provision of clearly designated and labelled containers.

Note: All putrescible or offensive waste should be in lidded containers.

Bins are overflowing and there is no option for recycling

As the availability of appropriately licensed waste disposal depots is often limited in remote outback areas, it may be necessary to consider alternative options. The Environment

Protection Authority should be contacted in this eventuality. The Outback Areas Community Development Trust may also be contacted for assistance (refer to Section 18).

NEEDLE AND SYRINGE DISPOSAL

Illegal and prescription drug use at events must be considered and planned for. The presence of injecting equipment may pose a safety hazard for patrons and staff. Sharps containers should be provided at the event. Generally these are located within toilets, however other locations may be considered appropriate.

Cleaning and security staff must be briefed on the dangers associated with used injecting equipment and instructed on safe handling methods.

DUST CONTROL

A common problem at outdoor events is dust control. Large amounts of dust may develop as a result of the event itself. Dust caused by large crowds or vehicle movement can contaminate food, create a nuisance, and cause problems for performers and patrons, especially asthma and allergy sufferers. Consideration must be given in the planning stages to the need for lawn or grass mowing, light watering, and ground covering (artificial or otherwise) – when it is to be carried out, how and by whom. For dust caused by frequent or heavy vehicle movement, event organisers should consider laying a gravel road, compacted rubble, and/or frequent wetting down.

WATER SUPPLY

An adequate supply of water must be provided at public events, the quantity and quality appropriate to the intended use. All water for drinking and use within food premises must be of potable quality, that is, it must be suitable for human consumption. The quantity of water supplied will depend on a range of factors including:

- the nature of the event and crowd activities
- event duration
- location of event and the time of the year
- environmental conditions such as temperature, wind, rain, etc.
- number of people (patrons, performers and other staff) attending the event
- proportion of persons camping on the site
- flush toilets and other ablutions
- food handling arrangements
- dust control.

Event organisers should refer to the NHMRC/ARMCANZ Australian Drinking Water Guidelines for information in relation to microbiological and chemical standards for drinking water.

The Emergency Management Australia Manual, Safe and Healthy Mass Gatherings, recommends twenty litres of potable water per person per day, of which four litres is the drinking water component. Event duration, location and expected ambient temperatures should be considered in determining the quantity of drinking water required.

Non-potable water supplies may be used for toilet flushing, fire fighting or dust suppression. Where camping is permitted, water for showers needs to be bacteriologically safe although not necessarily of potable quality. Non-potable supplies, including piped outlets, are to be clearly identified as not suitable for drinking.

Water supply must be constant and at a sufficient pressure to withstand peak demands at all outlets. Water should be readily accessible at all food premises, toilets, ablutions, laundry facilities, designated standpipes for patron use, fire fighting and first aid posts.

TOILETS AND ABLUTION FACILITIES

Depending on the nature and duration of the event, event organisers need to ensure that adequate toilet facilities are provided for patrons, entertainers and support staff. These facilities should include water closet pans, urinals and hand basins. Showers are required where camping is proposed in conjunction with the event. Facilities should be adequate in number, conveniently located and suitable for the event. The toilet facilities must have the necessary provisions for the collection, treatment and disposal of sewage and wastewater. The facilities must be operated and maintained in a clean and tidy manner so that insanitary conditions do not occur.

Unless otherwise permitted by the relevant health authority, all toilets will be water flush and have hand basins provided, connected to a cold water supply. Portable water flush toilets must be provided when existing toilet facilities are inadequate. When planning for public toilets, the following should be taken into consideration:

- type of event
- duration of the event
- crowd type and activities
- number of patrons
- alcohol and food consumption.

Toilet and ablution facilities should be:

- clearly designated for each sex with unisex toilets for disabled persons
- separate from food service preparation and storage areas
- cleaned and maintained for the duration of the event
- well lit and clearly identified
- situated and screened to ensure privacy
- preferably having separate approach for each sex
- provided with handwashing basins with cold running water, soap (bar or liquid), disposable towels or air dryers and waste containers
- provided with toilet paper
- provided with provisions for disposal and removal of sanitary napkins, nappies and incontinence pads, condoms, needles and syringes and other refuse
- provided to enable feeding and or changing of infants.

Where showers are provided, suitable provisions for holding of clothing during shower use are needed.

In hot areas, shade should be provided in conjunction with the facilities.

Event organisers should ensure that all support staff are briefed on the proper procedure for handling needles and syringes, on the risks of needlestick injuries and the correct procedures should a needlestick injury occur.

To maintain facilities in a sanitary condition they must be cleaned at least daily or more frequently where necessary to prevent nuisance or offensive conditions and infestation/harbourage by nuisance insects or pests. A cleaning schedule should be established for toilet facilities and ablutions to cover frequency of cleaning, monitoring, equipment and chemicals to be used. There must be adequate maintenance personnel available to repair any blockages, and sufficient supplies need to be available for use by the cleaning staff, including soap, toilet paper, buckets, mops, brooms, protective clothing, etc.

At least one unisex toilet for patrons with a disability should be provided at each group of toilet facilities. Refer to the Building Code of Australia as a guide for further information.

As a means of alleviating long line-ups, particularly at female toilets, event organisers should consider the provision of additional unisex toilets.

Portable toilets must be situated so that they can be pumped out during the event. Vehicles pumping out portable toilets must not block access for emergency services.

Signs directing patrons to toilet facilities should be prominently placed at locations where patrons can see them. Toilet and ablution facilities should also be sited to allow easy access and minimum queuing. Toilet locations could be included on site maps that are provided with tickets to the event and at information centres.

If an event is to be held within a building, for example in a building that is specifically built for the purpose of entertaining or holding an event, then the number of toilets must comply with the requirements for South Australia as set out in the Building Code of Australia.

Toilet and ablution facilities must not give rise to insanitary conditions. The Public and Environmental Health Act prohibits insanitary conditions which includes conditions posing a risk to health; conditions where offensive material or odours are emitted, and conditions that could cause justified offence. The Act also prohibits the unlawful or inappropriate discharge of wastes into a public or private place.

SEWERAGE AND WASTEWATER

When the event site is not served by a sewerage system, or the sewerage system is inadequate, the relevant health authority or agency must be contacted to determine the requirements for all types of sewage and wastewater disposal. This includes sewage, wastewater from handwashing, food stalls, ablution blocks and from any crowd comfort measures such as spray tents and foam parties.

Sewage and wastewater collection, treatment and disposal systems must be constructed and operated to prevent contamination of the food or water supply or other water bodies, or insanitary conditions. In areas administered by local government contact the local council.

The Minister for Health through the Environmental Health Service of the Department of Health is the relevant health authority in all other areas of the State (see also Section 11.3).

Source: Guidelines for the management of public health & safety at public events (2003)
Department of Health PO Box 6, Rundle Mall, Adelaide South Australia, 5000.

PLANNING A WASTE WISE EVENT

A Waste Wise Event is one where the event organisers integrate simple and cost-effective waste, recycling and litter management systems in their events. The NSW Government Department of Environment, Climate Change and Water provides outstanding guidelines for planning such an event. Its guidelines for planning prior to the event are given below.

Communicate and gain support for your intentions to host a Waste Wise Event with your relevant stakeholders by focusing on the benefits of being involved. Your key stakeholders will most likely be:

Councils

Most events in NSW are held on council-managed public land. Your local council can help achieve Waste Wise aims for an event through policy initiatives, waste management and resource recovery experience. By doing this the council will be more able to fulfill community expectations and give positive reinforcement to their residents by mirroring the at home recycling behaviour when away from home.

Event site owners

The benefits to them of a Waste Wise Event can easily be explained, such as reduced costs for waste management, a positive environmental image, and public acceptance of recycling strategies. The site owners may need to establish the costs and benefits of running their site differently—from social, economic and environmental perspectives. Once gained, the commitment from the site owner can be formalised by putting some Waste Wise clauses in your contract/agreement with them.

Sponsors

Sponsors can gain promotional benefit, and are attracted to events that send a sound environmental message. They need to be made aware of exactly how their brands will be enhanced by being involved with or endorsing a Waste Wise Event. It's wise to check whether the landowner has a policy about sponsors or branding. Be careful of sponsors whose products may not be consistent with Waste Wise aims.

Stallholders and vendors

Stallholders and vendors' commitment can be gained by inserting a short standard clause in their agreement, permit or contract that commits them to using certain materials for packaging and to following Waste Wise procedures. They need to be informed early of the goal to minimise waste and packaging, and their expected compliance with the Waste Wise aims. The businesses could even develop their own Waste Wise Plan for their operations throughout the event. Using less costs less.

Waste services

Waste service contractors will usually be private contractors, but may be council's own staff. They are critical to the success of your Waste Wise Event. The best way to gain commitment to Waste Wise aims is to insert a short standard clause in their contract/agreement. Included in this should be a commitment to providing accurate data of quantities taken to both landfill and recycling facilities, probably in the form of a weighbridge receipt. (Check what data is available at no extra charge.)

Other contractors

Other service contractors, including businesses supplying fencing, portable toilets, power supply, sound systems or marquees, need to fully understand the Waste Wise aims of the event. It is advisable to negotiate a mutually agreeable clause in the agreement or contract for waste avoidance well in advance.

The public

The public will respond positively to a well organised Waste Wise Event. Mention the benefits of being Waste Wise in all promotional material through clear communications and signage during the event. Messages of encouragement and support will have a positive impact by reinforcing their at home Waste Wise behaviour. It may also be worth conducting a survey during the event to gauge their commitment to being Waste Wise.

Source: Pearson Australia acknowledges the use of the Department of Environment, Climate Change & Water NSW (DECCW) 'Waste Wise Event Guide' (2008)-DECC2008/257 in the preparation of this document. For further information on waste wise events go to: www.environment.nsw.gov.au/warr/WWE_Home.htm

Figure 20.1 opposite shows a useful waste management flowchart for before, during and after an event.

The website of the Department of Environment, Climate Change and Water also provides many templates, including clauses that could be included in legal contracts with suppliers and other stakeholders. Similar guidelines are available for South Australia— Waste Minimisation Guide for Events and Venues—together with waste labels (see below), and for other states and territories. The South Australian publication has particularly useful guidelines for exploring better catering options to increase the amount of environmentally friendly, compostable waste and reduce the waste that ends up as landfill.

LOGISTICS OF WASTE MANAGEMENT

Suppliers of waste bins and recyclable products are available through an internet search or via links on the two websites mentioned above. Event organisers need to plan the location

Handy labels for a Waste Wise Event

Source: Zero Waste SA, <http://www.zerowaste.sa.gov.au/About.mvc/RecyclingSignage>. Copyright Zero Waste SA 2010.

of bins and the best time to have them installed. Clearing bins and storing waste is another major consideration for event organisers. In many cases, clearing is done by the cleaning contractor and waste is removed by a recycling/waste contractor, and it is essential that these companies work in partnership. In other situations, councils may provide waste management solutions.

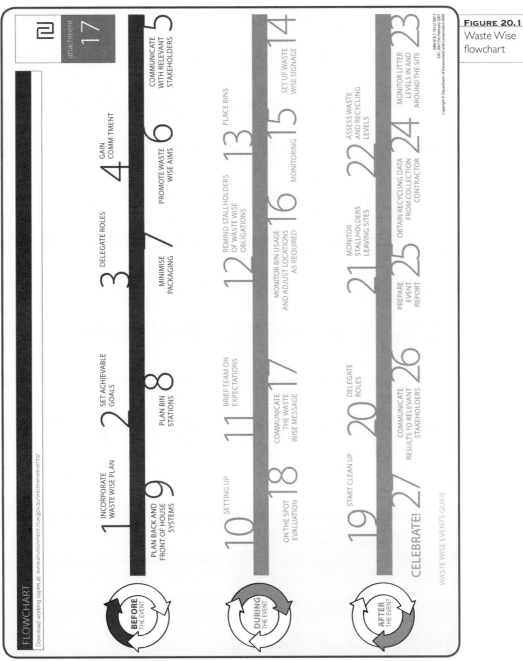

FLOWCHART
Download working copies at: www.environment.nsw.gov.au/wastewiseevents/

BEFORE THE EVENT

1 INCORPORATE WASTE WISE PLAN
2 SET ACHIEVABLE GOALS
3 DELEGATE ROLES
4 GAIN COMMITMENT
5 COMMUNICATE WITH RELEVANT STAKEHOLDERS
6 PROMOTE WASTE WISE AIMS
7 MINIMISE PACKAGING
8 PLAN BIN STATIONS
9 PLAN BACK AND FRONT OF HOUSE SYSTEMS

DURING THE EVENT

10 SETTING UP
11 BRIEF TEAM ON EXPECTATIONS
12 REMIND STALLHOLDERS OF WASTE WISE OBLIGATIONS
13 PLACE BINS
14 SET UP WASTE WISE SIGNAGE
15 MONITORING
16 MONITOR BIN USAGE AND ADJUST LOCATIONS AS REQUIRED
17 COMMUNICATE THE WASTE WISE MESSAGE
18 ON THE SPOT EVALUATION

AFTER THE EVENT

19 START CLEAN UP
20 DELEGATE ROLES
21 MONITOR STALLHOLDERS LEAVING SITES
22 ASSESS WASTE AND RECYCLING LEVELS
23 MONITOR LITTER LEVELS IN AND AROUND THE SITE
24 OBTAIN RECYCLING DATA FROM COLLECTION CONTRACTOR
25 PREPARE EVENT REPORT
26 COMMUNICATE RESULTS TO RELEVANT STAKEHOLDERS
27 CELEBRATE!

WASTE WISE EVENTS GUIDE

attachment 17

FIGURE 20.1
Waste Wise flowchart

ISBN 978 1 74122 590 3
DEC 2007/56, February 2007
Copyright © Department of Environment and Conservation NSW

Source: www.environment.nsw.gov.au/resources/warr/200756attach17.pdf
Pearson Australia acknowledges the use of the Department of Environment, Climate Change & Water NSW (DECCW) 'Waste Wise Event Guide' (2008)-DECC2008/257 in the preparation of this document. For further information on waste wise events go to: www.environment.nsw.gov.au/warr/WWE_Home.htm

SEEK OPPORTUNITIES TO IMPROVE RESOURCE EFFICIENCY

The most important element of any waste management program is effective communication with stakeholders to enlist their support in the implementation of green initiatives. Stakeholders include staff, contractors, volunteers and, of course, the event audience.

One of the biggest problems with recycling is contamination of the waste stream. This occurs, for example, when a load destined for composting is contaminated by plastic, foil or other non-biodegradable items having been placed in the wrong bin, necessitating its disposal as landfill.

The concept of a composting stream is new to most people attending events. As mentioned previously, only food scraps and biodegradable foodware (plates, cutlery and cups made from cornstarch and sugarcane) should be placed in the bin provided for this purpose. The important message is 'right rubbish, right bin'. When procedures work well, the amount of landfill resulting from an event can be reduced dramatically.

The following principles form the basis of the waste management plan and need to be communicated to both internal and external customers.

Reduction

Waste reduction can be achieved through purchasing strategies aimed at reducing the amount of material brought into a venue, for example, by ordering supplies in large boxed quantities rather than small plastic packages. However, there is sometimes a conflict between waste management and food hygiene—for example, where food safety authorities recommend provision of individual portions of sauces, butter and jam to customers. If individual portions are dispensed with in favour of jars, bottles or other larger containers in the interest of waste management, the caterer must be confident that the condiments can be dispensed in a hygienic way, in accordance with food safety legislation. The pumps illustrated on the Heinz stand meet this requirement. Using this system avoids small plastic sauce packages being included in the compost waste stream. The idea is that all food-related items are binned together in this one stream—a simple message for inattentive event fans.

Dispensing units for ketchup are more environmentally friendly than individual sauce packages

Reuse

Waste reduction can also occur if items are reused. A good example is polystyrene boxes in which some vegetables are delivered. These should not be allowed to remain on the site and should be removed for reuse if this can be done hygienically.

Recycling

Most members of an event audience will be familiar with recycling messages in relation to glass bottles, plastic bottles, paper and cardboard.

PLANNING SANITARY FACILITIES

Planning the correct number of toilet facilities for an event is very scientific. In fact, council guidelines can sometimes be very specific in respect of the number of toilet facilities to be provided for events. This is illustrated in Tables 20.1, 20.2 and 20.3. As you can see from these tables, there are a number of considerations for the event organiser, including the duration of the event, the number of males and females attending the event, and service of alcohol. Provision of toilets for people in wheelchairs and for baby change rooms also needs to

Table 20.1 Toilet facilities for events where alcohol is not served

| Patrons | MALES | | | FEMALES | |
	WCs	Urinals	Hand basins	WCs	Hand basins
<500	1	2	2	6	2
<1000	2	4	4	9	4
<2000	4	8	6	12	6
<3000	6	15	10	18	10
<5000	8	25	17	30	17

Source: Blue Mountains City Council, Event Application Form 2010/11, <www.bmcc.nsw.gov.au>.

Table 20.2 Toilet facilities for events where alcohol is served

| Patrons | MALES | | | FEMALES | |
	WCs	Urinals	Hand basins	WCs	Hand basins
<500	3	8	2	13	2
<1000	5	10	4	16	4
<2000	9	15	7	18	7
<3000	10	20	14	22	14
<5000	12	30	20	40	20

Source: Blue Mountains City Council, Event Application Form 2010/11, <www.bmcc.nsw.gov.au>.

Table 20.3 Reductions for duration of event

Duration of event	Quantity required
8 hours plus	100%
6–8 hours	80%
4–6 hours	75%
less than 4 hours	70%

Source: Blue Mountains City Council, Event Application Form 2010/11, <www.bmcc.nsw.gov.au>.

Note that in Tables 20.1, 20.2, 20.3 figures are a guide only. Each event needs to be assessed on a case-by-case basis.

be considered. Facilities provided can range from the most basic to the luxury complex described earlier in this chapter. There is no question as to which one the consumer would prefer.

No doubt this type of analysis will be refined even more, with more variables such as the number of intermission periods and type of seating being taken into account.

What is clear is that careful consideration must be given to this issue, particularly for events held out of doors or at temporary venues. Anyone who has spent some time in a long toilet queue at an event will agree that this important element of customer service is sometimes poorly planned. At one event, organisers forgot to turn on water supplies to the toilet facilities, causing dismay on the part of the event audience and incredulity on the part of the emergency plumber who was called in after most toilets had blocked up. The importance of using pre-event checklists is well illustrated by this story.

GENERAL CLEANING

The cleaning function for most events is handled by the venue staff or by a contract cleaning company. The staff involved must be trained in all areas of waste management and policies and procedures developed specifically for cleaning, including cleaning routines and inspections. Responsibility for specific areas needs to be clearly defined. For example, while public areas and toilet facilities are generally the responsibility of the cleaning contractor, the catering contractor may be responsible for cleaning in the kitchen, particularly during service. Staff involved in cleaning need to be very knowledgeable about the event itself as they are frequent targets for questions, the most common one being 'Where are the toilets?'

SUMMARY

This chapter has focused on how the event manager can comply with environmental laws, regulations and codes of conduct. To this end, an environmentally friendly approach to waste management at every event is recommended and, in many cases, a waste management plan is a requirement of local councils. Waste management is an important element of operational planning and one likely to cause dissatisfaction on the part of the customer if anything goes wrong. An increasing level of sophistication is evident at most large events in the provision of facilities, cleaning procedures and waste management, with customers having increasingly higher expectations. Effective communication with all stakeholders, including the audience, is imperative for the successful implementation of the waste management plan.

Chapter review questions

1 What does 'environmental sustainability' mean?
2 List three events which have environmental sustainability as a theme or message.
3 List five practices that can create a more environmentally friendly event.
4 Resource efficiency can be practised by event organisers. Explain this term and give three examples.
5 When registering for a conference it is possible to purchase carbon credits. Explain this concept.

Activity

Visit a waste management site in your state or territory to find bin labels. (Labels are also provided on the EcoRecycle and Department of Environment, Climate Change and Water websites provided in this chapter.) Using these labels, develop a communications strategy to train staff in the area of waste management.

Case study

Waste management

As the event coordinator for the Corumbah International Food and Music Festival, plan the type and number of bins needed as part of your waste management plan. Draw a site map showing the 20 food stalls and the location of public use bins and bins used by the stallholders. Show also the larger skip bins and illustrate how and when these will be installed and accessed by the waste management company during the three-day event. The event is expecting around 25 000 people over the three days. One of the case studies on the Waste Wise NSW website <www.environment.nsw.gov.au/warr/wwe_home.htm/> may provide some relevant ideas.

References

Getz, D & Andersson, T (2009), 'Sustainable festivals: on becoming an institution', *Event Management*, 12(1):1–17.

Jones, R et al. (2008), *Assessing the environmental impacts of special events: examination of nine special events in Western Australia*, CRC for Sustainable Tourism, <www.crctourism.com.au/WMS/Upload/Resources/bookshop/80042JonesEnviroImpactsWEB.pdf>, accessed 11 May 2010.

Robbins, D, Dickinson, J & Calver, S (2007), 'Planning transport for special events: a conceptual framework and future agenda for research', *The International Journal of Tourism Research*, 9(5):303.

CHAPTER 21

FINANCIAL INFORMATION

Unit descriptor

This unit describes the performance outcomes, skills and knowledge required to interpret the types of financial information used by operational supervisors and managers in their day-to-day work activities. The unit focuses on understanding key financial terminology, different types of financial reports and on how financial information is used in the management of a business. This unit applies in any industry context and to a wide range of individuals who need to interpret financial data to inform their work practice, including senior operational staff, supervisors and managers. This unit does not include the skills required to produce financial reports that would generally be created by senior managers, financial specialists or accountants.

Elements

■ Access and interpret financial information
■ Apply financial information to work activities.

Critical aspects for assessment

■ Understanding of the accounting process and of key accounting terminology
■ Ability to interpret financial information and determine the relationship between the information and the performance of a business.

FESTIVALS AUSTRALIA is an Australian Government program which funds Australian regional and community festivals to present quality cultural projects. Funding is available to add a new or special sort of cultural activity.

To be eligible for funding, an activity must not have been previously presented and must be one that could not be afforded without the funding.

Source: <www.arts.gov.au/arts/festivals_australia>. 'All legislative material herein is reproduced by permission but does not purport to be the official or authorised version. It is subject to Commonwealth of Australia copyright.' Copyright Commonwealth of Australia, reproduced by permission.

Applications must be made by organisations that manage regular festivals. Eligible organisations include local governments and councils, cultural organisations and regional arts councils that manage festivals. Applications must come from incorporated not-for-profit organisations, with annual audited financial statements, that have been in existence for at least 12 months.

If you are a new organisation or festival, or if your organisation is not incorporated, your application needs to be prepared under the auspices of an incorporated not-for-profit organisation, such as a local council.

Source: <www.arts.gov.au/arts/festivals_australia/who_is_eligible_to_apply>. All legislative material herein is reproduced by permission but does not purport to be the official or authorised version. It is subject to Commonwealth of Australia copyright.' Copyright Commonwealth of Australia, reproduced by permission.

Almost everyone understands the three concepts—income, expense and budget—because most people use them in their daily lives. Simplistically, income is money that comes in, expense is money that goes out and a budget is a plan to ensure that expenses aren't higher than income. Cash flow management is ensuring that you always have enough money to pay the big bills like the car insurance when they come in.

From the event management perspective, there are various forms of income, including grants, such as those from Festivals Australia described in the chapter opening. Funding is available from Festivals Australia for running events but only to not-for-profit organisations. As you can see, even not-for-profit organisations generally need to submit audited financial statements for past events when applying for new funding, so it is important that you understand the accounting process and how to interpret financial information. Both topics are covered in this chapter.

Running a financially viable event business with the ever-increasing challenges of the current business environment is not easy. These challenges include competition, economic uncertainty, increased government regulation and continuous change. In this context, it is imperative that today's event managers have an understanding of finance and management accounting. Effective operational management, marketing management and human resource management generally ensures excellent service, quality and other attributes of a successful business. However, sound financial management is necessary to ensure financial viability, which is the key to the success and longevity of a business. A manager who has an understanding of accounting and finance is better equipped to take management decisions based on objective data. Accounting and finance are important to every business, regardless of its nature.

The first chapter in this text highlighted some of the key differences between events, event organisations and more traditional long-life businesses. Understanding these differences is important as some events are one-off or annual activities and therefore from an accounting point of view are treated more as *projects* than ongoing business concerns. However, for other event operations, such as staging rental companies, wedding planners and conference organisers, the business is an *ongoing concern* with multiple events and activities occurring on a daily and annual basis. This type of event business looks much like any other business in any other sector.

ACCESS AND INTERPRET FINANCIAL INFORMATION

Usually non-accountants struggle to understand what figures mean. But, as mentioned earlier, to run any event or event business, an understanding of the key accounting concepts is essential, as is an ability to interpret this financial information. First we will discuss the main concepts you need to understand to be able to read an income statement.

INCOME STATEMENT

An income statement (previously known as a profit and loss statement) is a summary of an organisation's revenue, expenditure, gross profit and net profit (or net loss) for a specific period.

Profit

Profit is the positive gain from a business operation after subtracting all expenses from the income. Profit is what most businesses are trying to achieve. However, in the event industry there are two types of organisation: for-profit and not-for-profit. The first of these expects income to exceed expenses, thus making a profit, to be regarded as successful, while the second aims to break even, i.e. simply meet expenses.

The event manager also needs to be aware of a rather unique concept relevant to the industry: that is value in kind (VIK), known by Festivals Australia as 'assistance in kind' (see below).

KEY TERMS	
Accounting	The systematic recording, reporting and analysis of financial transactions of a business
Cash flow	Cash received minus cash payments over a given period of time
Expense	Any cost of doing business
Finance	Simplistically, finance deals with matters related to money; financial management has the aim of managing money well
Income	Also called revenue; simplistically, money earned
Profit	The positive gain from a business operation (or specific event) after subtracting all expenses from the income; the opposite of loss
Sales	Income received for the accounting period

This relates to contributions made by individuals and organisations to support an event. These contributions are not cash and are not purchased by the event organiser; they are goods or services provided free of charge as value in kind. At charity auctions, for example, many of the items are contributed by celebrities, businesses and other supporters of the event.

From an accounting perspective, the event organiser needs to place a value on such contributions so that the financial records give an accurate portrayal of the success or otherwise of the event. Festivals Australia provides the following advice:

> Assistance in-kind income is the estimated value of the work of volunteers, free access to venues or equipment, free advertising or other goods or services provided to the festival by local government or businesses without charge. It should appear under 'Assistance In-Kind' equally in both the income and expenditure columns of the Festival Budget and the Project Budget. This helps the Committee to understand what contribution the festival organisers and the local community is making towards the total cost of both the festival and the project.
>
> *Source:* <www.arts.gov.au/__data/assets/pdf_file/0012/81021/FA-Explanatory-Notes-Round-30.pdf>. 'All legislative material herein is reproduced by permission but does not purport to be the official or authorised version. It is subject to Commonwealth of Australia copyright.' Copyright Commonwealth of Australia, reproduced by permission.

This is unusual: VIK appears in the accounts as income and expense, with the outcome effectively being neutral. The idea is to show its value even though cash does not change hands.

So income should exceed expenses for a for-profit organisation and break-even (no profit and no loss: income = expenses) is the required outcome for a not-for-profit. Both could be in a loss situation, but that is best avoided. At the end of the day, an income statement shows these potential outcomes.

Income accounts

Income is revenue earned by the organisation, but also includes grants, donations, etc. as discussed above. For most events, income comes from the client (e.g. the parents of the bride) or from ticket sales. Sponsorship comes either in the form of cash or as VIK.

Typical income accounts for a small event organisation might include:

★ sales revenue (from ticket sales, etc.)
★ grants
★ donations
★ rentals
★ value in kind.

Adding them together yields **gross revenue**.

Expense accounts

Most companies have a separate account for each type of expense they incur. Typical expense accounts include:

★ salaries and wages
★ advertising
★ telephone
★ electricity and gas utilities
★ interest paid
★ rent paid
★ equipment hire paid.

So profit is the difference between the income of the business and all its costs/expenses. It is normally measured over a period of time.

$$\text{Profit} = \text{Income} - \text{Expenses}$$

For events that run as a one-off affair, this is adequate for the income statement. In a perfect world, the income statement would match the budget. The budget is the plan, and if everything went to plan this would be reflected in the income statement.

In the event industry, the budget is generally prepared before the event and the income statement afterwards, while in most ongoing business operations, budgets and income statements are done regularly and routinely. Budgets are covered in the following chapter.

The income statement for Wave Aid (which raised funds for tsunami victims in 2005) in Figure 21.1 illustrates the actual costs of running this event for which most services were provided free of charge, and then compares these with the final column, which shows the potential expenses associated with a commercial event of a similar scale. Note that talent fees were zero for Wave Aid; in normal circumstances, these fees and expenses would have amounted to approximately $1 million. Technically this represents VIK.

If you look carefully at the income statement for Wave Aid, you will see that it paid $596 727 in cash for goods and services (total expenses), while the 'normal' expenses for this event if run commercially (final column) would amount to $3 527 908. The contributions of all performers, contractors and other organisations amounted to $2 931 181 (potential cost of $3 527 908 less actual cost of $596 727), representing almost $3 million VIK. This example does not follow the recommended listing of VIK in income and expenses, instead using two columns. This also illustrates the unique nature of events and their reporting. However, this example does provide an exceptional insight into the commercial operation of a large-scale music concert.

Wave Aid brought together 50 000 people and 11 artists and raised $2.3 million for Oxfam, Community Aid Abroad, UNICEF, Care Australia and the Australian Red Cross.

Turning to more conventional layouts for reporting revenue and expenses, particularly for events businesses that are ongoing concerns, we need to look at some additional concepts, those of gross revenue (all sources of income), gross profit and net profit.

On the income statement, the most important source of revenue, such as sales of tickets, appears as the first item. If the event is paid for by a single client, this will be the first item as it is the predominant source of revenue. Gross revenue is the total revenue before any costs have been deducted. This is a similar concept to gross (not unpleasant) wages—the amount you would receive if there weren't all sorts of deductions such as tax before it reached your pocket.

If you deduct the direct costs (also known as cost of goods sold) from the gross revenue, you get the gross profit. If the gross revenue from an event were $750 000 and direct costs of $520 000 were deducted, this would result in a gross profit of $230 000. Cost of goods sold covers those costs which relate directly to the revenue earned. They might include cost of venue hire, labour and equipment rental. After calculating the gross profit, you would then deduct your overheads, such as administration costs and rent costs, of $165 000, and you would be left with an operating profit of $65 000. Finally, your net profit is your profit after

FIGURE 21.1
Income
statement
—Wave Aid

Wave Aid Tsunami Relief Concert—29 January 2005
Projected Profit & Loss Statement (exc GST)
as at 15 February 2005

DESCRIPTION	DETAIL	SUB-TOTAL WAVE AID	TOTAL	DETAIL	SUB-TOTAL COMMERCIAL	TOTAL
INCOME						
Concert						
Ticket Sales						
(45191 attendance)	2,220,362					
43150 @ $49.49						
385 @ $62.36						
716 @ $85.09						
940 @ $ 0.00 (suppliers)						
Corporate Boxes (18 × $5000)	90,000					
Merchandise	176,956					
BigPond Licence Fee	15,000					
Total Concert		$2,502,318				
Donations						
Public—1800 line	57,128					
Ticketek Donation	255,000					
Playbill Donation	65,706					
Showbiz Donation	2,500					
K2 Agency Donation	2,385					
Rode Microphones Donation	10,000					
ATS Donation	1,690					
Total Supplier Donations		$394,409				
TOTAL INCOME			$2,896,727			
Less **EXPENSES**						
Cost of Ticket Sales						
Credit Card Charges	43,318					
Total Cost of Sales		$43,318				
Talent Fees & Expenses						
Total Talent Fees & Expenses		$0			$1,200,000	
Production						
Production Management Team	8,350			17,000		
PA Hire & Crew	24,672			84,000		
Lighting Hire & Crew	2,520			56,000		
Screen Hire & Crew	9,500			40,000		
Stage Crew & Loaders	23,980			50,000		
Drivers & Runners + Petrol	6,014			12,000		
Risers	900			4,000		
Backline Hire	2,652			7,000		
Trucking	51,208			75,000		
Banners	8,101			9,686		
Total Production		$137,897			$354,686	
Venue						
Hire Fee	0			350,000		
Customer Service Staff	0			30,000		
Crowd Safety Staff	0			30,000		
Maintenance Staff	0			7,000		
Admin Staff	0			2,000		
Wage On-Costs	0			12,420		
Contractor Fees—A/C, Lifts	0			3,000		
PA Staff On-site	0			2,000		

(continued)

FIGURE 21.1
(continued)

DESCRIPTION	DETAIL	SUB-TOTAL WAVE AID	TOTAL	DETAIL	SUB-TOTAL COMMERCIAL	TOTAL
Cleaning Service/Waste Removal	29,800			49,000		
Skip Bin Hire	0			0		
User pays Police Charge	0			30,000		
Cash handling/Money	0			550		
Scrolling Signage Removal	7,940			3,300		
Sports Lighting	0			13,120		
Medical Charges	0			7,000		
Event Accreditation	0			250		
Turnstile Hire & Installation	0			0		
Barricade Hire	627			8,000		
Variable Message Boards	0			2,500		
Scoreboard & Operator	0			2,000		
EPA Charges	0			7,500		
Sound Monitoring Charge	0			6,000		
Trust Terraplas Hire	0			11,000		
Turf Replacement	0			13,000		
Radio & Headset Hire	0			2,300		
Venue Directional Signage	0			2,000		
Backstage Furniture Hire	2,850			12,000		
Phone Lines	0			1,000		
GA Wristbands	2,453			3,000		
Damages/Misc	0			30,000		
Total Venue		$43,670			$639,940	
Staging						
Engineering & Drafting	2,250			5,814		
Project Management	2,500			2,500		
ESS Crew	22,932			27,925		
Ground Support	0			30,000		
Waterproofing	0			12,000		
Rigging & Build Over	5,338			10,500		
FOH Scaffold Rental	0			2,000		
Decking & Scaffold Rental	2,000			30,000		
Staircase Rental	0			420		
Ballast Rental	600			2,500		
Equipment Prep	10,000			11,897		
Insurance	750			750		
Flights	2,500			2,500		
Set Specials	500			500		
Accommodation	3,500			3,500		
Mojo Barrier	0			8,000		
Incidentals	5,000			5,000		
Local Crew	42,989			56,746		
Catering	0			2,000		
Crane	3,000			5,000		
Hoeckers	4,127			8,500		
Total Staging		$107,986			$228,052	
Security/Site Administration						
Toilets, Basins, Cleaners	3,560			8,000		
Pro floor 9600m^2	43,524			96,000		
Bike Rack Fencing	0			4,000		
Plastic Barrier	0			6,200		
Waterfills	0			3,500		
Event Staff	500			1,500		

(continued)

DESCRIPTION	DETAIL	SUB-TOTAL WAVE AID	TOTAL	DETAIL	SUB-TOTAL COMMERCIAL	TOTAL
Forklift Hire/Fuel	0			6,900		
Fork Operators × 5	10,527			3,000		
Generator Hire/Fuel	15,507			26,000		
Letterbox Drop	0			1,200		
Lighting Towers	0			900		
Site Misc—Float	0			3,000		
Tools (Site Crew)	0			900		
Road Ply	5,310			5,841		
Black Plastic	1,086			1,400		
Cherry Picker/Scissors	2,479			4,770		
Security Staff	39,600			55,000		
Radios	746			4,000		
Site Manager Fee	0			6,000		
OHS Management Syst	500			4,200		
Safety Officer	2,300			6,700		
Water	4,275			4,000		
Wet Weather Contingencies	0			2,500		
1st Aid Marquees	500			2,300		
Contingency	13,291			20,000		
Site Labour	28,916			38,169		
Total Security/Site Administration		$172,621			$315,980	
Catering						
Load-in & Setup Days	0			10,000		
Artist Dressing Rooms	0			10,000		
Backstage Catering—Show Day	9,513			20,000		
Water for Crew	2,435			5,000		
Media Room	0			2,000		
Total Catering		$11,948			$47,000	
Travel & Accom						
Air Travel—International	1,900			15,000		
Air Travel—Domestic	12,009			30,000		
Accommodation	431			40,000		
Ground Transport—Hire Cars	1,924			1,000		
Total Travel & Accom		$16,263			$86,000	
Administration & Mngment						
Accreditation	1,928			3,750		
Office Costs	20,000			70,000		
Mobile Phones × 7	5,000			9,000		
Total Administration & Mngment		$26,928			$82,750	
Marketing & Publicity						
Logo Design	0			3,000		
Artwork	0			10,000		
Radio Ad—Production	0			5,000		
TV Ad—Production	992			15,000		
Press Ads—Production	0			10,000		
Street Poster Print	700			4,000		
Street Poster Distribution	0			3,000		
Street Press Advertising	0			5,000		
Metro Press Advertising	0			170,000		
Radio Campaign—Nova	0			5,000		
Radio Campaign—Triple M	0			5,000		
Radio Campaign—2Day-FM	0			5,000		
Foxtel Platform Campaign	0			100,000		
Free to Air TV Campaigns	0			50,000		

FIGURE 21.1 (continued)

(continued)

FIGURE 21.1
(continued)

DESCRIPTION	DETAIL	SUB-TOTAL WAVE AID	TOTAL	DETAIL	SUB-TOTAL COMMERCIAL	TOTAL
Publicists x 3—Fees	0			30,000		
Publicity Costs	6,704			7,500		
Press Launch —Venue/Prodn Hire	0			7,000		
Website & E Cards	0			25,000		
Total Marketing & Publicity		$8,396			$459,500	
Finance & Insurance						
APRA	0			35,000		
Insurance—Public Risk	25,645			59,000		
Accounting/Legal	2,055			20,000		
Total Finance & Insurance		$27,700			$114,000	
TOTAL EXPENSES		**$596,727**				**$3,527,908**
NET PROFIT		**$2,300,000**				

Source: Reproduced with permission of Wave Aid, <www.waveaid.com.au/about.html>.

FIGURE 21.2
Income
statement

Income Statement as at 30 June 20XX

Gross revenue	$750 000	
Less cost of goods sold	$520 000	
Gross profit		**$230 000**
Less adminstrative and other overhead costs	$165 000	
Operating profit		**$65 000**
Less other income expenses (such as interest)	$6 000	
Profit before tax		$59 000
Less tax	$18 000	
Net profit for the year/event		**$41 000**

all other costs (such as interest paid) and tax would be deducted, giving you your net profit, in this case $41 000. This is illustrated in Figure 21.2.

To summarise, gross profit takes into account the direct costs of sales, while net profit is the bottom line.

Gross profit

As we have seen, gross profit is the difference between **sales income** and the **direct costs** of the product. (In the event business the product is the 'show' or other event such as a surf carnival). Gross profit is used as a performance indicator to help the business make decisions on its pricing policies. For example, sales income would be ticket sales, and direct costs would be the cost of performers, staging and venue. Thus the most likely costs to appear as direct costs would be:

★ venue rental or site costs
★ performance costs (e.g. staging)
★ event operational costs (e.g. food and beverage)
★ talent costs (e.g. speaker, band, players).

Net profit

Net profit represents gross profit less all expenses associated with the normal running of the business. Net profit shows how well the business performs under its normal trading circumstances. Normal **running costs** for an event business generally include administration and office expenses, as well as advertising, as the key expenses.

Food and beverage costs relate directly to the numbers attending an event

Therefore, when producing an Income Statement the headings would be:

Sales income

Less cost of sales

GROSS PROFIT

Less administrative and other overhead costs

NET PROFIT

Figure 21.3 shows these terms for a normal business on the left and an event 'translation' on the right.

Having dealt with the idea of 'in', 'out' and what is left over—'profit', let us move on to another way to look at the financial status of a business. Here we take into account assets (things of value), and liabilities (usually bank loans or other debts).

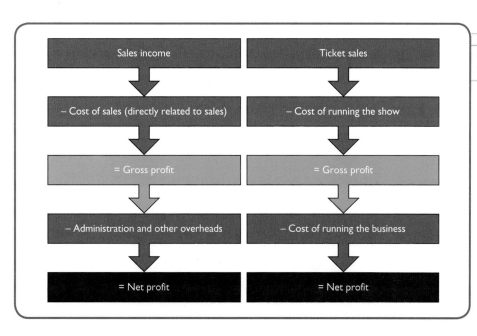

FIGURE 21.3
Illustration of net profit

BALANCE SHEET

If only life were so easy—now there are assets and liabilities to consider. An event company might own a vehicle and a store full of staging equipment. These items are assets as they have a value. On the other hand, the company might also have liabilities. These are amounts owed by the company (such as bank loans).

While the income statement (or statement of financial performance) captures results for a given period, such as a financial year, the balance sheet (or statement of financial position) gives you an idea of what a business is worth at a certain point in time. Where the owners of the business have acquired assets (e.g. sound and lighting equipment), this becomes very relevant; likewise, if there are outstanding bills to be paid. The balance sheet shows what the result would be if all bills were paid and everything were sold (assets minus liabilities). This result is the owner's equity in the business:

Assets – Liabilities = Owner's equity

The problem for many event management businesses is that many of their assets, such as their reputation, are intangible and difficult to value!

Figure 21.4 illustrates the concept of owner's equity for a normal business on the left, with another event 'translation' on the right. Generally, of course, the assets and liabilities are listed in detail. However, as mentioned previously, an event business is quite different from most others as it is service oriented and doesn't carry stock as does, for example, a

FIGURE 21.4
Illustration of owner's equity

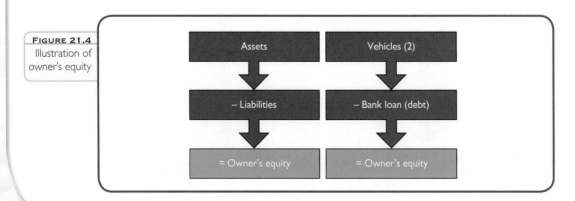

fashion boutique. Consequently, reporting is simpler as the owner generally has little equity. Assets and liabilities are often minimal for event businesses run by professional conference organisers or wedding planners for example.

APPLY FINANCIAL INFORMATION TO WORK ACTIVITIES

Now that the two main accounting statements have been outlined:

Income Statement or Statement of Financial **Performance** (Income – Expenses = Profit or Loss)

and

Balance Sheet or Statement of Financial **Position** (Assets – Liabilities = Owner's Equity)

we can look more closely at day-to-day activities where many financial transactions take place, all of which finally contribute to these reports. However, before doing so, it is important to understand that the net profit is calculated on the income statement and is then added to the owner's equity (see definition of owner's equity).

The accounting process records every financial transaction that a business makes. A financial transaction involves a transfer of money for goods or services. This gives rise to receipts and payments for the business. Financial transactions can take place on cash or credit terms. Cash terms imply that there is an exchange of cash for receipt of a good or service. Credit terms imply that there is a promise to pay within a specified time for the exchange of a good or service. This gives rise to debtors and creditors. Debtors (Accounts Receivable) are people or businesses that owe money to the business. Creditors (Accounts Payable) are people or businesses to which the business owes money. Debtors are assets to the business and creditors are a liability to the business. Assets are items of monetary value owned by the business or owed to the business. Liabilities are financial debt owed by the business to outside parties. This widens our understanding of the concepts, asset and liability.

Examples of financial transactions include:

★ purchase of staging equipment on credit
★ cash deposit into the bank from ticket sales
★ receipt of money from a donor
★ payment to a supplier, creditor X
★ receipt from a customer, debtor Y.

Every financial transaction generates a proof of transaction or documentary evidence for all parties involved in the transaction. The documentary evidence can be electronic copies or hard copies. They are known as source documents and are the first records in the accounting process.

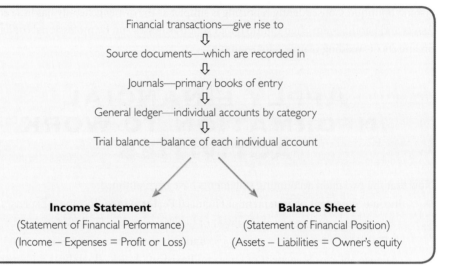

FIGURE 21.5
Flow chart of the accounting process

Financial transactions—give rise to
⇩
Source documents—which are recorded in
⇩
Journals—primary books of entry
⇩
General ledger—individual accounts by category
⇩
Trial balance—balance of each individual account

Income Statement
(Statement of Financial Performance)
(Income − Expenses = Profit or Loss)

Balance Sheet
(Statement of Financial Position)
(Assets − Liabilities = Owner's equity

Examples of source documents include:

★ invoices
★ receipts
★ statements
★ cheque butts
★ petty cash vouchers
★ bank statements
★ credit notes.

These source documents are entered in accounting records called journals and ledgers, and the process of record keeping of all the financial transactions is commonly known as bookkeeping. In today's world, bookkeeping is electronic through the use of accounting software. The basic rules of bookkeeping are the same whether recorded manually or electronically. A flow chart of the accounting process is illustrated in Figure 21.5.

JOURNALS

Information is summarised into journals before it is entered into ledgers. Transactions are sorted into similar groups and each group is entered into a journal. A journal is a **daybook** recording in date order the transactions of the business. There are five common journals:

1 Cash Receipts Journal—records all cash or cheque receipts of the business
2 Cash Payments Journal—records all payments made by cash or cheque by the business
3 Sales Journal—records all credit sales of the business
4 Purchases Journal—records all credit purchases made by the business
5 General Journal—records all other transactions not recorded in any of the specialised journals.

Ledger accounts are individual accounts for every asset, liability, owner's equity, revenue or expense item in the business. Ledgers require double entry.

What is double entry?

Double entry is the recording of financial transactions in two different places to form a system of checks and balances. An amount recorded as a debit has a corresponding amount recorded as a credit. The basic rule is that for every debit there should be a credit of equal value. The accounting equation is fundamental to the system of double entry.

Debits and credits

These are the essence of any accounting system. Every accounting entry in the general ledger contains both a debit and a credit. Further, all debits must equal all credits. If they don't, the entry is out of balance. That's not good. Out-of-balance entries throw your balance sheet out of balance.

Therefore, the accounting system must have a mechanism to ensure that all entries balance. Indeed, most automated accounting systems won't let you enter an out-of-balance entry. Depending on what type of account you are dealing with, a debit or credit will either increase or decrease the account balance. Figure 21.6 illustrates the entries that increase or decrease each type of account.

Account	Debit	Credit
Assets	Increases	Decreases
Liabilities	Decreases	Increases
Income	Decreases	Increases
Expenses	Increases	Decreases
Owner's equity	Decreases	Increases

FIGURE 21.6 Debits and credits for different account types

Notice that for every increase in one account, there is an opposite (and equal) decrease in another. That's what keeps the entry in balance. Also notice that debits always go on the left and credits always go on the right.

The recordings of financial transactions are entered by date, account name and the amount in one of two columns. The left-hand column is called the debit and the right-hand column is called the credit. In double entry, debit and credit does not mean good or bad, it just means left or right column entry. Debits and credits are determined in journals and then posted to the general ledger where the account balances are updated to reflect all the transactions for the period. An illustrated example of this is provided in Chapter 29.

Two ledger formats are illustrated on page 332 in Figure 21.7.

For most business operations there is a time delay before accounts are paid. To manage these processes we have accounts receivable (collecting money) and accounts payable (paying the business's accounts for goods and services purchased).

Accounts receivable (debtors)

These are amounts owed to the business by outside parties due to credit sales. For example, a longstanding client for whom the event company runs corporate lunches is allowed 30-day credit terms and may settle their accounts within that time. Until they settle their accounts they are debtors to the business.

Accounts payable (creditors)

These are amounts owed by the business to suppliers of goods and services. The suppliers, as part of trading, stipulate credit terms, again, say 30 days. Until they are paid they are

FIGURE 21.7
Formats for a
ledger account

1. T-account format

Account name

Debit			Credit		
Date	Account	Amount	Date	Account	Amount

2. Running balance format

Account name

Date	Account	Debit	Credit	Balance

creditors to the business. Credit purchases in events management might be for hire equipment, flowers or small-scale catering.

So let's return to the concept of double entry and look at examples.

In the first stage of the example we will record a credit sale to a customer for a catered lunch:

General Journal

Date	Details	Debit	Credit
	Accounts Receivable (Asset, increasing)	$1000	
	Sales (Income, increasing)		$1000

If you looked at the general ledger right now, you would see that Accounts Receivable had a balance of $1000 and Sales had a balance of $1000.

Now we'll record the collection of the money from the client:

General Journal

Date	Details	Debit	Credit
	Cash at Bank (Asset, increasing)	$1000	
	Accounts Receivable (Asset, decreasing)		$1000

In the end, the Accounts Receivable balance will be back to zero? That's as it should be once the balance is paid. The net result is the same as if we conducted the whole transaction in cash:

General Journal

Date	Details	Debit	Credit
	Cash at Bank (Asset, increasing)	$1000	
	Sales (Income, increasing)		$1000

Of course, very few business transactions are made in cash and there would probably be a period of time between the recording of the receivable and its collection.

LEDGERS

Financial transactions are recorded in ledgers, which are primary record-keeping books. All ledger accounts may be grouped under five categories:

1 Assets—items of monetary value owned by the business or owed to the business
2 Liabilities—money owed by the business to outside parties
3 Owner's equity—owner's share of the business
4 Income—revenue earned by the business
5 Expenses—costs incurred by the business to earn income.

The balances of the assets, liabilities and owner's equity group of accounts are reported in the **balance sheet**. The balances of the income and expense accounts are reported in the **income statement** for taxation purposes. The accounting period is one financial year, which generally starts on 1 July and ends on 30 June of the following year. Owners may also require weekly, monthly or quarterly reports depending on the nature and size of the business. Profit is the primary measure of business performance for most organisations and these reports help keep businesses on track.

As mentioned at the beginning of this chapter, these accounting processes are typical for an ongoing event company which presents annual reports. However, when reports are done for a single event, things are simplified, and the main report is the income statement, which shows whether the event has made a profit, a loss or achieved break-even. In the next chapter we will look at the budget, which forecasts financial performance.

SUMMARY

An ability to interpret financial information in order to understand business performance is an essential attribute of an event manager. In this chapter we have therefore looked at the accounting process, which involves collecting, classifying and recording financial data in journals and ledgers in order to produce an income statement and a balance sheet from which performance can be measured against the budget. Most accounting concepts, such as income, expense and profit, are easy to understand. But in business money does not generally change hands immediately as accounts operate on a 30, 60 or even 90 day credit cycle, so at any one time a business owes money for goods and services that have been purchased, and is also owed money for goods and services it has sold. Unless creditors are carefully monitored, cash flow problems will inevitably occur. And unless a close watch is kept on income and expenses, the result could be a loss to the business.

Chapter review questions

1 Explain the meaning of the following terms:
   (a) Accounting
   (b) Financial management
   (c) Expense
   (d) Income
   (e) Profit
   (f) Cash flow.
2 What are typical income accounts for an event organisation?
3 What is VIK (value in kind) and why is it important to deal with it from an accounting point of view?
4 What are typical expense accounts for an event organisation?
5 Using Wave Aid as an example, explain how so much money was raised for charity.
6 List four source documents for financial transactions.
7 Why is the system of double entry used?
8 Explain the meaning of the following terms:
   (a) Assets
   (b) Liabilities
   (c) Debts
   (d) Sales.

Activities

1 Visit three websites for venues used for parties and find out about their credit terms, if any. At what stage would you need to pay a deposit and a final payment?
2 Search for suppliers of event goods and services to see if any offer credit terms that imply a discount if the payment is made within a specified time.

Case study

Advantageous credit terms

Georgina has come up with a brilliant idea for an events catering business. She says that she can buy all her food and beverage products from a wholesaler on 30 days credit. She will be paid by her clients before the event, deposit on booking (20%) and full payment and confirmation of numbers one week before the event. Using the accounting concepts of income, expense, cash flow and credit, explain how this business has advantages over an events business that has several large debtors.

References

Lymer, A, Randall, J & Azmat, N (2010), *Basic accounting*, Hachette Australia, Sydney, NSW.
Tracy, J (2008), *Accounting for dummies*, 4th edn, Wiley Publishing, Hoboken, NJ.

22

BUDGETS

Unit descriptor

This unit describes the performance outcomes, skills and knowledge required to prepare and monitor budgets. While the nature of the budget may vary, the unit focuses on the key managerial skills of analysing financial information to inform developing a budget, drafting a budget and monitoring budget performance over time.

This unit requires researching and analysing financial and other business information and applying it to budget planning, development, negotiation and monitoring. It requires sound knowledge of accounting principles, budget development methods, and presentation formats for different types of budget.

Elements

- Prepare budget information
- Prepare budget
- Finalise budget
- Monitor and review budget.

Critical aspects for assessment

- Understanding of the technical processes and procedures that must be followed in budget preparation
- Sound analysis of the factors that impact the budget and budget development process
- Ability to prepare realistic and accurate budgets within relevant workplace context
- Preparation of multiple budgets to meet specific and differing workplace needs
- Project or work activities conducted over an operationally realistic period of time so that the planning and evaluation aspects of preparing and monitoring a budget can be assessed.

CHRISTMAS came early for some of Ballarat's major events this week. The bearer of gifts was state Tourism and Major Events Minister Tim Holding, who announced $170 000 in funds for three Ballarat events. The Australian Open Road Cycling Championships will be given $100 000 over the next three years and the Ballarat Begonia Festival will get $50 000 over two years. The Ballarat International Foto Biennale will get $20 000 towards its next event in 2011. Mr Holding said the funding was timely in what had been a difficult year for regional tourism. 'We've had the bushfires, the worst natural disaster in Australia's history, swine flu, the global financial crisis which effectively stopped spending,' Mr Holding said. He said regional events bring large numbers of visitors which boost the local economy and create jobs. 'What you can do is reinvest in the events that you've already got. That's exactly what Ballarat is doing and I think it will be a very successful strategy.' Ballarat Mayor Judy Verlin said the funding would provide certainty for the council in its management of events.

Source: Power, M (2009), 'Ballarat events share $170 000 funding', The Courier, 23 December,
<www.thecourier.com.au/news/local/news/general/ballarat-events-share-170000-funding/1712669.aspx>.

Many events are dependent on funding from government bodies as one source of income. This contribution of $170 000 by Tourism Victoria's Events Program to the three Ballarat events is a good example, potentially engendering higher levels of tourism visitation in this regional area, which in turn creates positive direct and indirect economic impacts in the region. Government funding for cultural and sporting events also has a positive social impact. For example, the International Sporting Events Program, a NSW Government initiative, is designed to assist in attracting international sporting events to NSW, and supporting these events. Only the following types of organisations are eligible for funding:

★ national and state sporting organisations
★ not-for-profit sporting and recreational organisations
★ other not-for-profit organisations
★ event organisers that have a contractual arrangement with a national or state sporting organisation.

As explained in previous chapters, event organisations fit into two key categories: for-profit and not-for-profit. A for-profit event is planned with a margin in mind in order to achieve a return on investment. However, a not-for-profit organisation has to budget just as carefully as a for-profit business, as it is essential that it covers all or most of its costs. Suppliers also expect a mark-up, except for charitable and other not-for-profit events for which they might provide goods and services at cost.

Event budgets differ in other significant ways. Some event budgets, such as those illustrated in Figures 22.3 and 22.4 at the end of the chapter are for a single event. The budget template provided in the Activity at the end of this chapter and on the website for this text is also for a single event, something we call a short-life or project organisation. Budgets are also developed by long-life event organisations, such as event suppliers of goods (stage rentals) and services (AV support) and conference and exhibition centres, which run events almost on a daily basis. Long-life event organisations need to develop more traditional budgets such as sales budgets, departmental budgets and cash flow forecasts. Reviews are then conducted on a weekly or monthly basis to check performance against the annual budget.

A conference and exhibition centre is a venue and charges for space and services. It manages the budget for the operation of the venue. A professional conference organiser (PCO) or exhibition organiser manages the event budget for a conference or exhibition held at the venue, and the client manages the budget for its organisation. This is illustrated in Figure 22.1.

Not all events have profit or break-even in mind; they have other non-financial objectives. For example, a promotion for a new product, such as a brand of perfume, would be part of a marketing initiative, with the expectation being a long-term return through sales. Similarly, a company awards ceremony or incentive event might be paid for by the organisation with the expectation that this would lead to increased employee motivation. In some cases the company expects a return on objectives (ROO) rather than a return on investment (ROI). These objectives are often marketing objectives where the event's purpose is to communicate several messages to the audience. In all cases, it is essential that the contracted event company has a clear idea of the financial and other objectives of the client, which may be a business, a government agency, or an individual, such as a bride!

According to Goldblatt (2002) there are three categories of event budgets:

★ profit-oriented events where revenue exceeds expenses (e.g. ticketed events)
★ break-even events where revenue is equal to expenses (e.g. community events)
★ hosted events where the client meets the cost of the event (e.g. product launch, 21st birthday party).

The first step in the financial management of an event is to ask the following questions.

Is the aim to make a profit?

As explained above, many events have a range of objectives that do not include making a profit. For example, street parades or music festivals may be offered to the public free of charge, the expenses being met by government agencies and/or sponsors. Or goods and

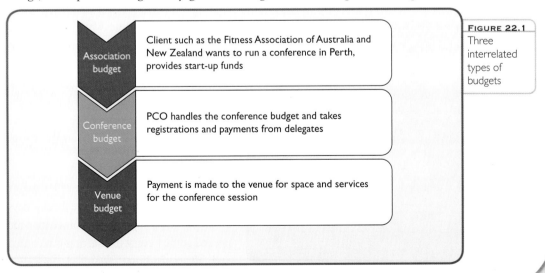

FIGURE 22.1
Three interrelated types of budgets

Association budget — Client such as the Fitness Association of Australia and New Zealand wants to run a conference in Perth, provides start-up funds

Conference budget — PCO handles the conference budget and takes registrations and payments from delegates

Venue budget — Payment is made to the venue for space and services for the conference session

services are provided by businesses and individuals to assist in the running of an event, thus making it difficult to accurately estimate the actual costs. However, it is still essential that all other expenses are properly approved and documented.

Where the objective of an event is raising money for charity, a target needs to be set and, once again, both the expenses and the funds raised need to be accounted for correctly.

How much will the event cost?

In the example of the fundraising event above, as indeed for any non-profit event, it is important to estimate how much the event will cost as well as to keep track of the actual expenses incurred. With every event, money changing hands must be properly documented and, in most cases, the financial records should be audited. Expenses, or costs, include fees, hire costs, advertising, insurance, and so on.

What are the revenue sources?

Generally, revenue is raised by selling tickets or charging admission or registration fees. Merchandise sales also contribute to revenue. Merchandising items, such as T-shirts and caps, may be sold by the event organiser or under arrangement with retailers whereby the event organiser earns a percentage of any sales. The same arrangement may occur with food and beverage sales.

How many tickets must be sold to break even?

This is a critical question. In essence, it relates to whether you decide on a large venue, large audience and low price or a small venue, small audience and high price. This will be discussed in more detail later in this chapter.

What is the cash flow situation?

Events are fairly unique in that, for many, revenue comes in only on the day of the event. This means that all costs, such as salaries, office expenses and fees, have to be met up-front from existing funds. When ticket sales occur long before an event is staged, as they do with major concerts, this puts the company in the enviable position of being able to pay for its expenses from revenue while also earning interest on this money until the remaining bills become due. Very few events fit this category. Cash flow planning is an essential part of the event planning process for the above-mentioned reasons.

Ten thousand emergency ponchos may be required for an outdoor event and should be included in the budget unless the supplier will take returns; if sold the margins could be high

What control systems are needed to avoid fraud?

All businesses are accountable and systems need to be put in place to ensure that moneys are accounted for. Systems and procedures are needed so that every transaction is recorded and all expenditure approved, including payment of invoices, cash payments, tax and so on. Cash management systems for the day of the event are often lacking and it is not uncommon for registers to be left open, for staff to take handfuls of change without substituting notes and for bags of cash to be left lying around. This is clearly unsatisfactory.

Equipment rental—a common expense item for events

How will legal and taxation obligations be met?

Employing the services of a properly qualified accountant will ensure that your organisation maintains accurate records and meets its legal obligations.

PREPARE BUDGET INFORMATION

Preparing a budget is part of the initial planning stage for any event. A budget includes projected revenue and expenditure from which an estimate of the net profit (or sometimes net loss) for the proposed event can be ascertained. It is a plan based on accurate quotes from all contractors and suppliers and careful research to ensure that no expenses have been overlooked. It provides guidelines for approving expenditure and ensuring that the financial aspects of the event remain on track. The budget is part of the event proposal or the basis of the quote by the event management company to the client.

An example of an event budget is provided in Figure 22.2 on page 340. This budget illustrates the difference between fixed costs (administration and overheads) and variable costs (those *directly* related to the number of customers, e.g. catering costs), which vary in relation to the size of the audience.

The following factors also need to be taken into account when preparing budgets.

INTERNAL AND EXTERNAL FACTORS

During initial budget discussions these internal and external factors need to be considered and clarified:

★ organisational and management restructures
★ organisational objectives
★ new legislation or regulations
★ growth or decline in economic conditions
★ significant price movement for certain goods or services
★ shift in market trends
★ scope of the project
★ venue availability and cost
★ human resource requirements.

Fixed Costs

Venue hire
Artists
   Speaker
   Actor/scriptwriter
   Singer/composer
   Choreographer
   Technical director
   Set designer
   Make-up designer
   Props designer
Production Team
   Stage manager
   Asst stage manager
   Asst technical
Costumes
   T-shirts @ $ (+10% extreme sizes)
Sound
   Copyright
   Hire
Lights
Vision (for presentation and speaker)
   Based on powerpoint presentation and video
   Preparation of visuals
Staging
   Preparation of production detail
   Set backdrop, paints etc.
   Props materials
   Expendables
   Posters for theatre × 6
   Props
   Laptop and printer
Printing
   Individual group labels
   Invitations
   Programs—shell plus insert
   Reviews
Onsite staff (catering)
Other hire (catering)
Gifts
Photography (digital camera)

Video recording
   Video camera hire
   Tapes
Set-up/dismantle
Freight
Airfares
   SYD–AKL return × 1
   SYD–AKL return × 1 (bus.class)
   SYD–MEL return × 5 @ $
Transfers
   Airport
   Coach—Hotel–theatre–hotel
   Coach—Office–theatre–office
   Coach—Airport–theatre–hotel
Accommodation and meals
   AKL 2 × 2 days
   MEL 4 × 2 days, 1 × 1 day
Miscellaneous
   Phone, fax, courier estimate
Contingency
Management fee

Total Fixed Costs

Variable Costs

Catering

Coffee on arrival	@ $
Morning tea with muffins	@ $
Lunch—working type	@ $
Afternoon tea	@ $
Pre-show canapé and buffet dinner	@ $
Beverage	@ $
Total	**$ per head**
Breakfast for interstate arrivals 15	@ $

Total Variable Costs

Total Each Location

GRAND TOTAL

Source: Reproduced with permission of Events Unlimited

The organisational objectives and human resource requirements for the Surry Hills Festival are illustrated in the extract below. The implications from a budget perspective are immediately obvious: the budget for this event would be largely built from value-in-kind (VIK) contributions and donations.

Organisation of the Surry Hills Festival is a major undertaking, and is effectively a 12-month process. We employ two professional part-time Festival Directors 6 months prior to the festival, but everyone else involved is a volunteer. A Festival planning committee meets monthly throughout the year, and on the day of the event about 100 volunteers are involved, not to mention the

100 or so performers, all of whom donate their time and talents to the Festival free of charge. Community members are invited to participate in the planning of the Festival and to volunteer their time in the weeks leading up to the Festival and on the day.

Source: <www.shnc.org/festival/SHFCommunity.htm>.

In contrast, it appears that nothing comes free in the wedding business. Choice magazine reports that the soon-to-be married couple pays a premium for their venue and services; in one case, the venue charged double for a wedding!

Here comes the bride: and up goes the price

Mention the word 'wedding' and events can cost you more

A CHOICE undercover shadow shop has revealed that if you mention the word 'wedding' when booking an event more than half of the venues and suppliers will charge more than for an identical birthday event. CHOICE sought quotes from 60 reception venues, cake makers, hire car businesses, entertainments, florists and photographers in Sydney and Melbourne. One shopper asked for prices for her wedding and another for her 40th birthday. Both events had the same number of guests and identical requirements in terms of cars, cakes, flowers, photographers, entertainment and venue. All the venues, bar two, wanted extra for the nuptials with one Melbourne business wanting to charge almost double.

Photographers were told shots were only needed at the reception centre. Of the ten approached five charged a higher rate for the wedding. One asked for $2200 extra. Seven of the ten hire car businesses quoted more for the wedding. Two Sydney operators upped the ante by 54%. Six of the ten DJs did likewise with one quoting 87% extra for the wedding.

Suppliers said that the demanding nature of weddings and 'sky-high' expectations meant higher costs and justified the more expensive quotes. The average cost of a wedding in 2008 was $33 349, with Australian couples expected to spend a collective $3.7 billion on their big days in 2009.

Source: <www.choice.com.au/Media-and-News/Media-releases>. 'Here comes the bride: and up goes the price', Media release, 11 December 2009, CHOICE.

MANAGEMENT FEES

In many cases, an event organiser charges a management fee to oversee an event. As a ballpark figure for planning purposes, this is generally in the region of 10–15% of total costs. While an event might have a low budget, it might still require considerable time and effort in its organisation and the lower end of the range, 10%, would simply not cover management costs. In this case, or in the case of smaller projects, clients can be billed on a per hour fee basis. In a fiercely competitive environment, there may be situations in which the event planner may look at business as a short-term opportunity with long-term gain.

Prior to contracts being signed, the event organiser should work out the tasks involved in the event, allocate staff to the various roles and determine their pay rates (plus on-costs such as superannuation, workers compensation insurance, payroll tax, and sick leave and annual leave (for permanent employees) in order to come up with a more accurate estimate of management costs and therefore the management fee to be charged. In some situations, the event organiser might wish to involve themselves in a collaborative entrepreneurial arrangement with the client whereby the management fee is based on income earned or sponsorship raised.

If a management fee is charged, the client is usually responsible for all pre-event payments to venues and subcontractors. The fee is for the management and coordination of the event by the event organisers, and for their expertise, from concept through to execution. By charging a management fee only (and not assuming financial risk), the event organiser is to some degree at arm's length. This in turn is linked to other risks, such as public liability risk. Since many events are structured with cascading responsibility through many layers of client, contractor and subcontractor, it is essential that all these contractual relationships are clear, including financial and legal responsibilities at each level.

CONTINGENCIES

Most event budgets include a contingency for unexpected expenses. This ranges from 5% of the costs (if the event organiser is confident that the costs are controllable) to 10% (if there are a number of unknown variables or the costs are uncertain).

PREPARE THE BUDGET

The budgeting process is as follows:

1 Draft the budget, based on analysis of all available information, ensuring that income and expenditure estimates are clearly identified and supported by valid, reliable and relevant information.
2 Analyse the internal and external environments for potential impacts on the budget.
3 Assess and present alternative approaches to the budget.
4 Ensure that the draft budget accurately reflects event/business objectives.
5 Circulate the draft budget to colleagues for comment and discussion.
6 Negotiate the budget with all relevant stakeholders, including the client where relevant.
7 Agree and incorporate modifications to the budget.
8 Complete the final budget in the required format within the designated time.
9 Inform colleagues of final budget decisions and ramifications in a timely manner.
10 Review budget regularly to assess performance against estimates.
11 Analyse and investigate deviations (variances).
12 Collect information for future budget preparation.

BREAK-EVEN POINT

To work out the break-even point, the event organiser has to estimate the number of tickets that need to be sold in order to meet expenses (see Figure 22.3 on page 343). These expenses include both fixed costs and variable costs. Fixed costs, such as licensing fees, insurance, administrative costs, rent of office space, advertising costs and fees paid to artists, generally do not vary if the size of the event audience increases and are often called overheads. Variable costs increase as the size of the audience increases. If food and beverage were part

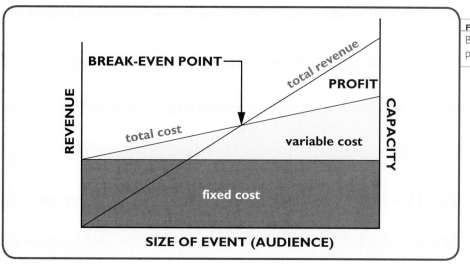

FIGURE 22.3
Break-even
point

of, say, a conference package, clearly these costs would escalate if the numbers attending the conference increased. Once the total revenue is the same as the total expenditure (fixed and variable), then break-even point has been reached. Beyond it, the event is profitable.

In the case of an exhibition, the organiser would be using the budget to establish how many exhibitors were needed to break even. The price charged for exhibiting could clearly be quite low if there were a lot of exhibitors; the price charged would have to be high if there were few exhibitors and if the aim were to meet the budget (particularly for fixed costs). However, this is not an altogether feasible way of setting prices or fees since there is a maximum price the market will bear and a minimum level at which the event becomes viable. This iterative process of analysing ticket prices or fees charged and the break-even point is part of the financial decision-making process.

INCOME STRATEGY

Income strategy is a most complex issue for both large and small events. Even the smallest school fete committee wonders whether to charge an entry fee at the gate, and how much, to meet all costs of running the event, and whether to allow stallholders and ride operators to charge individually and then to take a commission from these operators.

Event income can come from the following sources:

★ entry tickets
★ rental for stalls, stands and exhibitors
★ merchandise sales (hats, CDs, etc.)
★ licensing
★ sale of programs
★ sale of food and beverage
★ sponsorship or grants
★ parking fees.

Licensing the sale of products can be a major source of income. When, for example, there is significant demand for merchandise associated with a major event (such as the World Cup, Le Tour de France, *The Lion King*), an agreement may be reached with another organisation to manufacture and sell products such as toys, clothing, CDs, pins and souvenirs. This licensing arrangement will include a royalty for use of logos, names and images of the event on specific products, and the products will often be sold in retail outlets outside the event precinct, such as Kmart, as well as at the event. Each item sold will attract a royalty payment for the event organising body.

Food and beverage items are often sold by concessionaires who pay a retainer to the event organiser or client to operate on the event premises and sell at the event. This arrangement is also common for bars and coffee stalls.

Ticket pricing

All sources of income must be factored in when making a decision on ticket prices. Clearly, the higher the level of sponsorship and other income, the lower the ticket price.

Ticket pricing decisions also need to reflect the anticipated size of the audience, the potential for different pricing levels (e.g. seating allocations), the price the audience will bear, the opportunity for last-minute discounting, and many other factors. The logistics of ticketing include printing, distribution, collection and reconciliation, which all have implications for cash flow. A ticketing agency charges a commission on sales and distribution; however, pre-event ticketing does provide a source of cash when it is most needed.

Ticket sales and distribution on the day of an event can be problematic in terms of service and safety if not managed well—crowds forming at an entrance and long queues are to be avoided at all costs.

In addition to numbering of tickets and development of an interval pass system, the event organiser needs to consider the logistics of delivering cash for change and banking large amounts of money (often necessary when banks are shut) at the close of the event.

FINALISE THE BUDGET

Once the budget has been negotiated and approved, it needs to be monitored on an ongoing basis to see whether forecasts were accurate. Modifications may be necessary and these should be carefully documented, particularly if the client is paying the bills.

Management accounting refers to the establishment of the budget, while cost accounting (part of management accounting) refers to establishing the actual cost of operations. Management accounting also involves analysis of variance: that is, areas in which there is a variance between the budget and the actual cost. In the organic event environment (in which every hour brings a new idea—more lights, better sound, bigger stage), it is difficult to manage the budget. Every change requested needs new agreement and this should be done in writing. The formal processes (approvals) involved here depend on the nature of the event and the financial arrangements. As with the management structure, the financial structure of a large event can be very complex, involving, for example, promoter, venue, sponsors and suppliers.

PANIC PAYMENTS

This unusual accounting term is not exclusive to the event industry, but this industry is one in which inflated panic prices are often paid. In an ideal world, the event manager has all quotes sewn up and the budget locked in long before the event. There should be few unforeseen contingencies—but don't forget this line in your budgets!

In reality, Murphy's law dictates that something will always go wrong. And the closer it is to the event, the more difficult it is to negotiate a reasonable price for what you require to put it right. In fact, if it is a last-minute crisis, it could easily lead to a high premium price—a panic payment. Essentially, the supplier has the event manager over a barrel. Careful planning, budgeting and detailed contracts negotiated well in advance can prevent this situation occurring.

FINANCIAL CONTROL SYSTEMS

All purchases must be approved and usually a requisition form is used for this purpose. This means that the manager has the opportunity to approve costs incurred by employees. Once goods are ordered, or services provided, checks must be made that they meet specifications before the bills are paid. Fraud could occur if an employee had authority to make purchases, record and physically handle the goods, and pay the bills. This is why these roles are usually carried out by different people. In any case, the system should have checks and balances to make sure that:

★ purchases or other expenses are approved
★ goods and services meet specifications
★ payment is approved
★ accounts are paid
★ incoming revenue is checked and banked
★ revenue totals are recorded correctly
★ debts are met
★ all transactions are recorded and balanced
★ taxation requirements are met
★ financial matters are correctly reported to stakeholders.

MONITOR AND REVIEW THE BUDGET

As mentioned earlier, all stakeholders with a financial involvement in the event need to review the budget regularly to assess actual performance against estimated performance and to prepare accurate financial reports. The first of these steps is illustrated in the budgets for a family fun day and a multicultural food festival in Figures 22.4 and 22.5 on pages 246 and 247. In both of these, the difference between budget and actual expenditure is shown. As you can see from Figure 22.4, an essential item for NAIDOC week, a flag, was not included in the original budget and for some reason catering costs were not considered in the planning stages either. Fortunately, savings were achieved in some other areas.

Financial reports may include periodic reports showing budget versus year-to-date, actuals and financial commitments, periodic sales reports, taxation commitments, and funding acquittals in relation to grants received. Fundraising and charitable events are required to maintain accurate records of their financial affairs and in some cases these records are audited. Post-event, a report needs to be prepared, showing actual income and expenditure against the budget.

NAIDOC Week Family Fun Day

EXPENDITURE	BUDGET $	ACTUAL $
Promotion		
Promotion	2 500.00	103.50
Flyer Print (9000)	1 000.00	928.00
Roadside Signage—Design and Print	400.00	90.00
Flags (Indigenous)	–	159.00
Flyer Delivery	390.00	375.00
	4 290.00	**1 655.50**
Catering		
Biodegradable Cups	–	473.00
Luncheon and Consumables	–	883.00
		1 356.00
Infrastructure		
Cool Room	250.00	–
Stage/Stage Cover	4 600.00	4 273.00
Chairs/Tables/Marquees	250.00	6 718.00
Flag Poles	275.00	364.00
Generators/DBs/Cables	350.00	1 567.50
Mini Skip	243.00	182.00
Rubbish Pickup	–	126.50
Chemical Toilets	900.00	1 038.00
Barrier Tape/Gloves	–	91.70
	6 868.00	**14 360.70**
Entertainment		
Face Painting	–	800.00
Performers (DJ, NSA, Bassonovas)	2 392.00	1 254.55
	2 392.00	**2 054.55**
Day Labour		
Security Staff (× 2)	500.00	1 660.00
First Aid	200.00	540.00
Council Labour (P&G)	600.00	233.25
Event Assistance	750.00	600.00
Parking Coordination	500.00	–
Cleaning (Toilets)	200.00	80.00
Cleaning—Grounds	200.00	120.00
Contingency	1 000.00	180.00
Photographer	500.00	200.00
	4 450.00	**3 613.25**
TOTAL EXPENSES	**18 000.00**	**23 040.00**
INCOME	**BUDGET**	**ACTUAL**
Council Contribution		
Budget Allocation	15 170.00	19 202.00
Grants and Sponsorship		
Lotterywest		805.00
Healthway	2 000.00	2 000.00
Other Income		
Stallholder Fees	830.00	1 033.00
TOTAL INCOME	**18 000.00**	**23 040.00**

Source: <www.bassendean.wa.gov.au/3_your_council/agendas_minutes/cultural-2009-12-02-agn.htm>. © Town of Bassendean.

MULTICULTURAL FOOD FESTIVAL 2009

EXPENDITURE		BUDGET $	ACTUAL $
Promotion	PR Activities	2 000.00	2 140.00
	Brochure	1 000.00	928.00
	Brochure—Distribution	400.00	285.00
	Signage—Roadside	400.00	451.00
	Fireworks Notification	60.00	
		3 860.00	**3 804.00**
Infrastructure	Tables/Chairs/Marquees	2 800.00	4 500.00
	Generators/DBs/Cables	1 500.00	1 788.00
	Lighting Towers	1 000.00	840.00
	Cool Rooms	300.00	240.00
	Chemical Toilets	2 000.00	920.00
	Sound/Stage/Stage Cover/Op	8 500.00	7 600.00
	Bulk Bin	360.00	265.00
	Dance Floor		1 295.00
	Wheelie Bins	300.00	182.50
	Two-way Radio Hire		256.00
		16 760.00	**17 886.50**
Entertainment	Performers' Fees	5 000.00	4 910.00
	Community Art Project	2 000.00	3 500.00
	Activities	–	–
	MC	300.00	400.00
	A Kickett—Welcome to Country	0.00	300.00
		7 300.00	**9 110.00**
Day Labour	SES—Excl. Zone and torches	–	–
	Cleaning—Toilets	250.00	250.00
	Cleaning—Grounds	300.00	300.00
	First Aid	400.00	325.00
	Security	3 000.00	1 599.50
	Parking Coordination— Jnr Footy	700.00	700.00
	Council (P&G/Leisure)	750.00	500.00
		5 400.00	**3 596.00**
Other	Food Vouchers	200.00	200.00
	Contingency	655.00	0.00
	APRA Licence	125.00	125.00
	Photography	200.00	200.00
		1 180.00	**525.00**
TOTAL EXPENSES		**34 500.00**	**34 796.50**

INCOME		BUDGET	ACTUAL
Council Contribution			
	Budget Allocation	27 950.00	29 167.00
Grants and Sponsorship			
	Lotterywest	5 000.00	5 000.00
Other Income			
	Site Fees	1 200.00	465.00
	Parking Income	350.00	164.00
TOTAL INCOME		**34 500.00**	**34 796.00**

FIGURE 22.5
Budget items for a multicultural food festival

SUMMARY

This chapter has covered the important subject of preparing and monitoring budgets. We have learnt that the budget developed prior to an event must anticipate all revenue and expenditure and that steps should be taken to finalise contracts as early as possible to ensure that expenses do not exceed budget forecasts. The event manager also needs to take into account the cash flow situation in the lead-up to an event since most expenses occur early in the planning process while the bulk of the revenue is generally collected close to, or during, the event. In this chapter we have also emphasised the importance of financial control systems for managing expenditure. Reporting systems need to be in place so that complete and accurate records are available for the final post-event report.

Chapter review questions

1 Describe the three categories of event budgets using event examples:
   (a) Profit-oriented
   (b) Break-even (not-for-profit)
   (c) Invitation.
2 List and explain three possible revenue sources for a festival.
3 What is a management fee?
4 What is a budget contingency?
5 Describe the budgeting process.
6 Use a diagram to **illustrate and explain** the concepts of:
   (a) Variable costs
   (b) Fixed costs
   (c) Break-even point.
7 Establish (a) the break-even selling price; and (b) the selling price if the following event wanted to make a profit of $5000 to fund the purchase of new equipment for the association.

   Your business has been retained to stage the end-of-season celebration for the local softball association. It is to be held on grand final night, to celebrate the participation of players in the sport. It has been decided to hire the ballroom at the Sea Rider Hotel, which is in the heartland of the association's catchment area, at a cost of $1000. The association has requested a theme of 'Denim and Diamonds' to celebrate the tough game and environment, and the primarily female participation. It is expected that the decoration of the ballroom will cost approximately $2500 and that the entertainment will be a Mobidisk hooked into the ballroom's sound system at a cost of $1250. The event should break even if sufficient funding is raised via entrance fees to cover the hire of the room, the decoration, entertainment and a reasonable food/wine package at a cost of $25 per head. It is expected that approximately 300 players, officials and partners will attend the event.

Activity

Prepare a budget for an event using the following template (also available as an Excel file on the text website). You can add or delete items as required, depending on your event concept. Once completed, write a report explaining the concept and budget to the event committee.

EVENT NAME:

EVENT DATE:

All figures are to be GST Exclusive

Item	Description	Cash ($)	In-Kind ($)
INCOME			
I-1	Sponsorship Funding/Underwriting		
I-2	Sponsorship		
I-3	Ticket		
I-4	Merchandising		
I-5	Other Income		
I	**Grand total income (Items I–1 to I–5)**		

EXPENDITURE

Administration

Item	Description	Cash ($)	In-Kind ($)
A-1	General Administration		
A-2	Insurances—General & Event		
A-3	Travel & Accommodation		
A-4	Salaries & Fees		
A-5	Other Administration Expenses		
A	**Total admin expenditure (Items A–1 to A–5)**		

Event Expenses

Item	Description	Cash ($)	In-Kind ($)
E-1	Event Evaluation/Bid Costs		
E-2	Sanction Fees (e.g. fee paid to sporting association)		
E-3	Facility/Venue		
E-4	Ceremonies		
E-5	Entertainment		
E-6	Other Production Costs		
E-7	Merchandising		
E-8	Travel, Accommodation & Services		

continued

Activity

E-9	Communication		
E-10	Ticketing Production		
E-11	Other Event Expenses		
E	**Total event expenditure (Items E–1 to E–11)**		

Marketing & Promotion Expenses

M-1	Marketing/Advertising		
M-2	Promotions		
M-3	Other Marketing & Promotional Expenses		
M	**Total marketing expenditure (Items M–1 to M–3)**		

W	**Grand total expenditure (Items A + E + M)**		
X	**Add contingency (5% of total expenditure)**		**NA**
Y	**Total expenditure + contingency**		**NA**

Z	**Operating surplus (deficit)**		**NA**

Source: Guidelines for completing application for Temporary Event. <www.sunshinecoast.qld.gov.au/addfiles/documents/events/ Event_App_guidelines120110.pdf> Sunshine Coast Regional Council 2009.

Case study

Event budgeting

Your event business, Rave Reviews, has the opportunity to quote for two major parties. Having experienced some financial difficulties in your first year of operation, you want to ensure that you choose the most feasible of these for which to prepare a proposal and produce the winning quote.

The first party is for a top celebrity and will be held at her waterside mansion. The party will be outdoors and the brief is to transform the garden through the use of a spectacular theme. The party will be attended by 350 guests and a lavish dinner is expected.

The second party is much larger—500–600 people will be invited. The company is giving the party to celebrate its 50th year of tractor and farming equipment operations. The party will be held in a large airport hangar in the country. Food will be pretty basic and alcohol will be very plentiful. Decor is not important, but entertainment is.

Task

Discuss which of these two events you would choose in terms of its ease of financial management and its potential profitability.

References

Allen, J (2009), *Event planning: the ultimate guide to successful meetings, corporate events*, 2nd edn, John Wiley & Sons, Canada.

Goldblatt, J (2002), *Special events: twenty-first century global event management*, 3rd edn, The Wiley Event Management Series, Wiley, New York.

Melbourne Fringe, *Working out your costs/budget*, <www.melbournefringe.com.au/assets/working-out-your-costs.pdf>.

Wendroff, A (2003), *Special events: proven strategies for nonprofit fundraising*, John Wiley & Sons, New York.

CHAPTER 23

EVENT TRENDS AND PRACTICES

Unit descriptor

This unit describes the performance outcomes, skills and knowledge required to research and critically evaluate past, present and future event industry practices to enhance the quality of one's own work practice. This unit applies to individuals managing events in any industry context. It is particularly relevant to the cultural, community, hospitality, sporting and tourism sectors. The unit focuses on research, analysis and communication of information, ideas and concepts at a complex level, as well as the evaluation and extension of one's own professional development needs. It is therefore relevant to individuals who analyse, design and execute judgements in technical, conceptual or managerial areas.

Elements

- Research event industry ideas, practices and trends
- Evaluate information to inform work practice
- Extend event management skills and knowledge.

Critical aspects for assessment

- Ability to conduct research on a complex range of event industry issues, trends and ideas
- Ability to analyse, critique and synthesise complex sources to develop own positions and ideas
- In-depth conceptual, technical and management knowledge of the event industry
- Demonstration of skills through one or more pieces of event industry research.

LAST YEAR'S EVENT, despite forecasts of wet weather on event day, proved an outstanding success by attracting a large field of over 1450 entrants. There has been a 23.6% increase in the popularity of the event over the past four years in comparison to the previous four-year period, when the event won a national award from the Heart Foundation as 'Australia's Best Community Recreation Event'.

These results indicate that a local 'fun walk' is capable of attracting at least twice as many people as the average 'fun run'.

Last year, the number of local entrants had increased to 82.6% of the total field, yet over 17% of entrants continue to travel from outside the Macarthur region. The popularity of the event with residents of the greater Sydney metropolitan area, the Southern Highlands, the Blue Mountains, the Illawarra region and the South Coast indicates that the event could have a positive impact on non-health fields such as local tourism and the local hospitality industry.

It is significant that over 85% of the field selected the 6 km distance and that entrant details showed considerable involvement by family and neighbourhood groups, as well as teams from schools, clubs and workplaces.

These results indicate success in targeting participation rather than competitiveness and reinforce the findings of the entrant survey, which revealed that, when asked their reasons for participating, 28% chose 'family outing' as their first priority and 15% chose 'a fun day with friends/work colleagues'.

Source: Campbell City Council Health Promotion Unit.

This example of event evaluation demonstrates the council's achievement of its objectives, which were to raise awareness of walking as a viable form of exercise and to provide a motivational goal for commitment to regular exercise as an integral part of a healthy lifestyle. However, in addition to the findings that supported the health-related objectives, it was found that over 17% of the participants were from outside Macarthur, suggesting a positive economic impact for local tourism and the hospitality industry. More than a quarter of the participants saw the walk as a family outing, demonstrating a positive social impact as well.

In this chapter we will look at how to explore trends, ideas and practices in the event industry, as well as two other important aspects of event management: control and evaluation. Evaluation is the process of measuring the success of an event against its objectives. The data from performance measures is used in this analysis. Taking the example of the fun walk above, control systems would ensure that all participants were registered, while evaluation would involve an analysis of the questions on the registration form and feedback after the event. If a significant number of local residents joined the walk without registering, this would indicate a lack of control measures, and would naturally have an impact on the evaluation findings.

INITIATE MONITORING AND CONTROL SYSTEMS

Control systems are essential in ensuring that procedures are followed (for cash handling and recording entrants, for example) and that performance measures are achieved.

The challenge for the event manager is to delegate and monitor effectively and not to micromanage (become too involved with detail). While attention to detail is positive, this should be left to the event manager's team. A successful event manager needs to be aware that during the peak time of an event non-standard situations and incidents will require his or her time, which means that all routine procedures and control systems need to be in place before the event. Such control systems ensure that information filtering to the top of the event organisation will prompt management to make decisions to intervene only if things are not going according to plan.

The event environment has been described as being 'dynamic' and 'organic', requiring a great deal of flexibility in the planning stages. However, a systematic approach is needed to balance creative input in order to ensure that the event achieves its objectives and has a positive impact. According to Getz (2002) some of the reasons that festivals fail include problems associated with:

★ marketing/planning (lack of research, lack of strategic planning, inadequate promotion)
★ external forces (weather, competition, regulations, community opposition)
★ human resources (incompetent managers or staff, high turnover of staff and volunteers)
★ financial resources (lack of income, poor control of costs, cash flow problems)
★ organisational culture (lack of leadership and structure).

PREVENTIVE AND FEEDBACK CONTROLS

There are two types of controls: preventive and feedback. A preventive control is established early in the planning process. For example, checking the quality of incoming food for a banquet is a preventive control measure, as is monitoring food temperatures to avoid food poisoning. Signed requisition forms designed to curtail unauthorised spending and budget blow-outs and checklists for setting up equipment before sporting events are other examples of preventive control measures. For an international sporting event, the checklist for set-up would need to be designed to ensure that international specifications were met: if measurements were inaccurate, injury could be caused to an athlete or an athlete could be disqualified. An example of a site inspection checklist is included in Figure 23.1.

Venue Checklist

Plans to scale (all venue dimensions)	✓
Disability access	✓
Capacity for seating and standing	✓
Sight lines for event audience (no pillars, obstructions)	✓
Capacity for storage	✓
Appropriate number of toilets, suitable locations	✓
Suitability of food and beverage preparation and service areas	✓
Accessibility for delivery and installation of equipment, food, etc.	✓
Correct number of tables, chairs, plates, glasses, etc.	✓
Emergency evacuation plan	✓
Safety of venue (fire equipment, access and egress)	✓
Preferred contractors (e.g. security, catering)	✓
Fixed and hire equipment requirements	✓
Electrical supply	✓
Water supply (especially for temporary kitchens)	✓
Venue limitations	
Outstanding issues/actions	

FIGURE 23.1
Site inspection checklist

Feedback controls are put in place to assist with decisions during an event. For example, feedback would be required to decide on the point at which event merchandise should be discounted to avoid having stock left over. If you discount too early, you lose revenue. If you discount too late, you find yourself with stock that has no sale value after the event. Incident reporting is another form of feedback control: if a series of similar incidents occur, preventive measures need to be implemented. As an example, the reporting of a number of slips and falls in the kitchen over a period of days would require the implementation of one or more preventive measures, which might include thorough overnight cleaning, sandpapering the floor and painting it with a non-stick surface, or providing mats to cover the slippery areas.

In most industries, information from point-of-sale and stock control systems is the feedback used for measuring and managing sales and profit levels over a particular period. However, in the event industry, decisions about price and other product features are made before the event, with sales occurring over a very short time period, allowing little opportunity to respond to financial information during an event. This is why it is so important to collect and store information on aspects of an event, such as merchandise sales, for use as a precedent for the next event of a similar nature.

OPERATIONAL MONITORING AND CONTROL

There are a number of issues in relation to operational procedures that need to be addressed before an event begins. These include delegation of responsibility, flexibility in carrying out procedures, the effect of control systems on customers and the important issue of financial control.

Delegation of decision-making

A flat organisational structure is essential for the successful operation of an event, so some parts of the event manager's role must be delegated. At most events, the pace is so fast that it is crucial that staff be in a position to make decisions on the spot. This is particularly important for volunteers, many of whom are well qualified in other roles and generally like to know that they have a part to play in the problem-solving process. Only decisions on important matters need to be referred to the more senior staff on duty.

Event staff need to be trained to make decisions when minor incidents occur, and each of these incidents needs to be recorded in a logbook for analysis at the end of the shift or at the end of the day. Checking and monitoring will ensure that delegation is managed well, that quality service is provided and that costs are contained.

Flexibility in operational procedures

Flexibility is required in many aspects of event management, most particularly in the operational phase, so it is important that the desired outcomes are fully understood by all staff. Staff, too, need to be able to think on their feet and make quick decisions about changing non-critical procedures where circumstances demand it. This is in fact one of the most desirable attributes of event operations staff.

However, there are high-risk situations where procedures must be fixed, detailed and well documented. There can be no deviation from this type of procedure. It must be part of training and readily available to those who need to use it. The procedure for emergency evacuation is a good example. Posters and signs must be erected to assist staff to remember their training on evacuation, and controls must be put in place for checking on emergency systems, such as exits, fire fighting equipment, announcement and crowd management equipment (e.g. loud hailers), and access for emergency vehicles.

Customer satisfaction vs customer safety

In some cases, control systems can serve to frustrate customers and, at times, customers will endeavour to circumvent the system by trying, for example, to:

★ enter areas without accreditation
★ purchase alcohol for underage drinkers
★ change their seating to a better area
★ break the rules for rides (about height, attire or use of safety equipment, for example)
★ cut across crowd control barriers
★ stand or sit in the aisles.

In each of these cases, a decision needs to be made by event staff as to what to do. If a customer is refusing to wear safety equipment for a ride, for example, customer safety considerations should come before customer satisfaction. On the other hand, if you were confronted by customers frustrated by having to walk an extra distance as a result of crowd control barriers, when there were clearly no crowds, you may decide to move the barrier to allow them through.

Financial control

Financial control can be assured by:

★ using a requisition system for purchases/expenditure that limits those authorised to spend over a certain dollar limit
★ ensuring that all expenditure is documented and accounted for
★ checking goods against requisition and order forms
★ checking stock levels
★ using financial systems that maintain up-to-date information on income and expenditure
★ using financial systems to forecast cash flow
★ ensuring that everyone understands the budget and current financial position.
    Control of point-of-sale systems, or registers, can be achieved by:
★ checking and securing cash floats
★ checking that cash received is accurately recorded and/or processed through the point-of-sale system/register
★ checking that point-of-sale terminal/register print-outs have been balanced against cash takings (after removing cash float)
★ checking that cash and documents have been securely transported and stored
★ checking that banking documentation has been retained and balanced against statements issued by the bank.
    The following suggestions for monitoring and controlling event operations have been provided by experienced event organisers:
★ CHECK everything, over and over.
★ Write everything down, including promises made by your contractors and requests made by your client.
★ Develop checklists for everything possible.
★ Check the venue before you move in and note any existing damage.
★ Never leave the venue until the last staff member has finished.
★ Check the venue before leaving—some things may be left on (gas) or left behind (including people).
★ Pay attention to detail at every stage.
★ Schedule carefully as the audience has little patience with, for example, long-winded speeches.
★ Maintain a contingency fund for unexpected expenses.
★ Involve the sponsor at every stage.
★ Get approvals for use of logos before printing.
★ Don't take safety knowledge for granted; repeat often.
★ Train staff to be observant.
★ CHECK everything, over and over.

EVALUATE INFORMATION TO INFORM WORK PRACTICE

Evaluation is frequently neglected following an event although there are many benefits to be gained from event critiques. It allows those involved to learn from their experience and to improve operations. For those not involved, it provides a body of information for future planning of events. If you can't learn from your own experience, at least you can learn from someone else's.

Evaluation needs to be planned before the event, the event objectives generally guiding the evaluation process. In Chapter 2, the concept of developing event aims and objectives was introduced, and in Chapter 27 the importance of understanding the target audience will be discussed, together with the consumer's decision-making process. As an example, see the history and detailed audience analysis of the Melbourne Comedy Festival below.

THE MELBOURNE INTERNATIONAL COMEDY FESTIVAL

THE Melbourne International Comedy Festival is one of the three largest comedy festivals in the world, alongside Edinburgh Festival Fringe and Montreal's Just for Laughs Festival.

An annual event, the Melbourne International Comedy Festival literally takes over Australia's comedy capital, Melbourne, each autumn with an enormous program of stand-up comedy, cabaret, theatre, street performance, film, television, radio and visual arts.

The Festival was launched in 1987 by Barry Humphries and Peter Cook. Twenty festivals later, with attendances of over 400 000, it has grown to be Australia's largest cultural event. With an average ticket price of just $22, the Comedy Festival is not only a hugely popular event but an extremely accessible one. When the Melbourne Town Hall precinct is converted into a giant comedy hub, there is something for every comedy lover, from the very best local and international comedy acts in venues of all shapes and sizes.

The Melbourne International Comedy Festival aims to:

- showcase and celebrate the best of Australia's comic artists
- nurture and develop new comic performers and comedy works
- present the finest overseas comedians to Australian audiences

Audience Profile

Proving once again that we love nothing more than a good chuckle, the Melbourne International Comedy Festival had record attendances and box office for the 2010 Festival.

With a total attendance of over **508 000** and paid attendance of more than **425 000**, with **15%** new attendees, it goes without saying that the Festival is much loved by Melbourne audiences, as well as interstate and international guests and remains one of the biggest events in the cultural calendar of Australia. Interstate and regional visitation was up by 1% (9%) with the biggest increases from NSW (43%, up 3%) and Queensland (23%, up 4%). The average spend of each visitor was $704.

For lovers of numbers, there were **369** shows, **4947** performances by **1764** performers helped by **1527** support staff in **120** venues. The average ticket price was **$25.75**. The 2010 Festival recorded **$10 971 653** in box office—an increase **of 3.9%** on last year's record-breaking Festival. The Festival's free public events played to over **82 000** people, up more than **10%** on 2009. Said Virginia Lovett, General Manager:

The Festival is unique in its sheer breath of activities. We reach broadcast audience of over 3 million through the Galas, opening night broadcasts, RAW Grand Final, The Great Debate and other broadcasts. Our virtual audience increased 25% from 292 594 in 2009 to 392 411 augmented by 15 000 downloads of our new iPhone application. And our national development programs, RAW, Class Clowns and Deadly Funny throughout the year nurtures and trains the next generation of performers and producers.

EVALUATION METHODS

When planning evaluation, it is very important to work out what information you require. For example, participants entering a cycling race may be asked for their age and address, which would allow an analysis in terms of their general demographics. What a pity if they were not asked if they had participated before, how they had heard about the event and when they had made the decision to take part. This information would greatly assist the organisers of the next event.

Customer surveys, staff debriefings and financial records all provide information that can be used in event evaluation.

Customer surveys

The type of information described above can be obtained from surveys conducted before, during and after an event by completion of forms or through personal interviews. Alternatively, a small focus group of participants can provide valuable information through group discussion.

The following are examples of questions that may be included in a customer survey for an informal post-evaluation report. However, to obtain a more reliable report, the survey would need to be designed and analysed by a market research company.

★ How did you find out about this event?
★ Why did you decide to come to the event?
★ When did you decide to come to the event?
★ Did you come to the event with other people?
★ Who was the main decision-maker?
★ How did this event meet your expectations?
★ Was the transport/parking adequate?
★ Did you get value for money?
★ Was the food and beverage adequate?
★ Were the seating, sound and vision adequate?
★ Would you attend this event again?
★ Why would you recommend/not recommend the event to others?
★ How could the event be improved?
   In the case of an exhibition, the questions would be something like:
★ Why did you come to this exhibition?
★ When did you decide to come to the exhibition?

★ Did you come to this exhibition last year?
★ Do you have the authority to purchase at this exhibition?
★ Did you place any orders at this exhibition?
★ Do you plan to place any orders as a direct result of the exhibition?
★ Have you travelled interstate to visit the exhibition?
★ What were the best features of the exhibition?
★ How could the exhibition be improved?

Staff debriefings

Meetings of event staff and other stakeholders can generate valuable information for the evaluation report. Some of the questions addressed in this type of meeting include:

★ What went well and why?
★ What went badly and why?
★ How could operations be improved?
★ Were there any significant risk factors that we did not anticipate?
★ Was there a pattern to any of the incidents reported?
★ Are there any legal issues concerning, for example, injuries or accidents?
★ Are there any implications for staff recruitment and training?
★ How would you describe the organisation and management of the event—in the planning and the operational phases?
★ What can we learn from this event?

Financial records

Audited financial records, together with a number of planning and other documents, are an essential component of post-event analysis and reporting. These include:

★ audited financial statements
★ budgets
★ revenue, banking and account details
★ point-of-sale reconciliation
★ payroll records
★ the risk management plan
★ incident reports
★ minutes of meetings
★ insurance policies
★ contracts with other agencies and organisations, such as hire companies and cleaning companies
★ asset register
★ promotional materials
★ operational plans
★ policies and procedures
★ training materials
★ database of attendees/participants (where possible)
★ record of results of competitions

★ event statistics (including attendance)
★ event or sponsor report.

It is one thing to know that you have managed a successful event but quite another to prove it. The event manager needs more than informal feedback from the after-event party. A summary report evaluating the event against specific aims and objectives is an absolute necessity.

SPONSORSHIP EVALUATION

Evaluation of sponsorship outcomes is required in order to provide accountability to sponsors in relation to their investment. This post-event report needs to include the aims and objectives of the sponsorship and the measures used to evaluate them. Sponsors such as brewers, communications companies and banks will have a presence at the event, some selling their products and others advertising their organisation and its products. Sponsors want more than intangible benefits; they want evidence that the sponsorship dollar has achieved a return on investment. There are a number of measures that can be used:

★ *Demographics*—of both event attendees and television viewers (to tie in with the sponsor's strategic marketing plans).
★ *Signage*—the range of exposure, such as website, posters, T-shirts, screen displays, directional signs, tickets and all places where the sponsor's logo appeared.
★ *Audience response*—the number of products sampled or purchased at the event as a percentage of the total audience attending.
★ *Surveys*—audience opinions regarding the sponsor's product (how the product was evaluated on site, whether the product was recognised, whether future purchase was intended).
★ *Publicity*—number of times the sponsor was named in publicity. This involves collection and copying of all media, estimating the time of television coverage and its dollar value, and analysing print media exposure and its dollar value. Samples should be included in an appendix to the report.
★ *Image*—surveys can be undertaken with the non-attending public to demonstrate their response to the sponsor's image.
★ *Sales*—an analysis of pre- and post-event sales can be done to estimate the impact on sales. This is an estimate only as a number of other variables might influence sales in the short term. For example, sales of beer might drop soon after the event due to unseasonally cold weather, but this would have nothing to do with the promotional effort.
★ *Employee benefits*—to the sponsor organisation.
★ *Corporate hospitality*—identification of business networks and the value of new alliances.

Poon and Prendergast (2006) have provided a new framework for evaluating sponsorship opportunities. They suggest that the fit between the sponsor and the activity can be evaluated in terms of two mutually exclusive categories: function-based similarity (the product is used in the event) and image-based similarity (the image of the product is enhanced by the event). However, they do note that the two can co-exist using the construct of 'integrated product relevance' (p. 25).

BROADER EVALUATION OF EVENTS

Events are often evaluated in terms of the triple bottom line: economic, social and environmental impacts (Fredline et al. 2005). The Melbourne Commonwealth Games were evaluated in these terms, as shown in Figure 23.2.

Economic impact

The Co-operative Research Centre (CRC) for Sustainable Tourism has a number of useful publications on the subject of event-related tourism and impact analysis. In particular, it provides standardised tools so that comparative studies can be undertaken.

Business events attract tourism visitors with a high yield (big spenders) and as such are a valued sector. One event that had a significant economic impact was the Amway Greater China Seminar, held in Melbourne in 2008. The seminar involved more than 7000 Chinese delegates. The Melbourne Convention and Visitors Bureau estimated that delegate expenditure was $18.6 million and that the total economic impact was $35 million. The event represented 20 000 room nights for Melbourne hotels. Of delegates surveyed, 78% indicated they would return to Melbourne for a holiday and 96% would recommend the city to their friends and colleagues. The economic impact generated by Amway in regional Victoria, including Phillip Island and Ballarat, exceeded $2 million. The tracked retail expenditure generated at two shopping outlets (Myer Melbourne and JR Duty Free) totalled

FIGURE 23.2 Triple bottom line assessment of the Commonwealth Games, Melbourne

	Economic	Social	Environmental
Opportunities for better delivery of major events	Earlier rollout of business leveraging programs		Better recycling at venues building on Melbourne 2006 lessons
Lasting benefits of the Games achieved	*Lasting relations* • Increasing local capability • Enhanced economic relationships, export sales and foreign awareness of Australian business opportunities • Indications of future tourism • Promotion of Melbourne as a 'can do' place	*Behavioural change* • Volunteering legacy • Greater social inclusion and connectedness • Greater social awareness	*Behavioural change* • Greater awareness of environmental issues • Greater willingness to benefit environment • Knowledge transfer in construction trades • Increased update of technology
Immediate benefits of the Games achieved	Tourist targets were met. Businesses reported feeling prepared for Games. Significant economic stimulation	Significant participation in sporting and Festival Melbourne2006. Strong family involvement. Mix of metro and regional events	Games were low waste. Games were water wise. Games achieved carbon neutral targets

Source: Reproduced with permission of Department of Planning and Community Development, State of Victoria, 2010. Material was produced by Insight Economics Pty Ltd. <www1.dvc.vic.gov.au/ocgc/news.htm>.

$65 000 (with one free day for shopping in Melbourne CBD). As a result of the Amway event, other large incentive groups have since shown interest in hosting their event in Melbourne (MCEC 2009).

Traffic police monitor a protest march

According to a report by Access Economics, the economic benefits of staging major events such as international sporting competitions are often exaggerated. While the report, which was commissioned by the Commonwealth Department of Resources, Energy and Tourism, had not been released at the time of publishing, it is expected to recommend a series of rigorous principles which governments should use to evaluate the economic impacts of events for which they bid, including the FIFA World Cup (Davis 2010).

Social impact

The economic impact of World Youth Day (WYD), held in Sydney in 2008 (with around 500 000 young Catholic visitors, including 135 000 pilgrims from overseas) was matched by its social impact (the first visit of His Holiness, Pope Benedict XVI). The first WYD was officially celebrated in Rome on Palm Sunday in 1986. It was then repeated in 1987. WYD is promoted as an opportunity 'for young people from throughout the world to make a pilgrimage in faith, to meet, and experience hospitality and the love of God'. Since then, WYD has been held every two to three years. It was held in Argentina in 1987, Spain 1989, Poland 1991, the US 1993, the Philippines 1995, France 1997, Italy 2000, Canada 2002 and Germany 2005.

Other events that have had a social impact include Wave Aid, held as a benefit for tsunami victims, and handing over $2.3 million to three charities in 2005. Earthday events and Live 8—'Make poverty history'—also aim for direct social impacts as well as communicating important messages. The bushfire appeal in 2009, Sound Relief, raised the grand total of $9 million over two events, including CD sales. The initial sum raised by the concerts, over $8 million, went straight to the Bushfire Appeal for distribution by the Victorian Government to affected people and communities.

On a smaller scale, most community events have social impacts as their main aim (e.g. celebrating the arts, maintaining cultural heritage, or strengthening the community). Many, many others raise funds for charities and social causes.

A protest, such as the one illustrated, is also an event with a social impact, requiring the same level of planning, risk management and notification of traffic authorities.

Environmental impact

More and more events are demonstrating environmental awareness. For example, the Peats Ridge Festival is a well-established, environmentally friendly event, while another music festival, Regrowth, held in the Southern Highlands, runs on sustainable energy, a mix of solar power and biodiesel. Food is organic and toilets are composted. While music plays at night, the audience is expected to plant native trees by day. The best example of an event with an extremely positive environmental impact is Clean Up Australia Day, which now operates in countries throughout the world. This event has a practical orientation and a very clear public message.

However, events can have a negative environmental impact by causing damage or creating offensive noise; for example, the debate over the use of Albert Park in Melbourne for the Grand Prix continues unabated.

RESEARCH EVENT INDUSTRY IDEAS, PRACTICES AND TRENDS

As with all other industries, knowledge of the event industry and its practices can be enhanced by both formal and informal research. Formal and informal research strategies may include:

★ reading current literature, including specialist journals and industry magazines
★ participating actively in relevant industry associations
★ participating in professional development and other learning opportunities
★ participating in and contributing to discussion through conferences, meetings, seminars, courses and journals
★ formal study.

Over the past decade there has been much debate about the event industry as an entity and during this time a number of publications specific to this question have emerged. In particular, Donald Getz (2007) provides readers with an understanding of how various disciplines and other professional fields view planned events and the contribution they make to understanding events. He also provides a detailed evaluation of research issues and challenges, and of methodologies and theories applicable to event studies.

New ideas and concepts form the basis of many of the emerging trends, and these need to be followed closely too. For example, the annual arts festivals make every effort to include new and contemporary components in their programs. Sport, too, changes over time. For example, cricket comprised only the test match prior to the emergence of the one day match, World Cup Cricket in 1975 and, more recently, the Twenty20 game, a real crowd pleaser. Such concepts may relate to the country's overall philosophy about events and the role of events in the broader social, economic and political environment.

Research into new trends, including emerging and future technologies as they impact on events, is now essential for every event manager. In the conferencing area, these technologies have already brought about major changes and will continue to do so into the future. And for trade exhibitions, more sales are likely to take place online over the next decade.

For the more creative event planner, ideas can be triggered by a study of artists and designers, photographers and film makers, historians, authors and entertainers.

Management and operational practices, particularly relating to safety and risk management and environmental sustainability, are now a significant consideration for all event planners.

EXTEND EVENT MANAGEMENT SKILLS AND KNOWLEDGE

Several controversial issues relating to the future of event management are raised below, with the expectation that readers will continue to follow these topics in their readings and research.

Can events be defined as a sector of the economy?

Events cross many sectors, including sport, the arts, entertainment, community and business. They also vary a great deal in size and scope, ranging from a few hundred attendees to hundreds of thousands. They also have vastly different aims and objectives, some being profit motivated and others not.

Is event management a profession?

Many industry practitioners suggest that a professional body would enhance the status of event managers. This would require registration and professional development, which already occurs in some associations such as MEA (Meetings and Events Australia).

Does event management require a separate project management system?

Undoubtedly, the terminology of the Project Management Body of Knowledge (PMBOK) is already widely used in event management (e.g. scope, work breakdown, critical path, milestone), as discussed in Chapter 14. Its planning tools are used extensively too, including the Gantt and PERT charts.

So is EMBOK necessary? Several writers have proposed an event industry body of knowledge (go to <www.embok.org> to evaluate this proposal).

Are too many people being trained for the industry?

The current popularity of event management courses has some people worried, particularly since event industry positions are not clear-cut, nor do they provide long-term stable employment for many people in the industry. Others argue that the project style of management and deadline-driven approach is common to many emerging business environments.

WHY IS IT IMPORTANT TO IDENTIFY THE CRITERIA FOR A 'MAJOR EVENT'?

This is important when applying for government funding in the form of support (grants) or value in kind (VIK). It is best to address in advance government criteria that must be met as disputes can arise over which events should be, and should not be, supported by the public purse. Support in the form of VIK (e.g. policing, traffic management or waste management services) may be provided free of charge for any event meeting the criteria for 'major event'. Allocation of funds, whether cash or VIK, has to be equitable and in line with public interest. This is why specific criteria have to be met in order to qualify. Tourism bodies may also promote and advertise a major event, saving the event organisation considerable money.

Do music festivals lead to socially unacceptable behaviour?

The behaviour of young people at music festivals can be a problem: we have all seen newspaper reports of inappropriate behaviour, binge drinking and drug use by underage teenagers at these festivals. The original Woodstock festival was held as far back as 1969, but remains an example of an event that attracted thousands more than expected, creating many problems for the organisers in controlling, among other things, alcohol and drug use. The 2009 death of a 20-year-old Sydney woman after taking ecstasy from a bad batch following attendance at a local music event raised the community's expectations of event organisers, who are now implementing stricter controls concerning ticketing, policing and security, alcohol availability and drug searches.

Are events safe places for children, even those with families as their target market?

Parents are increasingly reluctant to let their children and young teenagers out of their sight. How can event organisers provide for the entertainment needs of children while providing a safe environment and meeting the community's expectations for child protection?

Are volunteers exploited?

Many events use volunteers to expand their workforce. Some suggest that this should not occur and that people should be paid for their work, particularly at commercial and ticketed events. Mistreatment stories abound, even though most volunteers for large-scale events say that it was the 'opportunity of a lifetime', and for small community events report a high level of enjoyment.

Will events continue to grow in size and popularity?

In a buoyant economy with high disposable income, the size of crowds at sporting and entertainment events continues to escalate, with many sporting matches and music tours being sold out. Can this level of growth be sustained?

Do events really contribute to environmental awareness?

While most events provide biodegradable plates and cups, many customers still ignore the relevant signs on bins, resulting in waste that is so seriously contaminated it cannot be recycled. However, it can also be argued that raising awareness of the importance of waste management is a slow process and gradually people are taking in this message and are starting to see it as a serious issue.

How much control should government bodies have over the staging of safe events?

It used to be quite simple to run a road race, for example, and expect cars to slow down and take care. Current risk management practices, however, are now forcing the closure of many small fun runs as police and traffic authorities insist that roads must be closed completely

THE Colosseum is an ancient amphitheatre in the centre of the city of Rome. Originally capable of seating 55 000 to 87 000 spectators, it was used for gladiatorial contests and sometimes bloody public spectacles. The amphitheatre was completed in 80AD. The Colosseum remained in use for nearly 500 years, with the last recorded games being held there in the 6th century. As well as the gladiatorial games, many other public events were held there, such as mock sea battles, animal hunts, executions, re-enactments of famous battles, and dramas. As the photograph illustrates, the stage was built over many tunnels and cages used to hold men and beasts or used to channel water for the mock sea battles. Among the other major innovations was the unique roof system that featured ropes and pulleys to change its sail-type roof structures so that it could draw in wind to cool the audience.

In more modern times the site has been used for quite different purposes:

- 2002 Rome's Colosseum staged its first music concert in its 2000-year history. The concert was hosted by legendary musician Ray Charles and was aimed at promoting world peace.
- 2003 Sir Paul McCartney played a rare show inside Rome's historic Colosseum. A crowd of just 400 people paid up to 1295 euros ($2000) in an internet auction to witness the charity show. It was a warm-up for a free concert for over 300 000 fans outside the Colosseum.
- 2004 Simon and Garfunkel closed out the European leg of their Old Friends tour with hundreds of thousands of adoring fans. Rome Mayor Walter Veltroni told the crowd that 600 000 people had turned out for the free concert.
- 2005 Sir Elton John delighted 200 000 fans with a free show outside the Colosseum. Fans started gathering at dawn to see the singer, who performed the show on the Via dei Fori Imperiali boulevard.

to avoid any incidents. Will safety become so big an issue that many good ideas are dropped during the risk assessment process?

How successfully do events meet their aims in terms of attitudinal impact?

In the current media environment, events are increasingly being used as a means of creating awareness and attitudinal change on a range of topics such as the environment, global warming, AIDS and poverty. Sponsors are linking their brands to these messages and in some cases designing and running the events themselves as a thinly disguised marketing campaign. Is the public aware of the ways in which events influence social change?

SUMMARY

In this chapter we have looked at two neglected aspects of event management: control and evaluation. Control systems are necessary to ensure that plans are carried out, yet often the event deadline draws near too soon for these systems to be developed. Preventive controls are established during the early planning phase of an event, while feedback controls help with decisions during the event. If control systems meet best practice standards, they reduce risk and ensure that there is ample evidence if a court action should arise. Evaluation is required to ensure that an event has met the aims and objectives identified in the planning strategy. The capacity to show that the objectives have been met is one way of guaranteeing that the event management team will be selected for future events and that sponsors will continue to give their financial or in-kind support. The impact of events from a wider point of view—economic, social and environmental—has also been considered.

Chapter review questions

1 What is the difference between control and evaluation?
2 Describe three ways in which an event can be informally evaluated.
3 What is the triple bottom line?
4 Describe current trends in environmental sustainability for events.

Activity

Investigate a control system to be put in place at an event OF YOUR CHOICE and evaluate its effectiveness (or lack of it). This system may relate to:
- registration of participants
- cash handling
- safety
- food hygiene
- purchasing and control
- staff accreditation.

Case study

Event evaluation

The Red Bull Air Race World Championship is a world renowned event, with the Australian round of the championship held in Perth, Western Australia.

Perth offers one of the best locations the Red Bull Air Race has ever seen—the city's Langley Park transformed into the Air Race 'airport' merely metres away from the aerial race track over the Swan River, the city skyline providing the perfect backdrop.

This is one of the most innovative world championships on the sporting calendar. Spectacular backdrops teamed with jaw-dropping stunts guarantee spectators an exhilarating and exciting experience.

Precision flying through an air gate at speeds up to 400 kph is tough ... doing it 10 metres off the ground is what makes the Red Bull Air Race the most challenging motorsport in the world.

Source: <www.westernaustralia.com/redbullairrace/pages/about_the_race.aspx>. © Tourism Western Australia.

Case study (continued)

Questions

1 Explain the concept of triple bottom line.
2 Discuss each of these in relation to the above event.
3 Review the media for discussion and controversy relating to this event.
4 Describe how the potential impacts of this event can be evaluated.
5 How does this event exemplify new approaches by sponsors to management of the events they sponsor?

References

Davis, M (2010), 'World Cup not such a golden goal', *Sydney Morning Herald*, 17 March.

Dwyer, L, Forsyth, P & Spurr, R (2005), 'Estimating the impacts of special events on an economy', *Journal of Travel Research*, 43(4):351.

Fredline, E, Raybould, M, Jago, L & Deery, M (2005), *Triple bottom line event evaluation: a proposed framework for holistic event evaluation*, Australian Centre for Event Management, Lindfield, NSW.

Getz, D (2007), *Event studies: theory, research and policy for planned events*, Butterworth–Heinemann, Oxford, UK.

Getz, D (2002), 'Why festivals fail', *Event Management*, 7:209–19.

Jackson, J, Houghton, M, Russell, R & Triandos, P (2005), 'Innovations in measuring economic impacts of regional festivals: a do-it-yourself kit', *Journal of Travel Research*, 43(4):360.

Melbourne Convention and Exhibition Centre (2009), 'Melbourne's biggest incentive event sees Amway's best enjoy Victoria', <www.mcvb.com.au/LinkClick.aspx?fileticket=mEqQ7_lhR3k%3D&tabid=79>, accessed 24 May 2010.

Poon, D & Prendergast, G (2006), 'A new framework for evaluating sponsorship opportunities', *International Journal of Advertising*, 25(4):471.

24

LEGAL KNOWLEDGE

Unit descriptor

This unit describes the performance outcomes, skills and knowledge required to ensure business compliance with legislation across a broad range of operational areas. Ability to research and apply relevant legal information to business operations is the key focus of the unit. This is combined with a general knowledge of the legal framework in which businesses in different contexts operate.

This unit applies to senior personnel and operational managers responsible for ensuring overall business compliance with legislative and regulatory requirements. The unit does not cover the specialist skills and knowledge required by legal experts or managers whose primary role relates to compliance.

Elements

- Research the legal information required for business compliance
- Ensure compliance with legal requirements
- Update legal knowledge.

Critical aspects for assessment

- General knowledge of the legislation and the powers of delegated authorities such as councils that affect business operations in a particular industry sector
- Knowledge of how to access and update the legal information required for business compliance or seek professional assistance on legal matters
- Demonstrated application of legal knowledge to specific workplace situations and problems.

UNRULY and disruptive patron behaviour is often an indication of intoxication which may result in penalties for licensees under the Act. A number of licensees have been successfully sued for failing to demonstrate the necessary duty of care towards their patrons. An event manager may also be liable for an incident resulting from a poorly organised event or irresponsible serving of alcohol. There is increasing government and community awareness of the legal responsibilities of event managers, specifically in relation to duty of care, negligence and workplace health and safety issues. Event managers need to be aware of these responsibilities and, as much as possible, ensure that event management plans account for the health, safety and comfort of event patrons and staff, and minimise the disruption and harm caused to the community.

Source: <www.olgr.qld.gov.au/resources/liquorDocs/PlaningGuideEventManagement.pdf>, p. 4. © The State of Queensland, 2010, (Department of Employment, Economic Development and Innovation).

This extract illustrates the overlap between compliance considerations, in this case between alcohol service and public safety. In Chapter 9 many legislative compliance topics were introduced, and guidelines have been provided on the companion website for many different types of events, including sporting events. However, this extract also refers to 'duty of care' and 'negligence' and it is these and other legal concepts that will be explored in this chapter.

It is unnecessary, and indeed almost impossible, for event managers to fully understand all laws pertinent to their industry and all their ramifications. For professional legal advice, most managers would contact their professional association or their organisation's own solicitors. The key issue for managers in the event industry is knowing when to seek professional legal advice.

In order to be able to make such a judgement, the event manager must remain abreast of general changes to legislation that could have an impact on daily operations. For example, public liability issues have brought about many legislative changes in the Australian states and territories, so anyone operating an event business would need to carefully research the implications of those changes. They would also need to seek advice from their insurance company, as well as from their solicitor, regarding appropriate indemnity forms that their customers may need to sign. Indemnity forms can reduce or remove liability in certain circumstances but they must be carefully prepared by a competent legal person. Sudden increases in insurance premiums may be the stimulus needed to research this issue further.

The aims of this chapter are therefore to provide a general understanding of the legislation that could have an impact on event operations and to underline the importance of updating knowledge on any changes to this legislation.

RESEARCH THE LEGAL INFORMATION REQUIRED FOR BUSINESS COMPLIANCE

Creating the right environment to minimise litigation is every manager's and every supervisor's role. Indeed, every staff member has a part to play in this regard. Reporting safety issues, for example, can help prevent accidents, often the cause of customer complaint and, at times, legal action. One major change to the law was in the OHS legislation that introduced the need to report incidents as well as accidents. Dealing with incident reports and fixing them will usually result in reduced accidents. It is therefore the responsibility of management to create awareness of legislative compliance requirements, to develop appropriate policies and procedures, to undertake induction and training of employees, and to provide leadership that motivates employees to meet the highest professional standards.

Up-to-date information can be obtained from:

★ print and news media
★ reference books
★ internet
★ industry associations
★ industry journals and magazines
★ clients and suppliers
★ legal experts.

Most event industry associations run seminars to update their members on any changes or trends and these are recommended to anyone working in the event business. Associations are listed in Appendix E.

SOURCES OF LAW

In Australia, the law consists of:

★ *Acts* passed by the *Federal Parliament* within the scope of its powers under the Australian Constitution (Statute Law)
★ *Acts* passed by *State Parliaments* and the *Legislative Assemblies* of the Northern Territory, the Australian Capital Territory and Norfolk Island (Statute Law).
★ Australian *common law*, which developed from English common law and is interpreted and modified by the *courts*. This results in decisions of courts that interpret the law and these decisions are called precedent cases. These precedent cases usually alter the interpretation of the law or legislation and a number of important precedent cases are generally decided every year. Lawyers are required to stay up to date on all these relevant cases.

The Australian Constitution does not allow the Commonwealth Parliament the power to make laws on all subjects. Instead, it lists the subjects about which the Commonwealth Parliament can make laws. These include taxation, defence, external affairs, interstate and international trade, foreign affairs, trading and financial corporations, marriage and divorce, immigration, bankruptcy, and interstate industrial arbitration. Economic considerations have resulted in all the states agreeing that income tax be imposed solely by the Commonwealth.

Although the State Parliaments can pass laws on a wider range of subjects than the Commonwealth Parliament, the Commonwealth is generally regarded as the more powerful partner in the federation. If a Commonwealth law is clearly within the powers of Section 51 of the Constitution and is inconsistent with a law of a State Parliament, the Commonwealth law operates and the state law is invalid to the extent of the inconsistency.

The *Racial Discrimination Act 1975* is an example of a Commonwealth Act, and is an important Act for event managers to take into consideration. This is the principal Act and there have been numerous amendments. Section 9 of the Act states that:

> This Act is not intended, and shall be deemed never to have been intended, to exclude or limit the operation of a law of a State or Territory that furthers the objects of the Convention and is capable of operating concurrently with this Act.

It states further that:

> It is unlawful for a person to do any act involving a distinction, exclusion, restriction or preference based on race, colour, descent or national or ethnic origin which has the purpose or effect of nullifying or impairing the recognition, enjoyment or exercise, on an equal footing, of any human right or fundamental freedom in the political, economic, social, cultural or any other field of public life.

Related Acts have been passed in the states and territories, which cover a range of issues in more detail. Under the *Anti-Discrimination Act 1991* (Qld), for instance, it is discriminatory to refuse to allow a guide dog onto premises.

As we learned in Chapter 9, local governments and various government agencies (such as the transport authority) are responsible for implementing Acts and regulations under their jurisdiction. Examples of such regulations are building codes, signage limitations, lighting, street closures and noise restrictions, all of which are important considerations for the event coordinator. Local council offices generally give advice on their requirements but they are not permitted to give advice on legal compliance and they will request the event organiser not only to comply with council requirements but also to contact the police or the Environment Protection Authority, for example, if applicable. Some councils have event planning templates which cover all relevant council regulations, as well as higher level legal compliance requirements. As councils provide consent for an event to take place, they place great emphasis on the positive and negative impacts of the proposed event. In approving an event to proceed, the council is making a decision on behalf of the community. This is why they have extensive planning guidelines that must be satisfied, these guidelines being based on the Acts and regulations pertinent to event management.

The NSW Department of Local Government provides a comprehensive document called *Major and special event planning: a guide for promoters and councils* on its website (see Appendix E). Similar guides are available in other states and territories. In Appendix C, the outline for an event proposal provides prompts for a range of legal compliance requirements, some of which may not be applicable, for example, to the organisation of an indoor event. However, this general outline gives you the main cues for event planning, and for meeting legal obligations.

The three levels of government discussed above are illustrated in Figure 24.1 opposite.

It must be made clear that local government powers are all delegated from the state and do not rank in the same level of law as State or Commonwealth legislation. However, from the viewpoint of an event organiser, the requirements of the local council are usually the most important parts of the law that need to be dealt with.

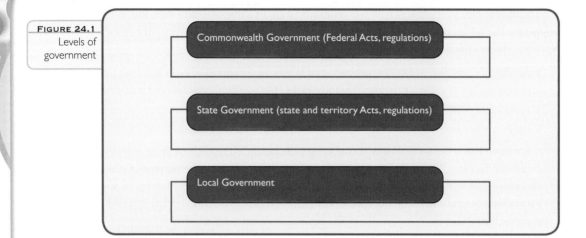

FIGURE 24.1
Levels of
government

Commonwealth Government (Federal Acts, regulations)

State Government (state and territory Acts, regulations)

Local Government

COMMON LAW

The third source of law in Australia, as mentioned above, is common law. Common law was introduced in Chapter 3 with the illustration of the venue hire agreement/contract. For a contract to be valid there must be an offer, an acceptance and a consideration (an exchange, usually money, for goods and services rendered). Where there is a dispute about a contract it is taken to court. In this circumstance, a judge needs to make a decision, largely based on precedent. Precedent cases vary and interpret the common law so it is critical that event organisers are aware of all relevant precedent cases that may affect them. Contracts will be covered in detail in the second half of this chapter.

One of the most fundamental areas of common law for event organisations is *duty of care*. Where lack of *reasonable* care can be shown in court, the resulting claim for *negligence* can lead to an award for damages being made by the judge. Accidents occurring at events are usually brought to court with the plaintiff arguing negligence. This argument could be made against the event organiser, the venue management, the security company, or the ride operator. In fact the claim might be made against all four, and it would be up to the courts to judge whether the defendants had shown the appropriate duty of care. Risk management strategies and contingency plans demonstrate that all reasonable steps have been taken to prevent an accident. A theme recurring through this book is therefore concern for the safety and welfare of everyone on the event site, with policies and procedures to reduce or eliminate risks where they are foreseen.

A situation such as the one described here demonstrates the legal concepts of duty of care, safety and negligence. The coroner made the following recommendations:

Fox Studios was ordered to improve its public safety yesterday after a coroner found the death of a nine-year-old boy was foreseeable and preventable.

David Selinger was crushed to death on January 15, 2001 when metal fence palings fell on him during a storm as he walked to the toilets. Despite an extensive search his body was not discovered until the next day.

The senior deputy state coroner, Jacqueline Milledge, found yesterday the failure of a site supervisor at Fox Studios to remove unsecured metal fencing, inadequate protocols for dealing with missing children, and poor lighting contributed to his death.

While she said there was no criminal negligence, she made nine recommendations, directing Fox Studios to improve its public safety by revising its protocols for dealing with lost children, establishing a storage area for fence panels, and appointing a person to oversee safety issues.

She said floodlighting should be available at the complex for use in emergencies, noting that inadequate lighting meant David's body lay under the fencing for 13 hours …

Ms Milledge said the inexperience of Lisa Webb, site supervisor for the Fringe Festival, who left the unsecured fencing, was a contributing factor. Ms Webb testified that the panels were intended to be there briefly, and she had thought the fencing contractor would have dealt with them. Ms Milledge said Fox Studios should not have allowed the fencing to be stored in a public area near toilets.

Source: Ellen Connolly, Sydney Morning Herald, 15 February 2003.

Recommendations to:

The Minister for Fair Trading:

That all service providers for temporary fencing provide all users with appropriate information regarding safe use and storage of their product. That the Department of Fair Trading consider reviewing the standards applicable to shade cloth and other materials attached to temporary fencing with regard to wind resistance and fence stability.

The Minister for Police:

That all operational police be personally issued with torches as part of their official appointments.

The State   Management Board:

That the board consider the possibility of the search coordinating role at high risk incident searches be undertaken by Police Rescue Squad in the Sydney Metropolitan Area or by the State Emergency services and volunteer rescue associations in regional areas.

Fox Studios Australia:

- That the protocols for dealing with 'lost children' be immediately revised to ensure all contingencies are catered for. The current protocol is based on the assumption that the majority of 'Lost Children' are found within a very short time frame. Within the protocol, there needs to be an emergency plan catering for children that may have been forcibly dealt with.
- That a compound be established to store equipment such as bollards, fence panels and other removable items used within the public areas of the complex.
- Advise each event production manager that only experienced personnel are to erect and dismantle temporary structures.
- That Fox Studios Australia ensure all licensed events submit a 'Risk Assessment and Management Plan' prior to approval being granted. It is suggested that a pro-forma be developed by Fox to ensure consistency of approach, particularly when temporary structures are being used.
- That Fox Studios Australia provide flood lighting for all Public Areas for use in emergency situations.

Source: <www.lawlink.nsw.gov.au/lawlink/coroners_court/ll_coroners.nsf/vwFiles/Recommendations%20-%20Glebe%20 2003.doc/$file/Recommendations%20-%20Glebe%202003.doc>. © State of New South Wales through the Department of Justice and Attorney General.

Organisations have a duty to take reasonable care not to cause foreseeable harm to other people or their property. This is also known as the law of negligence. A large number of civil law cases involve what are called 'torts', which are legal wrongdoings. The term 'tort' is derived from the Latin word *tortus*, meaning 'a wrong'. Tort law exists to protect an individual's bodily safety and security, to protect tangible property and intellectual property, and to protect an individual's reputation. If any of these things are compromised or damaged by another person or organisation, a remedy can be sought by an action for negligence that will result in an order to pay damages and *compensation*, which usually takes the form of monetary damages. Civil law, for example, covers accidents, contract disputes, or the dividing up of a will. In general, civil law deals with private disputes between private people or organisations. The standard of proof required to succeed in negligence is one of *balance of probabilities* as opposed to criminal law, which is *beyond reasonable doubt*. The level of compensation decided in a court case in which a plaintiff is seeking compensation is decided by a judge, or in major claims by a jury, the findings and compensation being based on precedent. In contrast, a breach of a statute, such as the OHS Act, can lead to fines and these are clearly stipulated. WorkCover inspectors are given inspection powers for the purpose of the Act, including the taking of samples, and the carrying out of a range of tests. There are very clear sentencing guidelines, and specific fines for breaches of the Act, thus illustrating the difference between legislation enacted by parliaments and common law negligence, which is judged in the courts and based on precedent.

LEGAL TERMS

Agreement (legally called a contract)	Parties reach an agreement in contract law when an offer is accepted that creates rights and obligations enforceable by law.
Breach of contract	Failure by one of the parties to a contract to satisfactorily perform the service or action agreed to in the contract.
Common law	This is a collection of rules based on the decisions of judges in the most important courts. It is also called precedent law.
Compliance	Following the Acts and regulations of government bodies.
Consideration	Usually money (price), something of value that is exchanged in contracts.
Copyright	The rights belonging to the owner or licensee of literary, artistic and dramatic works, films and sound recordings, to reproduce, perform or otherwise deal with these works.
Duty of care	The obligation of a person to exercise reasonable care in the conduct of an activity. Breach of a duty of care which causes damage or loss to another may give rise to an action in tort.
Implied terms	Terms set out in legislation that are automatically part of a contract, without having to be stated in the contract document.
Indemnity	Compensation for a wrong done, or an expense or loss suffered as a result of the act or default of another. Verb: indemnify.

Jurisdiction	The laws of a particular state; the power to define unlawful conduct, enforce laws and adjudicate disputes.
Legislation	Laws made by Parliament, referred to singly as an Act.
Mandatory	Having to be strictly complied with. Mandatory reporting: obligation to report cases of child abuse, for example, to authorities. Mandatory sentencing: automatic gaol term for certain offences.
Negligence	A tort involving the breach of a duty of care resulting in loss or damage to another person.
Regulations	Laws which are not made by Parliament but by other bodies to whom the power to make law is delegated in legislation.
Sue	To take legal action.
Tort	A civil wrong; an act which causes harm, intentionally or otherwise, for which the remedy is an action for damages.

ENSURE COMPLIANCE WITH LEGAL REQUIREMENTS

The principles of the major Acts and regulations relevant to event management are covered below, in general terms.

LOCAL GOVERNMENT REGULATIONS

As mentioned previously, councils play an important role in approving a public event. Some councils have detailed guidelines, while others have less formal requirements. The size of the event largely determines the detail required in the submission since smaller events tend to have a lower impact on the community.

If an event has already been held in one council area, with approval, it is still usually necessary to obtain approval for a second similar event in another location. Likewise, if the event covers more than one jurisdiction, additional proposals may need to be submitted.

If the event requires the building of permanent structures, a development application would most likely be required, and this would link to the Local Environment Plan (LEP), which is the community's vision for the future of the area. Application for the use of the premises and property for entertainment may also be necessary. Plans would need to be developed for the erection of temporary structures and approval would need to be sought for them.

Approvals are required by most councils for:

★ using loudspeakers or amplifiers in public spaces

★ installing amusement devices

★ singing or providing entertainment in public places (fees would also apply)

Street fairs must be approved by council and local authorities

★ using a building or structure for entertainment (change of approval classification)

★ building a temporary structure.

Councils are also very concerned about cleaning programs during and after an event, noise and disturbance of local residents, and traffic management.

Street fairs such as the one illustrated require local councils to undertake extensive planning and consultation with stakeholders, including traders in the affected areas. Tourist buses are more likely to stop off during a festival period, which can have a significant impact on provision of services and facilities.

BUSINESS REGISTRATION

Every business must be registered with an Australian Business Number (ABN) for taxation and Goods and Services Tax (GST) purposes. The name of the business must also be registered. A business can take the form of a sole trader, a partnership or a company.

A *sole trader* is an individual who is trading on their own. That person controls and manages the business. The income of the business is treated as the person's individual income, and they are solely responsible for any tax payable by the business.

A *partnership* is a legal relationship between two or more people to carry on a business with the intention of making a profit. There are many problems associated with partnerships and they must be carefully documented by a partnership agreement that covers profit sharing, work practices, death and divorce, etc. This should be prepared by a legal person.

A *company* is a legal entity separate from its shareholders. It is a separate legal body created under the Corporations Act but does not include a partnership. Companies are regulated by the Australian Securities and Investments Commission (ASIC). New companies must be registered with ASIC. The first step in the registration process is to ensure that the proposed name is available for registration as a company. The ASIC National Names Index can be used to check if a proposed company name is identical to another name already registered.

There are also *associations*, which are similar to companies but are non-profit, and there are also *cooperatives*, which are also similar to companies but are registered under state law. To decide which legal entity is best suited to your needs, you need to consult a lawyer and an accountant.

TAXATION

For anyone running a commercial business (fee for service), compliance with taxation rules is essential. All businesses must be registered and this can be done by contacting the Australian Taxation Office (ATO). Advice will be provided on all types of taxation applicable, including deductions of PAYG for paid employees. Deductions for superannuation must also be made. All commercial businesses must pay GST, although charitable bodies and some educational institutions are exempt from GST.

INDUSTRIAL RELATIONS

Employers and employees have certain obligations or duties to each other under common law and legislation. These obligations or duties are regarded as legal standards of behaviour in the employment relationship.

Some rights and obligations of employers as interpreted and applied by the courts are to:
★ pay wages
★ reimburse employees for work-related expenses
★ ensure a safe working environment suitable for the performance of the employee's duties
★ not act in a way that may seriously damage an employee's reputation or cause mental distress or humiliation
★ not act in a way that will damage the trust and confidence necessary for an employment relationship
★ not provide a false or misleading reference (should one be provided)
★ forward tax instalments to the Australian Taxation Office.

The employee's main obligations are to:
★ obey the lawful and reasonable commands of the employer
★ exercise due care in the performance of the work and to do it competently
★ account to the employer for all moneys and property received while employed
★ make available to the employer any process or product invented by the employee in the course of employment
★ disclose to the employer information received by the employee relevant to the employer's business
★ be faithful to the employer's interests, for example, by not passing on to a competitor information about the employer's business or denigrating the employer's products.

The employment relationship between employers and employees is also covered by legislation at Commonwealth and state/territory level. The legislation deals mainly with the framework for negotiating working conditions, including wages, holidays and other leave. In particular, employees may be paid under industrial awards (which tend to cover an industry or occupation, such as the catering industry) or workplace agreements (which cover a particular place of work). For more information regarding awards or agreements relevant to the event industry, the Fair Work website (for which details are provided in Appendix E) is a good starting point. Departments of industrial relations in the states and territories will also provide information relating to employment.

ENTERTAINMENT INDUSTRY LEGISLATION

Licences for the entertainment industry apply to agents, managers and venue consultants. The disbursement of fees and trust accounts for performers are covered by this type of legislation. There is also a code of ethics. Entertainment industry legislation allows for complaints to be heard and resolved regarding payments to performers, agents, managers and venue consultants.

COPYRIGHT

The right to use music in a business or commercial operation requires a licence from APRA (Australian Performing Rights Association) for the copyright in the song, composition or lyrics. A licence is also required from PPCA (Phonographic Performance Company of Australia), the association representing music publishers and record companies. Therefore, if a sound recording were to be played at an event, the event company would need to apply for licences from both APRA and PPCA. The fees, while nominal, recognise the copyright and commercial value of the music. They vary according to the use of the music (from background music, live performance, music played or sung at sporting venues or function centres, to karaoke).

To clarify, there are two copyrights in each recording: first, the copyright in the sound recording of the recorded performance and, second, the copyright in the song, composition or lyrics. There are usually at least three copyright issues in a music video clip, namely, copyright in the cinematographic film that embodies the recorded performance, copyright in the recorded performance itself and copyright in the song (i.e. composition or lyrics).

Copyright on text is generally held by the writer, artist or publisher, and permission is required from the copyright holder of any text or image that you wish to reproduce. In the same way, you hold the copyright in your own work. Logos and trademarks must be registered separately.

LIQUOR LICENSING

In general, this legislation covers the age of drinkers, the venues and the situations (e.g. with meals) in which alcoholic drinks can be served, as well as the legal hours of alcohol service. Liquor must be correctly labelled and sold in legal measures. A sign must be displayed to say that it is an offence to sell or supply liquor to, or obtain liquor on behalf of, a person under the age of 18 years. The licensee must be able to show that reasonable steps (including requests for identification) have been taken to ensure that minors have not been served alcohol. Every person serving alcohol must hold a current Responsible Service of Alcohol (RSA) certificate. It is the obligation of event organisers to ensure that this is verified. Complaints about noise or indecorous behaviour can be made to the Licensing Board.

A liquor licence is required to serve alcohol

TRADE PRACTICES

The Trade Practices Acts aim to ensure that advertised goods and services are provided in accordance with the advertising. For example, at one concert in Sydney featuring an overseas performer, the stage design was so poor that many members of the audience could neither see nor hear. As a result, the event management company was forced to refund the money paid for the tickets to those who had been affected. The staging problem was resolved to everyone's satisfaction before the next performance.

The *Trade Practices Act (Clth) 1974* and the various state Fair Trading Acts protect the consumer against misleading advertising and deceptive conduct. A consumer (or a client) can sue under common law, under the Trade Practices Act or under the relevant Fair Trading Act. This means that conduct that is liable to mislead the public as to the nature, the characteristics, the suitability for the purpose or the quality of any services must not occur. The contract for services to be provided in the organisation of an event thus needs to be extremely explicit.

PRIVACY

Information kept on a database provided by a client, exhibitor or spectator can only be used for the purpose for which it was given, i.e. registration or ticketing. This data cannot be used for any other purpose, or used or sold to another business for direct marketing. The event business works closely with celebrity performers and athletes and a breach of confidentiality should never occur. Thus all employees should know that personal information should not be given to the media.

ANTI-DISCRIMINATION LEGISLATION

The Human Rights and Equal Opportunity Commission investigates discrimination on the grounds of race, colour or ethnic origin, racial vilification, sex, sexual harassment, marital status, pregnancy and disability. A case can be made for unlawful discrimination if management or staff refuse entry to a premises on the basis of any of the above factors. Equal employment opportunity legislation is a subset of anti-discrimination legislation referring specifically to workplace discrimination. It is unlawful to discriminate when advertising for new staff, when selecting new staff, when offering training opportunities, and when selecting staff for promotion and other career development opportunities.

ENVIRONMENTAL PROTECTION LEGISLATION

This legislation aims to prevent pollution, including air and waterways pollution. Discharge of sewage, oil and other waste into water systems is illegal and our waterways are protected by a number of state and territory Acts, all relating to protection of the environment. Noise is covered in this category. Noise is a troublesome problem for festivals and events since by their very nature they attract crowds, entertainment events being particularly problematic. It is therefore essential to check noise limitations in terms of allowable decibels and the times during which loud music is permitted.

FOOD SAFETY

Food Acts provide guidelines for safe food handling. Every contract caterer is required to develop a food safety plan covering food safety at all stages of delivery, preparation and

Safe plating of food—these trolleys are designed to be stored in refrigerators

service. This is necessary to guard against bacteria which may develop if food is left standing after delivery, or during preparation and service, and not kept at an appropriate temperature. Buffets where food is left unrefrigerated are notorious for high bacteria levels. Generally, food needs to be kept cool or heated to a hot temperature. The mid-temperature range is the most dangerous. A qualified caterer should know all about food hygiene and should follow correct procedures to avoid contamination. A food safety plan should be part of any catering contract, which should also include menus and prices. It is also important that all menus clearly indicate if there are any products included in them that may cause allergic reactions (e.g. nuts).

CHARITABLE FUNDRAISING LEGISLATION

The aims of this legislation are to:
★ promote proper management of fundraising appeals for charitable purposes
★ ensure proper record-keeping and auditing
★ prevent deception of members of the public who desire to support worthy causes.

A person who participates in a fundraising appeal that is conducted unlawfully is guilty of an offence. Authority is required to conduct a fundraising appeal; this is obtained by applying to the relevant body in your state or territory.

SECURITY LEGISLATION

This legislation provides for the licensing and regulation of persons in the security industry, such as crowd controllers, bouncers, guards and operators of security equipment. In general, there are different levels of licences requiring different levels of training.

SUMMARY OFFENCES ACT

Summary Offences legislation covers issues such as desecration of public and protected places, shrines, monuments, statues and war memorials. One very common offence is urinating on or in these protected places.

OCCUPATIONAL HEALTH AND SAFETY

This legislation is designed to prevent workplace accidents and injuries. The legislation has specific requirements for employers to provide safe workplaces and safe work practices. This topic is covered in detail in Chapter 9.

WORKERS COMPENSATION INSURANCE

Workers compensation insurance, which is obligatory, covers treatment and rehabilitation of injured workers. There are penalties for businesses that do not insure their employees for work-related accidents and injuries. Through workers compensation schemes, claims may be made for medical expenses and time off work. It is also important to ensure that the various categories of workers are correctly designated in the insurance proposal. If you say a worker is merely taking tickets when in fact they are a bouncer, the insurance company can cause major problems when there is a claim by the worker because they can say that the risk of injury to the worker had not been correctly assessed.

Where rehabilitation is necessary, redeployment to another role may occur until the person is fit to return to their original position. Employers have a responsibility to:
★ register with WorkCover
★ pay insurance levies by the due date
★ send end-of-year reconciliation statements to WorkCover
★ submit all claims for compensation on the prescribed forms
★ assist with rehabilitation of injured workers.

When an event is organised, all contracting organisations on site (employers) should carry this type of insurance for their workers and a certificate of currency is generally required when negotiating such contracts with service suppliers of security, maintenance, staging, catering and so on.

Volunteers and spectators are covered, in most cases, by *public liability insurance* since they are *not paid workers*. In some cases, event organisations take out specific insurance for volunteers to cover accidents and injuries. In the absence of this type of cover, volunteers fall under the umbrella of public liability.

BUSINESS INSURANCE

The various different types of insurance are summarised below, some being obligatory, others voluntary.

Public liability insurance

The most important insurance required by an event management company is public liability insurance. This covers a business owner's legal liability to compensate any person who is not an employee or a family member (a third party) for injury, damage to property or death as a result of the business operations should the owner and/or employees/volunteers be shown to be negligent.

Claims against this insurance can be reduced by careful risk analysis and prevention strategies. One council requires a $10 million level of insurance for minor events and a $20 million level of insurance for major events. As with most local government requirements, these may change from one council or municipality to another. Assets and motor vehicles also need to be insured.

Event organisers sometimes require participants to sign a disclaimer to reduce their liability. Essentially, the person who signs a disclaimer is taking responsibility for his or her actions. However, from a legal point of view, there is nothing to stop the contestant from making a case for negligence against the race organiser. Clearly it would have to be shown that this negligence led directly to the injury, and the extent and impact of the negligence would then be investigated. In other words, an event organiser cannot avoid liability for negligence by having participants sign an indemnification agreement. The person has the right to sue in any circumstances and the case would be judged on its merit.

In addition to public liability insurance which must be taken out by the event management organisation, all contracts signed with subcontractors, such as a company that erects scaffolding, should also include a clause requiring the subcontractor to hold a current policy covering them against liability for incidents that may occur. As you can see, there are a number of different stakeholders who are potentially liable and the event organiser needs to limit their own liability by managing risk and ensuring that subcontractors are also insured. It is also essential that the event organiser actually sees a current insurance policy covering the required areas and preferably takes a copy of the policy to put in their file.

In the following article, the honorary vice-president of Clowns International advised 70 members to take out insurance against potential claims for custard pie injuries!

> Clowns gathered at a special Big Top conference last week—to discuss the legal risks of chucking pies. They got serious as they discussed whether circus audiences sitting in the front row were wilfully placing themselves in the line of fire. Clowns fear they could be liable for compensation if a member of the public got it in the face.
>
> *Source: International Express*, 10 April 2001.

Sports injury

This type of insurance provides injury protection during sanctioned practices, games and related travel that is approved and under the supervision of a proper authority. The policy can cover all participants, managers, coaches, trainers or officials, volunteers, auxiliary workers and employees.

Professional indemnity

Another policy which should be considered is professional indemnity insurance. This indemnifies the insured against any claim for breach of professional duty through any act, error or omission by them, their company or their employees. It is essential cover for lawyers and accountants who may be sued for their 'unprofessional' advice, as well as for anyone providing consultancy advice in the area of event safety, security and fire risk.

Product liability

Product liability is another type of insurance, essential if selling tangible products such as food or beverages and event merchandise, particularly toys, but not generally required as the event experience is intangible. With product liability insurance, damages arise out of product failure. However, should the scaffolding collapse, the event company would expect that the hire company and manufacturer of the scaffolding carry this insurance. As with all other insurance, make sure the policy is current and adequate.

Superannuation

It is now compulsory to provide for employee superannuation.

Fire insurance

Fire insurance covers the building, contents and stock of the business against fire, lightning, storms, impact, malicious damage and explosion. It is critical that all insurance cover is current market value. If you are underinsured you will be paid only a percentage of your claim. So if your cover is for $1 million and the insurance company decides the true value is $2 million, you will only be paid half of any claim you make!

General insurance

General insurance covers property, including equipment, fixtures, fittings and miscellaneous property.

Business interruption or loss of profits insurance

This insurance provides cover if a business is interrupted through damage to property by fire or other insured perils. It ensures that a business's net profit projection is maintained and pays employee wages and additional working costs if alternative facilities have to be used.

Burglary insurance

Theft of property and damage caused by burglars breaking into property are covered by this type of insurance. It does not cover theft by shoplifters or staff.

Fidelity guarantee

Fidelity guarantee insurance covers losses resulting from misappropriation of goods or cash (i.e. embezzling or stealing).

Money in transit

This covers loss of money on the business premises or when being taken to and from the bank. It can be extended to cover money taken home overnight or deposited in a bank night safe. Responsibility for money in transit should be made very clear when negotiating with stallholders, concessions or merchandise outlets. Security organisations can provide cash management services, including delivering change, receiving takings, transportation, counting and banking. The event organiser should make it clear to contractors that they should take out their own insurance for money in transit.

Machinery breakdown

Designed to cover breakdown of all mechanical and electrical plant and machinery at a work site, this type of policy can be extended to cover spoilage of foodstuffs consequent of such breakdown.

Cancellation or non-appearance (contingency insurance)

Where the cause is beyond control, such as the non-appearance of the main performer or abandonment by financial supporters of the event, this insurance would cover the costs incurred through cancellation of the event.

Weather

While insurance can be obtained for event cancellation due to weather conditions, this type of cover is extremely costly and claims are hard to fully substantiate.

STAKEHOLDERS AND OFFICIAL BODIES

While mention has been made of industry bodies, tourism authorities and professional associations (some of which are listed in Appendix E), the number of government authorities that may need to be involved in the planning of a major event can be quite daunting. A number of these are outlined below.

Traffic and transport authorities

Any potential impact on traffic by an event must be discussed with the relevant traffic authority. If a road closure is necessary, this would involve preparation of a detailed plan and a lengthy period of consultation. Transport authorities may also need to plan for additional or alternative public transport. Most councils require that, where possible, you ensure that all parking is off the street and either on the venue property or some adjoining parking venue.

Emergency services

Emergency services need to be alerted to the risks associated with an event. As a minimum, lines of communication and incident reporting procedures would have to be submitted,

as well as plans for dealing with potential emergencies and crowd control (see
Chapter 18).

Preparing for
the Monaco
Grand Prix—
an event
of this size
would need to
comply with
the regulations
of many
official bodies

Police

It may be necessary for additional police
to attend an event and often a charge is
incurred by the event organisers for these
services.

Authorities for parks and public places

Depending on the venue or site selected, it may be necessary to find out about the rules
and regulations governing use of the site. A submission to the authority is generally necessary, together with a set or negotiated fee. This is true even for the smallest wedding at most
city beaches.

Government authorities may include:

★ sport and recreation
★ facility managers (e.g. stadium, city hall)
★ licensing (including alcohol, transport, storage and handling of food)
★ waste management
★ utilities (use of additional or temporary supplies of electricity, gas or water)
★ information services (such as tourism information centres).

The level of involvement of these authorities is determined by the scope of the event, the
nature and complexity of the event, the requirements of regulatory bodies, the level of safety
risk, and the potential impact on the physical environment (including noise). Essentially, the
more complex the event, the wider the range of stakeholders that need to be consulted.

CONTRACTS

This topic is the most important in this chapter and could become a book in its own right.
A contract is an agreement between two or more parties which is enforceable at law. There
are three sources of contract law: common law (case law); statute; and the specific agreement between the parties. Statutes such as the Trade Practices Act apply to contracts. The
effectiveness of the contracts between the parties involved in an event is crucial. Specifications need to be incredibly detailed in order to avoid disputes. Clarity and agreement
between all parties is essential. The contract provides the basis for variation in price every
time the customer has new demands. For this reason, time invested in the writing of the
contract will reap rewards and often resolve legal disputes. Professional legal advice is essential for a new event management business.

The bulk of contracts used by event organisers are legally referred to as simple contracts.
Figure 24.2 gives an outline of the inclusions in a simple contract. These should be in writing
but legally do not need to be written to be enforceable. Formal contracts are written documents referred to as 'a contract under seal'. For a contract to be valid there has to be an offer,
intention to be legally bound, acceptance and consideration (usually money).

FIGURE 24.2
Content of contract/agreement

- Parties to contract
- Deadline and deposit
- Specifications (e.g. space booked, timing, food and beverage, accommodation)
- Services to be provided
- Special requirements
- Schedule of payments
- Insurance
- Cancellation
- Termination/non-performance
- Contingency
- Consumption
- Confidentiality
- Arbitration
- Warranties
- Signatories
- Date

Many events involve a range of contractors for services such as catering, cleaning, sound, lighting and security. While it is tempting for an event organiser to take on all roles, the benefits of employing contractors are many. Specialist organisations generally have more expertise and better equipment, they generally carry their own insurance and they have a lot of experience in their particular field. By dealing with a range of contractors and using professionally prepared, well-negotiated contracts, the event organiser can dramatically reduce risk and liability. On the day, the main role of the event organiser is to monitor the implementation of the agreed contracts.

Many different types of contract are entered into by event organisers, including the implied conditions of a ticket held by the participant. Contracts are made between the event organiser and:

★ participants (any member of the event audience, ticketed or registered)
★ funding bodies (any donor, sponsor, contributor, bank or financing institution)
★ the owner or controller of the site
★ employees (the employment relationship is a form of contract, with many elements determined in law, but not usually in writing)
★ providers of goods and services (plumbers, scaffolding and staging suppliers, caterers, security companies, including preferred providers).

Contracts also cover:

★ licences (music, liquor, rides, fireworks)
★ trademarks/branding (logos, trademarks, images)
★ transfers of contracts or rights (such as rights to a musical performance)
★ franchises (operational guidelines, branding and marketing agreements).

Where there are chains of contracting parties, it is essential to identify who is acting as principal and as agents down the chain. The event organiser is potentially liable all the way down the chain and this is why insurance certification is advisable.

A standard contract for a live performance by a musician is provided on the companion website to this text. Specifications particular to this type of contract might include the following clarification:

Set Up and Load Out: The Hirer will provide the Artist and personnel with reasonable access to the venue before the performance to load in, set up, do sound checks and load out after the performance. The Hirer will provide secure on site parking for the Artist and personnel.

Staging: The Hirer will provide safe working conditions and ensure all equipment and facilities are in good working order. The Hirer will be in compliance with all statutory requirements (including adequate staging with protection from sun and bad weather) and will obtain all permits, consents and licences necessary for the performance.

Power Supply: The Hirer will provide safe and adequate power supplies operated by competent persons in accordance with all statutory requirements. If any of the Artist's or the personnel's instruments or equipment is damaged by malfunction or improper operation of the power supply the Hirer will reimburse any cost incurred to repair or replace the instruments or equipment.

Source: <www.alliance.org.au/resources/musicians/?mosmsg>. Republished with the permission of the 2010 Media, Entertainment and Arts Alliance.

Most contracts include generic terms and conditions such as cancellation or insurance. However, the specifications are an essential component, clearly delineating responsibilities to help prevent operational problems.

POLICIES, PROCEDURES AND STAFF TRAINING

As the previous discussion illustrates, events are a legal minefield! This is why industry professionals are highly sought after for their understanding of compliance issues and, more importantly, their understanding of the implications of the legislation for undertaking risk analysis and developing policies and procedures. In summary, compliance with legislation can be improved by:

★ developing policies and procedures

★ recruiting knowledgeable staff

★ inducting and training new staff

★ reinforcing legal responsibilities in meetings and in written communications

★ conducting ongoing risk assessments in relation to non-compliance

★ developing a culture of commitment by employees, volunteers, supervisors and managers.

UPDATE LEGAL KNOWLEDGE AND MAINTAIN DOCUMENTATION

Maintaining up-to-date legal knowledge is essential and it is also necessary to be aware that in many instances specialist advice is required from a legal professional or an insurance company. Government agencies, such as the taxation department, can also provide assistance. Record-keeping is equally important as there are many documents that must be kept for legal and insurance purposes. Any claims or disputes are likely to occur after the event, so documents such as certificates of currency for insurance for all contractors must be kept on file. So, too, with risk assessments, action plans and incident reports. All approvals, permits and licences should be filed logically. With so many stakeholders involved—committee members, sponsors, suppliers, contractors—attention to detail is essential. As the agency quoted at the start of this chapter suggests, 'compiling a file will demonstrate that the event manager has been prepared and organised before the event and this could assist in any lawsuit brought against the event manager or organising committee. There are also obvious benefits for future planning in keeping a record. Any subsequent events will be easier to plan if there are records and examples of documents to be used as a starting point' (Queensland Government Department of Tourism, Sport and Racing, Liquor Licensing Division, p. 27).

SUMMARY

In this chapter we have outlined the legislation and related issues, such as licensing and approvals, that must be considered during the planning of an event. Legal compliance is one of the major risk issues for organisers of an event and research into relevant legislation is essential. Tight contractual arrangements with the client and subcontractors are equally important as these can ensure the financial viability of an event or completely derail it. Insurances of various types are also required, including workers compensation and public liability, while workplace health and safety should always be a major consideration of the event organiser. Finally, the importance of staying abreast of changes in legislation and filing all relevant legal and other documentation has been noted in this chapter.

Chapter review questions

1 Explain the meaning of the following terms:
   (a) compliance
   (b) duty of care
   (c) indemnity
   (d) negligence.
2 Explain the three sources of law in Australia.
3 List five different types of insurance and explain which of these is compulsory.
4 Briefly explain the intention of the following legislation:
   (a) Summary offences
   (b) Occupational health and safety
   (c) Food safety
   (d) Anti-discrimination
   (e) Privacy
   (f) Trade practices.

Activity

Investigate two venues offering weddings and compare their advertised services/products, contracts and checklists from the point of view of the customer and the owner of the business. In addition, compare the contracts of the two venues in terms of the potential for misunderstandings to develop and legal disputes to follow.

Case study

Legal implications of holding a party

You and your friends are planning to have a party to celebrate the end of the college year. Your plan is to hold the party at the local football oval, but if it rains you will hold it in your garage. Invitation has been informal and your whole year has been invited. Everyone will bring their own alcohol, although a few of the attendees will be under eighteen. A friend is bringing their sound system along. You have decided to charge everyone who attends $10 to cover your costs. Another friend who runs a catering company will do a spit roast and charge $3 for a beef roll.

Questions

1 Is permission required to use the football oval? If so, from whom?
2 What are the implications of charging an entry fee? Would you recommend this?
3 Should the police be told about the party? (Is there any chance that uninvited people may turn up?)
4 Do you need a liquor licence if alcohol is not sold?
5 Who is responsible for underage drinking?
6 What would happen if a fault in the wiring caused someone to be electrocuted?
7 What are the limitations on the use of a sound system, either at home or at the football oval?

References

Allen, J (2003), *Event planning ethics and etiquette: a principled approach to the business of special event management*, Wiley, Etobicoke, Ontario.

Murn, C (2008), 'Council regulations crash street parties', *Review—Institute of Public Affairs*, 59(4):12–13.

Queensland Government Department of Tourism, Sport and Racing, Liquor Licensing Division, *Alcohol safety and event management*, <www.olgr.qld.gov.au/resources/liquorDocs/PlaningGuideEventManagement.pdf>, accessed 17 May 2010.

Vickery, R & Pendleton, W, with contributions by Flood, MA (2009), *Australian business law: compliance and practice*, 6th edn, Pearson Australia, Frenchs Forest, NSW.

CHAPTER 25

EVENT FEASIBILITY

Unit descriptor

This unit describes the performance outcomes, skills and knowledge required to assess the viability of a proposed **complex event** comprising multiple components, and to develop recommendations and models for its future planning and operation. This unit applies to individuals managing events in any industry context. It is particularly relevant to the cultural, community, hospitality, sporting and tourism sectors.

The unit focuses on research, analysis and communication of information, ideas and concepts at a complex level, as well as the evaluation and extension of one's own professional development needs. It is therefore relevant to individuals who analyse, design and execute judgements in technical, conceptual or managerial areas.

Elements

- Analyse event context and rationale
- Assess resource requirements and opportunities
- Evaluate planning and operational requirements
- Develop recommendations and models.

Critical aspects for assessment

- Ability to critically evaluate a wide range of complex information and to develop substantiated positions and recommendations to inform event planning and management at both a strategic and an operational level
- In-depth conceptual, technical and management knowledge of the event industry
- Demonstration of skills through the completion and presentation of a detailed feasibility analysis for at least one complex event concept.

FIREWORKS supremo Mr Syd Howard has been dumped from London's New Year's Eve celebrations after London's Lord Mayor cancelled the evening's festivities over transport and security concerns. A dispute erupted between transport organisers, police and the office of the Mayor, which was coordinating operations. A director of Howard Fireworks, Mr Garry Suprain, said it had been an 'unfortunate incident'. 'We're philosophical about it but it's a shame for London because they could have had the biggest and the best New Year's Eve [but] they were scared of "could have's" and "mights"'.

Source: Sydney Morning Herald, 5 December 2000.

This article clearly illustrates the issues associated with feasibility and risk. There are many events worldwide that are cancelled as a result of risk, not least financial risk. Careful analysis of feasibility and detailed analysis of potential risks are essential when looking at the feasibility of an event. Anticipating risk and planning preventive measures can reduce the liability of the event management company. In the end, however, the event should not go ahead unless there is an unequivocal 'Yes' to the question: 'Is this event feasible?'

This chapter introduces the concept of feasibility and the chapter that follows will cover more strategic and systematic approaches to management of business risk.

In order to consider the concept of feasibility, we will look at three very different types of event: a games competition held during each school holiday period for up to 200 teenagers; a monthly organic food market; and a concert raising awareness of (and contributing funds to) youth suicide prevention with an audience of 10 000 (the Life Concert).

ANALYSE EVENT CONTEXT AND RATIONALE

To analyse the event rationale, it is essential to understand the event purpose. In the case of an **organic food market**, its purpose may be to raise the profile of the area and its products, to raise funds for charity, or to make a profit as a commercial venture. Sale of organic produce arriving direct from the farm is consistent with the trend towards healthier lifestyles. Other major considerations for this event would be competition from any other markets in the region, certification that products are indeed organic, and the rental fee charged to cover management and venue expenses.

The *rationale* for the organisers of this event is: commercial venture allied with a personal interest in health issues.

The **Life Concert** to raise awareness of youth suicide prevention could be a success, depending on the support of volunteers and performers being persuaded to appear at no cost to the organisers. A high-profile celebrity band would certainly attract an audience. Ticketing would be a major consideration for this event—advance ticketing would be costly (commissions). A small entry fee on arrival would be more palatable for the event audience. With a low budget and a charitable/community outcome, the expenses, sponsorship and VIK (value in kind) for this event would have to be worked through very carefully indeed.

The rationale for the organisers of this event would be community benefit.

Games events using consoles and PCs are not new. While many teenagers play games online and virtual gaming competitions occur all the time, this concept would formalise these meetings, enabling parents to leave younger teenagers (aged 13–16) under supervision and provided with a range of services such as PC and game support, security and catering. The program would run over three nights each week of the school holidays (5–11 pm) and would be aimed at families staying in a major tourist city as well as children on school holiday from the city and surrounding areas, allowing parents to visit attractions, eat out or just relax while 'the kids are at play'. This event could therefore have a significant tourism impact. It could also attract sponsors keen to reach this target market.

The rationale for organisers would be commercial (including merchandise, Xbox, PlayStation, Nintendo sales) and tourism impact.

Regardless of whether the organisers think their idea is good or not, the organising committee must consider whether they have the human resources and skills to run these events. This is one of the internal factors to consider. The skills required to run an **organic food market** are largely administrative. If, however, the concept were developed as a charitable fundraising event, it would be necessary to carefully consider the ongoing time and commitment required by the volunteers to sustain the event on a monthly basis. If an ongoing event, it would certainly need to be managed by paid staff.

Staging a **concert** is a real challenge, requiring extensive equipment and technical support. Bands' management and road crew will often support the staging and music performance, although other professional skills in lighting and sound, for example, would also be essential to the success of this event. The event organiser or committee would still be responsible for such areas as ticketing, perimeter fencing, security, safety, toilet facilities, catering and cleaning. Ticket sales, donations and other income would need to be channelled into professional staging and security, the two main skill considerations.

The technical expertise of the organisers of the **games** event would be key to a successful outcome. Staff would need to understand and be able to solve problems with gaming consoles and PC games. Venue planning, networks, power supply and various other logistics issues would need to be considered. Management and supervision of a large group in this age bracket would be a critical consideration.

Finally, in analysing the event context, one of the most important considerations is whether the host community is supportive. This is an external factor. A monthly **organic food market** would probably generate little opposition from residents unless stallholders were noisy when setting up early in the morning. However, local food retail stores might be quite antagonistic, since the market would not be faced with the same overheads and could thus provide competition through lower pricing. On the other hand, the market could attract visitors from outlying areas and a few tourists, which could lead to increased trade for the retail outlets. Most studies show, however, that tourists visiting festivals and markets tend to do so on impulse, so it would not make sense to base planning on the tourism potential of such markets.

Since the **concert** is supporting a good cause, the host community would be far more likely to be supportive than if it were a commercial production. Local councils would be likely to provide permission. On the other hand, there would be a long lead time for this event, given the profile of possible celebrities. Publicity would be a key element and a good relationship with local media would be essential. If church and other community groups were involved, this would provide a solid base of volunteers, free promotional opportunities and expertise that would otherwise be costly.

The **games** concept should be discussed with the local tourism office as it would be necessary to ensure that it did not clash with other events on the calendar. The proposed event would also have to fit with plans for marketing the city as a tourism destination. To attract the local school holiday market, fliers could be distributed in appropriate outlets.

Positioning the proposed event on the event calendar may require consideration of its relationship with other similar events, competing events and events with similar objectives. Consideration would also need to be given to wider industry directions (e.g. targeting business events, generating environmentally friendly practices), the philosophy of the host organisation and previous similar events.

In addition to analysing the host community, the potential event audience would need to be profiled to determine the proposed event location's suitability. In the case study at the end of this chapter, you are given a list of potential events and asked to rank them in terms of their feasibility. All are located in different towns and cities and a study would need to be made of the local population, as well as domestic and international visitors who may be attracted to the event. Identifying the audience is a key issue for event managers in planning an event.

Market research into current trends is also essential for event feasibility planning. An extensive range of reports is available from tourism authorities, at both state and federal level. For example, findings from a report on the seniors market show that this age group is a tourism market segment with significant potential (Glover & Prideaux 2009). These statistics, combined with Australian Bureau of Statistics reports on the changing demographics (including age groups) of the Australian population, clearly point to the size of this market now and its potential in the future (ABS, cat. no. 3101.0). In the next 10 years the seniors population will swell from 3 to 4 million, while the 15 to 45 age group will experience zero growth (ABS, cat. no. 3222.0). Seniors from Australia, as well as seniors from international source countries, are living longer than ever before.

According to the above research, then, the feasibility of an annual event with seniors as a target market would seem to be far higher than one planned for the zero growth age group. However, this is a simplistic approach to market segmentation. For the purpose of illustration, Tkaczynski, Rundle-Thiele and Beaumont (2009) caution that a 'one size fits all' approach is not suitable because different tourism stakeholders within a single destination attract different tourists.

Having said that, with the seniors market in mind, let us return to the example of the **organic food market**. This concept could be expanded to include the whole spectrum of health products to become a highly feasible event targeted specifically at seniors. The

Organic food markets are increasingly popular

location would need to be in an area in which this demographic group was large and growing, and the venue or site should have facilities for seniors. Most councils can provide this type of information.

For example, analysis of the age structure of the Warringah Council area at the last census in 2006 compared to the wider Sydney area shows that there was a larger proportion of people in the older age groups (60+). At that point in time, 11.8% of Warringah Council area's population was aged between 60 and 74 years, compared to 10.6% in the Sydney area.

While the Warringah Council area has a relatively higher proportion of adults aged 60 to 74 years, it is important to note that this varies across the different suburbs within the council area. Proportions range from a low of 8.3% in North Balgowlah to a high of 16.1% in Killarney Heights. The five areas with the highest percentages are:

★ Killarney Heights (16.1%)
★ Forestville (15.4%)
★ Belrose–Oxford Falls (15.4%)
★ Davidson (14.2%)
★ Allambie Heights (13.9%).

Further analysis of income levels shows that 36.3% of the Warringah Council area's total households were classed as high income compared to 29.5% in the Sydney area.

While the Warringah Council area has a relatively higher proportion of high income households, it is important to note that this also varies across the suburbs within the council area. Proportions range from a low of 24.6% in Narraweena to a high of 52.2% in Davidson. The five areas with the highest percentages are:

★ Davidson (52.2%)
★ Killarney Heights (49.5%)
★ North Balgowlah (45.5%)
★ Frenchs Forest (44.4%)
★ Queenscliff (42.3%).

From this, we can conclude that Killarney Heights has the highest percentage of people aged 60–74 and the second largest proportion of high-income households. This information could be used effectively to indicate the feasibility of an event designed

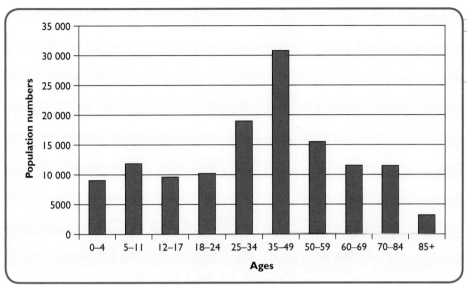

FIGURE 25.1

Age structure
Warringah
Council area

to attract a local audience with this demographic profile. As the current age structure of Warringah Council area shows in Figure 25.1, the proportion of people in this age range is likely to continue to grow in future, ensuring the long-term sustainability of the event concept.

Thinking now about the **concert** example, the demographic profile of teenagers would be a significant consideration, especially if planning an alcohol-free event. The promotional material would need to indicate the target age group and, if targeting the 15–17 age group, would need to address the safety concerns of parents. If targeting an older age group (18+), this concept may have less appeal since the entertainment alternatives for over 18s are far more extensive.

Careful market research would be required to evaluate the messages developed for promotional literature. While you may wish to appeal to a young audience that is attracted to a rave, their parents are more likely to want nothing more than a supervised playground with a little low-key entertainment. Carefully balanced messages would be required here. Also, any small mistakes could turn the potential audience away very quickly and just as likely alienate the parent group who would be providing permission, entry fee and spending money.

The audience for the **gaming** event concept would be boys at high school since studies of computer game users show a largely male demographic. The organisers would need to ensure that the age group was targeted carefully. As with the concert for young teenagers, it would be important that the audience not be 'contaminated' by older, more sophisticated (or badly behaved) visitors/gatecrashers. This brings to mind the complaints about older men being attracted to Schoolies Week (end of school celebrations) and spoiling the fun.

Figure 25.2 summarises the steps involved in analysing the event context and rationale.

FIGURE 25.2
Analysis of
event context
and rationale

Confirm overall event rationale and goals through consultation with key stakeholders
⇩
Assess the proposed event in relation to other events, the industry and the community context
⇩
Assess and determine the marketability of the proposed event through research and consultation
⇩
Evaluate the internal and external factors that may impact on the viability of the proposed event

FIGURE 25.2
Analysis of event context and rationale

ASSESS RESOURCE REQUIREMENTS AND OPPORTUNITIES

Determining event feasibility also requires an assessment of the necessary resources and the opportunities presented by the event. Figure 25.3 shows the steps involved in this process. (The budget template from the Sunshine Coast Regional Council on the companion website to this text is a good example of a tool for analysing the resource requirements for an event attracting a significant level of sponsorship.)

As Figure 25.3 illustrates, it is necessary to identify potential sources of revenue and other resources and develop realistic estimates of revenue and then to develop estimates of primary event expenses based on a thorough breakdown of all event components. Primary event expenses may include:

★ venue
★ catering
★ equipment
★ transport

★ security
★ staffing requirements
★ materials
★ marketing costs.

Potential sources of revenue and other resources may include:

★ industry bodies
★ government funding
★ grants
★ sponsors

★ participating organisations
★ community organisations
★ general public.

FIGURE 25.3
Assessment
of resource
requirements
and
opportunities

Identify potential sources of revenue and other resources and develop realistic estimates
⇩
Develop estimates of event costs based on a thorough breakdown of all event components
⇩
Test and explore different revenue and expenditure scenarios using a range of event models

FIGURE 25.3
Assessment of resource requirements and opportunities

For most event organisers, the cost of venue rental is a key consideration. Many are tempted to save money by hiring marquees and using temporary accommodation, but this can prove a false saving since the cost of decor, lighting, catering and the like is generally more expensive and more risky. The benefits of function rooms include tried and tested facilities, safety plans and insurance, as well as numerous other features. The expertise of venue managers cannot be underestimated and can contribute to the technical success of an event. With an entertainment event, the location and cost of the venue can have a critical impact on pricing and promotion.

The cost of the venue is also dependent on the time for which it is required. In some cases, the time needed for bump-in and bump-out (setting up and dismantling) is quite long, necessitating higher than expected rental costs. Motor car and boat shows are good examples, with huge demands on the logistics of setting up. Goldblatt (2002) refers to these as time/space/tempo laws, pointing out that the actual physical space governs the time required. He cites the example of a Superbowl at which 88 pianos had to be moved onto the field during half-time. Loading area access and storage are other considerations. Security is of particular concern because high-priced items can go missing: it was reported that a new model car disappeared from the floor of the 2001 Sydney Motor Show and was taken for a 600 kilometre joyride!

The costs incurred by the **organic food market** for its venue would be minimal compared with the cost of purpose-built venues suitable for major events. Nevertheless, these costs are just as important a consideration for the markets as they are for the organisers of larger events since they are generally a proportion of income earned.

If it is assumed that the **concert** is being held outdoors, the venue cost would not be high if it were held on council property. The cost of a stadium or covered venue would be insurmountable. Venue issues would relate mainly to placement and cost of temporary structures.

As mentioned above, the most sensible venue for the **games event** would be a room or rooms already set up with computers and gaming consoles. This could be prohibitive if this was a one-day event. However, if run each week over the school holidays at an empty educational facility, the picture would be quite different.

For the event manager, careful attention to budgeting will provide a reasonably accurate idea of the costs involved in running the event, which is essential in making a decision as to what to charge for tickets. This judgement is also informed by knowledge of the particular consumer market and likely perceptions regarding value for money.

In Chapter 22 the concept of break-even point was discussed. This is the point at which there is enough income to meet expenses. After reaching break-even point, the event organiser will make a profit. Even for a community event that is not aiming to make a profit, break-even is the target.

The two models illustrated in Figures 25.4 and 25.5 on page 400 and 401 show how variable costs impact on event planning. Variable costs change according to the number of customers. For the conference in Figure 25.4, daily delegate costs are $79 (including conference room and meals) and accommodation is $150 per night. One night's accommodation

	Number of delegates		
	150	250	300
INCOME (delegates charged $550)	$ 82 500	$137 500	$165 000
Variable costs			
Delegate fees paid to venue per head	$ 23 700	$ 39 500	$ 47 400
Hotel accommodation per night	$ 22 500	$ 37 500	$ 45 000
	$46 200	**$ 77 000**	**$ 92 400**
Fixed costs			
Office and related costs	$ 15 000	$ 15 000	$ 15 000
Commissions	$ 4 500	$ 4 500	$ 4 500
Speaker accommodation and fees	$ 15 000	$ 15 000	$ 15 000
	$34 500	**$ 34 500**	**$ 34 500**
TOTAL COSTS	$ 80 700	$111 500	$126 900
PROFIT OR LOSS	**$ 1 800**	**$ 26 000**	**$ 38 100**

and two days' delegate fees are used to calculate the variable costs based on the number of delegates. Delegates are charged at a rate of $550 for the conference.

As this example shows, the organisers cannot break even unless they have just under 150 delegates. Once they have over 300 delegates the conference is extremely viable. As bookings for the conference come in by telephone, email and online, the organisers are in a good position to estimate the number of hotel rooms and the size of the conference room needed. Therefore, they may be able to negotiate a lower delegate fee with the conference centre and lower room rates with the hotels based on volume, thus contributing to better bottom-line performance. This level of financial flexibility is envied by other sectors of the industry.

In contrast, for a music festival nearly all costs are fixed and there are few, if any, variable costs. This makes it much more difficult to assess financial viability, particularly if tickets are sold just before, or on the day of the event. In the simplified model shown in Figure 25.5 all costs are fixed, including the fees paid to the artists. Unless audience numbers reach 2000 the production will run at a loss. The total costs are almost the same for the final model in both figures, but the music festival is more profitable. On the other hand, the level of risk is much higher. Anyone looking at the two events in terms of financial feasibility would conclude that the possibility of losing money would appear greater with the music festival (with a potential loss of $29 000 if ticket sales were not high enough), while the profit would be higher if a large audience was attracted.

As these models demonstrate, feasibility analysis—looking at the best and worst case financial scenarios—is extremely useful. The timing of the event audience's decision-making will impact on cash flow and cause significant anxiety for the event organiser if these decisions are made at the last minute. Picture the sleepless nights of the music festival planner if only 1500 tickets had been sold a week before the event! The conference organiser's task seems less financially stressful in this example as there is a heavy reliance on variable costs. These costs can be closely monitored and linked to deadlines for delegate

	Number of tickets sold		
	1500	**2000**	**3000**
INCOME (tickets charged at $65)	$ 97 500	$130 000	$195 000
FIXED COSTS			
Artists	$ 70 000	$ 70 000	$ 70 000
Travel and related	$ 15 000	$ 15 000	$ 15 000
Office and related	$ 15 000	$ 15 000	$ 15 000
Marketing	$ 12 000	$ 12 000	$ 12 000
Equipment and rental	$ 15 000	$ 15 000	$ 15 000
TOTAL COSTS	$127 000	$127 000	$127 000
PROFIT OR LOSS	**–$ 29 500**	**$ 3 000**	**$ 68 000**

FIGURE 25.5
Modelling a music festival with high fixed costs

registration. While to some extent these models are oversimplified, they do demonstrate the importance of making assumptions and using these to look at the break-even point and various feasibility scenarios.

Unlike retail stores that can discount merchandise that is slow to sell, event organisations must sell before the event and as far ahead as possible. Tickets cannot go on sale the day after an event is over, nor can the merchandise produced for the event. If T-shirts, caps, CDs and DVDs are not sold, this too will mean lost revenue. Even the concession outlets that sell food and beverages do not get a second chance at sales. For these reasons, the decision on price point is extremely important in ensuring that the event audience reaches a viable level.

However, not all events are ticketed. An exhibition, for example, involves renting stands to exhibitors, and the price charged for exhibiting is based on the cost of staging the exhibition and the likely number of exhibitors. For non-profit events, financial decisions involve keeping within the budget, which may be established by another body (e.g. the local council). Where a client is paying for the staging of an event, the event management company will develop a budget for the event based on very clear expectations from the client as to the benefits expected from the event. Often the event management company earns a fee and the client is ultimately responsible for the cost of the budgeted items and any variations.

EVALUATE PLANNING AND OPERATIONAL REQUIREMENTS

Operational requirements differ markedly from one event to another, depending largely on the complexity of logistics and the existing or absent infrastructure.

Transport and parking are generally important considerations. However, in the case of the **organic food market**, these would not be problems if held in a country town. If the market were held close to a railway station and timing were matched with peak arrivals and departures, this could in fact be advantageous.

Transport and parking for the **concert** would be a significant consideration. Advice would be needed from the local council and the roads and traffic authority. Since most attendees would be transported by parents, drive and drop areas and public transport would be priorities.

Canberra would be a good location for the **games** event since it is midway between major cities and accessible from many country areas. There are also many other attractions for the rest of the family, including the Australian National Gallery.

Specific operational requirements for each event component may relate to staffing by specialists, paid staff requirements and the contributions of volunteers. It must be remembered that there are costs associated with volunteer management, including recruitment, training, uniforms, meals and recognition programs. There are also the all important production costs such as staging, as well as all the operational costs such as infrastructure, security and transport.

In summary, it is necessary to evaluate all operational requirements and the cost implications of these. In doing so, it is essential to remain mindful of the key regulatory requirements and their impacts, particularly safety, licensing, insurance and environmental sustainability. Figure 25.6 illustrates this phase of the process.

FIGURE 25.6
Evaluation of planning and operational requirements

Analyse overall event planning and management requirements
⇩
Evaluate specific operational requirements for each event component
⇩
Identify all key regulatory requirements and their impacts

DEVELOP RECOMMENDATIONS AND MODELS

In this phase the financial viability is the critical consideration and one that has crushed many a good concept. An event that is financially viable and brings benefits to the community can defeat any objections. One that is not viable will have a short life span.

It is traditional, and important, to do a SWOT analysis for every event. This involves analysing the strengths, weaknesses, opportunities and threats of the event or event concept.

S   **Strengths** are the internal strengths of the organisation, for example, the enthusiasm and commitment of volunteers, the specialist knowledge of the lighting engineer or the wide range of products available for planning themes and decor.

W   **Weaknesses** are the internal weaknesses of the organisation, for example, the skills and knowledge of the management committee or their lack of availability for meetings.

O   **Opportunities** are the external favourable things that may occur, such as new sponsorships or unexpected positive publicity.

T   **Threats** are also external: competition, poor publicity and poor crowd behaviour would all be classified as threats.

Essentially, the idea of improving the feasibility of an event is to improve the strengths of the organisation (and the concept) and to maximise the opportunities. Likewise, acknowledging potential weaknesses and dealing with them will minimise the risks. Assessing potential threats and introducing contingency plans to circumvent them will also improve the feasibility of an event.

Once an event concept's feasibility is agreed, it is then possible to create a number of financial models. In the example in Figure 25.7 there are two models, one in which the main source of income is ticket sales and the other in which ticket sales projections drop from 66% of income to 42% of income. In Model B, there is a much stronger push for sponsorship and fundraising is abandoned. However, as a result, the festival is in a loss situation. Given the difficulty associated with raising sponsorship, the first model would appear to be the better. These models are simplified and do not take merchandise or fixed and variable costs into account (more on this in Chapter 22). However, for this purpose, they illustrate the value of modelling techniques.

Another form of modelling, based on historical data, is very useful for annual events or events that are reasonably predictable in terms of demand. Differential ticket pricing is

Income	Model A	% of Income	Model B	% of Income
Ticket sales	$175 758	66%	$102 301	42%
Memberships	$ 12 036	4%	$ 25 123	10%
Sponsorship	$ 10 230	3½%	$ 52 146	22%
Grants	$ 32 156	12%	$ 32 513	14%
Donations	$ 12 351	5%	$ 12 351	5%
Fundraising events	$ 9 856	3½%	$ –	–
Stall rentals	$ 15 623	6%	$ 15 623	7%
Total Income	**$268 010**		**$240 057**	
Expenses		**% of Expenses**		**% of Expenses**
Artist performance contracts	$ 68 952	28%	$ 68 952	28%
Festival production	$ 35 612	15%	$ 35 612	15%
Marketing and fundraising	$ 22 613	9%	$ 22 613	9%
Salaries and wages	$ 62 133	26%	$ 62 133	26%
Office and related costs	$ 22 613	9%	$ 22 613	9%
Postage	$ 5 021	2%	$ 5 021	2%
Other	$ 27 591	11%	$ 27 591	11%
Total Expenses	**$244 535**		**$244 535**	
Net Income	**$ 23 475**		**–$ 4 478**	

FIGURE 25.7
Financial modelling

based on a concept of revenue management initially popular in the airline industry and now used widely in many other service industries.

Using information systems, it is possible to allocate different prices for different shows, seats, sessions and market segments. It is also possible to monitor advance sales and offer special deals. For example, if it is anticipated that an event is going to be a sell-out, then more tickets can be sold at A prices than for a match that is unlikely to fill the stadium. In the case of mega events, many tickets are allocated to overseas bodies or sold as part of tour packages. Consequently, these tickets may return unsold at the very last minute, causing much consternation when some of the best seats come onto the market very close to the event. To manage differential pricing well, historical data is required to predict demand. McMahon-Beattie and Yeoman (2004) describe this well: 'Revenue management (RM) or yield management marries the issues of supply, demand and price, and is considered to be a method of managing capacity profitably (p. 202)'.

Figure 25.8 shows the steps in reaching decisions regarding feasibility of an event.

To finish, let's take a look at how our three case studies might fare.

The **organic food market** would be unlikely to make huge profits, but it might contribute to community spirit and provide intangible benefits to the local population. For example, it might enhance the reputation of local agricultural products, thus attracting investment in the organic concept. Fees charged to stallholders would need to cover all expenses associated with the event since there would be no charge to visitors. It appears that this concept would be viable, with long-term potential, but the margins would be very low for an entrepreneurial venture.

The **concert** needs to break even in terms of operating costs. Depending on the range of donations, sponsors and VIK support, this could be achieved. However, it would be dangerous to underestimate the time and effort needed to get this level of support. A modest entry fee could help this event to break even, but the weather and other factors would make it hard to estimate gate revenues. Cash flow would be another major consideration.

The viability of the **games** concept is most questionable, since the ticket sales for three-night attendance at this event would be unlikely to cover the venue and technology-related costs. This audience, being young, would be unlikely to have any income, other than

FIGURE 25.8
Development
of models and
recommen-
dations

Develop positions and recommendations based on the outcome of analysis
⇩
Develop specific planning, management and operational recommendations
⇩
Clearly articulate contingency planning requirements
⇩
Present accurate and complete income and expenditure estimates to inform decision-making
⇩
Offer different models and options, including clear details of the benefits and risks
of suggested models
⇩
Present key stakeholders with feasibility outcomes in an appropriate format

pocket money, and parents would have to wear the cost. A high price, even if the event were packaged with accommodation, would probably be too much for this family market to bear. The concept would be feasible only if extensive sponsor support could be obtained. The sponsors, including games companies, might well wish to make in-roads into this market by providing software and hardware for the event audience to sample. Developing brand loyalty at a young age is a priority for these suppliers. However, in the view of the author, this event has little merit for all the reasons described. The event would succeed only as a publicity exercise fully subsidised by the games companies and supported with a carefully targeted online promotional effort and media campaign.

In summary, the feasibility of an event project involves detailed analysis of all production and operational elements, a complete income and expenditure estimate, and a review of benefits and risks of various models.

SUMMARY

In this chapter we have compared three very different types of events and in the process have shown that asking simple questions can help you to determine the feasibility of an event concept. Questions need to be asked about the financial viability of the concept, the demographics of the audience, the infrastructure required to stage the event and, very importantly, the potential risks. We have also discussed the contribution of community and media support to the success of an event. An evaluation of an event's success or otherwise, based on criteria established in the planning stages, should be carried out after the event. Some events are measured by profits, others by their social impact and the level of community support they attract.

Chapter review questions

1 Using the following framework, describe how you would work through your analysis of an event's feasibility. This can be an event you have attended or one for which you have created the concept.
   • Confirm overall event rationale and goals through consultation with key stakeholders.
   • Assess the proposed event in relation to other events, the industry and the community context.
   • Assess and determine the marketability of the proposed event through research and consultation.
   • Evaluate the internal and external factors that impact on the viability of the proposed event.
2 How does the concept of 'break even' help to decide whether an event is feasible or not?
3 Explain the concept of an event calendar and how this is used to manage destination branding and visitation for a tourist destination.

Activity

List the advantages and disadvantages (and thus the feasibility) of the following event durations:

- one session on one day
- multiple days
- annual.

Use an example for each in your discussion, which should be based on some of the concepts in this chapter and Chapter 2.

Case study

Discuss the feasibility of the following event concepts. Then rank them in order, from most to least feasible.

- Agricultural Show in June in the town of Nerang, Queensland
- Flower Show in Renmark, South Australia, in August
- Wedding on an island in Sydney Harbour in January (with marquee)
- Red Earth Arts Festival in Alice Springs, Northern Territory, in February
- Aboriginal Dance Festival at Cooktown, Queensland, in January
- Marathon in Hobart in July
- Food and Wine Festival in Geelong, Victoria, in June
- Wildflower Show in Albany, Western Australia, over the Easter weekend
- School-leavers celebration at Merimbula on the New South Wales coast in December.

References

Australian Government Productivity Commission (2005), *Economic implications of an ageing Australia*, <www.pc.gov.au/__data/assets/pdf_file/0006/13587/ageing1.pdf>, accessed 17 May 2010.

De Groote, P (2005), 'Economic and tourism aspects of the Olympic Games', *Tourism Review*, 60(1):12–19.

Glover, P & Prideaux, B (2009), 'Implications of population ageing for the development of tourism products and destinations', *Journal of Vacation Marketing*, 15(1):25–37.

Goldblatt, J (2002), *Special events: twenty-first century global event management*, 3rd edn, The Wiley Event Management Series, Wiley, New York.

McMahon-Beattie, U & Yeoman, I (2004), 'The potential for revenue management in festivals and events', in Yeoman, I et al. (eds), *Festival and events management*, Elsevier, Oxford.

Tkaczynski, A, Rundle-Thiele, S & Beaumont, N (2009), 'Segmentation: a tourism stakeholder view', *Tourism Management*, 30(2):169–75.

26

BUSINESS RISK

This unit describes the performance outcomes, skills and knowledge required to actively identify risks to business operations, assess the associated consequences and take measures to eliminate or control the risks. It requires the ability to monitor business risks on an ongoing basis. This unit focuses on business risk and not on the risk management strategies that a business applies to the management of OHS issues. OHS management practices are covered in separate specialised units. A risk to business operations can be faced by any type of organisation, including non-profit businesses, whether they are micro, small, medium or large. Managers within these businesses require skills to ensure the success of the operation, meet budget, minimise losses or ensure a profit, depending on the focus of the activities.

This unit reflects the active participation of any personnel in the identification, assessment and control of risks to business and operational activities. This activity would normally be undertaken by unsupervised senior staff members who have significant responsibility in the workplace, owner–operators and managers. It could also be undertaken by frontline operational personnel who work with some level of autonomy or under limited supervision and guidance from others. Assessments of business risk are commonly conducted as a team effort and a person achieving competence in this unit could either actively participate in group assessments or could take a lead role in coordinating a group approach.

Elements

- Identify risks to business operations
- Assess risks to business operations
- Eliminate or control the business risk
- Monitor and evaluate business risk management practices.

Critical aspects for assessment

- Project or work activities that show the candidate's ability to systematically identify risks to business operations, assess the associated consequences and take measures to control the risks for a given service industry operation
- Ability to develop or access and use business risk identification and assessment template
- Project or work activities conducted over a commercially realistic period of time so that the monitoring and evaluation aspects of business risk can be assessed.

EXHIBITION PARK in Canberra is where street machine enthusiasts meet, display and strut their mechanical stuff. It's the place to find the most highly customised, modified and faithfully restored cars from early model street machines through to the cutting edge, late model 'techno' cars.

Exhibition Park offers the opportunity to cruise the kilometres of roadways, and stretch performance to the maximum, in the outrageous Burnout and Go-Whoa competitions on the world's first and only purpose-built burn-out facility. Entrants' cars, tortured on the Chassis Dyno, search for the Summernats Horse-power Hero, while grass driving events provide the stage to demonstrate those proudly held driving abilities.

The Top 80 Show, Car Audio Sound Off, and Miss Summernats combine with entertainment and displays to bring Exhibition Park to life with a high-spirited, automotive, New Year atmosphere.

While not everyone's choice of event, this car festival is extremely popular, attracting a crowd of enthusiastic rev heads to the world's only purpose-built burn-out facility. This crowd has been described as high spirited, so the organisers insist on the following rules in an effort to minimise risk: no alcohol to be brought in; no glass bottles; no pets; no fireworks; no weapons; and no illegal drugs.

However, as this chapter will show, business risk is about much more than safety. In the case of the Summernats Car Festival, no doubt one of the business risks that the organisers would have initially needed to consider would have been the response from the local community. The selection of Exhibition Park (outside the CBD) as a venue would have assisted in mitigating business risk to the organisers caused by a disgruntled community calling for the closing of the event. The 'Save Albert Park' movement, for example, is against holding the Grand Prix in Albert Park, Melbourne, arguing that it is an inappropriate and very costly venue and suggesting that the race should be held at a permanent purpose-built track well away from residential areas.

In Chapters 2 and 25 we stressed the importance of establishing a clear event purpose and specific, measurable objectives. The focus of risk management should be the attainment of the event's objectives through identifying any foreseeable risk that might prevent these being achieved. The following list, while not exhaustive, covers the key objectives for most events and event organisations:

The Summernats Car Festival

★ meeting budget (e.g. when an event is managed for a client or charity)

★ minimising losses (e.g. due to cancellation by a key player or artist)

★ making a business profit or contribution to a charitable cause

★ meeting project deadlines (extremely important when the event will be broadcast live)

★ achieving a positive environmental impact (e.g. reducing landfill).

This chapter provides guidelines for identifying and assessing risks to business operations, controlling these risks, and monitoring and evaluating risk management practices.

IDENTIFY RISKS TO BUSINESS OPERATIONS

Australia can be justifiably proud of its early initiatives in the area of risk management as they have now been used in the development of an international standard. In 1995, Standards Australia and Standards New Zealand developed a risk management standard: AS/NZS 4360:1995 Risk Management. The emergency management sector recognised the value of this approach and contextualised risk management guidelines were published by Emergency Management Australia in 2000. Its online learning program introduced the concept of risk and hazard analysis in a community environment. This approach also formed the basis for the many event management guidelines provided by organisations listed in Appendix E.

In 2005 the International Standards Organisation decided to create an international ISO standard, based on the later version of the standard, AS/NZS 4360:2004. The new international standard, ISO 31000:2009 Risk Management, has an increased focus on corporate governance, no doubt due to the causes and impacts of the global financial crisis in 2009. This chapter will use this risk management approach to look beyond safety to the wider scope of business risk, include financial and other risks.

Risk is now defined in terms of the effect of uncertainties on objectives, while previously the standard focused on risk as being the chance of something happening that would have an impact on objectives. The process of managing risk in the new standard remains the same as in the old standard and involves:

★ establishing the risk context by defining the environment in which the organisation's processes take place, describing external and internal influences and identifying risks

★ undertaking a risk assessment, which involves risk identification, analysis and evaluation

★ treating the risk, either by avoidance (by discontinuing a specific activity), taking on or increasing the risk in order to pursue an opportunity, removing the risk source, changing either the likelihood or consequence, sharing or transferring the risk (either partly or fully outsourcing the activity), or retaining the risk by informed decision

★ monitoring and reviewing risk treatment plans.

The emphasis in the international risk management standard is on continual improvement through a systematic and structured approach, which is used in all aspects of management. The benefits of such an approach include:

★ improved legal and regulatory compliance

★ improved corporate governance (financial management)

★ improved stakeholder relations

★ improved organisational learning.

This framework and process, which was introduced in Chapter 17 in relation to safety and security, will now be discussed more broadly here. The framework is illustrated in Figure 26.1.

As this diagram shows, the event risk management *framework* guides the risk management *process* from which procedures can be developed.

Before looking at policy and procedures, let's look at several generic sources of risk.

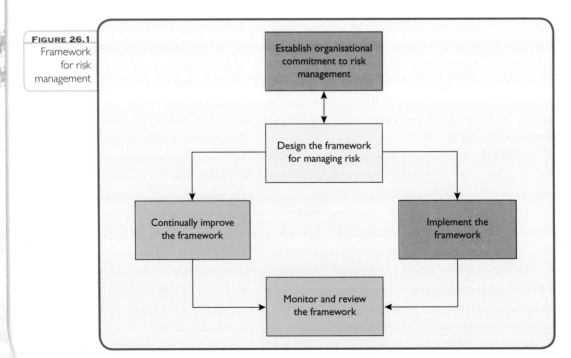

FIGURE 26.1
Framework for risk management

Source: Adapted from draft International Standard ISO/DIS 31000, 2008.

NATURAL DISASTERS

Heavy rain is a disaster for an outdoor event, as too are hail, snow and extreme heat. Flooding can affect event venues, particularly temporary ones, and it can also cause damage to electrical wiring—potentially a very serious risk. Of course, fire is one of the risks venue managers fear, and must plan for, since evacuation of large crowds is extremely difficult.

FINANCIAL RISK

Financial risk may involve unforeseen costs, lower than expected revenue, high exchange rates, general decline in economic circumstances and disposable income, fraud, fines and cash flow problems.

LEGAL RISK

Legal risks include disputes over contracts between the event organiser and the client and/or between the event organiser and a subcontractor. These can occur if expectations are unrealistic or if a gap develops between the expectations of the client and the product the event organiser can produce for the price negotiated. Disputes can also occur if the venue hired does not meet the required standards in terms of such things as reliable electricity supply and suitable access for delivery vehicles. Breach of legal requirements is another form of legal risk, an example being a venue losing its liquor licence for a violation of the liquor laws.

TECHNOLOGY-RELATED RISKS

Technological failure is an increasing risk for high-profile events that are extremely reliant on computer programming and computer networks operating successfully. For example, a problem with guest registration at a trade exhibition would prevent the successful capture of attendee data, which is essential information for all stallholders. For the exhibition organiser, the attendance list (generated during registration) is their most valuable asset. It is made available to current exhibitors wanting to follow up contacts, as well as being used by the event organiser in the advertising drive for the next event of a similar nature.

New Year's Eve fireworks displays are probably one of the events that are most reliant on highly sophisticated technology. Pyrotechnics planners for major firework displays need many back-up systems. If an event is simulcast live around the world, preparation and planning have to be flawless. Every possible contingency has to be anticipated, such as a delay to the telecast or even cancellation of the event.

Technology-related risks of this magnitude are of increasing concern for the event management team

MISMANAGEMENT

A successful event requires good management, detailed planning and sound interpersonal relationships at all levels. Mismanagement can prevent an event reaching its objectives, so too can people-related problems, such as disputes at top management level, leading to the dismissal of key personnel. Both are potentially serious risks.

SAFETY AND SECURITY RISK

Accidents, riots, terrorism and sabotage are all safety and security risks. Safety and security risk management measures are described in more detail in Chapter 17.

RISK AT SPORTING EVENTS

While the risks associated with most community, commercial and entertainment events are largely financial, with sporting events there is the additional risk of danger to the sports-people involved and, in some cases, to the audience. For example, most bike and car races carry the risk of injury to both drivers and spectators, whether on the track or off-road. Bike races, and even fun runs, generally experience a number of medical emergencies and the occasional fatal heart attack.

Bike races carry risk for the competitors—one mistake can cause a pile-up

Well-designed sporting venues such as this one help to improve safety

The challenge for organisers of such events is to reduce risk to an acceptable level by careful planning and by introducing new procedures and technologies where available, as safety standards change over time. Working out the safety standards for a particular sporting event at a particular time involves looking at a number of factors:

★ perceived level of acceptable risk for participants and audience
★ current legislation and legal precedents
★ availability of risk management solutions
★ development and implementation of plans, procedures and control mechanisms.

The last of these is extremely important for event organisers, for if they can show that their procedures for managing risk were well considered and well implemented, this will stand them in good stead if a charge of negligence is laid.

Another important risk issue for sporting event organisers concerns temporary fencing and seating. Recently, a theatre company was fined $40 000 for two breaches of the Occupational Health and Safety Act because a temporary seating stand collapsed at a play, resulting in four people being hospitalised. According to *WorkCover News*, Issue 16, the judge determined that the theatre company had not obtained a report from a structural engineer and had not taken steps to ensure that correct safety standards had been met.

From the discussion of the types of risk the event organiser could face, it is clear that a first-rate risk management strategy is essential.

ASSESS RISKS TO BUSINESS OPERATIONS

Strategic risk management is not only about dealing with threats, it is also about dealing with opportunities. Both concepts were introduced in Chapter 25 and will be discussed in relation to marketing in Chapter 27.

There are many situations in which an event business may be poorly placed to capitalise on opportunities, for example, when an unexpectedly high number of people turn up for an event. Or when an annual show is expecting approximately a million visitors over five days, and rainy weather for the first three days sees attendance at a record low, followed by a huge surge on the fourth day when the sun comes out. While it may have been feasible to manage this number if the event audience was fairly evenly spread over this period, it would be almost impossible to do so under the above conditions unless planning and procedures were in place to deal with such an occurrence. In these situations, venues could be stretched beyond capacity, leading to dissatisfaction on the part of those attending, long queues, delays and, in the worst case, risks to safety. Spectators arriving at soccer matches that have been oversold have been known to storm the stadium, leading to fatal crowd crush.

The risk management process is shown in Figure 26.2 on page 414. Risk management is fundamental to the event manager's role. Indeed, the capacity to think strategically and to plan at micro level is a valuable attribute for an event manager.

Risk management strategies must be put in place during the following developmental phases of an event:
★ concept and marketing strategy development (identify strategic risk)
★ logistics planning, e.g. development of registration or ticketing policies (identify operational risk at macro level)
★ equipment safety and food safety planning (identify operational risk at micro level).

Having identified the potential risks to the event or the event business, the next step is to assess these risks in the relevant context.

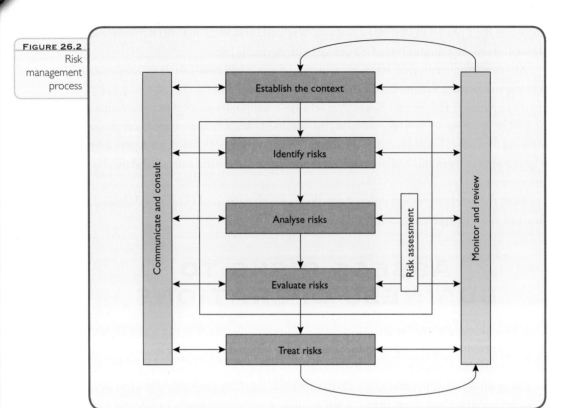

FIGURE 26.2
Risk
management
process

The process of establishing the context for the risk management process provides guidance for decision-makers, as well as establishing the scope for the development of risk management policies and plans.

STRATEGIC CONTEXT

The focus of the strategic context is on the external environment. For the event manager, this means looking at the global economy, the local economy, tourism trends, political initiatives, competitive forces and social trends. As the world becomes globally oriented, consideration must be given to scheduled competitive major events (particularly sport and entertainment events).

ORGANISATIONAL CONTEXT

The size of the event or the event business and its dependence on market segments creates the organisational context. All factors involving markets, products and timing are part of the organisational context. For example, an event business that specialises in conference organisation for the accounting profession (with associated tours, entertainment, etc.) may find that new probity guidelines will limit the scope of all future events and, in turn, have a major impact on profit margins. Reliance on any one market, including a particular source country for overseas tourists, is another aspect of organisational context that might need to be reviewed with a view to diversification. Extreme sports events clearly carry a higher risk than many others, as do some music concerts. However, these may be niche markets for a particular event company and they may need to accept (to some degree) the level of risk involved. Effort would be made to treat these risks, rather than avoid them, by planning different types of events.

RISK MANAGEMENT CONTEXT

Specific security threats, such as terrorism, would be a significant factor in the risk context. Close liaison with relevant authorities and task forces would provide more specific information about the level of threat for different types of public event.

As a further example, a dramatic increase in insurance premiums may necessitate a review of all organisational and operational activities, the level and type of insurance coverage the organisation holds and the level of risk the organisation is prepared to bear. The issue for the organisation would be to decide on the appropriate level of insurance cover. This would mean looking at replacement costs and policy limits. Insurers can provide quotes on relevant insurances, such as:

★ public liability (for corporate and community events)
★ volunteer personal accident and weather cover (for community events and large events like the Olympic Games)
★ prize indemnity insurance (for hole-in-one tournaments, sporting events and corporate promotions)
★ equipment cover (for performers and artists, event organisers and promoters).

The different types of insurance were covered in Chapter 24.

The process of identifying risk can be undertaken by brainstorming the following questions:

★ What are the worst things that could happen?
★ Where are we exposed?
★ What are the best things that could happen?
★ How would we cope?

There are a number of sources of risk. Table 26.1 includes a framework for looking at the generic sources, together with specific examples from the event industry.

When considering generic sources of risk, an event organiser needs to look at a range of potential risk events which could conceivably impact on their specific operation. For example, a major breakdown of lighting equipment at an event could be nothing short of catastrophic. If preventative measures and contingency plans were in place, this risk could be minimised (as will be discussed later in the chapter).

When identifying risks it is essential to consult with and involve key people to achieve broad input into the risk assessment process, to use a systematic hierarchical process to conduct the risk assessment, and finally to document this ongoing process.

Risks need to be assessed from various viewpoints. First, what is the *consequence* or impact of the risk event likely to be? Second, what is the *likelihood* of the risk event occurring? Fires tend to have a major or even severe impact, but they are extremely rare. A long,

Table 26.1 Generic sources of risk

Source of strategic risk	Examples of event risk
Human behaviour	Celebrity endorses an event unexpectedly, resulting in wide positive media exposure and crowd crush.
	Security staff member critically injures fan.
	Senior management disguises significant losses.
Technology and technical issues	Videoconferencing facility at conference centre fails during high-profile session with global audience.
	IT specialist leaves company.
	Lighting and sound systems are incompatible with local conditions.
Occupational health and safety	Excessive noise and hearing damage claims impact on workcover insurance premiums.
	Negative media exposure resulting from an accident causes damage to reputation.
	Rides declared unsafe by authorities.
Economic	Decrease in family disposable income due to rapid increase in interest rates leads to lower patronage.
	Budget tightening results in cancellation or downsizing of all corporate Christmas functions.
Legal	Public liability costs lead to cancellation of a community festival.
	Contractual arrangements, such as naming rights, result in disputes between the organisers and competing sponsors.
Political	Emphasis and support for regional events in overseas advertising on Australian tourism has negative impact on capital city events.
	Funding sources for festivals and events dry up.
Financial/market	Economic recession in overseas source country impacts on a major inbound tourism market, impacting on ticket sales.
	Financial institution refuses to cover cash flow crisis.
Property and equipment	Gas supply fails over a sustained period rendering cooking equipment inoperable.
	Rented equipment does not meet safety standards.
Environmental	Fans damage the environment at the Botanic Gardens.
	The local community protests about the approved decibel level of a music concert.
Natural events	Constant rain during event leads to cancellation of performances/games.
	Cyclone devastates marquees and temporary buildings.
	Heat exhaustion causes problems for tennis players and spectators.

rainy holiday season could have a moderate financial impact, and in the life of certain event businesses the likelihood of this is almost certain.

Once the consequence and likelihood have been evaluated, it is then necessary to look at the *level of risk* and decide which risks need treatment. Clearly a potentially catastrophic risk, such as fire, while having a low probability, would still be rated as a high-level risk.

The level of risk is calculated by finding the intersection between the likelihood and the consequences (see Table 26.2).

The final rating can be calculated as the product of the two numbers for likelihood and effect, ranging from 1 (low) through to 25 (extreme). See example in Table 26.3. For each of the combinations, there is an overall risk rating of Low (L), Moderate (M), High (H) or Extreme (E) as shown in the matrix.

Table 26.2 Level of risk determined by likelihood and consequence

LIKELIHOOD	EFFECT (CONSEQUENCE)				
	Insignificant 1	Minor 2	Moderate 3	Major 4	Catastrophic 5
5 (Almost certain)	M	H	E	E	E
	5	10	15	20	25
4 (Likely)	L	M	H	E	E
	4	8	12	16	20
3 (Possible)	L	M	M	H	E
	3	6	9	12	15
2 (Unlikely)	L	L	M	M	H
	2	4	6	8	10
1 (Rare)	L	L	L	L	M
	1	2	3	4	5

Key
Extreme (E) An extreme risk requires immediate action as the potential could be devastating to the organisation.
High (H) A high level of risk requires action, as it has the potential to be damaging to the organisation.
Medium (M) Allocate specific responsibility to a medium risk and implement monitoring or response procedures.
Low (L) Treat a low level of risk with routine procedures.

Source: Based on Tables 6.3, 6.4 and 6.6, Risk management guidelines: companion to AS/NZS 4360:2004.

ELIMINATE OR CONTROL BUSINESS RISKS

The next steps are to assess the organisation's capability to eliminate or control the risk, to determine specific elimination or control measures, to develop and document contingency plans, and to communicate these to key people involved in operational activity. Of course, it is preferable to eliminate the risk, but if this is impossible control measures must be put in place to minimise the risk. The event management team needs to continually monitor specific risks and controls to ensure the effectiveness of the control measure.

Risks can also be transferred by outsourcing the risk to professional organisations. The most obvious example is transferring the safety risk of a high-profile VIP to a security company. Financial risks can likewise be shared by, for example, increasing the number of investors in a production. Insurance is another way to transfer risk.

The possibility of failure also has to be countenanced, as it needs to be when a performer cancels. Contingency plans are designed to deal with risks like this that cannot be avoided or controlled.

A risk analysis form similar to that illustrated in Figure 26.3 opposite might be used, although for most events they are larger and more complex. The columns in this form that are most important are 'Control' and 'Contingency'. From this form it is evident that a number of risks can be expressed in generic terms.

An organisation can take steps to prevent a risk event. Such steps may be based on legal obligations for example, the installation of a fire detection system.

Contingency planning is necessary in case the risk event occurs. Fire fighting systems would be put in place for such contingency, as would evacuation procedures. Contingency plans need to be developed for all of the following emergency situations:

★ prohibited access to a facility or venue
★ loss of electric power
★ communication lines down
★ ruptured gas mains
★ water damage
★ smoke damage
★ structural damage
★ air or water contamination
★ explosion
★ chemical release
★ trapped persons.

Security risks could include:

★ cash stolen in transit
★ hold-up at ticket booth
★ goods stolen from site
★ illegal entry (e.g. climbing fences)
★ illegal entry to performance or VIP areas
★ vandalism to facilities and equipment
★ insufficient number of security personnel on duty to control crowds
★ untrained and unqualified security staff
★ use of excessive force by security staff.

It must be stressed, however, that not all risks are physical or tangible. For each event, risks need to be categorised and evaluated. Figure 26.4 on page 420 provides a risk analysis for human resource management, illustrating again that this approach can be used with all generic sources of risk and not just safety.

Risk treatment involves identifying the range of options for treating the risk, assessing those options and preparing risk treatment plans. There are a number of options for most risk events:

★ Avoid the risk by abandoning the activity (e.g. abandoning children's rides).
★ Reduce the likelihood of the occurrence (e.g. by implementing prevention programs such as a maintenance program).
★ Reduce the severity of the consequences (e.g. contingency planning for first aid training).

Identified risk	Likelihood	Consequence	Level of risk	Control	Contingency
Main sponsor withdraws support	Possible	Major	High	• Sign long-term contracts with blue chip business partners • Maintain ongoing business intelligence activities • Maintain ongoing communication to develop business relationship with sponsor	• Approach other sponsors • Approach government bodies for assistance • Take out a short-term loan • Extend other sponsorship involvement • Cancel the event
Cash flow crisis	Possible	Major	High	• Careful budgeting • Short-term contracts • Monitoring and control of expenses • Review pricing • Review promotional activities	• Increase borrowings • Search for new markets • Extend promotion • Discount tickets • Find more sponsorship or funding
Major fatal accident	Unlikely	Catastrophic	High	• Safety policies and procedures • Staff training • Insurance coverage • PR crisis plan	• Implement crisis management plan • Provide accurate information to the media
Maintenance systems failure	Rare	Major	Low	• High-calibre staging/engineering staff • Systems and procedures for preventative maintenance • Insurance	• Contingency plans for breakdown of major plant or equipment

FIGURE 26.3
Risk analysis for an event management company

Identified risk	Likelihood	Consequence	Level of risk	Treatment	Contingency
Unable to recruit critical staff with specific technical experience	Possible	Moderate	Medium	• Workforce planning • International recruitment • Database of applicants	• Use agencies, network of contacts, head hunt • Meet relocation expenses • Provide incentives
Key staff member resigns or becomes ill shortly before the event	Likely	Major	Extreme	• Document policy and procedure • Maintain records • Work in teams • Appoint assistants • Provide incentives for staying until close-down	• Restructure • Recover lost ground • Reshape plans • Reassign responsibility
Volunteer and staff attrition during the event	Likely	Moderate	High	• Provide a reason to be there • Reward attendance • Acknowledge support	• Ensure rosters allow for attrition (inevitable) • Have a redeployment team
Contractor defaults on service immediately prior to or during the event	Possible	Major	High	• Appoint contractors based on selection criteria including past performance • Contracts to have penalty clauses • Work breakdown extremely detailed • Monitor activities	• Invoke penalties • Hire another contractor • Undertake work using own staff

(continued)

Identified risk	Likelihood	Consequence	Level of risk	Treatment	Contingency
Misconduct by staff member causes bad press	Rare	Major	Low	• Code of conduct • Disciplinary policy • Counselling and dismissal processes	• Dismissal • Press release
Fatal safety incident resulting from inadequate staff selection and training	Unlikely	Catastrophic	High	• Job analysis • Safety risk analysis • Selection based on experience and, in some cases, specific licences • Training in safety procedures • Documented procedures and signed checklists • Supervision	• Incident reporting system • First aid services • Communication system • Crisis management team • Press release
Non-compliance with industrial legislation	Unlikely	Minor	Low	• Assign responsibility for HR compliance • Monitor compliance including of contractors	• Resolve with authorities

Source: Van Der Wagen (2007), p. 32.

Risk treatments are linked to the management functions of planning and control. Planning for prevention includes many of the processes described in this book, such as development of sound contractual arrangements, inspection processes, training, supervision, technical controls and compliance programs. Contingency plans for emergency situations have likewise been discussed at length in Chapters 17 and 18.

It is important to note that waivers do not release an organisation from its duty of care to the person who signs the waiver. They do not protect organisations which act negligently or fail to act when they should have. Disclaimers (statements that responsibility is not accepted for certain incidents) also do not exempt organisations from their duty of care.

Risk treatment generally identifies the following:

Source of risk	How could the risk arise?
Risk event	What could happen?
Priority	What priority does this risk have in relation to others?
Likelihood	Almost certain, likely, possible, unlikely, rare?
Consequences	Insignificant, minor, moderate, major, catastrophic?
Level of risk	Extreme, high, moderate, low?
Risk treatment	What will be done to eliminate the risk, control the risk, transfer the risk or retain the risk?
Responsibility	What is the name of the person who will implement the risk treatment option?
Resources required	What physical and human resources are needed to implement the risk treatment?
Performance measure	How will it be known that the risk treatment is working?
Timetable	When will the treatment option be implemented?

The outcome of a risk analysis is a prioritised list of risks for further action. The cost of managing the risk needs to be commensurate with the benefits obtained. Often large benefits can be obtained for a reasonable cost, but to continue to strive for reduction incurs an escalating cost disproportionate to the result. This is called the Law of Diminishing Returns, and is illustrated in Figure 26.5.

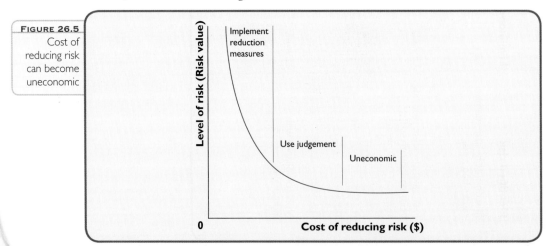

FIGURE 26.5
Cost of reducing risk can become uneconomic

The event or organisation's capability to eliminate or control risk requires access to accurate information, expertise within the organisation to determine and implement appropriate control measures, analysis of legal liability, and consideration of the financial or other resource constraints on implementing sufficient control measures.

MONITOR AND EVALUATE BUSINESS RISK MANAGEMENT PRACTICES

Finally, it is essential to continually monitor operational activities for a changing risk profile and identify, assess and control business risks on an ongoing basis. The importance of consulting with key people and stakeholders to elicit feedback on the effectiveness of all risk management practices cannot be stressed enough.

Clear documentation of identified risks and the outcome of assessment of these risks may include:

★ checklists
★ completed risk identification and assessment reports
★ comprehensive file notes
★ correspondence with customers, suppliers or specialist advisers
★ reports
★ meeting notes or minutes
★ action plans.

Several event planning guides which cover this topic in detail are available on the companion website to this text, and there are many more examples of forms and templates on the internet. The most useful are those provided by local government agencies.

DEVELOP A RISK MANAGEMENT POLICY

One final consideration for event managers is that of policy development. This goes beyond the steps of process and procedure to ensure that risk management forms a core element of policy in event planning. Policy development ensures that all stakeholders work together to mitigate risks. Feasibility analysis, discussed in Chapter 25, involves business risk assessment.

The following steps are recommended for developing a risk management policy:

★ Obtain the support of senior management for ongoing risk analysis, evaluation and treatment.
★ Decide who is responsible for managing risks.
★ Develop the required documentation.

★ Develop a timeline for implementation and ongoing review of the policy.
★ Integrate risk management with strategic and operational planning.
★ Communicate with staff on an ongoing basis.
★ Manage the program at each relevant level and integrate with all other management responsibilities.
★ Monitor and review the policy, procedures and outcomes.

In the following situation a policy was developed to stop participants over the age of 50 from participating in an event. In light of the feedback obtained with regard to this policy, no doubt it will be reviewed.

Peter Biscoe reckoned he was in good shape for yesterday's Rough Water swim at Bondi Beach. But the former champion swimmer, lifesaver and water polo player didn't get his chance. He was among about 90 swimmers aged over 49 who were excluded from the 1-kilometre swim because of rough surf.

Organisers said they had made the decision based on the greater health risks—particularly of heart attacks—among older swimmers. It didn't sit well with Mr Biscoe. '[Age] is an extremely arbitrary and irrational basis on which to exclude people,' he said. 'Any of my children could go in the race, even though I am a much stronger swimmer than any of them.'

Last night, the head of the Anti-Discrimination Board, Chris Puplick, said such a decision based on age, not fitness, might breach the state's discrimination laws.

Source: Geesche Jacobsen, *Sydney Morning Herald*, 13 January 2003.

Risk management is an iterative, ongoing process. It occurs during the event planning phase, but must also become part of the minute-by-minute management of an event. Activities must be monitored on an ongoing basis using an incident report form (illustrated in Chapter 17). These incidents must be analysed and 'near miss' incidents given special attention. Likewise, any incidents that indicate a risk to health, safety or security should be given special attention and action taken immediately to reduce or eliminate the risk.

SUMMARY

The event industry has experienced many economic downturns that have had a serious impact on business, including most recently the global financial crisis. Extreme weather has also resulted in cancellation of events. Internal forces such as lengthy contract disputes or serious accidents can also impact negatively on a business in this industry. For these reasons, this and other chapters in this book stress the value of risk management planning during all stages of event planning, from concept through to execution. This chapter has also outlined the steps in identifying, assessing, evaluating, controlling and monitoring risk, with emphasis on the ongoing nature of this process. Strategic and operational risk management can prevent damage to a company's financial status and/or reputation, enhance opportunities and improve relationships with stakeholders.

Chapter review questions

1 Summarise the risk management process.
2 Explain the concept of risk treatment.
3 Explain, with examples, five sources of strategic risk for an event organisation.
4 Identify one event that has not properly evaluated the level of risk, with serious consequences.

Activity

Consider some of the social and legal issues relating to the use and abuse of alcohol and drugs at events. Identify some of the factors that increase the level of this risk for the event organiser, and ways in which this risk can be minimised and managed.

Case study

Conduct a risk management analysis using a table format and appropriate headings (see Figure 26.3 on page 419 as an example) for at least two of the following events:
- Outdoor launch of a soft drink product, with entertainment, for a target audience of children aged nine to fourteen.
- Surf carnival (run, swim, paddle) for all age groups, with a handicapping system based on heat times.
- School swimming competition for high school students of the Asia-Pacific region with finals in a major city.
- Global warming conference and concert involving politicians, scientists, activists and the media.

References

ACT WorkCover (2006), *A guide to risk management of public events*, <www.ors.act.gov.au/workcover/pdfs/WorkSafe/Guides/Guide_Public-Events.pdf>, accessed 18 May 2010.
ISO 31000:2009 *Risk management: principles and guidelines*, SAI GLOBAL, <http://infostore.saiglobal.com/store/Details.aspx?ProductID=1378614>, accessed 25 May 2010.
ISO/IEC 31010:2009 *Risk management: risk assessment techniques*, SAI GLOBAL, <http://infostore.saiglobal.com/store/>, accessed 25 May 2010.
Van Der Wagen, L (2007), *Human resource management for events*, Elsevier, Oxford, UK.

CHAPTER 27

MARKETING STRATEGIES

Unit descriptor

This unit describes the performance outcomes, skills and knowledge required to develop and manage marketing strategies, including developing a marketing plan. The actual conduct of activities that generally takes place within the framework of marketing plans is covered in various other units such as SITXMPR004A Coordinate marketing activities. This unit applies to individuals operating in a management capacity who are responsible for developing marketing strategies and plans. This may include managers whose primary role is marketing related or those for whom marketing is a part of the overall job responsibility. Marketing strategies could be developed for a specific new or existing product or service, a small or medium-sized business organisation, a destination or a specific project, such as an event.

Elements

- Collect and analyse information on the internal business environment
- Collect and analyse information on the external business environment
- Develop marketing strategies
- Prepare a marketing plan
- Implement and monitor marketing activities.

Critical aspects for assessment

- Ability to develop a marketing strategy and plan for a specific event product, service or organisation that identifies current and relevant marketing issues and includes a detailed, realistic implementation program
- Knowledge and understanding of specific implementation and monitoring issues
- Project or work activities conducted over a period of time to allow the candidate to develop and implement a marketing strategy for a given product or service
- Development and implementation of a marketing strategy that targets and involves individuals or businesses with a genuine interest or potential in purchasing the product or service.

THE OPTUS FESTIVAL BUDDY is your official pocket guide to all Sydney Festival 2010 events. You can create your very own festival planner, read event descriptions, view trailers and image galleries, purchase tickets and interact with each event on your favourite social networks.

You also have comprehensive venue information, including maps, directions and public transport details. The search function allows you to find an event by date, genre or venue. If you can't decide, the Inspire Me section will recommend something to you.

Optus Festival Buddy is a community initiative from Optus to support the Sydney Festival.

Source: <http://itunes.apple.com/au/app/festival-buddy/id346086467?mt=8#>. © Optus.

This interactive mobile phone application illustrates the pace at which marketing efforts are changing. The application enables visitors to the Sydney Festival to view the calendar of events, see trailers and purchase tickets.

At World Expo 2010 in Shanghai, China Mobile, global partner of the event, customised similar applications for that event. Visitors were able to choose between 100 shows daily; over the six months of the Expo there were 2000 performances over 35 venues. After booking online, visitors received a picture of a barcode on their mobile phones. When they arrived at the entrance, they just opened the file, placed the mobile phone on the sensor and all the information was read by a scanner. They could also make purchases of food, beverage and merchandise using their mobile phone. And Radio Frequency Identification (RFID) card visitors were able to go to certain terminals on the Expo site to find their location and check which pavilions they had already visited. They could also see in advance if pavilions they planned to visit were crowded. Organisers were able to control LCD advertising with their mobile phones.

These innovations are likely to change the face of event marketing in future, with customers having better information just in time, potentially delaying their decision-making. It is therefore clear that staying abreast of current and new trends in marketing and consumer behaviour is essential for the event manager.

In this chapter we will look first at the nature of event marketing and then at the external and internal business environments in which marketing takes place. The next step covered is the development of marketing strategies on which to base the event's marketing plan, and the final step in the process is implementing and monitoring the plan.

NATURE OF EVENT MARKETING

The UK Chartered Institute of Marketing defines marketing as:

The management process responsible for identifying, anticipating and satisfying customer requirements profitably.

The American Marketing Association provides the following definition:

Marketing is the process of planning and executing the conception, pricing, promotion, and distribution of ideas, goods, and services to create exchanges that satisfy individual and organizational goals.

Another definition involves satisfying customer needs and wants through an exchange process. In this definition the concept of profit is not included, suiting many non-profit community events. Most people think that marketing is only about the advertising and/or personal selling of goods and services. Advertising and selling, however, are just two of the many marketing activities. Marketing activities are all those associated with identifying the particular wants and needs of a target market of customers, and then going about satisfying those customers better than your competitors. This involves doing market research in relation to customers, analysing their needs, and then making strategic decisions about product design, pricing, promotion and distribution.

When marketing something purely intangible, such as a performance, show, festival or competition, there is a large service component. In some respects it is far more difficult to market something that the customer cannot take home or physically consume. Thus promotional efforts might suggest that the audience will be entertained, have fun or learn (e.g. from a conference presentation). Zeithaml and Bitner (1996) define services as 'deeds, processes and performances'. The definition relates well to the event business, whether the event is a conference, street parade, sporting contest or festival, and clearly places event marketing in the field of services marketing.

The first feature of services marketing that makes it challenging is its *intangibility*. Services are much more difficult to evaluate when they are intangible: 'excitement' is very much a subjective experience and much more difficult to evaluate than, say, a personal computer, which is a tangible item. Other tangible goods include cars, food and household furniture. While many goods are sold in conjuction with services, there are some services with little or no 'goods' component. The intangibility of various event products is illustrated in the continuum in Figure 27.1.

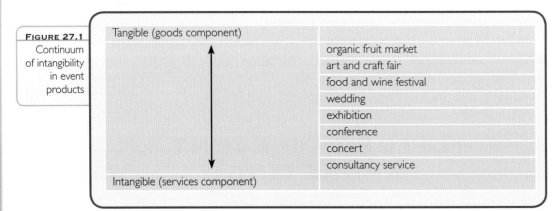

FIGURE 27.1
Continuum
of intangibility
in event
products

Tangible (goods component)

organic fruit market
art and craft fair
food and wine festival
wedding
exhibition
conference
concert
consultancy service

Intangible (services component)

The service and the service provider are also distinguished by their *inseparability*. This means that, as an event organiser, you are very reliant on your staff, performers and athletes to meet the needs of the audience. You have far less quality control than you would over tangible goods (such as soft drinks)—unless your training is first rate. Interaction between the customer and the various service providers occurs at four stages:

1. **Pre-purchase**
   - ★ interactive website
   - ★ email
   - ★ telephone enquiry
2. **Purchase/pre-event**
   - ★ ticket sale
   - ★ transportation
   - ★ parking
   - ★ queuing
   - ★ entry
   - ★ security check
3. **Event**
   - ★ seat allocation/usher
   - ★ food and beverage
   - ★ entertainment
   - ★ performance/participation (e.g. concert/fun run)
   - ★ information
   - ★ first aid
   - ★ merchandise sales
   - ★ lost and found
4. **Post-event**
   - ★ exit
   - ★ queue
   - ★ transport
   - ★ online results
   - ★ photographs/memorabilia.

Another feature of services marketing is its *variability*. This means that there is little consistency since the service performance is delivered by different people whose performance can vary from day to day, and indeed from customer to customer. The consumer is also involved in the service communication, thus influencing the transaction with the service provider.

In summary, the main features of services marketing are:

1 Intangibility (e.g. fun, entertainment, information)
2 Inseparability (e.g. the usher's service approach to the customer where product and provider are inseparable)
3 Variability (e.g. the different levels of service provided by different service personnel or the different responses from two or more customers to the same experience).

There is one final important consideration for the event marketer. A restaurant in a good location can rely on a level of passing trade. So, too, can a general store. This is not the case with an event, as the decision to attend or not to attend is generally made shortly before the event and is irrevocable. If a customer decides not to attend, revenue to the event organiser is completely lost. This is not the case for the restaurant owner or shopkeeper who may see the customer at a later date.

An event, whether it is one-off or annual, is highly *perishable*. Unsold tickets cannot be put out on a rack at a reduced price!

Services provided at events, then, are intangible, inseparable, variable and perishable, presenting a number of marketing challenges as value for money is an issue for most consumers.

COLLECT AND ANALYSE INFORMATION ON THE EXTERNAL BUSINESS ENVIRONMENT

The first stage in event marketing research involves identifying and analysing relevant information on the external environment. This may involve looking at the economic climate in which the event will be staged, as well as the expected market growth or decline for the particular type of event, together with associated risk factors. In particular, it is essential to identify and analyse industry and customer trends and developments, including technological advances, to see how they could be incorporated into the marketing effort. Environmental issues would also need to be considered. Finally, you would need to be aware of changes in legislation, regulations and codes of practice that may impact on a particular event, as well as any relevant cultural influences.

The viability of a business is affected by any number of factors in the external business environment beyond the owner's or manager's control. For example, a decline in economic growth can have a negative impact on domestic tourism, while threats of terrorism overseas can boost this sector. Trends in international and domestic tourism can also have a significant effect on events that attract tourists. Sports tourism is a growing field, with more and more spectators travelling the world to watch matches, with other attractions being secondary. England's Barmy Army started with 1000 enthusiastic cricket supporters in 1994–95 travelling to Australia to support their team. The group has grown rapidly since then, also supporting many international events in their thousands. The cessation of the SARS virus in 2003 had significant positive impacts on a range of local events.

It is therefore necessary to analyse all pertinent factors in the external business environment when developing a new marketing strategy. The steps to take are outlined in Figure 27.2.

FIGURE 27.2 Analysis of external business environment

Identify and analyse information on expected market growth or decline and associated risk factors
⇩
Analyse projected changes in the labour force, population and economic activity
⇩
Gather and analyse comparative market information
⇩
Analyse industry and customer trends and developments, including emerging issues, fashion and technology
⇩
Analyse the legal, ethical and environmental constraints of the market and potential business impacts
⇩
Report information and develop action plans for marketing

The following are examples of factors in the external business environment that could provide either opportunities or threats to a new enterprise or event or new marketing strategy.

THE ECONOMY

Both the domestic economy and the international economy have a strong impact on the event business. For example, when these economies are strong, leisure travellers have access to a high disposable income and sports enthusiasts will travel vast distances to watch matches. Conversely, when they are in decline, tourism drops and event attendance by international visitors drops off, as does related expenditure in the event sector. During times of recession, companies reduce their spending on product launches, promotional events, sponsorship and company celebrations. Business during the Christmas season (with extravagant parties for clients) is highly dependent on the state of the economy.

DEMOGRAPHIC CHANGES

Any event business that does not pay attention to demographic change cannot plan strategically. Analysis of demographic change in Australia predicts that the age structure of the population will change noticeably by 2051. According to the Australian Bureau of Statistics, by 2051 there will be a much greater proportion of people aged 65 years and over than in 2004, and there will also be a lower proportion of people aged under 15 years. In 2004, people aged 65 years and over made up 13% of Australia's population. This proportion is projected to double to between 26% and 28% in 2051. The number of people aged 85 years and over in Australia in 2004 made up 1.5% of the population and this group is projected to more than quadruple to 7%–10% by 2101 (ABS cat. no. 3222.0). Figure 27.3 shows projected increases in population numbers between 2006 and 2056.

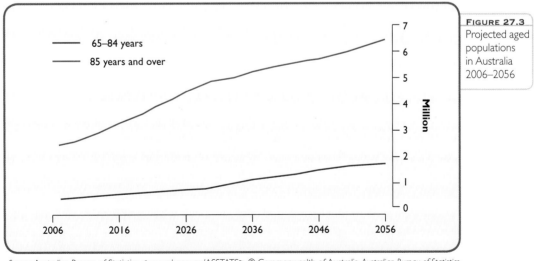

FIGURE 27.3
Projected aged populations in Australia 2006–2056

Source: Australian Bureau of Statistics <www.abs.gov.au/ASSTATS>. © Commonwealth of Australia, *Australian Bureau of Statistics, Population Projections*, Australia 2006_2101. Cat No. 3222.0.

Meeting the needs of these market segments is a consideration for almost any event planner, whether organising a writers festival, outdoor opera or regional food and wine promotion.

SEASONAL FACTORS

Australia and New Zealand are fortunate in that most areas are suitable for tourism all year round, whereas in other parts of the world seasonal factors have a major impact on tourism, effectively closing some operations in mid-winter. This is a positive factor for event planning in temperate climates with many good months for outdoor events. Sporting calendars are, however, more complex to manage, with effort needed to ensure that there is no clash between significant games. This is relevant for attendance and television broadcasts.

GOVERNMENT ACTIVITIES

Federal government websites, as well as those of the states and territories, all provide short- and long-term business plans for tourism, including priorities and general directions. (The website for Tourism Victoria's Business Plan 2008–2011 is listed in the references at the end of this chapter as an example.) These are useful resources when preparing a new event marketing strategy. Outstanding research data on international market segments from Tourism Australia can assist with marketing Australian events to overseas markets. Government subsidies and grants also need to be considered. Government subsidies for the arts underpin the running of many arts festivals, and government grants for community events can have a significant impact on event planning.

TOURISM TRENDS

Very often a target market can be identified using information on tourism trends. Tourism forecasts predict fluctuations in visitor numbers, both international and domestic. When a trend is clear (e.g. an increase in visitors from China), then an event can be promoted to this market via tour wholesalers. Tourism bodies conduct regular research to monitor such trends.

SOCIAL AND CULTURAL CHANGE

Social change is reflected in the conceptualisation of new events. For example, a recent event was labelled as a 'grown up music concert with the vibe but without the mosh pits and porta loos'. This reflects the needs of a more sophisticated consumer who has enjoyed outdoor concerts as a teenager. The popularity of different music genres such as folk, country, blues, jazz, latin and world fusion, rap and hip hop follows fashion trends linked to social and cultural change. Short film festivals and outdoor cinema are also reasonably new entertainment 'products'. Some products have a long life cycle (e.g. Opera in the Park), while others might lose popularity quite quickly. Young children are a particularly fickle market, dependent on who is popular in current television programming.

ECOLOGICAL AND ENVIRONMENTAL FACTORS

Developing community awareness of ecological and environmental issues has led to the creation of such events as Waste Wise. Indeed, environmental awareness has led to the development of one of Australia's most famous events, Clean Up Australia, which is now staged annually in other countries around the world.

TECHNOLOGICAL DEVELOPMENTS

Developments in technology have transformed the event environment in ways not generally envisaged even 20 years ago. The big screen is one of the industry's best innovations, extending the size of audiences dramatically. The internet, of course, has had a major impact on how the event industry operates, and also on marketing, with even the smallest event advertising on their website.

INDUSTRIAL RELATIONS LEGISLATION

Many aspects of industrial relations legislation, such as pay provisions, have an impact on event operations, and must be taken into account during the planning phase. Initiatives such as enterprise bargaining also need to be considered for human resources planning, as these in turn can impact on the level of service and labour cost. And occupational health and safety is a major consideration for staff, contractors and volunteers.

LEGAL AND ETHICAL ISSUES

A range of legal and ethical issues were covered in Chapter 24 from which it is possible to see that laws and regulations can place restrictions on business ideas and marketing strategies. Marketing departments need to be particularly aware of trade practices legislation to ensure that, for example, all products and services are accurately represented in the advertisements they create. The aim of a marketing campaign is to raise, meet or exceed customer expectations, but it is essential that expectations created in the consumer mind can be fulfilled. For example, tickets should not be oversold or overpriced. Public safety is a current concern with many outdoor events moving indoors to safer venues because insurance cannot be secured.

COMPETITION

Whether running a single event or an event business, the issue of competition is paramount. Finding a new niche is becoming increasingly difficult. Sand sculpture competitions, mini marathons, food and wine festivals, and craft fairs are fairly commonplace. Party planners are a dime a dozen—everyone thinks they can plan a good party! Exhibition companies are highly competitive. Research into current competitive companies and events is therefore an essential element of marketing planning.

COLLECT AND ANALYSE INFORMATION ON THE INTERNAL BUSINESS ENVIRONMENT

When developing a marketing plan for a specific type of event (such as a conference), a new business enterprise (a wedding planner) or a single event (such as a street parade), it is essential to analyse the internal business environment. The process of analysis is illustrated in Figure 27.4. Keep in mind that the focus is the internal business environment, as well as the strengths and weaknesses of that environment.

When analysing the strengths and weaknesses of the internal environment, there are a number of resources and capabilities that may need to be considered, depending on the particular business or event. Some of these are outlined below.

LOCATION

For most event businesses, location is a key factor. The central business district is a good location for a professional conference organiser (PCO). The organising body of most major events is generally close to or within the venue or general precinct.

CLIENT BASE

An existing client base is a valuable resource for a new marketing initiative. It is also an important consideration when purchasing an existing business. In direct selling, the response rate from existing clients is likely to be higher than from a more generalised marketing campaign. For an existing business, a client base is useful only if customers are likely to return or to organise new events. If the majority of customers of a business are transient, and there is no likelihood of repeat business, then targeting a client list would be a waste of money. One would expect this to be the case with wedding planning!

FIGURE 27.4
Analysis of internal business environment

Identify core activities, customer base, business values and current business direction
⇩
Analyse current and past marketing and its effectiveness
⇩
Review performance of the business to identify strengths, weaknesses and critical success factors
⇩
Identify current capabilities and resources, including the need for specialist assistance
⇩
Identify any underperforming products and services and analyse and report on reasons for underperformance
⇩
Record and report information and develop marketing action plans

HUMAN RESOURCES

The existing staff of a business, from frontline service personnel to management, can be the key to its success. An excellent office administrator can be the making of an event business, encouraging loyalty among the existing clientele and attracting new customers. A reliable source of skilled labour is also an important factor when planning new events or expanding operations. For example, if expanding to include catering, an event business would need access to qualified chefs who may be in short supply.

FINANCIAL RESOURCES

The current and future financial performance of a business is critical, as significant budgets are required for new marketing initiatives. Reaching a target market can be very costly, with the visible return occurring over a lengthy period. Sometimes businesses simply do not have the cash flow to sustain involvement in new types of events and major advertising campaigns. Specialisation is a critical consideration, whether in the incentives market or the exhibitions sector. Arts festivals, in particular, tend to make five- to ten-year financial projections, sometimes expecting earlier losses to be made up over the long term.

FACILITY AND EQUIPMENT CAPACITY

Access to a range of facilities is essential for most event managers as these are generally hired for the period of the event. The props and staging equipment are also hired. Few event businesses carry stock such as curtains, crockery, lighting or costumes. When these requirements are unique to an event and cannot be hired, the costs escalate quickly. If an outright purchase is made, the stock in hand is seldom used again, leading to issues of storage and disposal.

HOURS OF OPERATION

Council regulations might limit the hours of an event, while noise regulations might render a concert a non-event from a feasibility point of view.

COMMUNITY PROFILE

Most existing event businesses have ongoing communication with a wide range of customers, potential customers and suppliers. These networks and the community profile of the business are key factors in its success. Popular beaches, small towns and central parks generally have an existing calendar of events, making it difficult for the newcomer.

E-BUSINESS CAPACITY

Nearly every event or event business is listed on the web, with many offering online ticket sales or registration. The range in sophistication, and thus cost of e-business, can vary.

DEVELOP MARKETING STRATEGIES

The next step is to develop the marketing strategy, which needs to be consistent with the mission, aims, objectives and business direction of the organisation.

Generally the aims are to enhance the profile of the event (and its associated sponsors), to meet the needs of the event audience and, in most cases, to generate revenue. Some festivals are fully funded by government bodies, and although they are not expected to raise revenue, they aim to attract a high level of attendance or interest as a minimum expectation. When these are quantified in the form of measurable targets they are objectives.

The following processes are essential to the development of an effective marketing strategy.

IDENTIFY CUSTOMERS

Planning is a cyclical process in which target market segments (customers) are identified, events are developed to suit their needs, and the event is competitively positioned. The aim is to develop a perception on the part of the customer that the event is desirable, indeed more desirable than the products and services of competing organisations. Fun runs and craft fairs, for example, attract completely different target markets.

Market segmentation is the process of analysing customers in groups. Some groups may enjoy a particular type of country and western music. Others may enjoy line dancing. Yet others may visit a music festival just for the excitement and the atmosphere. It is absolutely essential to analyse the different motivations of the event audience and to develop a profile for each of these groups.

As the Mayor of Tamworth, Warren Woodley, said about the festival audience at the Country Music Festival:

> The festival is a cultural event the whole nation can be proud of. That's why tens of thousands of fans and families come here every year— the young, the old, the diehards and the curious.
>
> It's a safe haven with a carnival atmosphere made even more enjoyable by the alcohol-free zone in the heart of the city.
>
> Tamworth is an amazing soundscape of different styles: contemporary, traditional, acoustic, bush music, country rock, rockabilly, blue grass, western swing, blues, urban country, comedy and gospel—not to mention astonishingly popular bush poetry.

Motor sports and music concerts are pitched at different audiences

PLAN TO MEET AUDIENCE NEEDS AND WANTS

Once customer groupings have been identified, it is then necessary to ensure that all their needs are met. With the Tamworth example, there may be a generation of older music enthusiasts who are looking for a certain type of entertainment as well as a younger group (say aged 10 to 14) which needs to be entertained, too, so they can gain something from the experience. As another example, a Symphony under the Stars concert would attract many fans of classical music. However, many others would come 'for the atmosphere' and some just for the fireworks at the end. None of these customer segments' needs can be ignored. All audiences need food and facilities, but food and beverage may or may not be a high priority of a particular event audience. For some the fairy floss is the highlight; for others the food is unimportant.

ESTABLISH THE PRODUCT FEATURES

Each event offers a range of potential benefits to the event audience. These may include one or more of the following:

★ a novel experience

★ entertainment

★ a learning experience

★ an exciting result

★ opportunity to meet others

★ chance to purchase items

★ dining and drinking

★ inexpensive way to get out of the house

★ chance to see something unique.

Many marketing experts are unable to see past the main motivating factor for the event, which may be the opportunity to watch an international cricket match. There may, however, be some members of the audience who have little interest in cricket, but are motivated by some of the other features of the product such as the opportunity to see and be seen. Generally, people attending an event see the product as a package of benefits. Convenience and good weather, for example, could be benefits associated with an event product. Most products also carry negative features. Like a pair of jeans that is just the right fit but not the perfect colour, the event may have features that are not desirable such as crowding, heat and long waiting times.

When marketing an event, therefore, alignment between the product benefits and the needs of the audience is necessary to guide the design of the event and the promotional effort. Pre-match and mid-match entertainment are good examples of adding value to the main benefit offered by a sporting event product.

DEVELOP PRODUCT/S AND PRICE/S

It should be clear by now that there is an important difference between marketing and selling. Selling is only one aspect of marketing and is primarily concerned with promoting the organisation's products and services through sales calls (personal and telephone) and direct communication with the customer by frontline staff. Marketing is a much broader concept, starting with an analysis of the internal and external environments, as we have discussed above, targeting specific markets and developing products that people will pay for. Briefly, marketing involves:

★ ascertaining the needs and wants of the customer
★ creating the appropriate product/service to satisfy the customer
★ promoting and selling the product/service at a profitable level.

As discussed earlier in this chapter, one of the most neglected market segments is the 65–85 age group. Developing an event product that would suit this market would involve careful selection of the type of event. For example, it may be worth investigating the feasibility of an outdoor symphony. In this case, ease of access to the event site would be an important element of the product to consider and would be closely related to the choice of venue. A beach or outdoor venue would not provide the same level of comfort or accessibility for those in wheelchairs or with walking sticks. For this event, price sensitivity would be high since many of this age group would be pensioners with little disposable income, so obtaining sponsorship for the event would be worth considering to reduce the ticket price. Consideration would also need to be given to the cost of transport and food, and the choice of food available.

ANALYSE CONSUMER DECISION-MAKING

The next step is to analyse the customer's decision-making process. Research conducted here will produce information which is very useful in guiding the marketing strategy. There are many features of the event product, some valued by the audience more than others. Masterman and Wood (2006) suggest pre-testing messages with the audience before moving on with the plan: 'the message concept, images and words can be tested using a variety of techniques including focus groups, interviews, experiments and observations' (p. 74).

Below are some of the things that may need to be considered.

Competitive pressure (positioning)

Competition from other forms of entertainment for a person's disposable income would need to be taken into account. The economic environment would also need to be scanned in order to understand factors that might have an impact on discretionary spending on tickets, as well as possibly on travel and accommodation.

Motivation

Potential customers may have positive responses to some aspects of an event and negative responses to others, such as the distance to be travelled, crowding and the risk of bad weather. Customers can be divided into decision-makers, followers, influencers and purchasers. While in most cases the person who decides to attend (and perhaps take his or her family or friends) is the one who makes the purchase, there are situations in which the decision to spend money on an event is influenced by others. For example, if a teenager wanted to go to a concert, they might exert pressure on their parents to make the purchase on their behalf. In this case, both the needs of the teenager and those of the parents would need to be met. As teenagers would generally discourage their parents from attending, promotional efforts should ensure that parents perceived the concert to be a 'safe' environment.

The influencer, the decision-maker, the follower (those who tag along to an event) and the purchaser generally have different expectations of the event and evaluate it differently.

Timing

This is the most important aspect of consumer decision-making since it has implications for the promotions budget. The issue is: when does the consumer make the decision to attend? If the decision will be made two months before the event, all promotional initiatives need to be deployed at that time. If, on the other hand, the decision will be made the week or the day before the event, this will have important implications as to how and when the advertising and promotions dollar will be spent.

Purchase or attendance

Finally, the desire to attend needs to be translated into a purchase action. If it is perceived that getting good tickets is going to be difficult, some consumers might not make the effort. In fact, for some festivals, there are no advance sales of tickets. This means that the decision to attend is considered impulsive and would generally be made on the day. Clearly, advance ticket selling means a better opportunity to plan for an event as well as a substantial boost to cash flow.

PLAN THE DISTRIBUTION SYSTEM (TICKETING)

Ticketing is a key consideration in event planning. If done through a conventional ticketing agency commission is payable on each ticket sold. For community events, online ticketing and door or gate sales are the best options.

Another consideration is whether event attendance will be tied to tourist travel to the destination. In this case, negotiations would need to take place with a tour wholesaler, extending the timeline for planning. Plans would need to be finalised long before the event, with price determined, brochures printed and advertising done (sometimes overseas) well in advance. This type of package tour might also include airfares and accommodation.

PREPARE A MARKETING PLAN

With all this in mind, the process of developing and implementing a marketing action plan can be initiated. A marketing action plan can be developed for an event business or a single event. An event business might regularly organise several concurrent events and would thus develop a marketing plan in a traditional format with a focus on the business, its services and profile. Developing a marketing action plan for a single event (whether annual or not) follows the same guidelines but in most cases the plan carries higher risks.

Figure 27.5 provides an example of a marketing plan for a product launch.

THE MARKETING MIX

Marketing action plans can be considered in terms of the marketing mix (see Figure 27.6). In other words, how will the event be positioned well, priced well, promoted effectively and distributed through different channels efficiently. All these factors must work together if success is to be the outcome.

The considerations of product, price, promotion and place (the four 'P's), which were discussed more broadly regarding strategic planning earlier in this chapter, need to be finalised at an operational level, ready for implementation.

FIGURE 27.5
Simplified marketing plan for launch of an alcoholic beverage

Event Launch: Alcoholic Beverage

Target Audience

Direct target audience: 'A list' celebrities and key television media.

Indirect target audience: 20–30 year olds, mainly female, responding to associated promotion and publicity.

Marketing Objectives
- Achieve 80% attendance by invitation-only guests, VIPs and celebrities.
- Attract two of three key television channels for publicity purposes.
- Achieve $3000 publicity value in print media write-up.
- Achieve 15% increase in retail and wholesale beverage sales within the first three months.
- Establish the brand as first choice for 5% of target market segment.
- Achieve 45% brand sampling or recognition by target audience.

Action Plan
- Conduct market research in February (pre-event).
- Plan launch and obtain budget approval by 31 March.
- Prepare promotional brief and objectives by 4 April.
- Employ PR company to achieve publicity objectives by 12 April.
- Finalise promotional campaign plans by 29 April.
- Approve promotional material, including advertising, invitations and guest list by 30 April.
- Issue invitations and press releases by 10 May.
- Implement promotional campaign as per schedule.
- Launch advertising campaign on 15 May.
- Follow-up RSVPs by personal calls by 25 May.
- Stage launch 31 May.
- Conduct market research (post-event) in June.
- Media coverage final report due 3 July.

Event Marketing Budget
- Public relations campaign $95 000.
- Advertising campaign $250 000.
- Invitations—design, printing and postage $8000.
- Marketing staff and administration $60 000.

Monitoring and Evaluation
- Media monitoring done by PR company.
- Market research conducted pre- and post-launch.
- Value of retail and wholesale liquor sales monitored.
- Follow-up telephone survey of invited guests.

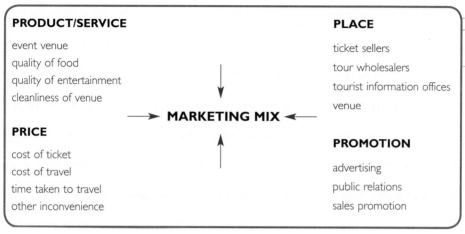

FIGURE 27.6
The marketing mix

Product

Product features were discussed on page 429. While the product/service may be intangible, it is not difficult to analyse some of its features from the consumer perspective. One example is the 'performance' of the keynote speaker, entertainer, athlete or dancer for instance. Elements of performance are also present in street parades, exhibitions, conferences and competitions. Interestingly, the level of participation by the audience is a significant consideration: at an operatic concert the audience is largely passive, while at a mini-marathon the audience participates more. The timing of this participation can be extended to include the build-up to the event, as anticipation is an important element of the event product.

Prior to the 2010 FIFA World Cup, for example, many enthusiastic supporters visited the website daily. In this case, the website was a key element of the product, bordering on a virtual event (there are quite a few—such as virtual dating!).

The ambience, food, lighting and many other features also form part of the product. For a conference, the program of events or speakers is the main product. The members of the audience, and their behaviour, contribute to the audience perception of the product, albeit peripherally.

Transportation, seating, shelter against the elements and nearby tourism attractions are other potential features of the product. All these detailed elements need to be finalised so that the audience is provided with the information required to make an informed decision.

Price

Pricing for an entertainment event is very tricky. It depends on the size of the potential audience and the selected venue. If the ticket price is too high, and the featured artist not as popular as expected, then the half empty venue will result in a dismal financial outcome. Pricing of food and beverage items is also an important consideration because customers become annoyed if mark-ups are excessive. For events involving travel the price often includes the cost of transportation and accommodation. Decisions must therefore be made in a timely manner regarding 'early bird' purchases, last-minute discounting and special prices for groups.

Promotion

Promotional activities need to be chosen carefully and timed effectively. There are many forms of promotion, including personal selling, brochures, posters, banners, internet advertising, news, radio and television advertising, and press releases. Balloons and crowd pleasers (people balloons with moving arms) are examples of eye-catching promotional strategies that can be incorporated in the marketing plan. Promotion is a costly exercise, radio and television advertising being two of the most expensive. Overall, the most cost-effective methods of promotion for many events are feature articles in local newspapers and banners. Events are also promoted by tourism bodies and tourism information offices at minimal cost.

Place/distribution

Tickets can be distributed as part of package tours, through ticket sellers (who take commission) or at the venue. In many cases, the event product is produced, distributed and consumed at the venue. This contrasts, for example, with goods that are imported for sale and ultimately consumed by the customer at home. The effectiveness of the channels through which an event is promoted and sold is a crucial aspect of its success.

The event venue is the location at which the product is enjoyed, playing an important part in meeting the needs of the consumer. Easy parking, good seating, excellent visibility, cleanliness and provision of suitable facilities are often determined by the physical location of the event.

The example of a motor show below illustrates the four Ps for an exhibition of the latest wheels on the road:

Product

★ featured motor vehicles (high-tech concept cars)
★ number and variety of exhibitors/brands
★ dates and hours of exhibition
★ associated events (such as seminars)
★ prizes (door prizes, competitions)
★ entertainment
★ decor, lighting, special effects
★ staffing
★ parking
★ transportation

Price

★ price of admission
★ free tickets for sponsors and exhibitors

Promotion

★ website
★ motor magazines
★ print news (e.g. motoring supplements)
★ direct mail

Place/distribution

★ city location (capital city, distance to travel)

★ type of venue (and proximity)

★ accommodation options (and proximity)

★ tourist attractions (and proximity)

★ ticket purchase (online, at venue, from dealers)

SPONSORSHIP

Many events are substantially subsidised by sponsorship, with marketing plans closely linked to sponsorship. For example, Red Bull has created a niche for itself in the energy drink category by aligning with extreme sports and events. Exclusively produced in Austria and exported worldwide, the brand is wildly popular in 70 countries around the world.

While sponsorship was covered in detail in Chapter 7, it is worthwhile looking at some of the marketing issues associated with sponsorship.

The sponsor can have part or absolute control over an event, which in turn influences marketing and operational planning. Sponsorship is one of the most common funding sources for events. In some cases, the sponsor is happy to provide funds to support the event in exchange for enhanced profile and sales of their products. In other cases, the sponsor provides value-in-kind support. This means that the sponsor donates free goods and services, again with the expectation that this will have a bottom line benefit. For example, a newspaper sponsor may provide free advertising space. Sponsors sometimes use an event to promote a new product, so in this case the whole event is aimed at developing customer awareness and loyalty. In all of these situations, the marketing messages must be consistent with the event and must be clear to the audience. An expensive party to celebrate the release of a new product is a waste of money if the audience cannot recall the name of the product a few weeks later, much less purchase it.

Essentially, the sponsor identifies with the event, mainly through the use of their name and logo, and expects a return on their investment. It is thus essential to evaluate both the sponsor profile and the sponsor's sales, or any other sponsorship objectives, after the event to ensure that the sponsorship has been successful and that the sponsor's relationship with the event will continue.

There are a number of questions to ask before approaching a potential sponsor.

What are the benefits for the sponsor?

Can the sponsor's involvement lead to some benefit for them in terms of enhanced profile or increased sales? What other benefits are there? At what cost? Will it be time-consuming for their staff?

How long will the association last?

Is it possible to build a long-term alliance with the sponsor? Can an agreement be reached for perhaps a five-year sponsorship?

How much exposure will the sponsor achieve?

Will the sponsor's logo appear on all advertising? Will they have naming rights to the event or will specific prizes be awarded for particular events by their senior staff? Will the winning athlete wear one of the sponsor's caps when interviewed by television crews? Will the sponsor be named in the prize-giving ceremony?

Will the sponsorship be exclusive?

Will this sponsor be the only one and thus clearly associated with the event? Or will there be a large number of sponsors?

Is there compatibility?

Have the potential sponsor's competitors agreed to provide sponsorship and will this lead to a conflict of interest? Is there compatibility between the sponsor's product and the event purpose (e.g. if the purpose of the event was promoting a healthy lifestyle)?

Will there be ambush marketing?

Are there organisations which will attempt to gain advertising mileage and sales from the event, despite their lack of sponsorship or other commitment? Will competitors' products be on sale at the event or in a nearby area?

Ultimately, the most important question of all concerns the sponsor's benefit from their involvement in the event. This needs to be negotiated early in the arrangement and a process for measuring sponsor objectives, such as recognition or purchase of their products, needs to be put in place prior to, during and after the event. Where clearly audited records or professional surveys can demonstrate sponsorship outcomes, renegotiating sponsorship arrangements for subsequent events, or different events, will be much easier since success has been demonstrated in a tangible way. At the end of the day, the sponsor needs a report detailing all promotional efforts and the ensuing benefits, as well as photographs and success stories for post-event publicity.

IMPLEMENT AND MONITOR MARKETING ACTIVITIES

Having developed specific marketing objectives, action plans and corresponding budgets, as discussed earlier in the chapter, the event manager can be more confident that the event will attract a good audience and meet customer expectations. Success must be monitored to identify whether the marketing plan is working, and modifications made to the plan if necessary.

Generally, the timeline between developing the event concept and implementing the marketing plan is quite long, relatively speaking. It may therefore be necessary to revisit the external and internal factors to see whether there are any changes that need to be taken into account. These could be changes to attendance levels, which might require modifications to the layout or venue. If it is a ticketed event, lower than anticipated sales may require plans for discounting or other measures to increase sales. Monitoring of all aspects of marketing needs to continue on a daily basis and research needs to be conducted so that the event can be properly evaluated.

With an annual event, for example, customer responses to the various types of marketing activities undertaken will guide marketing and promotional efforts in future years. Evaluation needs to be done systematically by asking questions such as 'Where did you find out about the event?' or 'When did you decide to attend this event?'

There are three stages at which research can be conducted: prior to the event, during the event and after the event. The research can be qualitative, such as focus groups and case studies, or quantitative. In the latter case, the research generates statistics such as customers' expenditure at the event.

Both formal and informal techniques can be used for the ongoing evaluation process. Informal staff meetings can be held to discuss customer satisfaction with the event product, while ongoing analysis of sales figures provides valuable financial data on the event business or event.

A market research company can be contracted to conduct formal field research, surveying event attendees using questionnaires. Sampling of the survey group is particularly important to ensure valid results. Statistical analysis and reporting are all part of the professional services provided by market research specialists. Consulting organisations can arrange mystery customer programs that will provide ongoing feedback on customer satisfaction and focus groups, another technique for developing, reviewing and modifying products or improving services.

A useful management tool, the Marketing Information System (MKIS), can be used to systematically gather information about prospective and current customers to enhance marketing decision-making, providing both quantitative and qualitative information. The reports generated should be distributed to all involved, including frontline employees.

As mentioned previously, the event marketing and promotional campaign is carefully planned in collaboration with major sponsors. Approvals are needed from all sponsors when using their logos, developing promotional material and writing publicity material. These approvals must be obtained in writing. This is time consuming and must be written into the timeline. Events involving multiple sponsors are particularly challenging since all relevant groups and individuals must be involved at every stage of planning. A marketing risk analysis should be undertaken to look at potential situations such as loss of a major sponsor, a clash between sponsors, or ambush marketing by a competitor. The topic of risk management was covered in the previous chapter and these methods can be used to analyse the level of risk and develop contingency plans.

SUMMARY

In this chapter we have discussed strategic marketing, preparing marketing plans, and implementing and monitoring marketing activities. As we have seen, an analysis of both internal and external business environments is an essential stage in developing marketing strategies. Other activities include identifying customers, establishing product features, developing products and prices, and planning distribution. Identifying consumer interest in the product and their decision-making processes forms a key part of planning the marketing effort. Since most marketing budgets are limited, the expenditure must be timed carefully to ensure maximum impact. Monitoring should occur on a daily basis during implementation of the plan, and adjustments made to the plan as needed. Research conducted during and after the event is essential for sponsors and for informing improvements to future events.

Chapter review questions

1 What do we mean when we say that the event experience is intangible?
2 Explain why marketing an event is more challenging than marketing a tangible product.
3 Using an event such as Big Day Out, explain the importance of the event program.
4 Which aspects of the external environment play a part in planning the event marketing strategy? Give five examples with your explanation.
5 How will technological change impact on events marketing over the next decade?

Activity

Visit the websites of one of each of the following companies or events and use the information provided to explain the marketing mix (the four Ps) for each one:
(a) Party hire company
(b) Staging company
(c) Festival
(d) Conference.

Case study

Marketing plans

Using the concepts in this chapter, develop a very brief marketing plan for two or three of the following events. When complete, analyse the differences in the approaches you have suggested.

1 Melbourne International Flower and Garden Show
   Features displays designed and constructed by some of Australia's most talented landscape designers.
   www.melbflowershow.com.au
2 Melbourne International Comedy Festival
   Long-running annual festival of fun and laughter, rated as one of the world's three major comedy fests (with Edinburgh and Montreal).
   www.comedyfestival.com.au

continued

Case study (continued)

3 Melbourne Writers' Festival

Annual event featuring workshops and talks by Australian and international writers.

www.mwf.com.au

4 Moonlight Cinema

Movies under the stars in Sydney, Melbourne and Adelaide.

www.moonlight.com.au

5 Perth International Arts Festival

Western Australia's leading cultural event.

www.perthfestival.com.au

6 Alice Springs Camel Cup

Event organised by Lions Club Alice Springs.

www.camelcup.com.au

References

Australian Bureau of Statistics (2005), *Population projections, Australia, 2004 to 2101*, cat. no. 3222.0.

Gelb, B, Andrews, D & Lam, S (2007), 'A strategic perspective on sales promotions', *MIT Sloan Management Review*, 48.

Liu, Y & Chen, C (2007), 'The effects of festivals and special events on city image design', *Frontiers of Architecture and Civil Engineering in China*, 1(2):255–59.

Masterman, G & Wood, E (2006), *Innovative marketing communications: strategies for the events industry*, Elsevier, Oxford, UK.

Tourism Victoria Business Plan 2008–2011, <www.tourism.vic.gov.au/images/stories/Documents/StrategiesandPlans/Tourism-Victoria-Three-Year-Business-Plan.pdf>.

Zeithaml, V & Bitner, M (1996), *Services marketing*, McGraw Hill, New York.

CHAPTER 28

PUBLIC RELATIONS STRATEGIES

Unit descriptor

This unit describes the skills and knowledge required to develop and implement
a plan for public relations activities within an organisation. It focuses on the skills
and knowledge required by managers, owners/managers of small businesses and
marketing personnel. As such the unit does not reflect the depth and breadth of skills
required by specialist public relations professionals.

Elements

■ Prepare public relations plan or strategy
■ Generate organisational identity
■ Manage the implementation of a public relations plan
■ Evaluate and review the public relations plan.

Critical aspects for assessment

■ Development and implementation of a public relations plan for a specific
organisation or area of an organisation
■ Detailed knowledge of public relations protocols, resources and activities as
relevant to the industry sector.

WORLD'S FUNNIEST ISLAND

FOR TWO DAYS ONLY World's Funniest Island crams around 200 brilliant comedy performances on one amazing Sydney Harbour island. One insane weekend and ONE ticket buys you comedy with the lot ... the best comics in the world – circus – burlesque – sketch shows – standup – sit down – fall over ... and probably that guy wearing something really stupid on the ferry over.

There's music, art, booze, food, camping out and spectacular harbour views to calm you down in amidst all the mayhem.

Come for one day, two days or even stay for a night or two. Special ferries run all weekend and are included in the ticket price.

World's Funniest Island gives you the opportunity to enjoy one of the funniest days out ever on a single ticket! Some of the biggest names in comedy will mix it up with dozens of up and coming young comedians.

World's Funniest Island is a celebration of comic diversity and hilarious talent—when it comes to great comedy, billing size really doesn't matter.

Source: <www.worldsfunniestisland.com>.

Developing effective public relations strategies, whether for an organisation, special event or other group, is an important part of managing an organisation's relationship with its audience. Public relations can also play a major role in the marketing and promotion of an event, as would have been the case for the World's Funniest Island, where pre-event public relations activities would have been key to ensuring strong awareness and interest in the event, which would help drive ticket sales.

In essence, public relations describes the process by which an organisation communicates with their audience in a meaningful way. In this context, the 'audience' is anyone that the organisation wishes to reach, and for many events this involves the viewing audience at home. The concept is similar to 'target market' except that public relations messages often reach an even wider audience than the target market, including, for example, other businesses or government bodies. The term 'audience' is widely used in public relations and should not be confused with the more usual use of the term in events or the theatre. In public relations the audience encompasses any recipient of messages emanating from the organisation.

There are many reasons why an organisation would want to communicate with their audience. It may be to build relationships with important decision-makers within the organisation's industry, raise the profile of an organisation or individual, educate an audience on an important issue, raise awareness for a cause, consult with communities, position the organisation as a leader in their field, or to foster a closer and mutually beneficial relationship with its audience. For example, events such as Earth Day aim to educate, while events such as Sorry Day have social and political motivations and messages.

Having addressed the coordination of marketing activities in Chapter 6 (which also included an overview of public relations and promotions activities), in this chapter we will explore in greater detail the role, knowledge and processes required by managers, owners or managers of small businesses, and marketing personnel to develop and implement a plan for public relations activities.

Managers or marketing personnel who are responsible for overseeing and implementing a public relations program must start with a strategic understanding of the event organisation's vision and its identity. On that foundation, a public relations strategy can be devised, implemented and later evaluated against this vision.

GENERATE ORGANISATIONAL IDENTITY CONSISTENT WITH ORGANISATION'S VISION

The first step in generating an organisational 'identity' (also referred to as 'brand' or 'reputation') that matches the vision of the organisation is to gather as much existing information as possible. Think of this stage as a fact finding mission. This information will help inform all future decisions relating to public relations.

Relevant internal and external information that informs the public relations strategy may include business plans, community activities, competitor activity, current market conditions, current trends/developments in the relevant industry context, financial plans, government activities (whether federal, state or local), marketing plans and the legal environment.

Information gathered relating to the above areas may raise important issues or business contexts within which any public relations activities will be made. Without this important step, a public relations plan could miss the mark or, worse, cause damage to the organisation's identity or to the industry in which it operates. If an organisation's public identity is not consistent with its vision, then the public relations program will result in confused or mixed messages that are not valuable to the organisation as a whole.

IDENTIFYING IMAGES AND MESSAGES

Another reason to review the organisation's core activities, business values and current business direction is to identify potential images and messages.

Images and messages may relate to any or all of the following:
★ the nature of products and services (e.g. performances, exhibitions, sales)
★ operational style (e.g. efficient, honest, ethical, fair, responsive)
★ relationship to the public (e.g. leading edge, responsive)
★ service provision (e.g. hours of operation, range of facilities, services, access)
★ stylistic direction (e.g. innovative, contemporary, classical, folk, indigenous, international)
★ track record of organisation as well as visual identity (e.g. logo, signage, public appearance, colour).

For example, the images and messages relating to a major car rally event would differ significantly from those for a green-living family festival. Images for the car rally could include fast cars, dirt clouds, bright colours, flags and loud spectators. Messages could include words like revved-up action, thrills and spills, and pedal to the metal. Conversely, for a green-living family festival, the images would more likely include chilled out families and children, natural materials, parklands and greenery. Messages could include green lifestyle choices, alternatives to polluting, carbon-friendly, climate change, environment, and making a difference.

Images and messages identified at this stage can help inform the public relations strategy, and may also be incorporated into specific key messages for media materials and briefing documentation for spokespeople.

INFORMING STAKEHOLDERS

Another step is to identify and then consult with key stakeholders in relation to public relations issues. Key stakeholders may include funding bodies, sponsors, patrons, visitors, promoters, representatives from boards and committees associated with the event organisation, and staff.

If complex, it may be helpful to develop a 'stakeholder map', on which these groups or individuals are represented visually in a diagram to indicate any overlapping of their interests, issues and relevant messages.

Consulting with these key stakeholders will provide another source of useful information to help inform the public relations plan. It is important to understand their existing perception of the organisation, their relationship with it and, therefore, what they feel the organisation needs to address or achieve.

PREPARE PUBLIC RELATIONS PLAN OR STRATEGY

Having now been well informed of the organisation's vision and identity, the next stage of preparing a public relations plan is to consider the audience with which you are hoping to communicate.

IDENTIFYING TARGET GROUPS

Target groups for public relations activities may include event organisers, media representatives (e.g. journalists, editors, producers, directors), patrons, sponsors, funding bodies, promoters, staff, volunteers, suppliers, vendors, related businesses, visitors and audiences.

Each of these different target groups is likely to have different communications needs or expectations. It is important to bear them all in mind when considering a public relations strategy, as well as to consider specific communications activities to ensure each important group is addressed. For example, suppliers and vendors operating at a large festival or sporting event will be interested in quite different aspects of an event or organisation than a visitor. A supplier or vendor wants to make sure an event is being well managed, with clear guidelines, agreements and planning. They want updates regarding anticipated visitor numbers, right down to guidelines relating to site access and waste disposal. A visitor, on the other hand, has no interest in these practicalities. They will want to know the 'what, where, when, who and why' of an event in order to be interested and make a decision to buy a ticket or attend. Communications with each of these groups may differ significantly, but all are important in ensuring a successful public relations program.

Later, when planning the communication methods or channels to reach these audiences, it is important to remember that some groups have particular communication needs or restrictions (e.g. non-English language speakers), or low-level access to the internet, or some other limitation. For this reason, as well as identifying target audiences, it is worth spending some time understanding them also.

SETTING GOALS AND OBJECTIVES

Setting goals and objectives at the outset, based on information gathered on organisational and/or marketing objectives, is key in any public relations plan. It will not only provide the context for developing the public relations strategy, but will also provide the ability to measure the success of the public relations plan at its conclusion.

Goal setting is an effective way of ensuring that all internal parties have a clear understanding of the 'big picture' and desired outcome for the organisation, division or event. Any new idea or opportunity should be considered against the set goals.

A helpful rule to apply when setting the public relations plan's objectives is to consider the well-known management tool, SMART objectives, developed by management authors Doran, Miller and Cunningham (1981).

The SMART method specifies that all goals or objectives must be:
★ Specific
★ Measurable
★ Attainable
★ Realistic
★ Time-bound.

For example, a goal may be to increase the number of unique visitors to the event website during the two-month period prior to the event by 20% compared to the same period last year.

This goal would be helpful in driving the public relations strategy and assisting with measurement as it is specific (focused on driving people to the event website), measurable (website hits are recorded by web hosts), attainable (a 20% increase could be viewed as attainable depending on the previous year's results and the upcoming planned level of activity), realistic (since successful public relations efforts, which would raise awareness of the event, should help lift website hit rates) and time-bound (as the period to be measured is specified as the two months prior to the event—the key time to help drive visitor numbers or ticket sales for the event).

DEVELOPING PUBLIC RELATIONS STRATEGY

Time should be spent brainstorming, or identifying, and then selecting strategies that will enhance and promote the organisation's identity to the target groups and achieve the goals that have been set for the public relations plan. A strategy hinging on celebrity involvement, compared with one focused on an important cause, may have a different impact upon different target audiences. Having said that, a strong strategy should be as inclusive as possible of all groups.

Public relations plans and strategies can vary widely, depending on for whom or what they are devised. A public relations plan may be developed for a department, a program of events, a single event, a specific product or service, an organisation—or even a mixture of these.

Public relations plans developed for different purposes can look very different. For example, a public relations plan for a single event or a specific product or service launch may have a much shorter life span, or cycle, than a plan for an organisation or department which may be very long-term in view and ongoing. This is certainly the case for the major festivals held in capital cities.

Depending on what the public relations plan has been developed for, the strategies and activities included in the plan may relate to, or cross over, with the following:

★ direct advertising
★ gifts
★ logos
★ media materials (e.g. press releases, articles, reviews)
★ membership and loyalty programs
★ planned activities (e.g. launches, openings, guest appearances, charitable support, cocktail parties)
★ signage, banners
★ sponsorship.

Some of the elements above may have already been planned as part of a marketing or promotions plan, in which case the public relations plan must work in partnership. For example, a significant sponsorship may dramatically affect the direction and target market of the event, and this should be reflected in the public relations planning.

Other elements, such as media releases, articles or backgrounder documents (broadly described as media materials), should be thought of as tactical tools in the PR toolbox. While differing in format and purpose, each public relations resource should be considered for each element of the public relations programs. Do you want to announce a significant development, milestone or launch, or report on major research findings? Then a media release will be most useful. Is the topic very detailed or complex, requiring contextual knowledge of which a general news or even specialist journalist may not be aware? This is where a fact-filled media backgrounder or fact sheet document is very helpful.

Media releases and backgrounders are often gathered together with other helpful resources, such as a USB loaded with photography or video footage files, and presented to media in a folder as a press kit or as a downloadable package of documents and files. Press kits should be considered within the public relations strategy to determine on which occasions such a resource would be warranted and most successful, such as during a press conference, launch event or media familiarisation tour.

Media familiarisations (or 'famils' as they are known in the industry) are a way of enabling a journalist to experience first hand the subject of interest. They also allow a media outlet to take its own photography or footage, which is often vital for television outlets as well as most print media.

The structure and function of a range of print, electronic and social media should be understood and considered in relation to the public relations strategy. A concept that may be compelling for print media may be much less successful with television media if it doesn't provide the 'vision' or footage that is essential for any television news report.

Again, for social media, if there is no high interest level, humour, social cause or other compelling reason that would warrant it to be shared among friends or like-minded communities, then it will have limited success.

Depending on the objectives of the organisation, and the target audience that is being sought, some or all of these different types of media and media relations resources should be considered in the public relations strategy.

PLANNING IMPLEMENTATION

An important part of public relations strategising is to determine how the plan will be implemented. While the term 'strategy' is used to describe the overarching plan or idea to communicate effectively with the target audience, 'tactics' is the term to describe how you will actually go about achieving it.

For example, a public relations plan to promote a fundraising event may have as its goals to raise awareness for the cause and to encourage visitors and donations. The strategy may be to raise awareness through the real-life stories of people affected by the cause and the difference made by awareness, support and donations. Alternatively, the strategy may be to position the main celebrity ambassador as the champion for the cause and inspire others to get involved. In this example, the tactics could include prepa- ration of media materials (press releases quoting the celebrity, or a backgrounder

Some media broadcast directly from the event

on the real-life story), holding a small media event briefing, launching a competition for primary-school children to write short stories inspired by 'making a difference', seeking to arrange exclusive radio interviews for the celebrity partner, holding small photo opportu- nities (or photo calls) for the local newspapers to photograph local people affected by or championing the cause.

A public relations plan would likely include the following elements, in order to address implementation:

★ objectives
★ target audience
★ strategy
★ key messages
★ tactics (including media materials to be used, spokespeople, media targeted, social media activities)
★ timeline
★ responsibilities
★ budget and anticipated costs.

Each element of a public relations plan should be thoroughly thought through and should describe the process in which that activity will be executed. For this reason, public relations plans are often very detailed, specifying exact dates, all parties involved, and all the tools or resources required.

CRISIS MANAGEMENT

Crisis management is an important part of public relations planning for any event or organisation. Plans need to be prepared as a contingency measure to minimise the impact of any unfavourable press or respond to unforeseen operational issues (e.g. shortages), major incidents, accidents and other crises.

Many things can go wrong and the media are ready and willing to report on interest- ing, dramatic, tragic and controversial stories. For mega events the media may actually actively search for negative stories that would reflect poorly on the event organisers, sponsors and, in particular, the government bodies involved. These can range from stories about the mismanagement of the event (particularly about wasting public money) to stories about crowd misbehaviour. While most organisations cannot predict the exact nature of a crisis, it is useful to develop a communications strategy for each of the following scenarios:

★ spontaneous and unexpected crisis (security threat, failure of water supply, cyclone, fire, rain, extreme heat)
★ slowly emerging crisis (doping issues)
★ sustained crisis (pandemic illness, airline strikes).

A crisis protocol for what to do, who to alert, what to say and who should say it needs to be developed. These steps are recommended:

★ notify emergency services (if required), e.g. police, ambulance, fire department.
★ notify senior management and other key stakeholders.
★ obtain information direct from the source, witnesses (unless being handled by authorities) and staff.
★ continue to consult with emergency services or other authorities.
★ reach decisions on statements and actions.
★ set up a media centre, plan a regular media briefing schedule and provide contact details for media enquiries.
★ send journalists' questions up the line to the appropriate spokesperson and respond promptly with a prepared or rehearsed response.
★ provide accurate, reliable and timely information to the media.
★ brief and counsel employees.
★ maintain a watching brief as the issue emerges/develops.
★ provide information to the public via the organisation's/event's website or advertising.

Additionally, the spokesperson should:

★ show deep concern
★ avoid speculation
★ avoid attributing blame, making excuses or passing the buck
★ avoid providing information unless sure of the facts
★ explain the steps to be taken and authorities involved.

Protests emerged during a recent Tamworth Country Music Festival when the original founding musicians for the event challenged the organisers of the event, who had decided to include rock and pop performances in the festival in order to widen the audience demographic. At the Beijing Olympic Games a media storm erupted because the child singer at the opening ceremony had been replaced due to her crooked teeth. And an alleged lip-synced performance by Britney Spears also caused a media frenzy.

However, the most serious crises for events managers involve emergencies, disasters and fatalities. This is particularly the case for sporting events, with soccer being one of the more likely games to lead to violence between fans. A crisis management plan should be in place for this type of situation in order to be ready to deal with a worst case scenario. Public events generally involve several arms of the emergency services, including the police service. In the event of a major incident these bodies will manage their own media messages. It is vitally important that the event organisation defers to and liaises closely with these stakeholders in this type of situation.

In addition to being prepared to respond to a potential negative issue or crisis, a public relations plan should also specify the unexpected but positive situations to which an organisation may need to react or respond. These could include capitalising on favourable publicity, or unprecedented or overwhelming support/attendance. In essence, all possible scenarios, whether positive, minor or a major crisis, should be anticipated and planned for.

LEGAL AND ETHICAL CONSIDERATIONS

Legal and ethical considerations must always be incorporated in the planning process. A public relations program or activity that is illegal or unethical risks major reputation damage to the event organisation and possibly its sponsors, and leaves the organisation open to litigation or charges from authorities.

Legal and ethical considerations may relate to:

★ codes of ethics
★ cultural expectations and influences
★ legislation (consumer, copyright, trade practices)
★ social responsibilities.

For example, nearly all industry bodies promote codes of ethics for their particular industry. The Public Relations Institute of Australia (PRIA) lists a code of ethics on its website. This code of practice suggests that its members should be prepared to identify the source of funding of any public communication they initiate or for which they act as a conduit. Furthermore, in advertising and marketing their skills and services and in soliciting professional assignments, they should avoid false, misleading or exaggerated claims and should refrain from comment or action that may injure the professional reputation, practice or services of fellow members.

In addition to industry or organisational codes of ethics, cultural expectations and influences, legislation (consumer and copyright) and social responsibilities must also be met. These could include expectations to treat minority groups in a fair and equitable manner, or to seek permission and authorisation from local councils for the use of public spaces or local promotional activities. Consumer legislation relates to the delivery of goods and services, and consumer advocate groups can take action if consumers are misled by the organisation. Copyright infringement is another very serious offence and can result in legal action or financial recourse against the organisation. Employment legislation should also be addressed, including the organisation's duty of care for its employees. Social responsibilities, such as the expectation that an event designed for families (a community fair, for example), would not allow X-rated stallholders to set up shop at the event. All such legislated, industry accepted or community expectations and responsibilities must be met.

CONSULTING INTERNAL STAKEHOLDERS THROUGHOUT PLANNING

Colleagues and other important internal stakeholders should be provided with timely opportunities to contribute to public relations planning. As mentioned previously, a public relations strategy is not created or implemented independently of other management processes. In particular, senior executives or founders of the event should be consulted to contribute to the public relations goals, overarching strategy, resourcing, budget and evaluation plans. The media spokesperson/s should be consulted in relation to key messages and the sponsorship manager should be aware of the public relations plans in order to ensure they will not conflict with agreements made with sponsors and supporters. Those involved in the 'nuts and bolts' of the event management should be consulted in relation to feasibility of the plans. All key stakeholders should be consulted prior to the finalisation of the public relations plan.

The public relations plan must then be submitted for approval, where appropriate, in accordance with organisational policy. This includes sign-off on the budget, strategy and all elements of the public relations plan.

MANAGE IMPLEMENTATION OF THE PUBLIC RELATIONS PLAN

Implementation of the public relations plan must also be managed, with all priorities, responsibilities, timelines and budgets defined and clear communications with all appropriate colleagues. This could take the form of group or one-on-one briefings, sharing of documentation, teleconferences, emails, or likely a mix of these.

Unless clear responsibilities are communicated, important tasks can be easily forgotten or missed. Constant communication is required among team members to ensure all elements of the activity have been addressed and assigned responsibility, otherwise team members may simply assume someone else is taking care of them.

Careful monitoring of the plan and checking back with colleagues to make sure tasks are completed on time is also vital in ensuring all activities are being implemented as planned and within the correct time frame.

Throughout the implementation process, public relations reports produced in accordance with the organisation's policies will ensure everyone are kept up to date with progress. That may involve monthly meetings with key colleagues and frequent reports and updates, which may increase in frequency in key periods of the public relations program.

Sharing public relations information with colleagues will help to maintain awareness of current organisation direction and priorities. While a public relations plan may have been through a successful consultation process, and have been approved and finalised with the endorsement of the organisation, regular communication and reporting should be maintained throughout as organisational priorities may change significantly over a short period of time, and the public relations plan may need to be adjusted quickly in response.

Imagine if the keynote speaker for a major conference cancelled their speaking engagement and had to be replaced. The timeline, or even public relations strategy, may need to change in light of such a significant change. A public relations plan should be created in order to be executed as planned, but with enough flexibility to allow for adjustments or radical changes as situations unfold.

Media coverage should also be reported on daily or weekly (or as frequently as appropriate) and shared among key colleagues. By reporting on positive media coverage, colleagues and spokespeople are kept abreast of the success of media relations activities. Keeping colleagues informed of any emerging issues or negative reporting in media coverage is also vital, as it may impact organisational direction, key messages or the public relations strategy.

Throughout the implementation of the plan, it is important to go back to the objectives that have been set in order to remind yourself and others of the goals and targets you are all working toward. Despite a busy schedule of daily activities, it is vital that a strategic vision of the campaign is maintained.

EVALUATE AND REVIEW THE PUBLIC RELATIONS PLAN

During the public relations planning stage, particularly during goal setting, appropriate mechanisms should be established to obtain feedback about public relations activities and strategies. Feedback mechanisms may include:

★ consultation with colleagues
★ direct questioning
★ formal/written feedback
★ measurement of level of support (e.g. attendance, sponsorship, patronage)
★ media monitoring (e.g. number of media hits, media impressions—the size of audience reached, share of voice, inclusion of key messages, tone of reporting, mentions on blogs and Twitter).

At the conclusion of the event, or period in which the public relations plan has been implemented, public relations activities must be evaluated using agreed methods and benchmarks. Overall success of the public relations plan should be measured against the goals set.

For example, if one of the goals was to achieve positive media coverage, including frequent reporting of key messages among target media, then media monitoring and analysis would be used to evaluate the public relations program's success. The number of media hits (articles, TV interviews, TV reports, blog write-ups, etc.) should be quantified by number, as well as the total media impressions (circulation/audience figures) achieved by those hits. Graphs can also be created to demonstrate where the media hits were achieved, whether by media type (print, online, television or radio) or by geographical reach (e.g. international, national, metropolitan, local), and then assessed against the set targets.

Deeper analysis of media coverage, including frequency of key messages, tone of reporting and prominence of the event or organisation's name in the coverage, is more time consuming and costly; however, it does provide in-depth and meaningful measures.

Remember that unless measurements are assessed against original goals, they hold little value. For example, achieving positive international media coverage may be an impressive feat, but if the event is held in a local community with the goal of increasing volunteer numbers from among local residents, then that achievement has little value. On the other hand, a front-page article in the small local newspaper would be viewed as a great success.

Benchmarking results achieved against the previous year's efforts or against those of comparable competitors is another valuable tool for evaluation. Achieving a million media impressions might sound impressive, but if over three million media impressions were achieved the year before, or by a competitor, then the figure would be assessed differently.

Other hard figures, such as ticket sales, number of visitors and their feedback on the event, are also important measures. However, it is important to bear in mind that many other organisational initiatives are likely to have also affected those figures. Public relations may have played a vital role in contributing to organisational success, but be careful not to overstate its role.

Important learnings should also be gathered based on feedback and evaluation. Perhaps some elements of the public relations plan were more successful than others. This information is incredibly valuable in informing what adjustments should be made, whether immediately for ongoing public relations activities, or recorded to ensure next year's plan is adjusted accordingly. All learnings should be shared among key colleagues, with recommended changes agreed to and communicated to all involved parties.

In these ways, the evaluation of a public relations program is not only valuable for assessing success in the short term, but is also a key way of ensuring ongoing or greater success in future programs. Often it is the most seasoned public relations professional who sees the greatest value in learning from past experiences.

SUMMARY

In this chapter we have addressed the major elements involved in the development and management of a public relations program, in order to understand the important stages, requirements, methods and best practices involved in public relations. We have seen how pivotal a role public relations plays in the relationship between an organisation and its publics, and the contribution successful public relations can make to an organisation seeking to achieve its goals. Being well informed by the organisation, key stakeholders, the industry and other sources is important in ensuring a public relations strategy is in keeping with the strategic direction of the organisation, its images and its messages, and will be well received by its publics. We have also discussed the range of processes involved in keeping stakeholders informed, consulted with, and managed throughout the planning, implementation and evaluation stages. A successful public relations program will not only be well strategised, but also well executed, ready to respond to issues or crises as they arise. Hard work, organisational skills, flexibility and persistence are key attributes of public relations professionals.

Chapter review questions

1 What is public relations?
2 Give examples of three events that have a strong organisational identity.
3 List and explain five potential elements of a public relations strategy.
4 Provide guidelines for crisis management in the event context.
5 How can one evaluate the success of a public relations campaign for an event?

Activity

Search for all items of media coverage for an upcoming event, and then quantify and analyse the results achieved. Be sure to measure and report on:

* number of media hits or articles
* tally of where those hits were achieved (e.g. national, metropolitan or local)
* the entire audience reached—calculate by adding the circulation figures of each article or audience number of each TV segment, and then calculate the total figure (circulation figures can nearly always be found on media websites, particularly in their advertising sections)
* in-depth analysis of one chosen article, reporting on the tone of the article (negative, neutral or positive) as well as the prominence of the event or organisation.

Case study

Public relations campaign

Movember sprouts for a cause

Movember is an annual, month-long celebration of the moustache, highlighting men's health issues, specifically prostate cancer and depression in men.

Mo Bros, supported by their Mo Sistas, start Movember (November 1st) clean shaven and then have the remainder of the month to grow and groom their moustache. During Movember, each Mo Bro effectively becomes a walking billboard for men's health and, via their Mo, raises essential funds and awareness for Movember's men's health partners—The Prostate Cancer Foundation of Australia and beyondblue, the national depression initiative. At the end of Movember, a series of Gala Partés are held to thank Mo Bros and Sistas for their support and fund raising efforts.

The idea for Movember came about in 2003 when a few mates were having a beer in a small bar in Fitzroy, Melbourne. Inspired by

continued

Case study (*continued*)

the women's health movement, it was recognised that men were lacking a way to engage and actively involve themselves in their own health. During a conversation about fashion and past trends, the idea came up to bring the moustache back for one month, and in doing so, have some fun, raise a small amount of money and hopefully encourage men to talk about their health with each other.

Since this time, Movember has continued to grow each year, both in terms of participation numbers and funds raised. In its first year, 30 Mo Bros took part in Movember and last year, in Australia alone, 125 000 Mo Bros & Sistas got on board, raising more than $8 million for each of Movember's men's health partners.

Source: Information and photography provided by and property of The Movember Foundation.

Task

Use the above background information, and any other information you can find on the history of this event, to develop the following public relations campaign elements:

- communications strategy (detailing the communications objectives, measurable goals, target audience, stakeholders, target media, traditional and social media relations strategy, tactics, timeline and budget)
- a social media strategy to utilise Facebook, blogs, Twitter, etc. to raise awareness for Movember (this should be included in the communications strategy)
- a press release regarding the latest commercial partnership/sponsorship in support of Movember
- a letter to the Federal Health Minister, providing background on Movember and seeking government support
- a fact sheet for media explaining the specific men's health issues that Movember is seeking to address.

Note: It is not necessary to contact the organisers to complete these tasks; there is sufficient information on their website.

References

Doran, G, Miller, A & Cunningham, J (1981), 'There's a S.M.A.R.T. way to write management's goals and objectives', *Management Review*, 70(11), November.

Masterman, G & Wood, E (2006), *Innovative marketing communications: strategies for the events industry*, Elsevier, Oxford.

Miller, A & Cunningham, J (1981), 'How to avoid costly job mismatches' *Management Review*, 70(11), November.

Smolianov, P & Aiyeku, J (2009), 'Corporate marketing objectives and evaluation measures for integrated television advertising and sports event sponsorships', *Journal of Promotion Management*, 15(1/2):74, January.

CHAPTER 29

FINANCIAL OPERATIONS

Unit descriptor

This unit describes the performance outcomes, skills and knowledge required to manage day-to-day financial operations of a small organisation, a department within a larger organisation or a complex project. The unit is not intended to cover detailed specialist accounting skills that are undertaken by qualified accountants or financial controllers, but does include the awareness of accounting issues and concepts needed by managers for effective communication with accountants or other specialists on financial matters.

Elements

- Develop approaches to financial management
- Develop and monitor financial procedures and systems
- Monitor financial performance
- Make pricing decisions
- Prepare financial reports.

Critical aspects for assessment

- Understanding of the total financial management process within a business
- Ability to integrate the financial management activities of a business into overall business operations
- Knowledge of financial control, reporting and monitoring systems
- Establishment and management of financial systems over a period of time so that the monitoring and implementation aspects of the unit can be assessed.

Summernats boost in support

Friday, January 08, 2010 » 09:05pm

ORGANISERS of the annual car festival Summernats say business support's been boosted by the easing of the financial crisis, new management and a secure future in Canberra. The four-day event started yesterday featuring restored and modified cars, competitions, car parades, fireworks and a Miss Summernats competition. Co-owner Andy Lopez says trader and exhibitor numbers are up 10 per cent and major sponsors have re-signed after last year's financial uncertainty.

Source: <http://bigpondnews.com/articles/Finance/2010/01/08/Summernats_boost_in_support_415462.html>.

Financial management is the process of managing the financial resources of an event business or specific event, including accounting and financial reporting, budgeting, collecting accounts receivable, risk management and insurance. From this it is clear that financial management is strategic: it involves making decisions that will impact on the organisation five or ten years down the track. Unlike events around the world that have failed, the annual Summernats event in Canberra has survived an economic downturn, established a niche market and become financially viable.

Many conference and exhibition centres which operate on a year-round basis find it much harder to deal with economic peaks and troughs—they have large venues with significant operating costs, and on some occasions they have too much business and on others too little. Financial management involves careful attention to the external factors that might impact on the future viability of the business. Decisions such as diversifying the business to cover a wider scope of event types, or targeting new markets, are examples of strategic thinking.

The finance function requires specialist knowledge. It varies from business to business, but it is essential that an event manager have an understanding of this function. Financial management is required in all of the following areas:

★ strategic business management (planning five to ten years ahead)
★ research and development (investigating potential markets)
★ mergers and acquisitions (joining with other businesses)
★ ownership structure (sole trader, partnership, incorporated)
★ capital efficiency (use of funds for long-term growth)
★ risk management (deciding on which risks to take and how many)
★ working capital management (managing day-to-day capital; the enterprise's ability to pay its debts, or short-term liabilities, when they fall due)
★ auditing and reporting (keeping records in order)
★ taxation (meeting ATO requirements)

★ pricing and cost volume profit analysis (break-even)
★ budgeting (forecasting income and expense)
★ regulatory requirements (Australian Investment and Security Commission, ASIC).

The Energy Events Centre in Rotorua has benefited from the opening of a new international airport

Research into funding available from government sources shows that there is more funding for regional events than for urban events. This is because there are economic and political gains to be made from regional events. A new concept is much more likely to get off the ground in a regional area mainly because urban areas are already saturated with events.

Getz (2002) suggests, however, that resource dependency is a concern for organisers of public festivals. In some cases, organisers are almost solely dependent on stakeholder contributions to ensure the financial viability of their events. Sustainability of the event depends on the reliability of this contribution over many years. However, many festivals do fail and this is one of the reasons why they do.

In the commercial (for-profit) sector, strategic relationships with clients and sponsors are equally important, often being more tenuous than those with government bodies. We have all noticed the constant changes to naming rights to events and stadiums and other sponsorship arrangements. This highlights the importance of ensuring continued support from government and/or sponsors and in this regard the importance of good financial management.

DEVELOP APPROACHES TO FINANCIAL MANAGEMENT

Previous chapters have stressed that event management can refer to the management of an event as a project (one-off occurrence) or management of an ongoing organisation or business enterprise. Enterprises may include party hire companies, wedding planners, function centres, entertainment companies, even speed dating businesses! For the one-off event, the budget (forecast income and expense) and the income statement (actual income and expense) are the main focus of financial management. For the long-life event organisation, however, the financial aspects of the business are similar to those of any other business so that the balance sheet (assets and liabilities), among other reports, is also important. There are few benchmarks in the event business, but several common accounting ratios and performance measures are used, and these will be discussed later in the chapter. Depending on the type of event—public festival, private function, conference or exhibition—the event committee or management needs to identify any specialist accounting assistance required.

The section that follows describes financial management systems and procedures needed by event organisations and enterprises. These are based on the overall objectives and goals of the organisation or project.

DEVELOP AND MONITOR FINANCIAL PROCEDURES AND SYSTEMS

The dynamic and pressured event planning environment is not one that lends itself easily to careful monitoring of systems and procedures or, indeed, moments of quiet reflection over budget variances. However, financial procedures and systems are vitally important. They encompass the following tasks:

★ developing financial procedures and systems to meet relevant statutory and internal control requirements

★ communicating the importance of financial objectives and management controls and systems to all staff

★ developing practical procedures and systems for monitoring income and ensuring payment of accounts

★ researching and integrating the use of current industry practices and technology in systems where appropriate

★ checking compliance with procedures and systems on a regular basis

★ monitoring the flow of financial information within the organisation in terms of currency, accuracy, level of detail and relevance

★ regularly reviewing financial management systems and making adjustments according to organisation needs.

This section reviews much of the information in Chapter 21 by taking another quick look at the accounting cycle that produces reports and ratios used for financial analysis, starting with analysis of transactions and posting to ledgers. This process is illustrated in Figure 29.1.

ANALYSIS OF TRANSACTIONS—LEDGER ACCOUNTS

Each group of accounts has individual accounts and code numbers. The chart of accounts lists numbers for each account. A list of the balances of each of these ledger accounts of the business is known as a trial balance. The basic building block to good books is data entered in the right place. To begin with, the business needs a system to *identify* each item and note its account number. For example, this can be done for accounts payable (e.g. an invoice from the stage supplier) by going through invoices and marking each one with the right account name or number.

Common ledger accounts for most event operations are listed below.

Bank

This is a record of all transactions (incomings and outgoings) that should match the bank statement.

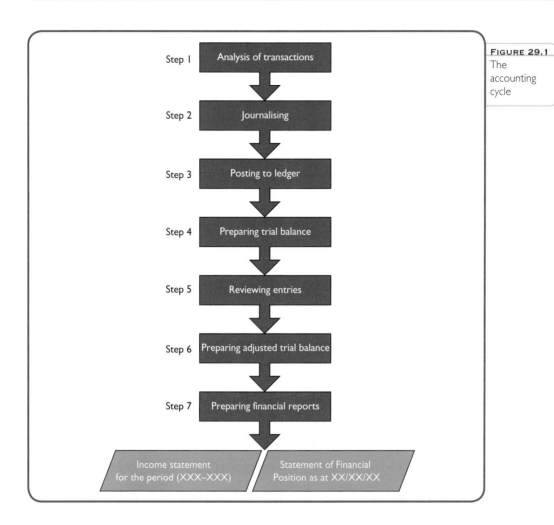

FIGURE 29.1
The
accounting
cycle

Step 1 — Analysis of transactions

Step 2 — Journalising

Step 3 — Posting to ledger

Step 4 — Preparing trial balance

Step 5 — Reviewing entries

Step 6 — Preparing adjusted trial balance

Step 7 — Preparing financial reports

Income statement for the period (XXX–XXX)

Statement of Financial Position as at XX/XX/XX

Equipment

Equipment is all equipment purchased by the business, such as staging or lighting equipment. These will be assets of the business.

Rent

Rental paid for business premises is recorded in this ledger.

Office expenses

Since a significant part of event management involves planning, office expenses need to be carefully recorded. These include stationery, printing, telephone, etc. Salaries and wages of the event team fall into this category. However, this is not usually the case for the casual staff employed on the day of the event as their wages fall into the 'event operational expenses' category.

Energy/utilities

Electricity and other energy bills generally fit into this ledger account.

Marketing and promotion

These are costs associated with, for example, advertising or direct sales.

Insurance and other specialist services

Public liability, workers compensation and other insurances might fit into this category, as well as accountancy and legal fees.

Accounts receivable

These are amounts owed to the business by outside parties due to credit sales. For example, account customers who book corporate meetings are allowed credit terms and may settle their accounts within an agreed lapse of time, usually 30 days. Until they settle their account they are debtors to the business. Collectively they are called accounts receivable.

Accounts payable

These are amounts owed by the business to suppliers. The suppliers as part of trading stipulate credit terms and until they are paid they are creditors to the business. Collectively they are known as accounts payable. Credit purchases could be for food, beverage or decor items.

Capital

Capital is the investment the owners or shareholders bring into the business. The owners of a business bring in start-up capital and may also inject further capital progressively.

Sales

This is a record of all the sales made by the business, and in the event business this can take the form of ticket sales, conference or sporting event registrations, exhibition or function bookings.

Event production

Event production costs are those costs that are required to 'put the show on the road', such as the cost of performers, musicians, etc. Staging costs such as lighting and sound would also come into this category.

Event operations

Event operations costs include the costs of hiring the venue or site, installing fencing, scanning entry tickets, providing security, etc.

Travel and hospitality

Travel may be required for event staff or performers, and hospitality would include food and beverage costs.

In the event industry it is difficult to have hard and fast rules about which of these costs to identify as *direct costs* in order to calculate cost of sales. For a conference, the cost incurred for each delegate (which covers catering and room hire) is clearly a direct cost. This cost varies according to the number of delegates. For the event business illustrated in the case study at the end of this chapter, an organic food market, the cost of hiring the event site is included as a direct cost linked as it is to the payments by the stallholders for their spaces. However, for the most part, the cost of a stadium (fixed) and a high-profile performer or team (fixed) are overheads, unrelated to the number of people who buy tickets. In all situations, it is useful to differentiate between rental for office premises (overhead) and rental of an event venue or site. In the budget pro forma provided for the Activity in Chapter 22, the major expenditure categories were administration, marketing and event expenses.

Let us refer again to the definitions: in financial accounting, *cost of goods sold (COGS)* includes the direct costs attributable to the production of the goods sold by a company. This amount includes the materials cost used in creating the goods along with the direct labour costs used to produce the goods. As there is no inventory in the events business, we refer instead to the *cost of sales (COS)* which includes the costs associated with generating reported sales, including direct labour and other costs attributed directly to the sales activity.

Having entered all transactions into the appropriate ledgers, at the end of an accounting period the account balances are itemised and listed to ensure that the records are correct. This itemised list is called a 'trial balance'. Adjustments are made to the trial balance if necessary and an adjusted trial balance is prepared. The final reports are generated from the adjusted trial balance at the end of an accounting period.

For taxation purposes, the accounting period is one financial year, which in Australia starts on 1 July and ends on 30 June of the following year. A financial year is used to measure profit as owners cannot wait until the end of the life of the business to establish if the business has been profitable. The financial year also coincides with the tax requirements in Australia, although many businesses prepare financial reports more regularly because of the reporting requirements for GST. Other countries have different financial years and sometimes these are used by Australian businesses, particularly where the business is owned by an overseas business/individual.

ACCOUNTING SYSTEMS

Every business needs to adopt an accounting system that recognises when to recognise a transaction— when the transaction is made or when the actual cash is exchanged. The two systems are *cash accounting* and *accrual accounting*. Cash basis accounting recognises an accounting transaction when cash is paid or received. It is a simple straightforward system. However, its application is limited to very small businesses and does not allow for the complexities of a large business where the majority of the business transactions are on credit terms. Accrual accounting, in sharp contrast to cash accounting, recognises expenses *when incurred*, not when they are paid and revenue *when earned* not when received. It incorporates the matching principle—matching expenses incurred for the revenue received during a particular period. Accrual accounting is more realistic for a medium to large event business.

Once again, there is a difference between the project-based reporting of a single event and the reporting requirements of an ongoing event business where the following adjustments are more likely to be necessary.

Adjustments

A business is an ongoing entity and transactions do not cease exactly at the end of an accounting period. In accrual accounting, adjustments are required due to the matching principle, which states that expenses incurred are matched with revenues generated. Income and expenses should relate to the same accounting period in order to get a true picture of the net profit. If payments for advance bookings are included in sales, the net profit will be greater than what it should be, resulting in more tax payable. Similarly, if credit sales revenue not received is not included it will reflect a lower net profit as expenses to generate the sale have been incurred and less tax will be payable due to the lower profit reflected. Incorrect accounting defeats the purpose of accounting. Financial reports are generated from ledger accounts with the assumption that the records are correct. Adjustments are necessary to make the income and expense accounts relate to the accounting period for which financial reports are generated. Management decisions are based on these financial reports and their accuracy is therefore vital. However, it is important to bear in mind that the cost of making the adjusting entry should not be greater than the benefit realised from any accuracy achieved. Some common examples of adjustments in revenue and expense items are either because they are *prepaid* or *accrued*—prepaid meaning paid or received in advance and accrued meaning yet to be paid or yet to be received by the business. Examples of these follow.

Prepaid expense

A prepaid expense is an expense paid in advance before it is incurred. For example, Event Concepts paid an annual business insurance of $3600 on 1 June 2010. The monthly premium is $300. When the income statement for the month of June is prepared, the insurance expense should be $300, not $3600, even though it was paid in the month of June 2010. Following the double entry principle a debit entry of $3600 would be made in the insurance account and a credit entry of $3600 in the bank account. An adjustment would therefore need to be made to show the correct expense incurred. A $3600 insurance expense makes a $3300 difference in the monthly profit. The adjustment also results in an increase in the assets on the balance sheet. This is just as important as it is the balance sheet that will be used to determine the financial stability of the business when assessments are being performed for loans and suitability for grants, etc.

Accrued expense

This is an expense that has been incurred but is yet to be paid. For example, Event Concepts had several expenses owing at the end of the financial year in 2010. It had received alcohol to the value of $5500 in the month of January 2010. The goods were received and used for an event but the supplier had not sent in an invoice by error. Event Concepts had not paid for it either as they only received a delivery docket and not an invoice or statement. However, an adjustment of $5500 needs to be made to reflect the accurate cost of goods sold, and the fact that the business has a sizeable liability of $5500 owing to the supplier.

Prepaid revenue

Prepaid revenue is unearned revenue (when an advance payment is made for a future service). An advance deposit for a function or venue booking is not uncommon in the event industry. This amount should not be reflected as sales if the services have not been rendered. If it has been recorded as sales, an adjustment should be made to record it as prepaid revenue and not sales. If recorded as sales revenue, the resultant profit in the income statement would be inaccurate. For example, Event Concepts showed an excess profit of $10 000 for the financial year ended June 2010 due to the inclusion of $10 000 advance payment for the September 2010 room bookings for the Clean Up Australia fundraiser. This was corrected by adjusting entries.

Accrued revenue

This is revenue that is earned but not received. Commissions and interest on deposits are common examples. Interest on deposits is paid at maturity of the deposits, which may not necessarily coincide with the end of the accounting period. For example, Lillian and Joe, owners of Event Concepts, realised that they had earned a lot more than expected at the end of the financial year as they had over $7500 of commission revenue unpaid by the Equine Association. They had no expenses related to this revenue other than the time taken by reception staff to take bookings and coordinate activities for the association. There is no time lag with payment of wages and therefore no outstanding expenses, only an increase of $7500 to income and thus to net profit.

These are some of the common adjustments to income and revenue items. Bad debts and depreciation are two other expenses that need to be included if they are not accounted for in the records. When debts are unrecoverable they are known as *bad debts*. They then become expenses to the business. *Depreciation* is a non-cash expense. It is not payable by the business, as there would have been a cash outflow when the asset was purchased. Rather, it is a cost of doing business, as an asset reduces in value over its useful life. Depreciation is the wear and tear of an asset over its useful life.

All adjustments need to be authorised. Final reports are generated when adjustments have been made.

Table 29.1, on page 472, outlines the different adjustment types, together with examples and the required adjustment entries.

In order to analyse and interpret financial reports it is necessary to have a basic understanding of the underlying principles and the formats used for presentation.

MAKE PRICING DECISIONS

The first important decision facing many festival organisers is whether or not to charge an entry fee. The Surry Hills Festival, for example, relies on gold coin donations. Major festivals such as the Adelaide Festival generally have a free opening night followed by

Table 29.1 Examples of adjustments

Adjustment type	Examples	Adjusting entry
Prepaid expense	• Rates paid to the local council for a whole year • Building insurance for the full year	**Debit** Prepaid expenses (Assets increasing) **Credit** Expense account (Expense decreasing)
Prepaid revenue	• Deposit for a future function • Advance payment for a booking	**Debit** Function revenue account (Income decreasing) **Credit** Accrued revenue account (Liability increasing)
Accrued expense	• Electricity expense incurred but not billed as yet • Telephone bill not received though telephone charges apply • Wages not yet paid	**Debit** Expense account (Expense increasing) **Credit** Accrued expense (Liability increasing)
Accrued revenue	• Business has a term deposit investment: interest earned for the accounting period but not received • Commission earned for sale of merchandise but not received	**Debit** Accrued revenue (Assets increasing) **Credit** Interest revenue (Income increasing)

many ticketed events: opera, theatre, dance and visual arts. In 2008, the Adelaide Festival attracted an audience of 600 000 and exceeded box office targets to achieve more than $2.5 million in ticket sales. Total income from the festival and its associated events reached nearly $6 million. The original Adelaide Festival was set up by two people in 1960 and the first festival cost just over £15 000 to run. The sustainability and growth of this festival are evident from these figures.

In the business events sector pricing is very competitive. A conference package for a Melbourne hotel can cost as little as $69 per delegate (based on a minimum of 15 delegates) and includes the following:

★ Meeting room hire
★ Tea and coffee on arrival—freshly brewed coffee and a selection of teas
★ Morning tea—freshly brewed coffee and a selection of teas with chef's selection of freshly baked muffins, danish pastries and scones
★ Buffet lunch—with chef's daily selection of antipasto, salads, vegetables, hot dishes, fruit and desserts, plus soft drinks and freshly brewed coffee and tea
★ Afternoon tea—freshly brewed coffee and a selection of teas, homemade biscuits.

Whether for hotels or convention or exhibition centres, prices in the business events sector are competitive during quieter periods such as the summer holidays. Pricing decisions need to be based on current, accurate and relevant financial and marketplace data. In some cases it might be appropriate for a hotel or conference centre to lure a customer using a bargain basement price (called a loss leader) with the hope of securing long-term business. In other situations it may be appropriate to hold standard prices and avoid discounting. However, the conference organiser is likely to view service assurances (such as AV support) as more important than small savings.

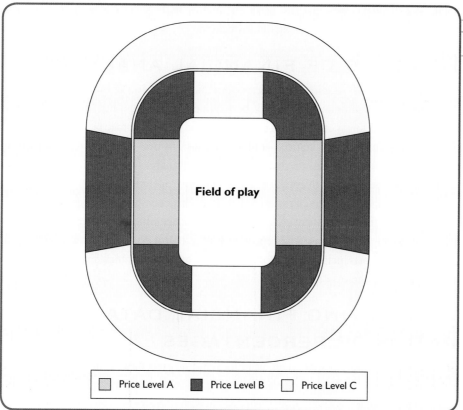

FIGURE 29.2
Ticket plan

Field of play

☐ Price Level A   ■ Price Level B   ☐ Price Level C

Chapter 25 on feasibility discussed the benefits of running events with high variable costs. Because these costs are directly related to income they are more easily managed than overheads (fixed costs) which are largely unavoidable. For example, if you were running a conference with a deadline for registrations a month before the event, you would know by then how big a function room was needed and the level of catering required. As the pricing is done on a per head basis, bookings with hotels for functions like this can be managed fairly easily. In contrast, organisers of an event with high fixed costs (overheads) selling tickets mainly during the fortnight before the show enjoy far less flexibility and certainty.

Differential ticketing pricing, mentioned in Chapter 25, allows organisers to allocate different prices for different shows, seats, sessions and market segments and thus manipulate the yield. Depending on the popularity of the event, price levels A, B and C in Figure 29.2 might vary. For a potential sell-out event, the organisers might drop category C entirely.

MONITOR FINANCIAL PERFORMANCE

When monitoring financial performance there are a number of reports and ratios that can assist management in deciding whether a proposal is sound or whether a business is on track. The first step is to prepare the accounts, and the next step is to analyse the figures in order to gain a better understanding of the business.

BENEFITS OF FINANCIAL ANALYSIS

Financial analysis tells us a lot about the performance of a project or business and helps to determine the overall financial health of both. Issues such as liquidity (does the business have enough cash to pay its debts on time) and profit (the percentage of net profit to total sales) are only part of the financial analysis of your business that puts the information from the financial statements into perspective. Financial analysis helps to identify problems, implement the necessary corrective actions, and improve operations.

These 'snapshot' measures of the event project or business should be regularly reviewed and analysed. In the management cycle, the budget is the planning phase, accounting systems are the implementation phase and reporting is the control phase. The people who need access to these reports include operational managers, owner–operators, financial controllers and external accountants or auditors.

CONVERTING FINANCIAL DATA TO RATIOS OR PERCENTAGES

Comparing the absolute dollar values over time is not very meaningful and does not provide a complete view of the business or event project. It does not correct for inflation or allow you to make comparisons with other businesses in your industry. We can overcome many of these shortfalls when we convert the financial data to ratios or percentages.

A ratio by itself means little unless it is benchmarked. A ratio needs to be compared to some expected or required outcome. For example, ratios might be compared to budget, different time periods in the same business or to industry expectations to determine whether there has been a significant change.

Some common ratios used in financial analysis are outlined below.

Debt ratio

Debt ratios measure the ability of the business to repay long-term debt. The debt to equity ratio shows the proportion of capital invested by the business owners to the funds provided by external lenders. It gives a comparison of how much of the business was financed by owner's equity and how much was financed through debt or liabilities.

The formula used to calculate the debt to equity ratio is:

$$\text{Debt to equity ratio} = \text{Total liabilities} \div \text{Owner's equity}$$

The higher the ratio, the more the business relies on debt to finance its operations and the greater the risk to external lenders. A debt to equity ratio of 1:1 indicates that the external lenders and the owners are bearing the same degree of risk.

A debt to equity ratio in the range of 1:1 to 4:1 is acceptable, depending on the individual business. However, most banks will have guidelines and limits for the debt to equity ratio. A ratio of 2:1 is often used for small business loans (a limit of up to $2 loaned for every $1 of owner's equity). Too much debt can put your business at risk and may cause difficulty in meeting interest and principal repayments.

Liquidity ratio

Liquidity ratios measure the capacity of the business to meet short-term financial commitments as they become due. The current ratio (also called the working capital ratio) is a measure of the solvency or liquidity of the business. It shows whether the business has enough current assets to meet its short-term financial obligations (current liabilities) as they become due. Current assets are those assets that can be converted into cash within 12 months. Current liabilities are those that will be repaid within a year.

The formula used to calculate the current ratio is:

$$\text{Current ratio} - \text{Current assets} : \text{Current liabilities}$$

The higher the current ratio, the better the capacity to meet short-term financial commitments. A current ratio of 2:1 (which means the business has current assets of $2 for every $1 of current liabilities) is regarded as desirable for a healthy business. A current ratio that is too high may indicate investment in current assets that could otherwise be used to produce income. A current ratio that is too low means there may not be enough current assets to meet short-term financial obligations when they are due.

Return on investment (ROI)

Various bodies that contribute to the event's income will want to see if there is a return on their investment. If, for example, the sponsor is using the event for publicity purposes, then an estimate can be made of the print, broadcast and television exposure (in print lines, minutes, etc.). The value of promotional efforts is quantified (through media monitoring) and compared with the investment made in the event. Thus the value of publicity is compared with the sponsor's financial contribution to the event.

The formula used is:

$$\$\text{Value of media exposure}/\$\text{Investment}$$

Other objectives such as reputation (return on objectives, ROO) are not as easily quantified.

Per head cost

The simplest ratio used in the event business, which is similar to the hospitality concepts of REVPAR (revenue per available room) and REVPASH (revenue per available seat hour in restaurant) is REVPAX (revenue per head). This quite simply is the profit margin per head, and can be calculated for many different types of events, particularly corporate events, but also ticketed events. Clearly, from the CHOICE research discussed in Chapter 22, there is a high REVPAX for weddings. Allen et al. (2008) refer to a similar concept, but from the client's perspective: 'perceived value compared to the cost per head'. Here, the corporate is expecting a perceived value of, say, $80 per head, but only paying, say, $60 per head. Per head costs are quoted for conferences, banquets and many other hospitality functions.

Yield

Yield management is the practice of pricing to maximise the amount of revenue received per unit sold—in the case of events, the revenue per ticket sold or per booking made for a conference delegate. This follows on from the above concept of REVPAX. However it goes further. A yield manager analyses categories of ticket prices (A, B, C seating), monitors bookings and offers discounts at strategic times for consumer decision-making, often based on sophisticated computerised analysis of previous ticket sales. The release of tickets to the world's most sought-after sports events, such as the Olympic Games or the FIFA World Cup, is timed and priced using complex formulas, with last-minute releases by some stakeholders such as tour organisers who may not have made their planned premium sales. An increased yield of 50 cents on a capacity crowd of 60 000 is $30 000.

MONITORING CASH FLOW

Events are fairly unique in that, for many, revenue comes in only on the day of the event. This means that all costs, such as salaries, office expenses and fees, have to be met up-front from existing funds. When ticket sales occur long before an event is staged, as they do with major concerts, this puts the company in the enviable position of being able to pay for its expenses from revenue while also earning interest on this money until the remaining bills become due. Very few events fit this category.

Cash flow planning is an essential part of the event planning process for the above-mentioned reasons. As Figure 29.3 illustrates, there may be a cash shortfall in the early period when contractors and venues need to be paid (expenses), while income is slow to come in due to ticket sales occurring closer to the event.

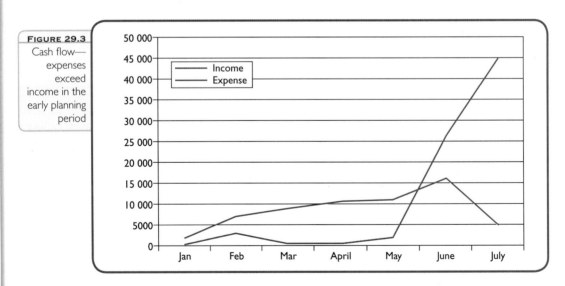

FIGURE 29.3
Cash flow—
expenses
exceed
income in the
early planning
period

PREPARE FINANCIAL REPORTS

Accurate and regular financial information allows the business to monitor success or failure. Useful information about the business depends on complete, accurate and timely record-keeping practices. Financial records allow managers to:

★ identify income and expenses to create a profit and loss statement
★ identify business assets and liabilities to create a balance sheet
★ identify the timing of income and expenses to create a cash flow forecast
★ compare business operations with industry benchmarks
★ prepare accurate business activity statements and tax returns.

RECORD-KEEPING OBLIGATIONS

By law, the Australian Tax Office (ATO) requires all business operators to keep certain business records for tax purposes. You are required to keep records for five years after they are prepared, obtained or the transactions completed (whichever occurs later), and in English. Certain additional obligations regarding keeping business records exist for different types of businesses, including companies.

REPORTS

The balances of the assets, liabilities and owner's equity group of accounts are reported in the *balance sheet*. The balances of income and expense accounts are reported in the *income statement*. These were discussed in Chapter 21 and are discussed again briefly here and illustrated in Figure 29.4.

Income statement

Accurate, concise, relevant and sufficiently detailed financial reports should be prepared to schedule, in a format appropriate to the audience and according to organisation and statutory requirements that show a true and fair view of the financial affairs of the business. By producing regular income statements the business will be able to work out how much (if any) money is being made and review the following:

★ compare projected (budgeted) performance with actual performance
★ compare performance against industry benchmarks
★ use past performance trends to form reasonable forecasts for the future
★ show business growth and financial health over time
★ detect any problems regarding sales, margins and expenses.

	Debit	Credit
Income	Expenses	Income
Balance Sheet	Assets	Liabilities & Owner's equity

FIGURE 29.4
The double entry grid

And for tax purposes:

★ provide proof of income and financial stability if a loan is needed
★ complete the Instalment and/orBusiness Activity Statement as required
★ calculate income and expenses when completing and submitting the tax return.

As the name indicates the Income statement (also known as a statement of financial performance) measures the profit or loss of a business over a specified period. It summarises the income for a period and subtracts the expenses incurred for the same period to calculate the profit or loss for the business. The main components of the income statement are revenue, cost of sales, gross profit and expenses. Each component influences the determination of net profit, and each is used in the two basic equations on which an income statement is based:

$$\text{Gross profit} = \text{Sales} - \text{Cost of goods sold}$$
$$\text{Net profit} = \text{Gross profit} - \text{Expenses}$$

Balance sheet

The balance sheet is a statement of what a business owns (assets) and owes (liabilities) and what is the owner's investment in the business (owner's equity) at a specific point in time. The balance sheet is also known as a statement of financial position because it shows a summary of the business's financial position at a particular point in time.

A balance sheet enables a business to:

★ review its level of assets, debt and working capital
★ compare the increase or decrease in value of the business over time
★ see the relative liquidity of the business.

It is called a balance sheet because assets minus liabilities (net assets) must equal the owner's equity (they must balance).

A balance sheet is based on the formula:

$$\text{Owner's equity} = \text{Assets} - \text{Liabilities}$$

Taxation

Goods and services tax (GST) is a broad-based consumption tax of 10% on most goods, services and other items consumed in Australia. (Items sold in Australia but consumed overseas are not subject to GST.)

Generally, registered businesses include GST in the price of goods sold to their customers. In effect, the business collects GST from the customer. The GST must then be paid by the business to the Australian Taxation Office after offsetting credits for the GST included in the price of their business purchases. So, while GST is paid at each step in the supply chain, businesses do not actually bear the economic cost of the tax. The cost of GST is borne by the final consumer, who cannot claim GST credits. If you carry on a business, you must register for GST if your turnover (income) is at or above the GST turnover threshold, that is, $75 000 or more ($150 000 or more for non-profit organisations).

SUMMARY

This chapter has illustrated the importance for the event manager to understand concepts used in managing financial operations. It has also discussed the differences in financial management between a one-off event project and an event organisation which operates as an ongoing reporting entity. In both cases, compliance with standard accounting and reporting principles is essential, but in the case of the short-term project, the focus is generally on the budget, variance from the budget and the income statement. Financial management for the ongoing event business may require more stringent analysis, requiring an understanding of debt, liquidity and return on investment ratios, as well as the income statement, balance sheet and owner's equity, which are covered in Chapter 21 and in this chapter. In both project and ongoing business management, lack of careful pricing, record-keeping, cash flow management and financial control can lead to financial failure.

Chapter review questions

1 List and explain 10 reasons why knowledge of financial management is useful to event organisers and event managers.
2 This chapter has talked about events as *projects* and event organisations as *ongoing enterprises*. Give an example of each and explain the difference between the two from a financial management point of view.
3 This chapter lists the seven steps in the analysis of transactions. Summarise your understanding of each of these steps.
4 Explain the concepts of pricing and yield management as applied to the event industry.
5 Explain why cash flow is an important consideration at the concept development stage of event planning.

Activities

1 Visit the small business website for your state or territory and explain the different business structures (sole trader, etc.) and how to register a business.
2 Investigate and explain the tax concessions for a registered charity and how these are accessed.
3 Discuss the following statement from a financial management perspective: 'The event industry is extremely diverse and from a financial management point of view provides fewer guidelines and ratios than exist for businesses in other related industries.' In your response, explore this diversity by explaining financial management considerations for two types of events or event businesses using the following concepts: stakeholder contributions; pricing; cash flow; record-keeping; and reporting. You could also discuss the benchmarks that are common in the accommodation and food and beverage sectors of the hospitality industry. A reference for this is *Hospitality Management* (Van Der Wagen & Goonetilleke 2008).
4 Using the example provided in the Case Study, prepare a trial balance for an event of a different type, such as a surf carnival or charity dinner.

Case study

Organic Food Market

This case study shows the accounting process for a small events business. (The useful table below indicates how double entry works.)

Account type	Increase balance	Decrease balance
Asset	Debit	Credit
Liability	Credit	Debit
Owner's equity	Credit	Debit
Revenue	Credit	Debit
Expense	Debit	Credit

Natalia has started a new business—a weekly organic food market (OFM). The main source of income is 'rental' paid by each of the stallholders. Some stallholders bring their own tents and tables, while others rent a stall structure from Natalia. So a secondary source of income is the rental on hired stall structures. The main expense is the rental Natalia pays for the site on which the market is situated, an industrial car park.

This is the first event for OFM. Five hundred food enthusiasts turn up on the day (no entry charge). There are 30 independent stallholders (who bring all their own equipment) and who pay $50 for the day. The remaining 20 hire the stall structure and each pays $75 for the day. The stallholders who need an electrical supply pay an additional $30.

The pricing structure is thus as follows:

Space only $50

Space and stall structure rental $75

Electrical supply $30

Natalia starts her business with a $10 000 investment of her own money. She deposits the money into the new OFM business cheque account.

	Debit	Credit
Cheque account (Asset increasing)	$10 000	
Capital (Owner's equity increasing)		$10 000
Owner contributes cash to business		

Natalia purchased 20 stall structures @ $250 each on account (credit, due in 30 days) after paying a $2500 cash deposit.

Note this smart move—she only has to hire them out 10 times to get her money back!

	Debit	Credit
Stall equipment (Asset increasing)	5 000	
Cheque account (Asset decreasing)		2 500
Accounts Payable (Control)		2 500
Purchase of 20 stall structures on credit, due in 30 days		

continued

Case study (continued)

Natalia pays $200 for advertising using the business's cheque book.

	Debit	Credit
Advertising (Expenses increasing)	200	
Cheque account (Asset decreasing)		200

Natalia pays a deposit to the industrial estate in case there is any environmental damage ($500) (refundable) as well as the rent for the car park for the day ($1000), and she also has to pay a supplement of $200 for the electrical supply, total $1700.

	Debit	Credit
Site hire (Expenses increasing)	1 200	
Cheque account (Asset decreasing)		1 700
Environmental deposit (Asset increasing)	500	
Payment for hire of industrial estate including a $500 deposit, $1000 car park rent and $200 electricity		

Natalia finds that one hire structure has been damaged. She informs the supplier, EVENT HIRE, and they agree to give her credit off the amount payable in 30 days if she returns the damaged stock.

	Debit	Credit
Stall equipment (Asset decreasing)		250
Accounts payable control (Liability decreasing)	250	
Credit for damaged stall structure returned		

As mentioned, there are 30 independent stallholders (who bring all their own equipment) and who pay $50 for the day. The remaining 20 hire the stall structure and they each pay $75 for the day. The stallholders who needed an electrical supply (10) pay an additional $30.

Sales
30 stalls × $50 = $1500
20 stalls × $75 = $1500
Electricity supply charge (10 stallholders × $30) = $300
(expecting $3300 for the day)

Recording the sales
All stallholders are expected to pay in cash on the day and this amount is deposited in the cheque account. However, one stallholder (Fred) forgets to bring enough cash for the electricity supply and agrees to pay the amount at the next food market next week.

	Debit	Credit
Cheque account (Assets increasing)	3 270	
Accounts receivable (Assets increasing)	30	
Sales (Income increasing)		3 300
Monies received and owing for stall hire and electricity supply		

continued

Case study (*continued*)

Cost of running the food festival (*excluding purchase of food stalls and the environmental deposit as these are assets*)

Rental of site		1 200
Musicians		100
Total cost of sales		1 300

When written in the general ledger, each account will look like the following.

Account	Transaction	Debit	Credit	Balance
Cheque account	Beginning deposit	10 000		
	Down payment for stalls		2 500	
	Payment for rental of site and environmental deposit		1 700	
	Payment for advertising		200	
	Payment for musicians		100	
	Deposit cash from stallholders	3 270		
	Totals	13 270	4 500	
	Balance			8 770 Debit
Debtor control	Fred owes	30		
	Totals	30		
	Balance			30 Debit
Stall equipment	Stall equipment purchased	5 000		
	Damaged, returned		250	
	Totals	5 000	250	
	Balance			4 750 Debit
Creditor control	Stall purchase		2 500	
	Damaged stall, returned	250		
	Totals	250	2 500	
	Balance			2 250 credit
Owner's equity	Natalia's investment		10 000	
	Totals		10 000	
	Balance			10 000 Credit
Sales	Payments from stallholders		3 300	
	Totals		3 300	
	Balance			3 300 Credit
Cost of goods sold	Rent and payments for site	1 200		
	Musicians	100		

continued

Case study (*continued*)

Account	Transaction	Debit	Credit	Balance
	Balance	1 300		1 300 Debit
Advertising	Advertising	200		
	Totals	200		
	Balance			200 Debit

From the account balances a trial balance can be prepared.

Trial Balance for OFM as at 30 May 20XX

Trial Balance	Debit	Credit
Cash in bank	8 770	
Debtor control	30	
Stall equipment	4 750	
Environmental deposit	500	
Creditor control		2 250
Owner's equity		10 000
Sales		3 300
Cost of sales	1 300	
Advertising	200	
Totals	15 550	15 550

As you can see, the trial balance allows us to see all the account balances. It also shows that the debit account total equals the credit account total, as it should.

With the trial balance information, the financial statements can be prepared.

Income Statement for OFM for the week ended 30 May 20XX

Sales		3 300
Less Cost of sales	1 300	
Gross profit		2 000
Less expenses		
Advertising	200	
Total expenses		200
Profit/(Loss)		1 800

Note: A loss would be shown as a bracketed or negative amount.

Once the profit or loss is known, the balance sheet can be prepared.

continued

Case study (continued)

Balance Sheet for OFM as at 30 May 20XX

Assets		
Current assets		
Cash in bank	8 770	
Debtor control	30	
Environmental deposit	500	
Total current assets		9 300
Non-current assets		
Stall equipment	5 000	
Total non-current assets		5 000
Total assets		14 300
Liabilities		
Current liabilities		
Creditor control	2 500	
Total current liabilities		2 500
Non-current liabilities	–	
Total non-current liabilities		–
Total liabilities		2 500
Net assets		11 800
Owner's equity		
Capital	10 000	
Plus net profit	1 800	
Total owner's equity		11 800

As you can see, Assets – Liabilities = Net Assets = Owner's Equity. The net profit shown on the balance sheet is the total profit for the period from the income statement.

Task

Natalia decides that the business could be producing more revenue if she ran one or two stalls herself. The event now attracts 3000 people every Sunday. In particular, Natalia has seen the long queues at the two coffee stalls and has been wondering whether to start a mobile coffee business of her own which would run at the OFM and at other locations during the week. Provide some financial advice to Natalia on this proposal by producing a financial forecast for her using the figures provided as a starting point. Bear in mind the capital expense required for this initiative.

References

Allen, J, McDonnell, I, O'Toole, W & Harris, R (2008), *Festival and special event management*, 4th edn, Wiley, Brisbane.

Anderson, T & Getz, D (2008), 'Stakeholder management strategies of festivals', *Journal of Convention & Event Tourism*, 9(3):199–220.

Bergamin Barbato, M & Mio, C (2007), 'Accounting and the development of management control in the cultural sphere: the case of the Venice Biennale', *Accounting, Business & Financial History*, 17(1):187–208.

Getz, D (2002), 'Why festivals fail', *Event Management*, 7(4):209–19.

History of the Adelaide Festival of Arts (n.d.), <www.adelaidefestival.com.au/servlet/Web?s=22 90869&action=changePage&pageID=792949593>, accessed 21 May 2010.

CHAPTER 30

EVENT PROPOSALS AND BIDS

Unit descriptor

This unit describes the performance outcomes, skills and knowledge required to plan and develop proposals and bids for the staging of complex events comprising multiple components. Development of event proposals and bids at this level requires the application of business writing as well as document and bid presentation skills, combined with sound knowledge of the event management process and the particular context for the staging of a given event. The unit is broad in focus to capture the application of skills in an event context and does not include advanced writing or visual communication skills. Depending on the event context and scope, specialists (e.g. graphic designers) are often employed to undertake particular aspects of proposal preparation.

Elements

- Interpret event brief
- Develop proposal or bid details
- Develop proposal or bid materials.

Critical aspects for assessment

- Ability to undertake the proposal or bidding process for a specific complex event, including effective assessment of the brief, coordination of all details and resources to meet the proposal or bid requirements, and professional presentation of proposal or bid materials and documents
- Knowledge of typical proposal or bid requirements and formats
- Development of a proposal or bid for a specific complex event in a competitive bidding environment.

BIDDING for the right to host a national or international convention or event can be an excellent opportunity to bring recognition and world experts in your field to Melbourne. Melbourne Convention + Visitors Bureau (MCVB) has the experience and resources to assist you in securing an event. Our services for helping local host organisations in bidding for national and international conferences, events and incentive programs include developing a complete strategic marketing plan to assist in securing the event; coordination and preparation of bid documents to present to the International Committee; obtaining letters of endorsement pledging support for the event from key people/bodies such as the Prime Minister of Australia, Premier of Victoria, Victorian Government Ministers, and other relevant industry leaders; and locating suitable venues within Melbourne or regional Victoria that meet the event's specified criteria.

Source: <www.mcvb.com.au>. © Melbourne Convention + Visitors Bureau MCVB).

Major events are generally subsidised by public funds because governments recognise that these events have a positive economic impact on the city and country in which they are held. Expenditure by major event organisers can stimulate the local economy, producing increased demand for goods and services and higher levels of employment. As we have mentioned, events often have a significant tourism benefit, too, as they attract both domestic and international visitors. And the long-term impact on tourism can be significant if the event has international exposure in the media, raising the city's and country's tourist destination profile. This has certainly been the case for Barcelona, Sydney, Athens and Beijing since hosting the four Olympic Games. All media attending a major event are issued with photographs of the city showing it in its best light, and it is common for visiting journalists to develop documentary material about the city and the country in the lead-up to the event. This media coverage (measured in minutes) is worth millions of dollars.

Other events have a social impact on the community. One example is The Croc Festival™, an innovative event that builds partnerships in regional and remote communities by celebrating youth culture. Involving young Indigenous and non-Indigenous Australians in visual and performing arts, sports clinics and careers markets in a 100% drug- and alcohol-free environment, the festival promotes health, education and employment in a spirit of reconciliation. An evaluation of the festival demonstrated that 'there was an overwhelming consensus that The Croc Festival™ was beneficial for the participants, communities, and for Weipa as a town. The Croc has become a symbol for a host of activities conducted in schools and communities as far apart as Cairns and the islands of the Torres Strait' (Allard et al., 2001). This quote comes from a post-event

Media attention— highly valued by events

evaluation report and illustrates the important link between the aims of an event and its outcomes. The subject of evaluation is covered in more detail in Chapter 23.

The main topic for this chapter is bidding and tendering for events. When bidding, the event organisation must establish credibility by submitting previous event evaluation reports and references to support the bid. Effective use of grant funds, successful fund-raising efforts and sponsor return on investment all demonstrate an organisation's solid reputation for planning, management and evaluation of events.

Table 30.1 provides a simplified outline of the potential impacts of an event and the measures by which they might be monitored. For a major event, a professional event evaluation report would be required, indicating the measures used for monitoring and reporting. Market research and testimonials would also be included in the report.

With this wider focus on the potential impacts of an event, the event organisation is in a better position to bid for larger events and compete with other organisations. A bid document for an event to be held in a park showing how environmental issues would be managed, for example, would be looked upon favourably by the potential client.

Table 30.1 Monitoring event impacts

Impact	Monitoring
Social and cultural	Visitor surveys Audience participation Professional judging Media exposure, publicity
Economic	Expenditure by event organisers Infrastructure development Employment
Tourism	Visitor movements Visitor expenditure (event and non-event) Survey of destination awareness Return visits Media exposure, publicity
Environmental	Environmental impact analysis (noise, waste management, damage to natural environment, use of energy and water)

BIDS, TENDERS AND GRANT APPLICATIONS

While bidding for sporting events, meetings and conventions is commonplace, this process is increasingly being used for other events as well. A *bid* is a document describing the event concept and proposed planning for the event which is submitted to the event organiser or organising committee. Sometimes the submission is prepared collaboratively by the event partners, which may include:

- ★ sponsors
- ★ donors
- ★ providers of goods and services
- ★ marketing company
- ★ venue
- ★ government bodies
- ★ convention/event bureaus and associations
- ★ tourism and hospitality partners
- ★ voluntary organisations.

Bidding for events such as the summer and winter Olympic Games is a lengthy and complex process. In the conference sector, too, bids are called for long before the meetings will be held. An annual conference with an expected attendance of 5000 might be planned 10 years ahead of time, and bids would be sought from across the world. Generally, larger conventions like to move the event from one continent to another to provide interest and tourism opportunities for delegates.

Bids to host international events are usually put together by a consortium of government authorities and the event management organisation. Tourism Events Australia has been developed at federal level to support Australia's branding as an events destination and to coordinate international bids. For many large events the bidding process is fiercely competitive. Issues surrounding the staging of the Rugby World Cup in 2003 created ill feeling between organisers in Australia and New Zealand when the event took place exclusively on Australian soil after earlier plans had games scheduled for both countries.

Many state organisations also bid against each other for national events, all competing for high profiles in sport, business and arts/entertainment. Motor races, major conferences and performing arts festivals are just a few areas in which the states are competitive. And event organisations compete with one another on a local level for the same event.

Where events come within the orbit of government, the event may be put out to tender. Most government-initiated events are listed as government tenders for which the process is highly regulated. A *tender* is very similar to a bid, but usually involves a procedurally specific and complex submission to the relevant government body. As probity is a significant concern in government tendering, it is essential that each tender document is carefully ranked against select criteria.

For a smaller event, an *expression of interest* (or quote) may be requested from several event companies. This is a more informal process, with fewer objective success criteria. While cost may be an important factor to the client, they may also be swayed by a highly creative concept.

A *grant submission* is a request for government funding for an event. However, the amount of the grant does not cover all costs associated with the event; it is only one component of the event funding, in most cases supporting non-profit sporting event initiatives or artistic endeavours. However, grant applications are dealt with in a very similar way to bids and tenders, with specific criteria to be met. At the end of the event, a report showing how the grant money was spent would need to be submitted to the grant provider.

The general principles for bid, tender and grant submissions are the same, although the level of detail differs widely according to the size and scope of the planned event.

WOODFORD FOLK FESTIVAL WINS $650 000 BOOST

The Queensland Government says a funding boost for the Woodford Folk Festival will help secure the event as a major tourist attraction. The festival is held at Woodford north of Brisbane each year between Christmas and New Year. Premier Peter Beattie, who is on the Sunshine Coast for a community Cabinet meeting, has announced $650 000 for the festival over two years. He says the internationally recognised event attracts about 80 000 people each year. 'The good thing about that, almost a third of them ... were from interstate and just under 4 per cent were from overseas—that's good news for Queensland', Mr Beattie said. 'It has an estimated economic impact of just under $11 million to the state and so what we want to do is work with the organisers and the Sunshine Coast community to build on that.'

INTERPRET THE EVENT BRIEF

When preparing a bid document, it is essential that the stated criteria remain the central focus of the bid, as it is against these criteria that the bid will be judged. In some cases, the criteria are listed in general terms; in others, each criterion is given a particular weighting. For example, the application for a local council grant shown in Table 30.2 has an assigned value for each section of the submission.

It is very important to clarify with the potential client any information in the brief that is unclear. Bid documents must appropriately address all criteria. They must also be accurate and flawlessly presented. Most importantly, they must be received on time—the deadline for bids and tenders is immutable.

The funding guidelines from Arts SA in Figure 30.1 for grants to develop the arts content within community festivals provide specific evaluation criteria on which grant submissions will be assessed.

In contrast, to attract funding a sporting event may need to show how the event would:

★ meet the needs of participating players, volunteers and officials
★ meet the needs of the event audience/spectators
★ enhance the profile of the sport in question
★ generate visitors to the city/town
★ attract a key market segment (e.g. retirees)
★ provide an ongoing competition
★ attract media exposure
★ provide direct and indirect dollar returns to the community
★ sit within the current calendar (be compatible with other events)
★ show potential for long-term self-sufficiency
★ utilise existing facilities

★ create minimum environmental impact
★ reinforce community health messages relating to sport and fitness.

Table 30.2 Weighting of criteria for a grant application

Criteria	Points
Fit with current event calendar—utilising date not currently being used	10
Innovative ideas and match with community profile, feasibility analysis	20
Event impacts, including social and environmental	10
Level of contribution to the event by other supporters: • sponsors • applicant • other grants or subsidies	10
Budget including cash flow	10
Planning, including business plan, marketing plan, timelines	20
Legal compliance, stakeholder consultation	10
Risk management plan	20
Potential value to the district economy $25 000 – $50 000 $50 001 – $100 000 $100 001 – $200 000 Over $200 000	20
Tourism visitation to the region 200–500 500–1000 1000–2500	20
Level of community support	20
Community legacy	10
Previous event reports, referees	20
TOTAL	

2010 Community arts development guidelines

FIGURE 30.1
Bid for festival funding

The Government of South Australia has a strong commitment to social inclusion and building stronger, more cohesive communities.

The priority of this program is to support community engagement and celebration, cultural diversity, social inclusion and increased access to the arts for targeted disadvantaged communities.

The Government also understands the special place of festivals in the South Australian community and is keen to support small to medium regional and metropolitan festivals. Funds are available to assist community-based festivals to develop or enhance their arts content.

(continued)

FIGURE 30.1

Bid for festival funding *continued*

Overview

The program is divided into three categories:
- Project
- Festival
- Development

Project category

To support innovative projects/activities developed by communities and organisations in consultation with artists and arts workers.

Funding of up to $30,000 is available for arts and cultural activities that:
- address issues of community engagement, equity, access, cultural diversity, social inclusion—these activities may include a one-off event or initiative or a one-off workshop series or exhibition
- introduce new audiences to the arts or extend the arts experiences of existing audiences.

Project category assessment criteria

Priority will be given to projects which address the increased participation in creative activity by members of the community who are disadvantaged due to geographic, economic or social factors, and best demonstrate:
- high quality artistic work and processes
- greater community awareness, appreciation of and participation in arts and cultural activities
- the development of partnerships between arts and non-arts organisations
- the capacity of the selected artists to deliver the project/activity outcomes
- evidence of community interest and involvement in the project's/activity's development
- viable planning, and effective use of resources, including cash and in-kind funding from sources other than Arts SA.

Festival category

To support small scale regional and metropolitan festivals to develop and enhance their arts content.

Funding of up to $15,000 is available for:
- the employment of professional artists to program, perform or exhibit
- the development of new work in collaboration with professional artists, local artists and communities
- the employment of festival staff including artistic directors, coordinators, and event managers
- the infrastructure associated with presenting a festival such as technical requirements, marquees and site dressing.

Please note that festivals in receipt of annual or triennial funding from Arts SA are not eligible to apply to the festival category but may apply to the project category.

Festival category assessment criteria

Successful applications will be those that best demonstrate:
- high quality artistic work and processes
- greater community awareness, appreciation of and participation in arts and cultural activities
- evidence of community interest and involvement in the activity's development
- some tourism opportunities
- the capacity of the selected artists to deliver the project outcomes
- viable planning, and effective use of resources, including cash and in-kind funding from sources other than Arts SA.

Your application for **Project** or **Festivals** funding will be stronger if you can show that your project will:
- increase the employment of South Australian artists and artsworkers
- include fair rates of pay or professional fees for artists
- increase access to the arts by disadvantaged communities
- encourage lively cultural activities in South Australian communities through cultural engagement
- encourage new audiences to attend or extend the arts experiences of existing audiences.

(continued)

FIGURE 30.1
Bid for festival
funding
continued

Development category

Funding of up to $4000 is available to develop a project or festival that supports the aims of the Community arts development program. Funds may be used to employ an artist or arts worker to consult with a community to develop a project and source resources.

Applicants will be assessed under the assessment criteria for the project or festival categories. Applicants **must** discuss their project with the Manager, Community Arts Development prior to submitting a proposal.

There is no closing date for this category.

Advice for applicants

The following information is related to applications to the **Project** and **Festival** categories.

Who can apply?

- arts and cultural organisations (including those in receipt of ongoing Arts SA funding)
- State and local government agencies
- not for profit and community organisations and groups
- festival and event committees.

Applicants must be legally constituted and based in South Australia.

Funded activities must be delivered in South Australia to provide direct benefits to South Australians.

The following are **not** eligible:

- individuals
- unincorporated groups
- schools
- major organisations in receipt of triennial Community arts development funding
- commercial, for-profit, fundraising, competitions, awards and prizes
- general funding for annual programs of activity
- projects already completed, or due to be completed, before the funding period
- projects without professional arts outcomes—such as amateur productions and the self-publication of literature
- infrastructure costs associated with running an organisation
- equipment, capital works or maintenance projects.

Organisations that have not fulfilled previous funding obligations, including the provision of appropriate evaluation and acquittal reports, will not be provided with funding until these obligations are met.

Source: <www.arts.sa.gov.au/site/page.cfm?u=179>.

It is evident from the assessment criteria in the above two examples that the grounds on which grants, bids or tenders will be decided will be specific to the particular event or grant. So the first rule in bidding or tendering for events or grants is to be mindful of the criteria!

DEVELOP THE BID DETAILS

With most event bids, an extensive range of information needs to be accumulated. What information is required depends, of course, on the bid document. Most importantly, you need to establish as much information about the bidding organisation as possible, as well as who your competitors are likely to be. An analysis of the potential audience for the event, as described in Chapter 27, is also essential. This may involve a detailed investigation of local demographics and tourist visitation to the region.

Local councils have a range of plans and policies (such as the local environmental plan) and it is essential to indicate in the bid how these guidelines will be addressed. It is also necessary to be mindful of the event organisation's sponsorship policy as you would not want to suggest a sponsor (or activity) that was inappropriate in terms of the organisation's community profile.

The event concept and plan, including the budget, play an important role in establishing the credibility of the bidding organisation. The professionalism of bids varies widely and selection of the successful bidder is easier when professional expertise is immediately apparent in the bid document. However, no amount of professionalism is going to allow a bid to be accepted if the criteria in the brief are not accurately addressed.

Following is an outline of the type of information that would be included in a bid document or proposal:

★ covering letter
★ cover sheet
★ executive summary
★ event concept or theme
★ event dates and program
★ event city, tourism infrastrucure, event infrastructure, attractions, accessibility, etc.
★ marketing and promotional activities
★ event audience
★ venue/s and floor plans, capacity
★ event organisation/management
★ budget
★ ticketing, fees
★ tours, travel and accommodation
★ social activities
★ event staffing
★ staging and logistics
★ special features
★ event services
★ technical requirements
★ risk management plan
★ impacts and evaluation methods.

Clearly, not all would be relevant to every event. Bid documents for conferences, incentive tours, sporting events, arts festivals and community parades would all be quite different. For more detail, refer to Appendix C, which includes a checklist for an event proposal.

The following items would be included as appendices:

★ letters of support (particularly from high-profile politicians or heads of government bodies)
★ testimonials from previous satisfied clients
★ previous event evaluation reports
★ financial records/audits
★ specified documents such as business registration and insurances.

DEVELOP THE BID MATERIALS

It is absolutely essential that the bid document is prepared in a timely manner so that there is sufficient time for professional desktop publishing, printing and binding. When bidding for major events, the services of a graphic designer would generally be employed to ensure that the bid document is eye-catching.

A complete project plan with timelines is needed for assembling the bid document to ensure that the bid is delivered on time.

When the document is prepared in a hurry, simple mistakes or failure to address all assessment criteria can ruin any chance of success with the assessment panel. For example, if the tendering specifications required a copy of the business registration or the public liability insurance policy and this was not included, the document would not reach the committee/panel for assessment.

At times, the event bid is presented to the client (or committee) in person. Once again, the presentation needs to be highly professional and supported by a multimedia presentation of the event concept. Artist impressions, maps, diagrams, models and other visual aids help clarify the event concept and look impressive—they might even help clinch the deal.

SUMMARY

Bids for events must show that the bidder has the qualifications and management skills to ensure the success of the event. In most cases, the event organising committee establishes the criteria for success and the bidder must address those criteria in the bid document. The same applies for grant applications and tenders. Understanding the aims and objectives of the event (economic, tourism, social, environmental) is essential since the final evaluation of the event must demonstrate that the aims and objectives have been successfully achieved. Indeed, a bid document must include a range of past successes as evidence that the bidder has the essential know-how. Bidding for events is fiercely competitive, particularly in the international sphere, so all bid documents and materials need to be professionally produced and attractively presented.

Chapter review questions

1 What does the process of bidding involve?
2 What does the process of obtaining a grant involve?
3 Suggest ways in which you could present a bid document and communicate your ideas.
4 Discuss the pros and cons of using unusual ideas to communicate an event concept to a committee.

1 Visit the website for the Department of Sport and Recreation in your state or territory and find out whether there are grants for sporting events. Look for the criteria on which these grants are assessed.
2 Visit the websites of five events listed in Appendix E and find out whether each event has been supported by government or similar grants.
3 The Australasian Special Events website <www.specialevents.com.au> has an archive of magazine articles and media links. Read some of the articles and analyse two events in recent times that have struggled financially or recovered from a slump to become more financially successful.

Case study

Hidden Valley (your local) Council would like to expand its event calendar while at the same time achieving a wide range of other objectives, including:
• promoting a sense of pride and community identity
• increasing access to community events to everyone in the community
• promoting cultural and disability awareness in the community
• contributing to the profile of the council
• creating an environment for innovation and creativity within the community
• leaving a lasting legacy to the community.

The council will provide funding to the value of $60 000 and this must be earmarked for specific components of the planned event. You will need other sources of funding to launch the whole concept.

Investigate the calendar of events in your local area and develop an event concept and bid which will meet the aims listed for Hidden Valley. Use the criteria and points allocated in Table 30.2 when preparing your submission. Ideally, you should work with other students, some playing the role of the council and assessing each of the bids presented, and then rotating roles. Detailed feedback should be provided on each bid document and presentation. This mirrors the real-life experience of bid presentation.

References

Allard, A, Fitzclarence, L, Nakata, M & Warhurst, J (2001), 'Evaluation of the 2000 Croc Eisteddfod Festival in Weipa', Australian Curriculum Studies Association, South Australia.

Dunphy, A (2006), 'Common success factors when bidding for sporting events in New Zealand', Australasian Digital Theses Program, AUT University, <http://aut. researchgateway.ac.nz/handle/10292/278>, accessed 22 May 2010.

EventsCorp WA, *Special events: a managed approach*, <www.tourism.wa.gov.au/ Publications%20Library/Events/Special%20Events%20A%20Managed%20Approach %20_2_.pdf>, accessed 22 May 2010.

Shone, A & Parry, B (2004), *Successful event management*, 2nd edn, Thomson Learning, London.

APPENDIX

A

EVENT OBSERVATION AND ANALYSIS

These lists of questions and event elements are provided as a guide for a structured observation and analysis of an event of your choice. This exercise should be limited to your own observations. It is not necessary to contact the particular event organisation for information. Making comparisons across a number of events can also be very productive, as this will demonstrate the many different dimensions of events and the different solutions offered by event planners.

OVERVIEW

1 What is the name of the event?
2 What type of event is it?
3 Who is the audience for this event? Can the audience be described in terms of market segments? Does the event have a tourism impact?
4 Who are the participants/players/performers in this event?
5 Can you identify the stakeholders in the event (local council, police, traffic authority, etc.)?
6 Is there evidence of sponsorship of the event in naming rights, signage or product sales?
7 What type of pre-event promotion has been done?
8 Has there been a system of pre-event registration or ticket purchase?
9 What is included in the event program?
10 What do you see as the main purpose of the event?

OPERATIONAL ANALYSIS

Comment on the following operational arrangements:
1 Suitability of venue
2 Accessibility of venue (wheelchairs, prams, etc.)

3 Parking

4 Public transport

5 Access for emergency vehicles

6 Directional signage

7 Maps, plans

8 Fences and perimeters

9 Admission control system

10 Location, size and type of entries and exits

11 Pass-out system

12 Spectator flow through the venue

13 Crowd management (e.g. mosh pits)

14 Provision of information

15 Cooling and heating systems, shade

16 Decor and furnishings

17 Lighting

18 Catering provision (what food is on offer to event audience)

19 Beverage provision, including alcohol and drinking water

20 Refrigeration and other cooking and food storage facilities

21 Cleaning services

22 Toilet facilities

23 Waste management, including recycling

24 General condition and maintenance of facility

25 Staging

26 Seating, aisles, tables, etc.

27 Sound systems, sound spill/acoustics

28 Seating and line of sight for audience (obstructions such as pillars)

29 Visual or special effects

30 Staffing (adequate number for tasks)

31 Uniforms

32 Service provision

33 Security system/staff

34 Safety (hazards)

35 Merchandise for sale

36 Lost and found

37 ATM

POST-EVENT ANALYSIS

1 Has there been any media comment on the event, positive or negative?

2 What are the primary reasons for the success or failure of this event?

3 What are five recommendations for improvement you would give to the event organiser?

In this assessment you will be submitting a grant application to your local council or governing body using the grant guidelines for Hobart City Council as your template. However, you may assume that it is your local area and your council.

The application is for a grant to support the staging of a community event such as a street parade, food and wine festival, fun run or a more imaginative concept of a similar scale. This event must meet the criteria specified in the bid document and align with the council's strategic direction.

The competency units being assessed here require application to a 'complex' event. This is described as an event comprising multiple components that must involve:

★ the need for a comprehensive and multifaceted event plan
★ the need for a formal internal or external communications strategy
★ a dedicated and diverse event budget
★ multiple administrative and operational components
★ a wide range of stakeholders
★ an event operations team.

Please note that although the grant may be for a specified amount, this should be only **part of your operations budget** and there should be other sources of income or value in kind from stakeholders such as sponsors.

In completing this assessment you must demonstrate that you can:

★ interpret the grant guidelines
★ research and develop details and options for inclusion in the application
★ assess current and emerging factors and trends
★ seek support for the proposal from relevant individuals and agencies
★ evaluate competitors and develop strategies to address competitive issues
★ conduct a risk analysis (including, if relevant, potential community opposition to the staging of the event)

★ prepare proposal materials (props, multimedia presentations, models, plans, etc.)

★ present the proposal using professional presentation and promotional techniques.

HOBART
CITY COUNCIL

COMMUNITY Grants
CULTURAL Grants
EVENTS and Festivals Grants

GRANT GUIDELINES

Community Grants Program

This program provides financial assistance for community groups and organisations to develop projects or events, or specific elements of ongoing programs, which aim to build community through fostering opportunities for access, participation, and responding to community issues and concerns.

In previous years, **cash grants** between $100 and $5,000 have been approved under this program, with an average of $1,730 per grant paid last financial year.

Cultural Grants Program

This Program provides financial assistance for:

- **Community Cultural Development projects**: Projects which involve artists and communities in the creation, direction and/or management of a project
- **Arts projects:** including visual art, craft and design, literature, new-media and the performing arts.

In previous years, **cash grants** between $250 and $10,000 have been approved under this program, with an average of $2,470 per grant paid last financial year.

Events and Festivals

This program provides assistance for events and for festivals. Details of the economic benefits to Hobart in supporting the event or festival are sought as part of the application process. Last year **cash and in-kind grants** ranged from $400 to $10,000 with an average of $3,750.

Council Services

Council is able to offer a range of services including assistance with road closures, waste management, or fees for hire of Council venues. These need to be costed and entered in your budget on the application form. You may however choose to include these services within your cash request so that you have the option to either purchase these separately from Council or other service providers.

ASSESSMENT OF GRANT APPLICATIONS

Eligibility

All applications will initially be assessed against the following compulsory eligibility criteria.

Eligible Organisations

Only organisations and groups are eligible to apply. Organisations or groups eligible for funding are:

- incorporated, or auspiced by an incorporated organisation
- financially viable
- able to demonstrate the capacity to successfully manage and administer their proposed project on time and within budget.

Projects which are eligible for funding

Projects or activities eligible for funding will:

- improve the quality of life for the Hobart community by providing access to a range of activities, events and festivals
- not duplicate or overlap with existing similar activities
- have outcomes which are delivered in the Hobart City Council area, or are accessible to Hobart City Council residents
- demonstrate that suitably qualified and experienced people are involved in the project
- be financially viable
- appropriately recognise the Council's support.

Assessment Criteria for Eligible Projects

Projects assessed as eligible for funding will then be assessed against the following criteria. Projects or activities do not necessarily need to meet all criteria, nor is meeting all the criteria a guarantee of funding. Each application will be assessed on its individual merit and against all other applications.

Projects will be assessed in terms of their capacity to:

- align with or support the Council's strategic outcomes (as outlined below)
- respond to demonstrated needs and concerns of the community
- produce innovative, quality outcomes which benefit the community
- demonstrate wide community support
- support and enhance the cultural life of Hobart and acknowledge and celebrate its cultural diversity
- enhance the image of the city as a vibrant place to live and visit
- involve local communities and individuals in the development and implementation of the project
- enhance community life by providing opportunities for participants to build relationships and networks
- for major events, deliver economic benefits to the city through increased visitation and promotion, and align with the Council's city marketing strategy
- for activities which are to be ongoing, have the capacity to develop self-sustainability.

Consideration will also be given to the outcomes of funding provided in the past.

While applications can be made for projects which have been funded in previous years (some have received funding on more than one occasion), the Council does attempt to direct funding to assist new projects.

Strategic Outcomes as outlined in the Hobart City Council Strategic Plan

A livable city
- is a safe and convenient place for people, encouraging creativity and lifestyle opportunities

Management of our environment
- protects and conserves its environment and natural beauty

Protection of our heritage
- conserves and enhances its significant built and cultural heritage

Growth of our economy
- encourages the sustainable growth and prosperity of the community

Gateway to Tasmania
- as the state capital, commits itself to the development of the economic, tourism, cultural and social life of Tasmania

Management of our resources
- prudently manages its affairs and the delivery of quality affordable services.

Supporting or Additional Information

The application forms provide space for most of the information required including a budget, however applicants should also attach:
- a financial statement for the organisation for the previous year
- a financial statement for the project, if held previously
- a brief curriculum vitae for any principal project manager, professional, artist, curator, craftsperson, writer or performing artist who will play a significant role in the project.

Support material may also include:
- research supporting the need for the event, festival project or activity
- a marketing plan for the project
- letters of support
- photographs or 35mm mounted slides
- DVD (max. 10 minutes)
- audio tape, CD or CD Rom (max. 10 minutes)
- copy of relevant publications.

Assessment Process

Assessment

Separate Assessment Teams will assess applications under each program. The Community Grants team will include a representative from the community sector and Council Officers. The Cultural Grants team will include a representative from the arts sector and Council Officers.

The teams meet separately to assess applications against the assessment criteria.

If the Assessment Team requires additional information in relation to your application you will be contacted by the relevant Program Officer, who may wish to discuss your application with you.

Recommendations

The teams make recommendations to the Hobart City Council's Community Development Committee as to which applications should receive full, partial or no funding based on decisions made as a result of the assessment process. The Committee approves the recommendations and/or makes amendments to recommendations.

Please Note: The decision of Council is final.

Communication

Applicants will receive written notification of receipt of application and notification of the assessment results. It is anticipated that applicants will be informed of the outcomes of their applications by no later than the end of July.

Feedback

Unsuccessful applicants may discuss their application with the relevant Program Officer.

Successful Applicants

Agreement

Successful applicants will need to complete a Grants Agreement prior to funding being provided.

Grants made for Events and Festivals will be subject to a separate Grant Agreement stipulating reporting requirements against the selection criteria specific to Events and Festivals detailed in this document.

Inability to comply with these Agreement's Conditions of Assistance may result in withdrawal of support.

Recognition of Council Assistance

Successful applicants must acknowledge Council's assistance for the project. This must include at a minimum:

- Council logo on **all** promotional and advertising material, including posters, flyers, newsletters, programs and advertisements
- display of Council banners at event or activity (to be provided by Council)
- opportunity for the Lord Mayor or nominee to participate in the project at the launch or any media opportunities, if applicable.
- invitations extended to all Aldermen to attend the event or project launch, if applicable.

Acquittal

All grant recipients are required to provide an acquittal upon completion of the project or within the financial year of funding. The information required includes:

- a financial report
- a brief assessment of the event/project
- details of your organisation's acknowledgement of Council's support, including documentation.

Organisations that do not satisfactorily acquit their grant may not be eligible for funding in the following year.

Again, grant recipients for Events and Festivals will be subject to additional reporting requirements as specified in the Grant Agreement for these activities.

GST & Grants

When a grant is paid to your organisation for a specific purpose or with any conditions, GST is payable on the grant.

Where grants are provided to GST registered organisations, the Council will increase the grant by 10 per cent. This is dependent on the submission of a tax invoice from the organisation.

Where your organisation is not registered for GST, GST is payable on goods and services and the grantor (Council) is not entitled to an input tax credit. **Council therefore reserves the right not to increase the grant to compensate for an unregistered organisation having to pay GST.**

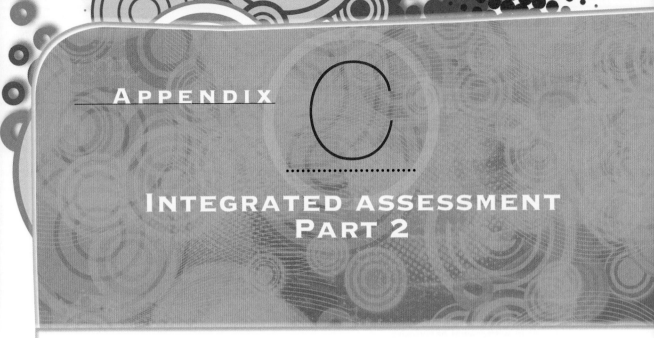

EVENT PROPOSAL AND OPERATIONAL PLAN

Develop a detailed event proposal covering all aspects of your planned event from concept to risk analysis, marketing strategy, budget, human resources and evaluation strategy. This is an opportunity to fully develop a concept in an area of interest to you, whether in business (corporate), the arts, entertainment, sport, community or outdoor public festivals.

The following guidelines for a detailed event proposal are not prescriptive. In some cases the individual elements will not apply to your project and can be ignored. For the purposes of assessing the knowledge gained in this text, the event needs to provide scope to illustrate your ability to plan in detail. For this reason, an event such as a meeting or a wedding held at a hotel venue is an example of one that offers little scope since the venue would provide staff, catering, security, etc.

Furthermore, the competency units assessed here require application to a 'complex' event. This is described as an event comprising multiple components that must involve:

★ the need for a comprehensive and multifaceted event plan
★ the need for a formal internal or external communications strategy
★ a dedicated and diverse event budget
★ multiple administrative and operational components
★ a wide range of stakeholders
★ an event operations team.

A simple event such as a small in-house conference, school fundraiser, sports carnival or awards ceremony would not meet the requirements of a 'complex' event.

The level of difficulty will be a consideration when grading this assessment. Events that would be considered difficult include the following:

★ outdoor event, no infrastructure

★ event with multiple stakeholders

★ multi-session event

★ multi-venue event

★ new concept event

★ event with tourism impact

★ event with higher than average risk (such as financial, safety)

★ event with operational or logistical challenges.

You are expected to present your proposal using the outline below, which in many respects follows the text chapters. The proposal should be in report format with a matching folder containing relevant appendices. It is up to you to decide what should appear in the main report and what should be included as an appendix. For example, an overall risk management plan and budget are essential parts of the main report. More detailed plans, job descriptions, volunteer advertisements etc. should be included as appendices. Imagine that the report will be read by a major client, sponsor or government body. It should be more detailed than usual, and it should be readable and flawlessly presented.

Read through the following sections carefully, as you will need to select an event that will provide the scope to cover many of these elements.

EVENT CONCEPT

In this section you need to describe the event concept. The reader should have a clear picture of the event before moving on to the planning details. Note: It is surprising how many assumptions are made in this section, so make sure that you paint a good picture.

Some of the elements you might cover include:

★ event name

★ event type

★ location, suburb and council

★ date(s)

★ duration/timing

★ event overview and main purpose

★ aims

★ measurable objectives (e.g. audience size).

EVENT FEASIBILITY

This is a brief justification for the event (probably easier if summarised later when more detailed planning has been completed) covering the following as an overview for the reader:

★ management responsibility for the event

★ major stakeholders and agencies

★ physical requirements (venue/route/layout)

★ marketing strategy

★ financial management strategy (including income generation)

★ human resources strategy

★ event impacts (social, environmental, economic)

★ risk management plan (overview)

★ operational planning (overview)

★ evaluation strategy (overview)

★ timelines (Gantt chart of macro-level plans; more detailed timelines can be provided in later sections).

Approvals and consultation

This section should describe all relevant compliance issues and insurance requirements, as follows:

★ state and federal government

★ council

★ Roads and Traffic Authority/ Department of Transport

★ liquor licensing

★ police

★ building

★ health

★ environmental

★ entertainment

★ music licensing

★ security

★ contracts for service

★ insurances (including public liability).

Marketing

In the marketing section you look at marketing the event product (promotion comes later) and need to carry out:

★ competitive analysis

★ market analysis and planning

   – customer segmentation

   – meeting audience needs

   – consumer decision-making

   – price and ticket program

★ event promotion (overview).

Sponsorship and other forms of income

If these are sources of income for your event, they need to be covered in detail:

★ sponsorship (minor, major, cash or in kind)

★ grants

★ donations

★ merchandising

★ other.

Financial management

You should present more than one budget model, based on different assumptions (e.g. different ticket pricing, choice of indoor/outdoor venue). You need to justify both income and expenditure.

For financial operations you need to provide:

★ financial procedures (to meet relevant statutory and internal control requirements)

★ sources of income, including capital funding requirements, sponsorship, grants, ticket sales, entry fees, merchandising, etc.

★ detailed budget with itemised expenses, including insurances

★ pricing plan based on break-even analysis of fixed and variable costs

★ cash flow analysis

★ methods for approval and payment of accounts

★ other relevant control systems (e.g. cash handling)

★ strategies for communicating financial objectives and systems (including graphs as illustration)

★ taxation information

★ income statement.

RISK MANAGEMENT

In this section you will need to look at the strategic risks, such as the loss of a key sponsor (this section is not about detailed health and safety planning) according to the recommended process:

★ establish the context

★ identify the risks

★ analyse the risks

★ evaluate the risks

★ treat the risks.

When you have completed this section, you might like to look at Chapter 30, 'Event proposals and bids', to ensure that you have covered all strategic elements of planning before focusing on operational planning.

OPERATIONAL PLANNING

In this section you will look at the operational and logistical challenges of the event and start to provide more detail about the site and the services required:

★ site/venue maps and plans

★ logistics and schedules (bump-in, bump-out)

★ services
  – electricity
  – water

★ transport (including air travel, access to venue)
  – traffic management
  – street closure
  – impact on local traffic
  – notification of affected businesses, etc.
  – diversions
  – marshalling
  – support vehicles
  – parking
  – disability access

★ catering
  – providers
  – facilities
  – food safety plans

★ waste and environmental management
  – toilets
  – waste management (e.g. recycling)
  – noise
  – water pollution

★ cleaning.

EVENT PROMOTION

Your promotional plan might include developing a website, advertising in the press and a publicity campaign. The content, cost and timing of all these strategies need to be elaborated:

★ advertising (messages, look, media)
★ public relations (who, where)
★ event program design and printing
★ website design.

EVENT STAGING

Staging covers the peformance, entertainment or competition aspect of the event and most of the terms are theatrical terms. For example, the stage manager is responsible for the stage when the show is being performed and is the director's right-hand person in the lead-up to the performance. In this section you need to show how the event will be delivered to the audience, finishing (or starting if you wish) with the production schedule, which shows how the performance will come together. While earlier sections covered mainly public areas and audience issues, the focus for this is on the cast and crew and the physical area in which they will perform. Other events, such as conferences and sports competitions, also require similar considerations, including MC, stage manager and other production roles. For a sporting competition, substitute field of play for stage.

You should consider:

★ theme
★ decor
★ layout/seating
★ stage

★ entertainment
★ special effects, lighting
★ sound
★ production schedule.

STAFFING

This section describes your human resources strategy and approach to management of a temporary or volunteer workforce. Job analysis is vitally important so that roles are clear. Organisation charts should show all stakeholders and contractors, as well as full-time, temporary and volunteer staff. This is what you would include in the staffing section of your event proposal:

★ organisational charts (pre-event, event and post-event)
★ work breakdown and job descriptions
★ selection and recruitment
★ rosters
★ training (including OHS)
★ briefing
★ recognition strategies
★ workplace relations
★ volunteer management.

SAFETY AND SECURITY

In this section you address some of the issues in more detailed risk management plans:

★ safety of the event audience
★ safety and security of the performers, VIPs, etc.
★ health and safety of the staff
★ security for premises, equipment, cash, etc.
★ communications
    – meetings
    – reporting relationships
    – emergency reporting relationships
    – communication methods (radio)
★ emergency access and emergency management
★ first aid.

SPECTATOR MANAGEMENT

This section emphasises policy, procedure and contingency planning:

★ signage, way-finding
★ spectator flow planning
★ admission control
★ policies (e.g. complaints, lost children, violence)
★ contingency plans
    – weather
    – electrical supply, lighting
    – fire
    – accident
    – crowd crush
    – delay or cancellation
    – bomb or other threat
    – security incident.

EVENT EVALUATION

As we have discussed throughout this book, evaluation is a very important part of every event, informing future events of a similar nature. It is a process of measuring the outcomes against the objectives using a variety of methods (such as customer surveys, focus groups, etc.). The evaluation report prepared for the customer should include all information used in its preparation, including statistical summaries.

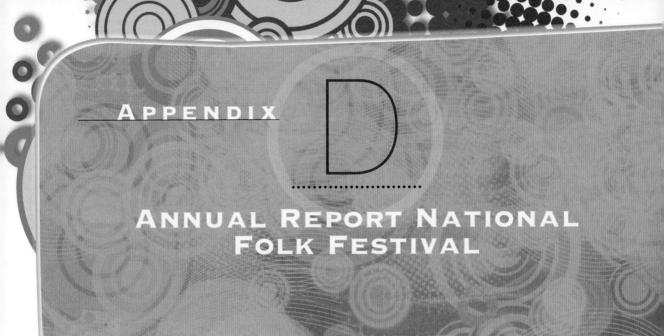

APPENDIX D

ANNUAL REPORT NATIONAL FOLK FESTIVAL

National Folk Festival Ltd

Annual Report

2006 - 2007

Managing Director's Report

The National Folk Festival used the 2006 – 2007 financial year to continue moving forward and doing some restructuring of the organisation.

There were new appointments to the Board of Directors that brought experience in Folk Culture, Business, Marketing, Media and a fresh view of the Festival. It had been almost four years since the last appointment to the Board and the new members promptly set about bringing their experiences and strengths to the Festival.

A Staff restructure saw the creation of the Managing Director and Artistic Director positions and a new Production Manager hired to complete the team. I have been the Managing Director for over a year now and have been proud to oversee the entire National Folk Festival team, from Volunteers to Board Members and all the Staff, bring about such a successful period over the last twelve months.

Attendance

The Festival achieved modest growth in attendance figures for the 2007 Festival with more Season, Day and Evening Tickets sold than the previous year. The growth was 6% on the 2006 event but this has been identified as both a comfortable amount of growth and a regular figure each year. We are conscious of the limitations that the site at EPIC has and have planned for this steady growth most noticeably by the large site expansion that occurred in 2006.

The National Folk Festival has a policy of subsidising the ticket price for people attending the event from some of the feature states. This policy exists to recognise the distance that needs to be travelled and the cost to do so. For 2007 people who were able to provide proof of residency in Western Australia were granted free entry to the event through pre-purchase ticketing. The result was an increase from 20 to almost 400 attendees from WA.

We have seen an increase of young people attending the Festival and, most importantly, taking an active part in the event through volunteering, workshop participation and performing through the Blackboard venues. These people are the future of the event and we look forward to seeing them take up, promote and give back to the Festival over the years.

Finances

The NFF entered the 2006 – 2007 financial year with a plan to produce a moderate surplus as a result of better fiscal management. The increase in attendance combined with no operational costs exceeding their budgeted expenditure has seen the Festival produce an operating surplus above expectations.

After recording three consecutive losses this result has enabled the Festival to recoup some ground and to add to the Rainy Day Fund. The Rainy Day Fund exists to self-insure the organisation in event of the Festival being cancelled and is vital to the health and longevity of the National.

The Festival continues to offer tickets at the minimal price possible with highly discounted tickets for youth and children. An Adult Season Ticket at the Gate Price works out at around $35 a day and a Child Season Ticket at $7 a day. This remains exceptionally good value and as a result of a higher expected surplus ticket prices will be increased only $1 or $2 in 2008.

Partnerships

The National Folk Festival continues to build new partnerships, bringing more people into the community that is the Festival. The partnerships formed by the Festival are seen as two-way streets with both organisations bringing something to the table and gaining something from the experience.

The National Folk Festival is a celebration of national culture and as a result the Festival works closely with a number of national institutions to highlight and provide other experiences of the Australian identity. With the National Library of Australia (NLA) the Festival presents the National Folk Fellowship providing funding, access and performance outcomes for a research project developed from the NLA collection. The National Film and Sound Archive had a presence at the Festival by providing a program of old TV footage that was shown in the Palladium venue each night along with hosting the Artists Signing Tent. For the first time the National Archives of Australia had a presence at the Festival through part of their touring exhibition about water being present at the event.

The Festival continues its relationship with the Australian National University School of Music through the hosting of the Masterclass program. Through this program high quality tutors of traditional music are brought into the school to teach across three days. The Masterclasses are open to all musicians and included students from the School of

Music Traditional Music course. The Festival also works with the Canberra Institute of Technology Department of Communication and Media by providing an opportunity for students to take part in fieldwork.

A new partnership with Youth in the City, a Canberra based integrated youth services centre, saw refreshed and better provided Axis Youth Venue become a hub of activity for young people at the Festival.

The National continued its work with local community groups such as 2XX community radio, Artsound radio, Butt Littering Trust, NoWaste, Pedal Power, Monaro Folk Society, Rotary, Woodcrafters Guild, Deafness Resource Centre and the ACT Cancer Council.

The Construction, Forestry, Mining and Engineering Union (CFMEU) has been a supporter of the Festival for more than 10 years supplying training for Volunteers and other resources. Other supporters and partners include the ACT Government through Australian Capital Tourism, ACT NoWaste and ACT Health Promotion Grants, Barlens Event Hire, Coopers, the Embassy of the United States of Australia and Infinite Networking.

The Festival commenced a new Licence Agreement for five years with Exhibition Park in Canberra (EPIC). This will provide the Festival with a steady home for the event and allow for some planning towards 2013.

Artistic Program

For 2007 Western Australia held the mantle of Feature State and the Artistic Director, Dave O'Neill, was able to present a diverse and high quality selection of acts such as the country styling of *The Pigram Brothers*, the blues rhythms of *Andrew Winton*, the cornucopia of *David Hyams and the Miles To go Band*, choir *Working Voices* and the youth based *Just Fiddling* along with much, much more.

The programming theme of *The Music of the Middle East* opened up a little known, or understood, part of Australian culture. *Sirocco*, *Yalla*, *Ismail Bektas*, *Paul Koerbin* and *Camoon* are all Australian based acts playing music of middle-eastern origin who performed at the Festival. The Festival tries to increase the knowledge and diffusion of the diversity of culture that forms the unique Australian culture and the introduction of a musical theme will enable us to present what this country has to offer as well as bringing artists from overseas.

The international acts present at the Festival included *Apodomi Compania, The Mammals, Chris Smither, Dougal Adams and Ormonde Waters, Jez Lowe & Kate Bramley, Keith Donnelly, Kevin Burke & Ged Foley, Madviolet* and *Winston Wuttunee*. Combined with local legends such as *Anne Kirkpatrik, Keith Potger* and the new talent of

CC, *Dahahoo* and *Pettibone* along with the almost 200 other acts that took part the 2007 National Folk Festival the artistic program was diverse, entertaining and enthusiastically received by all.

The Future

We have identified education as a focus point for the next few years. We want to expand the Masterclass program and develop an In Schools program to bring traditional music into schools in the Canberra region. This will ensure that the National Folk Festival has participants well into the future.

The 2008 Festival will feature two new venues. The Henley Theatre will host theatre performances, film and concerts in a dedicated 'black-space' venue. The Flute & Fiddle will provide the Feature States with a venue to highlight what folk clubs operate in the state and to showcase the performers who are appearing at the National.

Amongst these additions remains the true heart of the Festival, the place where people can continue to come together to share their stories and to continue to celebrate our diverse national cultural heritage. We will never loose sight of this as we broaden the range of what the National Folk Festival can offer.

2006- 2007 was an exciting and successful year and we will endeavour to make 2007-2008 just the same.

I look forward to seeing you at the National in 2008.

Jared Wilkins
Managing Director

Festival Review

Attendance

The Festival continues to attract a national audience.

In recognition of Western Australia's position as the feature state the Festival decided to offer free tickets to any WA residents who made the long journey to Canberra at Easter. The response was phenomenal with 226 tickets being provided in pre-purchase ticketing. In 2006 21 people from WA bought pre-purchase tickets and in 2005 only 18 bought tickets.

The Festival continued to have a manageable increase in attendance with an average daily attendance of 11,946 across the Friday, Saturday, Sunday and Monday of the Festival and around 6,000 on the Thursday. This was a 6% increase on 2006 attendance figures and was the upper level of the management plan.

There was 6% growth across interstate attendance however international attendance saw no growth over 2006 figures.

Media Coverage

Print Coverage (pre-, during and post- Festival)
- Daily Feature articles, what's on guide and photo art stories in The Canberra Times.
- Feature articles and photo art stories in The Chronicle.
- Feature article in Virgin Blue in-flight magazine.
- Feature in QANTA in-flight magazine
- Editorial in Sydney Morning Herald
- Editorial in Melbourne Herald Sun
- Feature article in Financial Review
- Feature article in CFMEU Journal
- Feature articles in interstate youth and music publications.
- Feature article in Macafferty's in-bus magazine
- Feature articles in national folk publication Trad & Now
- Feature photo article in The Canberra Review
- Feature article in Capital Magazine
- Features in various trade union magazines
- Features in various interstate folk magazines
- Cover story Yass Tribune

Radio Coverage
- National 3-hour on- site OB broadcast on Good Friday on ABC metropolitan and regional station network (78 stations).
- Local 3- hour on- site OB broadcast on Easter Sunday on 666 ABC Radio Canberra
- National 3-hour outside broadcast over CBAA network by 2xx Community Radio
- National coverage on SBS Radio
- Daily interview with Managing Director on Canberra FM station MIX106.
- Interview with Managing Director on Canberra FM station FM104.7
- Assorted interviews on Community Radio Station Artsound FM
- Assorted interviews on community radio station 2XX
- Assorted interviews on Australia -wide interstate community radio stations
- Daily interviews on national community radio
- Interview with Artistic Director on community radio station Radio Adelaide
- Interview with Managing Director on ABC Rockhampton
- Interviews with Managing Director and others on ABC Hobart

TV Coverage
- Interview with Managing Director on local station WIN TV.
- Interview with Managing Director on local ABC station.
- Interview with Managing Director on Prime TV
- Interview with Managing Director on State Focus (Southern Cross Network)

Internet Coverage
- The Program online magazine (theprogram.net.au)
- The Session musician forum (www.thesession.org)
- Go See Australia (www.goseeaustralia.com.au)
- The Green Man (www.thegreenman.net.au)
- Yahoo!7 News (au.news.yahoo.com)
- News.com.au (news.com.au)
- ArtsHub (artshub.com.au)

Waste Reduction

- With the decrease in operational capabilities at ACT NoWaste the Festival has forged onwards regardless.
- The Festival is the only major event within the ACT that attempts a wide scale waste reduction process. The Festival continues to work on the process with the aim of having zero waste sent to landfill.

- In 2007 the Festival set and achieved the goal of 75% of all waste produced before, during and after the Festival sent to recycling facilities. The Festival was also able to reduce the overall amount of waste produced.
- Again provided an on-site cup washing service with a bank of 6,000 cups that cycled through an average 5 times, providing an estimated 37,000 cup-fulls for serving at food stalls.
- The Festival commenced a partnership with the Butt Littering Trust to minimise the amount of cigarette butt litter being generated at the Festival. This was a successful pilot year and will improve in 2008

Survey Report

First Time Visitation
- **36%** of attendees were visiting the Festival for the first time

Return Visitation
- **80%** of attendees indicated they would return for the 2008 Festival.
- **15%** indicated that they would like to but were unsure if they could.

How attendees are introduced to the Festival

Magazine	**0%**
Newspaper	**1.7%**
Radio	**1.7%**
TV	**0%**
Other People	**60%**
NFF Materials	**1%**
Just Know	**30%**

Where attendees are from

ACT/Queanbeyan Region	**34%**
NSW	**33%**
Other States	**28%**
International	**4%**

Why attendees came to Canberra
- **84%** of interstate attendees come to Canberra for the National Folk Festival.

Audience

Male	**45%**
Female	**55%**

Age of Attendees

>15	**7%**
15-24	**22%**
25-34	**10%**
35-44	**10%**
45-54	**24%**
55-64	**23%**
65 +	**4%**

Accommodation

- Camping onsite at EPIC   **63%**
- Motel/Hotel   **12%**
- Camping offsite   **1%**
- Hostel/Backpackers   **2%**
- Caravan Park   **1%**
- Private Home   **19%**
- Other Accommodation   **1%**
- Staying outside ACT   **1%**

NATIONAL FOLK FESTIVAL LIMITED
ABN 96 058 761 274

FINANCIAL REPORT FOR THE YEAR ENDED 30 JUNE 2007

INCOME STATEMENT FOR THE YEAR ENDED 30 JUNE 2007

	Note	2007 $	2006 $
Revenue from government and other grants	2	65,808	93,491
Other revenue	2	1,550,611	1,361,852
Employee benefits expense	3	(283,816)	(215,181)
Depreciation and amortisation	3	(15,710)	(20,938)
Finance costs	3	-	(100)
Doubtful debts	3	(1,405)	(1,405)
Repairs, maintenance and vehicle running expense		(5,732)	(4,951)
Fuel, light and power expense		(17,184)	(16,221)
Rental expense		(9,217)	(9,155)
Training expense		(1,858)	(2,199)
Audit, legal and consultancy expense		(6,350)	(3,972)
Direct Festival Costs		(965,731)	(915,744)
Other expenses		(150,310)	(286,240)
Profit before income tax		159,106	(20,763)
Income tax expense		-	-
Profit after income tax		159,106	(20,763)

NATIONAL FOLK FESTIVAL LIMITED
ABN 96 058 761 274

FINANCIAL REPORT FOR THE YEAR ENDED 30 JUNE 2007

BALANCE SHEET AS AT 30 JUNE 2007

	Note	2007 $	2006 $
CURRENT ASSETS			
Cash and cash equivalents	4	434,777	359,437
Trade and other receivables	5	113,874	81,260
Inventories	6	1,800	651
Other current assets	7	8,388	7,021
TOTAL CURRENT ASSETS		558,839	448,369
NON-CURRENT ASSETS			
Property, plant and equipment	8	59,453	71,209
TOTAL NON-CURRENT ASSETS		59,453	71,209
TOTAL ASSETS		618,292	519,578
CURRENT LIABILITIES			
Trade and other payables	9	97,201	163,357
Short term provisions	10	23,251	21,830
TOTAL CURRENT LIABILITIES		120,452	185,187
NON-CURRENT LIABILITIES			
Trade and other payables	9	2,000	2,500
Long term provisions	10	10,693	5,850
TOTAL NON-CURRENT LIABILITIES		12,693	8,350
TOTAL LIABILITIES		133,145	193,537
NET ASSETS		**485,147**	**326,041**
EQUITY			
Retained Earnings		340,977	181,871
Reserves		144,170	144,170
TOTAL EQUITY		**485,147**	**326,041**

NATIONAL FOLK FESTIVAL LIMITED
ABN 96 058 761 274

FINANCIAL REPORT FOR THE YEAR ENDED 30 JUNE 2007

STATEMENT OF RECOGNISED INCOME AND EXPENDITURE
FOR THE YEAR ENDED 30 JUNE 2007

	Retained Earnings $	General Reserve $	Total $
Balance at 1 July 2005	202,634	132,491	335,125
Profit attributable to the entity	(20,763)	-	(20,763)
Transfers to and from Reserves	-	11,679	11,679
Balance at 30 June 2006	181,871	144,170	326,041
Profit attributable to the entity	159,106	-	159,106
Transfers to and from Reserves	-	-	-
Balance at 30 June 2007	340,977	144,170	485,147

NATIONAL FOLK FESTIVAL LIMITED
ABN 96 058 761 274

FINANCIAL REPORT FOR THE YEAR ENDED 30 JUNE 2007

CASH FLOW STATEMENT FOR THE YEAR ENDED 30 JUNE 2007

	Note	2007 $	2006 $
CASH FLOW FROM OPERATING ACTIVITIES			
Receipts from customers		1,509,203	1,445,053
Receipts from grants		65,808	93,491
Payments to suppliers and employees		(1,509,186)	(1,446,480)
Interest received		17,634	16,795
Dividends received		-	-
Finance costs		-	-
Net cash generated from operating activities	17(b)	83,459	108,859
CASH FLOW FROM INVESTING ACTIVITIES			
Proceeds from sale of property, plant and equipment		-	-
Payment for property, plant and equipment		(8,119)	(10,943)
Proceeds from sale of investments		-	-
Payment for investments		-	-
Net cash used in investing activities		(8,119)	(10,943)
CASH FLOW FROM FINANCING ACTIVITIES			
Repayment of finance lease commitments		-	-
Increase in finance lease commitments		-	-
Net cash generated from (used in) financing activities		-	-
Net (decrease) increase in cash held		75,340	97,916
Cash at the beginning of the financial year		359,437	261,521
Cash at the end of the financial year	17(a)	434,777	359,437

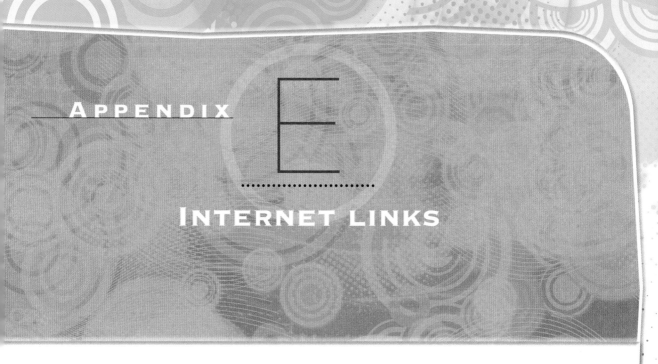

EVENT PLANNING

Australasian Legal Information Institute
   www.austlii.edu.au

Australasian Promotional Marketing Association
   www.apma.com

Australasian Special Events
   www.specialevents.com.au

Australia Council for the Arts (Indigenous protocol)
   www.australiacouncil.gov.au/research/aboriginal_and_torres_strait_islander_arts

Blue Mountains City Council, event guidelines
   www.bmcc.nsw.gov.au (search events)

CrowdSafe
   www.crowdsafe.com

CRC for Waste Management
   www.crcwmpc.com.au

Emergency Management in Australia
   www.ema.gov.au

Executive Planet
   www.executiveplanet.com

Fair Work Online
   www.fairwork.gov.au/index.cfm?pagename=agreementsfind&norightcol/

Guidelines for Event Organisers (Southern Waste Strategy)
   www.southernwaste.com.au/community/organiserguidelines.html

Nowaste ACT, Guidelines for Recycling at Public Events
   www.nowaste.act.gov.au

NSW Department of Environment, Climate Change and Water,
   www.environment.nsw.gov.au/warr/wwe_home.htm/

NSW Department of Local Government, *Major and special event planning: a guide for promoters and councils*
> www.dlg.nsw.gov.au/dlg/dlghome/documents/information/97-65.pdf

NSW Department of Premier and Cabinet, Community Engagement and Events Division
> www.events.nsw.gov.au/

Our Community
> www.ourcommunity.com.au

Party Oz
> www.fancydresshire.com.au

Playbill Venues Safety Centre
> www.playbillvenues.com

Queensland Liquor Licensing
> www.liquor.qld.gov.au/ourproducts/brochures/planning_guide/page_1.asp#obtain

Safe Work Australia
> www.safeworkaustralia.gov.au/swa/

Standards Australia
> www.standards.org.au

State Government of Victoria Department of Health (Food Safety)
> www.health.vic.gov.au/foodsafety/

Sustainable Tourism Cooperative Research Centre
> www.crctourism.com.au/

Traffic and transport for special events (available through the Roads and Traffic Authority)
> www.rta.nsw.gov.au

TravelSmart Australia
> www.travelsmart.gov.au

Volunteering Australia
> www.volunteeringaustralia.org

TOURISM

Canberra Tourism
> www.visitcanberra.com.au

Northern Territory Tourism Commission
> www.nttc.com.au

South Australian Tourism Commission
> www.southaustralia.com

Tourism Australia
> tourism.australia.com

Tourism New South Wales
> www.tourism.nsw.gov.au

Tourism New Zealand (market research)
> www.tourisminfo.govt.nz

Tourism New Zealand (travel)
> www.newzealand.com/travel

Tourism Queensland
   www.queenslandholidays.com.au/pfm/index.htm
Tourism Tasmania
   www.discovertasmania.com.au
Tourism Victoria
   www.tourismvictoria.com.au
Western Australia Tourism Commission
   www.westernaustralia.com
World Tourism Organization
   www.unwto.org.

TOURISM TRAINING

Tourism Training ACT & Region
   Email: ttact@interact.net.au
Tourism Training Australia
   www.tourismtraining.com.au
Tourism Training QLD
   Email: info@ttq.org.au
Tourism Training SA
   Email: ttsa@ttsa.com.au
Tourism Training TAS
   Email: tourtraintas@bigpond.com.au

STATISTICS AND FORECASTS

Australian Bureau of Statistics
   www.abs.gov.au
Commonwealth Department of Resources, Energy and Tourism
   www.ret.gov.au
Festivals Australia
   www.arts.gov.au/arts/festivals_australia
The World Factbook
   https://www.cia.gov/library/publications/the-world-factbook/
Tourism Research Australia
   www.ret.gov.au/tourism
World Tourism Organization
   www.unwto.org
World Travel and Tourism Council
   www.wttc.org

GOVERNMENT

Austrade
   www.austrade.gov.au
Australian Commonwealth Government Information and Services
   http://australia.gov.au

Australian Local Government Association
   www.alga.asn.au

City of Sydney
   www.cityofsydney.nsw.gov.au

Fair Work Australia
   www.fwa.gov.au

New South Wales Government
   www.nsw.gov.au

Northern Territory Government
   www.nt.gov.au

Queensland Government
   www.qld.gov.au

South Australian Government
   www.sa.gov.au

Tasmanian Government
   www.dpac.tas.gov.au

Victorian Government
   www.vic.gov.au

Western Australian Government
   www.wa.gov.au

MEETINGS AND EVENTS ASSOCIATIONS

Australian Amusement, Leisure and Recreation Association
   www.aalara.com.au

Australian Conference & Events Bureau
   www.aceb.com.au

Australian Tourism Export Council
   www.atec.net.au

Exhibition & Event Association of Australasia
   www.eeaa.com.au

International Congress and Convention Association
   www.iccaworld.com

International Festivals & Events Association
   www.ifea.com

International Special Events Society
   www.ises.com

International Association of Exhibitions and Events
   www.iaee.com

Media, Entertainment & Arts Alliance
   www.alliance.org.au

Meetings and Events Australia
   www.meetingsevents.com.au

Meetings, Incentives, Conferences and Exhibitions
   www.miaanet.com.au

Pacific Asia Travel Association
   www.pata.org
Venue Management Association
   www.vma.org.au

CONVENTION BUREAUS

Business Events Cairns and Great Barrier Reef
   www.businesseventscairns.org.au
Business Events Sydney
   www.businesseventssydney.com.au
Canberra Convention Bureau
   www.canberraconvention.com.au
Conventions & Incentives New Zealand
   www.conventionsnz.co.nz
Melbourne Convention & Visitors Bureau
   www.mcvb.com.au
Perth Convention Bureau
   www.pcb.com.au

INTERNATIONAL EVENTS

Clean Up the World
   www.cleanuptheworld.org/en/
Edinburgh International Festival
   www.eif.co.uk
National Football League (Superbowl)
   www.nfl.com/
Tourism Thailand
   www.tourismthailand.org
Wimbledon
   www.wimbledon.org/en_GB/index.html

AUSTRALIAN EVENTS

Adelaide Horse Trials
   www.adelaidehorsetrials.com.au
Australia Day
   www.australiaday.org.au/experience/
Australian Grand Prix
   www.grandprix.com.au/
Australian Motorcycle Grand Prix
   https://bikes.grandprix.com.au/
Australian Open
   www.australianopen.com/en_AU/index.html
Australian Science Festival
   www.sciencefestival.com.au

Big Day Out
   www.bigdayout.com/home.php
Camel racing
   www.austcamel.com.au/acn_race.htm
Canberra Floriade
   www.floriadeaustralia.com
City to Surf Sydney
   http://city2surf.sunherald.com.au
Classic Car Rally
   www.classicrally.com.au
Clean Up Australia
   www.cleanup.com.au
Gay & Lesbian Mardi Gras
   www.mardigras.org.au
Goodwill Games
   www.goodwillgames.com/2001/2001_index.html
Henley-on-Todd Regatta
   www.henleyontodd.com.au
Hobart Fringe Festival
   http://hobartfringe.com
Hunter Valley events
   www.atn.com.au/nsw/syd/event-e.htm
Juvenile Diabetes Research Foundation events
   www.jdrf.org.au
Melbourne Cup
   www.melbournecup.com/150%5FMelbourne%5FCup/
Melbourne Flower Show
   www.melbflowershow.com.au
Melbourne Food and Wine Festival
   www.melbournefoodandwine.com.au
Melbourne International Comedy Festival
   www.comedyfestival.com.au
Mt Isa Rodeo
   www.isarodeo.com.au
National Days of Commemoration
   www.awm.gov.au/commemoration
National Folk Festival
   www.folkfestival.asn.au/the-festival/
Perth International Arts Festival
   www.perthfestival.com.au
Reef Festival
   www.whitsundayreeffestival.org.au
Rosemount Australian Fashion Week
   http://rafw.com.au/

Royal Melbourne Show
    www.royalshow.com.au
St Kilda Film Festival
    www.stkildafilmfestival.com.au
Summernats
    www.summernats.com.au
Surf Lifesaving Championships
    www.slsa.asn.au
Sydney events listing
    www.whatsonSydney.com
Sydney Writers Festival
    www.swf.org.au/about/
Womadelaide
    www.womadelaide.com.au
Woodford Folk Festival
    http://woodfordfolkfestival.com
World Solar Challenge
    www.worldsolarchallenge.org

NEW ZEALAND EVENTS

New Zealand Events
    www.nz-events.co.nz
New Zealand International Arts Festival
    www.nzfestival.nzpost.co.nz
Queenstown Winter Festival
    www.winterfestival.co.nz
Rally New Zealand
    www.rallynz.org.nz
Royal Easter Show
    www.royaleastershow.co.nz/
Volvo Ocean Race
    www.volvooceanrace.com

OTHER EVENT SITES

Eventclicks
    www.eventclicks.com
Special events ideas
    www.bizbash.com
Special Events magazine online
    www.specialevents.com.au
Visual Event Management
    www.vem.com.au

INDEX